More Praise for Michele Borba—
America's Trusted Parenting Expert

"Award-winning educator and author Michele Borba heads to the top of the class again with a comprehensive go-to guide for parents looking for advice on behavior and development. These 101 practical solutions to parenting cover all ages and stages of childhood and address traditional problems like temper tantrums and sibling rivalry as well as issues unique to the Internet generation of kids. *The Big Book of Parenting Solutions* should be at every parent's fingertips for no-nonsense, straightforward answers about childhood behavior challenges."

> —**Jennifer Shu, M.D.**; editor, American Academy of Pediatrics' *Baby and Child Health*; and coauthor, *Heading Home with Your Newborn* and *Food Fights*

"*The Big Book of Parenting Solutions* is a comprehensive resource packed with real-life parenting solutions that you can really trust!"

> —**Bobbi Conner**, host of the nationally syndicated public radio show *The Parent's Journal*, and author, *Unplugged Play*

"Michele Borba offers insightful, realistic, and straightforward advice that is sure to get immediate results."

> —**Sally Lee**, editor-in-chief, *Ladies Home Journal*

"Michele Borba has gathered together some of the finest ideas and activities ever collected in one volume for parents. Consistently using the ideas Michele suggests will help your kids lead more successful lives not only now but also for the rest of their lives."

> —**Jack Canfield**, coauthor, *Chicken Soup for the Soul*®

"This step-by-step, here's-how manual is almost like having Michele Borba as your personal parenting trainer."

> —**Thomas Lickona**, author, *Educating for Character* and *Raising Good Children*

"Michele Borba is an inspiring educator, an experienced parent, and a terrific writer. She has identified the core issues for parenting moral kids and presented them with passion, wit, and enormous practicality."

—**Michael Gurian**, author, *The Minds of Boys, The Good Son,* and *The Wonder of Boys*

"A sensitive, thoughtful, and eminently practical book that will help parents help their children change behavior—and improve the well-being and happiness of the child and the entire family. A wonderful contribution!"

—**Alvin Rosenfeld, M.D.**, child psychiatrist, and coauthor, *The Over-Scheduled Child*

"*12 Simple Secrets Real Moms Know* is a godsend for all the anxious, stressed-out mothers who worry that they're not 'doing enough' (and that's pretty much everyone!)."

—**Christiane Northrup, M.D.**; author, *Mother-Daughter Wisdom* and *Women's Bodies, Women's Wisdom*

"A practical, easy-to-read guide, full of great examples to help mothers teach their children the skills that will eventually be invaluable for great success and happiness in college."

—**Richard Kadison, M.D.**, chief, Mental Health Service, Harvard University Health Services

"I hope this book finds its way into homes all across the country. I know that the strategies, ideas, and activities it provides can make a tremendous difference in the lives of our children."

—**Thomas Armstrong**, author, *Awakening Your Child's Natural Genius* and *In Their Own Way*

"I appreciate the message that this book champions and the guidance it provides to mothers struggling to foster a brighter future for their children."

—**Mary Bono Mack**, member of Congress, California's 45th District

"This smart and helpful book integrates much of what we know about raising moral children."

—**William Damon**, professor and director, Stanford University Center on Adolescence

"A revolutionary, wonderful, and welcome answer to a mother's prayers. Michele Borba has shown us all how to be loving moms who raise great kids, without losing our peace of mind, our lives as adults, or our true selves."

> —**Phyllis George**, former Miss America, pioneer female sportscaster, former first lady of Kentucky, and mother

"While many people in public life decry the lack of character and moral development among our kids, few take this concern further, into the realm of practical steps to address the issue in the lives of real children and youth. Michele Borba has done so in her book *Building Moral Intelligence.*"

> —**James Garbarino**, author, *Lost Boys: Why Our Sons Turn Violent and How We Can Save Them*

"Every reader of this book is sure to have an ah-ha! moment and rediscover the simple joys of parenting."

> —**Peggy Fleming Jenkins**, 1968 Olympic champion and ABC sports commentator

"Michele Borba articulates the core traits that build and promote responsible citizenship among the young and old alike. Her book is a must-read for parents, educators, and community leaders."

> —**Ronald D. Stephens**, executive director, National School Safety Center

"A must-read, user-friendly collection of stories, facts, and practical suggestions that will help parents who want their children to become competent, confident, and contributing adults."

> —**Jane Bluestein**, author, *Parents, Teens and Boundaries* and *The Parent's Little Book of Lists: Dos and Don'ts of Effective Parenting*

"Michele Borba has done it again—she's written another must-have, must-read book! I highly recommend this book to anyone who cares about kids."

> —**Hanoch McCarty**, coeditor, *A 4th Course of Chicken Soup for the Soul®* and coauthor, *Acts of Kindness*

THE BIG BOOK OF
PARENTING
SOLUTIONS

THE BIG BOOK OF PARENTING SOLUTIONS

101 Answers to Your Everyday Challenges and Wildest Worries

Michele Borba, Ed.D.

JOSSEY-BASS
A Wiley Imprint
www.josseybass.com

Published by Jossey-Bass
A Wiley Imprint
989 Market Street, San Francisco, CA 94103-1741—www.josseybass.com

Jossey-Bass books and products are available through most bookstores. To contact Jossey-Bass directly call our Customer Care Department within the U.S. at 800-956-7739, outside the U.S. at 317-572-3986, or fax 317-572-4002.

Jossey-Bass also publishes its books in a variety of electronic formats. Some content that appears in print may not be available in electronic books.

Library of Congress Cataloging-in-Publication Data

Borba, Michele.
 The big book of parenting solutions : 101 answers to your everyday
challenges and wildest worries / Michele Borba.—1st ed.
    p. cm.
 Includes bibliographical references and index.
 ISBN 978-0-7879-8831-9 (pbk.)
 1. Child rearing. 2. Parenting. I. Title.
 HQ769.B652 2009
 649'.1—dc22

                                        2009017415

Printed in the United States of America
FIRST EDITION
PB Printing   10 9 8 7 6 5 4 3 2 1

Contents

101 Tough Problems Parents Face and How to Deal with Them

Part 1 **Family   1**

Part 2 Behavior 45

Part 3 Character 139

Part 4 **Emotions** 231

Part 5 **Social Scene** 313

Part 6   **School**   423

Part 7   **Special Needs**   465

Part 8   **Day to Day**   **531**

Part 9   **Electronics**   **597**

With love to my father, Daniel Ungaro, who instilled in me the love of writing and research, and the belief that a misbehaving child is discouraged and really needs a caring adult to show a different way

Note to the Reader

All the examples in this book are based on cases of children and their families with whom I have worked over the last years or gathered from my actual observations. A few stories are composite cases of children I have treated. All e-mails are personal queries received in my iVillage blog, Parenting Solutions, or posted on my Web site, micheleborba.com. I also presented many of these solutions in over seventy parenting segments as contributor for NBC's *Today* show.

As the mother of three boys, I have a natural tendency to overuse the male gender in my examples, so in the interests of maintaining a reasonable gender balance throughout the book, I have somewhat arbitrarily alternated the gender between topics, boy-girl, boy-girl. However, some issues—such as cliques and video gaming—do tend to be gender specific; these circumstances obviate against a strict alternation of the genders within each part of the book. Overall, however, the number of entries using the male gender is equal to the number using the female.

Acknowledgments

Countless people have helped shape my writing and philosophy and the scope of my work in child development over the past few decades. I could never have written this book without their help. I'm sure many are not even aware of just how great their influence has been. To all I extend profound appreciation. In particular . . .

To the dozens of teachers and administrators who allowed me the privilege of conducting research at their school sites to analyze the effectiveness of implementing these ideas with their students. I am grateful to each and every one of them for so honestly sharing their concerns and successes with me.

To the publishing staff at Jossey-Bass—having the good fortune to produce seven books with this dedicated group is a true privilege. To Alan Rinzler, executive editor extraordinaire and friend: wise, meticulous, and always ready with support. Words can't express my gratitude for having him as an editor for seven of my books. To some of the finest publishing staff around, who clearly made this book far better: Jennifer Wenzel, marketing manager; Nana Twumasi, editorial assistant; Erik Thrasher, marketing director; Carol Hartland, production editor; and Mike Onorato and Lori Sayde-Mehrtens, Wiley publicists. In particular, I thank Debra Hunter, the president of Jossey-Bass, and Paul Foster, the publisher, for their faithful support and the privilege of writing for them over these many years together. And to Michele Jones, the world's most meticulous and competent copyeditor. Thank you. I could not have finished the process without you.

To Joelle DelBourgo, my agent, for her stellar competence and for lending an ear at always just the right time. Believe me, every writer should have this woman in her corner.

To the folks at NBC's *Today* show, in particular Jim Bell, executive producer, and Marc Victor, senior producer, for the honor of working with the NBC family. To producers Rainy Farrell, Antoinette Machiaverna, Debbie Kosofsky, and Jaclyn Levin for their support and for suggesting many of these challenges as segments. And especially to Dana Haller for producing over fifty of my segments, constantly stretching me to find real solutions and always an absolute joy to work with.

To the iVillage staff—both past and present—including Diane Randall Jones, Sheila O'Malley, Christian Martin, and Betsy Alexander. Most especially I thank Pat Sandora for his constant support and always "being there" behind every e-mail.

To Diane Debrovner, senior editor of *Parents* magazine, for ongoing support but also for helping me develop and conduct the *Parents* magazine "Joys of Motherhood Survey." Those results are what really planted the seeds for this book. To Dana Point, editor in chief, and to all the *Parents* editors for the privilege of speaking with so many of your great writers about these topics and the honor of serving on your advisory board.

To Anne Leedom, founder of Net Connect Publicity and Parentingbookmark.com, for her incredible publicity skills, eternal optimism, and steadfast friendship; and to Steve Leedom, founder of digitalmindmedia.com and my Web designer, for having such a gift for putting my vision onto paper and always making it far better than what I could ever imagine. To Dottie DeHart, of DeHart and Company, for teaching me everything I needed to know to survive media and publicity hurdles and being such a great pal who never ceases to give me unending encouragement.

To the numerous researchers, therapists, and educators whose work has contributed enormously to my philosophy about child development over the years. In particular I thank a few individuals who offered valuable insights about their expertise during conversations—though they probably aren't aware of just how much they helped me formulate my own beliefs. Thanks go to David Fassler (stress), Gay Norton Edelman ("accessory parenting" and tweens), Barbara Turvett (motherhood and maintaining balance), Sally Talala (Autism Spectrum Disorder), Jerry Perez (creative play and "benign codependency"), Marilyn Lane and Sheryl Deeds (gifted), Tom Lickona (character development), Tamar Chansky (negative thinking patterns), Kenneth Ginsburg (redefining success), Peter Scharf (Kohlberg and morality), Harold Koplewicz (depression), Deborah Roedder John (materialism and self-esteem), Thomas Armstrong (multiple intelligences and ADHD), Caryl Miller (secondary parenting), Linda Acredolo (early child development), Michael Gurian (gender), Eric Staub (empathy), Michael Vitelli (electronic gaming), Parry Aftab (cyberbullying), Bobbi Conner (play and creativity), Marvin Berkowitz (moral reasoning), the folks at the Thompson Child and Family Focus (adoption and attachment disorder), Phil Vincent (parenting), and especially Hal Urban, teacher extraordinaire, friend, and the voice of reason when it comes to book titles. All these folks are not only great thinkers but also fabulous cheerleaders who have helped me get through this writing process far better than they know. Your work has been a godsend to children and of extraordinary help to me. I only hope I've done it justice.

And to my family, who have really made the difference in my life. To my husband and best friend, Craig, for his unending support and love through every phase of my life—but particularly this project; to my parents, Dan and Treva Ungaro, for epitomizing that miraculous concept, "unconditional love"; to my mother-in-law, Lorayne Borba, for her continual encouragement and optimism; to my darling daughter-in-law, Tiffany; and to the true joys of my life: my three great sons, Jason, Adam, and Zach, for keeping me so grounded in reality and for the constant love and fun they have brought to my life.

During the time I was writing this book, my son Jason was deployed to Iraq. The experience affected my parenting like no other, as I'm sure is the case for so many other mothers and fathers of sons and daughters who serve. Profound gratitude to Lucille

Alosi, Murf Ryan, Tom Lickona, and Hal Urban for their unending support and prayers (they worked!) and to Ester Khubyar, an extraordinary woman who I chanced to meet for no more than three minutes and who became my guardian angel, helping me get through those days with her astonishing acts of kindness. Finally, to the incredible guys of the 187th 3rd platoon: bless you, thank you, and stay safe.

Introduction

From June Cleaver to Desperate Housewives— How Did We Get Ourselves into This Mess?

Your six-year-old and his pal are playing the video game Conker's Bad Fur Day about a cute little squirrel. Your kid begged for it, so you gave in. But now you're horrified: the sweet little squirrel is getting drunk at a bar, throwing up, and then blacking out, swearing profusely all the while.

The pediatrician begins, "I'm concerned that your daughter is anorexic." This must be a mistake, you think. She's only eight, but deep down you know the doctor is only confirming what you've suspected for some time.

Your twelve-year-old barrels into the kitchen. "Sorry I'm late, Mom," she begins. "Some eighth grader threatened to kill the teachers because he flunked a test. And he even had a gun! Can you imagine?" No, you can't imagine at all.

Ah, the joys of raising our next generation! Frankly, I can't imagine any other job that is more challenging and rewarding, frustrating and joyous than parenting. It's perhaps the most significant role we'll ever have (we're talking about raising a human being, for Pete's sake) and also the only one that doesn't require a single credential. And it's the kind of job that you can finally sort of figure out how to do right—by the time you're done. From the everyday challenges like getting your kids to brush their teeth, say "please," or make their beds, to the more worrisome issues, such as drinking, sexual promiscuity, or eating disorders, raising kids has never been easy. But many people feel that it has gotten harder over the last few years.

In a recent poll, 76 percent of the respondents said they felt that parenting is getting much tougher and that it is far more difficult to parent now than when they grew up. You probably won't get an argument with most folks on that one, but here is a statistic of greater concern: about 60 percent of adults also feel that today's parents are not measuring up to the standards set just a generation ago.[1] In fact, most Americans feel that moms are doing *a far worse* job than their own mothers did just twenty or thirty years ago. (If I haven't hit a nerve so far, this next one should do it.) What's more, the majority of moms and dads today agree with their low performance ratings and feel that they've been unsuccessful in their parenting endeavors.[2]

But the situation gets even more troubling: many parents confess that they aren't even enjoying their kids! One-third of the parents in one survey said that if they were to do it all over again, they would *not* start a family.[3] For the past few decades, I have watched this troubling parenting trend unfold, and I have to tell you that I'm greatly concerned about the state of the American family.

I've spent my professional life in the field of child development, and all those varied experiences helped form my beliefs. I earned a doctorate in educational counseling and psychology and a master's degree in learning disabilities. I have taught emotionally and physically challenged kids and kids with learning disabilities; I have also taught gifted and talented students, and briefly had a private practice for troubled kids. I've worked as a consultant in hundreds of schools and organizations around the globe, spoken to thousands of parents at workshops, personally worked with scores of kids, wrote a number of parenting books, and raised three great sons (spoken like a proud mom and by far my best training). Through those years, I focused on infants through tweens.

Then I became a contributor to NBC's *Today* show, and I suddenly gained a whole new perspective that dramatically stretched my views. The topics I was asked to report on often dealt with tough, news-breaking issues facing adolescents, such as depression, stress, sex, and risky teen behaviors. Preparing for each segment (over seventy at this point) allowed me an incredible opportunity to comb stacks of new research. What I saw was a very troubling trend in the lives of American kids: they were having problems coping, bouncing back, and handling life—particularly as they left home and had to fend for themselves.

One segment confirmed it all. I was on the *Today* set with Meredith Viera. It was December, and students who had finished their first college semester were coming home for the Christmas and New Year's break. I was there to warn parents that new research showed that more than 50 percent of freshman college students felt so depressed that it was difficult for them to function.[4] Suicide rates were soaring—in just that one year alone, there was a 114 percent spike among adolescents, girls in particular. Counselors predicted many freshmen would never graduate because their mental health needs were so severe. Ironically this was the same group that experts said had the closest relationship with their parents: much loved, indulged, coddled, and unable to deal with life independently.

That was my "aha" moment: how these young people had been parented hadn't done them any favors. Each additional *Today* segment I did showed the same troubling trends: stress rising, risky behaviors increasing, peer pressure and bullying skyrocketing. Something was amiss in American Kidsville. But it turned out that parents' weren't fairing well either.

NBC asked me to be a parenting contributor for the iVillage online community and write a blog called Dr. Borba's Parenting Solutions. I've since posted dozens of articles and also received scores of e-mails from moms seeking advice. But there was a clearly discernible difference between these queries and those I had received in the past. These mothers were more stressed and worried—even overwhelmed. They were trying so hard.

Wanting so for their kids to be happy and successful. Their love and intentions were there, but they were also *doing* so much for their kids that they were forgetting to take care of themselves.

What I saw over and over was a lack of confidence in their mothering. These moms were always second-guessing themselves and seemed to spend a lot of time comparing themselves and their kids with other moms. Around the same time, I reported results from a *Parenting* magazine survey on the *Today* show, and it was déjà vu. In that survey, 96 percent of mothers admitted feeling stressed; 73 percent felt that yesterday's moms had it easier; and 67 percent felt that yesterday's mothers were happier.[5]

Don't get me wrong: we clearly are doing some things right. For starters, today's children are smarter. Their IQ scores are even increasing.[6] (Really!) All those extra tutors and pricey extracurricular activities seem to be paying off (by the way, American kids are now the most scheduled in the world[7]), but at a stiff price. By all benchmarks, today's children are sadder;[8] more materialistic,[9] narcissistic,[10] anxious,[11] stressed,[12] disrespectful,[13] and ill behaved; and poorly prepared to cope with life.[14] And that's just for starters.

Deep down I think most parents realize that their kids aren't turning out as well as they'd dreamed. It's a big reason why many feel so darn guilty and stressed out and are just not enjoying their family life. It's also why so many lack confidence in their job performance and are turning to others for reassurance and pointers on parenting. (We'll get to those a bit later.) But for now let's explore how we got ourselves into such a sorry state—what's causing the breakdown of our children's mental health, behavior, and character, and the rise of our own stress, the lack of confidence in our parenting abilities, and our unhappiness in our role.

THE PROBLEMS WITH MOST MODERN-DAY PARENTING APPROACHES

Over the last few decades, there has been a major change in how we raise our kids, and the descriptions of modern-day parenting are far from flattering. Try these for starters: helicopter parenting, incubator parenting, snowplowing, paranoid parenting, hyperparenting, and accessory parenting. I can't help but envision kids on their knees praying for someone to stop the insanity. In just a matter of a few decades, we've morphed ourselves from Marion Cunningham of *Happy Days* to characters in *Desperate Housewives*. No wonder Judith Warner called modern motherhood "perfect madness."[15]

In all fairness, our more frantic, super-octane-charged mode is at least partly due to today's culture. June Cleaver or Carol Brady didn't have to deal with such hair-raising issues as cyberbullying, school shootings, online predators, and Facebook when they raised their broods. Nor would Clair Huxtable or Laura Petrie have read any parenting book including such serious issues as school-age children's eating disorders, depression, and worrying about the world. But let's get beyond the culture for a minute, because that isn't the only thing that has changed. We're also raising our kids differently, and our new approaches aren't doing them any favors. In fact, many of these approaches contradict over fifty years of solid research that shows what kids really do need for solid character, emotional health, and fulfillment. Several modern-day child-rearing approaches are so toxic to effective parenting that I call them the Seven Deadly Parenting Styles. I am convinced that using them is a big part of why we're so darn dissatisfied, stressed out, and lacking confidence in our parenting.

THE SEVEN DEADLY PARENTING STYLES

Take a minute to review each style and be brutally honest. Might any of these be what you're using as a parenting approach? If so, here is a crucial point to know: *before you can change your child, you must first change how you respond to your child.* Might your parenting approach need altering first?

Deadly Style 1: Helicopter Parenting

Hovering over your kids, hurrying to smooth every one of life's bumps

It's a bird . . . it's a plane . . . it's a helicopter parent![16] These parents constantly hover, and stop at next to nothing when it concerns their kids. They finish their homework, do and redo those science projects, and make sure their kids have every advantage. After all, they've invested too much energy into parenting; nothing should stand in the way of their kids' success. And if it does, watch out. Helicopter parents go into Black Hawk mode, swooping in for the rescue and solving each and every problem.

But all that parental involvement can backfire. This style can keep kids in a perpetual state of dependency through adulthood, leaving them unprepared to handle the many curve balls that life is sure to throw at them. If you've always been rescued or micromanaged, you may have had too little practice in developing such critical life skills as self-reliance, decision making, and problem solving. It's why large numbers of "copter kids" often suffer from what has been called "problem-solving deficit disorder"[17] and have trouble developing confidence in their own capabilities and coping out there in the real world.

The Change to Parent For   Learn to be involved but not intrusive in your child's life so that she develops a healthy sense of independence and can cope someday without you.

Deadly Style 2: Incubator "Hothouse" Parenting

Pushing your kids into learning earlier than appropriate for their cognitive age and developmental level

There's nothing new about parents wanting their children to excel, but these days their quest is all about raising the Superkid (aka "a mentally superior child").[18] Hothouse parents start in early: piping classical music into the nursery, using flash cards and Baby Einstein tapes (which have *no* proven value) to prepare their infant for reading, giving violin lessons to toddlers, and enrolling kindergartners in chess classes. Forget what developmental guidelines, based on years of scientific observation, recommend as suitable to your child's age and stage. Time is of the essence, so these parents push, push, push, all so their kids will (they hope) achieve, achieve, achieve.

A part of this push is the current standard of "success" determined by a portfolio of numbers, and these days there is no child left untested. From preschool admission tests to LSATs—it's making us crazy worrying that our kids aren't going to be good enough. So there's no time for play. It's all about tutoring (which is now a billion-dollar industry), using educational toys (another billion-dollar industry), doing extra "mind-building" activities, and studying. But we're seeing an impact from this parenting style that isn't pretty.

Kid stress, anxiety, and perfectionism have never been higher; their honesty quotients, never lower. Kid cheating is now of epidemic proportions, all because we've pushed character and developmental appropriateness out of our child-rearing formula.

The Change to Parent For   Learn to appreciate your child's natural talents and abilities, and fit your parenting to your child's developmental stage.

Deadly Style 3: (Quick-Fix) Band-Aid Parenting

Relying on fast solutions to temporarily fix a problem instead aiming for real, lasting change

We're tired. We're harried. We're short on time, and we're trying to make ends meet. We need everything to be easy and quick, including our approach to discipline. We'll do anything to get our kids to act right—as long as it'll work *right now.* So we use that "1-2-3 Method" ("That's warning one . . . warning two . . . warning three") to head off a tantrum, buy those fancy behavior charts, promise our kid a new Lexus if he's good, and even give out pills. Seriously.

Experts warn that this pill-popping craze is a big reason that the use of drugs designed to curb hyperactivity have tripled since 1993.[19] It's just easier to give the pill than to teach kids a new way to behave, eh? Now don't get me wrong. I'm a former special education teacher, and I bless the pharmaceutical industry. There are some kids who do need prescribed medication to help them control their impulses. My concern is about those times when we rely on this Band-Aid approach really just to make life easier for ourselves. Let's just admit it.

Besides, these quick-fix strategies only teach kids to act right based on warnings, rewards, or pills. Effective discipline *always* is instructive and helps the child learn how to right his wrong. A quick-fix style may bring temporary relief, but almost never creates real, lasting change, which is why many of our kids keep relapsing back to those same bad behaviors and we end up more exhausted and discouraged.

The Change to Parent For   Learn that the most effective way to discipline is always to take a few minutes to help your child understand what was wrong and how to make things right.

Deadly Style 4: Buddy Parenting

Placing popularity with your child above establishing limits and boundaries or saying no

Nearly half of parents today admit that deep down they want to be their "child's best friend,"[20] and there sure is no bigger friendship ender than saying no. We can't stand the idea of making an unpopular decision, turning our kids down, or (heaven forbid) disciplining our kids if doing so might cause them to resent us in any way.

And it appears that our kids have our number. One survey of grade school kids found that when they crave something new, most expect to ask nine times before their parents give in.[21] Of course we want our kids to like us—and someday they will become our friends. Right now they need a parent who sets rules and boundaries and doesn't blur the line between buddy and adult. Besides, the truth is that our inability to turn our kids down isn't helping them grow to be secure, responsible, resilient, and compassionate. Instead, it is creating what most adults believe is the most spoiled and ill-behaved generation ever. Over 80 percent of adults think kids today are more spoiled than kids were just ten or fifteen years ago.[22]

The Change to Parent For   Learn to set clear boundaries and firm limits, take back your control, and realize that what your child needs most is a parent and not a friend.

Deadly Style 5: Accessory Parenting

Measuring your worth and success as a parent on the basis of your child's accolades

Forget healthy and well adjusted—over the past two decades, what has taken precedence is spawning the "perfect" child whom we can proudly show off. And thus dawned the era of the Trophy Kid Syndrome. Every little accomplishment, test score, or hockey goal suddenly became bragging rights, and oh, how parents using this style love sharing those accolades. Just in case anyone missed hearing about little Buford's latest achievement, refrigerators are always plastered with all his achievements, certificates, and gold star papers. The newest trophy—among thousands—is sure to be displayed proudly on the mantel.

Showing them off is all part of the style, as every new trophy and recently earned award is a direct reflection of how well the child has been parented. And a child's success is a living representation of a parent's own worth.

Gay Norton Edelman, senior editor of *Family Circle,* aptly termed this style "accessory parenting." All is fine and dandy if a parent can share something meritorious to the rest of the world or at least with the neighbor next door. ("Susie is in the gifted program, you know." "Can you believe it? Keithy made captain *again.*") But if the child fails or receives a less than perfect score, it can only mean that the parent somehow flunked. This style of parenting is really about making our children an extension of our own wants, needs, and dreams. It fuels excessive competitiveness among parents and creates enormous guilt and stress if we feel that our kids aren't measuring up, leaving our kids feeling as though they've let us down. If the accessory parenting style continues, the child's identity is threatened, and an unhealthy codependency emerges, with both parent and kid depending on each other for their sense of self-worth.

The Change to Parent For   Learn to see your child as a unique individual separate from yourself, and tailor your parenting to her own special traits, talents, and needs.

Deadly Style 6: Paranoid Parenting

Obsessively keeping your child safe from any physical or psychological harm

Keeping kids safe is always a top parent priority, but these days there is a heightened fear of letting our kids out of our sight for even a nanosecond. The best name for this over-the-top always worried style is *paranoid parenting.*[23] Of course, turning into a nervous wreck isn't hard when we're constantly reminded of dangers looming everywhere and threatening our children's safety and well-being. Kidnappers. Terrorism. School shootings. Sex predators. Cyberbullying. Online pedophiles. Tainted food. Lead-painted toys.

It's scary out there, so we rein our kids in a little tighter. We watch them closer and we protect far more—and sometimes to the extreme.

"Don't do that! You could get hurt!" "Don't talk to strangers!" "Don't go too far!"

We provide our kindergartners with those new cell phones lined with sweet Disney characters "just in case they're snatched by a child molester." We install webcams in our homes so we can peek in to ensure that our children aren't being abused by the nanny. We purchase kid jackets embedded with GPS trackers and hand sanitizers to keep them germ free. We even think about buying those backpacks lined with a bulletproof plate that protects against gunfire (designed by a couple of very concerned dads).[24]

But constantly fretting about dangers that "might" happen only breeds fear into kids. In fact, the more we tighten our safety net, the more obsessed we become and the more anxious and less confident our kids turn out. Is it any wonder that today's kids are more anxious than any other generation?[25]

The Change to Parent For   Learn to relax a bit more, realize when you're being too protective so that your child learns to face life, and handle your own worries so that you don't pass your fears to your child.

Deadly Style 7: Secondary Parenting

Relinquishing your influence such that your children's world is controlled more by outsiders, including corporations, marketers, and the media[26]

In case you haven't noticed, today's kids are media driven. Computers. Wii. You-Tube. Video games. TV. Facebook. iPods. DVDs. Cell phones. It's no wonder they're called the plugged-in generation. Many kids spend more time involved with media than with anything else but sleeping.[27] Research shows that 99 percent of boys and 94 percent of girls ages twelve to seventeen play computer, Web, portable, or console games.[28]

Television viewing has increased by more than an hour a day from just five years ago. Considering that almost two-thirds of all eight- to eighteen-year-olds have a TV in their bedroom, that's an easy accomplishment.[29] Even two- to seven-year-olds are putting in an average of about three hours per day of "screen time."[30] Children are especially vulnerable because they believe what they see. And make no mistake: they are bombarded with an incessant parade of images—of sex, alcohol use, violence, vulgarity, and commercialism—that are pushing them to grow up too fast too soon.

But there's another danger: all that "plugged-in" time means less face-to-face time with us. Once we take a "secondary" role in our child's eyes, we begin to lose our power, and the prevailing culture becomes our substitute. Your child becomes more vulnerable to outside pressures; he is more likely to rely on someone other than you to guide him, and more likely to adopt others' values.

The Change to Parent For   Realize that you are the most powerful influence in guiding your child's values, attitudes, and behavior as well as in protecting him against risky behaviors; intentionally find ways to stay more involved in your child's life.

SO HOW DO WE CHANGE?

We've made parenting much too hard. We've gotten ourselves further away from solid, basic parenting, throwing out the core principles of effective parenting established by more than fifty years of research in the child development field. We began relying on what everyone else thought and less and less on our own instincts. Our quick-fix endeavors only fueled those annoying behaviors. One thing is clear: staying stuck in our present "autoparent" mode won't do our kids or ourselves any favors.

It's time that we change. Take back parenting. Use our instincts. Roll up our sleeves and dig in. No more quick fixes: let's take on one issue at a time and turn things around until we get the change we want in our kids. For the sake of ourselves and our families . . . it's time.

GEARING UP FOR REAL AND LASTING CHANGE

> "My four-year-old's tantrums are nuclear. Time-outs work at the moment, but a few hours later he has another meltdown. How do I stop these exorcisms once and for all?"

> "My daughter is such a pessimist. Is there a way to change her attitude so she has a more positive view about life instead of such a doom-and-gloom mentality?"

> "My son's teacher says he has ADHD and should be on Ritalin. Is there anything we can do to help him without pills?"

> "Mealtime is a nightmare because my daughter is such a picky eater that I'm worried she'll develop an eating disorder. How do I help her develop healthier eating habits?"

Did you ever think child rearing could be so darn difficult? If you're feeling a tad bit confused or even at your wit's end about your kid's behavior, believe me: you're not alone. I receive dozens of e-mails every week from parents asking for help.

"When should I worry?" "Is my child's behavior normal?" "Nothing works!" "He just keeps doing the same thing!" "What am I doing wrong?"

It isn't as if you haven't tried finding ways to stop those annoying behaviors, implement strong values, and teach your kids to "Just say no!" You've bought every parent book off the shelf and checked countless others from the library. You've read dozens of online articles (which are certainly ample these days; I just Googled the word *parenting* and got 84,300,000 hits in 0.16 seconds). You've talked to your pediatrician and almost (well next to almost) had the courage to ask your mother-in-law. You've sought out those experts but are even more confused—each one gives you a different approach. You've tried all those cute solutions that your girlfriends swear work for her kid, but they don't work for yours.

Despite your efforts, there is no change. Oh sure, the time-out or that newest discipline fad may have curbed your kid's annoying behavior at the moment, but the following day, that same old bad behavior returns.

Why? Well, the reason is that you really didn't parent for *change*—real, lasting, permanent change. After all, your parenting goal is to help your children learn to act right, behave, develop healthy lifestyle choices, and make wise decisions on their own someday. The problem is that most parenting manuals these days aim for the quick fix. All those books and articles give lots of tips and advice, but they fall short in that their approach doesn't show you how to parent so that the problem is replaced with a new and improved behavior or attitude *and doesn't return*. Now that's a different approach to parenting. And that's really what we want for our kids. Right?

My goal is to help you parent for that lasting change you want in your child. That's a big part of how this book is different from any other parenting manual. This book provides step-by-step strategies based on proven scientific findings as to how to make that desired change a reality. No more hiring an outside therapist or parent coach to do so. I'll guide you through the steps. I'll ask you questions to help you figure out what's really going on with your child. I'll give you emergency intervention strategies as well as more effective responses for you to try. I'll warn you when you should worry and tell you when it is time to get outside help. I'll also provide new habits to teach your child that will replace her current inappropriate behavior or attitude.

I'll be your personal coach in helping you take on that parenting challenge that concerns you right now. Your job is to commit to making that change, be willing to alter your current response and adopt a more effective one, and hang in there with me. But above all, what I want you to do is use your instinct and common sense about what really will work best for your child. And if you do, here's what I guarantee: a changed child and a more confident and satisfied parent—you! So let's get started.

ANSWERS TO COMMON QUESTIONS ABOUT PARENTING FOR CHANGE

I've provided all the tools you need to help you deal with the top 101 contemporary child-rearing challenges. All these strategies are based on sound psychological principles and proven scientific research. I'll show you step-by-step how to achieve the change you want.

Before we begin, however, here are answers to a few of the most common questions you may have as you parent for the change you desire for your child:

When can I begin using the strategies for change in this book?

This book is designed to be used immediately. In fact, as soon as you finish reading this Introduction, you'll have everything you need to start parenting for change.

I know you don't have time to wade through pages of child development theory about problems that don't concern your child at this moment. So don't read about issues that don't apply to your situation or child. Instead, refer to the table of contents and identify the challenge that concerns you now. Then flip to those pages, where you will find step-by-step strategies and solutions that tell you what to do and how to make that change happen. Not only will this approach save you time by focusing on only one issue at a time, but you'll be more likely to succeed with the goal you set for yourself.

How were the 101 parenting challenges in the book selected?

I wanted to ensure that the topics addressed parents' most pressing concerns, so I used a variety of sources. I combed the contents of leading parenting magazines, especially *Parents,* as I'm on their advisory board, which helps me stay current with upcoming features. I asked five thousand parents in workshops in twenty-five cities to write their top concerns. I sifted through dozens of e-mails sent to my Web site and iVillage blog, and I also reviewed my *Today* show segments over the past two years because they are based on late-breaking news. The 101 top-ranked parenting challenges from those sources became the contents of this book.

Will these strategies work for all kids?

The strategies are especially designed for children three to thirteen years of age and will work for all genders, races, religions, and cultures. I know so because I've tested these strategies with parents on four different continents, from Hutterite colonies, Lutheran ministries, and Native American longhouses to Catholic schools, Jewish synagogues, and Muslim charter schools. Even so, keep this rule in mind: effective parenting is always tailored to a child's specific needs and stage of development, so feel free to alter any strategy to fit your kid.

What if I can't find the challenge or problem I want to change in my child?

Although there are 101 issues, you may not find your particular challenge, so look in the table of contents to find the issue most similar to your concern. For instance, if you want to curb interrupting, you can go to Demanding for insights and techniques. You can flip to more than one issue to find helpful strategies. For example, if your child is hitting, try Angry and Biting. Each issue also provides recommendations to refer to other challenges elsewhere in the book as sources of additional strategies. Let's suppose you wanted to help your child with her shyness. Go to the contents and find Shy. Once you've turned to that entry, you will see that Rejected, Sensitive, Stressed, and Teased are recommended for review.

Do I have to use all the solutions for each issue to see change?

I've intentionally listed more solutions than you'll need in order to parent for the desired change. So select only those strategies you feel will work best for your child. If the problem is new or not severe, focus on strategies listed in the first step, Early Intervention. Strategies in the second step, Rapid Response, are designed to help you change a more entrenched issue or one that needs immediate intervention. The final step of change, Develop Habits for Change, provides strategies that teach more appropriate behaviors or habits to replace the inappropriate behaviors or attitudes. Be sure to teach your child at least one replacement. Without teaching a new habit (or replacement), you'll find that your child generally reverts to the old behavior, and you're back where you started from.

How many challenges can I take on at a time?

I strongly recommend that you take on only one—but no more than two—challenges (or areas needing improvement) at a time. You'll be able to put more energy into the change instead of spreading yourself in too many different directions. You'll also be more likely to reap positive gains because you are more focused on what really needs altering.

How do I know how big of a change I should take on?

It's critical that you set expectations that are both realistic and attainable for your child. Unrealistic goals overwhelm kids, creating only frustration and tears. So identify what needs changing, then ask yourself one critical question: *What was my child capable of doing yesterday?* For a picky eater, that may be tasting one tiny portion of a vegetable. For an impulsive kid, it may be doing homework without help for only five minutes. Next think in terms of "one step more," then aim your expectations accordingly. For example, help your picky eater by giving her just two tiny vegetable portions, or have your impulsive child do homework without your help for six minutes. The trick is to break expectations into smaller, more manageable chunks so that your child can succeed, then gently stretch your expectations to fit his capabilities. Imagining a rubber band may help: just *stretch* your child gently toward that new positive change without *snapping* her spirit!

Should I tell other caregivers about the plan?

Absolutely! The more that caregivers are on the same page with your change plan, generally the easier and faster the change. So always seek the counsel or support of spouses, partners, immediate and extended family, and all those other adults who care about your child (such as teachers, coaches, relatives, babysitters, day-care workers), even if the person sees your child just a few minutes a day. That doesn't mean you have to divulge your plans to the rest of the world, but if you can get at least one person to reinforce your endeavors, there is a greater likelihood that you will succeed.

Why doesn't punishment make my child want to change?

Punishment usually only stops the inappropriate action in the moment, but doesn't help the child learn what to do differently. Real change requires that a child understand what's wrong; why it's worth the effort to adopt a new approach, action, or lifestyle; and what to do as a replacement. Further, the child needs opportunities to practice the new behavior or belief and be reinforced for good efforts until he finally adopts the change for good.

Is it okay to use rewards or stickers to get my child to try harder?

If you think your child will respond to rewards or a sticker chart, then go for it. Some kids need a little jump-start to get started on the road to change. The trick is in knowing when to stop doling out monetary rewards, stickers, or prizes; you don't want your child to learn to rely on them to act right or even to expect you to up the ante. Wean your child of tangible reinforcements as soon as she no longer needs them. Keep in mind that research shows that smiles, hugs, and verbal praise work just as well—and often are even more effective—in changing a child's behavior.

Why does my child work so hard not to change?

Let's face it: it's just easier for all of us to do what we're used to doing. Change isn't easy and can even be a bit scary. Learning a new behavior or adopting a new attitude pushes us out of our comfort zone into unknown territory. It's easy to revert to our old, more comfortable ways. So you should expect your child to test you to see if you are really serious about your new approach. But habits, behaviors, and attitudes *are* changeable—so hang in there. A big part of change is not just teaching a new habit but also helping your child "see herself" in the new image. The former image may remind her of that same "old" kid who was afraid, who was a bad sport, or who lies (or whatever behavior you're trying to change).

How long will it take to see the desired change?

A general rule is that the longer a child uses an inappropriate behavior or attitude, the harder it is to change (which is why you always want to nip those bad behaviors in the bud). But each issue is different, just as each child is different. You may be surprised to see that some issues are much easier and faster to "fix" than others. The key is not to give up until you see the desired change.

Why don't the strategies work the same for each of my kids?

The plain truth is that strategies, discipline, and parenting responses that worked for one child often won't work for another—even if your kids are identical twins. That's because when it comes to raising kids, nature as well as your nurturing matters, so all those factors like temperament, genetics, and even learning styles enter into the picture. It's why your oldest might need only to see you raise your eyebrows and know that enough is enough, whereas your middle child may require a lot more reinforcement and stern reminders to get his act together. A big part of parenting for change is to figure out the response that works best for each child. Once you figure that out, you've struck gold—you've discovered the secret of effective parenting.

How do I know when I've succeeded in making the change?

When your child can finally use the new skill, lifestyle, habit, attitude, or behavior in real life, you know you have succeeded. She'll no longer need an adult to guide or reinforce the desired change. You'll also find that you no longer have to put so much energy into reminding or correcting your child. Your child's self-image will also change. He'll notice the change in himself. "I'm not biting so much." "I'm not afraid of the dark." "Don't worry. I know how to be a good sport now if I strike out." Once your child adopts a change, you may be in store for an added surprise and see additional positive transformation in your child. There is some truth to that old saying, "Success begets success."

What if I don't get the desired change?

Change usually comes in little spurts. So don't assume that change isn't happening just because you don't get instant results (which are quite rare, believe me). But you should see a gradual reduction of the inappropriate behavior or slow adoption of the new belief. If you don't see that gradual change, then here are a few factors to consider that might be standing in your way:

> Are your expectations realistic for your child?
>
> Are you consistent with your new response?
>
> Are you delivering the new response in a cool and calm way?
>
> Are you teaching a new habit to replace your child's inappropriate response?
>
> Are you providing opportunities for your child to practice that new response so that she feels comfortable using it?
>
> Are you reinforcing your child's efforts and giving at least five positive comments to every negative comment?
>
> Are other important caregivers on board with you or reinforcing your efforts?
>
> Are other factors (for example, depression, illness, stress, trauma, learning disabilities) contributing to the problem?

If you suspect that something more serious might be going on with your child (for instance, depression, stress, an eating disorder), please seek the advice of a trained professional. Usually the longer you wait, the more serious the problem becomes and the more difficult it is to turn around. The longer you allow the problem to continue, the more serious the damage to your child's self-esteem and the more family harmony is destroyed. Get help!

JUST ONE REMINDER: DON'T FORGET TO USE YOUR COMMON SENSE

Here is a recent letter I received from a distraught mom. Humor me: read the note and play child psychologist for a minute. What advice would you give Mom?

> *All my two-year-old wants to do is play in the cat litter box. I tell him no. I give him time-out. I try distracting him. I spank him. Nothing works and I'm at my wit's end! How do I stop my kid from playing in the cat litter box?*

If you said, "Move the cat litter box," you win. If you thought this was a trick question, not at all. It's the exact same answer I gave the mother. Just a simple solution that certainly didn't need any expert advice. No discipline. No new parent response. No new skill to teach. No new parenting book to read. No need to hire a parent coach. Just move the darn box! But I can't tell you how many queries I get from distraught parents about problems that require only basic common sense. And it seems that Using Your Common Sense is the one strategy in our parenting toolbox that we forget to use.

And remember, no one knows your child better than you do. My mother's own parenting guru, Dr. Benjamin Spock, years ago offered this timeless advice that we should tape on our bathroom mirrors:

> *Trust yourself. You know more than you think you do.*[31]

I couldn't agree more!

HOW TO GET A NEW KID—AND STILL KEEP THE ONE YOU HAVE

The Secrets for Parenting for Real and Lasting Change

> *I hate to admit this, but our kid is driving us crazy. We've tried just about every parenting technique, and they work for a little while, but sooner or later we're back where we started with the same annoying behaviors. We've thought about putting him for sale on e-Bay, but the truth is we love him to death. Please help! What's the secret to really changing behavior?*
>
> —SUSAN AND RICK, FRUSTRATED PARENTS
> OF A MUCH-LOVED EIGHT-YEAR-OLD

If you haven't figured this one out, here's the update: *kids don't come with a return policy.* And parenting really is a life sentence. You'd be a rare mom or dad if you couldn't admit that there isn't at least a day or two that you'd like to put your kid up for auction.

Then reality sets in when you realize there's nobody who would take the kid. Let's face it: you're stuck with this critter who may be causing you a few sleepless nights due to his latest antics. But come on—this the same kid you also love more than life itself. So the real question is this: How do you get a new kid without turning in the one you have?

I learned these basic principles of change in my doctoral studies in psychology. But it was when I was a special education teacher dealing with students with behavioral and emotional needs that I knew the principles worked. The school psychologists warned me that these kids were "hopeless." "You'll never change them," they said. But I found otherwise. The trick was in tailoring a plan and strategies to the child's needs and applying the ten basic principles I'm going to describe next. The change process always took time, but if I hung in there, used the right response, and didn't give up, change happened. I continued to refine my methods and began teaching them at workshops to parents and educators. To date I've shared them with over a million participants on four continents. All the strategies and proven techniques you need for the top 101 parenting challenges are in this book. And all are based on the latest scientific findings, easy to use, and tried and true.

Ten Principles of Change You Need to Know

Here are the ten most important principles about change you need to know to help your child:

1. *Most behaviors and attitudes are learned.* Granted, some behaviors may be influenced by biological factors, but most are learned. Our children learn those behaviors, attitudes, and habits from what we teach them about the world and from their experiences. Although there are some things we *can't* change (such as our child's personality and physical characteristics), we can teach new behaviors and habits and values and skills so that our child can handle her world and deal with the genetic hand she was dealt. For instance, the shy kid can learn social skills to become more confident in groups; the aggressive kid can learn anger management skills; the impulsive kid can learn skills and techniques to stop and think before he acts.

2. *Most behavior can be changed.* Because behaviors and attitudes *are* learned, they can be changed. Most can be changed by using proven, research-based techniques.

3. *Most behaviors need intervention.* Don't expect your kid to change on his own. His behavior will most likely only get worse without your intervention. Also, don't think poor behavior is "just a phase that he'll outgrow." You're just providing more time for your kid's bad behavior to become a habit. And then it will be even tougher to change. That's why the first step of every change in this manual is called Early Intervention. That first step can help you nip the problem before it becomes a habit.

4. *Change agents must alter their response.* You must be willing to use a more effective way of responding so as to produce the desired change. After all, what you're currently doing isn't working, right? An important change formula is "Change yourself so you can change your child." I'll give you effective new responses, but you must commit to using them and change your current interaction. By doing so you'll also be less likely to just *react*; instead, you will respond more effectively. Your child is more likely to change if in responding you

   - *Stay calm.* Be cool and calm in your tone and posture.

   - *Be respectful.* Start requests with "Please." When your child complies say, "Thank you."

   - *Get in close proximity.* Being physically closer to your child increases the likelihood that he will comply. So move closer to your child. Get down to eye level when you make a request.

   - *Be direct.* Explain what you want in a clear and direct way, and then expect nothing less than full compliance.

   - *Model.* Your child is watching you. Model the behavior you want her to copy.

   - *Be consistent.* Use the new response everywhere and everywhere.

5. *You are more likely to succeed if you target one change at a time.* Don't overwhelm yourself or your child by trying to change too many behaviors at once. Instead focus your energy on only one challenge at a time. That way you can develop a much more specific behavior plan to eliminate the bad behavior.

6. *Identifying the desired change is essential.* Most parents have no problem naming what they want to stop, but to achieve change you must also identify what behavior you *want instead.* Usually the desired change is for the child to be doing the exact opposite of what he is currently doing. The behavioral term for that is the "positive reverse." Only when you identify the positive reverse will you be able to create a plan to turn things around. Use the "Goldilocks Question" to help you identify the positive reverse: "What is my child using *too* much?" (The problem: a whiny voice.) Next ask: "What is my child doing *too little or not enough*?" (The desired change or positive reverse to aim for: "Using a more respectful tone.")

7. *Every unacceptable behavior needs a replacement.* For every desired change, always think: "If my child is to stop doing one behavior, what will she do instead?" No behavior or attitude will change unless you teach another behavior, skill, or habit to replace the current, inappropriate one. Without this step, chances are that the child will revert to using the old misbehavior, and no change will take place.

8. *Children need to rehearse the new behavior.* Learning any new behavior takes practice. And rehearsing or practicing the new skill, behavior, or attitude enough

times is what makes real change possible. The goal is for your child to be able to use the replacement confidently in real life without your help. Psychologists call that principle "reinforced practice," and it is a crucial step for change. Science shows that if the new replacement behavior is repeated enough, it actually rewires a child's brain such that she is far less likely to revert back to the troublesome former behavior.[32]

9. *You need to reinforce the right action.* Research shows that giving kids the right kind of praise (called "positive reinforcement") is one of the best ways to shape new behavior. Science also shows that parents are more likely to point out the negative behavior they don't want. Result: no change. So catch your kid doing the action you want. Just make sure your praise is *specific* and tells your child *exactly* what she did right. (Adding "because" or "that" takes your praise up a notch. "I'm so impressed that you started your homework all by yourself this time.") Research also proves that kids don't need all those fancy and pricey rewards to change. They do need acknowledgment for their efforts.

10. *The Rule of 21 will keep you on course.* Change takes time. Don't expect your thirty-minute Saturday night lecture to make more than a dent in your kid's behavior on Sunday. Give yourself and your child time to make that change really happen. Learning new habits usually takes a minimum of twenty-one days of repetition. A big parenting mistake is not sticking to a behavior plan long enough. So whatever change you want, commit to your plan for *at least twenty-one days.*

Above all, here's the most important principle to know: research proves that it's *never too late to change.* Even if the problem has been going on for a long time, don't despair—and never give up. Help is on the way. Small, temporary changes in what you do can have lasting effects in changing your child's behavior at home and at school.[33]

So you have everything you need to know. It's time to turn back to the table of contents, find the first challenge you want to take on, turn to that page, and take the first step toward real change.

The *Parents* Magazine
"Joys of Motherhood Survey"

What Mothers Really Feel and Their Advice to Help Us Raise the Next Generation

For the past several years, I've been on the board of advisers for *Parents* magazine and worked with their superb editors and writers. (My actual relationship started much earlier when I read those magazines cover to cover as a new mom.) While in the process of writing this book, I had an enlightening talk with Diane Debrovner, *Parents*' health and psychology editor, who graciously offered to connect me with the magazine's research department. For the next weeks, its team helped me develop questions that became the *Parents* magazine "Joys of Motherhood Survey."[1] I hoped the results would help me understand what moms feel are the joys and challenges of parenting today as well as gather their advice to other mothers.

The survey was conducted online over a two-week period among readers of *Parents* and *American Baby*. In all, 2,140 mothers responded and shared their views about parenting.

Those responses confirmed my other research findings, specifically:

- Today's moms are stressed, and they feel that parenting is more difficult than in the past.

- They're frustrated about the conflicting advice they receive from experts.

- They use books, magazines, and online sources to get their parenting advice.

Here is a sample of the most interesting findings from the "Joys of Motherhood Survey."

Qualities Moms Want Most in Their Child

Moms were asked to rate the importance of ten traits they'd like their child to possess. It is no surprise that *healthy* and *happy* are foremost, but what is interesting is that more moms rated *secure, caring, confident,* and *moral* as "very important" than they did *smart*.

Here are the ten traits, in the order of the percentage of moms who rated them as very important:

Trait	Percentage
Healthy	98
Happy	97
Secure	95
Caring	94
Confident	94
Moral	91
Resilient	66
Smart	65
Social	61
Spiritual	52

Where Moms Seek Advice

When a problem arises, moms say their best sources for advice are "parenting books and magazines" (23 percent) and their own mom (22 percent). The next best sources are "pediatrician, nurse or other health professional" and other moms. Baby and parenting magazines are also cited as the resource moms would not want to live without. Conversely, topping the list of "worst" sources for advice is their mother-in-law. (Some things never change.)

Using New Child-Rearing Research

Eight in ten say they are very (14 percent) or somewhat likely (69 percent) to pay attention to the latest research about raising babies. More than half (55 percent) admit feeling frustrated sometimes because different sources of parenting information contradict each other.

Motherhood Stress

The majority of mothers feel that being a mother is more difficult today than when their mother raised them. More than three-quarters (81 percent) agree that today's moms are too concerned about how their baby compares to other babies. Half feel that parenting today has gotten away from the basics of the natural mother-and-child relationship (48 percent), and they admit to feeling stressed during baby's first year to do all the right things to make baby smart (47 percent).

Motherhood Experience

Respondents were asked to choose one of six movie titles based on which one best characterized their past or present experience of day-to-day life as a mom of a baby one year or younger. Their responses follow, in the order of the percentage of moms who chose them. As you review them, reflect on your present parenting experience. Which title would you pick?

Movie Title	Percentage
It's a Wonderful Life (confident in my mothering)	46
Sleepless in Seattle (exhausted most of the time, never get enough sleep)	37
Guilty as Charged (always guilty or worried I'm not doing the right things)	16
Titanic (feeling completely overwhelmed)	6
Mommy Dearest (depressed or emotional)	3
Clueless (lacking confidence, always asking others for advice)	2

"What One Tip or Piece of Advice Would Have Helped You Become a Better Mom?"

I received pages and pages filled with comments that were remarkably similar. Whether the moms were younger or older, college educated or not, married or single, working or stay-at-home, suburban or urban, their top piece of advice is this: *use your instincts and stop relying on everyone else.* It seems that somewhere in those child-rearing years between cradle and prom, too many parents lose some of their confidence and joyful notions about parenting. Here are other pearls of wisdom offered by these moms:

It's okay not to know everything.

Be patient and slow down.

Ask for help when you need it.

Listen to your "Mommy Voice" . . . that instinct that calls to you when you know something is wrong with your child.

Treasure every moment you have with your children. It goes by fast!

Each child is different. So let them guide you.

Relax! Don't stress the little stuff!

Get to know your child as an individual.

Balance your priorities.

Let your child develop at his or her own pace.

Take each day at a time.

Roll with the punches and keep an upbeat outlook on everything.

Nothing is more important than being a mom. Everything else can wait!

Don't lose sight of the joy in mothering!

Simple, powerful, right on, and the exact advice we need most in raising our next generation. It's also how to bring back the joy in mothering and help our kids turn out the way we want most: healthy, happy, secure, confident, caring, and moral. So gear up. It's time to parent for real and lasting change for your child and family.

THE BIG BOOK OF
PARENTING
SOLUTIONS

Part 1
Family

**OUT OF THE MOUTHS OF BABES
WHY GOD MADE MOMS**

Answers given by second-grade schoolchildren to the following question:

Why did God make mothers?

1. She's the only one who knows where the scotch tape is.

2. Mostly to clean the house.

3. To help us out of there when we were getting born.

Adopted

SEE ALSO: *Angry, Communicating, Depressed, Fearful, Grief, Homesick, Stressed*

THE PROBLEM
Red Flags

Feelings of loss or abandonment by the birth parent, shame and humiliation about unknown origins of birth and early life, emptiness; inadequate sense of identification with adopted family, extended family, and community; feelings of competition and of always being a loser with any natural birth siblings or extended family kids; fears of being thrown out and abandoned by adopted family

The Change to Parent For

Your adopted child feels secure, loved, and attached to his new family. He may ultimately be curious about his birth family, but he remains connected to his adopted family as well.

Why Change?

Each year some 120,000 children are adopted in the United States. Recently about 40,000 children in one hundred countries have replaced domestic adoptions due to a shortage of local adoptees. The latest news shows that the vast majority of adopted children are doing just fine, thank you. One big reason is that adopting parents are a special breed. Research finds that most are highly motivated, better educated, and better off financially than parents who do not adopt. They are also more likely to get help from mental health professionals for their adopted child when behavioral problems arise.[1] But there are unique challenges in parenting an adopted child. The most serious of those issues have nothing to do with when the child comes into your home but rather what happened before his adoption. Genetic factors, the health and habits of the biological parents, and any trauma the child may have experienced can affect mental health. That's why the more knowledgeable you are, the better prepared you'll be in making the right decisions for your child. Although not born of your flesh, this child is definitely born of your labor of love.

LATE-BREAKING NEWS

Minneapolis: One of the largest studies of adoption, "Growing Up Adopted," was conducted by the Search Institute.[2] The study included more than 880 adolescents who were adopted as infants, and found that most developed psychological well-being that was about equal to that of twelve- to eighteen-year-olds who were not adopted. What's more, 55 percent of the adopted teens reported high self-esteem and self-understanding compared with 45 percent of the nonadopted teens. Their acceptance of their adoption was reflected in their response to the question, "Which of the four different ways young people might feel about adopted is most like you?"

- "Being adopted has always been easy for me": 68 percent
- "Being adopted used to be hard for me, but now it's easier": 15 percent
- "Being adopted used to be easier for me, but now it's harder": 12 percent
- "Being adopted has always been hard for me": 5 percent

This research should put your mind a bit more at ease if you've ever had that gnawing concern as to how adoptees turn out.

THE SOLUTION

Seven Strategies for Change

1. *Know the law.* The process of adoption can be difficult and confusing at best, so it's critical that you become knowledgeable about laws and regulations to prevent any heartache down the road. Some determined parents who want to adopt kids bump into obstacles and then try to ignore or circumvent domestic and international laws. Those laws will vary depending on the original place of birth; the sex, health, and age of the child; and whether you are pursuing a public agency adoption, foster care adoption, independent adoption, or international adoption. Gather as much information as you can about laws, regulations, guidelines, required training, documentation interviews, home visits, the time frame for the process, and the cost. For information, seek out the National Council for Adoption.

2. *Gather as much history as possible.* The more you know about your child's past history, the better you'll be able to handle potential behavior, education, or medical problems. Try to find out these details, with the understanding that data may be sketchy or lost:

Child's history. Instances of early trauma or child abuse; contacts for all previous placements; an older adopted child's social, developmental, medical, behavioral, psychological, and educational history.

Previous placements. Foster parents and sibling names and addresses; an older child's temperament, interests, activities, concerns, and fears, as well as what soothes him and helps him cope. Ask questions of every agency and demand as much data from previous homes as you can access.

Birth parents. Medical information: alcohol, drug addiction, sexually transmitted diseases, possible genetic liabilities, or lack of prenatal care; cultural, religious, medical, genetic, and social background or anything else that you think your child may one day want to know.

3. *Talk about adoption from the beginning.* The general thinking is that parents should tell their child about his adoption early on. Here are a few principles to use in talking to kids about adoption.

- *Start early.* Begin using the term "adoption" during your child's early toddler and preschool years to help you feel at ease. Just look for natural ways to bring up the topic, such as mentioning a friend who is considering adoption, or a book, TV show, or movie about adoption. Your child always needs to hear this information from you in a context of approval, love, and commitment.

- *Create an open-door policy.* Peter L. Benson, lead researcher of one of the largest studies on adoptees, says that "Quiet, open communication about adoption between adopted kids and their parents seems to be the key" to helping kids thrive and take their adoption in stride.[3] Your child needs to know he can come to you in ease and comfort with any question and at any time.

- *Be honest.* Never hide the fact that your child is adopted or cover up the tougher parts about your child's "past life." Doing so can create serious trust issues between you and your child when the truth comes out later.

- *Stick to what has been asked.* Although you should be honest, only give your child what he needs to know at the time. Too much information is overwhelming. Leaving out certain facts due to the age of your child is okay. Use words and language that are suitable to your child's age and ability to understand.

- *Use literature.* Books are a great way to discuss adoption with your child. Here are a few tailored to different ages.

  Preschooler: *Tell Me Again About the Night I Was Born,* by Jamie Lee Curtis; *The Day We Met You,* by Phoebe Koehler

  School age: *A Place in My Heart,* by Mary Grossnickle; *How Families Are Made and How Kids Feel About It,* by Marc Nemiroff and Jane Annunziata; *My Adopted Child,* by Kevin Leman and Kevin Leman II

Tween: *It Happened to Me: Adopted: The Ultimate Teen Guide,* by Suzanne Buckingham Slade; *Today I Was Adopted,* by Yvonne Drew; *All About Adoption: How It Feels to Be Adopted,* by Jill Krementz; *Maybe Days: A Book for Children in Foster Care,* by Jennifer Wilgocki and Marcia Kahn Wright

- *Be reassuring.* The central fear of adopted children is that they will be "given up" again. Your child needs assurance—both now and forever—that your relationship is permanent. Reassure your child that his feelings (whatever they may be) and quest for information about his past are normal and that you will do whatever you can to fill in those details.

- *Keep an ongoing dialogue.* Kids grasp the concept of adoption in gradual stages over time. Be prepared to repeat an explanation as your child's understanding evolves. Be patient and answer what he asks each and every time as though your child has asked for the first time. Most teens who have adjusted to their adopted status say they report two or fewer conversations about their adoption with either parent in the past year, but feel comfortable talking with parents about such issues.[4]

4. *Watch for attachment problems.* Strong emotional bonds between child and parent are crucial for healthy psychological development, but especially for adoptees. Early adoption (at least before the age of six months) is usually easiest.[5] Your child may have been exposed to trauma during his early years that could curtail healthy attachment. New studies reveal how early infant-caregiver interactions affect brain development and a child's future neurological, physical, emotional, behavioral, cognitive, and social development. Familiarize yourself with the work of Daniel Siegel, Stanley Greenspan, Daniel Stern, or Bruce Perry; read *Ghosts from the Nursery,* by Robin Karr-Morse and Meredith S. Wiley; contact the adoption agency for information; or seek out the Association for the Treatment and Training in the Attachment of Children (ATTACh.org). If you have any problems bonding, get help immediately. You will need highly specialized and proven advice so that you can provide the best help for your child.

5. *Keep some things secret.* Painful details about your child's past (such as sexual and physical abuse, a parent's criminal background, the birth mother's alcoholism or drug addiction, or that the pregnancy was caused by rape) should be kept confidential. Besides you and your parenting partner, only the child's doctor or mental health professional needs to know those details for now. If anyone asks, simply say, "When Devon is old enough, he can choose to share about his past. We have all the information we need." Then say no more and protect your child. You also do not need to address those issues with your child until he is old enough to understand. A few resources to help you prepare for discussion of more difficult topics with adoptees are *Making Sense of Adoption,* by Lois Ruskai Melina; *Great Answers to Difficult Questions About Adoption: What Children Need to Know,* by Fanny Cohen

Herlem; and *Telling the Truth to Your Adopted or Foster Child,* by Betsy Keefer and Jayne E. Schooler.

6. *Make it normal!* All kids have the same basic needs: to feel safe, loved, and accepted. The last thing they want is to feel "different." So never introduce your child as anything other than a member of your family. Don't say "He's our adopted child" or "He's from China," regardless of how different he looks from you or his siblings. I'd also caution against your using such terms as "our chosen child" or "the special one" as well. The terms may make your child feel as though he stands apart from your family or that he always has to somehow measure up to your expectations.

7. *Help your child work through emotional issues.* Your adopted child may feel abandoned because a birth parent gave him up, angry at the parent who deserted him, or responsible for what he perceives as causing past pain, though it probably was not the case. Those negative feelings might materialize any time (often at the anniversary of the adoption or at other significant events) despite all your love and effective parenting. Know that your child will ultimately ask about his birth parents at some point. One study found that 70 percent of adopted girl teens and 57 percent of adopted boys admit that they'd like to meet their birth parents (though the majority said they "seldom or never wished to actually live with their birth parents").[6] Don't take your child's desire personally. It doesn't mean that he doesn't love you or want to keep living with you. Express empathy for your child's quest to discover his identity and be prepared with a loving and supportive response. An adopted child's feeling of loss is a serious issue that often needs to be resolved. If this is the case for your child, seek the help of a certified mental health professional—particularly one trained in adoption issues.

Pay Attention to This!

University of Minnesota: Margaret Keyes, a University of Minnesota research psychologist, led a first-of-its-kind study of 692 adolescents who had been adopted before age two, conducting in-depth psychological interviews.[7] Researchers found that "Most adoptees are doing fine" and are just as psychologically healthy as kids the same age who are not adopted. The study did report that adoptees are at a "slightly increased risk" for behavioral problems, such as Attention-Deficit/ Hyperactivity Disorder (ADHD) or Oppositional Defiant Disorder (ODD). But the youths were found to have no increased risk for depression, anxiety, or any form of serious delinquency that involves aggression and vandalism.

WHAT TO EXPECT BY STAGES AND AGES

Research at Rutgers University found that all kids develop a gradual understanding of adoption in these predictable stages.[8]

Preschooler Preschoolers don't have the ability to distinguish between being adopted or born into a family or comprehend "blood ties." They are usually quite accepting of adopted status, especially if adopted at infancy. They may seem to understand more about adoption than they actually do; when they explain how they joined your family, they tend merely to paraphrase your explanation no matter how many times it is explained.

School Age Understanding of adopting slowly evolves as children now begin to understand conception and how children join a family. By age six, most kids can distinguish between birth and adoption. By age eight, they begin to have a notion of "blood ties" and how adoption differs from other relationships, though they still don't grasp the legal system, so they may think the biological parent could possibly reclaim them.

Tween The paramount concern of this age group is for peer acceptance, so adopted kids may perceive themselves as "different" and worry how peers view their adopted status. At ages nine to eleven, a common fear is of losing parents; because adopted children have already experienced this loss, they worry that it could happen again. The realization hits them that someone gave them up, so adopted kids at this age may experience symptoms similar to, though usually not as severe as, grief. (See *Grief*, p. 255.) Ten- and eleven-year-olds begin to understand the legal system that makes adoption (and relationship with you) permanent.

One Parent's Answer

A dad from Charlotte shares:

Our son was eleven and had lived in five foster homes when we adopted him. It was hard enough for Jake to keep his previous families straight, but next to impossible for my wife and me. But knowing our son's past life and the trauma he had endured was essential if we were to understand him. We began piecing together major chronological events and milestones in an album. We gathered photos and mementos, such as a lock of hair, report card, or ticket stubs, and if pictures of a family weren't available—as often was the case—we substituted with graphics, such as maps showing the town or hand-drawn pictures of his past foster family. When Jake saw how serious we were, he got involved and began dictating missing pieces of his childhood. The more we learned about our child's troubled past, the more our love grew. Reliving some of troubling memories has been tough on Jake, but the process helped him recognized that he finally has a family who loves him for keeps.

NOTE: For more information, refer to *Lifebooks: Creating a Treasure for the Adopted Child*, by Beth O'Malley, or go to www.adoptionlifebooks.com.

Divorce

SEE ALSO: *Angry, Communicating, Depressed, Grief, Sibling Rivalry, Stressed*

THE PROBLEM
Red Flags

Feelings of anger, betrayal, guilt, abandonment, immense sadness

The Change to Parent For

Your child learns that her feelings are normal, understands how divorce will affect her, and develops skills to cope with a new major life change *in her family.*

Question: "I am a divorced dad of three kids ages four, eight, and twelve. I have custody every weekend, but how can I stay involved in their lives on the days I'm not there?"

Answer: Research shows that ongoing positive involvement is the best way to help kids adjust to a divorce.[9] In fact, children of divorced families with fathers who assist with homework, provide emotional support, and listen to their kids' problems have more positive academic achievement and fewer behavioral problems.[10]

Why Change?

One of the most stressful events in a child's life is the news that Mom and Dad are divorcing—only the death of a parent is ranked higher. Even so, a *Parenting* magazine survey found that 81 percent of parents believe that an unhappy couple should not wait until their child is a certain age before getting a divorce.[11] Almost 40 percent of all kids are exposed to parental divorce before reaching the age of eighteen.[12] What impact it will have on those children depends on many factors, including their age and gender (adolescents and boys seem to suffer the most); the presence of other disruptions, such as changes in home or school; the degree to which they were brought into the conflict; the quality of the relationship they had with each parent; their temperament; and the intensity of parental conflict before and after the divorce.[13]

I'm not going to tell you whether you should stay together or split up. Those are adult decisions that you need to weigh carefully. My concern is solely with how your children cope, and that should be your foremost concern as well. There's no doubt that this is going to be a rough ride for your kids, but how you and your ex talk to your kids before, during, and after the breakup will have a lot to do with how they fare both today and tomorrow. This entry offers some of the most well proven solutions to help your children cope and significantly reduce the negative effects of divorce.

Signs and Symptoms

Although each kid responds differently, here are common symptoms to expect:

- *Anger:* defiance, uncooperativeness, refusal to comply, short fuse, impulsivity
- *Shame:* embarrassment about the divorce, embarrassment about being seen with you
- *Anxiety:* stress, tension, trouble sleeping, nightmares
- *Altered peer interaction:* withdrawal from peers, more conflict, retreat to the home of the peer
- *Diminished self-care:* poor grooming, excessive disorder in a formerly neat bedroom, poor hygiene
- *Dependence:* clinginess, refusal to let you out of sight, regression
- *Academic problems:* trouble in school, decline in work or grades, trouble focusing
- *Parent-child conflict:* breakdown of your relationship, blaming or criticism of one parent
- *Altered life view:* discontent, feelings of betrayal, rejection, cynicism about the institution of marriage
- *Low self-esteem:* feelings of worthlessness, comments about being stupid or unimportant
- *Sadness:* profound sense of loss, frequent crying or sobbing, depression

Pay Attention to This!

If your child's excessive sadness or anger lingers beyond three weeks or affects other areas of her life, such as school, peer relations, or other family relationships; if she develops sleeping or eating problems, appears depressed, becomes oppositional or defiant, develops irrational fears or compulsive behaviors, or starts to engage in risky behaviors—call for help. This is a tough time for all of you, and there are trained professionals who can guide you as well as provide strategies for reopening communication and helping children cope. Get help if you think you need it.

THE SOLUTION

Step 1. Early Intervention

- *Get a handle on your life.* The best predictor of how kids cope with the stress of a divorce is the way their parents handle it. Your child will be watching you closely to see how you cope these next few days, weeks, and months—especially when things get tough. Eat a balanced diet, exercise to relieve stress, build a support group for yourself, and if you need counseling to help you get through this, get it. The more you take care of yourself, the better you'll be able to take care of your child.

- *Get a reality check.* Research has yielded remarkably different results on how kids fare, so there is no predicting how your children will respond. Go into this fully aware that a family breakup will impact your kids emotionally. Read about the effects of divorce (refer to the More Helpful Advice box). Seek the advice of trained professionals. Base your decisions only on sound knowledge so that you can help your children cope with the negative short- and long-term effects.

- *Keep your kids as your main focus.* Do whatever you can to avoid arguing in front of your kids. Conflicts and bickering are a big reason why divorce is so difficult on kids.[14] Take a pledge—even if it's one-sided—that you will not bad-mouth your child's other parent. That doesn't mean you have to fake an unrealistic picture of the other parent. It just means that you stick to the facts and leave your judgments behind. Also, do not use your child to be your messenger to convey your financial woes or problems to your ex. Stay civil! Whatever your feelings about your ex, he or she is your child's parent.

- *Plan the time and place to tell your kids.* Once you make a decision to separate or divorce, schedule a time to tell your kids shortly before they will notice the change. Don't wait until the papers are about to be signed. Plan with the other parent what to say. This information should come from both of you, with all kids present so they hear it at the same time.

- *Anticipate concerns.* Take time to predict your child's concerns—no matter how trivial—so that you can provide answers when you announce your decision. It will help reduce some of your child's anxiety about this major change. Here are typical concerns that need solutions:

  Living: Where will I (Mom, Dad, siblings) live? Will I have two separate places, one with Mom and one with Dad? Do we have to move? Do I have to take sides? Do I have to go to court? Can I see Dad? Can I talk to Mom?

  Siblings: Will we be together? Does that mean I have to have my new step-mom's kids for my sisters?

Holidays: Will we be together for holidays or my birthday? Whose house do I go to?

School: Will I go to a new school? How will you take me? When will I start? Who signs my report cards and goes to the parent conference? Who does the teacher call?

Pets: Can I keep my pets? Where will they live? Can I see them every day?

Care: Who takes care of me when I'm sick? Who will feed me and get my clothes?

Activities: Can I still do my activities (go to summer camp, be on the soccer team)? How will I get to my piano lessons or practice?

Peers: Will I still get to see my friends? How will I tell them? Will they accept me?

Parents: Will I have a new dad? Is that woman going to move into our house?

- *Connect with grandparents.* A famous twenty-five-year study of children of divorce found that a key factor that helped them fare better before, during, and after the family breakup was their grandparents' support and stability.[15] Bring your kids' grandparents up-to-date on what is happening. Stress that you need their help for the sake of your children.

- *Be really clear about where your child will be sleeping at each of your homes.* Setting up safe and comfortable living places in the primary and also part-time parent's home is so important. Be sure to have some familiar furniture (a bedside light, a stuffed chair) or drawing on the wall, a beloved pillow, toys, or a stuffed animal in *both* homes so that your kid feels cozy and familiar. With older kids, be sure both homes have a place for books, schoolwork, sporting equipment, musical instruments—whatever is necessary.

Step 2. Rapid Response

- *Calmly announce your intention.* Set aside time for a family meeting when it is most convenient for everyone (not when your child has to cancel a game or someone has to dash off). Eliminate interruptions: take the phone off the hook, turn off the television, put a "please don't interrupt" sign on the door. Your children deserve to hear that you are separating or getting a divorce in a calm, uninterrupted manner tailored to their developmental level. Here are a few openers for each age:

Preschooler: "Mommy and Daddy are going to live in different houses. We love you very much and will help you get through this together."

School age: "Mom and Dad have spent a long time thinking about what is best for our family. We decided that we can no longer stay married and live together."

Tween: "As you know, your dad and I have not been getting along and are not happy together. We've tried going to a marriage counselor to help us, but it just hasn't worked. We have decided to divorce and live separately."

Kids do not need to know details about finances, legal matters, or extramarital affairs. And make sure your child does not overhear phone conversations about these matters either.

- *Stay unified.* If possible, talk as a unified front. Your ideal is to keep the emphasis on "we." *"There is something we need to tell you." "We will always be there for you." "We love you very much." "Your family will always be your family even though we will not all be living under the same roof."* Stress that although the two of you cannot live together, your love for your children will never change, and both of you will remain in their lives forever as their parents. It helps if you take turns in your talk, each of you covering one or two points of information. If your child gets upset, both of you comfort her. If your child runs to his room, both of you go to him. The message kids need most is that they will be able to maintain a quality relationship with each parent and that they still have your unconditional love.

- *Give essential information.* The goal is not to overwhelm your child with too much information. Doing so will be confusing, especially for a younger child. Kids want to know the essentials: what will happen and the changes they should expect. Be forthcoming and tailor the facts to their level. By the end of the talk, your kids should know the following:

  Why you made this decision and why you think it is the best choice. Hint: When a child asks, "Why?" it usually means "Why is this happening to me?"

  When the separation or move or divorce will take place.

  Where everyone will be living, particularly the parent who is leaving.

  Who each child will live with and who is responsible for each part of her day (who will make her breakfast, tuck her into bed, take her to school).

  How they will see or connect with the other parent and under what circumstances.

- *Ask to hear their concerns or fears.* Take any questions seriously, regardless of how trivial they might seem, and answer each and every query in a matter-of-fact tone. Some kids ask the same question repeatedly as a way to process what they are hearing; others might not ask anything. Let your kids know that their feelings will be taken seriously: "I know you feel sad [lonely, afraid], but we will get through this."

- *Reassure them that they are not to blame.* Beware that children often assume that they or a sibling are to blame for your breakup, especially if one child's behavior was a point of contention: "If Mike behaved better, Mom and Dad wouldn't fight." "They were always unhappy because of me." "If I got better grades, they would be happier." Be very clear that they were not responsible for the separation and that there is nothing they can do to "fix" things. You may have to repeatedly assure your kids that your decision is not about them.

- *Be prepared for any reaction.* If there have been problems in your marriage, your disclosure may come as no surprise, but it may also be a shock. Some kids are relieved that the fighting will be over; others will do anything to keep their family together. Stress that you know this is a sad occasion and understand how they feel, but that you struggled quite a while trying to make things work, and there is just no other option. If they need a breather, allow time for them to calm down. If your children get angry, stay calm and don't yell. It does no good.

- *Explain the difference between separation and divorce.* If you are separating and haven't made a decision to divorce, tell your children you're taking a break to work on your relationship. Don't use the word "divorce" unless you and your spouse are absolutely certain. Then explain that you don't know what's going to happen, but that you'll keep them informed as soon as you know. If you have decided to divorce, then in a gentle but matter-of-fact way, explain that your decision is final and you will not be getting back together again.

- *Give time to adjust.* Explain that you will plan to meet again as a family to continue discussing the changes and deal with their concerns. Emphasize that they should come to either of you at any time with any questions. Over the next few days in particular, be available and offer a lot of attention and reassurance. Watch closely how each child copes.

- *Contact immediate caregivers.* Talk with the teacher, babysitter, day-care worker, counselor, coach, or any other significant caregivers in your children's life so that they are in the loop. These next few weeks can be difficult, so ask them to keep you apprised of any behavior or emotional changes that they may spot and to offer support to your kids.

One Parent's Answer

A dad from Reno shares:

I had custody of my son, but he blamed me for the breakup of our marriage even though his mother had an affair and left us both for her new relationship. I swore I wouldn't tell him the truth and ruin his image of her. He refused to speak with me for weeks, but every day I left a note on his pillow saying how much I loved him. One day I found him sobbing and sitting on the floor with a small box on his lap. He was reading all my notes that he'd saved in that box. I never even knew he even read them. I grabbed onto him and we sat and cried together. He said he always thought he caused his mom to want to leave him and caused the divorce. I'm just so grateful I never stopped writing those notes. I always tell everyone who is going through a divorce to do whatever it takes to stay connected with your child and never give up!

Step 3. Develop Habits for Change

- *Emphasize continuity.* There can be many changes involved in the breakup of a family, including new living arrangements, school, or neighborhood, so the trick is to help your kids see that although everyone may not be living together, most day-to-day things will be the same. Stick to your regular eating, homework, and bedtime schedule. Help your child maintain friendships and continue participating in her favorite activities. Keep those special family traditions like Sunday dinners with Grandma, going out for yogurt on Wednesdays, and hanging up the birthday flag. Assure your child that the turmoil will be temporary, that all the kinks will be resolved as best you can, and that daily life will go on.

- *Offer choices.* A divorce or separation leaves kids feeling powerless, so help them gain some semblance of control. Listen to what they consider important, and give them options (that you consider acceptable), but don't allow the choices to disrupt routines or your child's well-being. Examples might include choice of food or clothing, visitation days, bedspread color, or where the dog sleeps.

- *Stay connected.* Here are ways to keep in touch on noncustodial days:

  - Give your younger child something to keep in her pocket so that whenever she touches it, she knows you're thinking of her.

  - Record yourself reading her favorite bedtime story so she can listen each night.

  - Leave notes in your eight-year-old's backpack, wishing her luck at practice or school; put the notes in individual envelopes marked with the date that your child should open each one.

  - Leave messages on your tween's cell, or learn to text so that you can communicate by text message 24/7.

  - Give your kids a video camera and teach them how to use it so that they can video their school events or practices to share.

  - Show them how to scan artwork and e-mail it to you.

  - Tell them to fax troubling homework assignments or set up webcams on your computers so that you can talk face-to-face.

  - Be sure that both places they live have everything they need for comfort and uninterrupted social, educational, athletic, or musical activities—whatever they're into.

- *Create positive new family memories.* Try to work in time for regular family fun—doing inexpensive things as a group that you can look forward to doing together. It will help your kids adjust to the new living arrangement, break tension, and create positive memories. The family can suggest and vote on each upcoming event (going to a museum or movie) or rotate turns so that each member chooses (a younger child may want to bake cookies or play Chutes and Ladders; an older kid may choose to go bike riding or watch a video). A longitudinal study found that children from divorced families rarely talk about their fun childhood times, but instead recount feelings of sadness, loneliness, or preoccupation with the logistics of driving from one home to another for holidays.[16] Build in time for fun family memories!

- *Help work through their emotions calmly.* A majority of kids view a divorce as the "most devastating event of their childhoods, if not their lives" and say it generates a range of painful emotions—sadness, confusion, anger, guilt, and shame.[17] Those raw emotions can easily turn discussions into yelling matches and destroy family relationships. So help your kids find healthy ways to release negative feelings. Start by acknowledging that your child is understandably upset and that it's important for her to tell you she's frustrated, angry, sad, or resentful. Listen and remain nonjudgmental. But also state clear talking boundaries: kids may describe their feelings and concerns but not criticize family members. Create a hand sign for "time out," to be used when discussions get too tense, giving participants permission to walk away and come back when they're calm. And above all, you need to stay calm to help your children stay calm. If things get too tense, seek the help of a counselor trained in communication skills to help you and your kids.

- *Use children's literature.* Kids are sometimes more apt to talk about their feelings and concerns if they hear a story about someone going through a similar ordeal. Here are books about divorce you can use for kids at different stages and ages:

  Preschooler: *Dinosaurs Divorce: A Guide for Changing Families,* by Laurene Krasney Brown and Marc Brown; *Two Homes,* by Claire Masurel; *It's Not Your Fault, KoKo Bear: A Read-Together Book for Parents and Young Children During Divorce,* by Vicky Lansky

  School age: *Kids' Divorce Workbook: A Practical Guide That Helps Kids Understand Divorce Happens to the Nicest Kids,* by Michael S. Prokop; *How Do I Feel About: My Parents' Divorce,* by Julia Cole; *I Don't Want to Talk About It,* by Jeanie Franz Ransom; *The Divorce Helpbook for Kids,* by Cynthia MacGregor; *What Can I Do? A Book for Children,* by Danielle Lowry; *Where Am I Sleeping Tonight? A Story of Divorce,* by Carol Gordon Ekster

  Tween: *Divorce Is Not the End of the World: Zoe and Evan's Coping Guide for Kids,* by Zoe Stern, Evan Stern, and Ellen Sue Stern; *Pre-Teen Pressures: Divorce,* by Debra Goldentyer; *What in the World Do You Do When Your Parents Divorce? A Survival Guide for Kids,* by Kent Winchester and Roberta Beyer

- *Keep communication open.* Find a way to keep a dialogue going with your kids even if they are defiant or if they blame you or do not want talk. One mother said she and her daughter wrote to each other in a diary until their relationship reopened. Another mom learned to text so that she could leave short messages on her son's cell; one dad left notes in his son's backpack. If things get too tough, enlist the help of a family counselor or mediator. The Sandcastles Program, developed by marriage counselor M. Gary Neuman, is a onetime group session for kids six to seventeen that helps them express feelings about their divorce. Parents are included in the last half hour. Look for trained counselors in the Sandcastles Program in your area.

- *Emphasize stability.* A long-term study involving hundreds of kids found that although a stable family situation after divorce does not erase all the negative effects of divorce, it is the core aspect that helps kids adjust.[18] Make sure that regardless of what happened prior to your divorce or separation, your current home environment is a place of warmth, structure, and consistency. As much as you'd like to make things easier, don't let your kids off the hook for inappropriate behavior. Also, buying them things to alleviate your guilt or to "make them feel better" will backfire. You're better off giving them your attention and love. Keep up the same discipline and enforce the same rules; stay on the same page with your ex if at all possible. The American Psychological Association combed dozens of studies and found that key factors that contribute to healthier adjust-

LATE-BREAKING NEWS

Kids in Joint Custody—Either Physical or Legal—Fare Best

American Psychological Association: Robert Bauserman, a psychologist in Maryland's Department of Health and Hygiene, analyzed thirty-three studies involving almost three thousand families and discovered that children in joint custody arrangements were as well adjusted as those kids raised in intact families.[19] Bauserman pointed out that children do not necessarily need to be in joint custody to show better adjustment; sharing legal custody while still having the child maintain primary residence with one parent also works. What really matters is the amount of time spent with *both* parents. It appears that kids fare better if there's a joint custody agreement where there is ongoing close contact with both parents. So find ways for your child to stay connected with both of you.

ment for your child after divorce include appropriate parenting, disciplining authoritatively, providing emotional support, monitoring children's activities, and maintaining age-appropriate expectations.[20]

- *Make visitations easy.* The easier you make visitations, the easier it will be on your child and her adjustment. Make sure each parent knows all necessary contact information (teachers, pediatricians, coaches, scout masters), homework and practice schedules, school routines, and doctor's appointments. Keep some of the same toys, toiletries, and clothes in each home to eliminate packing stress for your child. Designate a transfer place and time (where and when your child should be waiting each time). Get a cell phone so that your child can communicate easily with the other parent. Your goal should be to make change as trouble free as possible.

WHAT TO EXPECT BY STAGES AND AGES

Preschooler   It's hard to express concerns and have trouble comprehending divorce, so preschoolers may be confused and anxious. Because they have difficulty distinguishing between make-believe and reality, they may have strong fantasies about you reuniting. They sometimes feel responsible for the breakup and may believe that if they are really good (or stop "misbehaving"), their parents will get back together. Watch for nightmares and for regression, such as thumb sucking, wanting their security blanket or old toys, baby talk, clinginess, or bedwetting. Kids this age may also become uncooperative, angry, or defiant.

School Age   At this age, children have a better understanding of loss and know that their parents' marriage has ended, and so may experience grief or even depression. They are mature enough to recognize that they are in pain, but too immature to know how to cope; they need strategies. Their pressing concern is how their own lives both now and in the future will be affected. Common reactions

More Helpful Advice

Between Two Worlds: The Inner Lives of Children of Divorce, by Elizabeth Marquardt

Ex-Etiquette for Parents: Good Behavior After a Divorce or Separation, by Jann Blackstone-Ford

Helping Your Kids Cope with Divorce the Sandcastles Way, by M. Gary Neuman

Making Divorce Easier on Your Child: 50 Effective Ways to Help Children Adjust, by Nicholas Long and Rex Forehand

Surviving the Breakup: How Children and Parents Cope with Divorce, by Judith S. Wallerstein

What About the Kids? Raising Your Children Before, During and After Divorce, by Judith S. Wallerstein

Why Did You Have to Get a Divorce and When Can I Get a Hamster? by Anthony Wolf

include sorrow, embarrassment, shame, resentment, regression, or anger. School-age kids may also act out; display regression, clinginess, or insecurity; or seek a lot of attention. They may feel rejected by the parent who left or feel that the parent "divorced them."

Tween   Tweens may take sides with the "good" parent against the "bad one who caused the divorce," blame one parent, or feel pressure to "choose" one parent over the other. They can struggle with uncertainty about how to stay in a relationship with the parent who they feel was the cause. Watch out for withdrawing from longtime friends and activities and for risky behaviors. Tweens often experience anxiety, anger, fear, loneliness, depression, and guilt, and may feel abandoned by the parent who moves out of the house. Don't let the older child feel the need to take on more adult responsibilities at home or worry about such issues as financial security and younger siblings.

Middle Child

SEE ALSO: *Argues, New Baby, Oldest Child, Sharing, Sibling Rivalry, Youngest Child*

THE QUESTION

"My wife and I have three kids: a three-year-old girl, six-year-old boy, and the oldest boy, who's ten. Our middle boy is always saying things like *It's like I'm stuck in the middle. But I don't want to do things like my sister! I want my own stuff, not these hand-me-downs. My coach always asks why I can't play like my brother.* What can we do to help get out of this 'stuck-in-between' complaining?"

THE ANSWER

Let's face it: middle kids often do get a bad rap. But it seems these middle children also learn valuable skills and perspective because of their unique family position. The re- nowned psychologist Alfred Adler was one of the first of scores of researchers to study the effects of birth order on siblings. He found that middle kids are generally more cre- ative and flexible because they are trying to be different from their elder and younger sibling. They are also often more relaxed, independent, diplomatic, and resourceful, as well as more balanced and generous than their other siblings. They can make excellent negotiators and have great people skills if we let them forge their own way. Here are some ways we can help the situation:

- *Watch out for favoritism.* Although we may think we treat our kids equally, research shows otherwise. One survey found that 65 percent of moms and 70 percent of dads exhibited a preference for their older child.[21] So here's your test: Do your eyes light up with the same intensity for each of your kids? Beware: middle kids do pick up on which sibling is your favorite. So tune in to your in- teractions and how they might be perceived. Try hard not to express or leak out or even give a clue as to which of your offspring you favor even the tiniest bit more. Best yet, find a way to say what is special and loveable about each child: "You're my diplomat" or "You'll always be my little cuddler."

- *Make "first times" special.* Every "first" (word, step, recital, and so on) is a momentous occasion with our eldest; big moments for our youngest are special because we know it will be our last time. The middle children's "firsts" can get slighted. Be sure to make a big deal over your middle kid's first loose tooth, soccer trophy, holiday pageant, and slumber party so that he knows you're just as elated about his accomplishments. Katherine Conger's research at the University of California at Davis found that second-tier kids often tend to have more self-esteem questions and feel not quite as worthy as firstborns.[22] Those little slights, usually quite unintentional, can dig deep.

- *Halt the comparisons.* A big complaint of middle kids is being compared to their older sibling. "Your brother did that when he was three." "Your sister practiced diligently." Bite your tongue. Your cardinal rule is *Never compare siblings.*

- *Encourage them to share their thoughts.* The firstborn is notoriously more verbal simply because he had "alone time" with us before the second child's arrival, when we listened and talked more.[23] (In fact, firstborns on average have an almost three-point IQ edge over their other siblings, and researchers say that it is solely due to more parental one-on-one talking time with that child.) As a result, the middle kid often keeps things to himself and doesn't reveal his feelings. So draw that child out. Ask how he's feeling. Deliberately take that extra minute at the dinner table to make sure he's not being overlooked: "How was your day, honey?" "How did that project turn out?" Let him know you want to hear his thoughts. And make the older sib listen to his ideas.

- *Don't let him be taken advantage of.* Middle kids are often the diplomat in the family and smooth things over because they hate conflicts. They also give in to their siblings just to keep the peace. Watch out that your middle child isn't taken advantage of for his diplomacy. Aside from causing resentment, that's just not being fair.

- *Beware of hand-me-downs.* Every once in a while is fine, but watch out for always handing down those second-hand items. "The coat is still perfectly fine." "Your sister never even played with that doll." Middle kids hate getting the older kid's used items.

- *Allow individuality.* Research also shows that middle kids tend to be creative and individualistic. Whereas the oldest child is generally more ambitious (and some of that is due to the one-on-one attention and early parental push) and strives to keep or regain her parents' attention through conformity, the middle kid often has to carve out his own distinct identity. So tap into his unique strengths and provide opportunities to develop his talents. He shouldn't have to follow the path of his older sibling.

P.S. By the way, as a mom of a middle kid let me assure you that they turn out not only fine but just plain wonderful, thank you—especially if you let them march to their own drum.

New Baby

SEE ALSO: *Dependent, Middle Child, Oldest Child, Sharing, Sibling Rivalry, Stressed, Youngest Child*

THE QUESTION

"My wife is in her ninth month of pregnancy, and now that she can tell pretty clearly what's going on, our seven-year-old daughter is not such a happy camper. She constantly hits us with a real guilt trip with comments like *What did I do to make you want another baby? Will you still have time for me? Do I have to give up my stuff? Why does the baby get all these new presents? My friends won't come over when there's a stinky baby in the house!* What can we do to help our daughter adjust to the new baby?"

THE ANSWER

Although you may be thrilled about a new baby, the siblings-to-be aren't always so excited. After all, they realize you are no longer exclusively theirs, and their world is turned suddenly upside down. It isn't always easy being the big sibling, especially if you think you are no longer the most important or only person in Mommy and Daddy's lives. So jealousy, anger, and a bit of resentment are to be expected. But have faith: there are things you can do so that your child realizes there's always enough love, which will help make this transition smoother both before and after the birth. Here are a few key things you can do:

- *Discuss what* won't *change.* Your child is bound to tune in to all the impending changes you're discussing, so talk instead about what will remain the same. It will help make the adjustment easier.

- *Involve your child in decisions.* Let her take part in choosing the baby's name (or having a vote; and if not the first name, why not the middle one?). She might also help you chose the crib location or the paint color for the baby's room, or even do such things as set up the mobile or stuffed animal display.

- *Play up the "big sibling" role.* Tell your child *why* she will be a great big sibling. *"You can teach him to play baseball." "The baby will love hearing you read to him."* Just don't set up false hopes that she'll have a new playmate. She'll be disappointed to discover that all the baby does is sleep, cry, eat, and poop.

- *Stick to routines when the baby arrives.* Yes, there will be somewhat of a change, but if you try to maintain daily routines as much as possible, your older kid won't feel that the baby is infringing too much on her life.

- *Temper those oohs and aahs.* Of course you're elated, but use a little restraint when the new big sibling is around. You don't want your older child to feel left out, and all that attention centered on that new little critter can fuel her resentment. Ask guests please not to ignore your other kids.

- *Involve the older sibling.* Ask your child to help you with the baby. A younger child can push the stroller, wind up the mobile, pack the diaper bag, sing a lullaby, recite favorite nursery rhymes, and draw a picture for the baby. An older child can read a book, help with a diaper change, or even (if she appears interested) dress the new sibling. You might ask the sibling for advice: *"Do you think the baby would like the teddy bear or the stuffed rabbit?" "Should I put her in the red or pink jumper?"*

- *Find one-on-one time.* Tell her what it was like when she was a baby: which toys and stories she loved, how she preferred to be held, and how you loved to rock her all night long. Let her know that when the baby is sleeping, it's your time together—then use it! Set a special chair next to your rocking chair for your child to sit on, and read or sing or talk to her while you nurse.

Help your child understand that no one—ever, ever—can take her place in your heart.

Oldest Child

SEE ALSO: *Argues, Bossy, Middle Child, New Baby, Only Child, Sharing, Sibling Rivalry, Stressed, Youngest Child*

THE QUESTION

"My son is the oldest of our three kids, and he's always complaining: *Why does everyone always depend on me? Why is Mom so much stricter with me? Why do I have to take care of my dumb younger brother?* This is disturbing to his younger brother and sister and to both of us parents. What can I do to help him recognize that there are advantages to being the oldest child? There's no way we can change his birth order!"

THE ANSWER

Did you know that almost all of the U.S. presidents were either the firstborn child or the firstborn son in their families? All but two of the first astronauts sent into space were firstborns, and the other two were "only children." The eldest child is more likely to be confident, organized, intelligent, determined, eager to please, and a leader. This is also the sibling more prone to become a CEO, win a Nobel Prize, and be more academically successful as well as financially secure.[24] There's no doubt that being the firstborn has clear advantages. This is the only child who will receive our undivided attention and one-on-one time, and research shows that this makes a big difference in how they turn out.

A Norwegian study led by psychologist Petter Kristenson meticulously analyzed IQ scores of 250,000 men and found that the oldest child is smarter than the next oldest sibling by an average of 2.3 points (who in turn beat the third-born brother by 1.1 points).[25] Although 2.3 points may seem measly, in today's test-crazed society they can be just enough to give a child an academic edge and be the difference between earning a B+ or an A, going to a state school or a university. But here's the real kicker: if the eldest child dies, the second sibling becomes the smartest one. That means it's not just the birth order that boosts those IQ points but the dynamics in the family and how the firstborn is treated. It appears that our parenting really does make a difference when it comes to giving our eldest a clear intellectual edge.

With all those positives, how could there possibly be a problem with being the oldest kid? Well, consider things from your eldest's view. There is a downside to being the oldest, and even though you can't change his family rank, there are a few solutions to help this kid turn out the best he can be (as well as relax and enjoy life just a tad more).

- *Focus on your other kids.* Watch out! A few researchers find that parents *do* have favorites, and as much as we'd never admit it, we often favor our firstborn child. After all, that first birth is a life-changing, incredible event. And although that's a huge boost for your elder kid's self-esteem, it also can fuel sibling rivalry. Those jealousies can linger for a long time and cause a wedge between your eldest and his younger sibs. So beware of your interactions with your kids and ask yourself now and then, "Does each child feel I love him best?"

- *Watch those responsibilities.* We give our elder kids more responsibilities, and we just plain expect more of them at a younger age. But are you expecting *too* much? The eldest kid hates being told, "You're in charge of the house until I get back" or "You're the oldest, so I expect more of you." Every now and then take a reality check to make sure you're not imposing too many responsibilities on this kid or treating him as if he were older than his chronological age. (And do temper those "You're the man around the house" comments at least until he (or she) comes of age.)

- *Relax and take ten.* Although the firstborn has the clear advantage of having our undivided attention (at least until the next sibling comes along), he also stands the chance of being the most stressed. We really are stricter with our eldest child and let their younger siblings get away with far more.[26] We do inflate our expectations a bit for our first and expect more from him. Because this is our first-time parenting experience, we're more overly anxious in our response to this kid.[27] It's one reason the firstborn child usually is more anxious—our expectations and stress rub off on him. Take a few deliberate breaths before responding to your first (he is also more clued in to your reactions and feeds off your stress). And maybe pare down those expectations just a wee, wee bit.

- *Let your child go his own way.* Birth dynamics play an interesting role in how our kids turn out. We are tenser and have higher expectations for our oldest, and he tends to be a less of a risk taker, sticking to the path we've forged for him. Research also finds that we encourage our eldest child to pursue more cognitive and analytical interests that could lead to more prestigious careers like law or medicine.[28] (We also tend to be more open and relaxed with our younger child and far more receptive to letting him stray off that "straight and narrow" path to follow his more artistic and creative interests and become the poet or graphic artist.) The key is to identify from the get-go your oldest child's unique passions and strengths so that he can become his own person and develop those interests that may lead him to the career of *his* dreams. And while you're at it, encourage him to deviate a bit from the norm, take a risk, and think outside the box as his younger siblings do.

- *Let your child tutor his younger sibling.* The eldest child has another benefit: he has a younger sibling to help. *"Can you teach your brother how to read?" "Will you show your sister how to turn on the computer?"* Teaching someone a skill helps not only the tutored but also the tutor. In fact, in many cases, the oldest child gains the most (IQ-wise, anyway) from teaching his younger sibling. So, assuming he's willing and has the time, encourage your eldest to mentor and teach. Just remember to use the same strategy for your other kids so they can benefit as well.

- *Watch out for allergies.* A review of over fifty studies found that the oldest kids are more likely to suffer from hay fever, eczema, and other allergies.[29] One hypothesis: the eldest is overprotected and not exposed to those germs and bacteria, and so is far more susceptible to colds and likely to develop a weaker immune system (whereas the younger siblings battle the bugs at home before they start school and develop a stronger immune system to fight off those germs later on). Some doctors contend that all those colds firstborn kids tend to catch are really allergies in disguise. (The most pronounced symptom of an allergy is an itchy nose and no fever, ache, or chills.)

Now if we could just figure out a way to redefine success so that we don't get so crazed thinking it's all about IQ. Research shows that in the real world, IQ doesn't make much of a difference in achieving success. (Really!) What does matter for our oldest child is making sure he takes time to enjoy life and smell the roses.

Only Child

SEE ALSO: *Argues, Sharing*

THE QUESTION

"Sometimes my husband and I feel awful about bringing up our daughter with no siblings and only two busy adults in the house with her. It feels like such an adult-centered home, with not enough fun or youthful energy. At other times, I'm afraid we focus on her with too much attention and energy. How can I help our only child feel like a kid, not spoil her, and fill her childhood with wonder and spontaneity?"

THE ANSWER

Spoiled. Arrogant. Bossy. Selfish. Maladjusted. Lonely. Bratty. Just a few terms people often use to describe only children. But are those terms accurate, and if so, is your only child really doomed? Not according to the latest studies, which (thankfully) refute most of those old stereotypes and myths. Recent research gives a far more accurate as well as positive view of only kids that should allow parents sighs of relief. Here are just a few of those recent findings:

Onlies appear to have a huge advantage when it comes to achievement and intelligence. A twenty-year study found that only kids have higher education levels, higher test scores, better vocabularies, and higher levels of achievement. Research also concludes that for the most part, only kids grow up to be happy, with a closer parent-child relationship, and they are no more selfish, lonely, or maladjusted than if they had siblings.[30] In fact, a battery of studies show that onlies are no more bossy or spoiled than children in other birth orders.[31] In fact, hundreds of research findings show that only children are really no different from their peers.[32] Although some issues do pose special problems for onlies, there are simple solutions to help these children become the best they can be. Here are a few:

- *Dethrone your only.* Only children do have a huge advantage in the self-esteem department because they have all your attention and love. Consequently, they also stand the risk of acting a bit entitled, which is a huge peer turnoff. So beware that you don't put your kid on center stage or give her the impression that the world revolves around her (even though in your eyes I'm sure she does).
- *Help your child consider others.* Because only kids do spend much time alone (or in adults' company), they stand the risk of getting stuck in that "me-me-me"

mentality. So find ways to help your child think of others. Buy her a pet (and then make her responsible for taking care of it). Do charitable actions—such as making cookies for the lonely neighbor next door, helping paint the homeless shelter, or tutoring a younger child through your church group—as a family so that she can experience the joy of doing for others. And because onlies have the luxury of not having to wait to be heard, help your child learn to wait and listen to others.

- *Take your expectations down a notch.* All kids want to please their parents, but especially only children because they are so aware that they are your "one and only." That role can be a burden. Only kids usually already are more achievement oriented, do have those perfectionist tendencies, and are more likely to succeed. They tend to perform[33] better on standardized tests, earn higher grades, and stay in school longer. So check your expectations now and then and resist the urge to step in and redo what she's done or correct her mishaps and mistakes. Make sure you aren't too involved and that your aspirations aren't too high for this kid. Onlies need to learn not to put so much pressure on themselves, so they need not to feel that pressure also coming their way from you.

- *Provide social skill opportunities.* A study of over twenty thousand kindergartners found that teachers rated students with at least one sibling as better able to form and maintain friendships, get along, comfort and help others, express feelings in a positive way, and show sensitivity.[34] That doesn't mean you need to have a second child simply to help improve your child's social skills. But it does mean you should find opportunities for your child to be with other kids so that she can learn those friendship-making traits. Playdates, playgroups, a babysitting cooperative, scouting, church groups, family gatherings with cousins, holidays with friends, neighborhood kids, T-ball, summer camps, Boys and Girls Clubs, and sleepovers are just a few of the many options to be on the alert for.

- *Help your child learn to solve conflicts.* Only kids often have trouble solving conflicts, handling teasing, and negotiating or compromising because they don't have brothers and sisters to help them learn those skills in day-to-day tiffs. Try not to raise your only child with kid gloves. And make sure you find ways to help your only resolve conflicts and negotiate hot-button issues so that she has those skills to handle the real world. Intentionally (and in a fun way, of course), tease her so that she learns to laugh at herself. Don't get so caught up in the myth that you should never fight in front of your kid. I'm not suggesting a knockout match, but get your parenting partner to help you model how to disagree amicably.

- *Let your child forge her own path.* Make sure you don't expect this lone offspring to "complete" you because she is your one and only. Instead reflect on your child's unique talents, interests, passions, personality, and temperament. Then look at the activities and interests in which she currently partakes. Do they match her natural nature? Do they stretch her unique talents and strengths? Or are those activities more in sync with what *you hope* she will enjoy or *your own* talents, strengths, skills, or memories? Help your child become her own person. She deserves that right.

Whether you have one child or many, the key parenting secret is always the same: treat each child as if she were an only child. On a personal note, I'm an only child, and I married an only child. The two of us would be the first to admit (at least to one another) that we turned out just fine.

Sibling Rivalry

SEE ALSO: *Angry, Argues, Bossy, Bullied, Bullying, Middle Child, New Baby, Oldest Child, Peer Pressure, Teased, Youngest Child*

THE PROBLEM

Red Flags

Fighting words and actions between brothers and sisters; resentment and competition; constant or intense intermittent friction and hurt feelings; family disharmony due to constant sibling bickering

The Change to Parent For

Your children will appreciate one another and battle less by learning habits to help them get along, share their concerns, and solve their conflicts peacefully.

Question: "My kids constantly bicker, but whenever I try to help out, they complain that I'm not fair and accuse me of favoring the other sibling. I can't win! How do I help them get along?"

Answer: Don't go crazy trying to make things equal among siblings—it's impossible! And don't have unrealistic expectations for continued harmony, because resentment is inevitable and sometimes unavoidable. The truth is, your kids don't have to like each other or even get along every minute of the day, but they do have to respect each other's feelings and be considerate of the need for empathy and stability in the entire family. If you stress that principle, you will increase the likelihood that they will get along. (After all, the benchmarks of any strong relationship are empathy and respect.)

Why Change?

"Mahhhmmm, Jacob's touching me!" "Can't we give Jennifer away?" "I hate my brother!" "Why can't Sara find her own friends?"

Ah, the blissful sounds of siblings struggling to get along. Most of us have visions of our offspring being the world's best buddies, but with kids living under the same roof, some bickering is bound to be the outcome. The closer your kids are in age, the more likely there are to be squabbles. Keep in mind that research shows that kids spend about a third of their free time with siblings—that's more time than they spend with parents, teachers, or friends.[35] Although you can't force your kids to like each other, there are ways to fend off some of those battles, and some skills you can teach that will minimize jealousies and help your kids appreciate one another, so that they are more apt to get along (and just maybe learn to like each other).

Signs and Symptoms

All siblings will squabble and have tiffs every now and then, but here are signs that their rivalry and battles are in need of an outside kick in the you-know-where.

- *Escalating arguments.* Name-calling, yelling, or aggression (hitting, kicking, punching) are intensifying; you can't leave the kids alone with one another.
- *Increased animosity.* Siblings are destroying each other's possessions or relationships.
- *Deteriorating emotional well-being.* One sibling or both feel less loved or favored; self-esteem and feelings of belonging as a member of your family are affected.
- *Family disharmony.* Despite your best efforts, the relationship between the siblings is strained or the rivalry is escalating, and the conflict is having an impact your family's happiness and stability.

LATE-BREAKING NEWS

University of California at Davis (UCD): Katherine Conger, a family sociologist at UCD, visited the homes of 384 adolescents and their siblings three times over three years to see how well they interacted as a family.[36] She also videotaped family members working through sample conflicts and then concluded that 65 percent of moms and 70 percent of dads showed a clear preference for one child. In most cases it was the oldest sibling. What's more, the kids could identify the favorite to the researcher. Although the "unfavored" tried to brush it off as not a big deal, they clearly were sadder and felt somehow unworthy. Beware: kids do pick up on parental feelings and preferences—especially when it comes to sibling favorites—causing a lifetime of resentment.

THE SOLUTION

Step 1. Early Intervention

- *Discover the reason.* Here are common causes of sibling rivalry and battles. Check any that may apply to your family and then consider if there is any simple solution to try.

  ☐ Your kids' temperament, personalities, abilities, priorities, and styles are very different.

  ☐ Siblings have different parents; you are a blended family.

  ☐ Siblings are not given opportunities to share feelings of discontent, so animosity builds.

  ☐ Siblings are not allowed to explore their individual interests or have privacy; they have no "alone time" to develop relationships.

  ☐ Financial difficulties, marital conflicts, illness, or trauma lead to strained family dynamics.

  ☐ Siblings lack vocabulary, skills, or maturity to solve problems or share concerns.

  ☐ Siblings are imitating adult behavior. (You are fighting with your spouse, sibling, mother, boss.)

  ☐ One sibling has special needs or is overly aggressive or impulsive.

- *Identify the trigger.* Try to witness—without their awareness—a sibling conflict. Tune in to their behaviors *before* the fighting starts.

  What behaviors, perpetrated by one or both kids, escalate the situation, such as insulting, hitting, swearing, or biting?

  What are the common battle issues? (For instance: both kids want to play with the same item or use the computer at the same time; each wants to watch a different TV program.)

  Is there *any solution* you could implement that might minimize or prevent the problem? (For example, you might buy duplicate toys, arrange a computer schedule, teach a skill that might defuse the conflict before it becomes full blown.)

  Once the conflict began, how did you respond, and how did your kids react to your response? Did you escalate, reduce, or neutralize the conflict?

  Is there one simple solution you can implement to reduce the chance that the same problem will arise in the future?

- *Take a reality check.* Might you be playing favorites or putting too much pressure on one kid or another? Be honest. Do you . . .

  Expect more of one child?

  Give one kid more attention?

  Take sides?

  Listen to one kid's side more or assume one kid is right?

  Compare your kids in front of each other?

  Encourage rivalry in academics, sports, or popularity by acknowledging one kid over another?

  Pay equal attention to each child's hobbies, friends, school, and interests?

  Distribute chores, rewards, and opportunities fairly?

  Light up with the same intensity when you see each of your kids?

  Take time to write a list of what you like most and what you like least about each child. If your list is more slanted to one side or the other, it may signal that you have a potential problem. Do you need to change *your* response? How?

- *Reduce sibling competition.* Watch out for daily moments that may actually be setting your kids up as rivals. Here are a few things to avoid because they can lead to resentment:

  - *Never compare.* Don't say, "Why can't you bat like your brother?" A child may begin to think that he is inferior to a sibling in his parents' eyes. "When your sister was your age, she always got all A's."

  - *Avoid those labels.* Follow this parenting rule: unless a label or nickname is respectful or builds the child up, don't use it. Those labels ("Klutz," "Slowpoke," "Chubby") can be self-fulfilling; they can derail self-esteem and remain with your child through adulthood.

  - *Encourage teamwork.* Stop those contests that force siblings to compete against each other. ("Who can get dressed the fastest?" "Who will brush his teeth the most this week?") Play more cooperative games where there are no winners and losers. Instead of making sibs compete, challenge them to beat the clock.

  - *Nurture unique strengths and differences.* Each sibling's competing to define who he is as an individual often exacerbates sibling rivalry. So acknowledge each child's special talent that sets him apart from his siblings. For example, if you have a child who excels in art, he's the sibling whom you supply with colored pencils and sketchbooks and encourage to take art classes. The trick is to cultivate each child's natural talent and then find opportunities to show it off so that both kids aren't vying for the same "fame."

- *Give a little privacy.* If siblings spend *too much* together time (and it's not their choice), then find ways to separate them or give them each a bit of his own space. If they share a bedroom, then divide the closet and even the room in half; give each his own desk, bulletin board, bookshelf, clothes, drawers, and toy bins. If possible, arrange their schedule to keep them separate (without your going crazy): different playdates, different swim schedules. Is there *anything* you can do to give these two "alone time"?

- *Acknowledge cooperation.* When you notice your children sharing or playing cooperatively or trying to resolve issues peacefully, let them know you are proud of their behavior. If the children know that you appreciate their efforts, they are more inclined to repeat them. *"I really appreciate how you two worked things out calmly this time. Good for you." "I noticed how you both made an effort to help each other figure out how to put the DVDs away. Nice job."*

Step 2. Rapid Response

- *Stay neutral.* Most research finds that the more involved you get in your kids' tiffs, the more likely they are to engage in sibling rivalry. Siblings need to learn how to work out problems on their own. So intervene *before* an argument escalates. If the conflict does get heated, stay neutral and make suggestions only when your kids seem stuck.

- *Find time alone for each child.* Depending on your schedule, set aside blocks of time when each of your children can have your exclusive attention. While the other siblings are gone or another adult watches them, take turns taking each of the children on special outings, such as shopping, seeing a movie, or getting ice cream.

One Parent's Answer

A mom from Portland shares:

My eight- and six-year-old fought constantly. I tried everything from refereeing, separating, bribing, and punishing them, but they just kept at each other. Then it dawned on me that maybe I was too involved with their squabbles. Instead of curbing their rows I was aiding and abetting. So I stepped aside and insisted they work things out. The amazing thing is, my kids fought less.

- *Let each kid tell the story.* In the case of hurt feelings or a battle, ask each kid to take turns explaining what happened. Doing so helps each child (especially a younger or less verbal one) feel that he has been heard. As each child speaks, ask the other sibling to focus on him and really listen. No interrupting is allowed, and everyone gets a turn. You might need to set a timer for "equal talking time." When the sibling is finished, briefly restate his view to show you do understand. You might then ask, "What can you do to solve this problem?" Hint: Don't ask "What happened?" or "Who started it?" You'll only get a one-sided version, which can escalate the conflict even further.

- *Anticipate and distract.* When you see their tempers rising or one kid's patience maxed, it's time to use the "distract or separate" method: *"Let's get out that Monopoly game." "How about a Popsicle?" "How about you two take a break from each other for five minutes?"* Just use this strategy *before* their conflict has escalated to the point of no return.

ONE SIMPLE SOLUTION

The Five Simple House Rules to Curb Sibling Bickering

Here are five house rules to curb sibling tiffs. Each rule must be enforced consistently for results.

1. *No yelling.* Family members must use calm voices only—*no yelling allowed.* If talks get heated, anyone can make a "time-out" hand sign hinting that he needs to cool down.

2. *No taking without asking.* Permission of the owner must be granted before borrowing, using, or taking property. (This is a major cause of sibling conflict, especially with tweens.)

3. *No hurtful behaviors.* Hitting, name-calling, and hurtful behaviors are *never* allowed and will result in a consequence (time-out for a younger child; loss of a privilege for an older one).

4. *No involvement without evidence.* Get involved only if you actually *saw* or *heard* the conflict. If your kids seek your help with no evidence, suggest that they use Rock, Paper, Scissors. It keeps you neutral, and your kids just might adopt the strategy for themselves.

5. *No tattling.* This works wonders in curbing sibling resentment with younger kids: *"Unless you tell me something to keep your brother out of trouble or from being hurt, I won't listen."*

Step 3. Develop Habits for Change

- *Encourage outside friendships.* Each sibling needs his own group of friends outside your family. In some cases you may want to be sure that if one child's friends are coming over, the sibling doesn't interfere or annoy them. This is especially important for your tween.

- *See it from the other side.* Kids often get so caught up in feeling they're being treated unfairly that they don't stop to think how the other person might be feeling. So ask, *"See it from the other side now. How does your sister feel?"* You could also ask, *"How would your sister describe what happened?"* Some parents even ask each child to describe the conflict in writing from the other sibling's point of view and then compare the two versions.

- *Start family meetings.* Don't let animosity build up among siblings. It will only lead to more conflicts and resentment. Instead, provide the opportunity for each child to be able to express his feelings and concerns and work through issues he considers unfair. Family meetings are one way to air differences and talk though siblings' problems. This is a great time to teach your kids to use the Fair Fighting Rules (see the One Simple Solution box below). A fun way to begin the meeting is to have each member say something nice about each other. (Yes, it's hard at the beginning, but if you keep it up, kids actually start thinking of nice things to say before the meeting.) Some families set up a "Concern Box" where kids can request a "mediation" with the family member and a parent present to help them work things out. The secret is to find a way for kids to vent their feelings in a healthy way.

ONE SIMPLE SOLUTION

Teach "Fair Fighting Rules" to Help Siblings Solve Conflicts

University of Michigan Medical School: Research shows that siblings will fight more in families where there is no understanding of acceptable ways to solve conflicts. So help your kids learn the four crucial "Fair Fighting Rules" they need to resolve their bickering and keep things FAIR.

F – **Focus on facts.** Tell your brother or sister what he or she did that bothers you. Stick just to the facts so that you don't put down the other person and cause hurt feelings.

A – **Agree on a fair alternative.** No more going to Mom or Dad unless someone is hurt or it's just too big to solve on your own. Instead, think up options until you can agree on one solution that is fair for both.

I – **Use an "I" message to say what's bothering you.** Start your message with "I" and then say what's bugging you. *"I get mad when you take my stuff without asking."*

R – **Remain respectful.** No name-calling. No put-downs. Take turns listening respectfully to each side without interrupting until you can work things out fairly.

WHAT TO EXPECT BY STAGES AND AGES

The rule of thumb is that more conflicts transpire between siblings closer in age and of the same gender. Here is what to expect by age, according to the noted Gesell Institute.[37]

Preschooler   Children at this age are egocentric and impulsive, and lack the maturity to solve problems, so sibling conflicts are at their peak. Preschoolers can begin to start brainstorming solutions with your guidance. Siblings between two and four years old engage in a conflict about every ten minutes; three- to seven-year-olds have some kind of clash about 3.5 times an hour.[38]

School Age   Peak for potential sibling jealousy is during the ages of five to eleven. Five-year-olds are less bossy and can "mother" a younger sibling; they're better able to take turns and share. Six-year-olds are more domineering and have difficulty compromising; they're prone to have conflict with *all* siblings. They are very competitive and can't handle losing; they often complain of unequal treatment. By age seven, kids are less aggressive and less competitive; they are protective of younger siblings but often in a contentious relationship with those siblings closer in age. Eight-year-olds often argue; they have a tough time forgiving or overlooking a sibling's mistakes; they can be very resentful of a younger sibling "tagging along"—though they want to accompany older siblings (who tend to reject them).

Tween   Peer acceptance and independence are paramount: tweens need their *own* friends and *own* interests, so don't let younger siblings "hang around" with your tween and his pals. Kids' sibling relations begin to improve at around age nine; they are often protective of a younger sibling and proud of older ones; they tend to fixate on "who started it" in a battle. Ten-year-olds show noticeable gains in sibling relationships. Eleven-year-olds can be a bit more temperamental; tiffs and teasing are common. Sibling relations often improve for twelve-year-olds due to a more mature understanding of fairness. True friendships start to emerge when kids are thirteen, usually with the sibling closest in birth order. A sibling borrowing or damaging the child's possessions is one of the biggest conflict issues.

More Helpful Advice

Beyond Sibling Rivalry: How to Help Your Children Become Cooperative, Caring, and Compassionate, by Peter Goldenthal

Loving Each One Best: A Caring and Practical Approach to Raising Siblings, by Nancy Samalin

Siblings Without Rivalry: How to Help Your Children Live Together So You Can Too, by Adele Faber and Elaine Mazlish

Understanding Sibling Rivalry: The Brazelton Way, by T. Berry Brazelton and Joshua D. Sparrow

Twins and Multiples

SEE ALSO: *Argues, Sibling Rivalry, Tattles*

THE QUESTION

"My wife and I are expecting twins, though the doctor has said there might be triplets. We went through expensive fertility treatments and waited a long while, but couldn't be happier. Neither of us have been around twins before, and now we wonder if there are any special parenting concerns we should consider. Any advise would be appreciated. Also, just how common are multiple births these days? It seems as though they are suddenly all the news."

THE ANSWER

Did you know that 1 in every 250 births in the United States is now a multiple: twins, triplets, or higher-order multiples? Multiple births have increased almost 65 percent in the last three decades.[39]

There are many reasons for the increase; key among them are advancements in infertility treatments and maternal age. (As women get older, their chance of having multiples doubles, and these days many women are waiting to have their first baby later in life.) Despite the joy of giving birth, the reality is that there are unique parenting challenges in raising multiples (in addition to probably being more exhausted and financially strapped than other parents). Among them: How do you help your children develop their individual identities? Should twins share the same classroom? Should they have the same friends? What about those language delays that studies show are prevalent with twins? Here are few proven solutions to parenting multiples.

- *Get knowledgeable.* Although the basics of good parenting work for any child, there are unique issues when raising multiples. So start by gaining a perspective on the special challenges you may face. Here are a few of the best resources:

  Emotionally Healthy Twins: A New Philosophy for Parenting Two Unique Children, by Joan Friedman

  It's Twins! Parent-to-Parent Advice from Infancy Through Adolescence, by Susan Heim

  Raising Twins After the First Year: Everything You Need to Know About Bringing Up Twins—From Toddlers to Preteens, by Karen Gottesman

Raising Multiple Birth Children: A Parents' Survival Guide, by Bill and Sheila Laut

Twins 101, by Khanh-Van Le-Bucklin

Multiples magazine, www.multiplesmag.com

TWINS magazine, www.twinsmagazine.com

- *Encourage individuality.* Multiples often look, act, and even think alike, and because they share similar interests, classrooms, scout troops, friends, and even birthdays, others often see them as "package deal." What's more, because they share so many similarities, they are constantly compared to one other, which fuels competition among them. That's a huge disservice to their emotional growth. After all, these kids are also separate and unique and deserve to be treated as individuals. Here are six factors that encourage individuality and reduce the possibility of sibling competition:

  Different appearance. Same-sex multiples often look alike, but always being mistaken for the other can cause sibling resentment. Find ways to make each look slightly different so that other folks—and you—can easily tell them apart: a haircut, shoe style, or backpack color.

  One-on-one parent time. Find ways for each child to spend quality "alone time" with you, even if it's no more than a few minutes. For example: a minute at bedtime to hear each child's separate prayers; an extra minute at dinner so each can share her day; or a one-on-one lunch date, movie, or ball game every so often.

  Separate time. Multiples spend so much time together that friction can build. So look for ways they can spend brief times apart—a walk to the park with an older sibling, alone time with Grandma, a summer camp.

  Different activities. Parents often sign multiples up for the same activities or sport team, which may force them to compete against each other. Instead, encourage them to try at least one separate activity. Although it will no doubt complicate the carpool schedule, the benefits will outweigh the stress.

  Unique talents. Find the unique talent or strength in each sibling—singing, karate, guitar, jazz dancing, or whatever. Then provide individual opportunities to nurture each child's talent so that she is recognized for her special abilities.

  Separate friendships. Multiples often share the same friends, but the danger is that one child may monopolize the relationship, leaving the other sibling out. Nurture at least one separate friendship and let each sibling attend an occasional sleepover or playdate alone.

- *Make things fair, not equal.* Don't try in your parenting to make everything equal by treating each child the same. It's impossible! Instead, parent for fairness, which means treating each child justly by adjusting your standards and expectations on the basis of each individual child's needs. For instance, lay down the same rules, but discipline each child separately. (Hint: never punish them as a unit when only one is responsible.) Establish the same computer times, but if one needs more time for homework, the other knows that school comes first. Set clear bathroom schedules, but if one sibling has an upcoming event, the siblings switch their times. Buy toys for both of your kids to share, but make sure that each child has her own and that each item is clearly labeled. The same goes for books and clothes.

- *Talk to your children.* Multiples spend more time with one another and sometimes even develop a private language. Because they rely on one another, they also spend less talking time with parents and are at a greater risk for language delays than singletons.[40] That could have a negative impact on their language development, IQ, and academic potential. The influence of parent-child conversation—particularly in the early years—has a profound impact on your children's language development. So look for ways to talk to your kids during normal, everyday activities. Read to them and find time for frequent family meals (which offer great opportunities for talking and listening). Speak out loud about the things you are thinking—whether it's your to-do list, dinner menu, or plans to visit your mother—so that they can hear your inner dialogue. Or invite your friends and family over. Just having more adults around will help increase each child's exposure to speech.

- *Weigh the classroom scene carefully.* Although you want to help each sibling develop her unique individuality and have separate experiences, that parenting premise doesn't apply when it comes to school. In fact, *all* twin development research in the past twenty years finds that "twins who are allowed to be together in *preschool* and as long as they want to be in the *early elementary years* seem to make a much better adjustment both academically and socially than those who are arbitrarily separated. Once the adjustment to school is accomplished, separation in later grades happens naturally and easily."[41] Of course, decide what you think is best for your kids, but do be aware of the research. Here are other academic considerations:

  - *Watch for learning disabilities.* Some research suggests that twins, especially twin boys, are more likely to suffer from learning disabilities. Fraternal twins have a 40 percent chance of sharing learning disabilities; identical twins have been found to have a 68 percent chance.[42] Be alert, and consider having one or both children assessed for learning disabilities if there are academic difficulties.

  - *Don't label.* Refrain at all costs from calling one child more "gifted" or "our student."

- *Beware of competition.* If you notice that your kids are being pitted against each other academically and one is more successful than the other, separate them to different classrooms or teams.

- *Let them choose.* Middle school provides more options as well as teachers. If you haven't already separated your multiples, now may be the time to put them in different classes. This is the age when peer pressure and competition soar, so separating them may be best for their self-esteem. Ask them what they think is best.

- *Take care of yourself.* Multiple kids may double your pleasure, but they also double the stress. Some research suggests that the added stress of multitasking can put a strain on not only you but also your marriage. Here are ways to ease that strain:

  - *Join a "mothers of multiples" group.* Find other parents of multiples either on online or in your community and ask their advice. Join an organization of multiples such as the National Organization of Mothers of Twins Clubs, www.nomotc.org, or Multiple Births Canada, www.multiplebirthscanada.org.

  - *Carve out couple time.* Spending time with your spouse and away from your kids is a necessity. Take a short walk, hire a babysitter so you can go to a movie, join an exercise club, or just ride bikes together. The activity doesn't have to cost a dime.

  - *Find ways to relax.* Find what helps you stay balanced and relaxed—whether it's taking a hot bath, listening to Mozart, talking to your girlfriend, or popping in that Buns of Steel tape—and ink that into your daily routine. Setting aside just ten minutes a day may be all you need, but those minutes will help you take on the challenge of parenting multiples.

One touching and widely circulated article described how twins born prematurely were placed in separate incubators. A short while later, one twin was fighting for her life, and no treatment seemed to help. A concerned neonatal nurse decided to put the twins together in one incubator and then watched in awe as the healthy twin snuggled up and wrapped her tiny arm around her sick sister. Within minutes, the sick twin's blood oxygen rate stabilized, and the child recovered.[43]

Nothing else I've ever seen describes the extraordinary bond of multiples. Remember that regardless of the complications and special challenges, you are parenting a most unique relationship. Enjoy!

Youngest Child

SEE ALSO: *Argues, Dependent, Middle Child, New Baby, Oldest Child, Sharing, Sibling Rivalry*

THE QUESTION

"We have three kids, and our youngest boy always seem to get the short end of the stick. My husband and I aren't home as much as when we had our first kids, the older ones take a lot of our time and energy, and we're just not exactly as jazzed about parenting as we used to be. I'm worried that our youngest is neglected, underserved, and left on his own too much. What can I do to make sure he's getting everything that he needs?"

THE ANSWER

The renowned psychologist Alfred Adler was one of the first of scores of researchers to study the effects of birth order on siblings. He found that their order of birth—and how children are treated in that position—have a significant influence on our children's personality as well as their life choices and intelligence. Of course each child is different, but youngest kids do tend to share some common traits due to their birth order and how we treat them: they are often comical and entertaining, creative, spontaneous, highly social and outgoing, and more laid back and easygoing. They are generally less educated, intelligent, and financially successful than older siblings. But there are also interesting benefits to being the youngest.

A study of more than eight thousand schoolchildren found that later-born kids are much less likely to be overweight;[44] another study reports that they have far lower incidence of allergies and eczema.[45] They also tend to be more creative and unconventional; they are good team players; and they are more willing to see the other point of view (think Ronald Reagan, Charles Darwin, Harriet Tubman, Copernicus, Edward Kennedy, Descartes, and Mozart—all youngest kids who left a distinct mark on the world). There are also a few traits that can cause parents some sleepless nights. The youngest child can become the family rebel. He is sometimes more of a risk taker and is the kid in the family most likely to question authority.

Other studies show that this is also the sibling who goes through puberty the earliest and the one most likely to have the most sexual partners! (Maybe those are the reasons we decide that this will be our final child?) One thing is for sure: your youngest child is going to be fun, more relaxed, a bit healthier (at least when compared to the elder), and just possibly a bit of a challenge. He also will be well loved. Here are solutions to help your youngest thrive in his unique place in your family:

- *Talk and talk and talk.* Studies show that the oldest child has at least a 2.3-point IQ lead over his younger siblings, which in today's test-crazed educational system gives a huge academic edge.[46] But those extra IQ points are due not to genetics but to parents' spending more one-on-one time with the eldest. Talking is one of the best ways to enhance our children's verbal ability, and unfortunately our youngest kids lose that undivided time. *What* you talk about has no bearing on IQ; that you *do* talk is what matters. Here is proof: Joseph Price, an economics professor at Brigham Young University, analyzed data on twenty-one thousand people and found that firstborn kids get about three thousand more hours of solo time with their parents (roughly twenty to thirty more minutes daily) than their siblings. That increased parent-to-child talking time—found to increase intelligence and verbal ability—is how Price explains that the elder kids get more education, make more money, and score higher on IQ tests. The youngest receive the least amount of one-on-one time with parents. (They do spend more time with parents than their elder sibs do between the ages of four and thirteen, but the time is spent watching television![47]) So don't skimp on quality time with your youngest.

- *Fill in his baby book.* We spend hours completing our firstborn's baby book, photo albums, and scrapbooks. But don't forget your baby! It's disheartening to pull out your photo album and find little evidence that substantiates life beyond the first year. These can be time-consuming projects, so consider getting your youngest involved in finding those photos and gluing them into a scrapbook. This project would also give you time to talk one-on-one about how much you cherished your time together and to recall those special memories of when he was growing up (even though there may not be as many photos to prove it!).

- *Don't let the youngest get away with murder!* Our eldest keeps telling us, but now research proves it: the last-born kid does get away with more and is disciplined far less. Researchers from University of Maryland, Duke University, and Johns Hopkins University analyzed more than eleven thousand subjects in the National Longitudinal Study of Youth and found that parents are indeed far less strict with their youngest.[48] And because parents discipline less, the youngest is also far more likely to be a great risk taker, to be rebellious, to have unprotected sex, and to drop out of school and bend the rules as he gets older. Mom and Dad alert: listen to your older kid and don't be lax in your discipline with your youngest.

- *Watch out for attention-getting antics.* The reality is that we tend to be a bit more relaxed with our youngest child and don't watch his every move. It's no wonder that last kids are usually less stressed and more relaxed and often find their way to get attention by becoming the family comedian. (It's probably no coincidence that Billy Crystal, Whoopi Goldberg, Drew Carey, Steve Martin, Goldie Hawn, Eddie Murphy, Jim Carrey, and Rosie O'Donnell were all youngest kids.) Although a sense of humor is a great trait, make sure your baby doesn't use it at inappropriate moments (such as in school, at restaurants, and at the family dinner table). The trick is to help your little comedian decipher when a joke or some comic relief is appropriate and when it isn't. You may need to develop a private signal between you two for when it's an inappropriate moment to show off his hilarious Robin Williams routine or other entertaining antics.

- *Treat your youngest as capable.* We give our elder kids more responsibilities, and we just plain expect more of them at a younger age. Our expectations for our children do become self-fulfilling prophecies. Need proof? Eldest kids are more likely to become president of the United States or a CEO, land more prestigious jobs, and earn more money.[49] Almost all of the first astronauts were firstborns. Let's just not underrate our youngest and limit our expectations for their future. Be sure that your child hears that crucial parenting message—"You can do anything you put your mind to"—just as his older siblings have heard.

- *Raise the expectation bar.* Limited financial resources are often one reason the youngest doesn't earn as many degrees and diplomas, but aside from that, we are less likely to push that child to excel academically. Talk to your youngest in the "positive tense" about his education (*"When you finish college"*) and push his future goals (*"When you achieve your dreams"*). Don't curtail this child's academic success by lowering your expectations.

- *Keep up the responsibilities.* Make sure your youngest does his fair share of chores and gets to take out the trash just as his elder siblings were privileged to do. Those chores do teach responsibility as well as boost achievement scores.

- *Let your child tutor someone younger.* Parents often rely on the older child to help out with a younger sibling: "Can you teach your brother to tie his shoes?" "Will you show your sister how to use the computer?" Those little "tutoring" sessions appear to greatly benefit our older child. In fact, new research contends that one of the reasons the oldest child has a slightly higher IQ than her siblings (besides having had more one-on-one time with us) is from tutoring them. So find ways your youngest child can teach an even younger child a special skill so that he can have the same advantage as his older siblings. What about a younger neighbor, the babysitter's child, a cousin, or even his dog? It makes no difference whom or what he teaches, as long as he gets the opportunity to tutor.

- *Don't baby your baby.* The youngest kid has older siblings as well as parents who baby and take care of him. How great to be so coddled, right? But the problem is that the youngest kid can get locked into that "baby" role and become dependent on others. And there's the possibility that he will also lower his expectations for himself. So halt the labels ("He's our baby"). Watch out that this kid doesn't get stuck, become "too comfortable" as youngest and cutest, and depend on others to bail him out and do things for him. Research shows that younger kids can have difficulty establishing independence out there in the real world if they've never been taken seriously or required to be responsible for themselves.[50]

Part 2
Behavior

OUT OF THE MOUTHS OF BABES
WHY GOD MADE MOMS

Answers given by second-grade schoolchildren to the following question:

Why did God give you your mother and not some other mom?

1. We're related.

2. God knew she likes me a lot more than other people's moms like me.

Argues

SEE ALSO: *Angry, Biting, Communicating, Decision Making, Defiant, Dependent, Depressed, Sibling Rivalry, Stressed*

THE PROBLEM

Red Flags

Bickers constantly, has disagreeable attitude, alienates friends and family, can't solve problems

The Change to Parent For

Your child can express his opinion and concerns without bickering and is able to resolve conflicts so everyone is satisfied.

Question: "My son is constantly bickering and quarreling with the neighborhood kids. What can I do to help him learn to solve his own problems without me having to step in and referee? Right now he just runs to me and expects me to solve the problem."

Answer: Although it's tempting to step in and play negotiator, if you want your child to stop arguing and learn to solve his problems, then you must step back. Start by teaching him conflict resolution skills (such as "no yelling," "listen," "use the I word") and then the next time he comes running for help, say, *"You go right back there and work things through with your friend. I know you can solve this without me."*

Why Change?

Arguing. Quarreling. Yelling. Door slamming. Crying. Hurt feelings. Arguments are a big part of why kids can't get along with others. Of course, conflict is also a part of life, but some kids sure seem to get through it all a lot more smoothly. Usually that's because they have learned a few conflict resolution skills that help them get along more successfully with others.

You can teach children those same strategies, starting when they are quite young. These skills will not only help minimize arguments and tiffs with your children's peers but also serve them well for the rest of their life. Best yet, they will improve harmony on the home front. And wouldn't that ever be a plus?

Signs and Symptoms

Remember, all children argue, but here are a few symptoms of kids who bicker so constantly that it's become a problem in their daily life.

- Always comes to you to solve a problem
- Uses aggression to get his point across (bites, kicks, fights, shoves)
- Hears only his side of an issue; only wants his needs addressed
- Shouts or yells to air his views
- Puts down the other person's opinion
- Often loses his temper when trying to voice his views
- Doesn't "hear" where the other person is coming from or attempt to listen
- Takes things personally; overly touchy or sensitive
- Feels the need to retaliate because needs aren't met
- Blames others for the problem
- Can't identify or describe the problem or source of friction
- Can't think of solutions or alternatives or weigh the consequences

THE SOLUTION

Step 1. Early Intervention

- *Dig deeper to uncover the real reason.* Usually there are deeper issues involved: What's really triggering these arguments? For instance, is this a new behavior? If so, have there been any big changes in your child's life lately? Does

Pay Attention to This!

The American Psychiatric Association advises that if your child *frequently* displays *four* or more of the following characteristics *for at least six months,* you should seek the help of a trained mental health professional:

- Loses temper
- Argues with adults
- Actively defies or refuses to comply with adults' requests or rules
- Deliberately annoys other people
- Blames others for his mistakes or misbehavior
- Is touchy or easily annoyed by others
- Is angry or resentful
- Is spiteful and vindictive

your child quarrel with everyone or just certain friends or family members? Do the arguments usually happen at a certain time or day of the week (such as when he's hungry, stressed, or tired?). Ask friends, teachers, and coaches who know your child well for advice until you can discover the real reason for the constant bickering. Then commit yourself to changing one thing to start turning things around. Could any of these be the reason your child always argues? Check those reasons that may apply to your child:

- ☐ Lacking conflict resolution skills or ability to solve problems
- ☐ Jealous or resentful of the individual
- ☐ Experiencing unfair treatment; being taken advantage of; always slighted; trying to stick up for himself
- ☐ Copying what he sees and hears: everyone else in the family argues and yells
- ☐ Selfish or materialistic: always wants what others have
- ☐ Quick-tempered, easily frustrated, or stressed
- ☐ Overly sensitive and easily gets rubbed the wrong way
- ☐ Overly competitive, afraid to lose, perfectionist, or just a poor loser; arguments usually crop up when your child is in a competition
- ☐ Overdependent: always comes to you or someone else to solve the problem
- ☐ Domineering or bossy; craves control, attention, or power
- ☐ Bullied, teased, or picked on; trying to defend himself

- *Let him witness the right way to argue.* It's important for kids to see that two people can disagree calmly and respectfully. And what better way than watching the two people he loves most "fight fair"? So tune up your own conflict resolution skills and find the right moment to show your kids the "cool" way to solve conflicts. (Hint: if you notice that you're having heated arguments with adult family members, friends, and colleagues, start tuning up your own conflict resolution skills before trying to teach them to your child.)

- *Set a "no yelling" rule.* If arguments are becoming too heated and are turning into yelling matches, then consider making a family "no yelling vow." The pledge is written on a piece of paper, signed by all members, and posted as a concrete reminder. Then honor it! The second any arguer's voice goes up a notch, any family member can give a nonverbal "time-out" signal (like a referee) reminding the yeller to speak in a calmer tone.

- *Let your child be heard!* One of the biggest reasons kids argue is that they want their feelings and needs to be heard—but no one listens! Whether or not that's the case with your kid, he does need experience with voicing his opinions in a calm manner as well as listening to other family members do the same. Find ways for your family to get their needs across and disagree peacefully. Consider using family meetings or family dinners, or even set aside a half hour every Sunday for everyone just to debrief each other about the week.

- *Switch "You" to "I."* Derogatory comments usually begin with "You" (You never . . . You're so stupid . . . You don't know what you're talking about . . . You never listen). A quick way to help your kids learn how to get their needs across *without* downing the other person is for them to switch from "You" to "I" and then simply tell the other person how some unacceptable behavior makes them feel. Doing so focuses on the issue that is bugging the kid without putting the recipient down: *"I get really upset when you take my stuff." "I don't like to be kicked. It hurts."* Just stress to your kids that their job is to attack the problem and not the person.

- *Get your kid to see the other side.* Kids often get so caught up in their own point of view that they lose sight of where the other person is coming from. *"How does your sister feel?" "Did you hear what she actually said?" "What would she think is fair?"*

- *Call for time-outs.* Even a few seconds can be enough to stop a big quarrel, so help your child come up with a few ways to back off from an argument ready to blow. "When you feel like you and your brother are starting to argue, try to cool things off. You could say: *"You know I'm too mad to talk right now.' 'Give me a minute to cool off.' 'I need to take a walk.' 'Let's go shoot some hoops.'"*

Step 2. Rapid Response

- *Be sympathetic.* Arguments are tough for everyone—but especially so for kids. Chances are that your child or the other kid or both are hurting. Keep in mind that your goal isn't to solve the problem—that's up to them—but you can acknowledge the hurt. *"I can see why you're upset." "Arguments are never fun. They get everybody hurting."*

ONE SIMPLE SOLUTION

Teach Kids to Argue Respectfully

Kids needs to know that it's okay to disagree—just as long as they do so without bashing the other person. The problem is that most kids don't know ways to argue their point respectfully, so teach a few phrases they can adopt to get their views across, such as *"That's one idea; here's another . . ." "I don't agree. Here's what I think." "There's another way to look at it." "Have you considered . . . ?" "That's one way to look at it, but here's another . . ."* You might even write such phrases on a chart to hang up on the fridge as a reminder and then find a way to naturally use a different phrase each day with your kids so that they get in the habit of using them. Do stress that they must deliver the line calmly and then listen to the other person's opinion.

- *Don't ask why, ask what.* Asking the right questions can help your child think about what triggered the argument and might even prevent the next one. Asking "why" questions ("Why are you arguing?" "Why can't you get along?") are almost guaranteed to confuse your kid and yield an "I don't know" response. Instead ask "what" questions: *"What was your quarrel about?" "What did your friend say?" "What did you do?" "What do you want to happen now?"*

- *Encourage them work it out themselves.* Ask the kids involved what they plan to do to solve "their" problem. After all, real-life practice is the best way for children to learn skills. *"I know you two can solve this. If you need me, I'm in the other room, but don't leave the table until you can work this out fairly." "Let's see if you two can work this through calmly for three minutes. You've been friends far too long not to solve this."*

- *Intervene if necessary.* If you hear an argument brewing, stay within earshot, but jump in only before emotions get too heated and that argument escalates. A gentle reminder might be called for, such as a previously agreed-on private signal (tugging on your ear, for example). With younger kids, you might say: *"I see two angry kids who need to cool down. You go to the other room, and you to the kitchen until you can talk calmly and work things out."*

- *Encourage amends.* If there are hurt feelings and your child is the cause, encourage him to make amends. Have him call the friend, apologize, and tell the friend he's sorry, or suggest a way the two can get beyond the hurdle and on with their relationship.

- *Suggest a compromise.* A great way to reduce arguments is by compromising. Start by describing what it means: *"When you compromise it means you're willing to give up a little of what you want, and the other person is too. It's a fair way to solve a problem because everyone is more satisfied: each person can have at least part of what he wants."* Your kid should understand that each person

One Parent's Answer

A mom from Lake Tahoe shares:

My youngest kid never had a chance to voice his view against his older very-verbal sister. The arguments and tears drove me crazy. I finally gave him an egg timer and made a house rule that he must be able to talk—without interruption—until the buzzer went off after a full three minutes of expressing himself. He carried that timer around for days, but it worked. Not only did the tears stop, but he actually learned to state his case against his sister quite well.

always has the opportunity to present his side, and when he does, he should be listened to: "I need to practice soccer. I have a game Saturday." Then find ways to help your child learn to apply the skill to real-life situations.

Step 3. Develop Habits for Change

Teaching your child the five new habits described here will reduce those arguments and help your child resolve conflicts so that everyone is satisfied. Teach each habit separately (for instance, to solve a conflict, kids first need to learn to stop and calm down) and tailor your lessons to the developmental capabilities of your child. Then make sure you look for real-life opportunities to help your child practice until he can use each habit without you. By the time your child has learned the five parts to solving problems, he will be able to stand up for himself and solve his own conflicts. (The five parts spell out STAND to help your child remember the crucial habits.)

S – **Stop and Calm Down.** The first step to conflict resolution is to calm down. The reason is simple: it's impossible to think about how to solve a problem if you're upset. Once in control, you can begin rationally to figure out why you're upset and then find an answer to your dilemma. So teach your kid to take a slow, deep breath to calm down if the argument is getting heated. If people look or sound tense, encourage him to call for a time-out or suggest that everyone stop to stay calm, get a drink of water, leave for a minute, and then come back. Only when everyone is calm can you talk about what's bugging you.

T – **Take Turns Telling What the Problem Is.** The trick here is to enforce these critical rules: no put-downs or name-calling; you must listen to each other respectfully. No interrupting: each person gets a chance to talk. You might ask each kid to say what happened, summarize each view, and then end with, "What can you do now to solve this problem?" Make suggestions only when your kids really seem stuck. Tell kids to start their explanations with the word "I" instead of "You" and then to describe the problem and how they want it resolved. Doing so helps the speaker focus on the conflict without putting the other kid down. For instance: "I'm ticked because you never give me a turn. I want to use the computer, too." If emotions are high, give kids the option of writing or drawing their view of the problem instead of saying it to each other. This approach is particularly helpful for younger or less verbal kids. The goal should be to help each child try to feel what it's like to be in the other child's shoes. One way to do this is by having each kid put into his own words what the other kid has told him.

A – **List the Alternatives for Resolving It.** Next, kids need think of alternatives so that they have ways to find a resolution. Whether your child is a preschooler or an adolescent, the basic rules for thinking of solutions are the same: (1) say the first thing that comes into your mind; (2) don't put down anyone else's ideas; (3) change or add on to anyone's idea; (4) try to come up with ideas that work for both sides. Don't offer your help unless the other person really seems stuck! To keep kids focused, say they must come up with five different solutions before you return. Then leave for a few minutes. Stretch the time depending on the children's age and problem-solving skills.

𝒩 – **Narrow the Choices.** Now narrow the options down to a few choices. Here are two rules to help kids get closer to resolving the problem: (1) eliminate any solutions that are unacceptable to either kid because they don't satisfy his needs, and (2) eliminate any solutions that aren't safe or wise.

𝒟 – **Decide on the Best Choice and Do It!** The final part of conflict resolution helps kids learn how to make the best decision by thinking through the consequences of their choices. You can teach kids to think about the consequences of their remaining choices by asking, *"What might happen if you tried that?"* Another way to help kids decide on the best choice is by helping them weigh the pros and cons of each remaining possibility: *"What are all the good and bad things that might happen if you chose that?" "What is the one last change that would make this work better for both of you?"* Once they decide, the two kids shake on the agreement or take turns saying, "I agree."

WHAT TO EXPECT BY STAGES AND AGES

Preschooler   Though their vocabularies are emerging, preschoolers still need help putting their problem into words. Controlling impulses is still difficult, so boys in particular are prone to find physical ways to solve their problems. Kids this age are able to grasp

LATE-BREAKING NEWS

Philadelphia: Over twenty-five years of research conducted by renowned psychologists George Spivack and Myrna Shure found that children as young as three and four years old can be taught to think through their problems.[1] They also discovered that children who are skilled in problem solving were less likely to be impulsive and aggressive when things didn't go their way; tended to be more caring and less insensitive; were better able to make friends; and tended to achieve more academically. Spivack and Shure's research, and scores of other studies, confirm that learning problem-solving skills greatly enhances our children's chances for success and will reduce those arguments!

that angry feelings can cause hurt, so they should be encouraged to "use their words." Arguments focus almost exclusively on what they want and need, and they have difficulty seeing the other person's point of view.

School Age   Resolving conflicts get easier as language develops. A simple prodding question, such as "What's the matter?" is usually all kids need to identify the problem, though they will need help identifying possible outcomes of decisions. They can now better understand others' feelings and perspectives as well as patterns that occur in disagreements. Beware: boys in grades 4 through 6 are more likely than ever to use aggression to resolve differences.[2]

Tween   In a national survey, 43 percent of tweens said they have conflicts with other kids at least one or more times a day;[3] 80 percent said they see kids having arguments.[4] Top conflict areas for boys include who's right and who's wrong, bragging, who does better at sports or in school, game rules, and insults and name-calling. Top conflict areas for girls are gossip and rumors, having secrets told, boyfriends, feeling jealous or left out, and mean remarks made behind people's backs.[5]

More Helpful Advice

Peaceful Parents, Peaceful Kids: Practical Ways to Create a Calm and Happy Home, by Naomi Drew

Tired of Yelling: Teaching Our Children to Resolve Conflict, by Lyndon D. Waugh

Waging Peace in Our Schools, by Linda Lantieri and Janet Patti

The Kids' Guide to Working Out Conflicts: How to Keep Cool, Stay Safe, and Get Along, by Naomi Drew (ages nine to fourteen)

BEHAVIOR

Back Talk

SEE ALSO: *Bad Manners, Bossy, Communicating, Defiant, Swears, Whining*

THE PROBLEM

Red Flags

Uses a flippant, smart-alecky, or sassy comment, tone, or gesture in response to a request

The Change to Parent For

Your child curbs her back talk and flippant manners and learns to voice her concerns and needs in a respectful and appropriate manner.

Question: "Our sweet daughter has suddenly become smart-mouthed. If somebody heard her speak to me with her sassy tone I'd die. What's the best way to stop back talk?"

Answer: The best quick fix to ending back talk is simply not to allow it the very next time your child uses it. Calmly say, "Please use a polite tone." And then *do not respond to what the child says until she can talk to you in a respectful tone.* You may need to leave the room, but don't back down or compromise—not just the first time, but each and every time your child uses a flippant, disrespectful tone. Your reaction must be consistent and persistent. I don't care if your child wants to tell you something important or desperately needs your help; you must make her realize that back talk is intolerable and will no longer be indulged. This approach goes for little kids and big kids, too.

Why Change?

Consider these scenarios. You politely say to your son, "Robby, remember I want you home by four," and your sweet little darling in a flippant tone retorts, "Get real." Or you calmly ask your daughter, "Can you please make your bed?" and your prized offspring retorts, "Make it yourself!" Do these responses sound at all familiar?

Back talk and sass are on the rise, and these behaviors seem to bother every adult—and rightly so. The behavior usually starts at about four years of age, but if you allow back talk to continue, negative results can spread like wildfire. Believe me: no teacher, coach, scout leader, or other child's parent appreciates a disrespectful kid. Luckily, disrespectful behaviors such as whining, back talk, and sassiness are some of the easiest inappropriate behaviors to get rid of. In a survey quoted in *Child* magazine, only 12 percent of the two thousand adults polled felt that kids commonly treat others with respect; most described them as "rude," "irresponsible," and "lacking in discipline."[6] That's all the more reason we need to nip this behavior in the bud ASAP.

Signs and Symptoms

"Back talk" is any comment delivered in a flippant, sassy, smart-alecky, and disrespectful tone. Although it is normal for any child to use back talk a few times, here are five signs that it is time for a more intense parenting plan to change this unbecoming behavior:

1. Your child does not stop using the behavior at your simple request.
2. The back talk is increasing in frequency and intensity.
3. The back talk is ruining your family tone or your relationship with your child.
4. Children or adults are complaining or are concerned about your child's rude behavior.
5. Your child is using the behavior with other adults and children outside your home.

THE SOLUTION

Step 1. Early Intervention

- *Identify the reason.* Your first step to preventing back talk from escalating is to identify the reason your child is resorting to this rude behavior. Here are the most typical causes of back talk. Check those that apply to your child:
  - ☐ Copying other kids, TV, movies, or *you*
  - ☐ Getting attention
  - ☐ Feeling unappreciated
  - ☐ Testing limits
  - ☐ Proving independence or feeling "grown up"
  - ☐ Seeking control
  - ☐ Trying to fit in with kids or gain peer acceptance
  - ☐ Feeling angry or frustrated

- *Check your behavior.* Are you, your parenting partner, or an older sibling using a flippant or sarcastic tone that your child is picking up on? If so, tune up your behavior so that you model respect to your child—and suggest other family members do so as well.

- *Expect respect.* Announce your new talking rules:

  "In this house we only help and encourage each other."

  "Carey may talk to her mom like that, but you may not talk sassy to me."

  "I've heard your friends, but you live in this house, and we have different rules."

  "When I talk to you, you roll your eyes. It looks disrespectful, and you need to stop."

  "Telling me to 'chill out' when I talk to you is unacceptable. You may not talk that way."

  Notice how these messages address only the disrespectful behavior and *not* the child's character.

- *Monitor the TV.* Sitcoms and reality shows are laced with sarcasm and back talk. Kids do pick up on that language. Set clear viewing guidelines so that your kid knows which shows are not permitted. Then turn off that TV whenever the language is unacceptable; discuss your objections.

- *Boost character.* Stress the virtues of compassion, respect, and courtesy in your daily actions and discuss over and over why you believe in them. Tune up the family values you stand for, and your child will have a stronger understanding of why you object to back talk and disrespectful tones.

Step 2. Rapid Response

- *Intervene ASAP.* Back talk usually starts in the early years and then increases as kids become more verbal and confident. Regardless of your child's age, the second she uses a sassy tone or word, call her on it. Using a calm, firm "teacher" voice, tell your child what she did or said that was unacceptable. Here are a few examples:

  "That tone is disrespectful."

  "You may not tell me to 'shut up.'"

ONE SIMPLE SOLUTION

Use the Freeze-and-Replay Method

The very next time your child talks back, say: *"Freeze. Do not move until you can talk in a nice voice"* or *"I'll listen when you can ask politely."* Then turn a deaf ear or even walk away. Be careful not to send *any* nonverbal responses (sighing, rolling your eyes, shrugging your shoulders, or looking exasperated). The trick is to "respectfully ignore" your kid until she treats you politely—which you deserve. When kids see you are not going to give in, they usually stop the sass.

"Stop. Telling me that I don't know anything is disrespectful. We'll talk when you talk right."

"I don't listen to sass. If you want to talk to me, talk respectfully. I'll be in the other room."

"We'll talk when you can listen respectfully without rolling your eyes and smirking."

- *Stay calm.* Your best response to sassiness is to stay calm. Yelling or sounding irritated only shifts the focus from your child's inappropriate behavior to your anger, and sets you up for a power struggle. It also gives your kid what she may have been looking for: attention and reaction.

- *Be consistent.* Your goal is to let your child know that back talk will not be tolerated.

- *Don't take it personally.* Generally kids don't plan their comment—their words just slip out as an automatic response to what you said. Your child is probably expressing her honest, strong feeling about what you're asking. So relax and don't take the comment personally.

- *Get others on board.* Talk to other adults who care about your child and might encounter back talk—your parenting partner, day-care workers, Grandma. Let them know your plan so that you're on board together and can nip back talk before it escalates.

Step 3. Develop Habits for Change

- *Set a consequence.* If your child continues to talk back or the behavior escalates, it's time to take things up a notch. Here are four logical consequences for deliberate sass to help your child recognize that the behavior is not going to be tolerated.

  - *Mandate an apology.* A sincere apology for the hurt should be required. A young child can draw a picture apology; an older child can write or say one, or do something to make up for the hurt she caused (picking flowers from the yard, doing a chore for the offended party).

Pay Attention to This!

You should see a gradual diminishment in your child's back talk in two or three weeks if you stick to your no-back-talk rule. If you don't see any improvement, if your child is talking back to other adults or is becoming more defiant, then something else is setting off the behavior. It's time to dig deeper to determine the cause. Talk to others who know your child well for a "second opinion."

- *Send the friend home.* If your child talks back in the presence of a friend, explain your policy: *"You know our rule: Unless you talk nicely, you may not play."* Then briefly separate the two kids. If back talk continues, send the friend home.

- *Use a privilege poster.* Effective consequences cause a bit of discomfort to the child. So photograph or draw things your child can't live without and that you can control, such as her phone, TV, dessert, rollerblades, or MP3 player. Your child loses one privilege starting from least to most favorite for each back talk infringement.

- *Remove the child from the family activity.* Firmly remind your child that back talk is unacceptable and shows that she does not want to be with the rest of the family. Send your child to her room for the rest of the activity.

- *Nurture your relationship.* Continued back talk may mean that your child is feeling devalued and is lashing out with words. If this could be the case, put in more one-on-one time to reconnect with your child and repair the strain in your relationship.

- *Encourage respectful behavior.* One of the simplest ways to increase the frequency of a desirable behavior is to reinforce it when we see our child doing it right. Studies have shown, however, that the majority of the time we do the opposite: instead of "catching" our kids being respectful, we point out when they are acting incorrectly. So any time you see or hear your child practicing respectful behaviors and using a polite tone, acknowledge her and express your pleasure. Here are a few examples:

"Danny, I like that respectful tone."

"Jenny, thank you for listening so politely when I was talking."

"That's a nice voice, Theresa. Good for you for remembering how to say your words right."

"I know that you were frustrated, but you didn't talk back that time. It's hard changing a bad habit, but you're really trying."

One Parent's Answer

A mom from Cleveland shares:

I figured my kid would try out a sassy tone sooner or later. I just didn't want him to know he could get away with it. So when I asked him to do his chores and he responded with a sassy remark, I called him on it. Later when he asked for a ride to go skateboarding with his friend, I told him he'd need to find another driver. I was hurt the way he'd talked to me earlier and really played it up. The look on his face was priceless! It was the last time he used back talk.

WHAT TO EXPECT BY STAGES AND AGES

Preschooler Young children are little copiers and will try out new words and intonations for attention. If your child does use a sassy tone, your best response is to simply say, *"We don't talk like that in our house."* This is also the age when kids behave because "parents know best," and rules that you've set are likely to be followed.

School Age This is the stage of experimenting and limit testing, so expect your school-age kid to try back talk, but don't allow her to treat you disrespectfully. If you hold your ground now, your child will be far less likely to use a sassier tone as a tween or teen, which can destroy not only your relationship but also your family harmony. Also, don't overreact. Kids at this age will use you as their example for how to handle tense situations.

Tween These are prime years for back talk as tweens try to gain independence and want to see how you'll respond if they exert control. This is also the age when kids want to "fit in" and to appear "cool," so they may copy their peers' behavior. If things start to get too heated, call a time-out and tell your tween you'll talk to her later so that you both have time to cool off. Getting into an argument only takes the focus off the issue that should be addressed (such as the bad grade, disobeying the curfew, abusing the cell phone privilege) and gets the kid off the hook.

More Helpful Advice

Backtalk: Four Steps to Ending Rude Behavior in Your Kids, by Audrey Ricker and Carolyn Crowder

Discipline Without Shouting or Spanking: Practical Solutions to the Most Common Preschool Behavior Problems, by Jerry Wychoff and Barbara Unell

Raising Respectful Kids in a Rude World: Teaching Your Children the Power of Mutual Respect and Consideration, by Gary D. McKay

Say Goodbye to Whining, Complaining, and Bad Attitudes . . . in You and Your Kids, by Scott Turansky

Setting Limits with Your Strong-Willed Child: Eliminating Conflict by Establishing Clear, Firm, and Respectful Boundaries, by Robert J. MacKenzie

Biting

SEE ALSO: *Angry, Fearful, Sibling Rivalry, Stressed, Tantrums*

THE PROBLEM
Red Flags

Bites others due to impulsivity, frustration, attention getting, or need for protection; is unable to verbalize needs and feelings

The Change to Parent For

Your child learns new habits that help control aggressive urges, uses words to express feelings and needs, and learns healthier ways to manage frustrations.

Why Change?

Of all the common aggressive kid behaviors—scratching, slapping, pinching, spitting, hitting, shoving, and hair pulling—biting tops the parent concern list. If it's any consolation, the behavior is common during those early years, especially among boys. In fact, it's the most common reason kids get expelled from day care. But it should never be taken lightly. Although similar to hitting, biting is actually more dangerous.[7] That's because

Pay Attention to This!
Check Out the Child-Care Policy for Biting

Biting is the most common reason children get expelled from day care.[8] Do check the "biting policy" at the child-care facility as to what it will do if a child bites. (If the administrator says they've never had that problem, be leery!) A good facility has warm, involved workers who monitor children closely and have a clearly thought-out, consistently enforced policy for handling aggression. They also know that biting is typical in young kids, so they are trained in how to handle the situation.

young children have more power in their jaw muscles than in their arms, so the damage from those chompers is more severe.

Although biting usually tapers off once children learn to express their needs and cope with frustrations, it can become a vicious habit that continues even as the child gets older.[9] So don't sit idly by and expect this behavior to go away on its own. Whatever the cause, it is clearly unacceptable and will quickly make any kid (and his parents) very unpopular. Your job is to stop this aggressive behavior before it becomes a habit and help your child learn healthier ways to cope with frustrations and express his needs.

THE SOLUTION

Five Strategies for Change

1. *Figure out the reason and then anticipate.* Your first step to solving this problem is to discover why your child is biting. Do talk to his teachers. Here are a few possibilities. Check those that might apply to your child:

   ☐ *Jealous:* wants what someone else has; quick way to get needs met

   ☐ *Impulsive:* lacks self-control; quick-tempered; easily frustrated; shorter attention span

   ☐ *Protective:* uses self-defense against an aggressive or intimidating kid

   ☐ *Lacking skills:* has limited vocabulary to verbalize needs, says "It's mine"; has few coping skills

   ☐ *Seeking control:* tests limits or trying to gain power

   ☐ *Frustrated:* is with too many kids playing in too close quarters, not enough toys or supplies

   ☐ *Trying to get attention*: thinks biting is a quick, sure way to become the center of attention

   ☐ *Imitating:* copies the biting behavior of others (watch who your child hangs around with)

   ☐ *Stressed:* experiences friction at home, illness, pressure, a divorce, a death, new school, a move

   ☐ *In the habit:* has been allowed to get away with it

2. *Step in ASAP.* The next step is critical. Don't wait: move quickly.

   • The second your child bites, swoop in and say, *"No biting."* Then in your stern voice say, *"You may not bite people! Biting hurts!"*

   • Immediately remove your child to a more secluded spot away from other kids to give him time to calm down. This works particularly well if the biting was a ploy to gain attention. (See *Time-Out*, p. 118.)

- Stay calm and try not to overreact. No matter what anyone says, do *not* bite your child back! It is not helpful, and you're only sending the message that kids can't bite, but adults can.

- Caution siblings and other children not to laugh. Doing so will give your child attention he may be seeking. If your child has developed a pattern of biting, then supervise play times closely so that you can intervene *before* he bites.

- Watch for a frustration buildup. For these times, distracting him from the situation or offering an alternative is sometimes helpful: *"Let's go play blocks!"*

3. *Console the injured.* Center your attention on the victim: *"Oh, that must hurt!"* *"I'm so sorry. What can I do to help?"* Focusing on the injured helps your child realize that biting hurts and that his behavior has consequences. He will also be learning from your modeling how to convey sympathy. When your child is calm, you might suggest hints to make someone feel better: *"Why don't you . . . get Sammy a Kleenex, give him a washcloth, find the teacher, give him a stuffed animal."* Do notify the injured child's parents. Better that you make the call than someone else. Do relate what type of first aid was administered and what plans (if any) are in place to prevent future biting incidents. (See First Aid for Bites.)

4. *Replace biting with words.* Once kids learn to say what they want or need, biting starts to decrease. You can speed up the process by teaching your child to "use his words" when he is calm. Start by modeling appropriate words for your child to copy: *"Looks like you're mad. Tell your friend, 'I'm mad.'"* You can also teach phrases to reduce typical peer conflicts: *"I want to play."* *"May I have a turn?"* *"You need to share."* Then help him practice "using his words" until he can use them in real social settings. Remember to let your child know how proud you are when he tries to use control or express his needs appropriately. It's progress!

5. *Get other caregivers on board.* Take emergency action if your child has developed a history of biting. Set up a private conference with the school, day care, or playgroup so that the adult in charge is aware of the behavior and you all agree on the consequence (such as a brief time-out or going home). The plan *must* be consistently enforced at school and at home. Also insist that you be informed, and record each incident so you can track the pattern. With an older child, hold a serious talk as soon as convenient. Be clear that biting will not be tolerated, that there will be a consequence each time, and that you plan to monitor his behavior closely. Stay in contact with his teacher until the behavior stops. If the biting does not gradually decrease over a few weeks, seek a professional's advice. The American Academy of Child and Adolescent Psychiatry says that although some biting is a normal developmental phase, *persistent* biting can be a sign of an emotional or behavioral problem.[10]

First Aid for Bites

The following are the recommendations of the American Academy of Pediatrics:

- Wash the bite immediately with warm, soapy water for about ten minutes.
- If the skin is broken, cover the bite with a sterile dressing.
- Keep an eye on the bitten area for a few days and immediately report any signs of infection (such as swelling, new redness, fever, soreness that extends beyond the norm) to the child's pediatrician.
- Make sure that the child's tetanus immunizations are up-to-date.
- Contact the parent of the child who is bitten and advise her to seek medical help. Human saliva contains bacteria that can cause infection.

One Parent's Answer

A mom from Reno shares:

When the preschool teacher told me my sweet daughter bit a boy, I couldn't believe it. But sure enough, I found out that this little boy started in on my daughter, grabbing things from her. She was trying to "be good," but this kid was a bully, and sure enough she took a chomp out of his arm. I saw how upset she was and told her that I knew she didn't mean to bite and that I'd help her so she wouldn't have to bite again. She broke down, so relieved that someone was going to help her deal with this bully. Every day, we practiced using a "strong voice" until she was able to stand up for herself. It was the last time she bit or that boy picked on her.

WHAT TO EXPECT BY STAGES AND AGES

Preschooler   Biting is common among preschoolers, especially boys, because kids lack skills to handle strong feelings or emotions, are playing in overly close quarters, or are imitating other kids' behavior, especially at day care.

School Age   Younger school-age children may bite out of frustration or anger. It is not typical for kids older than seven to bite. If they do, it is usually due to deeper emotional issues, impulsivity, or severe stress and requires intense intervention. Seek the help of the school or district psychologist ASAP. Request a psychological assessment and a monitored behavior plan.

Tween   Biting at this age is not common and is typically is due to intense anger, trauma, or an emotional issue. Seek the help of a mental health professional immediately.

Bossy

SEE ALSO: *Back Talk, Communicating, Demanding, Insensitive, Sharing, Won't Listen*

THE PROBLEM

Red Flags

Tells everyone what to do in a dictatorial and inconsiderate manner, is overly controlling, doesn't listen or consider friends' needs or desires

The Change to Parent For

Your child learns habits that temper her bossy streak, help her consider the needs of others, and channel her pushiness into effective leadership.

Question: "I hate to admit it, but our daughter is so bossy. She dictates orders to her friends and wants everything to go her way. If she doesn't temper her "overly assertive spirit" now, she's going to end up with no friends at all. She's always been controlling, so how do you change a kid like this so she will be more accepted by the human race?"

Answer: Although you certainly can't change your daughter's core temperament, you can temper her bossy streak and teach habits that will help her consider the feelings of others. A simple way to help jump-start that change is to insist that she always ask permission before imposing her agenda on others. For instance: "I'm going to play Chutes and Ladders. Do you mind?" or "I want to sit in the front seat. Is that okay?" Teaching that one little skill just may help her realize she has to stop and think about what others may want instead of always bulldozing ahead with her own agenda.

Why Change?

Bossy kids appoint themselves to be the ones in charge. They set the rules, choose the activities, and decide the game plan. And very rarely do they bother listening to their peers' or siblings' thoughts or concerns. Although their dictatorial skills may someday be the makings of a strong leader and CEO, right now these kids' bossy ways are usually highly unappreciated by peers.

Pay Attention to This!
Bossy Children Are Unpopular and More Likely to Be Rejected

University of Illinois-Urbana: If you're in need of a compelling reason to change your child's bossy ways, here it is: studies find that one of the five reasons kids are most likely to be rejected by peers is that they are bossy and domineering.[11] Kids just don't like it when peers aren't cooperative, helpful, or considerate of others. So by eliminating your kid's bossiness, you increase your child's chances for social success and happiness.

Although you certainly won't want to stifle your child's self-confidence or willingness to take charge and assume responsibilities, you will want to help change a dictatorial, domineering attitude so that your child is more considerate of others' needs and more respectful of their feelings and wishes. Doing so certainly will boost your child's "likeability quotient" and social success. There are definite ways to parent for this type of change. You may see your child as a born leader, and she may indeed be the kind of kid who likes to take charge, assume responsibilities, and get things done. But remember, a true leader considers others' needs, hears where they are coming from, and has a positive goal that can benefit everyone, not just herself.

Signs and Symptoms

Here are several warning signs that your child's bossiness just may be affecting her emotional and social development. For the most accurate appraisal, observe your child's interactions with different kids in a variety of settings (at day care, at the neighbors, on the soccer field, at scouts).

- Your child dictates the activities, makes the agenda, and creates the game plan.
- She starts to boss *you* and tell *you* what to do.
- Things have to go *her* way; she plays only by *her* rules.
- She rarely negotiates or alters her desires to accommodate others; compromise is unacceptable.
- Friends don't return her calls, invite her back, or want to come over.
- Parents, coaches, scout leaders, or teachers label her "bossy" or "domineering."
- Clueless that other people feel pushed or slighted by her behavior.

LATE-BREAKING NEWS

University of California, Berkeley: Research by pediatrician
W. Thomas Boyce found that bossier preschool kids tend to
be healthier.[12] In fact, less dominant preschoolers at the lower end of the pecking
order were found to have more health problems and to respond to stress with
higher heart rates and a greater output of stress hormones than their bossier
counterparts. Boyce drew these conclusions through observing and videotaping
sixty-nine mostly middle-class preschoolers in eight five-week periods. So
keep those findings in mind. Your little dictator is more than likely to have a
biological tendency to dominate, and that trait may help her stay healthier and
handle stress throughout life. Meanwhile, continue to temper that too-pushy
spirit when it comes to relationships, so that your child is also happier.

THE SOLUTION

Step 1. Early Intervention

- *Identify why this is happening.* Your first step is to figure out the reasons your
  child is a little dictator so that you can find the best ways to temper her behavior and improve her ability to get along. Check the reasons that may apply to
  your child:

  - ☐ *Mimicking.* Your child is used to being bossed around, so she's modeling
    what she's experienced.
  - ☐ *Receiving reinforcement.* Someone is intentionally (or unintentionally) rein-
    forcing the bossiness by labeling it as assertive, confident, or outgoing, or as
    a leadership capability; or someone is just letting her always get her way.
  - ☐ *Expected to take charge.* She's assumed responsibility for taking care of
    others; may be hanging around kids who lack direction and need someone
    to "take charge."
  - ☐ *Insecure.* Your child is covering up for insecurities, low self-esteem, or
    perfectionism.
  - ☐ *Needs power.* She needs to feel a sense of power to compensate for being at
    the bottom of a pecking order among family or friends.
  - ☐ *Picked on.* Your child is frequently dominated by others; she's attempting to
    even the playing field.

- ☐ *Lacks social experiences.* She really doesn't know how to get her opinions across in a friendly way.
- ☐ *Voiceless.* Her ideas, feelings, and needs are frequently ignored.
- ☐ *Lacks empathy.* Your child is still in an egocentric stage of development or lacks the ability to take another's perspective or to think of where the other person is coming from.

Talk to others who know your child well to get their opinion, and make your best guess as to why your child is so dictatorial. Is there one thing you could do to start the change?

- *Emphasize consensus.* Dictators need to learn about democracy, so emphasize that in your home. In fact, enforce a new rule that for certain family decisions (vacation and restaurant choice, DVD rental, which TV show to watch, which board or video game to play), all members should be surveyed. Your child needs to learn democracy in action, so that she can apply it with her own friends.

- *Expect cooperation.* Research shows that kids who demonstrate cooperative behaviors—sharing, taking turns, taking into consideration the requests of peers, and so on—usually do so because their parents clearly emphasized that they expected them to. So take time to spell out your ground rules for sharing and cooperation and explain them to your child. Then expect your kid to use them. Make sure you also emphasize *why* bossiness is not appreciated and how it turns people off.

Step 2. Rapid Response

- *Point out bossiness ASAP.* The minute you hear or see your kid bossing friends or siblings (or you!), pull her aside and quietly point out what you see: "I notice you keep taking the controller from David." Don't accuse. Stay calm.

- *Remain calm.* Domineering kids can be stubborn and strong willed, and if you are headstrong as well, the two of you may end up butting heads. So pick your battles, reduce your lectures, and remain respectful, so that you don't engage in a lot of unnecessary conflict. If you

ONE SIMPLE SOLUTION

Bossy kids put their agenda first. So tell your child to use the "you" word a bit more whenever she is with a peer: "What do *you* think?" "Which game do *you* want to play?" "What do *you* want to do first?" That simple tweak can start the change in your child so that she considers the needs and feelings of others.

are a more submissive type, don't let this kid boss *you* around. Watch how you respond to your child so that you can determine the best approach to helping change her dictatorial approach.

- *Teach simple solutions to curb bossiness.* Don't assume that your child knows how to change her domineering ways; instead show her a new response. Here are a few examples of solutions for bossiness to help you get started. Then watch your child a bit more carefully to identify the problem and then provide a solution.

    Problem: Doesn't share. **Solution:** Explain taking turns to your child, why it's important, and then remind her of the expected behavior. *"Remember, I expect you to share. If there's anything you really don't want to share, put it away before your friend comes. Otherwise you must let her have a turn."*

    Problem: Dictates the game plan. **Solution:** Your new house rule is "the guest chooses the first activity"; from then on, choices are alternated.

    Problem: Doesn't realize she sounds bossy. **Solution:** Show her how to turn a bossy comment into a more tactful statement. Bossy: "We're going to shoot baskets." Tamer: "What would you like to play?" Bossy: "We're doing it my way." Tamer: "How about if we try it my way?"

    Problem: Unaware she's being bossy with a peer. **Solution:** Develop a private signal (pulling on your ear or touching your nose) so that the moment her bossiness kicks in, you signal to her to turn down her dictator mode.

    Problem: Doesn't consider the other person's view. **Solution:** Turn the experience into a teachable moment: *"Kara never got a turn. How do you think she felt?" "You never asked Bill what he wanted to do. How do you think he felt?" "What do you think you can do next time so your friend has a say?" "What will you do to make sure Paul has a better time?"*

- *Set a consequence if dictating continues.* Your child needs to know you are serious about curbing her bossy streak. So if despite your efforts your child continues to be a dictator around peers, it's time to set a consequence. *"Unless you can be less bossy, you won't be able to have Matt come over. Let's work on ways you can treat him more fairly."*

Step 3. Develop Habits for Change

- *Teach nondictatorial strategies.* Bossy kids don't stop to ponder what the other kid may want. So here are a few strategies to help your child learn to consider the other kid's desires. Choose one or two strategies to teach your child. Plan to practice the strategy at home several times until she is comfortable using it with peers.

- *Use decision breakers.* These are great when two kids can't decide what rules to play by, who gets to choose what to do, or even who goes first. Drawing straws, picking a number, tossing a coin, and playing Rock, Paper, Scissors are oldies but goodies that help make things fairer.

- *Use "Grandma's Rule."* The rule is simple and works like a charm to makes things fairer: "If you cut the cake, the other person decides which piece to take." The rule can apply to lots of things. For example: if you choose the game, the other person gets to go first; if you pour the lemonade, the other person chooses his glass first.

- *Set a timer.* Teach younger kids to agree on a set amount of time—usually only a few minutes—for using an item. Oven timers, egg timers, or sand timers are great devices for younger kids to use. Older kids can use the minute hands on their watches or stopwatches. When the time is up, the item is passed on.

- *Compromise.* Describe what it means to your older kid: *"When you compromise, it means you're willing to give up a little of what you want, and the other person is too. It's a less bossy way to solve a problem because each person can have at least part of what she wants."* She should understand that each person *always* has the opportunity to present her side, and when she does, she should be listened to. That way everyone tends to feel more satisfied. Then look for opportunities to practice compromising in real situations.

- *Negotiate.* Show your older child how to work out the shared use of the family computer so that everyone's interests and goals are met in a timely manner. *"Let's work together to make a schedule that's fair for all of us and lets everyone get what she needs. That's what it means to negotiate."*

One Parent's Answer

A dad from Toronto writes:

Lectures and time-outs didn't do a thing to temper our son's bossiness. We realized that the only way to change his bad habits was through practice, so my wife and I mandated fifteen-minute evening family meetings. All family members—young and old—must have a chance to be respectfully listened to, and all ideas had equal weight. It took a while, but after a few weeks we saw a change: Justin was realizing he couldn't rule the roost and was actually learning to listen and think about others.

- *Reinforce cooperation.* Change isn't always easy. Do acknowledge your child's efforts to be more agreeable and be sure to tell her exactly what you appreciate so she'll do it again. *"I saw how you waited to hear your friend's idea. You didn't interrupt that time, and Alan appreciated getting all his words out."* *"I noticed how you asked Juan what game he wanted to play. That was thoughtful and considerate."*

WHAT TO EXPECT BY STAGES AND AGES

Preschooler   This is the developmental stage when kids feel that the world revolves around them, so "Me," "I want," and "My turn" are staples of their vocabulary. Their cognitive capacity limits their ability to realize that their bossy actions appear rude or hurtful, so be gentle; it's best not to discipline them for their bossiness but instead to show them what to do. By age five they gain a bit more introspection and are less focused on control, so you can begin to encourage them to consider the feelings of others.

School Age   At this age, children begin to recognize that bossiness has negative consequences: other kids don't appreciate being told what to do. Bossy kids are likely to be rejected by peers. Organized sports becomes a big part of daily schedules, and kids discover that their teammates don't want to be bossed by another player—regardless of her athletic abilities.

Tween   By now kids have spent a good deal of time receiving instructions, directions, and orders from adults and may express their resentment by bossing you. Don't allow it; expect to be treated with respect. Extraordinarily sensitive to being bossed by peers or siblings, tweens' favorite retort is "You're not the boss of me."[13] Those peers described as "cooperative, sharing, and caring" are more popular as well as happier in their peer relationships.[14] Bossy girls (unless they're the Queen Bee) are likely to be dropped by the clique.

More Helpful Advice

Parenting the Strong-Willed Child,
by Rex Foreland and Nicholas Long

Raising Your Spirited Child: A Guide for Parents Whose Child Is More Intense, Sensitive, Perceptive, Persistent, and Energetic, by Mary Sheedy Kurcinka

The Challenging Child: Understanding, Raising, and Enjoying the Five "Difficult" Types of Children, by Stanley I. Greenspan and Jacqueline Salmon

Books on Bossiness for Younger Kids

Bartholomew the Bossy, by Marjorie Weinman Sharmat and Norman Chartier

Franklin Is Bossy (Franklin Series), by Paulette Bourgeois

Little Miss Bossy (Mr. Men and Little Miss), by Roger Hargreaves

Bossy Anna (Silver Blades Figure Eights, No. 4), by Effin Older

Brags

SEE ALSO: *Materialistic, Peer Pressure, Perfectionist, Poor Sport, Sibling Rivalry, Tattles, Youngest Child*

THE PROBLEM

Red Flags

Acts like a know-it-all, brags and boasts, always talks about his accomplishments, compares possessions and achievements to others', fails to recognize that boasting is a turnoff

The Change to Parent For

Your child recognizes when it's appropriate (and not) to brag, tunes into how people respond to boasting, tones down the need for one-upmanship, and develops authentic self-esteem.

Why Change?

"I'm so pretty, Mommy, I'm going to be Miss America." "I knew that when I was five." "Get real. I'm the one here with the smarts."

When kids are little, we may think it's cute when they brag about their accomplishments and volunteer all the answers, but beware. If not put in their place, the younger bragger can turn into an older know-it-all, which is anything *but* becoming (not to mention very unpopular to all those poor souls on the receiving end). Don't get me wrong: I'm not debating your child's intelligence, beauty, talent, or skills, nor am I doubting your pride in your offspring. Your child could well be a budding Einstein, a young Wayne Gretsky, a future Miss America, a potential Itzhak Perlman, or even the next Picasso. He may well deserve recognition and acknowledgment for his strengths.

But this issue has nothing to do with your child's gifts and talents. Instead, it's all about his preoccupation with making sure everyone knows he's good or even better than the other kids, which can usually be quite tactless and a big turnoff. Believe me: no teacher, coach, scout leader, or other child's parent appreciates a kid who always boasts. What peer wants to be around another kid who always boasts and makes him feel inferior? Besides, the best self-esteem is internalized: the child must gain a sense of pride that he accomplished something for the joy of doing it, and it did it *on his own;* he does not have to share it with the rest of the world. So here are solutions for taming your child's "Look at me!" ways and helping him learn humility, graciousness, and modesty, which will go a long way toward making him a better as well as happier person.

THE SOLUTION

Six Strategies for Change

1. *Uncover the reason.* Your first step to change is to discover why your kid feels the need to brag. Once you've identified the cause, you can implement solutions. The following is a list of common reasons. Check those that may apply to your child:

☐ *"Center stage" upbringing.* Have you set a precedent of encouraging your kids to display their talents to friends, relatives, or one another?

☐ *Jealousy.* Do you favor one child, or does he feel that you do?

☐ *Low social status.* Does he feel that the way to make friends is by "impressing" them? Does he lack the social skills to find friends who accept him for himself?

☐ *Insecurity.* Is his boasting a way to gain your approval or time?

☐ *Emphasis on achievement and winning.* Do you emphasize the concept of "What did you get?" (for instance, the grade, gold star, or score) with your kid? Do you reinforce or reward your child's performance (such as with money or privileges)?

LATE-BREAKING NEWS

One study found that nine out of ten adults felt that as they were growing up, they had to display a skill, talent, or special ability in order to gain their parents' love.[15] Might your child be feeling this way? If so, it could very well be a reason for his bragging or know-it-all ways. Take heed: researchers also found that needing to demonstrate competencies learned in childhood remains a pattern well into adulthood. This time, though, the adult uses his profession as a means of gaining approval and accolades from loved ones. Once again, instead of feeling a sense of quiet, inner confidence in his talents and strengths, he must toot his horn and demonstrate them to others for approval. Such individuals are at risk for anxiety, low self-esteem, and the fear of disappointment. Make sure your child knows that your love is based just on who he is—and not on that gold star, goal, or SAT score.

☐ *Sense of being "above others."* Do you stress your family's status—economic, social, educational, professional—as being better than others?

☐ *Egocentricity.* Is he at the egocentric stage of development? Have you made your child feel as though no one is as intelligent, talented, or capable as he? Is he spoiled?

☐ *Feelings of inadequacy.* Is he trying to prove his capabilities to others because deep down he feels "not good enough" or has low self-esteem?

☐ *Perfectionism.* Is competition to be "the best" a priority in your house, so he feels the need to prove that he meets your expectations?

2. *Halt the horn blowing.* If you've been putting your younger kid on center stage to parade her talents and beauty (so that everyone "oohs and aahs" over her every move), then cut it out! If you've become a "praise-aholic" each and every time your kid kicks a goal, says a funny joke, ties his shoelace, and blows his nose—cease! If you've been tooting your horn about your family's status, fame, and fortune so that when people see you they run, call a halt. Then pass your new plan on to your spouse, siblings, relatives, and friends so that they can apply the same treatment and your child can learn a little modesty.

3. *Teach the rules for "civilized" bragging.* Reprimanding a young kid for bragging will only make him feel ashamed and less likely to tell you his achievements. So teach the "Private Rule": you will always be delighted to hear his proud moments, but he should tell you privately. Then explain why: *"Bragging in front of friends may make them feel as if they aren't as good."* Create a private signal (such as pulling on your ear) so that if he "forgets," you can signal for him to stop boasting publicly. Then teach the "After Rule": you can be proud and acknowledge your accomplishment (such as a soccer goal or art project) only *after* someone mentions it first, so wait for someone to bring it up. Always remember to thank the person for the compliment.

4. *Point out others' reactions.* Kids who brag may have used this habit so long, they're unaware that it's a real turnoff and doesn't win them any points from friends, teammates, or adults. So help your child recognize how others react to his boasting. Here are a few solutions:

   • *Ask: How would you feel?* "You spent a lot of time telling Tim how much better you are on the computer. How do you think he feels? Do you think he'll want to come and play with you again?"

   • *Point out nonverbal reactions.* "Did you see Sara scowl when you showed her your trophies?" "Did you watch Derek roll his eyes when you bragged about your grade?"

   • *Role-play the other side.* "I heard you tell Joni that you are smarter than her in math and show her your report cards. What do you think she'd like to say to you?"

5. *Encourage compliments.* A big part of tempering your kid's bragging and boasting is to help him recognize the accomplishments and achievements of others instead of always focusing on his own strengths, talents, and accolades.

- *Teach builder-uppers.* Start by teaching a few statements that focus on building others up, such as "Nice try!" "Super!" "Great job!" "Good game!" Then urge your child to use those statements on others when they are deserved.

- *Look for strengths in others.* Once he feels comfortable encouraging others, teach him how to take his comments up a notch by complimenting a person's *specific* strength, skill, or talent. You may have to help your kid recognize kinds of traits that can be praised: *"Did you notice what a great batter Lewis is? You should let him know!" "I never realized how artistic Ellie is. You should tell her."*

- *Teach the "Two Praise Rule."* The final step is to encourage your child to give at least two sincere and deserved compliments to others every day. I call this the Two Praise Rule. He can deliver the compliments to a family member, friend, or stranger, just as long as your child practices the art of praising someone other than himself. At the end of the day, ask your child whom he praised and how the recipient responded. This is also a great activity to do as a family: because everyone is on board using the Two Praise Rule, there are more examples to learn from.

6. *Reinforce humility.* Remember: true self-esteem is a quiet, inner contentment; the child doesn't feel compelled to let others know of his accomplishments and accolades. Nor does he feel the urge to compare himself to others or put the other guy down. So find ways to temper your child's boasting by acknowledging his moments of humility. "Jesse, I know how proud you must feel about your hockey game. I'm proud of how hard you practice. I also appreciate that you just told Dad and me and didn't call all your friends this time."

One Parent's Answer

A mom from Charlotte writes:

Our son was not only bragging to the world about his baseball skills but exaggerating them as well. The truth is, he's a great baseball player, but he certainly isn't as great as he makes himself out to be. Toning down his overblown claims without derailing his confidence was tricky, but he had to learn to be more realistic about his performance. Whenever he would exaggerate, we acknowledged his skills minus the superlatives and mentioned another team member's abilities as well. "You are a good player. Wayne is a good hitter also." It took a while, but he became a little more realistic about his playing ability and even started recognizing the abilities and strengths of others.

WHAT TO EXPECT BY STAGES AND AGES

Preschooler   Kids this age are egocentric by nature, so expect them toot their horn and want to share their achievements. They don't yet have the social finesse and empathy to understand that their bragging can be a turnoff. They begin noticing how they differ from peers and sensing their own limitations. Preschoolers also lack ability to distinguish reality from fantasy, so they will sometimes exaggerate or embellish their achievements. See it more as wishful thinking than as lying. Kids usually grow out of the "bragging stage" around kindergarten, when they recognize that other kids can do many things even better than they can.

School Age   Being around other school-age kids delivers a dose of reality and helps kids put their abilities and talents in perspective. Trophies, report cards, and certificates are awarded routinely, so kids increasingly measure their accomplishments against their peers. Sports become more competitive; they categorize kids and promote comparisons of who is "best" and "worst." Try to balance your child's activities so as not to emphasize just winning and losing but also teamwork and fairness. Take advantage of his newly developed empathy (*"How do you think your friend feels?"*) to help him begin to recognize the other person's views on bragging. Materialism starts to mount, so watch that your child doesn't begin comparing and bragging about possessions. If he does so, it's time to start boosting gratitude and charity.

Tween   Fitting in becomes paramount, and friendships are now based on genuine mutual understanding and affection for one another; each friend makes the other feel good. Bragging becomes a turnoff because the boaster considers only his own strengths, needs, and feelings; the other person will see the friendship as one-sided, which will probably cause it to fail. Academic competitiveness is at a height, further categorizing kids.

Defiant

SEE ALSO: *Angry, Attention Deficit, Back Talk, Communicating, Demanding, Not Knowing Right from Wrong, Time-Out, Won't Listen, Yelling*

THE PROBLEM

Red Flags

Constantly resists your simplest requests, questions authority, pushes every limit; is blatantly disrespectful, noncompliant

The Change to Parent For

Your child learns to voice her views more respectfully, and you both learn ways to develop healthier ways to communicate.

Question: "I know every kid is going to defy his parent every now and then, but how do I know when my son is defiant or just being a normal tween with raging hormones?"

Answer: Of course, kids will disobey Mom and Dad—as well as teacher, coach, Grandma, babysitter—every once in a while. But usually a stern look or a firm reprimand is all that is required to shape up a kid. Defiant kids push the envelope and exhaust your parenting. Here are four red-flag alerts that a child has crossed over the line and headed into "defiant territory":

1. *Disrespectful.* Defiant kids are way-above-average rude but also surly and blatantly disrespectful.

2. *Self-centered and blind to anyone else's feelings.* They want *their* needs met, and to do so means flat-out refusal to comply with (let alone listen to) anyone else's requests.

3. *Striving for control.* They put themselves in charge, basically stripping their parents of authority and pushing adults—and as far as they can push—to do what *they* want, stopping at nothing.

4. *Holding family harmony at bay.* Family members feel as if they're walking on eggs and are held hostage when these kids are around.

LATE-BREAKING NEWS

A nationwide survey published in the *New York Times* showed that 93 percent of responding adults believed that parents have failed to teach children honesty, respect, and responsibility.[16] Louisiana lawmakers were so concerned with the breakdown of basic civility in schoolkids that they recently passed legislation making the saying of "Yes, ma'am" and "Yes, sir" expected student behavior. Failure to address a teacher respectfully is now considered an offense that can bring detention. The lesson here: boost respect and courtesy in your kids early and you will reduce the defiant attitude.

Why Change?

Do you feel exhausted from the day-to-day challenges with your child? Do you struggle to get your child to obey? Are you hesitant to take your child out in public in case she questions your authority? Are you tired of the stares you get from others about the rude way your child talks to you? If any of those situations describe you, chances are you have a defiant child. And I'm sure you've tried a number of parenting strategies to change things, but to no avail. If it's any consolation, you are not alone.

Your child's defiant attitude and behavior are not part of a phase that will clear up overnight. Instead you will need a different approach from what you've tried in the past. You must be willing to change not only your child but also your own parenting response. It will take commitment, patience, and effort to do so, but it will be one of your most important parenting endeavors. Helping your child moderate her defiant ways and find healthier alternatives to expressing her needs will not only greatly improve your relationship and family life but also your child's chance for social success in the world, both now and later.

Signs and Symptoms

Every child resists a parent's request every once in a while, but look for a *pattern* in your child's behavior in which she *frequently* displays many of these signs:

- *Inflexible:* is seriously stubborn; won't bend and see things from another view
- *Disobedient:* refuses to do most routine tasks or chores
- *Challenging:* questions or is unwilling to accept your authority
- *Hot tempered:* is often angry; loses temper, yells frequently

- *Irritable:* is easily annoyed, often touchy, overly sensitive
- *Driven by authority issues:* argues with adults, is unwilling to accept authority
- *Engaged in power struggles:* pushes every limit and turns everything into an argument that she must win
- *Blaming of others:* won't accept ownership for her mistakes or misbehavior
- *Disrespectful:* is surly, contemptuous, rude, and disrespectful

Look for an ongoing pattern of behavior in your child and not a one-time event. If you're seeing *any* of these behaviors on a recurring basis, then it's time to parent for change.

THE SOLUTION

Step 1. Early Intervention

- *Dig deeper.* Defiant, disrespectful, rude attitudes should never be tolerated. But that doesn't mean you shouldn't try to understand why your kid is acting this

Pay Attention to This!
Could Your Child Have Oppositional Defiant Disorder (ODD)?

Although all children will display a defiant streak and try pushing the limits every now and then, when such behaviors persist for at least every day for six months and are intense, they may be the signs of a condition called Oppositional Defiant Disorder. The American Psychiatric Association estimates that about 16 percent of American kids have this condition.[17] These kids relentlessly push the boundaries set for them by authority figures, and consistently use bad language, talk back, and refuse to comply. If you have concerns about your child, seek the advice of a trained mental health evaluator. If your child repeatedly displays any of these behaviors and you feel your parenting is not effective, seek help ASAP.[18]

- Is physically aggressive with people and animals
- Destroys property
- Has problems with the law or flagrantly violates rules
- Runs away
- Starts fires

way. There are many reasons for a defiant attitude, but here are a few of the most typical. Check ones that apply to your child:

☐ *Faulty discipline.* Is discipline so harsh that your kid rebels, so lenient that she is allowed to get away with this defiant attitude, or so inconsistent that she doesn't know what to expect?

☐ *Relationship fallout.* Is there friction with a particular parent? Is there a lack of time with a parent? Does the child feel unloved or unappreciated?

☐ *Feelings of resentment and jealousy.* Could she be jealous of a sibling, peer, or your adult relationships?

☐ *Feelings of inadequacy.* Might she be compensating for low self-esteem, inadequacy, or a feeling of "I'm not good enough"?

☐ *Explosive or quick temper.* Does your child have difficulties controlling her anger? Is she naturally short fused? Has your child always been a more difficult kid?

☐ *Undue anxiety or stress.* Are there heavy pressures on her to succeed (academically, socially, athletically)? Is competition to achieve a big theme around your house? Is she so scheduled that she has no downtime?

☐ *Learning disability.* Could your child have a learning disability or attention deficit that causes difficulties in processing what she hears?

☐ *Depression.* Is she suffering from an emotional problem, depression, or trauma that is triggering this attitude?

☐ *Unfair expectations.* Might your expectations be unrealistic or unfair? Are they appropriate to your kid's developmental level?

☐ *Alcohol or substance abuse.* Could your older kid be indulging in alcohol or drugs?

☐ *Abusive treatment.* Is your child treated disrespectfully? Has she now or in the past been verbally or physically abused?

☐ *Permissive family dynamics.* Is she subconsciously or even explicitly asking for boundaries, rules, and limitations? Does she really just want you to be more of the executive authority, the boss of the family?

☐ *Mimicking.* Is she copying the attitude from someone else?

- *Check in with other adults.* Ask for input from those who care about your child, such as grandparents, nanny, teacher, and coach. What is their take on why your child is so defiant? Watch how your child interacts with other adults. Are there any adults whom your child responds to and with whom she doesn't use this defiant attitude? If so, analyze how they make their requests and respond to your child. Is there any lesson you can learn and adopt as a new response?

- *Identify defiant triggers.* Does your kid refuse to do *everything* you ask, or just some things? To help you figure this out, fold a paper in half and make two lists. On one side list issues that usually cause home-front wars: homework, chores, curfew, TV, getting up, computer, hanging out with certain kids. Then list items that she will at least sometimes comply with (or that produce less heated debates). Maybe this list includes going to soccer, coming to dinner, feeding the dog. Review your lists. Kids usually comply with requests they enjoy, feel less threatened by, or feel that they can succeed in accomplishing. Do you see any pattern that might fit your kid?

- *Pick your battles carefully.* Defiant kids turn everything into a power struggle, so be selective as to which issues you feel are important (school, homework, swearing, taking medication) and let go of issues that aren't so crucial (eating vegetables and making her bed). Is there anything on the high-friction list that you can cut? Is that friction in any way caused by the way you are asking your child to comply? Your first goal is to reduce defiance and get your child to comply. One way to do so is to be a bit less controlling by picking your battles wisely. And instead of trying to change so many behaviors (granted there may be quite a few), aim for ones that are most important (such as stopping the swearing or talking back).

- *Model respect.* Could your kid be learning her defiant ways from you? For instance:

  Do you insist that things go your way with your friends?

  Do you refuse to listen to your family's requests or negotiate any issue?

  Do you expect all family rules to be obeyed with no exceptions?

  Is conflict a part of your relationship with your partner or child's biological parent?

  Are you overly demanding and controlling?

  Does your child see you engage in yelling matches? Give the "silent treatment"? Walk away or even out the door?

  Bottom line: Are you presenting a model you'd like your kids to copy? Your kids *are* copying. Beware!

- *Check your current response.* How do you typically relate with that defiant kid of yours? Be honest now:

  How do you make your requests known to your child? Do you state them in a calm and respectful tone, or do you yell, chastise, debate, or threaten?

  Are you polite or disrespectful (or even a tad sarcastic)?

  How are your nonverbal cues? Do you roll your eyes, shrug, smirk, or wait politely?

Do you flat-out demand compliance, or do you listen to your child's requests?

Would your kid agree with your self-assessment?

Think about your most recent conflict. Was there one thing *you* could have done differently that might have prevented the outcome? If so, how can you apply that the next time?

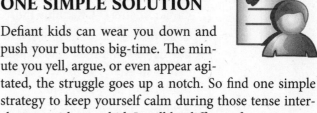

ONE SIMPLE SOLUTION

Defiant kids can wear you down and push your buttons big-time. The minute you yell, argue, or even appear agitated, the struggle goes up a notch. So find one simple strategy to keep yourself calm during those tense interchanges with your kid. It will be different for every parent, but here are a few options: take a slow, deep breath; visualize a calm spot in your mind; tell yourself, "Stay calm"; take a sip of water; excuse yourself and go to another room; pray; lock yourself in the bathroom. Find what works for you and then practice it until it kicks in when you need it most.

Step 2. Rapid Response

- *Bring down the intensity.* The very next time your child defies you, the most important thing you must do is *stay calm yourself.* If you yell or get agitated, the power struggle is almost guaranteed to escalate.

- *Spell out compliance expectations respectfully.* When both you and your child are calm, explain that from this point you expect her compliance. Be very clear so that there can be no doubt about what you mean. You might say, *"If I sound serious or say 'I'm serious,' I mean it."* Then make sure your kid knows your "serious tone" by modeling it. Explain that if she doesn't do what you ask, there will be a consequence.

- *Empower your child.* A defiant kid always wants control. So as you describe your new expectations, consider letting your child participate in creating her own consequence. Remember: you don't have to agree to her suggestions. This is just a way to involve her in the process.

- *Reduce verbal power struggles.* Defiant kids constantly push the envelope and your limits. They can take any little request and turn it into World War III. So a big piece of your new response is finding ways to reduce verbal power struggles. Here are options:

  - *Give ample warning.* It really is difficult for some kids to shift gears, so give a time limit or transition period: "I'll need your assistance in three minutes." "I have to talk to you in two minutes."

- *Give choices.* Giving just a bit of leeway sometimes breaks down a resister. "Your chores need to be done today. Would you like to finish them before dinner or after?" Offer only those choices you can live with.

- *Compromise.* "You're supposed to do your homework now, but you're practicing so hard on your dribbling. Do you agree to do your homework in half an hour?" Don't let your kid force you into a compromise you don't think is fair or appropriate.

- *Act like a broken record.* Tell why you want your kid to comply, then state your position: *"Mrs. Jones is coming in five minutes; you need to be at the door now."* Calmly repeat your request word for word each time your kid tries to argue. Don't get sucked into the argument, but instead keep repeating the words.

- *Whisper.* Try *lowering* your voice instead of raising it. Nothing turns a defiant kid off faster than yelling, so do the opposite: talk more softly, not louder. And it's hard to argue with a person who refuses to argue.

- *Learn to shrug (respectfully).* A great alternative to arguing is to shrug. It's a nonchalant type of message that can keep things cool and limit excessive emotional displays.

- *Try humor.* Don't be sarcastic (which will instantly backfire), but a little humor can help defuse a situation. The trick is to turn the joke on yourself or the event, but not on your child. Defiant kids are often hypersensitive, and although they can't handle a joke aimed at themselves, they sometimes can laugh about someone else.

- *Allow for legitimate excuses.* There always is the possibility that your kid has a legitimate excuse for not complying with your request, so hear her out. You might say, *"If you really have a good reason why you can't do what I ask you, tell me in a respectful tone."*

- *Expect compliance and don't give in.* Suppose your child still refuses to obey. Take a deep, cleansing breath to get yourself calm and then tell your kid in a controlled but firm tone that this is your bottom-line statement and there is no more negotiating. Warning: *do not plead, argue, bargain, beg, or coax.* Your kid may try every trick in the book to break you down: argue, turn your words around, and call you "unfair."

- *Enforce a consequence.* If you've been clear with your expectations, yet your kid continues to defy you, then it's time to set a consequence. Effective consequences are clear to the child, have a specified time, directly relate to the offensive attitude, *and* fit the kid's age and temperament. They must also cause a bit of misery so that the child is more willing to change her behavior than suffer the consequence. Your kid has to learn that you mean business. Here are consequences suitable for different ages of defiant kids:

Time-out. For kids generally up to age eight, time-out may be appropriate. This is when a child is immediately removed from an activity and asked to sit alone quietly for a specified time to think about her actions. The simplest rule for determining the time length is one minute for each year of the child's age (five years equals five minutes, eight years equals eight minutes, and so on). Customize depending on the age of your child, her temperament and personality, and the severity of the offense. For some kids it's an unendurable cruelty; for others it's no "fun" but not a big deal. Make sure that when your child completes time-out (and the time starts the second she complies with your time-out rules), she must still comply with your requests. (See *Time-Out,* p. 118.)

Loss of privileges. If the offense is particularly egregious or defiance continues, some parents remove entertainment privileges, such as TV, computer, video games, and cell phone. Or for a limited time the child loses the use of her favorite skateboard, scooter, bike, or even the common family area. *Make sure it's something you have control over.*

Grounding. Other than school or church time, your child must stay on the house premises for a specified length of time—generally a few hours for young kids and one to two days for older kids—and lose all social privileges except for education or church-related purposes. This should be spelled out ahead and is only for continued and deliberate defiance.

Giving to others. Find a service project your child can do (with an adult to oversee it), and then require duty for a set period. Maybe it's working in a soup kitchen, helping underprivileged kids, and tutoring children. Remember, defiant kids put their needs first, so requiring your child to do something for others may prove to be a meaningful punishment.

- *Get help.* If you've tried these options and altered your response, yet your child continues to display blatantly defiant behavior, then wait no longer and get help from a trained mental health professional. Something else may be triggering this behavior, and you owe your child and your family to get to the bottom of what is triggering this attitude. You may also need the help of a family counselor who can help you change your parenting response.

Step 3. Develop Habits for Change

- *Focus on the behavior you want.* If your child has been using this attitude for a while, then chances are that the majority of your attention has been aimed at the stuff she's *not* doing right. In fact, ask yourself what percentage of time on a typical day you are in a negative relationship with your child. Most parents admit that it is at least 75 percent of the time. The key is to start switching your focus to the behavior you want rather than the behavior you don't want. You might have to set up situations where your child is almost guaranteed to be compliant. But do so. Kids learn behavior (good or bad) from practice. At present, your child is only practicing (and learning) the defiant behavior. So find ways to help your child learn another way of responding to you and then acknowledge her positive behavior the second she responds appropriately.

- *Ask the Golden Rule question.* Emphasize the Golden Rule in your family: "Treat others as you want to be treated." Explain that a simple way to determine if you are acting respectfully is always to ask yourself before you act, "Would I want someone to treat me like that?" Once your child understands the meaning of the question, use it any time her attitude is disrespectful: *"Are you using the Golden Rule?"* It will help her think about her attitude and its consequences for other people's feelings.

- *Create new family rules.* Many families develop a set of "respect rules" that everyone agrees will govern how they treat one another. Though they are almost always ones you would choose yourself, because the kids have a voice in determining them, they become "their" rules, not just "yours" (so they're much easier to enforce). Begin by brainstorming together: *"What rules should guide how we treat one another in our family?"* Write all suggestions on paper and then use the democratic process and vote. The top suggestions become the Family Constitution. Here are a few samples I've heard:

Don't borrow without asking; listen to one another.

Don't pass on to others what is said in confidence.

Treat one another as you'd like to be treated.

One Parent's Answer

A mom from Tulsa shares:

Any little issue with my twelve-year-old turned into a full-blown argument. He had to have control. I finally realized I was playing right into him by screaming back, so I came up with a few phrases. The trick was to calmly deliver one line and keep repeating it whenever he pushed me. "I'm sorry, but that's the way it is." "I understand, but those are the rules." Or "Okay, but you'd better get started." The real trick was to not argue back and get into a power struggle. I knew I was doing something right when he said, "What's wrong with you? You're not the same." The difference was I wasn't giving in or screaming back, so he couldn't win.

Be considerate of one another.

Use calm, pleasant voices.

Say only things that build people up.

Respect each other's privacy.

Many families make their final version into a chart, have all members sign it, and post it as a continual reminder.

WHAT TO EXPECT BY STAGES AND AGES

Preschooler   Children this age will test boundaries and your rules, so stick to realistic expectations. Whining and tantrums are the most common ways to display defiance. These kids have limited emotional language, so describing intense feelings is difficult. You may hear "I hate you!" or "You're the meanest mommy in the world!" Don't take such comments personally, but explain instead a healthier alternative for verbalizing feelings. "I know you're mad, but that hurts my feelings. Tell me what you're upset about instead: 'Mommy, I'm mad because you won't let me watch TV.'" If your child is blatantly challenging your authority, there is no time to waste.

School Age   Put-downs and name-calling escalate at this age, so your child may try copying at home what she hears on the peer scene. Don't allow such negative talk, because it can destroy family harmony. Stop a defiant attitude now, before those tween and more difficult years kick in. Get on board with your parenting partner so that you're consistent and on the same page.

Tween   Depression, lack of sleep, mimicking peers, stress, and substance abuse can all lead to defiance. Hormones kick in and moodiness can mount, along with a surly attitude. Rolling eyes, shrugged shoulders, smirks, and other body language also send defiant messages. Peer pressure and the need to fit in and be included are paramount, so typical arguments involve their pushing your boundaries so they can do what the other kids do.

More Helpful Advice

10 Days to a Less Defiant Child, by Jeffrey Bernstein

Kid Cooperation: How to Stop Yelling, Nagging and Pleading and Get Kids to Cooperate, by Elizabeth Pantley and William Sear

Screamfree Parenting: The Revolutionary Approach to Raising Your Kids by Keeping Your Cool, by Hal Edward Runkel

The Defiant Child: A Parent's Guide to Oppositional Defiant Disorder, by Douglas Riley

The Explosive Child: A New Approach for Understanding and Parenting Chronically Inflexible Children, by Ross W. Greene

The Kazdin Method for Parenting the Defiant Child with No Pills, No Therapy, No Contest of Wills, by Alan E. Kazdin

Your Defiant Child: Eight Steps to Better Behavior, by Russell A. Barkley and Christine M. Benton

Demanding

SEE ALSO: *Back Talk, Bossy, Insensitive, Whining, Won't Listen*

THE QUESTION

"My kids are so demanding they drive me nuts. *Do it now, Dad. You're just sitting there. Mahhhmmm, I need to use the phone. Hang up!* It's so selfish and debilitating. What can I do to shut down the oh-so-frequent requests?"

THE ANSWER

Sound familiar? Demanding kids want things to go their way, and they want them now. And can these little critters wear you out. Demanding kids have one objective: to have their needs and issues met, and they can be quite relentless. Our biggest mistake is giving in. Sure, it's easier just to bow to what they want, but if we continue this pattern, our kids will turn into demanding adults only concerned about *their* needs and *their* feelings. That's why we have to tame their behavior ASAP, so that the really essential character traits of tact, empathy, tranquility, and consideration will have room to grow. Here are some solutions to help you tame your kid's demanding ways:

- *Get to the bottom of it.* Just why is your kid so demanding? Sure, the answer may be because he's used to getting his way, but there could be other factors. The following are some typical reasons; check the ones that apply to your child or situation:

  ☐ Have you been distracted, so he feels he needs attention?

  ☐ Does he feel that you favor another sibling?

  ☐ Does he feel the need for certain possessions to keep up status among his peers?

  ☐ Does he not know how to ask for something in a reasonable way?

  ☐ Has courtesy not been emphasized in your home?

  ☐ Does he feel that no one ever listens to him and that this is the only way he can get your attention?

  Identifying the specific source of your kid's demanding ways is the first step to turning it around, because you may be able to implement a simple solution. And if it's just that he's used to getting his way by being demanding, then you're the one who needs to find a better response.

- *State your new expectation.* Tell your kid that his demanding, pushy, self-centered "I want it and I want it now" behavior will no longer be tolerated. Explain in no uncertain terms that although it's okay to want something, he may not use a demanding voice to express his feelings. He must ask nicely and respectfully. Walk away and go about your business until he asks nicely. As long as he keeps demanding, keep walking. Warning: once you set this standard, you must not back down. Your kid needs to know you mean business, or he will never learn a new, more considerate attitude.

- *Teach the difference between needs and wants.* It is sometimes helpful to teach your kids the difference between a *need* (a necessity) and a *want* (not essential). Examples of needs include your signing the permission form for tomorrow's field trip or getting to soccer practice on time. Wants might be extra money to purchase a CD, a cookie before dinner, having you get off the phone so the child can call a friend. Once your child knows the difference, answer only those demands that are asked in a respectful, polite tone.

- *Require a courteous voice.* Many kids have learned to be demanding because they don't know how to state their needs in any other way. Their voice tones are usually loud, whining, or downright irritating. So teach a more acceptable tone to use. Then have him practice the new tone by repeating it back to you. *"Listen to how a nice voice sounds when I want something. Then you make your voice sound like mine." "No, before you interrupt anyone, you say, 'Excuse me.' Try your request again, please."*

- *Boost empathy.* Demanding kids rarely consider the other person's feelings; they're only thinking about their own agenda. They also can be completely oblivious to how inconsiderate their demands are. So the very next time your kid barrels ahead with his demands, make him stop and think about how the recipient is feeling. *"You be me right now. How would you feel if you were talked to like that? Would you want to agree to those demands?"* or *"Did you notice Dad was resting? Do you think he appreciated you interrupting him right then? Imagine you are Dad and you just came home after a long day. How would you feel if your son woke you up and demanded that you help him with his homework? So when would have been a better time to ask him to help you with your project?"*

- *Don't be afraid to say no.* The only way your child will realize that the world does not revolve around him and that all his desires will not be met is by setting limits that reduce his expectations. Decide now what your limits are and what is unacceptable, and then no matter how demanding, annoying, and obnoxious his behavior, do not give in when he crosses your line. It's the surest way for him to learn that demanding more than he deserves won't work.

Above all: don't let your demanding kid win. Make sure you also spread your message to all other immediate caregivers in your kids' life so that they know your new expectations, and then remain steadfast. The more you are on board together with your new response, the faster you will be in squelching your kid's demanding ways.

Hooked on Rewards

SEE ALSO: *Attention Deficit, Gives Up, Homework, Materialistic, Money, Perfectionist, Procrastinates, Selfish and Spoiled*

THE PROBLEM

Red Flags

Expects to be rewarded; relies on external control to motivate work, get started on a task, or behave; lacks satisfaction in doing something just for the sake of learning and does it for the rewards instead; always asks, "What do I get?" or "How much is this worth?"

The Change to Parent For

Your child develops self-reliance and internal motivation so that she no longer needs an external reward to act right and get her job done.

Why Change?

"What do I get if I do it?" "How much will you give me?" "I won't do it for less than ten dollars."

Heard any of these comments from your darling offspring lately? Don't get me wrong: there's no harm in a giving little incentive every now and then. I'll admit I've fallen victim to the infamous "Be good and you'll get a sticker" ploy. The key is to make sure we recognize that in the long run, continually giving out those rewards isn't beneficial in improving our children's behavior. In fact, over a hundred years of psychological research proves that rewards result in temporary obedience but not long-term change.[19] There is also the danger that our kids will get hooked on those rewards, then watch out: the stakes only get higher. That video game you offer if his grades improve no longer cuts it. He may want the Xbox instead.

One of our most important parenting tasks is to help our kids become self-reliant, recognize that they do have control over their lives, and learn to act right without the stickers or money. In the end our kids have to become their own cheerleaders and count on themselves. So as soon as you can wean your child away from rewards and bribes, do so! Meanwhile, use these solutions to help your child become responsible for reinforcing her own behavior and not expect something in return.

THE SOLUTION

Five Strategies for Change

1. *Stop giving material rewards for every little thing.* Take a firm stand against unnecessary incentives. Announce your new "no rewards for every and any little thing" policy and lay down the law that you just expect your kid to help out at home and do the best she can in school and other activities. Expect groans, arguments, and rolled eyes. So be it; this is the only way your child will learn to be self-reliant, independent, and self-motivated. And if your child asks, "Why do I have to?" Just say, "Because I said so."

2. *Reward the "right" way.* Research clearly shows that how you encourage your kids does make a difference in their behavior and in the development of internal motivation. If you must reward, here are the four big rewarding no-no's to keep in mind:

   - *Don't forgo expectations.* Remind your kids of your expectations *before* entering the store. "No whining—then you can earn a ride on the merry-go-round."

   - *Don't reward misbehavior.* Don't offer any incentive to stop a bad behavior ("If you stop that whine, you'll get a cookie.") It teaches kids to misbehave to get the treat. ("If I whine then stop, I'll get a toy. So I'll whine.")

   - *Don't reward unless deserved.* Never give a promised treat of any kind unless your kid displayed behavior you expected. (For example, "I know you won't hit your brother next time, so here's a cookie now" just isn't going to cut it.)

   - *Don't go overboard.* Make the reward reasonable. Giving out a Wii game for a soccer goal or paying big bucks to go to sleep, eat her veggies, or use the potty is not only unnecessary but also like dangling a carrot to get the kid to jump. Come on! No lures. Just a sincerely delivered "Good job!" or "I'm proud" will generally do the trick.

3. *Move to internal motivation.* Your ultimate parenting goal is to help your child develop internal motivation and no longer be hooked on the reward. Here are three ways to do so:

   - *Take it up a level.* Rewards can be divided into four basic categories: *material* (toys, candy, a ride on the merry-go-round); *tokens* (stars, stickers, certificates); *praise* (an adult's encouraging words); and *internal praise* (the reward of doing something for the joy in itself and because it feels good).[20] Identify the most common type of reward your child receives, then move to the next level and the next until she no longer needs external rewards. If your kid gets candy for sitting still, give stickers instead. If she gets a sticker for making her bed, use verbal praise in its place, and so on.

- *Stretch waiting time.* Increase the length of time between the act and the acknowledgment. Although a young child needs instant gratification, help your older child wait an hour, a day, or even a week for a reward.

- *Involve your child.* Make your child take ownership of her actions by helping her create solutions to her problems that previously required those rewards: *"You're forgetting to write down your homework. What do you think you can do to help you remember?" "Your math grade sure improved. How did you do it?"*

4. *Rethink material rewards.* If your child is used to material rewards (candy, toys, or money), then it's time to wean her away from expecting a prize. Here are a few rewards for getting good behavior out of kids that won't cost a dime—and will reap better results:

- *Be a cheerleader.* Rewards don't need to be purchased treats. Smiles, hugs, high fives, clapping, and cheers are all it takes to thrill some kids.

- *Use a pebble jar.* For each chore completed, kids put a pebble (or a marble or coin) into a small glass jar. When the jar is full, the family goes to the museum, a movie, fishing, or to some other fun place.

- *Go to special places.* Instead of giving food-related or monetary rewards (which signal that good behavior comes with a price tag or encourages unhealthy eating), reward your kids by going to a special place of their choosing, such as a roller-skating rink or park.

- *Offer one-on-one time.* Organize your day around spending time with your child, so that she doesn't have to compete for your attention with other siblings, even if you're just going shopping, to the library, or for a walk, or snuggling on the couch.

5. *Stress internal praise.* The very next time your kid does something noteworthy, don't reward. Instead try one of these tricks that nurture your kid's internal motivation by putting the success back in her corner.

- *State what you see—without a reward.* Begin by using a simple judgment-free comment that describes her success: "You rode your bike all by yourself!" or "Wow, you really put a lot of work into this report. Good for you!" or simply, "You did it."

- *Boost inside pride.* Instead of being so quick to reinforce your kid, find out what pleased her about the job she did. "How did you learn to balance yourself without the training wheels?" "What was the hardest part about writing that report?"

- *Emphasize self-acknowledgment.* Point out what deserved merit and then remind your child to self-acknowledge. Suppose your son has difficulty being a good sport whenever he loses at his soccer games, and this time he made an effort not to blame everyone for the loss. Acknowledge his success: "John, you really made an effort not to say anything negative about the other team today. You were being a good sport." Then encourage him to praise himself: "Did you remember to tell yourself that you did a great job?"

- *Switch from "I" to "You."* The simple pronoun switch in your praise takes the emphasis off of your approval and puts more on the child regulating her actions. So instead of saying "I'm really proud of how hard you worked today," switch to "You must be really proud of how hard you worked today."

- *Use accomplishment journals.* Once a week ask your child to spend a few minutes writing (or drawing) her successes in a small journal. The simple routine helps kids slowly recognize that they are their own best behavior guide and reinforcer.

One Parent's Answer

A mom from Cleveland writes:

My kids were always asking when they would get a sticker for "being good." One day I filled a box with marking pens, a hole-punch, stickers, construction paper, letter stamps, stencils, and glue. Now whenever my girls ask me for an award, I tell them to go to the box and make one for themselves. I also have one rule: if they want to hang the award on the refrigerator, they must identify and describe what they did to earn the certificate. It gradually weaned them away from expecting recognition from me and even improved their behavior!

WHAT TO EXPECT BY STAGES AND AGES

Preschooler   Young kids live in the moment and have shorter attention spans. If you're going to reward, then do so the minute your child is on her best behavior or very soon thereafter. "You'll get a treat later if you're good" just won't cut it. It's best to catch a preschooler the second she's good. It isn't until around age three that most children will truly understand a deal, are willing to cooperate, and can be a bit patient if they don't get their reward right now.

School Age   Self-control and reasoning skills increase, so kids can wait an hour, a day, or even sometimes up to a week to be rewarded for good behavior, depending on their age and personality. The goal is to gently stretch your child's self-control and attention span.

Tween   Instead of offering a reward, talk to your tween about what you think she needs to work on, whether it's doing a better job on homework or taking on more chores. Then discuss how you might honor her if she shows effort. Make sure the goal is clear (spending an extra half hour on homework or cleaning her bedroom once a week for a month). The practice instills the value of effort and teaches the crucial skill of goal setting.

LATE-BREAKING NEWS

Research confirms that rewarding kids for a job well done can backfire. Here's proof:

Arizona State University: Children of parents who rewarded their preschoolers for nice behaviors such as sharing or helping became *less generous and cooperative* over time than children raised without rewards.[21]

University of Nottingham: When preschoolers were rewarded with candy for performing a normal task, the children put their energy on the sweets and *stopped thinking about or enjoying the task.*[22]

Brandeis University: Experiments involving elementary school kids found that the *least creative projects* as rated by teachers were done by those students who had contracted for rewards.[23]

Impulsive

SEE ALSO: *Angry, Attention Deficit, Bad Friends, Biting, Bullying, Defiant, Lying, Not Knowing Right from Wrong*

THE PROBLEM

Red Flags

Acts without thinking, behaves recklessly, blurts out answers, is very impatient, lies impulsively, has difficulty waiting his turn, often interrupts, has frequent angry outbursts or temper tantrums

The Change to Parent For

Your child can anticipate his impulsivity and learns skills to regulate his thoughts and actions to the best of his abilities.

Why Change?

Impulsive kids are spontaneous and always on the go; they're always barreling ahead, and most of their actions are unpremeditated. They're fun and lively, but their inability to censor themselves and put the brakes on their behavior can cause a host of problems. They interrupt conversations, invade other people's space, ask irrelevant questions in class, and make tactless observations. Other kids and adults may view those behaviors as disrespectful or as a big turnoff, so the child's social status and reputation are affected as well.

One Parent's Answer

A mom from Memphis writes:

Our son had such trouble controlling his impulses that outings became a nightmare. What helped was when I anticipated a potential problem and then coached Zach over and over before a social gathering. "Remember, Grandma doesn't like her cat's tail to be pulled. Don't pull the cat's tail." "Before we go to your game, remember that the kids don't like you to grab the ball." "Remember it's Jimmy's party, so don't blow out his birthday candles." I felt like a broken record, but if I aimed for only one issue and kept coaching him prior to the event, it curtailed a lot of problems and became my sanity saver.

Staying in a classroom seat and following the coach's rules are tough. Safety is usually a concern, as impulsive kids don't think about consequences, often engage in riskier behaviors, and frequently end up in emergency rooms.

Although we can't change an impulsive child into one who is passive, we can help him learn to control his impulses. Doing so will be a gradual process and will take a lot of effort (and patience) on your part. But remember that many of the most important skills of self-control are learned, not inherited, and the very best training ground for teaching those skills is in our homes.

THE SOLUTION

Five Strategies for Change

1. *Learn your child's impulse warnings.* Tune in to your child a bit more closely and start to pick up his signs that he's maxed his ability to wait. Try to identify how your child behaves when he's moving into his zone of no return. What does he usually say or do when he gets overly stimulated, agitated, or frustrated? Often the best solution is to anticipate his impulsivity and then immediately intervene. For instance, one of my impulsive students used to start talking faster and faster and then tap his feet incessantly. That was my cue to intervene ASAP and help him gain control. Through trial and error, I found that putting my hand firmly on his shoulder and gently reminding him over and over that he needed to get himself together was what calmed him down best. Here are a few other strategies for impulsive kids:

   - Distract him (*"Have you seen the puzzle?"*) or change the focus.

   - Move him to another space (*"Let's go outside"*).

   - Speak in a calm tone to help him stay in control. (Hint: don't yell or be too dictatorial, which often makes an impulsive child oppositional.)

   - Remind him of a reward he's trying to earn (or the consequence if he barrels ahead).

   - Have him do something physical (tear a newspaper into shreds, knead a stress ball, do ten jumping jacks, jog around the yard).

   Remember that for the most part your child's impulsive behaviors are not deliberate. He really doesn't mean to get in trouble, but his lack of impulse control makes it difficult for him to regulate his behavior.

2. *Make safety a priority.* Impulsive kids often lack that internal brake system that helps them think before barreling ahead. That's why they are often accident prone and engage in risky behaviors, such as running into the street, climbing a fence with a High Voltage sign, or sticking scissors into an electrical socket. Here are ways to make safety a parenting priority and reduce the likelihood of those accidents:

- *Anticipate safety issues.* Put locks on liquor cabinets; cover electrical outlets; repair the torn fence; dump the toy weapons; remove fragile, breakable items; buy plastic and remove glass; move expensive, valuable items out of reach.

- *Reduce the danger.* If your child is a risk taker, then find ways to keep him safer. Purchase a helmet and extra knee and elbow pads if he's a daredevil on the skateboard. Get him swim lessons if he roughhouses around swimming pools.

- *Beware of certain "friends."* Know which friends agitate your kid or egg him to thrill-seek. Say no to social activities where peer pressure is too strong or could be dangerous.

- *Monitor him more closely.* Hold those playdates at your home where you can keep a closer eye on your child. Or make sure the adult in charge is aware of your child's impulsive traits.

3. *Boost boundaries and limits.* Impulsive kids don't have internal control, so they need you to create clear external boundaries. Here are your best discipline steps:

- *Set clear rules.* Impose structure with clearly spelled-out rules so that your child knows what he cannot do. Focus on only a few issues—those that involve safety or infringing on the rights of others—and ignore more minor misbehaviors; otherwise your child will always be in trouble.

- *Be realistic.* Impulsive kids are often less mature than their same-age peers, so set your expectations to his abilities and not his chronological age. If an accident occurs, downplay it. Explain that accidents happen and avoid reacting strongly.

- *Stay cool.* Yelling, grabbing, and spanking only make an impulsive kid more impulsive.

- *Act ASAP.* Step in immediately and enforce a consequence such as time-out or losing a privilege so that your child learns that he will be disciplined on the spot. Waiting to talk about the problem later won't help—he often won't recall it.

- *Provide a cool-down spot.* Have your child help you collect a few things that help him calm down (such as an Etch-a-Sketch, a wad of clay, or a CD player with favorite music) and put them in a basket. Leave it in a special spot where he can go to pull himself together and avoid escalating any conflict further. Of course your best option is to try to move your child to a calm-down spot before the impulsivity builds, but that is often impossible.

- *Reinforce any effort.* It is hard for an impulsive kid not to barrel ahead and into trouble. So acknowledge any positive effort: *"I know it was hard for you to wait, but you did. Good for you!" "You asked for a turn that time. Good going!"*

BEHAVIOR

4. *Find opportunities that boost success.*

Friendship Solutions

- Invite "calmer" friends that don't tax his impulse-control abilities.

- Reduce the number of playmates: start with only one.

- Find a pal who matches his abilities. (Impulsive kids often choose younger friends because they are usually more accepting and at the child's developmental level.)

- Decrease playtime to an hour instead of a half day.

- Prohibit aggressive toys—weapons, violent video games—that might increase impulsivity.

- Befriend parents of your child's pals. Let them know that they can call you if problems arise.

- Be an active participant in playdates and be ready to intervene before there is a problem. When visiting, take a quick scan of the room, then ask the parent if you might move any fragile or valuable items to an out-of-reach area.

School Solutions

- Become an ally with the teacher so that the two of you can be on the same page.

- Ask to have your child sit in the least distracting place possible.

- Set up a behavior chart where you can reward your child for on-task behavior.

- Ask if there is a quieter room he can go to during recess.

- Choose learning environments that are self-paced, active, and hands-on.[24] Some research suggests that children with ADHD do better in such environments.

Home Solutions

- Keep to a schedule that works best for your child and family.

- Set up opportunities to release energy (a basketball hoop, punching bag, weights).

- Use "On Your Mark" to build in time for your child to process your requests. Say, "On your mark. I need you to brush your teeth." Say, "Get set!" then give a moment to think. Say, "Go!" Repeat the task again: "Go brush your teeth!"

Community Solutions

- Encourage him to choose such sports as soccer, swimming, or track and field (where everyone runs as a pack and is less competitive) instead of being a shortstop on a baseball team (where the child must wait for the ball and stand out).

- Find an interest tailored to your child's quick-paced temperament, such as playing drums, marching band, skateboarding, scouting, 4-H, rollerblading, or snowboarding.

5. *Stretch "wait time."* Your child may barrel straight into every task right now, but your ultimate goal is gradually to stretch his ability to control those impulses. Start by timing how long your child can pause before those impulses get the best of him. Take that time as his "waiting ability" (even if it's only two seconds) and then slowly increase it over the next weeks and months. Here are a few strategies that help kids control impulses. Choose the one that works best for your child and then practice, practice, practice together until it kicks in and he can use when he feels those impulses taking over.

- *Freeze.* In calm voice, say this to your child: "Freeze. Don't move until you can get back in control."

- *Use a phrase.* Have him slowly say a phrase like "One Mississippi, two Mississippi."

- *Hold your breath.* Tell your kid not to breathe as long as possible and then to take a few long, deep breaths. (Just make sure he remembers to breathe!)

- *Count.* Join your child in slowly counting from one to twenty (or fewer with a younger kid).

- *Sing.* For a young child, ask him to pick his favorite tune, such as "Frère Jacques" or "Twinkle Twinkle Little Star" and hum a few bars.

- *Watch.* Have him look at his wristwatch and count set numbers of seconds (such as ten).

- *Use STAR: "Stop, Think, Act Right."* Research shows that what a child learns to say to himself (or "self-instruction") during the moments of temptation is a significant determinant of whether he is able to say no to impulsive urges.[25] You can teach these three steps to an impulsive child. Point out that when you put the first letter of each step together it spells STAR. The acronym often helps children recall the three steps.

  Step 1: <u>S</u>top. The first part to helping your child restrain impulses is the most important: he must learn to stop and freeze before acting. The split second he takes to freeze and not act on an impulse can make a critical difference—especially in stressful or potentially dangerous situations. And stopping is not easy for many kids to learn, particularly for those who are younger or more impulsive. So when you first begin, you may have to physically restrain your child by gently but firmly putting your hands on his shoulders and saying, "Stop and freeze." Then do it over and over and over until it becomes second nature.

Step 2: <u>T</u>hink. Kids next need to learn to think about the possible consequences of a wrong choice. So teach your child to look around him, see what's happening, and then ask himself such questions as: Is this right or wrong? Is this a good idea? Can someone get hurt? Is this safe? Could I get in trouble? Even very young kids can learn this step. Of course, your child will need you at the beginning to remind him of the questions, so be prepared to ask them repeatedly at first. When he hears you asking the same questions over and over, he will begin using them inside his own head without your prodding. Keep at it!

Step 3: <u>A</u>ct <u>R</u>ight. This last step helps your child think through what he might have done instead whenever he makes an unwise decision. Questions such as these (posed during a relaxed time) help impulsive kids sort out what happened: What did you want to happen? What happened instead? At what point did you think it might turn out right? Did you think about saying no? What made you keep going? What could you do the next time so it won't happen again? The process will take patience and repetition, but over time will help your child learn to "Stop, Think, Act Right."

LATE-BREAKING NEWS

Lehigh's College of Education: Research by George DuPaul found that those quick-fire images on computer and video games might help some kids with ADHD.[26] The games were found to be effective in preventing behavioral and academic problems, especially among preschoolers. So you might consider trying certain video and computer games—especially ones that teach educational skills—with your impulsive child. Watch to see if those games help him stay focused and more relaxed. Many educators believe that the high-speed behavior and thinking patterns of ADHD kids lend themselves quite well to cutting-edge technologies, such as hypertext and multimedia, and that these technologies can be powerful learning tools.[27] Just be sure not to use aggressive, violent games, which will increase impulsivity in certain kids.

WHAT TO EXPECT BY STAGES AND AGES

Preschooler   Kids at this age follow the rules set by the adults in charge and often talk out loud as a means controlling behavior. "I better not eat the candy because dinner is soon and Mom doesn't want me to eat snacks."

School Age   School-age kids use inner thoughts to direct behavior and manage impulses. They are learning beginning problem-solving skills and developing a stronger awareness of behavior. A seven-year-old is usually able to look at the bully and say to himself, "I need to stay calm. I always lose it when he starts teasing me."

Tween   Tweens are acquiring more sophisticated problem-solving skills and are much more aware of their own behavioral urges and triggers. Peer pressure to take risks becomes paramount and often pushes tweens to act impulsively and not think through the consequences.

Pay Attention to This!
Could Your Child Have ADHD?

Attention-Deficit/Hyperactivity Disorder (ADHD) is the term only a physician or psychologist can give to a child after a lengthy evaluation that combines medical, educational, and neurological tests as well as behavioral information gathered from the teacher and parent. The American Academy of Pediatrics (AAP) states that more than 6 percent of school-age children (boys far more than girls) are diagnosed with ADHD. Keep in mind that those symptoms of ADHD "must be present at least six months by age seven, evident in various situations, and be more intense than usually seen in other children of the same age and gender." Here are the characteristics of the disorder, as described by the AAP.[28]

Inattention

- Produces careless work at school
- Is unable to pay attention
- Does not seem to listen
- Is disorganized
- Avoids tasks requiring sustained effort
- Loses things
- Is easily distracted
- Is forgetful

Hyperactivity-Impulsivity

- Squirms and fidgets
- Is restless
- Is excitable
- Lacks patience
- Has uncontrollable energy
- Interrupts others
- Has trouble waiting his turn

Indecisive

SEE ALSO: *Argues, Dependent*

THE QUESTION

"My daughter has such a difficult time making a decision about just about anything. She changes her mind umpteen times, asks everyone what she should do and then usually begs me to decide. She goes through such stress that I worry about her. What can I do?"

THE ANSWER

Even young kids usually have little difficulty generating strategies to solve problems. The challenge is guiding them so that they know how to make the best choice. By helping them recognize that each decision has a consequence and both good and bad points, they'll soon learn to consider what might happen if they picked each possibility. Here are a few ways to help kids make decisions:

- *Model your decisions.* During the course of a typical day, dozens of opportunities come up where we must weigh choices and make decisions. Let your child hear how you make your choices by reviewing your problem-solving steps out loud. *"I thought a lot about whether to take the job. It would give us the extra money we needed, but I also knew it would mean I'd have to give up time with my family. I finally decided that there were only two hours each day when you'd be by yourself, and during those hours you usually were in after-school sports or at a friend's house. So I took the job."* Saying those steps aloud helps your child understand all the things you considered while making your decision.

- *Offer frequent decision-making opportunities.* If your child lacks confidence in making decisions, then find ways to increase the times she gets to choose. Start with simpler choices that you know she feels safe with and then increase the number of options and difficulty of the choice as your child gains confidence. The secret is to find your child's current comfort level and then gradually stretch her from that zone by gently encouraging her to make more difficult decisions.

- *Teach decision vocabulary.* Using decision vocabulary words, such as *choose, decide, prefer, pick,* and *select,* with younger children helps them learn to use the words in their own conversation.

- *Give "safe" choices that aren't life-and-death matters.* Start with making her choose between only two options: "Do you want to play Chutes and Ladders or Candyland?" "Do you want to go for a bike ride or a walk?" "Do you prefer the blue dress or the pink one?" Next try three options: "Do you want cake, ice cream, or pudding for dessert?" You can increase the options and work up to more sophisticated problems later: "Which college will you choose?"

- *Talk through outcomes.* A large part of making responsible choices is thinking about the immediate as well as long-term consequences of decisions. Predicting how decisions will turn out is not easy for many adults, let alone kids. One way to help your child think about possible outcomes is to ask, "If you pick that choice, do you think you'll still feel okay about it tomorrow?" "What about next week?"

- *Do cross-offs.* Too many choices can overwhelm a child, so teach her to eliminate some choices. Together list the possible choices on paper. Tell your child to "cross off" with a pencil any selection that she doesn't feel comfortable doing. Emphasize that if she feels she can manage the consequences of a choice, it's probably safe to keep it on the list. Any decision that she can't live with should instantly be crossed off. Suppose your child is invited to a party she desperately wants to attend, but it's at the same time as her soccer game. If her coach finds out she's at the party, she'll be kicked off the team. She's come up with these choices: (a) tell the coach I'm sick, (b) go to the party and then go to the game late, (c) play, then go late to the party, or (d) don't go to the party. Now guide your child in thinking about consequences. Reread each choice and say after each, "What would happen if you chose that?" It may take time the first few go-rounds, but it's worth it.

- *Set a time limit.* Some kids benefit from setting a time constraint on making a choice. "Decide before I count to ten." "Choose before I finish singing "Happy Birthday."

- *Don't rescue.* Once your child has settled on a choice, let it be. Don't rescue. Your child will never gain confidence if you continue deciding for her. Don't allow a second chance. And squelch your urge to mention the "you should of" or "I told you." One big part of learning to make a decision is just having the experience of doing so. It may take a while for your child's confidence to grow, but each experience helps her just a little more until she finally will be able to make a decision completely on her own.

Swears

SEE ALSO: *Angry, Back Talk, Bad Manners, Defiant*

THE PROBLEM

Red Flags

Swears; curses; uses profanity, "potty talk," bathroom jokes, or other inappropriate words

The Change to Parent For

Your child learns to understand which words and gestures are "off-limits" in your home based on your family's values, adopts your views, and learns to express intense feelings in an appropriate way.

Question: "Our 'well-mannered' daughter blurted the 'F-word' at dinner last night and sounded like a shock jock. We're petrified she'll do this in public. Should we be worried?"

Answer: It's not time to lose a good night sleep just yet, but do keep a closer eye on things. First, let your child know that she is not to use any such language in or out of the house, and let her know why it's offensive. Second, once you decide to squelch any particular bad word, be consistent and don't back down. Also, you didn't mention how old your child was, but do keep in mind that some kids throw out a term to gauge our reaction. Words can have power. So keep a straight face. And if your preschooler is the offending party, don't laugh. Letting your preschooler think for even a second that his cursing or potty talk is "cute" may encourage him even more.

Why Change?

We generally equate childhood with innocence, so it can come as quite a shock when a foul word escapes from the mouth of our sweet little darling. Experimenting with profanity, "dirty words," or "potty talk" these days is considered "almost a developmentally normal behavior."[29] After all, a big way our kids learn is by imitating others, and there's a lot of profanity for kids to hear these days, in music, movies, public places (60 percent of adults admit they swear in public[30]), and of course television. A Florida State University study found that profanity during prime-time hours has increased 58 percent in four years—nearly nine out of ten of those programs contained profane words.[31] Educa-

LATE-BREAKING NEWS

Swearing Is on the Rise Among Teens

Harvard University: Research shows that the use of swearing and obscene gestures is increasing dramatically on school campuses.[32] Fifty-nine percent of teachers in urban schools and 40 percent in rural areas said they daily face swearing and obscene gestures from students. A *USA Today* poll of high school principals found that 89 percent regularly deal with profane language and provocative insults toward teachers or other students. Chances are that your child is hearing profanity from peers, so be vigilant and keep parenting for the change you want.

tors are so exasperated that some high schools now fine students if they utter profanity on school premises.[33] And over 80 percent of Americans feel that vulgarity is getting worse.[34]

Regardless of the prevalence, it certainly doesn't mean you should allow profanity to become part of your children's everyday vocabulary—and most especially if those words are aimed in anger at a particular person. Swearing can become a hard-to-break habit that taints children's reputations, breaks down their character, and ruins family harmony. The best way to stop swearing is to nip it in the bud and to teach your child healthier ways to vent his frustrations. This entry provides some ways to parent for change.

Signs and Symptoms

There are five signs that swearing may be becoming a problem that does require swift change:

1. It has become a habit; bad words slip out any time and any place.
2. Your child's character or reputation is at stake because of his foul mouth.
3. Family harmony and relationships are being torn; respect is unraveling.
4. Your child is aiming those words at someone or some group in anger.
5. The problem is combined with other difficulties.

The American Academy of Pediatrics explains that by itself, swearing is not a sign of an emotional disturbance, but when other chronic problems are present (such as lying, hostility, depression, stealing, or trouble with peers), then it may be a symptom of a psychological or social disturbance.[35] Talk to a mental health professional.

Pay Attention to This!
Could It Be Tourette?

Tourette Syndrome, a neurological disorder characterized by involuntary tics, movements, or vocalizations, is often called "Swearing Disease" (though less than 30 percent of people with Tourette have the swearing tic). In children the tics usually start between three and ten years of age. For information, contact the Tourette Syndrome Association (http://www.tsa-usa.org); read *Children with Tourette Syndrome: A Parent's Guide,* edited by Tracy Haerle; or talk to your doctor.

THE SOLUTION

There are three steps to curbing potty talk, bad words, and swearing. You usually won't have to get beyond the first step with younger children. But with tweens and sometimes with older school-age kids, you may have to work through all three steps to parent for the change you desire in your child:

Step 1. Early Intervention

- *Identify the reason.* The first step is to figure out the reason your child is swearing so that you can tailor the solutions to that reason. Here is a list of a few of the most common reasons kids swear, tell inappropriate "bathroom jokes," or curse. Check any issues that may apply to your child:

  ☐ Copying what is heard from kids, TV, movies, other adults, or *you*

  ☐ Seeking attention or trying for "shock" value

  ☐ Testing limits and boundaries

  ☐ Proving independence or trying to feel "grown up"

  ☐ Attempting to "be cool" and impress others

  ☐ Trying to gain peer acceptance or "fit in" with the other kids

  ☐ Venting or letting off steam

  ☐ Intentionally hurting a person

  ☐ Behaving like others in his social group; swearing is a part of the culture

  ☐ Using the term in ignorance; he doesn't know the term is inappropriate and has never been corrected for using it

What is your best guess as to why your child is swearing or using inappropriate words? What is the first thing you will do to change this problem and turn things around?

- *Curb your tongue.* Be honest. Are you at all responsible for your child's new raunchy vocabulary? Could your child be replaying what he hears? Kids at all age are mimickers. So watch your mouth. And put a restraining order on any older sibling or adult in your home who is swearing. Those are not the first words you want younger kids to utter.

- *Have value talks.* Talk to your child about your family values and explain *why* you object to such language. *"I know other people may use those words in their homes, but we don't in ours." "Those are words that can hurt people's feelings. I expect you always to want to say and do things that make people feel good."* If these words are offensive to your cultural or religious beliefs, then say so: *"We don't ever use God's name in vain."*

- *Find the source.* If your child is saying more than an expletive or two, try to determine where the words are coming from. Is there anything you can to do to eliminate the source? For instance: curtail certain TV shows or CDs, tune in to the ratings on those movie rentals, watch your own cursing, curtail the play-date, talk to the older sibling.

- *Establish your house as a "No Swear Zone."* Set a rule that no swearing is allowed in your home. Just be clear with all family members about which words are considered off-limits and then follow through on your rule. (Mom and Dad—as well as their adult friends—must obey the home standards.)

Step 2. Rapid Response

If your child *does* use one of those "intolerable" swear words, here are the best ways to respond:

- *Stay neutral.* Your best response is a neutral retort. In fact, "underreacting" is far better than overreacting, which can mean to some kids that the term must be worth repeating. So remain calm.

- *Call out the unacceptable term or gesture.* Name

ONE SIMPLE SOLUTION

Increasing Vocabulary While Decreasing Swearing

My favorite consequence for swearing is to make the offender use the dictionary to look up a new, more appropriate word to replace the offensive one. The child must then use the word at least ten times (or some set amount) during the day. He could also be required to write the word on an index card to teach to other family members. You're not only eliminating curse words but also increasing your child's vocabulary skills.

the inappropriate word and then tell your child *why* the word is unacceptable: *"That word is impolite." "We don't say '#*!%' in our house." "That may be some- thing your friends say, but you may not in this house."* For older kids, make sure you state that the term also may not be gestured or written in a text or e-mail message. (See *Cyberbullying*, p. 602, and *Internet Safety*, p. 610.)

- *Explain the inappropriate term if needed.* Don't assume that your child under- stands the meaning of the four-letter word or other inappropriate term he's us- ing. Just keep the explanation at your child's level of understanding. If he's using the "F word" or a sexual term, it's time for an age-appropriate "sex talk" with your child. If he has picked up this term from school, chances are that the other kids are talking about sex, and you need to be the one to make sure your child is getting the right message. (See *Sex*, p. 394.)

Step 3. Develop Habits for Change

- *Teach younger kids the words for body parts.* Potty talk such as "Poopy Head" "Pee-Pee Face" or "butt" is quite innocent and should be expected with pre- schoolers. You can suggest that your child use more appropriate and anatomi- cally correct terms, such as "bottom" or "penis," and say them matter-of-factly. It will reduce the sensationalism and the potty talk. You don't want to discour- age your child from talking about his body.

- *Teach jokes to younger kids.* If you see that your preschooler is using "potty talk" because it makes people laugh, then teach him a few simple knock-knock jokes or funny sayings. *"Most jokes about going to the bathroom aren't funny; let's learn a joke that will make people laugh without being offensive."*

- *Offer appropriate word substitutes for older kids.* The biggest reason older kids (and adults) swear is to let off steam. If your child doesn't know an appropriate way to vent, it may be time for a family brainstorm session to find swearword alternatives. Just identify the word your child may *not* say and then think of other word options, such as *shoot, dagnabit, drat,* or *phooey.* Then use it until it becomes a habit. Remember, there's nothing wrong with yelling out, "I'm so mad!"

- *Reinforce "cuss-control" efforts.* Do acknowledge *any* efforts your child is mak- ing to stop the swearing. *"I know that you were frustrated, but you didn't swear that time. It's hard changing a bad habit, but you're really trying."*

- *Teach your child to track his behavior.* If your child is blurting out more than a few cuss words each day, then encourage him to keep track of the frequency. When habits set in, kids sometimes don't recognize just how often they are using the behavior. One simple technique is to give him a few pennies to put in one pocket each morning. Each time he swears, he removes one coin and puts it in his other pocket. At bedtime he counts the coins he moved. The goal is for him to gradually decrease the number of transferred coins until he stops the behavior. You might also challenge your child (or family) to see how long he can go *without* swearing. Offer a reward if he can go a certain length of time.

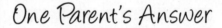

One Parent's Answer

A dad from Orange County writes:

My son accidentally left his CD in the car stereo that was loaded with the F word. That evening we went through his CD collection. If any CD had a Parental Advisory label, it was dumped, as well as inappropriate songs from his MP3 player. I told him to expect a random CD check every so often. He finally got the message that our family didn't approve of that kind of language.

- *Have your child "rip up" the words.* Every time your child uses a swear word, he should write it down on a piece of paper and perform a ritual in which he rips up the paper so that there's nothing left but scraps. Many a teacher has gone one step further with this task and has the offender "bury" the words under dirt somewhere outside to symbolically convey that the words are buried and "gone" for good.

- *Set a consequence if the problem continues.* If you've been clear with your expectations, yet the swearing still continues, then it's time to go up a level and set a consequence. Here are two things to do if you have a "repeat offender" on your hands:

  - *Create a swear jar.* Set up a swear jar—any jar with a lid will do. Your child should know which words will be fined and what the fine will be. Each time the child (and *any* member of the family—Dad and Mom as well) swears, he is fined and must put the set amount of money in the jar. When the jar is filled, donate the money to a charity of your child's choice. For kids short on money, post a list of chores that can be done to work off the fine. Warning: do *not* loan your child money to pay off the fine. It will defeat the purpose.

  - *Lose a privilege.* Profanity directed at another person should never be tolerated, and the offender should immediately be sent to time-out (*"If you can't talk nicely in the family room, you will go to your room"*) or lose a privilege (*"If you can't talk appropriately in this house, you will not be able to use your cell phone"*).

WHAT TO EXPECT BY STAGES AND AGES

Preschooler   Little experimenters will try out new words for attention, to gauge reactions, or to copy what they've heard from their peers or the TV. Preschoolers are starting to learn the vocabulary of bodily functions and parts, so potty talk such as "Pee-Pee Face" or "butt" is quite innocent and should be expected. They're beginning to understand humor, so creating words like "Poo-Poo Head" is just hysterical to them.

More Helpful Advice

Cuss Control: The Complete Book on How to Curb Your Cursing, by James V. O'Connor

How Rude! The Teenagers' Guide to Good Manners, Proper Behavior, and Not Grossing People Out, by Alex J. Packer

No More Misbehavin': 38 Difficult Behaviors and How to Stop Them, by Michele Borba

The Berenstain Bears and the Big Blooper (First Time Books), by Stan and Jan Berenstain

The Baffled Parent's Guide to Stopping Bad Behavior, by Kate Kelly

School Age   Expect experimentation with milder curse words, but don't let your child think they will be permitted. This age group needs guidance as to which words are unacceptable in your family and also needs to learn appropriate substitutes to express their frustrations. Don't be timid about reprimanding a friend who swears in your home: *"We don't talk like that in this house."* To allow cursing or other disrespectful talk by a friend sends a message to your child: *"He can do it. I can't."*

Tween   Appearing "cool" is huge for this age group, so expect experimenting with four-letter words to "fit in." Because image is a big concern, talk about how bad language affects others' impressions; most adults view cussing as uncultured, crude, uneducated, and plain "not nice." Set clear standards for media ratings and what is off-limits. (See One Simple Solution box.)

ONE SIMPLE SOLUTION

Stay on Top of the Ratings Game

Studies show that the media do affect our children's values, language, and behavior. So carefully check those advisory ratings listed on CDs, DVDs, television shows, video games, and movies, and then be clear to your child about which ratings are unacceptable to your family values.

Here is a quick review that *Parents* magazine created of the four ratings and how language is portrayed in each category:[36]

G	No cursing, but some crude language is fine if it's considered to be an everyday expression.
PG	Minimal profanity, but not the F-word or other harsh, sex-related words.
PG-13	The F-word can be used only once—but not at all if it's used in a sexual context—unless a two-thirds majority of the raters think it's okay because of how the word is used.
R	Hard language. Should be off-limits if you're eliminating profanity.

Tantrums

SEE ALSO: *Angry, Biting, Depressed, Grief, Stressed*

THE PROBLEM

Red Flags

Out-of-control crying and screaming, frequent meltdowns, inability to handle frustrations or calm down without intervention; outbursts for attention or to get her way

The Change to Parent For

Your child not only learns that tantrums are not appropriate and will not be tolerated but also acquires more appropriate ways to manage and express negative feelings.

Question: "When my three-year-old doesn't get her way, she puts on a tantrum that could win an Oscar. What is the best way to stop her meltdowns?"

Answer: Kids usually resort to temper tantrums because they don't know how to express their needs or to get what they want—and because they've learned it works. The secret to stopping them is not ever to give in to the outburst. The reality is that the more attention you give the behavior, the longer the tantrum lasts. So change your response to your child. Stay cool. Stay calm. And ignore, ignore, ignore. If you are consistent with that response, you should see a slow diminishment of this obnoxious behavior. Meanwhile, make sure you write a blow-by-blow account of your child's best performance in her baby book. These are the parenting moments that you never think you'll get through at the time, but later on you will sit back and relish the memories. (Really! I promise!)

Why Change?

"You won't believe what your 'angelic' daughter did at your mother's house! She looked like she trying out for a part in The Exorcist!*"*

"He kicked and screamed and yelled because I wouldn't give him what he wanted. The stares I got from other parents were so embarrassing I wanted to put a paper bag on my head!"

Tantrums are sure to be on the top of parents' list of "obnoxious, embarrassing kid behaviors."

These are Oscar-winning performances at their best: ear-piercing screaming, thrashing, and out-of-control behavior. And when your kid uses her routine at school, ballpark, or supermarket, it's just plain humiliating. So why do kids go through these exhausting dramatics? Simply because they've learned tantrums are a successful—though highly uncivilized—attention-getting antic.

You should expect your one- to three-year-old to try this behavior on you. And it's equally as common in girls as in boys. Older kids can also regress to the "tantrum stage" especially if there's been a recent stress or change in their lives. (We can all name an adult or two who's yelled, slammed doors, and broken something. Right?) But whether your kid continues using outbursts to get her way depends on how you react the first times she tries it. After all, a tantrum is simply a device kids use to get what they want because they've learned that it works. Once they learn that it succeeds—translation: they get their way—they're likely to try it again (and again and again). There goes any semblance of home, sweet home.

The truth is, there are no redeeming features to this behavior. Tantrums only cause stares and headaches, and teach kids a bad lesson: "Throw yourself on the floor, scream and yell, thrash about, and you'll get your way." That alone should be reason enough to commit to changing this annoying behavior.

Signs and Symptoms

Most kids resort to a tantrum or two, but here are signs indicating that maybe something more is going on and that you should seek the help of a trained mental health professional or your doctor:

- *Increase in frequency or intensity.* Despite your consistent efforts, the tantrums are increasing in number, lasting longer, or are more intense.

- *Safety issue.* Tantrums are so intense that your child's safety (or the safety of others) is in jeopardy, or your child appears to be deliberately hurting herself (banging head or fists).

- *Developmental inappropriateness.* The behavior is not typical for your child's age.

- *Emotional cause.* The behavior first began following a traumatic or stressful incident (a disaster, accident, divorce, deployment, death of a loved one).

- *Physical cause, neurological or mental affliction.* If you at all suspect that the tantrum may be due to a mental or neurological disorder, such as Bipolar Disorder, Oppositional Defiant Disorder, seizures, Attention-Deficit/Hyperactivity Disorder, or depression, use your instinct and seek the help of a mental health professional trained in child or adolescent psychology.

Pay Attention to This!

When to Worry About Tantrums

The American Academy of Pediatrics says you should consult with your pediatrician or mental health professional if the tantrums persist several times a day, have become a pattern whenever your child feels frustrated or angry, are severe, or last long, or if your child harms herself, others, or property during the episode.[37] Illness should also be ruled out. Seek help also if the tantrums are interfering with a normal, happy parent-child relationship. Your child needs emotional support and help in learning to control her anger.

THE SOLUTION

Step 1. Early Intervention

Your best defense is to anticipate a tantrum's onset *before* your child is in full meltdown mode. Here are some tips to try:

- *Identify the reason.* Temper tantrums are most common among toddlers, but preschoolers, older kids, and even adults resort to using uncontrolled outbursts. Here is a list of the most typical reasons for tantrums. Check those that apply frequently to your child:

  ☐ Demanding or self-centered attitude

  ☐ Immature temperament; lower frustration threshold

  ☐ Strong will; child wants independence, is upset when she cannot do what she wants

  ☐ Inability to express feelings, needs, or frustrations any other way

  ☐ Stress, trauma, illness, depression, or sudden life change

  ☐ Attention-getting: tantrums have worked before

  ☐ Strained home environment, stressed parents

  ☐ Failure to understand what you are asking or telling her to do

  ☐ Exhaustion, hunger, overstimulation, or boredom

  ☐ Too many or too few choices

  ☐ Biochemical imbalance, neurological impairment, mental health condition

  ☐ Sudden change in routine without warning

  ☐ Medication; do check those labels, as some medications exacerbate agitation in kids

- *Recognize your child's natural temperament.* Some kids are just more intense than others and have a tougher time calming down and handling frustrations. Could this be your child? If so, factor your child's temperament into your parenting. Give advance warning for an upcoming event; allow time to transition from one activity to another; follow an active activity with a calmer one; don't skip naps. Avoid those situations that might cause temper flare-ups.

- *Watch your behavior!* Be honest: What kind of a model are you or your parenting partner for your child? Do you handle frustrations coolly, or would your child say you have a bit of a temper yourself? Be careful—your child is watching and copying!

- *Check your expectations.* Asking your child to sit too long in a fancy restaurant, shopping cart, or car seat is just asking for trouble. Requiring a kid to do tasks beyond her developmental abilities (such as making a bed as a toddler, concentrating for long periods of time on homework) is unfair. Make sure your expectations for your child are in line with her capabilities.

- *Recognize your kid's tantrum signs.* Each child has unique stress or "I'm about to lose it" signs (clenched fists, a certain whimper or whine, waving hands). Watch for your kid's signs that a tantrum is on its way. Once you learn to identify your child's "tantrum is approaching" signs, you're in the best place to defuse or ward off the outburst.

Step 2. Rapid Response

What to do when a tantrum is **approaching.** You know the tantrum is approaching. You can see the signs. You now have seconds to ward it off. Try the tip that works best for your child:

- *Use calming techniques.* Try helping her calm down. Rub her back, hold her gently, rock her, or hum or sing a song. Get down eye to eye and talk in a soothing voice tone. Help her find a way to relax and self-soothe.

LATE-BREAKING NEWS

T. Berry Brazelton, the renowned pediatrician and author, shares this essential rule: *The more involved you are in trying to lessen the tantrum, the longer the tantrum will last.* So pay no attention to your wailing kid, and *never* give in to the outburst.[38]

- *Distract and redirect.* The second you know a tantrum is on the way, try to redirect your child's attention. *"Let's go get your teddy." "I bet you can't jump up and touch the sky!"* Or try distracting: *"Look at that little boy over there."* Your best bet is to try to divert a child's attention long enough to reroute her energy. This technique doesn't always work, but it's sure worth a try.

- *Describe feelings.* Put your child's feelings into words: *"Oh, you look tired. Are you tired?" "You seem frustrated. Are you frustrated?"* Pose a question that your child can answer with a yes or no nod. Your soothing tone along with labeling her feelings might help ward off a pending explosion (or not).

- *Be an interpreter.* Describe what you think your child wants or needs. You don't have to give in to the need (such as that extra cookie), but just acknowledging the child's concern can head off a meltdown. This is particularly helpful if your child has a limited vocabulary. *"You want Mommy to listen," "You are hungry." "Kevin is tired and wants to go home."*

- *Don't overcontrol.* Be careful about using the "too strict" approach. Spanking, yelling, or trying to be too controlling will backfire.

- *Give a warning.* For a verbal child, try giving a warning that lets your child know that her behavior is not appropriate and that if she continues, there will be a consequence. Using a firm teacher voice works best: *"Calm down now, Johnny, or we leave." "Stop, Dana, or you will go to the 'Calm Down Chair.'"* Sometimes a stern reminder is all it takes. Beware, though: warnings are effective only for kids at least three years of age. Your child must be able to understand the concepts of a warning and consequence, and have a speaking vocabulary of more than a few phrases.

What to do **during** *the tantrum.* Once a tantrum begins, you don't have much control. All you can do is ensure that your child is safe and then let the tantrum take its natural course until it winds down. Here are survival tips for during the tantrum:

- *Try to stay calm.* Shouting, shaking, spanking, or getting angry usually makes things worse. If you can't stay calm, turn your back to your child to get yourself in control, or leave the room. Your calmness will help your child get back in control.

- *Ensure safety.* Flailing kids can injure themselves or others (including you). Check out the surroundings. If there are sharp edges, glass objects, or anything else that could hurt your child, move her to a "safe zone."

- *Disengage!* Once the tantrum starts, *don't give it any attention.* No eye contact, no words; *do not react.* Ignore, ignore, ignore. Once your child learns that her outburst "works"—that is, she gets her way—she's likely to try it again (and again and again).

- *Don't try reasoning.* Forget trying to reason with a wailing, flailing kid. The child is out of control and incapable of responding to logic. It's like trying to reason with a goldfish. Once in tantrum mode, your child is beyond understanding. Also, don't coax or bribe. It doesn't help, and you're liable to escalate the outburst.

- *Remove when necessary.* There are cases when you may have to remove the child (she's destroying a public room, hurting another child, or using this antic for attention). Insist that she go to time-out (see *Time-Out*, p. 118) to calm down. You may have to escort her to another room. If you're out in public, stop what you're doing and remove your child to a secluded spot or take her home. Yes, it's inconvenient, but she'll learn that you won't tolerate inappropriate behavior.

- *Hold only if necessary.* Restraining a flailing child is generally not recommended unless absolutely necessary (when she may harm herself or others). Confining a child usually escalates the outburst, but with some highly sensitive kids, it is the only method that calms them down. Use a reassuring voice: *"You are very angry right now, and I am going to hold you until you calm down."* An out-of-control child is usually scared, and your taking charge may reassure her.

- *Concentrate only on your child.* Forget the stares and tune out any comments you might hear from other "well-meaning" (hmm!) adults. Your job is to focus only on your child.

- *Be consistent.* Once kids know that you will give their outbursts any attention, they will resort to using the same antics. Be consistent with your response. And tell other folks on the scene (grandparents, babysitter, neighbor) to follow your lead.

*What to do **after** the tantrum subsides.* Once the tantrum is over, take a breath. Then decide what your best course is for reducing future outcomes and helping your child learn healthier ways to express her frustrations. Here are tips:

- *Don't stress out.* Chances are you both are plain drained. So do whatever you need to do to recoup. Forget the long lecture or judgmental comments: "How could you!" "You know better!" They're valueless. You can deal with the issue later when you and your child are calm.

- *Check out your response.* Collect your thoughts and assess your response. Were you consistent in how you handled the outburst? Were you calm? Was there *anything* that seemed to work before, during, or after the outburst that you want to use again?

- *Identify triggers.* If the outbursts are frequent, consider tracking the episodes. Is there a pattern as to when or where the tantrums usually occur? For instance, just before naptime because she's tired, after day care because she's stressed, at noon because she's hungry? Does she have a tough time with change and need a warning that a transition is coming? Are there any issues at home that could be exacerbating the outbursts? For instance: arguing or yelling, going to stay with the other (divorced) parent, a parent leaving on a trip or evening meeting? Is there anything you can do to change your child's schedule that might help reduce her outbursts?

- *Set a consequence.* If you did give a warning and the tantrum continued, you *must* follow through with the stated consequence—for example, sending her off to a designated chair to sit (one minute per age of the child). The Calm Down Chair (also known by a variety of other terms, such as the Thinking Chair, Naughty Chair, or just time-out) is effective for children at least three years of age, sometimes for more mature two-year-olds, but *never before*.

ONE SIMPLE SOLUTION

Teach Feeling Words to Express Frustrations

Many kids use tantrums because they don't have the words to express their needs or feelings. So teach your child a few feeling words, such as *angry, mad, sad, tired,* or *frustrated*. It's best to choose just two or three words at most that describe the most common emotions that trigger her tantrums, so she'll be more likely to learn them. Start to use the emotion words at appropriate moments—for example, as you read that nighttime story (*"I bet Papa Bear feels really mad that Goldilocks is sleeping in his bed"*). Or use them in a real-life context: *"Let's be a little quieter tonight. Daddy is so tired and grumpy because he didn't sleep well last night."* When your child understands the words, encourage her at appropriate moments to label how she feels, such as *"I'm mad"* or *"I feel really cranky."* You probably will have to give word prompts in the beginning: *"Looks like you're getting cranky. Tell me how you're feeling."* Or *"Are you mad? Do you want to tell me you're mad?"* Once kids have a way to vent their feelings *and* are given permission to do so, those tantrums often slowly fade. In the meantime, continue to increase your child's feeling vocabulary and encourage her to use those words in place of the wailing, thrashing, and kicking.

Step 3. Develop Habits for Change

- *Talk about ways to handle frustrations.* It's essential that your child realize that it's okay to get upset, but that it's not okay to display it in such an uncivilized manner. So particularly with an older child, talk with her. Discuss what may have provoked the tantrum as well as ways she can handle it better next time.

- *Reinforce efforts.* Do praise your child whenever she tries to verbalize her needs or frustrations instead of resorting to a tantrum: *"You asked for help when you were upset. Good for you! Let's go see what to do."* In some cases a reward system may be worth a try. Offer some kind of material reward if your child can solve a conflict without throwing a tantrum.

- *Pass on your plan.* If your kid's using tantrums with other caregivers—such as your parenting partner, teachers, relatives, babysitters, or day-care workers— then establish a plan together for handling the behavior. Make sure you stay closely in touch with other caregivers to assess your kid's makeover progress. Consistency is critical in squelching out-of-control behaviors.

- *Reassess your plan and seek help if there is no change.* If you stick to your makeover plan and other caregivers are on board as well, you should notice a *gradual* diminishment of the tantrums. Positive behavior change depends on a number of factors, including the severity of the tantrums (the more frequent and intense the tantrum, the longer the change will take); how consistent you are with your new response and the reason for the tantrum (for instance,

One Parent's Answer

A grandmother from Palm Springs shares:

My grandson is adorable, smart as a whip, and throws absolute Oscar-winning tantrums to get his way. He throws his body onto the floor, kicks and screams so loud I was worried the neighbors would call the police. He's also knows his escapades work because his parents give in to his every whim just to keep him quiet. The day I babysat, I swore I wasn't going to let him get away with his little antics but didn't have a clue what the heck to do. Less than half an hour after his parents left, he was flailing and screaming because he couldn't have cake before dinner. His behavior was so absurd that I jumped down and started screaming and kicking with him. If my son had walked in he would have committed me on the spot, but it scared the pants off my grandson, and he locked himself in his bedroom. Later we talked about my fit, and he realized that I was showing him how ridiculous his tantrums appeared. It was also the last time he ever used them in my presence. I think he just needed a dose of his own medicine.

tantrums that are based in seeking attention are much easier to reduce than those that are stress related). So use a calendar to log the duration of the tantrums (how long they lasted) as well as frequency (which days and times they occurred). If you don't see a decrease in the frequency and duration in the next few weeks, then it's time to call for help from your doctor or a mental health professional. Something else may be triggering these outbursts.

WHAT TO EXPECT BY STAGES AND AGES

Preschooler   Tantrums are common and normal among toddlers and young preschoolers, but should begin to wane after the age of four. They are as common among boys and girls. About 80 percent of children between two and four years of age have tantrums mostly because they haven't developing coping or communication skills; about 20 percent of two- and three-year-olds and 11 percent of four-year-olds have two or more tantrums a day.[39]

School Age   Tantrums usually subside by school age, though they do persist with a small percentage of kids this age and beyond. Those who do have tantrums usually are impulsive, easily frustrated, and tightly wired; have experienced recent stress or change in their lives; or have emotional difficulties. Tantrums can also become an attention-getting device that has worked in the past to help the child get her way.

Tween   Most of us know an adult or two who still has tantrums, so a tween could as well (though such tantrums are quite rare). Recurring outbursts at this age need immediate professional help.

More Helpful Advice

The Everything Parent's Guide to Tantrums: The One Book You Need to Prevent Outbursts, Avoid Public Scenes, and Help Your Child Stay Calm, by Joni Levine

No More Tantrums: A Parent's Guide to Taming Your Child and Keeping Your Cool, by Diane Mason

Tantrums: Secrets to Calming the Storm, by Ann E. Laforge

Tears and Tantrums: What to Do When Babies and Children Cry, by Aletha J. Solter

The No-Cry Discipline Solution: Gentle Ways to Encourage Good Behavior Without Whining, Tantrums, and Tears, by Elizabeth Pantley

The Happiest Toddler on the Block: The New Way to Stop the Daily Battle of Wills and Raise a Secure and Well-Behaved One- to Four-Year-Old, by Harvey Karp and Paula Spencer

BEHAVIOR

Time-Out

THE QUESTION

"The other moms tell me using time-out is the best discipline to stop annoying behaviors, but it doesn't work with my son. I spend the time yelling at him to stay seated, and he begs me to let him go. I must be doing something wrong, so how do I make time-out work?"

THE ANSWER

Time-out is a discipline strategy in which a child is immediately removed from an activity for inappropriate behavior and asked to sit alone quietly to think about his actions for a specified time. The goal is to remove the attention from the child's inappropriate action and not reinforce that misbehavior (which could increase its frequency until it becomes a bad habit). It also gives both the child and the parent a chance to cool down and reduce angry outbursts. For some kids, time-out is an unendurable cruelty, and for others it's no "fun" but not a big deal. Here are general tips for using time-out so that you are more likely to reap the desired behavior change:

- *Target the "right" behaviors for the right kid.* Time-out is most effective in reducing such behaviors as hitting, biting, name-calling, whining, interrupting, or defiance in which the child directly disobeys an adult.[40] The time-out should always be directly correlated to the behavior that caused it. (If he hits, he gets a time-out.) *It's most effective for kids three to ten, and is rarely effective for children younger than two.* Time-out is not useful for children whose only problem behavior is excessive sulking or crying. Something else may be triggering the behavior, and you need to look into the real cause (which you should do no matter what).

- *Find a quiet, safe, well-lit part of the house.* Set aside an appropriate chair (no beanbag or recliner). Some parents call the location the "Cool Down Corner" or the "Thinking Chair." Make sure the area is one where the child is isolated; he should be unable to receive attention from others and have no access to distractions, such as games, toys, iPods, computers, pets, food, TV, friends, or phones. The spot should be out of the general household traffic, but you can still listen to make sure he is safe.

- *Set an appropriate time.* The simplest rule for determining the time length is one minute for each year of the child's age (three years equals three minutes, six years equals six minutes, and so on). Remember that these are the minimum times. Do *not* let your kid out earlier. The length of the time-out depends on the severity of the infraction and your child's age.

- *Be clear on the time.* Always tell your child exactly how long he is required to remain in time-out. Set a timer with a bell (placed near you so you maintain control—never give it to the child) so that you and the child know exactly when the time is up. Don't shave time off the time-out period once you announce the length. The clock starts as soon as your kid stops resisting and begins the time-out properly. Keep in mind that time-out need not be lengthy—usually a few minutes, and ten minutes at most is effective. *You must be calm and matter-of-fact when you administer time-out.*

- *Enforce it.* The child is not allowed to leave time-out until he behaves appropriately: sitting quietly to the best of his ability and remaining for the stipulated time. If he doesn't comply, add an extra minute of time-out from the moment he acts right. The American Academy of Pediatrics stresses that you should not drag or pull the child to the time-out spot.[41] Not only could you or your child get hurt, but the time-out will be ineffective. Do praise your child for complying with your request and for sitting quietly. *"Thank you for going to time-out."*

- *Ignore your child.* Don't peek in or respond to any attempts for attention. Keep in mind that one point of time-out is to remove the child from receiving *any* attention—whether positive or negative. Any interaction with your child will only reinforce whatever misbehavior he is displaying. This is the time for your child to think for himself and calm down. It is also critical that *you* remain calm. No long lectures. No yelling. In fact, no talking. One benefit of time-out is that it gives both the child *and parent* the opportunity to calm down. The single biggest parenting mistake is talking to the child during time-out. Ignore, ignore, ignore.

- *Use time-out anyplace and anytime.* Implement time-out *anywhere* your child displays the inappropriate behavior the minute the child misbehaves (or as soon as convenient): *"You are hitting; go sit on Grandma's bed for ten minutes."* Following the time-out, the child must still complete what you asked him to do (such as the chore or homework task). If he still doesn't comply, then double the time-out length and stay firm.

- *Do a quick debriefing.* A crucial part of discipline is helping your kid learn what he did wrong so that he won't be as likely to repeat the same misbehavior. So when time-out has been served, ask your child to describe what he did wrong and what he will do differently next time. With younger kids or those who have difficulty remembering, you will need to guide them with their answers. One of the biggest reasons kids continue using the same misbehavior is that they don't know another way to behave. Make sure you are clear about how you want your child to behave and that your child knows how to act in the way you are expecting. Make no assumptions: take time to role-play the "right way" with your child and then expect him to apologize for hurtful acts.

- *Remove a privilege if he refuses time-out.* If your child does not comply with your request to go to time-out or won't calm down, then tell him you are adding a minute more time to his time-out (from three minutes to four, or five minutes to six). You may up the time twice, but if your child still does not comply, then stop the time-out. The child now loses a privilege or the use of something he *really* cares about for a specified time period—an hour for little tykes and twenty-four hours for bigger kids. Simply state the consequence: "You didn't comply with time-out, so there's no television for the day." Then turn and walk away. Don't lecture. Just walk away. Make sure the possession or privilege is something you personally can control, such as use of the phone, computer, skateboard, video games, or TV. You should not drag or forcefully pull your child to time-out. Instead, remove a privilege if your child does not comply with your request.

You should see a gradual diminishment of the inappropriate behavior. Sometimes it is common for the misbehavior to slightly *increase*. If this happens, it means that your child is testing you to make sure you mean what you say. So be consistent. Do know that implementing time-outs successfully may take some practice, so hang in there. You should also track on a calendar how often you are using time-out to make sure there is a decrease. If you consistently use time-out according to these rules for a few weeks and see no improvement, or if the child refuses the time-outs or is physically damaging the room, seek the help of a behavior therapist, counselor, or psychologist. Something else may be triggering your child's misbehavior. Are there any new stresses or changes that might be affecting you or your child? Are you really implementing time-out correctly?

Whining

SEE ALSO: *Back Talk, Spoiled and Selfish, Stressed, Tantrums*

THE PROBLEM
Red Flags

Uses a grating, irritating voice that's a blend of crying and nagging for attention or to get her way

The Change to Parent For

Your child learns to use an appropriate and respectful voice tone and behavior to express her needs and desires, and accepts "no" from an adult or peer.

Question: "Anytime my daughter wants to get her way, she uses a whiny voice that is so embarrassing that we're afraid to take her out in public. Once she starts, I know she's going to keep on nagging until I give in. She's only four, but her behavior is driving me crazy!"

Answer: The top reason kids whine is to get our attention. Once they discover we will give in, they've learned that it works! *So don't give in! Don't pay attention or let her have the response she wants. Pretty soon, she'll learn it won't work.*

Why Change?

Whining is a loud, grating voice tone that is an exasperating blend of crying and nagging. And kids figure out early that using that grating sound is an effective means of getting their way. Probably because the sound is so darn irritating (the only two sounds more irritating are nails on a chalkboard or a dentist's drill), many parents admit they give in. In fact, even research verifies that the whining sound works: the average kid whines and nags us nine times before we finally yell "Uncle!" and give in.[42] And that's our big mistake when it comes to this behavior. You see, whining is clearly a learned behavior; it is also quite contagious and can turn into a household epidemic. If you don't nip it in the bud, siblings will pick up that it works and catch the whining behavior. It's also a huge peer turnoff. What kid wants to be around a whiner? But it also turns adults off as well. What

LATE-BREAKING NEWS

Kids Are Winning the Whining Wars

A national poll of 750 youngsters found that most refuse to take no for an answer and keep whining until their parents give in.[43] Most kids nagged their parents nine times to have their way. Twelve- to thirteen-year-olds were the worst whiners; they whined more than fifty times to get what they wanted. The parent lesson here is simple: *stand firm and don't let your kids whine you down!*

parent wants their kid to associate with a "whiner"? So there goes your kid's birthday party and sleepover invitations. And if those aren't reasons enough to beware: whining can escalate. It is often the first step to a tantrum. Whining ruins your kid's reputation and your relationship with your kid, and if not stopped only gets worse. The fact is, there is no redeeming value to this behavior. Absolutely none—all the more reason to stop your kid from resorting to using that grating, annoying tone. So let's get started on making this change happen ASAP.

Signs and Symptoms

Every child is going to use a whining, grating sound every once in a while to get her way, but here are four big signs that it's time to change this annoying behavior:

1. *Whining has become a habit that works.* Your child has learned to use that whining tone to get her way, and it usually works. (And you in turn usually say yes to your child more than you say no because it's easier than listening to that grating sound.)

Pay Attention to This!

Intervene ASAP or Whining May Increase

Most experts say whining almost never stops without parental intervention.[44] In fact, the rare kids who do stop on their own usually do so because they've found more efficient ways of getting their needs met—and those ways may include lying, stealing, or sneaking out after hours, or even more destructive behaviors like drug and alcohol abuse. So take this behavior seriously and stay committed to making this change happen.

2. *The whining is hindering your relationship.* Your child is now treating you in a disrespectful way. It's embarrassing to take your kid out in public.

3. *Your child's reputation is affected.* Adults roll their eyes when they hear your kid whine. Other kids have labeled her a whiner or have stopped associating with her.

4. *The whining has spiraled up a notch.* In addition to (or in place of) the whine, your kid is now resorting to back talk, rudeness, tantrums, or defiance to get her way.

THE SOLUTION

Step 1. Early Intervention

- *Identify the reason your child typically whines.* Here are reasons for whining. Your job is to figure out the most common reason why your kid resorts to using this tone so that you can put together a plan to stop it using the other information, tips, and resources provided in this issue. Here is a list of typical reasons kids whine. Check those that may apply to your child:

  ☐ Frustration

  ☐ Jealousy

  ☐ Fatigue, hunger, crankiness, or illness

  ☐ Testing limits

  ☐ Speech or hearing difficulties

  ☐ Attention getting

  ☐ Imitation

  ☐ Low frustration threshold

  ☐ Stress or emotional overload caused by recent events

  ☐ Impact of a number of changes (day care, school, a new baby)

  ☐ Success with using whining

- *Recognize your current response.* Think about how you typically respond to your kid's whining. If possible, discuss this with your spouse or another parent who knows you and your child well. Why hasn't your response succeeded in stopping the whining so far? Along with committing to no longer tolerating your kid's whining, you must plan how you will respond the next time your kid whines.

- *Identify the pattern, then anticipate it.* Usually there's a predictable pattern to kids' behavior in which certain situations are more likely to provoke that whining voice. For instance, is there a time of day when she is more apt to sulk? When she's hungry or tired? When you're on the phone and she wants your attention? When she's at the mall and sees something she wants? Identify the kinds of circumstances that might incite her to whine. Once you're aware of the pattern, you can anticipate when your kid is more likely to resort to using the behavior and can head it off before it starts.

- *Use a "nice voice."* Be sure your child knows the difference between a whining voice and a normal "nice" speaking tone. Whining may have become such a habit that she simply isn't aware of her annoying tone. Notice and point out when your child is not using a whining voice and say, *"That's it. Good. Thanks for not whining."* And take a moment to demonstrate what kind of a voice you expect. For example: *"Here's my whining voice: 'I don't wanna do this.' Here's my polite one: 'Can you please help me?' When you want something, make your voice sound like my polite voice. Now you try."* Hint: be careful not to mimic your child; your goal is to be instructional without ridiculing, so that she understands your expectations.

- *Try some distraction.* You might try directing a younger child before she starts to whine: *"Look, there's a gorgeous butterfly!"* or *"Listen. Doesn't that sound like Daddy's car?"* Beware: the first sign of a temper tantrum is often whining. So divert your child's attention or walk away ASAP before the whine escalates to an outburst.

Pay Attention to This!

Three Simple Solutions When Kids Whine in Public

Your kid needs to know you won't tolerate whining anytime or anyplace. So if your child tries that grating voice in public, try one of these simple consequences ASAP:

1. *At someone's home.* Designate a "Whiner's Chair" to use at the first whimper: *"Go sit in the Whiner's Chair for a few minutes so you remember to use your nice voice to ask for something."* Be sure to clue Grandma or Aunt Harriet into why you might be borrowing her chair.

2. *In the car.* Pull over to the side of the road (when safe), and wait until your kid talks correctly. Feel free to listen to the radio or even read. She'll get the point.

3. *In a public setting.* Just get up, take your child firmly but gently by the arm, and leave the scene immediately. You and your parenting partner may have to resort to driving in two cars, but your kid will get the picture that you won't allow this behavior anywhere. Period.

- *Acknowledge impatience.* Some kids just have a harder time waiting—even a minute can seem like an eternity. So they may resort to whining to get our attention. Responding promptly to a more impulse-prone child might fend off the whine. *"I'll be off the phone in two minutes. As soon as I'm done, let's read a book."* You might also try putting your hand gently on her shoulder or giving her a one-minute finger signal (*before* she starts those shrill tones) to let her know you see her and will help her momentarily.

Step 2. Rapid Response

- *Watch your tone.* The next time you catch yourself whining about the new hockey practice schedule or your child's teacher, check yourself. Kids are mimickers. Make sure your child hasn't learned this whining tone from you.

- *Lay down new rules.* Announce that from now on, she should expect an automatic "no" *any* time she whines. Then tell your child that you will flatly refuse to listen even to the first note of a whine uttered from your kid's lips. Your child has to realize that your rule is nonnegotiable.

- *Turn a deaf ear.* At the first whimper of a whine, say: *"Stop please. I don't listen to whining voices. Tell me what you want with a nice tone."* Then walk, turn, or do something else to appear as though you're occupying your time. But *ignore* the whine. Turn back when the whining stops (even for a few seconds) and say, *"I do listen to a nice voice. Can I help you now?"*

- *Do not overreact.* If your child's grating tone is getting to you, turn and look elsewhere, but don't get upset. You can escalate that whine to a full-blown tantrum. Stay calm. If you need to leave the room, do so. The trick is not to look irritated or to react. Watch your body language as well. Shrugging your shoulders, raising your eyebrows, and shaking your head are also reacting, and some kids actually use whining to irritate you. One mom passed on to me that whenever her child starts to whine, she pretends he's speaking in a foreign language that she cannot understand. She says that it helps her ignore the behavior and has really worked to reduce that whining tone.

- *Refuse to comply until your child speaks politely.* The best way to stop the behavior is to flat-out refuse to listen to requests unless they are spoken with a polite tone. Take heed: if you back down and surrender, your kid is likely to continue using the technique as a way to get what she wants. Worse yet, if not stopped, whining often escalates to back talk, arguing, and tantrums. So the bottom line is this: *don't let your kid think it works.* The moment your child uses a respectful, polite tone, do comply with the request (as long as it's reasonable, of course). *"Thank you. That's the tone my ears listen to."*

- *Tell your child that you expect better.* Just plain let your child know that you expect more of her behavior. *"We don't whine. I expect you to tell me what you need."*

Step 3. Develop Habits for Change

- *Hold respectful conversations.* Could it be that your child is resorting to whining because respect is missing in your conversation? If so, then it's time to put respect back into your daily interactions. Make sure you are talking to your child as you would to your best girlfriend. Be polite. Listen with your full presence. Smile and look as if you enjoy being with your kid. Thank your child for sharing her ideas. Don't take your relationship with your child for granted.

- *Reward the "right tone."* Do praise your child whenever she uses the right voice tone. *"I'd be happy to get you a cookie since you asked so nicely. My ears love that voice." "Thank you using your 'nice voice.' I love to help you when you talk that way."* The secret is to thank your child *every* time she uses the right voice. It may seem awkward, but you should see a dramatic decline in the whining.

- *Set a consequence.* Usually kids will stop whining if they know you refuse to listen to the tone. But if your child is caught up in the habit of whining, you might need to take your response up a notch and give a consequence. For a younger child, try a "Whining Chair" (*every* time she whines, she sits in the chair—one minute for each year of her life) or send your child to the "Whining Room" where she can whine, complain, and vent aloud as much as she likes. At least you and the rest of the family will be spared having to hear her. For older kids, remove a privilege (such as use of the Internet or cell phone) or require that they contribute part of their allowance to the family "Fees for Complaining Jar." Every whine, nag, or complaint is fined a preset amount, such as a quarter. If you don't follow through, the whining may actually increase, because your kid has learned that you just might give in. So *don't give in.*

- *Hang in there.* If your child has been in the whining habit for a while, don't expect instant change. Continue to be consistent with your same "no response" response, and you should see a decrease in the behavior. If not, then start thinking about what else could be contributing to this behavior. An illness? A speech delay or impediment? A low frustration threshold due to an attention deficit or emotional need? It may be time to seek professional help and get a second opinion.

One Parent's Answer

A mom from Calgary shares:

I tried everything short of buying earplugs, but nothing stopped my son's whine. One night my husband recorded our little darling in his full-blown whining mode. Then he played it back so Matthew could hear himself. Once he knew how obnoxious he sounded, his whining quickly faded.

WHAT TO EXPECT BY STAGES AND AGES

Preschooler   Whining starts around age three, when kids feel out of control or overwhelmed, or lack vocabulary to voice their frustrations. Crankiness, hunger, or fatigue can trigger the behavior because preschoolers have a low threshold for frustration. They also love to try out new voice tones and see just how far they can go to push your buttons.

School Age   Stress, big changes, and a need for attention (particularly with the birth of a new baby) can bring back the whining tone. Kids also learn to use a whine when hungry or tired but also when bored or when they're asked to do things they don't want to do. If not stopped, the behavior can continue well into the school years.

Tween   Kids this age often whine with not just a grating tone but also a disrespectful attitude. Watch also for body gestures. They usually deliver the whine with rolling eyes, smacking lips, or shrugging shoulders. They might use whining to pressure you for the latest products (gadgets, clothing, electronics) to fit in with peers.

More Helpful Advice

Taming the Dragon in Your Child, by Meg Eastman and Sydney Craft Rozen

Whining: 3 Steps to Stopping It Before the Tears and Tantrums Start, by Audrey Ricker and Carolyn Crowder

Winning the Whining Wars, by Cynthia Whitham

BEHAVIOR

Won't Listen

SEE ALSO: *Angry, Argues, Attention Deficit, Bad Manners, Bossy, Communicating, Defiant, Depressed, Procrastinates*

THE PROBLEM

Red Flags

Doesn't follow directions, listens only "selectively," doesn't pay attention, needs repeated reminders to do what you ask, can't recall directions

The Change to Parent For

Your child listens the *first* time to your request and follows your directions, as well as learns good listening skills that will help him pay attention and recall information.

Question: "I know my son can hear perfectly well, but whenever I talk he becomes 'selectively deaf.' I'm tired of telling him again and again what I want him to do. How can I get my child to listen to me?"

Answer: Make a pledge that you will not repeat yourself. Then get down to your child's level (if he's still smaller than you) and tell—*don't ask*—what you want done so that it is short and to the point. It's helpful to start with the word "The" so that your kid's ears hear exactly what you want him to do. "*The blocks need to be picked up.*" "*The TV needs to be turned off.*" Once you say your request and you're sure your child understands (you can ask him to repeat what you just said), then expect your child to listen and comply each and every time.

Why Change?

"*Why don't you listen?*" "*That's the fourth time I told you!*" "*Didn't you hear anything I just said?*" If you're frustrated in trying to get your kid to listen, take heart: you're not alone. *Parents* magazine polled moms and dads about their toughest discipline challenge, and the hands-down winner was "My kid doesn't listen to me."[45] There is an art to asking your kids to do something. The way you ask greatly influences the way they respond. The fact is, learning to give directions so kids will listen takes practice. And breaking a child's bad listening habits takes work and patience.

Improving your kid's listening skills will benefit every arena of his life—school performance, relations with friends, job performance, and family harmony. Many experts say that learning to listen is one of the most crucial habits our children need for handling life. Parenting for this change lays the foundation that fosters respectful communication as well as the acquisition of new knowledge.

Signs and Symptoms

Every kid tunes out and turns us off every now and then, but here are signs that listening and following directions are issues that need tuning up, or that your child may be having trouble listening for other reasons:

- Complies only after you have repeated your request several times
- Complies, but remembers only parts of what you said
- Doesn't understand what you mean or asks you to repeat yourself
- Responds only when you yell or threaten a punishment if he does not comply
- Refuses to comply with your request
- Tells you he'll do what you ask "later" (though rarely can be counted on to follow through)
- "Listens selectively" and ignores some requests (such as "Do your schoolwork" or "Make your bed") or feigns "I didn't hear you"

THE SOLUTION

Step 1. Early Intervention

- *Identify the reason.* There are many reasons kids don't listen, so your first job is to discover why your kid tunes you out. Could any of the reasons in the following list be the cause? Check those that may apply to your situation:

  ☐ You and your child (or other adults) are in a power struggle, or your relationship has broken down; your child is choosing to be noncompliant.

  ☐ You routinely repeat your directions several times before you sound serious.

  ☐ You usually give a bribe to get compliance or don't enforce listening, so your child waits until he is rewarded or for you to give up or do the task.

  ☐ Your child has a short attention span and is easily distracted.

  ☐ Your child is distracted by physical concerns, such as hunger, illness, sleepiness, or the need to use the bathroom.

☐ Your child is absorbed in a task when you give the direction.

☐ Your child has an auditory processing problem or trouble screening out background noise.

☐ Your child is avoiding the task due to laziness or fear that he will not meet your expectation.

☐ Your child has an earache, allergy, "swimmer's ear," illness, or hearing loss.

☐ Stress makes it difficult to concentrate: a recent trauma, too much yelling or stress in the family, or depression.

☐ Your delivery is too critical, preachy, judgmental, or threatening.

☐ Your directions or task expectations are not tailored to your child's stage of development.

What is your best guess as to what is triggering the problem? What is the first easy action you will take to remedy the situation?

- *Model good listening.* Kids can't learn to be good listeners if they don't have good models to copy, so make sure you show your kids what you expect them to do by being a good listener yourself. Show them that you listen to your spouse, your friends, and, most important, to them. An old proverb is a great reminder: "We have two ears and one mouth for a reason." Listen to your kid twice as much as you talk!

- *Avoid "listening stoppers."* Three words—*You, If,* and *Why*—said at the beginning of a direction can frequently cause a kid to go on automatic tune-out. "You" sets your message up to assault your child's character: "You never listen." "If" sends a threatening tone: "If you don't do what I ask . . ." "Why" expects your child to explain his behavior, and he may be clueless: "Why aren't you listening?" So just remove these three words from your requests and you'll be more likely to have your kid tune in and comply. (See *Communicating,* p. 545.)

Step 2. Rapid Response

A key to success is making sure you give directions and requests tailored to your child's ability and then expect compliance. Here are a few strategies that get kids to listen the first time.

- *Get his attention first, then talk.* If your kid is not listening, first get his attention and make sure he's looking at you before you speak. You might squat down to his level, lift your kid's chin up gently so he looks into your eyes, or give a verbal cue to get his attention. *"Please look at me and listen to what I have to say."* Give your request when you're eyeball to eyeball. You're more likely to have your child's full attention.

- *Lower your voice and speak more slowly.* Nothing turns a kid off faster than yelling, so do the opposite: talk softer, not louder. Or even try whispering. It usually catches the kid off guard, and he stops to listen. Teachers have used this strategy for years because it works.

> ## One Parent's Answer
>
> A mom from Nashville shares:
>
> *I got so tired of listening to myself give directions that I starting carrying a pack of Post-its and a pencil in my pocket. When I really wanted my child to do something ASAP, I'd write the word (toys, teeth, dinner) and stick it on him or the toy. Not only did he do my requests quicker, he thought it was fun and even learned to read the words!*

- *Keep it short, sweet, and to the point.* Tailor your directions to your child's attention span and cognitive abilities. Make sure you tell your child exactly what you want him to do. *"Please make your bed before you go outside"* or *"You need to get ready to go to school now."* Limiting your request to fewer words also helps. Sometimes saying one word does the trick: *"Homework!"* or *"Chores!"* Be sure you don't phrase your request as a question or a suggestion. If you want your child to comply, then tell, don't ask.

- *Get active.* If time is of the essence or your child needs you to "jump-start" him into action, don't say anything. Just gently grab his hand and take him to where you want him to go.

- *Give a little leeway.* Interrupting an occupied child can lead to resistance. So if you see that your child is really engrossed in something legitimate (his homework, texting his friend about homework, his Lego construction), be flexible. Wait until you see that your child is a little less engaged in his task. Then state your request. Just ensure that your child doesn't take advantage of the situation. (If he appears legitimately engrossed in an activity, give a time limit: "I need your attention in a minute.")

- *Expect compliance.* If you've been saying those directions two, three, or four times, then you're training your kid not to pay attention. You'll just keep repeating yourself. So use the parenting techniques already mentioned, but also expect your child to listen the first time. Walk over to him, say the request firmly, and then give no more reminders. If he doesn't obey, then apply a consequence. (See next tip.)

- *Allow consequences to kick in.* If you're sure your child has heard the request and you've given directions set at the level of your child's listening capabilities, then it is time to give a consequence. Not doing so sends a message to your kid that you're okay with his dismissing you. The way to set a first-level consequence might be to include it when you state your request: "If you want cookies for dessert, please come now." If he shows up later, just say in a matter-of-fact tone, "Sorry, it's too late." Don't back down or buy into your child's defense: *"I didn't hear you!"* Your answer is just a simple, *"Maybe next time you'll listen better."* Just be consistent so that your child knows you do expect him to tune in the first time.

Step 3. Develop Habits for Change

- *Teach memory strategies.* If the problem is that when you give a direction your child can't recall what he hears, then teach habits so your child learns to re- member what he hears without your reminders. Here are a few ideas:

  - *Use the rewind method.* To ensure that your child heard your directions, ask him to repeat your statement. But then go one step further and tell him to keep playing the direction in his head. A younger child can practice by telling his stuffed animal, puppet, doll, or family pet what you said. An older kid can repeat the direction over and over in a low voice until the task is finished.

  - *Write a note.* Some kids prefer to remind themselves by writing notes or putting a sticker on their hand that signifies the task.

  - *Picture it in your mind.* Tell your child to try "picturing the task in his mind." *"See your clothes on the floor and the hamper next to it. See yourself putting the clothes in the hamper. That's what you need to do."*

  - *Use your fingers.* Teach your child to use his hand as a "task counter": each finger represents one thing he is to remember to do.

- *Rethink your relationship.* You've tried better communication techniques and refined how you give directions. You've taken into account your child's age or attention span and considered whether he has any kind of hearing loss. Now consider another option: the child is blatantly choosing not to listen to you. This is a matter of noncompliance or disrespect. (See *Angry,* p. 232; *Argues,* p. 46; *Communicating,* p. 545; and *Defiant,* p. 76.)

WHAT TO EXPECT BY STAGES AND AGES

Preschooler   Preschoolers are able to answer simple questions, follow a story, and un- derstand most conversations. Attention spans steadily increase; most four- to five-year- olds can focus on an activity for twelve to twenty-five minutes.[46] Older preschoolers can follow a three-step direction (pick up your toys, brush your teeth, and put on your pajamas).

School Age Kids start to tune in to video and computer games and television—and tune out parents. Aside from their possibly making this attitude shift, do know that almost 15 percent of school-age kids have some kind of hearing loss;[47] 7 percent have auditory processing disorders and are often are accused of "Not trying hard enough to listen."[48] Could this be your child?

Tween Tweens have a tendency to tune out, whether out of defiance or rudeness or due to stress, sleep deprivation, hormones kicking in because of puberty, or just having "too much on their plate." This is also the age when kids start pulling back from parents and spending more time with peers. Use caution to avoid overuse of electronic devices, such as cell phones, video games, CD players, and MP3 players, as well as electric guitars and some other musical instruments. These devices played too loudly can cause hearing loss.

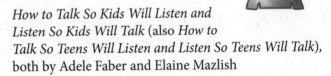

More Helpful Advice

How to Talk So Kids Will Listen and Listen So Kids Will Talk (also *How to Talk So Teens Will Listen and Listen So Teens Will Talk*), both by Adele Faber and Elaine Mazlish

Parent Talk: How to Talk to Your Children in Language That Builds Self-Esteem and Encourages Responsibility, by Chick Moorman

Parent Effectiveness Training: The Proven Program for Raising Responsible Children, by Dr. Thomas Gordon

BEHAVIOR

Yelling

SEE ALSO: *Angry, Argues, Chores, Defiant, Sibling Rivalry, Sleepless, Won't Listen*

THE QUESTION

"My daughter is only six years old but has a voice that can shatter glass. Her constant yelling gives the rest of the family a terrible headache. How can we stop her from yelling all the time whenever she gets crabby or doesn't get what she wants?"

THE ANSWER

Research shows that kids and parents alike are feeling far more stressed than just a decade ago, and yelling—though hardly a healthy or appropriate option—is one way to let off steam. But it's also a sure way to shatter patience and family harmony. Tolerating yelling just teaches a kid that the way to get what you want is by upping the volume. And beware: the more yelling there is, the more it must be utilized to be effective. In other words, family members get used to the screaming, the pitch gets louder, the frequency increases, and soon everyone starts using it so they can be heard.

Unless your child has a hearing problem—and please don't make any assumptions—yelling is a learned behavior. So this may be a good time to check in on your own behavior. Eliminating this behavior will do absolute wonders in creating a calmer and more peaceful family. So don't wait! Here are solutions to turn those screaming matches around:

- *Find the real cause, then commit to change.* Your first step toward change is to figure out what is going on. The following is a list of common reasons kids (and parents) yell. Check those that apply to your child:

  ☐ *Emotional distress.* Your child feels angry, frustrated, overwhelmed, in need of attention, stressed, physically tired or sick.

  ☐ *Powerlessness.* The youngest kid feels he isn't listened to.

  ☐ *Mimicking.* The child is *yelling back.* Everyone else yells. Is he yelling to get his needs across?

  ☐ *Feelings of being picked on.* Might he have a legitimate reason to yell? Is he picked on by a sibling? Is a sibling or another adult the real instigator?

  ☐ *Family stress.* Is the stress in your family at a boiling point? Is the problem between you and your spouse, and your kids are picking up on that stress?

☐ *Your problem.* How do you typically respond to your kid's screaming? Does your reaction calm him down or set him off further?

Identify what's really causing your kid or other family members to yell, then ask yourself what you are seriously willing to do. A study by sociologist Murray A. Straus, codirector of the Family Research Lab at the University of New Hampshire, found that half of parents surveyed had screamed, yelled, or shouted at their infants.[49] By the time a kid reaches seven years of age, 98 percent of parents have verbally lashed out at them. If you want to boost family harmony and reduce yelling, then something needs to be altered in your kid's environment, and now. What will you change?

- *Firmly and calmly convey your new rule: "No yelling!"* Begin by holding a State of the Family meeting and convey your "no yelling" expectations to all family members. Everyone must know that you mean business when you say that yelling will no longer be tolerated. Tell your screamers that although it's okay to be angry, they may not use a yelling voice to express their feelings. If the family member needs to take a time-out to calm down, she may do so. Ask everyone to take a "no yelling" vow. The pledge is written on a piece of paper, signed by all members, and posted as a concrete reminder.

- *Alter your response.* Yelling is contagious, so chances are that if your child or another family member has been screaming, you may have caught the "screaming bug." Try changing your response during those hot-button heated moments when arguments are most likely to transpire (maybe it's when you tell your kid it's time for bed or that she needs to do her homework). Here are four simple responses that reduce the need for screaming matches and keep things calm and cooler:

  - *Breathe.* If you have the slightest inkling that you're going to yell, take a deep, slow breath and get yourself back in control. If you need to walk away to calm down, do so.

  - *Whisper.* Instead of raising your voice (and yelling), lower it to a whisper. It's an old teacher technique that works almost magically. (Take it from a former teacher.) Your child is not only more likely to tune in but also less likely to yell back.

  - *Keep it down to one word.* Limit your request to one word: *"Homework!"* *"Dinner!"* Your child will get the hint, and you'll save your voice and be less likely to work yourself into a tirade. Or don't say anything. Write your request on a Post-it and just zap it on your kid's door, pillow, or forehead (what the heck). *"Bed!" "Toys!"*

  - *Take ten.* The quickest way to start a screaming match is to yell back. So don't. Tell everyone in your family that any time things get too tense, either person may "Take ten" (or walk away to get herself calm and cool again).

- *Teach healthier alternatives to express needs.* Many kids yell because they simply don't know how to express their frustrations any other way. So teach new, healthier ways.

  - *Model a new tone.* Teach your child to use an acceptable voice tone: *"That voice is yelling and unacceptable. Listen to how a calm voice sounds when I want something, then make your voice sound like mine."* Or *"Your voice is too loud. Are you angry? Tell Corinna why you're angry, using a regular voice."*

  - *Teach "I" messages.* Explain that instead of starting messages with "You," your child should begin with "I." It helps your kid stay focused on the person's troublesome behavior without putting the person down, thus lessening the chances for emotional outbursts (and yelling). The child then tells the offender what the person did that upset her. She may also state how she'd like the problem resolved. For example: "I get really upset when you take my stuff. I want you to ask me for permission first." Or "I don't like to be teased. Please stop."

  - *Teach problem solving.* Are your kids yelling because they don't know a way to resolve their problems? If so, it's time to help your kids learn conflict resolution strategies. (See *Angry,* p. 232.)

  - *Label emotions.* One way to reduce those screaming matches is for family members to acknowledge their feelings to one another. "Watch out. I'm really getting upset." "I'm so angry I could burst." "I feel so frustrated that you're not listening to me." Labeling the feeling helps both the yeller and the receiver calm down and get a bit of perspective. Give all members of your family permission to verbalize their feelings and then honor them by listening to their concerns.

- *Refuse to engage with a screamer.* Consider agreeing on a signal between you and the screamer—such as pulling your ear or giving a "time-out" hand gesture—signifying an inappropriate voice tone. Then the first moment that her voice goes one notch above a "normal range," give the signal. It means she needs to lower her voice immediately or you won't listen. If she continues using a loud, yelling tone, absolutely refuse to listen. Firmly (and calmly) explain, *"That's yelling. I only listen when you use a calm voice."* Walk away and go about your business until she talks right. As long as she yells, keep walking. If you have to lock yourself in the bathroom, do so. She needs to know you mean business, so be consistent.

- *Set a consequence for persistent yelling.* If you've tried all the methods and yet the yelling continues, then it's time to set a consequence. Make sure you explain the consequence at a relaxed time—not during a screaming match. Tell a younger kid that *each* time she yells, she will be sent to time-out for a few minutes to help her remember how to talk right. When the time is up (usually no more than a few minutes), help her express her concerns using an appropriate voice tone. An appropriate consequence for older kids is losing telephone privileges for a set length of time (an hour or the evening, depending on the circumstances). *"If you can't talk nicely to your family, then you won't be able to talk to your friends."* Once you set the consequence, then consistency is crucial! Use the same consequence every time she yells.

- *Get help.* If yelling continues despite your best efforts, then there is a deeper underlying problem. It's time to seek the help of a mental health professional for your child or a therapist for you and your spouse or family. Commit to following through.

It may take some time to create the change you are looking for in your family, but do not deviate from your goal. Reducing yelling is crucial to achieving a happier, more peaceful family. Don't forget that one of the simplest ways to change kids' behavior is to catch them being good. Any time you notice your kid (or spouse) handling a difficult situation calmly, expressing her frustrations without yelling, or keeping her temper in control, acknowledge her behavior and let her know you appreciate her efforts, and celebrate your success as a family.

Part 3
Character

OUT OF THE MOUTHS OF BABES
WHY GOD MADE MOMS

Answers given by second-grade schoolchildren to the following question:

What kind of little girl was your mom?

1. My mom has always been my mom and none of that other stuff.

2. I don't know because I wasn't there, but my guess would be pretty bossy.

3. They say she used to be nice.

Bad Manners

SEE ALSO: *Defiant, Materialistic, Selfish and Spoiled, Swears, Ungrateful, Won't Listen*

THE PROBLEM

Red Flags

Is discourteous, rude, flippant, or disrespectful; needs repeated "behave yourself" reminders; lacks social skills for certain settings; doesn't understand the need for common courtesy

The Change to Parent For

Your child learns age-appropriate etiquette skills and habits of civility and uses them in a respectful and courteous manner without reminders in everyday life.

Question: "Our 'sweet' son seems in need of a "manners makeover." We're going to a family reunion this coming summer and I'm concerned I'll be mortified. Is it too late???"

Answer: It's never too late to teach good manners—in fact, many businesses now require their adult employees to take etiquette courses. But the best way to boost courtesy is to work on just one or two manners at a time, then have your child practice them at home until he can use them *without* your etiquette reminders. If you start those courtesy lessons ASAP, your son can arrive at the reunion as your "well mannered" and sweet kid whom you'll be proud to show off.

Why Change?

A survey by *U.S. News & World Report* revealed that nine out of ten Americans feel that the breakdown of civility is a problem, and nearly half rate the problem as extremely serious.[1] Ninety percent of Americans polled said manners and good social graces have significantly eroded over the past ten years and that the situation is only getting worse. What's more, 93 percent of adults feel that the major cause of all rudeness is that parents have failed to teach respect to their kids.[2] By failing to deliver those lessons, we are doing our kids a huge disservice, and for a number of reasons.

Scores of studies find that well-mannered children are more popular and do better in school. Teachers speak glowingly of them; parents make sure they are on the top of their kids' invite lists. Polite kids are just plain nicer to be around. Because courteous kids are more considerate of others' thoughts and feelings, they are also more respectful and a less selfish breed. Courteous kids also have an edge later in life: members of the business world tell us that their first interview choices are those applicants displaying good social graces. Whether you think it's time your child has a more intensive rudeness makeover or just a quick manners tune-up, here are the proven solutions to cultivate courtesy in your child, make respect a priority in your home, and teach crucial habits that will help him both now and forever in all areas of his life.

Signs and Symptoms

Every child has an "off day" and forgets his manners, but here are signs that indicate that your child needs a more serious manners tune-up:

- A typical response is an impolite tone (sarcastic or surly) delivered with disrespectful body language (rolling eyes, smirking, shrugging shoulders).
- Impolite behavior is now more frequent or becoming a habit.
- Constant reminders are needed to reinforce manners that you thought you had already taught.
- Discourtesy is causing friction in your everyday relationship and breaking down your family harmony.
- Social experiences and peer interactions (birthday or slumber parties, dinners, and so on) are hindered because your child lacks certain social graces or doesn't feel comfortable using them.
- Discourtesy is ruining his reputation among friends, parents, teachers, relatives, and family.
- You are seeing increasing disrespect, poor character, and diminishing moral intelligence.

THE SOLUTION

Step 1. Early Intervention

- *Prioritize courtesy.* If you really want your child to be courteous (and what parent doesn't), then the first crucial step is to *commit* to raising a courteous child. The truth is, parents who raise well-mannered kids don't do so by accident. They are acutely conscious that they want their kids to become well mannered and polite, and simply put a bit more energy into that effort. Take a pledge from this moment on that you will look for simple everyday moments to reinforce politeness and the importance of good manners, so your kids will know that you just flat-out expect them to act in a civil, respectful, and courteous manner. Period.

- *Be an example of courtesy.* The easiest way for kids to catch good manners is by imitating others. So don't forget to say please when you ask your child for something and thank you when you receive it. And always treat your child with courtesy and respect so that he knows that's how you expect him to treat others.

- *Point out the value of courtesy.* Discuss the value of good manners and why you think your child should behave politely. *"Using good manners helps you gain the respect of your friends and teachers at school."* Also explain why he should use the new manner you're introducing to him: *"Shaking hands and introducing yourself is a great way to meet new friends." "Grandma always loves it when you show your good manners."* Once kids understand the impact good manners have on others, they're more likely to use them in their daily behavior.

- *Get others on board.* The best way to raise a courteous kid is to get other caring adults to reinforce your courtesy-building efforts. Ask the babysitter, the day-care worker, Grandpa, siblings, and your parenting partner to support your efforts. *"Please remind him to say 'thank you.'" "We're working on 'excuse me' this week. Make sure he remembers."*

- *Identify the underlying cause of incivility.* If your child has a more serious case of rudeness, then it's time to dig deeper and discover the reason. Here are the most common reasons kids backslide in the manners department. Check the ones that apply to your child or situation:

  - ☐ Manners are not modeled or made a high priority at home.
  - ☐ Your child was never taught particular etiquette skills.
  - ☐ Impolite peers or adults are being imitated.
  - ☐ Your child is fatigued, stressed, or ill.
  - ☐ Music, movies, or TV that flaunt rudeness are having a bad influence.
  - ☐ You're allowing him to get away with bad manners.
  - ☐ Your child is testing his limits.

Step 2. Rapid Response

- *Target manners that need tuning up.* The first step to your new response is to look over the Eighty-Five Crucial Manners to Teach Your Child (p. 145) and choose a few manners your child now lacks that would boost his courtesy quotient. Or just watch your child a bit more closely in social settings and assess which manners need tuning up. Feel free to make a long list, but select only one or two new etiquette skills to teach each week.

- *Model the new manner.* Kids learn new skills best by seeing an example of what you expect, not by hearing your lecture. So show your child the manner you want him to learn. Suppose you want to teach your child to make an introduction. *"I'll pretend I'm meeting you for the first time: 'Hi! I'm Jane. What's your name? Do you live in Reno?'"* Now he has a model to copy, and you can expect him to use it.

- *Hold manner "lookouts."* Point out others who are using the skill. That way your child will see when and how the manner should be used in action: *"When we go out to dinner, let's watch to see how many people remember to put their napkin in their lap before eating." "We're going to Grandma's today. Let's see how she meets us at the door like a good hostess."* (Just do remind your kids to keep their "manner discoveries" quiet so that they don't blare out their findings to the world.)

- *Acknowledge courtesy attempts.* Support your child's courtesy attempts by letting him know they are appreciated: *"Wow, nice manners! Did you notice the smile on Grandma's face when you thanked her for dinner?" "Waiting for the others to sit down before you began eating was polite."* Just remember to point out exactly what your child did that was polite so that he'll be more likely to repeat the courteous action again.

- *Be consistent!* Good manners do not develop naturally, but instead are the result of considerable effort, patience, and diligent training. There's no way around it. So keep encouraging your child's efforts and teaching new manner skills until you get the results you hope for. And don't settle for less.

- *Set a consequence for repeat discourtesy.* If your kid still uses bad manners despite your etiquette lessons, it's time to take things up a notch and enforce a consequence. Depending on your child's age and the severity of the offense, you might try requiring your kid to repeat the correct polite behavior ten times in a row on the spot, or to say or even write a sincere apology note to the offended party. For especially offensive discourteous behaviors, up the stakes by forbidding your child to attend social gatherings for an appropriate period of time. Doing so helps your kid get the message that you expect well-mannered behavior.

ONE SIMPLE SOLUTION

One of the simplest and most essential manners that every child should learn is a handshake, as it is a universal greeting. You can begin when your child is three years old. Just be sure to teach the two critical elements to a proper handshake: shake the person's hand with a firm grip and maintain eye contact. Practice the greeting with your child until he feels confident using it in the real world. You'll also be giving your child a jump-start for success: surveys show that one of the first things employers look for is whether a candidate knows how to use a proper handshake.[3]

Step 3. Develop Habits for Change

Kids learn any skill best through repetition; give your child lots of opportunities to practice the new skill so that he can use his new manners confidently in the real world. Here are a few ways:

- *Target a manner a week.* Some families practice a new manner each week. You might write the new manner (such as eating soup without slurping or waiting until the hostess sits before eating) on an index card. Then post the manner on your refrigerator as a family reminder so that everybody is practicing the same manner together.

- *Make mealtimes matter.* Dinnertime is the perfect place to practice conversation skills and table manners with kids, such as keeping your napkin on your lap, chewing with your mouth closed, and learning which fork to use with each course. Take advantage of those mealtime moments. Here are a few manners to get you started: *Please. Thank you. May I? Excuse me. Pardon me. I'm sorry. You go first. How was your day? How can I help? Please, may I be excused? Please pass.*

- *Practice good host skills.* Whenever your child has a friend over, use it as an opportunity to learn host etiquette. Remind your child of the "host basics": greet your guest at the door; ask the guest what he'd like to do; offer a snack; help him gather anything he left; walk the friend to the door; thank him for coming and say good-bye.

- *Teach tactful ways to decline an invitation.* One of the basic traits of well-mannered kids is that they are considerate. So saying no to an invitation is often a difficult task because they don't want to hurt the person's feelings or appear impolite. One of the easiest ways to get out of any tricky situation is to teach your child to say, "Gee, I'd like to, but I'll have to check with my parents first" or "I wish I could, but I'll have to call you back after I look up the date." Your child can then plan how he will turn down the invitation tactfully (if he chooses to) by thinking through exactly what to say so he doesn't seem rude.

- *Plan a party.* Start a monthly tradition like that of one of my friends in which you require your kids to help you plan a party just for your family. They can set the table—with the "company dishes"—arrange a centerpiece of hand-picked flowers, and then sit down in their "Sunday best." At party time, this mother helped her kids practice more sophisticated table manners and learn the right eating utensils so that they would feel comfortable eating out. It was well worth the trouble because so many people told this mom how well mannered her kids were.

WHAT TO EXPECT BY STAGES AND AGES

These descriptions of manners appropriate for each stage are from the prestigious Etiquette and Leadership Institute:[4]

Preschooler   Kids this age can grasp the differences between polite and not-so-polite behaviors; they will need gentle reminders for using correct etiquette in social settings. Manners to instill include saying hello, good-bye, please, I'm sorry, and thank you; washing hands; using an "indoor voice"; sitting with good posture; saying "Please, may I be excused?"; being a good host when the playdate guest arrives and leaves.

School Age   School-age children can be taught manners with an emphasis on everyday courtesies kids need for school, home, and activities, including how to answer the phone, give a firm handshake, greet someone, say hello to their teacher, thank the coach or parent for the carpool ride, use proper silverware at dinner, answer the telephone, host friends, show consideration for others, and use most etiquette basics without prompting (though you may still need to give occasional reminders).

Tween   Tweens can consider others' needs as basic to good etiquette, including conversing with those on their left and right at the table; not using a cell phone (at home, school, and public places) if it could disturb others; greet guests, ensure that everyone knows each other, and say good-bye as they leave; and know how to act at a fancier restaurant or social gathering. Kids at this age become more self-absorbed and may test family etiquette standards with crudeness or foul language (especially boys) and being inconsiderate (especially girls).

EIGHTY-FIVE CRUCIAL MANNERS TO TEACH YOUR CHILD

Here is a list of some of the most important manners etiquette experts say we should teach kids. Check off any your child already uses. Those that remain are ones you can slowly help your child learn.

One Parent's Answer

A mom from Salt Lake City shares:

I was mortified when my daughter used poor table manners at a recent family party, so when everyone left I made her set the table and practice the proper use of utensils. She wasn't dismissed until she could show me she knew how to hold and use each knife, fork, spoon, and serving utensil correctly. My etiquette session was so successful, I've haven't had to offer a "repeat lesson."

CHARACTER

Essential Polite Words

- ☐ Please
- ☐ Thank you
- ☐ Excuse me
- ☐ I'm sorry
- ☐ May I?
- ☐ Pardon me
- ☐ You're welcome

Meeting and Greeting Manners

- ☐ Smiles and looks the person in the eye
- ☐ Shakes hands
- ☐ Says hello
- ☐ Introduces self
- ☐ Introduces the other person

Conversation Manners

- ☐ Starts a conversation
- ☐ Listens without interrupting
- ☐ Looks at the eyes of the speaker
- ☐ Uses a pleasant tone of voice
- ☐ Appears interested in the speaker
- ☐ Knows how to end a conversation
- ☐ Knows how to maintain a conversation

Table Manners

- ☐ Comes to the table on time
- ☐ Knows how to correctly set a table
- ☐ Sits up straight
- ☐ Places napkin on her lap
- ☐ Takes his hat off
- ☐ Makes only positive comments about food
- ☐ Waits for the hostess to sit before serving or eating
- ☐ Puts modest portions of food on his plate

- ☐ Eats food only on his own plate
- ☐ Eats soup without slurping
- ☐ Knows proper way to cut meat
- ☐ Asks, "Please pass the . . ."
- ☐ Doesn't grab serving dishes or reach over someone for food
- ☐ Knows how to use utensils correctly
- ☐ Keeps his elbows off the table
- ☐ Chews with her mouth closed
- ☐ Doesn't talk with food in his mouth
- ☐ Places knife and fork sideways on the plate when finished
- ☐ Asks to be excused before leaving table
- ☐ Offers to help the hostess
- ☐ Thanks the hostess before leaving

Hospitality Manners

- ☐ Greets guest at the door
- ☐ Offers guest something to eat
- ☐ Stays with the guest
- ☐ Asks guest what he'd like to do
- ☐ Shares with the guest
- ☐ Walks guest to the door and says good-bye

Anywhere and Anytime

- ☐ Covers her mouth when she coughs
- ☐ Refrains from swearing
- ☐ Refrains from belching
- ☐ Refrains from gossiping
- ☐ Holds a door for a woman or elderly person

Visiting Manners

- ☐ Greets host's parents
- ☐ Picks up after himself
- ☐ If spending the night, keeps room straight and makes her bed
- ☐ Offers to help the parent of the host
- ☐ Thanks the host and her parents

Manners Toward Older People

- ☐ Stands up when an older person comes into the room
- ☐ Helps older guests with their coats
- ☐ Opens the door and holds it open when an older person leaves
- ☐ Offers his seat if no chair is available
- ☐ Is considerate of older people's physical needs (hearing, vision, and so on)
- ☐ Holds the car door and helps person into the car if necessary
- ☐ Is considerate and offers any help
- ☐ Doesn't address the person's shortcomings (wrinkles, hearing loss, cane, and so on)

Sports Manners

- ☐ Plays by the rules
- ☐ Shares the equipment
- ☐ Encourages her teammates
- ☐ Doesn't brag or show off
- ☐ Doesn't cheer mistakes
- ☐ Doesn't boo
- ☐ Doesn't argue with the referee
- ☐ Congratulates opponents
- ☐ Doesn't make excuses or complain
- ☐ Stops when the game is over
- ☐ Cooperates

Telephone Manners

- ☐ First greets the person and says her name
- ☐ Politely asks to speak to the person
- ☐ Answers with a clear and pleasant voice
- ☐ Asks the caller, "Who's calling, please?"
- ☐ Greets the caller by name if she knows him
- ☐ Politely says, "Please hold on" while she gets the intended speaker
- ☐ Takes and gives a message
- ☐ Politely ends a conversation
- ☐ Turns off cell phone or beeper at movies, concerts, or other public places
- ☐ If she must use a cell phone at a public place, she excuses herself quietly so as not to disturb others

More Helpful Advice

More Than Manners! Raising Today's Kids to Have Kind Manners and Good Hearts, by Letitia Baldrige

Move Over! Teenage Manners Coming Through, by Steff Steinhorst

Social Smarts for Today's Kids Ages 9 to 12, by Carol Barkin

The Gift of Good Manners: A Parent's Guide for Raising Respectful, Kind, Considerate Children, by Peggy Post and Cindy Post Senning

Cheats

SEE ALSO: *Homework, Lying, Not Knowing Right from Wrong, Overscheduled, Peer Pressure, Procrastinates, Steals, Test Anxiety*

THE PROBLEM

Red Flags

Copies test answers, sends or receives test answers via text message, plagiarizes a report from the Internet or other source, downloads quiz answers onto her iPod to listen to during a test, gives or sells homework to friends

The Change to Parent For

Your child understands the value of honesty and effort and adopts those virtues in her daily behavior.

Question: "Last night my twelve-year-old son showed me the A on his math test. I was really proud of him, figuring he had studied so hard. Then I noticed that he'd printed the answers on his hand. When I confronted him, he said that everybody else was doing the same thing and that it's no big deal so I shouldn't get so work up about it. Well, I happen to think it is a big deal—he cheated! So now what?"

Answer: My strongest piece of advice to parents on cheating is often the hardest one for them to follow through on: if you catch your kid cheating, don't let him take the good grade, blame his school, or excuse it as "something everyone else does." Instead, call the teacher and make your kid face the consequences. The short-term pain will be worth the long-term benefit to his character. Believe me, that one lesson is far more memorable and powerful than all the lectures and punishments. Let your child know you are serious about being honest, and then back up your words with your actions.

Why Change?

Concerned about your kid cheating? Well, you are not alone. Data clearly confirm that cheating is on the rise. Since 1969, the percentage of high school students who admitted to cheating on a test increased from 34 percent to 68 percent.[5] The 2002 Ethics of American Youth survey discovered that three of four high school students admitted to cheating on at least one test during the previous year, and 37 percent admitted they would lie to perspective employers in order to get a good job.[6] Cheating in school has also reached sophisticated new levels. Gone are the days when students tucked meticulously written crib notes inside their pants legs and coughed specially designed codes to peers. Pagers and cell phone text messages instantly transmit test answers without the hassle of note passing (and getting caught!). Plagiarism from the Internet has become so rampant that many teachers have to rely on a specially designed Web site to scan their students' papers to validate originality.

Make no mistake: cheating goes against the grain of integrity and solid character. After all, cheaters aren't concerned about whether their conduct was fair or how it affected others. Usually their biggest fret is worrying about whether they will get caught. Cheating is all about cutting corners and taking the easy way out. The good news is that parents *do* play a significant role in nurturing the virtues of honesty, integrity, and accountability in their kids. Let's just make sure we use that role wisely so that our kids do turn out right and this epidemic of cheating is stopped.

Signs and Symptoms

Here are possible signs of cheating in kids. Of course, there always could be another explanation, so listen, but keep a watchful eye on your child.

- *Your child has no test recall.* She can't tell you what questions were on the test from that morning.
- *There's a discrepancy between homework and grades.* Your child does little studying but receives exemplary marks; she performs poorly on in-class assignments but does superior work on homework assignments.
- *Your child can't describe the task.* She relies on the computer to do all her papers.
- *Your child nevver seeks help for schoolwork.* She brings home little or no homework, claiming that she finished it already or that teacher doesn't give it. Might be cutting corners and not doing the work. (Of course, she also may be brilliant, or the work is far too easy. Find out the facts.)
- *The teacher reports your child cheating.* Don't be too quick to dismiss an adult's complaint.
- *Your child can't explain content.* She has no understanding of the details in the paper she "wrote."
- *The work is just not her style.* Uses words that are too sophisticated and that she can't define; there's a large disparity between the child's writing style and the paper: this just isn't your child's writing.
- *Your child can't locate resources.* She's unable to find or describe the resources used for the report.
- *Your child is reluctant to show you her work.* She hides her work or doesn't want you to read it.

LATE-BREAKING NEWS

Watch Out for Organized Sports!

Those sports teams we hope are helping our kids become
better people may not be doing the job. A two-year study of 5,275 high school
athletes by the Los Angeles–based Josephson Institute of Ethics found rather
shocking results.[7] Two-thirds of the athletes confessed to cheating on a test at
least once in the previous school year (compared with 60 percent of the rest of
the student population). Boys cheated more, and football players were the worst.
Most also felt that it was okay for their coach to teach them ways to cut corners
and cheat so that the referees couldn't detect their illegal moves and their team
would have a better chance of winning. Another study found that hockey coaches
in particular encouraged aggressive, bully-like behavior in the players and taught
kids to challenge a referee's call if they were losing the game. The lesson here:
don't just drop your kid off at practice without turning up your honesty radar
and tuning in to what the coach is emphasizing. And while you're at it, make sure
your own expectations for your child emphasize honesty, fairness, and teamwork
and not a win-at-any-cost (including cheating) mentality.

THE SOLUTION

Step 1. Early Intervention

- *Identify the reason.* Reflect on why your kid might be cheating (or thinking she
  should be allowed to get away it) so that you can create the best solutions. The
  following is a list of common reasons. Check those that apply to your child or
  situation:

  ☐ Is overscheduled and overwhelmed, leaving not enough study time

  ☐ Fears failing; is perfectionistic, insecure about abilities; hates to lose, appear
  to be a loser, or fail in front of others

  ☐ Is incapable of doing the work, struggling to keep up; has a learning
  disability; academic expectations are set too high

  ☐ Fears getting in trouble or punished for poor grades

  ☐ Doesn't want to disappoint you; cheats to get the grade to make parents
  happy

  ☐ Is taking the easy way out, cutting corners by not studying or putting out
  the effort

☐ Has an "Everyone else does it" attitude; cheating is rampant, putting your kid at an unfair disadvantage if she does *not* cheat; cheating is easy to get away with; no one holds her or other students accountable

☐ Is bullied or caving into pressure from another student to give her homework or answers

☐ Doesn't understand that cheating is wrong; honesty has never been emphasized

☐ Has poor study skills, or doesn't know how to write that paper

What is your best guess as to why your kid cheats? Is there one thing you can do to change this behavior?

- *Don't ignore reality.* Don McCabe, a professor at Rutgers University, studied cheating over two decades. He found that 64 percent of twelve- and thirteen-year-olds admitted they "collaborated" with other students when they were supposed to be working alone; 48 percent confessed they copied homework from someone else, and 87 percent said they had let someone else copy their homework.[8]

- *Don't take a "not my kid" attitude—recognize that cheating is rampant.* Open up the dialogue with your kid and acknowledge the pressure: "I know you're worried about your grades, and cheating must be enticing, but it's still not right." You can let your child know you're aware of her stress, but she needs to get the message that cheating isn't acceptable. This is also an opportunity to assess if your child feels too overwhelmed; perhaps something needs to give to relieve that pressure. Is there one activity your child can give up?

- *Be an example.* Your kids need to know that everyone is tempted to cheat, but honesty and hard work are always the better policy. Refrain from telling your kids how you cheated on your taxes or in your tennis game, or exaggerated a bit on your resume. Your child will interpret those actions as signs that cheating is acceptable. Make sure your example stresses the values you want your kids to copy.

- *Step back!* A study by Public Agenda found that one in five adults say they've done part of a child's homework assignment and think doing so is fair.[9] Halt that urge to do—or redo—your kid's homework. Half of middle school kids think the practice is wrong.[10] Those everyday little behaviors you do send moral messages to your kids.

- *Emphasize effort.* The biggest reason kids cheat is to get a better grade. So switch your emphasis to the effort she puts into her practice, chore, or report instead of offering a reward simply for a good grade. Recognize your child for working hard and maintaining positive study habits. Rewarding effort has long-term benefits: the child understands that success is the result of effort and honesty and that the process of learning is as enjoyable as its result.

One Parent's Answer

A mom from South Dakota shares:

Cheating had become rampant at my son's school. The teacher graded by the curve, the majority of the students copied each other's tests and homework, and it was to the point that my child was at an academic disadvantage to not cheat. That's when I joined with a few other parents to address the cheating problem at the school level. We expected resistance from the administrators, but it turns out they were just as frustrated because many of the parents were doing their children's reports. It took a while, but the school instated a character education program to address the issues of honesty and integrity and established a Code of Honor, and the cheating problem has really declined.

- *Get savvy about the Internet.* A growing number of Web sites such as Schoolsucks.com provide free term papers on any subject; other sites offer them for a fee. One study found that almost half of all kids engage in "cut-and-paste plagiarism," and most parents are clueless.[11] So monitor your child's online experience. Keep the computer in a central place and track the sites your child is visiting. Watch your credit card for any unexplained Web site costs. And if your child does write a report, read it! Check the vocabulary; if her word choice is too sophisticated, it's a possible red flag. Ask her to define the words as well as show you her sources (books, encyclopedias). If she can't provide them or describe the topic without the paper, chances are she cheated.

- *Discuss the cons of cheating.* Thirty-four percent of parents don't talk to their kids about cheating because they believe their child would never cheat.[12] Don't make that mistake! Talk to your kid about the negative results of cheating. Here are a few important points to cover:

  Cheating can get you in serious trouble: probation, suspension, expulsion, or even criminal penalties, such as fines, tickets, and incarceration.

  People won't trust you, and you get a bad reputation. No one will want to be your friend or do business with you.

  It can become a habit, and you can reach the point where you feel you can't do anything without cheating both among your friends and in school.

  It hurts other people and isn't fair to other students or people who play fair and stick to the rules.

  If you get away with cheating, you can find yourself in a situation you are completely unqualified and unable to handle. Not only will you be in over your head, but you'll also know in your heart that you're a fraud.

  If you don't learn the work now, you'll have even more trouble at the next grade level.

Please don't make the mistake of thinking that a one-time talk on such a serious subject will convince your kid that honesty really is the best policy. State your views over and over and look for teachable day-to-day moments to review why cheating is wrong.

Step 2. Rapid Response

Do know that most kids will cheat at something, but whether they continue to do so often depends on how we respond. These responses help your child learn from this experience:

- *Stay calm and do not overreact.* Yes, it is hard, but it's the best way to respond. Chances are this is a minor, first offense and not some deep-seated psychological problem. Do let your child know you are disappointed and tell what you saw or heard. *"I just saw you move the ball. That's cheating." "I reread your report, and you copied most of it straight off the Internet."* Be brief: merely state your observation and stick to facts.

- *Be private.* It's best to cite your observations quietly in a one-to-one conversation rather than when your kid is with others. Public accusations of cheating usually only aggravate the situation, and your kid will most likely deny the accusation.

- *Do not label your kid "a cheater."* This is both unhelpful and counterproductive. Focus on the child's action, not her character. "Moving the ball is cheating." "Copying your friend's answers is cheating."

- *Tell where you stand.* Make it clear that cheating isn't how you want her to get the good grade or win the game, and that you expect honesty. *"I expect you to do your own work and not copy your friend's answers." "I expect you to play by the rules."*

- *Hear your kid out.* Try to determine the reason she copied her friend's work or plagiarized the report so that you can develop a solution if necessary. Does she feel overwhelmed with no time to study? Then create a solution by cutting one activity to make time. Does she say the class is way too hard? Set up a conference with the teacher.

- *Assess her moral reasoning.* Does she feel at all guilty? Does she apologize or say she will try not to let it happen again? Does she blame the teacher or peer and not take ownership? Does she say this isn't a big deal and that everyone else does it? If so, those are signals telling you to monitor not only your child's behavior but also her moral development. (See *Not Knowing Right from Wrong,* p. 191.) Your kid may need more intense honesty lessons. Although they will take time, don't deviate from that aim.

- *Set a consequence for repeat cheating.* If despite all your efforts your kid's cheating continues, or if this is a repeat offense, it's time to set a consequence and make your child accountable. For younger kids caught cheating in a game, simply stop playing. *"That was cheating again. It's not fun to play when you don't play fair. I'm going to stop playing now, and we'll try again later."* Older kids who cheat on tests or plagiarize reports should be required to redo the assignment. A *Redbook* magazine poll found that 65 percent of parents said they would alert the teacher if their kid cheated; 35 percent said they would keep quiet to protect their child.[13] If you catch your child, call the teacher and make your kid face the consequences.

- *Meet with the teacher.* Find out what is really going on. Is your child prepared? Is she struggling and in need of a tutor? Is this a past problem? Or is she just taking the easy way out? Let your child know in no uncertain terms that you and the teacher will continue to monitor her schoolwork and that she will be held accountable for cheating. If she is accused, don't be so quick to blame the teacher. Instead, step back, be open minded, and gather the facts. As tough as this may be to hear, your child may be cheating.

Pay Attention to This!
When to Worry

As much as we'd like our kids always to follow the straight-and-narrow path of honesty, the fact is that cheating is a common (but inappropriate) child behavior. Almost any kid may bend the rules, so your role is to help your child recognize that honesty really is the best policy and to make sure that cheating does not become a habit. But there are times you should seek help for your child from a mental health counselor, a child guidance clinic, or a psychologist to help you decipher what's really triggering this behavior:

- *Cheating habitual.* Despite your efforts, your child's cheating is a chronic problem.

- *Reputation at stake.* Peers, teachers, coaches, or parents see your kid as dishonest and label her a "cheater."

- *Other behavioral problems.* Your child exhibits other troubling behaviors, such as stealing or lying, setting fires, acting out, bullying or being mean to animals or peers, acting defiant or aggressive.

- *No guilt or remorse.* Evidence shows that your child is cheating, but she lies to cover it, sees nothing wrong with her actions, and displays no shame or guilt.

- *Seek help if the problem continues.* If cheating still continues, spend some serious uninterrupted time with your kid coming to an agreement on how further cheating will be prevented. Chronic cheating can be a symptom of an emotional struggle, peer problems, a learning difficulty, or even a more serious antisocial behavior issue that should be addressed. Seek the advice of a trained mental health professional if cheating continues or intensifies. (See the Pay Attention to This! box.)

Step 3. Develop Habits for Change

- *Teach the lacking skill so that your kid doesn't cheat.* Is your child plagiarizing because she *doesn't know how* to write a report? Does she cheat because *she doesn't know how* to lose? Does she copy the other kid's homework because she *doesn't have the study skills* to do it on her own? Ask the teacher for suggestions on how to teach the missing skill, and if you don't know how to do it, consider hiring a tutor.

- *Acknowledge honesty.* Certainly we should tell our kids that it is important to be fair and honest. We also should let them know how much we appreciate their being truthful whenever they are. So do acknowledge your kid's honest efforts: *"I really appreciate your honesty. I can count on you to say the truth."* Do be sure to recognize her especially anytime she refuses to give in to peer pressure: *"I know it was hard to say no to your friend. I admire how you stood up to him and told him he couldn't copy your paper."*

- *Teach ways to buck the temptation to cheat.* Tweens especially feel the urge to give their homework or test answers to a peer, usually because of the need to fit in. Bullying is also rampant these days, so check to make sure your child is not being threatened to supply answers. Standing up to a peer is hard at any age, but particularly during the years of ten to fourteen (when cheating also begins to peak). Discuss strategies to help your kid stand up to peer pressure or teach a few of the ones that follow. Just make sure you help her rehearse them over and over until she can confidently use them on her own. (See also *Peer Pressure*, p. 373.)

  - *Say no firmly, then don't give in.* Say no to the peer using a friendly but firm and determined voice.

  - *Repeat your decision.* Repeat your decision several times: "No, it's not right," "No, it's not right." It makes you sound assertive and helps you not back down.

  - *Tell reasons why.* Give the person the reason you're saying no so as to help strengthen your conviction not to proceed with what you've been asked to do: "I worked too hard to give you my paper." "It's against the honor code." "I could get a lower grade."

WHAT TO EXPECT BY STAGES AND AGES

Preschooler   Very young children do not understand the meaning of cheating and why they should stick to the rules, so they are prone to "bend" them in their favor. If you catch your child cheating, let her know you are aware of her tactics, and use gentle teaching (not punishment). Don't label the child a cheater, but instead emphasize why it is important not to cheat.

School Age   These are the years when cheating may start; kids begin to break rules to win competitive games, and there are also more opportunities to cheat. Boys cheat more than girls.[14] These kids are now beginning to understand right from wrong and fair and unfair, but not until the later school years will they really understand why it's wrong to cheat, though they may feel it is acceptable depending on the task. Although cheating is not unusual, act quickly so that it does not become a habit. Older school-age kids begin to feel pressure to "keep up" with extra activities (sports, lessons, chores, friends) and homework, so they may use cheating as a shortcut. If cheating becomes frequent, it is usually because of stress or another emotional issue that should be dealt with.

Tween   The ages of ten to fourteen are peak cheating years largely due to the emphasis on grades and test scores and mounting academic pressures.[15] Two-thirds of middle school students report cheating on tests, and 90 percent copy homework.[16] Cheating is often considered "cool" ("Everyone does it!"). Tweens may be intimidated into cheating because of their need to "fit in." Internet-related cheating and plagiarism become the quick way to do a report; kids also text test answers via cell phone or download answers to MP3 players. Over half the middle school students in one study confessed to having cheated on an exam in the past year.[17]

More Helpful Advice

Bringing Up Moral Children in an Immoral World, by A. Lynn Scoresby

Building Moral Intelligence: The Seven Essential Virtues That Teach Kids to Do the Right Thing, by Michele Borba

Character Matters: How to Help Our Children Develop Good Judgment, Integrity and Other Essential Virtues, by Thomas Lickona

Teaching Your Children Values, by Linda and Richard Eyre

The Cheating Culture: Why More Americans Are Doing Wrong to Get Ahead, by David Callahan

The Moral Child: Nurturing Children's Natural Moral Growth, by William Damon

Why Johnny Can't Tell Right from Wrong, by William Kilpatrick

Insensitive

SEE ALSO: *Autism Spectrum Disorder, Back Talk, Bad Manners, Bossy, Bullying, Materialistic, Selfish and Spoiled, Sharing, Ungrateful*

THE PROBLEM

Red Flags

Lacks sympathy to another's plight, doesn't show sensitivity or compassion

The Change to Parent For

Your child is more sensitive to others' feelings, shows concern for their distress, and reaches out to help others in need.

Question: "My son used to be so caring, but suddenly he's showing an insensitive side that really concerns me. He's started hanging with two boys and I'm wondering if this is where he's picking up this new behavior. Could these kids be influencing my son's character?"

Answer: Kids learn by copying, so any time your child begins displaying an out-of-character behavior like insensitivity, you should dig deeper to find the source. Monitor these boys closer. Invite them to your home so you can listen to their language and watch their behavior. And if you deem their behavior as inappropriate, observe your son to determine if he is mimicking or looking up to them. If you have evidence that your kid's friends may be contributing to your child's budding insensitivity, then guide him to a new social scene. If those peers are outwardly cruel and insensitive, refuse to allow your child to associate with them. Yes, this may be tough (and in extreme cases, you may need to move your child to a different classroom, school, or even neighborhood), but your child's character and reputation are at stake. The bottom line is that insensitivity is contagious, especially in that "peer scene" where kids want so to fit in, and being cruel is considered sometimes "cool" these days. When kids are allowed to get away with those insensitive acts, the behavior can become habit forming, and soon they develop the attitude that cruelty is acceptable. It's up to parents to keep their radar up so they can nip such behavior in the bud way before it gets to that level. But remember: there may be other sources of your child's insensitivity, so keep reading.

Why Change?

Sensitivity is the glorious ability to recognize another person's concerns. It's a powerful ability that halts violent and cruel behavior and urges us to treat others kindly. But whether our kids will develop this marvelous capacity to be concerned about others is far from guaranteed. Although children are born with the capacity to be sensitive, this feeling must be nurtured, or it will remain dormant. And therein lies the crisis: over the past years, many environmental factors that research has found to be critical to the enhancement of sensitivity and empathy are disappearing and are being replaced by far more negative ones.

Peer cruelty and bullying are escalating; the media—including music lyrics, video games, television, movies, and even real-world news—contain far crueler images; pop idols, sports stars, and political officials too often model shameful insensitivity; and let's face it, adult behavior doesn't always emulate the standards of civility.

But even so, none of those factors should excuse us from parenting for this change. Research shows that sensitivity is a trait that can be taught and nurtured. This entry offers a few proven solutions to sensitize your child's feeling for others and turn any insensitive behaviors around and pronto.

Signs and Symptoms

- Finds it difficult to see a situation from the other person's point of view
- Appears unconcerned if someone is upset or in pain; exhibits low level of empathy
- Laughs or seems to enjoy seeing that someone is in pain or upset
- Doesn't see the difference between friendly bantering and unfriendly teasing or recognize when teasing is going "over the line" and being hurtful
- Is unable to identify or misinterprets another's feelings
- Isn't moved or doesn't become teary-eyed when watching or listening to emotional movies or stories
- Makes crude, unkind, intolerant, or disrespectful comments or jokes to others
- Is unconcerned when someone else is treated unfairly, unkindly, or disrespectfully

THE SOLUTION

Step 1. Early Intervention

- *Identify the reason.* The following is a list of the most likely reasons kids are insensitive. What is your best guess as to why your child is displaying this behavior? Once you uncover the reason, you can develop a plan for change. Check those that apply to your child or situation:

☐ Has been chastised or made fun of for showing his feelings; emotions not acknowledged at home

☐ Lacks self-esteem; can't reach out to others when he feels he is an unworthy person

☐ Is copying cruel behaviors; part of a peer scene where "it's cool to be cruel" is the mantra

---

LATE-BREAKING NEWS

Nine Factors That Increase the Likelihood of Kids' Being Sensitive

Suzanne Denham, author of *Emotional Development in Young Children*, identified these nine factors that generally increase the chances that a child will be more sensitive to another's feelings:[18]

- *Age.* The ability to take the perspective of others increases with age, so older children are generally more empathic than younger kids.

- *Gender.* Children are more likely to empathize with a same-sex peer because they feel a greater sense of commonality.

- *Intelligence.* Smarter kids are more likely to comfort others because they are better able to discern other people's needs and devise ways to assist them.

- *Emotional understanding.* Children who freely express their emotions are usually more empathic because they are more capable of correctly identifying other people's feelings.

- *Empathic parents.* Kids whose parents are empathic are likely to become empathic themselves because the parents model those behaviors, which in turn are copied by their children.

- *Emotional security.* More well adjusted and assertive kids are more likely to assist others.

- *Temperament.* Kids who are by nature happier and more social are more likely to empathize with a distressed child.

- *Similarity.* Kids are more likely to have empathy for those who they feel are similar to them in some way or with whom they have shared a similar experience.

- *Attachment.* Kids are more likely to empathize with their friends than with those to whom they feel less closely attached.

☐ Has been allowed to be cruel: hasn't been reprimanded for displaying insensitivity or unkindness

☐ Is disciplined too punitively; is not treated warmly or respectfully at home

☐ Has difficulty identifying other people's feelings; lacks emotional vocabulary

☐ Is angry, depressed, or stressed; is dealing with his own trauma, such as divorce, death, or illness, so has trouble feeling for others

☐ Has been repeatedly bullied or harassed; has experienced trauma or cruelty; in seeking revenge, acts "insensitive" to cover up hurt

☐ Is continually exposed to cruelty in the media (television, movies, video games)

☐ Has a neurological or psychological condition such as Asperger's syndrome or Attachment Disorder that makes it difficult to read emotional cues

- *Be sensitive.* Your child learns a great deal about sensitivity simply by observing behavior. If you want your child to be sensitive, then consciously demonstrate kind, sensitive behavior whenever you are together. There are so many daily opportunities: phoning your friend who is down, soothing a child, cradling a baby bird, asking someone how she is feeling. After performing the action, be sure to tell your child how good it made you feel! By seeing sensitive actions in your daily words and deeds and hearing you emphasize how being sensitive makes you feel good, your child will be much more likely to follow your example.

- *Establish clear behavior expectations.* Research shows that parents who express their views about hurtful, insensitive behaviors and then explain why they feel that way tend to have kids who are more sensitive and who adopt those views. Begin by clearly laying down your new policy: "*In this house you are always to be sensitive to others.*" "*Jamie is going through a tough time right now, so be sensitive to how she's feeling and don't let Kevin pick on her.*" "*Jason is coming over. I expect you to be kind, or I will have to tell him that he can't play until you are.*" Then stand firm and be consistent.

- *Develop a warm, accepting relationship with your child.* In order for a child to reach out and be concerned about others, he must feel accepted. If your child has experienced any trauma, is suffering from depression, or has a stressful or tenuous attachment with a parent, he first needs to rebuild a connection with a caring adult. A warm, accepting relationship with you is what your child may need most right now. Devote your energy to that cause and seek the help of a counselor if needed.

LATE-BREAKING NEWS

Emory University, Atlanta: Renowned child psychologists Stephen Nowicki and Marshall Duke conducted tests with more than one thousand children and found that one out of ten, despite normal and even superior intelligence, has significant problems with nonverbal communication.[19] The psychologists found that this disability prevents kids from recognizing particular emotional signals that are so crucial in being sensitive to the feelings of others. If this might be the reason for your child's lack of sensitivity, then enhancing his skills in reading nonverbal messages may prove helpful. For more information, read *Teaching Your Child the Language of Social Success,* by Stephen Nowicki, Marshall P. Duke, and Elisabeth A. Martin.

Step 2. Rapid Response

- *Call out insensitive actions ASAP.* Each and every time your child is insensitive, call him on it. Tell him exactly what he did that was insensitive, and describe the impact of his behavior. *"That was insensitive: you didn't stop to think about your friend's feelings when you just left him there. Did you see how upset he was?"* Make sure your child understands what is wrong about his actions, why you disapprove, and why you consider insensitivity unacceptable. Then turn the moment into a learning experience to help your child recognize the hurt or pain registered by the other person: *"Look how sad you made Kara feel when you teased her about her new glasses. That was insensitive."*

- *Hold him accountable.* If your child continues to display insensitivity towards others' feelings, then it's time to set a meaningful consequence that's appropriate to your child's age and temperament. Your child must recognize that his actions caused pain and that he will be held accountable for his insensitivity. Ask: *"Was what you did helpful or hurtful?"* *"You're right. It was hurtful. And your friend's feelings are hurt. So what will you do to make up for what you did?"* Of course, making amends should be tailored to your child's age, temperament, and the "degree of intentionality." (Did your child *intend* to cause the other person pain? If so, to what degree?)

- *Demand an apology.* Insist that your child make amends for his insensitivity. Your child could apologize by calling, writing or drawing a note to say he's sorry, offering to try to make up for the unkind act, or even thinking of something to do himself, without asking. Don't assume your child knows *how* to sincerely and honestly apologize for an insensitive action. You may need to teach your child these three step to a sincere apology:

1. *Say exactly what you're sorry for.* "I [say what you are sorry for or what you did], and I'm sorry."

2. *Say how you feel about what you did.* "I feel really sad that I told Jenna what you told me not to tell." "I know it made you mad."

3. *Tell how you plan to right the hurt.* "I promise to keep what you tell me a secret."

Even if your child has apologized for an uncaring act, he needs to know that it may take time for the hurt to heal and for the hurt person to *accept* his apology and forgive him.

- *Curb consumption of violent media.* Be aware of those video games, TV shows, movies, and CD lyrics your child is listening to and watching. Research shows that children who have been repeatedly exposed to more violent television programming are less likely to demonstrate kindness by helping younger kids who are in trouble.[20] If you feel that media could be contributing to your child's insensitivity, set tighter standards as to what he may not play or watch.

- *Enlist the help of others.* Have a conference with your child's teacher or coach and state your concerns. Your child needs to know that you neither support nor tolerate this behavior and that other caregivers in his life are on board with you. The way to stop insensitivity is for everyone to be on the same page.

- *Seek the help of a mental health professional.* If your child's insensitivity increases or if he is intentionally treating children, adults, or animals in a cruel way, please seek the help of a mental health professional immediately.

Step 3. Develop Habits for Change

- *Expose your child to emotionally charged movies.* Robert Coles, Harvard psychiatry professor and author of *The Moral Intelligence of Children*, believes that one of the best ways to sensitize a child to the feelings of others is through emotionally gripping movies (and books).[21] The trick is to find the right selection for your child. A few favorite kid tearjerkers are *ET, Charlotte's Web, Stone Fox, Bambi, The Secret Garden, Old Yeller,* and *The Velveteen Rabbit.* Fill a bowl with popcorn and dig out the Kleenex. Remember to discuss the plight of the character and to describe what pulled your heartstrings.

- *Show the effect of sensitivity.* Sensitive, kind acts—even small ones—can make a big difference in people's lives, so point them out to help your child see the impact his actions made. *"Derrick, your grandmother was so pleased when you called to thank her for the present." "Suraya, did you see the smile on Ryan's face when you shared your toys?"*

- *Draw attention to nonverbal feeling cues.* Pointing out the facial expressions, posture, and mannerisms of people in different emotional states sensitizes your child to other people's feelings. As occasions arise, explain your concern and share what clues helped you make your feeling assessment: *"Did you notice Grandma's face when you were talking with her today? I thought she looked puzzled. Maybe she is having trouble hearing. Why not talk a little louder when you speak with her." "Did you see the expression on Meghan's face when you were playing today? She looked worried about something . . . Maybe you should ask her if everything is okay."*

- *Use the formula "feels + needs."* Michael Schulman and Eva Mekler, authors of *Bringing Up a Moral Child*, reviewed studies and found that an effective way to increase sensitivity is to ask children questions to help them discover people's needs and feelings.[22] Such questions were found to expand children's awareness of what people might be experiencing. As a result, the children became more sensitive to how they might be able to help. To use this approach with your child, look for occasions to draw attention to people's feelings and then ask him to guess what the person might need in order to remedy the feeling. Here is how a parent might use the method:

  Parent: Look at that little girl crying in the sandbox. How do you suppose she feels?

  Child: I think she is sad.

  Parent: What do you think she needs to make her feel better?

  Child: Maybe she could use someone to hug her because she hurt her knee.

- *Offer occasions to experience kindness.* Kids don't learn sensitivity by talking or reading about it, but by actually experiencing it. So look for opportunities for your child to do kind deeds for others that help sensitize him to a range of emotions. There are dozens of ways to get involved, lend a hand, volunteer, or show you care. Food drives, picking up trash in the park, painting shelters for battered women, serving meals at homeless shelters, delivering meals to sick and elderly folks who are housebound, and tutoring are just a few ways to help your child develop sensitivity and feel the joy of caring.

- *Praise sensitive, kind actions.* One of the simplest and most effective ways of enhancing any behavior is by reinforcing the action as soon as it happens. So whenever you notice your child acting in a sensitive and caring manner, let him know how pleased it makes you feel: *"Kyle, I love how gentle you are with your baby sister. You pat her so softly, and it makes me so happy knowing how caring you are."*

CHARACTER

WHAT TO EXPECT BY STAGES AND AGES

Martin Hoffman, a renowned authority on empathy, believes children slowly develop sensitivity to others' feelings in a series of stages.[23] The following stages are adapted from Dr. Hoffman's acclaimed work.

Preschooler   Preschoolers are egocentric and more concerned about their own feelings and needs. They begin slowly to develop role-taking capabilities. Young children recognize that someone's feelings may be different from theirs, start to decipher the source of another person's distress, and find simple ways to offer comfort or show support. *"You look sad. Your crayon broke. You can use this one."*

School Age   Kids gradually begin being able to see things from another person's perspective, so there is a noticeable increase in the child's efforts to support and comfort those in need. School-age children are able to identify and verbalize a wider range of emotions. The ability to use language to comfort others also substantially increases. *"That older woman looks frustrated. Maybe she needs help getting across the street."*

Tween   Children in this age group can now be sensitive to the plight of not only those they personally know or can directly observe but also groups of people they may have never met. *"The people in India look so hungry. If I sent some of my allowance each week, it might make them feel better."* Peer cruelty and bullying peak, and tweens are often immersed in a culture where it's "cool" to be insensitive and cruel.

One Parent's Answer

A mom from Seattle shares:

My mother pointed out that my son was "a bit insensitive." I was mortified and then recognized she was right. Though Jeff is a caring kid, he rarely displayed a sensitive side at home—but did with his friends and certainly with his grandmother. It finally dawned on me that the reason was because I kept my feelings to myself. How should I expect my son to be sensitive to my feelings? I started using situations to describe my feeling: "I'm so excited! My new computer is being delivered to me today." "I'm so tired. The barking dogs kept me up all night." It felt strange at first, but I knew my plan was working when my mother told me she'd seen a change in Jeff. He was more sensitive, and our relationship even improved.

More Helpful Advice

Building Moral Intelligence: The Seven Essential Skills That Teach Kids to Do the Right Thing, by Michele Borba

Raising Compassionate, Courageous Children in a Violent World, by Janice Cohn

Teaching Your Children Sensitivity, by Linda and Richard Eyre

Teaching Children to Care: How to Discover and Develop the Spirit of Charity in Your Children, by Deborah Spaide

The Caring Child, by Nancy Eisenberg

The Moral Intelligence of Children, by Robert Coles

Intolerant

SEE ALSO: *Bullying, Cliques, Cyberbullying, Insensitive, Internet Safety, Teased*

THE PROBLEM

Red Flags

Makes jokes or comments putting down others; focuses on "differences" like race, religion, age, gender, disabilities, culture; is closed to meeting others with backgrounds and beliefs unlike her own; judges unfairly, categorizes, or stereotypes others

The Change to Parent For

Your child learns to respect people, even those whose beliefs or behaviors she may disagree with, and begins focusing more on their positive traits instead of their differences.

Why Change?

Children aren't born to hate; intolerance is learned. Most experts agree that it is only when adults begin expressing differences, alleged weaknesses, and consequent prejudice that young children begin to adopt such bias. Many adults aren't curbing those remarks well enough, because today's kids are displaying intolerant actions at alarming rates and at far younger ages. In fact, researchers say that most hate crimes are committed by youth younger than nineteen.[24]

Hatred and intolerance can be learned, but so too can sensitivity, understanding, empathy, and tolerance. Although it's certainly never too late to begin, the sooner we start, the better the chance we have of preventing intolerant attitudes from taking hold of our children's minds and hearts.

The simplest way to start this change is for you to watch your own daily example to ensure that you walk your talk. Ask yourself each day one critical question: *"If my child had only my behavior to watch, how would I behave?"* There has never been a time when it was more important for parents to model tolerance than now. It may be the best chance our kids have for living peacefully and harmoniously in this highly conflicted, multi-ethnic twenty-first century.

LATE-BREAKING NEWS

Harvard social psychologist Gordon Allport explored the roots of intolerance and published his results in his renowned classic, *The Nature of Prejudice*. Allport reports that kids who grow up to become tolerant are generally raised in families where there are three conditions: strong parental love and warmth, consistent discipline, and clear models of moral behavior.[25] It's when those needs are not met that prejudice develops. Be honest: How you are doing in parenting for those three conditions?

THE SOLUTION

Five Strategies for Change

1. *Commit to raising a tolerant child.* If you really want your child to be tolerant of differences, then you must actively commit to raising her to be so. Once your child knows your expectations, she will be more likely to embrace your principles. Do examine your own prejudices and make a conscious attempt to temper them so that you don't pass them on to your child.

2. *Embrace diversity.* Knowledge boosts tolerance, so expose your child to positive images—including music, literature, videos, public role models, and examples from the media—that represent a variety of ethnic groups. Encourage your child, no matter how young, to have contact with individuals in your community of different races, religions, cultures, genders, abilities, and beliefs. Research finds that a big predictor of reduction in children's prejudice is cross-race friendships,[26] so involve your child in programs—whether they are in school, after school, or at a summer camp—that foster diversity. Make sure you display openness to people who represent a range of positive differences. The more your child sees how you embrace diversity, the more prone she'll be to follow your standards.

3. *Emphasize similarities.* Answering your child's questions honestly about differences is the first big step toward teaching tolerance. At about the age of four, kids begin asking questions because they notice that some people look different from them: "Why is his skin dark?" "Why is her hair lighter?" Just explain that people come in different sizes, shapes, and colors, and then encourage your child to see the beauty in everyone and to look for what she has in common with others instead of how she is different. Any time you hear your daughter point out how she is different from someone, you might say, *"Yes, isn't that a beautiful color for skin? It's kind of what you're trying for when you lie outside in the sun with your friends, except that*

she doesn't have to worry about getting skin cancer. There are lots of ways you are different from other people. Now let's try to think of ways you are the same." Help her see not only how similarities outweigh differences but also that we are all the same on the inside.

4. *Talk openly and honestly about prejudice.* Your kids will face intolerance. They will hear discriminatory comments, racial slurs, and hurtful jokes as early as first grade. So don't assume your kids will be immune. Talk openly and explicitly about what racism means and why it's hurtful and unfair to stereotype people. Make your talks about this issue as normal and relaxed as discussions about who will win the World Series or *American Idol.* New research from the University of Texas at Austin found that "racial fairness mattered more to both white and black school-age kids who learned about racial discrimination in school than to peers who weren't offered the same lessons, with the white kids becoming less likely to accept racial stereotyping."[27] So have those discussions about historical individuals like Harriet Tubman, Jackie Robinson, Barack Obama, and Martin Luther King Jr., who opened doors for African Americans and faced discrimination trying to break through the racial barrier.

5. *Counter prejudicial comments.* Kids are bound to make biased remarks, but whether they adopt the belief can depend on how you respond. The key is not to let such comments slide but to use them to change your child's views. Here are ways to respond to biased remarks:[28]

   - *Dig deeper.* Stay cool and listen without interrupting. Your goal is to find out why your kid feels that way and where this is coming from.

   - *Challenge biased views.* When you have the facts, point out why they are incorrect by providing countering examples, more information, or a different interpretation. Just do so in a way that is simple, nonjudgmental, and appropriate to your child's level of understanding. For example:

     Child: Homeless people are lazy and should get jobs.

     Parent: There are many reasons homeless people don't work. Some of them are ill and can't work. Some of them can't find jobs.

   - *Check for stereotypes.* A key part of ending prejudice is to listen for such statements as "You always . . ." "They never . . ." or "They're all . . ." because chances are that what follows will be a stereotype. Tell your kids that whenever a family member makes such a categorical statement, another member should gently remind him to "Check that."

     Child: Asian kids always get good grades in school.

     Parent: Check that! Do you think that's true for every Asian child? What about your friend Susan?

     The child should then rephrase his biased comment.

- *Don't allow bigoted remarks.* Kids are bound to slip with a biased joke or comment, but when they do, be sure to verbalize your displeasure: *"That's disrespectful, and I don't want to hear it."* Your child needs to hear your discomfort so that she knows you really walk your talk. It also models a response to copy if hurtful remarks are made in her presence.

One Parent's Answer

A dad from Omaha shares:

We've tried to raise our kids to be tolerant, so we were shocked when our youngest began spurting biased remarks about blacks and Latinos and how they were always in jail and doing bad things. Then one day we happened to catch them watching some cop reality show and there it was: policemen handcuffing blacks and Latinos. Once we tuned in to how other cultures were portrayed on sitcoms and even the evening news, we were aghast. It was a big wake-up call for us to start monitoring our kids' media consumption.

WHAT TO EXPECT BY STAGES AND AGES

Research by Marguerite A. Wright, a clinical psychologist and author of *I'm Chocolate, You're Vanilla,* shows that kids develop race awareness slowly in a series of predictable stages:[29]

Preschooler   At the age of three or four, children can identify skin color but don't see people as members of a particular racial group *unless adults draw their attention to them.* They see people without prejudice, though they will begin to form negative associations as they are taught to do. Be careful of your comments!

School Age   Between five and seven, children begin to pick up on social meanings attached to skin color and start to be aware of other physical differences, such as eye and body shape and hair color. They may begin to adopt skin color prejudices as well as the prejudices of family members and friends and those depicted in the media, although they do not fully understand them.

Tween   At this age, children can now accurately identify their race using such terms as *Native American, Chinese, Hispanic,* and *African American.* Unless they are taught not to prejudge people based on their race, children may adopt full-fledged racial stereotypes.

Pay Attention to This!
What to Do If Your Child Is a Victim of Prejudice

As much as we'd like to, we can't shield our kids from bigotry: it's too much a part of our society. Instead be prepared for what to do if your child is the victim of intolerance. Here are solutions:

- *Be calm and reassuring.* Be empathic: this hurts, and your child needs your support. Then calmly gather facts to discover who did this, what was said, and how often this happens.

- *Teach her how to stand up for herself.* Stress that your child has the right to be angry, but encourage her to stay cool and not insult back. It only intensifies things. She can let the person know she is offended by saying, *"Cut it out. I don't like you calling me that."*

- *Take action.* If the offensive incidents continue and are occurring at school, consider talking to the teacher or principal to find out their perspective and what can be done to stop the attacks.

- *Boost her identity.* Encourage your child to be proud of who she is. Provide role models who resemble her. Give her an appreciation of her heritage. Let her know it's okay to be different.

Lying

SEE ALSO: *Back Talk, Not Knowing Right from Wrong, Steals*

THE PROBLEM

Red Flags

Lies, exaggerates, or stretches the truth; can no longer be trusted; deceives out of habit

The Change to Parent For

Your child understands why honesty is the best policy, develops a healthy conscience, admits his deceptions, and knows he can come to you and others with the truth.

Question: "What do you do when your kid tells you he did his chores and homework when he didn't? I don't want to call him a liar, but I also don't want his truth-stretching to become a habit."

Answer: Kids lie for a number of reasons, but lying can become an easy way to solve problems if they are allowed to get away it. So whenever your child lies, sit him down ASAP and use it as an opportunity to teach honesty: *"I expect you to tell me only the truth, and I will do the same, so that we can always believe each other."* The trick is to find the right balance in your response so that your child knows lying is wrong but will still come to you with the truth.

Why Change?

Let's be honest. Nearly all kids—from tots to teens—stretch the truth, and for all sorts of reasons: to avoid punishment, make themselves look or feel better, get out of a task, keep their friend out of trouble. And they start lying as young as two or three. Occasional lying is an almost expected part of child development, but whether dishonesty becomes a habit depends largely on how we respond to that lie. And statistics show we may not be doing such a good job.

A *U.S. News & World Report* poll found that one out of four college students said he would lie on a job application; 84 percent believe they need to use deception to get ahead in the world today.[30] Another national survey found that 80 percent of high-achieving high school students admitted to cheating, and half believe deception is not wrong.[31]

LATE-BREAKING NEWS

Penn State University: Research by Nancy Darling, a developmental psychologist, found that 98 percent of teens admit that they lie to their parents.[32] But some do lie less and are willing to disclose more. The difference has to do with how they were parented. Darling analyzed these three parenting styles. Which style do you think minimizes lying most? Which is closest to your style?

1. *Permissive.* You dish out a lot of affection, don't set many rules or standards, and accept most of what your kids do. You wouldn't consider yourself a harsh disciplinarian. Your view is that by your being permissive with your kids, they will be more open with you and therefore more honest.

2. *Authoritarian.* You set a lot of rules and expect absolute honesty. Punishment is harsh if your child breaks your rules. Your view is that your kid must obey and needs a strong code of conduct to do so. You would rarely consider compromising or negotiating.

3. *Authoritative.* You set a few core rules, explain the reasoning behind them, expect your kids to obey them, and consistently enforce them. You encourage your child's input. Your view is that your child needs to have some independence but still must adhere to basic rules and will do so.

Answer: Kids raised by authoritative parents were far less likely to lie, were more open with their parents, and were less likely to hide details about their lives. The kids knew they could speak honestly and argue (respectfully), knowing their parent would at least listen.

Rather disturbing trends about the state of our children's honesty quotient, wouldn't you say? But it's even more puzzling when you consider that for over two decades, parents have rated honesty as the trait they most wanted in their kids.[33] But here's the real irony: the most accepted explanation of how kids develop the habit is that they learn from copying us. There's one bit of good news: it seems that parents still play the most significant role in whether their kids turn out honest—that is, as long as you stick to a few premises. This entry offers strategies to help you parent for the change you want.

Signs and Symptoms

Every kid fibs every now and then, but here are signs and symptoms that lying is becoming serious and that it's time to start parenting for change:

- *Untrustworthiness.* You can no longer trust your child to tell the truth.

- *Bad reputation.* Other adults or peers tell you he is lying and can't be counted on.

- *Habit of cheating.* Your child routinely plagiarizes or copies other children's work.

- *Frequent dishonesty.* Lying is not a one-time affair; it's becoming a routine habit.

- *No reason.* Your child lies for no reason; there is no gain and no motivation to lie.

Pay Attention to This!

An occasional fib is nothing to worry about, but if your child develops a habit of lying, it could be a sign of some deeper problem or, in rarer situations, Conduct Disorder.[34] Seek the help of a mental help professional for these reoccurring symptoms: stealing, lying, fighting, destroying property, truancy, deliberate infraction of rules, bullying and cruelty, or showing no sadness or remorse when confronted with the mistruth. See also *Bullying,* p. 332, and *Steals,* p. 218.

- *No guilt.* Your child sees nothing wrong with lying. ("Everybody else does.")

Hint: any sudden wave of lying or dramatic increase in lying is a warning sign.

THE SOLUTION

Step 1. Early Intervention

- *Pay attention.* If you're serious about stopping your child's "truth-stretching," your first task is to figure out why your child is using the behavior. Review the checklist here and check those that apply to your child or situation. Your kid may lie to

  ☐ Please you, gain your approval, not let you down, ease you from worry
  ☐ Fulfill a wish he hopes will come true (a younger child's "magical thinking")
  ☐ Vent frustration
  ☐ Get attention
  ☐ Solve a problem or find an easy way out of a dilemma
  ☐ Avoid punishment and stay out of trouble
  ☐ Brag as a way to assert status, impress others, appear good
  ☐ Overcome self-consciousness or low self-esteem
  ☐ Increase power and a sense of control
  ☐ Avoid an argument
  ☐ Get something he wants

☐ Find out what he can get away with

☐ Protect someone (such as a friend) so she won't get in trouble

☐ Avoid a task or get out of something he doesn't want to do

- *Solve the reason for deception.* Tune in a bit more closely to your child's lying. Is there a reason for the deception? If you can figure it out, you might be able to stop the lie with a simple solution. Suppose the problem is that your kid lies about doing his math homework. Is it because he is lazy, doesn't want to let you down, is overscheduled, or can't do the work? If he is lying because math is too hard, your solution is to hire a tutor and then stress that he tell the truth so that you can help.

- *Expect honesty.* Parents who raise honest kids expect their kids to be honest— and even demand that they be.[35] So repeatedly spell out your expectations for honesty: *"Everyone in our family is always expected to be honest with one another." "I expect you to tell me the truth even though it might be hard." "I need to know I can trust you to keep your word."* Once you lay down your honesty expectations, ask your child to promise to tell you the truth and tell him you promise to do the same. Research at McGill University in Montreal found that doing so was one of the most effective solutions in getting kids to tell the truth.[36] Some families develop a Family Code of Honor. Don't overlook that simple strategy!

- *Make it easy for your kid to open up.* Although you should *expect* honesty from your kid, he also needs to feel safe enough to come to you and admit his mistakes. A "too harsh" approach creates fear, and he may decide that lying is a better alternative than admitting the truth; a "too lenient" approach can make lying become a habit he gets away with.

- *Model honesty.* In one poll, 77 percent of parents admit they lie to their kids, and most feel guilty.[37] And so they should. One way our kids learn new habits is by modeling our example. (Translation: our kids are learning to lie by watching us![38]) So how are you doing? Do you ever . . . Ask your kid to tell a caller you're not home? LIE! Keep the change if you're given too much? LIE! Omit mention of some of those earnings when you're filling out your tax forms? LIE! Tell the cashier that your kid is younger to get a break on that ticket price? LIE! Beware: your kids are watching and will copy your behavior.

Step 2. Rapid Response

Although there is no way to stop lying immediately and entirely, how you respond can help minimize it and boost truthfulness. Here are the most effective, research-proven responses:

- *Do not overreact.* If you catch your kid in a fib, try to stay calm. Overreacting might scare your kid such that he will be afraid to come and tell you the truth next time. One of the biggest reasons kids lie is out of fear. Kids often come clean if they know parents aren't going to lose their temper. Give yourself a minute or two to decide where this lie is coming from and if punishment is really warranted. Your response should be based on your child's age and understanding of honesty. Take into account the nature and seriousness of the lie and whether this is a first-time or repeat offense. Beware: research shows that harsh punishment does *not* stop lying.

- *Don't entrap.* Accusations of lying only aggravate the situation, and kids will most likely deny the allegation. You're better off using a softer approach so that your child is more likely to admit the truth. Instead of saying, "Did you break the dish?" say, "Looks like an accident. Need help cleaning this? Gosh, what happened?" The kid will feel safer and will be less likely to lie.

- *Refrain from labeling.* Do not label your child "a liar." It is unhelpful and counterproductive. Besides, your kid may reason, "Mom says I'm a liar, so I might as well be one."

- *Focus on behavior.* Be brief, tell what you saw or heard, and stick to facts. *"Your coach told me a different version. Please tell the truth." "You didn't say what really happened at the party. I need to know the real facts." "Your bed was not made. I expect you to be honest."*

ONE SIMPLE SOLUTION

Use Moral Questions to Stretch Your Child's Honesty Quotient

Asking the right questions when your child bends the truth can be an important tool for stretching your child's honesty quotient. Here are a few questions to get you started:

- "Did you tell the truth?"
- "Was that the right thing to do?"
- "Why do you think I'm concerned?"
- "If everybody in the family [class] always lied, what would happen?"
- "If you don't follow through on your word, what will happen to my trust in you?"
- "How would you feel if I lied to you? How do you think I feel to be lied to?"
- "Why is lying wrong?"

The change you are aiming for is for your child to finally grasp that lying breaks down trust. It will take time, so use those teachable moments to help your child understand the value of honesty.

- *Set a consequence for repeat dishonesty.* The best consequences help kids think about how they'll change their misbehavior. If the lie was used to get out of a task, send him back to finish the job. If he cheated on a test or plagiarized the report, require the task be redone. If dishonesty continues, create a "Fibbing Jar" where any family member must put in a fibbing fine (a quarter or two, which later goes to a charity) for each fib. If he deceived you, he writes an essay explaining five reasons dishonesty is wrong. Or up the consequence to grounding or the loss of a desired privilege.

- *Teach the ideas of real and make-believe.* With younger kids, explain the difference between a real story (*really* true) and a make-believe story (you *wish* it were true, but it really isn't). Fairy tales can help illustrate your point. Then whenever your kid fabricates a tale, ask, *"Is that real or make-believe?" "Is that what you* wish *happened or what really happened?"* Usually kids will admit that their tales are make-believe when you call them on the tale in a calm, non-threatening way.

- *Stress that wishing can't make it real.* Deal with magical thinking matter-of-factly: *"I know you wish the scooter was yours, but it belongs to Jeb. You need to give it back." "I bet that's something you want to have happen, but you know that it can't."*

Step 3. Develop Habits for Change

- *Teach honesty with books.* Books can create great talks about honesty as long as you nail the lesson:

  For younger kids: *A Big Fat Enormous Lie*, by Marjorie Sharmat Weinman; *Liar, Liar, Pants on Fire!* by Miriam Cohen

---

 One Parent's Answer

A mom from Orlando shares:

We found out that our ten-year-old daughter and her friends were meeting every day at a mall instead of at the library where she said she was. Meghan admitted her lie, but it was clear the other parents were clueless. We invited them over for a chat. Our first decision was to ground them from seeing each other for a week. We also set up a phone tree to check up on their stories. It was a wake-up call that even our "little angels" could be dishonest, and we committed that evening to stay vigilant so their lying didn't become a habit.

For older kids: *Don't Tell a Whopper on Fridays!* by Adolph Moser

For all ages: *Pinocchio,* by Carlo Collodi; *The Emperor's New Clothes,* by Hans Christian Andersen; *The Boy Who Cried Wolf,* by Aesop

- *Provide good models.* One study found that lying was reduced 43 percent after kids discussed George Washington's confession of chopping down the cherry tree: "I cannot tell a lie."[39] His dad's line was the clincher: "Hearing you tell the truth instead of a lie is better than if I had a thousand cherry trees." Offer good honest heroes and heroines from the Bible and history, such as Honest Abe Lincoln, and current figures, such as whistle-blowers at the FBI, to teach honesty traits. Honest people admit when they do something wrong, tell the truth even when it is hard, return things they borrow, keep promises, can be counted on to keep their word, don't intentionally mislead others, don't lie, and can be trusted. Look also for examples in your community of people who stand up for an honest cause even when it isn't popular or convenient. Let your kid know you admire them.

- *Stress the repercussions.* Take time to explain why dishonesty is wrong; here are some possible arguments:

  Dishonesty gets you in trouble.

  You get a bad reputation.

  It hurts other people: cheating isn't fair to other students who did study.

  No one will want to be your friend or do business with you.

  It can get you in serious trouble (for example, probation, expulsion, suspension, or even criminal penalties like fines, tickets, and incarceration).

  It will hurt your family's reputation and break down your trust in one another.

  Save those news articles about dishonest actions of elected officials, sports stars, corporate executives, and celebrities (from impeachment to jail terms to fallen reputations) and use them to teach real-live "truth or consequences."

- *Create an honesty mantra.* Kids learn habits through repetition, so adopt a family motto about honesty, such as "A half-truth is a whole lie," "If it's not right, don't do it; if it's not true, don't say it," or "Honesty is the best policy." Then repeat it again and again until your child can say it on his own, which means he has internalized it.

- *Reinforce honesty.* Let your child know you appreciate his truthfulness, and acknowledge his honest efforts: *"I really appreciate your honesty. I can count on you to say the truth."* And give your kid credit for owning up to his mistakes and having the courage to admit a lie. Research shows that behaviors that are reinforced are more likely to be repeated, and repeated behaviors are more likely to become new habits.[40] So praise your child's honesty.

CHARACTER

- *Try an honesty challenge.* Mark Hyatt, superintendent of the Classical Academy in Colorado Springs, told me about how he challenged his high school students to go without lying for twenty-four hours. Not one was able to meet the challenge. Try a similar challenge in your home or discover the maximum time any family member (you included) can go without lying. Warning: a four-year-old lies about once every two hours; a six-year-old, about once every hour and a half.[41] You may need to start your challenge at a more realistic level (Can we go an hour?), then add time.

WHAT TO EXPECT BY STAGES AND AGES

Preschooler   Almost all kids start experimenting with lying to avoid punishment around three years of age and can distinguish between harmful lies and little white ones.[42] Vivid imaginations make it hard to separate real from make-believe, so expect kids this age to use "tall tales" to express things they wish were true but aren't ("I swam across the pool") or to stretch truth in their favor.

School Age   School-age children know that lying is wrong, but will test boundaries to see how far they can go in their truth stretching. Lies become more sophisticated, deliberate, and clever, and are used as a way to solve problems. Reasons for lying include avoiding punishment, impressing others, boosting their self-esteem, and getting something they want. If by age seven the child learns that lying works in handling difficult situations, lying will become a habit for the rest of childhood.[43]

Tween   Tweens understand that a lie is deception and that there are consequences, so lying takes on greater significance. Lies become more convincing, and the child is less likely to confess when caught. Usual reasons for a lie are to protect parents from worry and to avoid an argument;[44] tweens may also lie to protect a friend or if they feel that their privacy is being invaded. Be careful that lying doesn't become a habit.

ONE SIMPLE SOLUTION

Teach your child one or two of the following "honesty tests" to help him choose honesty whenever he considers twisting the truth. He just thinks about his dilemma ("Should I lie and tell Dad I already did my homework?"), asks himself an honesty test question, then listens to his conscience.

Assembly test: "Would I say it if my principal announced what I did at an all-school assembly?"

Newspaper test: "Would I say it if it made the front-page headlines?"

Parent test: "Would I say it if my parents heard about it?"

Grandma test: "Would I say it if my grandma heard about it?"

Fortune-teller test: "Would I say it if I could see into the future?

More Helpful Advice

Dealing with Your Kids' 7 Biggest Troubles: Lying, Cheating, Stealing, Sexual Acting Out, Drugs and Alcohol, Suicide, Violence, by Val J. Peter

Raising Good Children: From Birth Through the Teenage Years, by Thomas Lickona

Why Johnny Can't Tell Right from Wrong, by William Kilpatrick

When Good Kids Do Bad Things: A Survival Guide for Parents of Teenagers, by Katherine Cordy Levine

Materialistic

SEE ALSO: *Clothes and Appearance, Hooked on Rewards, Money, Peer Pressure, Spoiled and Selfish, Ungrateful*

THE PROBLEM
Red Flags

Is greedy and unsatisfied, unappreciative and ungrateful, overly brand conscious; bases her self-worth on what she owns; always wants more; spends impulsively

ONE SIMPLE SOLUTION
Turn Off the TV (No Kidding!)

Did you know that the average American child is exposed to forty thousand advertising messages each year and that corporations spend $15 billion annually advertising and marketing to kids up to age twelve?[45] Research also shows that *the fewer commercials kids see, the less materialistic they become.* When kids' TV viewing was cut by one-third, they were 70 percent less likely than their peers to ask parents for a toy the following week.[46] So monitor your kids' TV time, steer their viewing habits toward public television, pop in a video, or simply *turn off the TV!*

The Change to Parent For

Your child recognizes that what she owns does not bring happiness, puts a stronger value on relationships, and reduces her emphasis on material goods.

Question: "My son is six but already has a list of all the brand names and can quote almost every TV commercial for the stuff he wants us to buy for him. How can parents counter materialism in such a consumption-driven world?"

Answer: Television commercials have been proven to fuel materialism, so your first important task is to reduce the influence of those ads on your child's perceptions. Here are a few simple solutions. Hit the mute button on your television remote and talk to your child whenever those commercials are on. Turn him toward more commercial-free television shows, or even TiVo his "have-to-see" favorite so he can cut out the commercials altogether (you can teach him how) and fast-forward to the show. And teach your child how to resist those marketer's messages by playing the "What are they trying to sell?" game the second a commercial airs. Once kids learn that the motive of those ads is all about company profit and not their benefit, the product's desirability suddenly drops. And if a celebrity is the product's spokesperson, don't miss the chance to say, "I wonder how much she got paid to do that ad?" Helping our kids become more media literate may be the one strategy we've overlooked to curb their materialism.

Why Change?

In one poll, 89 percent of adults reported feeling that today's youth are far more materialistic and consumption-driven at much younger ages than previous generations.[47] In fact, two-thirds of mothers say that their kids ask for specific brands *before the age of three.*[48] Of course, raising kids in such a materialistic world, with advertisers constantly taunting children to buy-buy-buy, doesn't make matters easier. But let's face it: the biggest reason our kids are so darn materialistic is that we've allowed it. We've obliged their every whim, bought them only the best name brands, and tried motivating them to "do good" by rewarding them with possessions.

Sure, we do it because we want our kids to be happy and have what they desire, but the latest research shows that our good intentions are backfiring. Instead of being satisfied, kids with the materialism bug only want more and are actually *less* happy and *less* content. But even more dangerous: materialism also shatters our kids' character, sense of well-being, and outlook on life. If you're worried that your child is a little too brand conscious or materialistic, then it's time to change that attitude. This entry offers solutions to deprogram your child's materialistic streak and teach new habits that inspire charity and generosity, and help her be more appreciative of the nonmaterial everyday wonders of life.

Signs and Symptoms

Five problems—Brands Everywhere, Never-Ending Stuff, Exterior Focus, Selfish Self, and Unhappy Greed— best describe materialistic kids. Begin by thinking of your child's typical daily actions, then read the following

Pay Attention to This!

Researchers say that today's American kids are "the most brand-oriented, consumer-involved, and materialistic generation in history, and top the list globally."[49] Here are a few red flags about the growing spread of materialism in kids:

- More U.S. kids than anywhere in the world believe that their clothes and brands describe who they are and define their social status.[50]
- Ninety-five percent of adults say that kids are too focused on buying and consuming things.[51]
- Two out of three parents surveyed said that their kids measure self-worth more by possessions than the parents did at the same age.[52]

So how are your kids faring? If you're at all concerned about an unflattering trait called "materialism" taking hold of your kid, then it may be time for a serious parenting intervention.

descriptions. If even one description fits your child, it can mean that your child is slipping to the dark side of materialism. Once you recognize the signs and symptoms, you'll be in a better position to parent for change.

1. *Brands Everywhere.* Corporations and companies work night and day to keep their brands permanently stamped on our children's consciousness. The child is a walking, talking expert on brand names. Her desires become based solely on product name, brand, or logo and not on quality or even price considerations.

2. *Never-Ending Stuff.* The child is a consummate consumer and knows the total number of CDs, shoes, books, and any other "commodity" in her possession and announces it with pride. She rarely *needs* the newest item of desire—she just wants it.

3. *Exterior Focus.* The child evaluates people and situations based strictly on exterior appearances. What matters is what they're carrying or wearing, their clothes, gadgets, or accessories. Internal qualities and traits are overlooked and irrelevant.

4. *Selfish Self.* The child doesn't stop to consider that you may be stressed or inconvenienced by the price of the item. Everything is about *her* needs and desires for possessions. How hard you worked to pay for that privilege or possession is never considered. Who cares if those designer jeans cost the same as your two-week grocery bill?

5. *Unhappy Greed.* Despite everything she owns and all that you give her, deep down your child is really not content, satisfied, or happy and just plain wants more. It's the old and true saying: the more you get, the more you want.

THE SOLUTION

Step 1. Early Intervention

- *Identify the reason.* There is no gene for materialism, so where is your kid getting this desperate greedy streak? Your first task is to identify that reason. Check those items that apply to your child or situation:

  ☐ Is there an emphasis on materialism in your home? Do brand names have status in your home?

  ☐ Have her whims been too easily granted? Are you bribing her with stuff to do something or behave?

  ☐ Are you keeping up with the Joneses by bombarding her with things she doesn't need because you see your friends doing the same thing with their kids?

  ☐ Does she feel that the way to gain peer acceptance is by having the latest fashions or gadgets?

LATE-BREAKING NEWS

University of Minnesota: If you ever had even the slightest bit of guilt about saying no to your kids' materialistic whims, you can kiss those feelings away. New research confirms what we've known deep down: you're not doing your kid any favors by giving in to her every whim and buying her the latest stuff. The researchers found that materialistic kids are less happy, more anxious, less able to handle adversity, and less generous and charitable; they feel less secure and have lower self-esteem.[53] What's more, the study also found that materialistic kids have lower opinions of their parents and argue with them more.[54] Come up with a plan now to halt the gimmes in your home, and stick to it!

☐ Are all those TV commercials impacting her perceptions?

☐ Has a grandparent or other member of the family overindulged her?

- *Model restraint.* You're the best role model for helping your child cope with our complicated material world: What kind of example are you setting for your kid? Would you say that your typical day-to-day behavior is teaching your kid to be materialistic or charitable? Would your kid say that you demonstrate the idea that "It's not what you own but what you are"? Is she seeing you behave with restraint? Or might she be witnessing someone who wants what she sees and buys it on a whim? Are you stressing that it's what's "inside" that counts? Or might she see you flaunting your acquisitions, talking name brands, and always thinking about what you own and wear? Research shows that parents who are materialistic raise the most materialistic kids.[55] Be the model you want your kids to copy.

- *Dig deeper.* Is your kid a little depressed, shy, or lonely? Sometimes kids crave possessions to fulfill an emotional need. So watch for what is triggering your kid's materialistic urges, then dig a bit deeper to see if there's something more psychological behind the desire. For instance, ask your son, who never used to care about music, why he suddenly wants an iPod. If his answer is that his two best friends have one, so he has to keep up with the crowd, then you know it's time to boost self-esteem or use other techniques to buck peer pressure, not just cure his Band-Aid-level gimmes.

- *Spend more time than money on your kids.* A study shows that materialistic kids go on shopping outings with their parents far more than their less materialistic counterparts.[56] Be honest: How many of your family outings stress nonmaterial values? Make a conscious effort to spend time together doing things that don't cost a dime: go to the park and the museum, take bike rides, build forts, bake cookies, watch the clouds, play Monopoly. Try not to give your child things as a substitute for spending time with her.

- *Boost self-esteem.* Research shows that the more materialistic the kid, the lower her self-esteem.[57] And parents are often the biggest saboteurs. By caving into our kids' whims for clothes and electronics, we actually suppress their self-regard by sending the superficial message that their identity is in what they have—not who they are. After a while, our kids adopt that belief. But the researchers also found you can turn that message around by giving well-earned compliments that focus on such qualities as "smart" or "fun." Doing so reduced kids' materialistic tendencies immediately. So downplay appearance and possessions and emphasize your child's unique strengths and qualities. Just make sure that your compliments stress things that can't be purchased, such as sportsmanship, kindness, artistic, humor, or responsibility. That way your child's self-regard will come from those inside qualities she recognizes in herself instead of what she owns and wears.

- *Rotate stuff.* Materialistic children take pride in owning "stuff," and from their perspective, whoever owns the most wins. Instead of letting your child view her stockpile of matchbox cars, action figures, CDs, or whatever, store some away in a closet for a week or month. After all, she really doesn't use all those things—she just counts them. Your new rule is that when stowed items are returned, others are stored in their place. The simple solution of rotating stuff makes bedroom cleanups easier and helps kids learn they don't need so much to have a good time. Best yet, the returned items are more appreciated and treated like new. (Of course, the simpler solution is just not letting your kid buy all that stuff in the first place.)

ONE SIMPLE SOLUTION

Teach "Needs" Versus "Wants"

Materialistic kids often want things N-O-W and don't stop to consider if the item is even necessary. So whenever your kid pleads for some nonessential thing she just "must have," ask, *"Is it something you really need or just something you want?"* Ask the question each and every time your child makes a request. And then don't let her spend that hard-earned cash if the item is a nonessential, spur-of-the moment "have-to-have" want. She'll not only slowly recognize that you're not tolerating her impulsive requests but also learn to prioritize spending desires based on the essentials she really needs.

Step 2. Rapid Response

- *Don't fulfill every request.* How do you typically *respond* to your child's materialistic demands? Do you give in to your kid's desires and let her have her way? Talk to her about her materialistic attitude or ignore the request? Set a consequence or warn her what will happen if she continues her greediness? Always giving in to your kid's materialistic desires doesn't do her any favors. Say no to unending whims and consumer demands, even if that provokes tantrums at first. And do so without feeling guilty. Simply explain your concerns and the reason for your new policy, but most important: *do not give in.*

- *Curb those rewards.* "*I'll do it if you'll buy me those jeans.*" "*How much will you give me?*" "*But I wanted the Xbox!*" If you've heard those words from your kid, chances are she's been rewarded with monetary prizes and material possessions for behaving, working, or just breathing. Watch out: materialistic kids keep upping the ante, wanting more and pricier things. From this moment on, your new response is to just *expect* your child to do the job or behave without compensation. And instead of rewarding her with things or money (which only exacerbates materialism), give praise, hugs, and pats on the back whenever they are earned. No, she's not going to be happy with the new policy, but so be it.

- *Highlight people, not things.* Materialistic kids often believe that having stuff is superior to relationships. Reframing that notion will take your consistent, committed effort, but start by looking for experiences involving your child that stress people over things. Then point out to your child the emotional impact: "*You looked like you really enjoyed spending the day with Grandma. She sure loved being with you. Those are the kind of times you'll remember forever.*" "*Dad really appreciated your handmade card. It's so much more meaningful than something you buy. Did you see his expression?*"

- *Teach how to reduce the clutter and curb hoarding.* Materialistic kids tend to be pack rats, and the more stuff they stockpile, the better. It's time to break your child's hoarding habit. Start by giving your child three boxes labeled with one of these words: "Trash" (for ripped, torn, or broken items); "Memories" (items with special meaning); and "Charity" (gently used toys, accessories, or clothing that other kids may appreciate and she doesn't). Then encourage her to go through her drawers, closets, and shelves. Explain that she should keep what she *really* needs, uses, and wears, and put the rest into the specified box. Make sure that she comes with you when you take the charity box to an organization such as Goodwill, Red Cross, or the Salvation Army to realize that not everyone is so fortunate. You're teaching a great organizational habit that your child should use at least four times a year. But you're also helping her identify possessions by sentiment and not just price, and instilling generosity.

- *Prioritize waiting.* One solution to stop impulsive "have to have it" spending urges is to make your child wait before buying the latest object of desire. The waiting period can be one hour, day, week, or month depending on your child's age and maturity, but it gives kids time to think if they really, really need the purchase. If your child loses interest before the time is up, even she will probably agree that she didn't really want the item after all.

Step 3. Develop Habits for Change

- *Pass on your "no-frill" policy.* Enlist the aid of friends and grandparents who often delight in "spoiling" your child with stuff by encouraging them to scale down on lavish present buying at birthdays or holidays. Suggest they give money for your child's education fund or gifts that would cultivate your child's hobbies or talents or their relationship with your kid. The more you all stick together with your response, the more effective you will be in curbing your kid's materialistic streak.

- *Stress the deeper value of things.* Help your child value objects not for their cost or how trendy they are but for their inherent quality. *"This is a great skateboard because it's so sturdy and will last a long time."* Emphasize sentiment over cost: *"This chair means a lot to me because it was Grandma's when she was little."* Your child may not begin to adopt your reasoning right away, but over time she'll see that popularity, appearance, and high price tags aren't the only factors that make objects lovable.

One Parent's Answer

A mom from Charlotte shares:

Birthday parties in our town were becoming extravaganzas with clowns, magicians, and ponies, not to mention the huge, extravagant presents we're all supposed to bring. Each parent tried to outdo the last. The wake-up call was when we noticed our kids were complaining that the party favors were cheap. I invited five moms for coffee, and we agreed to call a moratorium on frivolous party spending. Gifts were capped to a certain price, and parties were to feature the birthday kid and not the stuff. What a difference it made on our kids. They started talking about the fun time they had and not about the price of the gifts and favors.

- *Teach ways to buck peer pressure.* Kids admit to feeling pressured to keep up with the latest trends in order to fit in and be accepted. And it plays a role their materialistic attitudes.[58] So teach comeback lines to prepare your child to counter a peer who is pressuring her to buy, buy, buy. For example: *"Not today," "I'll think about it." "I have to save my money." "I really don't need it." "Why don't you buy it?" "Nope. It's really not me." "I don't have enough money."* Then help your child practice the lines until she can deliver them with a strong, determined voice. Meanwhile, steer your kid and her friends out of malls or off Internet sites where the temptation to buy is strong.

- *Teach the habit of giving not getting.* "Hands-on" giving helps counter materialism more powerfully than almost anything else and helps gel that essential life lesson that it really is better to give than to receive. So take your kids with you to bring dinner to a sick neighbor or to volunteer in a soup kitchen. Require your kids to give part of their weekly allowance to needy kids. Choose a cause as a family—for example, adopting an orphan through Save the Children or befriending a lonely neighbor. Point out your child's charitable gestures so that she realizes the impact of her straight-from-the-heart, no-cost deeds: *"Grandpa loved your painting. He really appreciated your gift—much more than if you had bought something—because he knew it took time."*

WHAT TO EXPECT BY STAGES AND AGES

Preschooler   Kids are already "bonded to brands" by age three;[59] the average kindergartner can identify the logos of over three hundred brands. Preschoolers make their desires known by grabbing things off store shelves and whining or begging for certain name-brand toys or products.

School Age   Materialistic urges are motivated now by a basic desire for fun toys, an increasing awareness of what other kids have, and the desire to fit in by having the same things themselves. Viewing ads on TV fuels commercial urges. Their questions to peers after the holidays,

More Helpful Advice

Born to Buy: The Commercialized Child and the New Consumer Culture, by Juliet Schor

Branded: The Buying and Selling of Teenagers, by Alissa Quart

Consuming Kids: Protecting Our Children from the Onslaught of Marketing and Advertising, by Susan Linn

Kidnapped: How Irresponsible Marketers Are Stealing the Minds of Your Children, by Daniel Acuff

Packaging Girlhood: Rescuing Our Daughters from Marketers' Schemes, by Sharon Lamb and Lyn Mikel Brown

birthdays, or vacations shift from "What did you do?" to "What did you get?" Materialism increases significantly between ages eight and nine.[60]

Tween   Materialism rises sharply during the tween years when peer pressure and the need to fit in and be accepted are strongest. Materialism increases most dramatically when kids are between twelve and thirteen years of age,[61] and then begins to taper off and drop. Tweens believe that their clothes and brands describe who they are and define their peer status; a ten-year old has memorized almost four hundred brands;[62] 75 percent of kids this age want to be rich;[63] 36 percent of tweens feel pressure from peers to shoplift.[64] Those tweens with lower self-esteem tend to be significantly more materialistic than those with higher self-regard.

Not Knowing Right from Wrong

SEE ALSO: *Cheats, Cyberbullying, Drinking, Internet Safety, Lying, Peer Pressure, Sex, Steals, Steroids*

THE PROBLEM

Red Flags

Has difficulty deciphering right from wrong, chronically lies or steals, can't be trusted, blames others for wrongdoing, won't accept responsibility for wrongdoing

The Change to Parent For

Your child learns right from wrong, internalizes your family's good values, and develops a strong sense of morality that helps him act right even in the face of temptation or without your guidance.

Question: "I found a video game that doesn't belong to him in my eight-year-old son's room. I'm positive he stole it from the grocery store. He has everything he wants, so how do I handle it?"

Answer: How parents react to their child's misbehavior can be destructive or productive in helping him learn right from wrong. Responding appropriately to his wrongdoing makes a parent's job especially significant when it comes to stretching conscience. Here are my Four R's of Moral Discipline to help your son learn from his stealing episode. You can also use these four points with almost *any* misbehavior to help your child understand right from wrong.

1. *Respond so as to help the child think through his actions.* You might ask, "Explain what happened," "Why did you do it?" "What made you do it?" "How did you think it would turn out?" "Did it turn out as you had hoped?" "What would you do differently?"

2. *Review why the behavior is wrong.* You might ask, "Do you think stealing is right or wrong?" "Why shouldn't you take something from a store or anywhere else?" "Can you think of other reasons why a kid shouldn't steal?" "Why do you think I'd be upset?"

3. *Reflect on the victim.* Help your child imagine what it would be like to be in the victim's place. "Let's think about the man who owns the grocery store. How do you think he feels about his property being taken?" "How would you feel if you had to pay for things someone else took from you?" "Would it be fair if you had to use your salary to pay for it?"

4. *Right the wrong to stretch conscience.* Brainstorm together a few options that guide your son to right the wrong and return the game because he knows it's the right thing to do. "You know that what you did was wrong, so let's think of what you can do to make things right."

Your goal is to stretch your son's conscience so that he understands the full impact of his actions, including the victim's feelings. Moral growth evolves gradually, so don't expect overnight changes, but instead find simple daily ways to use the Four R's to boost his moral growth.

Why Change?

Strong conscience—that magnificent inner voice that helps us know right from wrong—is what lays the foundation for decent living, solid citizenship, and ethical behavior and what every parent wants for his or her child. But according to recent polls, the general public believes we aren't faring so well in nurturing our children's moral growth. A recent

---

LATE-BREAKING NEWS

Teach Kids That Conscience Can Be Stretchable

Columbia University: For the past ten years, psychologist Carol Dweck and her team at Columbia (she's now at Stanford) studied the effect of praise in a series of experiments on hundreds of school-age students.[65] Her research found that kids generally have two views about goodness, and those views can significantly affect moral growth. One group believes that goodness is basically fixed: people are invariably good or bad. The other group has a "goodness can be improved" mind-set, so that if a person does something wrong, it doesn't make him "bad," so long as he makes amends and resolves to do better next time. Dweck also found that kids in this group are less judgmental of others and try to set things right and learn from their wrong. The lesson from this research: *teach your child that conscience is like a muscle that can be stretched, and whenever he misbehaves, emphasize that he can right his wrong with a little effort and that doing so will also increase his potential for goodness.*

Newsweek poll found that almost half of Americans believe that we have grown lax about enforcing moral standards;[66] another survey revealed that 93 percent believe that parents have failed to teach children honesty, respect, and responsibility.[67] Those results are especially alarming these days because our kids receive so many conflicting moral messages in the media and among peers that too often counter our values. But research also clearly shows that parents play a significant role in nurturing their children's moral growth, because morality is learned, and that learning starts right at home.

This entry offers proven strategies to help your child learn right from wrong, develop a strong conscience, and act right even in the face of temptation. Only then will our kids really be able to do what Jiminy Cricket advises Pinocchio: "Always let your conscience be your guide." After all, the only real barometer of good parenting is for our kids to act right *without* us. So let's roll up our sleeves and get started.

Signs and Symptoms

Assuming that your child is developmentally capable of understanding right from wrong, the following are some signs of a weak or underdeveloped conscience:

- *Won't accept blame:* has trouble admitting mistakes or saying he's sorry when wrong; refuses to make amends or see the need to do so when he causes physical or emotional injury; tries to attribute his error to others
- *Has trouble deciphering right from wrong:* has difficulty identifying wrong behavior or understanding why it was wrong; needs admonitions or reminders as to how to act right; doesn't know how to turn a wrong action into a right one
- *Is dishonest:* lies and is frequently untrustworthy despite his understanding of honesty and his developmental maturity; can't be counted on to keep his word
- *Fails to see consequences:* fails to recognize consequences of improper behavior, makes unwise choices without thinking through the outcome
- *Is frequently in trouble:* knows how to act right but continues to behave inappropriately
- *Lacks guilt:* lacks a feeling of shame or guilt about wrongdoing
- *Is easily swayed:* knows the right way to act but is easily pressured by others not to act right

THE SOLUTION

Step 1. Early Intervention

- *Commit to raising a moral child.* Start by intentionally aiming to produce a moral child with solid character. Be mindful that you are influential and that

Pay Attention to This!
Could It Be Conduct Disorder?

Most kids will stretch the truth or take something that doesn't belong to them every now and then, but if such behaviors become a pattern, watch out. These *chronic* and *habitual* signs may indicate a more serious behavioral problem called Conduct Disorder, which requires an evaluation by a child or adolescent psychologist or psychiatrist:[68]

- Inability to give or receive affection; lack of long-term childhood friends; difficulty trusting

- Cruelty to animals; hurting peers or others emotionally or physically, relishing their pain

- Little or no remorse, guilt, or shame for wrongdoing or hurtful behavior

- Habitual stealing, lying, shoplifting, vandalism, truancy

- Eye contact abnormalities; won't look you in the eye

- Destructiveness: sets fires; is preoccupied with violence, blood, and gore

- Chronically disobedient; persistently displays little respect for you or other family members

conscience is formed by your repeated and purposeful daily efforts to raise an ethical child. After all, parents who raise children with strong consciences don't do so by accident.

- *Be a strong moral example.* Kids learn moral standards by watching your choices and reactions and hearing your casual comments. So what you do in those little ordinary moments of life are powerful conscience lessons for your child. For instance: how you treat your family, friends, neighbors, and strangers; what movies you watch and the kinds of books and television shows you choose; how you react to everyday moral conflicts, such as your child's cheating, his friend's lying, the neighbor's littering. These are all decisions and characteristics kids watch closely, so make sure the behaviors your child picks up on are ones that you want him to copy. One of the greatest questions to ask yourself at the end of each day is: *"If I were the only example my child has from whom to learn right from wrong, what would he have learned today?"*

- *Develop a close, mutually respectful relationship with your child.* Studies find that kids are most influenced by those persons toward whom they feel the strongest attachment and deepest respect. They are also more likely to copy these individuals' moral beliefs. So one of the surest ways to nurture your child's conscience is to develop a close, loving relationship. Just make sure the relationship is mutually respectful: you treat your child with love and respect, and he treats you the same way in return. Of course, building that kind of relationship clearly takes one-to-one personal, uninterrupted time, but doing so is the best way to ensure that your child's primary moral instructor is you. It's the stuff good parenting is all about.

One Parent's Answer

A mom from Denver shares:

Our six-year-old foster son, Tyler, seemed to always be in trouble and was developing a low opinion of himself. Every time I praised a "good" behavior, he would discount it and call himself a "bad boy." If he wouldn't "hear" his good qualities, I would show them to him. Using a small photo album, I made a scrapbook of Tyler's "goodnesses" using photos and magazine cutouts: his kindness toward animals, loyalty to his family, determination in soccer, assertiveness in saying his point of view, and prayerfulness in church. I presented the scrapbook to him and told him of all his virtuous qualities and pointed to the pictures in the book. My son kept the album under his pillow for weeks, and whenever he had a hard day he plopped himself on the bed and "read" his book about the "Good Tyler."

- *Expect and demand moral behaviors.* Experts find that parents who raise moral kids expect their kids to act morally and even demand that they do. Chances are that the kids will, simply because their parents require that they do. The best moral expectations are those that are high yet reachable and are explicitly communicated to kids. Once those expectations are set, parents must stick to them *and not back down.* Hang tough!

- *Identify your core family values.* Pretend that your children are grown. What are the two or three most important moral beliefs (such as perseverance, compassion, respect, integrity, honesty) you want them to remember from their childhood that will be etched in their conscience? Those are your core family values—the ones you hold most dear, reinforce most, and never deviate from.

- *Create family mantras.* Many parents create simple family mantras that incorporate your identified core values. Here are a few examples: "Everyone in our family is always expected to be honest with one another." "In this home, we will always treat one another kindly and act just as we would like to be treated by others." "We talk to one another respectfully with words that build each other up and don't put each other down." "We also honor and respect each other's privacy and property." The idea is to repeat your mantras over and over until your children not only can recite them without you but also internalize them.

Step 2. Rapid Response

- *Uncover the reason.* This is often the hardest part: stay calm and be objective to determine why your child's conscience is underdeveloped. Observe your kid in different settings and ask the opinion of adults you trust. Here are reasons for a weaker conscience. Check those that apply to your child or situation:

  ☐ *Immaturity.* Your child is not yet developmentally capable of moral reasoning or behavior.

  ☐ *Poor moral examples.* Parents, coaches, teachers, relatives, friends, or those your child looks up to—such as celebrities, sports heroes—exhibit weak conscience or poor modeling.

  ☐ *Weak parental influence.* The parent-child relationship is based on a lack of respect; there's a weak, distant, or ineffective parenting influence or an unstable or dysfunctional family life.

  ☐ *No accountability.* Your child has not been required to make amends for an obvious wrongdoing; he has never been held accountable for his actions, or is allowed to get away with moral infractions.

  ☐ *Flawed early attachment.* Your child experienced prebirth trauma or alcohol or substance abuse from mother, early childhood trauma, or extreme negligence; there was a lack of parental bonding or early parental love; the child has an attachment disorder.

  ☐ *Permissive parenting.* Your child has rarely been disciplined for wrongdoing; there are no rules or inconsistently enforced rules; he has grown up with conflicting parental discipline styles; he is poorly supervised, so he gets into trouble.

  ☐ *Experience or witnessing of cruelty.* Your child has been emotionally or physically abused, or repeatedly bullied; he has experienced severe cruelty, prejudice; he has witnessed or been coached in cruelty.

  ☐ *Neurological impairment or emotional disorder.* Your child's conscience has been hindered by brain injury or trauma, emotional disturbance, Fetal Alcohol Syndrome, or other cognitive handicap.

  ☐ *Too strict of parenting.* Your child has been raised with too harsh or corporal-style discipline; he has experienced "conditional" parenting, threatened with the withholding of love or approval if he doesn't behave; he's been shamed into acting right.

  ☐ *Attention getting.* Misbehaves, whether on purpose or unintentionally, as a cry for help or an attempt to gain approval or love.

  ☐ *Peer pressure.* Your child knows right from wrong but is easily swayed by peers and goes along with the crowd due to having few friends or weak social skills, or wanting to fit in.

☐ *Stress or hardship.* Your child is experiencing parental discord, financial or family instability.

☐ *Weak family values.* Family values, spirituality, religion, moral expectations, or even just discussion about knowing right from wrong has been infrequent, nonexistent, or deemed irrelevant.

- *Don't excuse wrong behavior.* If you excuse your child's behavior, let him off the hook, or allow him to get away with the wrong, he only learns that he doesn't have to be accountable. So never let your child get away with doing the wrong thing. Instead use moral discipline as your opportunity to stretch your child's conscience and make sure he understands that he will be held accountable. With a young child or first-time offender, just reasoning with the child may be enough. For some kids, setting a mild consequence is what is required for them to take your moral standards seriously. But just remember that conscience-building consequences should always fit the crime, be age appropriate, and help the child learn from the mistake so as to not repeat the offense.

- *Get on board with other adults.* If your child has a pattern of chronic or intentional wrongdoing, then you need a new behavior response. Call a meeting with his teachers and develop what you agree to be the best discipline approach. The key is to be consistent together so that your child recognizes that his wrongdoing won't be tolerated. For chronic and egregious behavioral offenses, such as lying, stealing, fighting, truancy, bullying, and deception, create a simple way (e-mail, phone, or note) to check up each day with the adult in charge (coach, day-care worker, grandparent, babysitter, teacher) so your child knows you are serious. (Do ask the teacher how she would like to be contacted.) For less serious offenses, the behavior can be monitored weekly, but don't let up until you see a steady improvement.

- *Get an outside opinion.* If your child continues to hurt others (and even relishes their pain), doesn't take ownership for serious wrong actions, or chooses to defy your family standards, or if the behavior pattern escalates, seek the immediate help of a trained mental health professional. Don't wait.

Step 3. Develop Habits for Change

- *Emphasize empathy.* Nurturing empathy is essential to stretching conscience because a child's heart and mind work together to help him do the right thing.[69] An easy way to develop empathy is to point out the impact of the child's behavior on the other person: "See, you made her cry when you said she couldn't play." Also highlight the victim's feelings: "Now he feels bad." The trick is to help your child imagine what it would be like to be in the victim's place. With a young child, try play-acting how a wrong action like stealing might feel by using a real toy.[70] After you "steal" the toy, ask, *"How would you feel if somebody really stole that toy from you? Would it be fair? Why not?"* With an older child, you could ask, *"Would you want somebody to steal from you?"* or *"Pretend you are your friend, and you just found out somebody took your toy. How would you feel? Why? What would you want to say to the person who took the toy?"*

- *Share your moral beliefs.* Speaking frequently to your child about values and beliefs is called direct moral teaching, and studies find that parents who raise kids with strong consciences do it a lot. Look for moral issues and talk about them as they come up. Use every source you can, from TV shows and news events to situations at school, at home, and with friends; tell your kids how you feel about these issues and why. Also use stories rich with moral examples, such as the Bible, Aesop's fables, *Pinocchio, Charlotte's Web, The Velveteen Rabbit,* or *The Book of Virtues: A Treasury of Great Moral Stories,* by William J. Bennett. Just make sure your talks are aimed at your child's level of understanding so that he grasps and learns from your moral-building lesson.

- *Require your child to "right the wrong."* One way to stretch conscience is by having your child recognize that his actions can cause other people distress. Although he can't undo his "wrong," he can let his victims know he is sorry. Here are a few conscience-building ideas that help kids make amends and realize that they will be held accountable for their actions, depending on their age and the severity of the wrong:

  - Write a note, draw a picture, call, or go to the victim personally to sincerely apologize.

  - List a few alternatives to the misbehavior, choose the best choice, and then practice doing it for a few minutes to ensure that he knows the "right" way.

  - Return what was taken, redo what was done under deception, replace or repair what was broken.

- *Reinforce the idea of "doing the right thing."* Your goal is to help your child ultimately act right without you, and the best way to do so is to reinforce those moments when he does "do the right thing." Praise that stretches conscience has these three elements:

  1. *The reinforcement is earned.* Do not ever praise unless it is deserved.

  2. *The praise names the virtuous behavior:* "That was honest . . . kind . . . responsible . . . respectful."

  3. *The praise describes the specific moral action in a sincere and enthusiastic way so that the child understands what was "right" and knows you approve.* "That was being honest. I know it's hard to admit mistakes, but you did. I'm proud of you."

WHAT TO EXPECT BY STAGES AND AGES

Conscience develops in a series of six predictable stages, and a child's experiences and abilities significantly affect its development.[71] Understanding those stages and how children acquire moral growth is enormously helpful in your daily parenting. Check out the recommendations in the More Helpful Advice box and commit to reviewing just one book about moral development so you can align your parenting to fit proven conscience-stretching practices.

Preschooler   Conscience starts to develop at this age, but preschoolers are egocentric by nature, so what they "want" is usually what's "right." They will try to get their way without considering the feelings or thoughts of others: *"Mommy, get off the phone. I need my lunch now!"* They are also prone to thinking of morality in terms of either reward and punishment or what will bring them pleasure, regardless of consequences: *"I'm not teasing Jena so I won't have to miss* Barney." Preschoolers act right to avoid punishment (*"I won't do this, or Mommy will send me to time-out"*) and to please Mom and Dad. They often believe that thinking about something can make it come true, and most will lie—or stretch the truth in their favor—in order to appear good to the people they love most.[72]

School Age   Younger school-age kids are still concrete thinkers, and though they won't admit it, they need to be told what's right and wrong. They are prone to behave morally when it meets their needs and occasionally the needs of others, and only then if there is an exchange of favors. *"I'll let you use my bike if I can use your scooter."* A big concern is still "What's in it for me?" Media (especially movies and television) begin to become moral influences, so monitor what your child consumes. By the age of six or seven, children make moral judgments on the basis of how much damage was done regardless of intention. By the age of seven or eight, they begin to make moral judgments based on intention.

ONE SIMPLE SOLUTION

Create a "Conscience Test" for Your Child to Use

One way to help plant a strong voice inside your child's head is to use the example of a real person who exemplifies conscience and your family's spiritual or religious beliefs (such as Jesus Christ, Buddha, Gandhi, or Mohammed). Teach your child about that person's life and what he or she stands for. Then anytime your child is confronted with a moral dilemma, encourage him to ask his conscience what the person would do in that situation. For instance: "What would Jesus [Buddha or Mohammed] do?" Some parents just say the initials: "WWJD?" ("What would Jesus do?") The key is to pose that one test over and over until your child has internalized it as his own inner reference and can finally use the test to guide his actions without you.

More Helpful Advice

Building Moral Intelligence: The Seven Essential Virtues That Teach Kids to Do the Right Thing, by Michele Borba

Raising Good Children: From Birth Through the Teenage Years, by Dr. Thomas Lickona

Right vs. Wrong: Raising a Child with a Conscience, by Barbara M. Stilwell, Matthew R. Galvin, and S. Mark Kopta

The Moral Child, by William Damon

The Moral Intelligence of Children, by Robert Coles

Why Johnny Can't Tell Right from Wrong, by William Kilpatrick

Tween Friendships and "fitting in" are dominant influencers, so tweens begin to seek social approval. Good behavior is what makes others happy and is also approved of by them. *"I'm going to be really nice to Joshua because it makes Mom happy. Then maybe she'll rent me a movie."* Peer pressure peaks and can cause kids to stray from what they know their conscience says is wrong. Tweens start to pull away from parents and toward friends, but home values are still paramount *if parents continue to stay connected and influential.* Beware: kids at this age are quick to notice hypocrisy and moral inconsistency in adult behavior, so be careful to practice what you preach. Capitalize on their strong sense of justice by involving them in community service or exposing them to unfairness or injustice, which will help activate conscience.

Poor Sport

SEE ALSO: *Cheats, Peer Pressure, Perfectionist, Rejected, Selfish and Spoiled, Steroids, Stressed, Teased*

THE PROBLEM

Red Flags

Changes rules midstream; can't accept defeat; blames others, makes excuses, cries, or loses temper; criticizes others

The Change to Parent For

Your child learns the skills of good sportsmanship as well as the crucial lesson that winning isn't everything—it's how you play the game.

Question: "My eight year-old is one of the best baseball players in the league. But if his team loses he throws a fit and blames everyone else. At this rate all anyone will remember is his poor sportsmanship. What can I do to help him?"

Answer: You can start by pointing out traits of "good losers." While watching the Olympics, a quiz, or even a reality TV show, say, "There's only going to be one winner. Let's watch to see what the losers do. See—they're shaking hands with their opponents." "That was a tough competition. Did you notice how some of the kids acted who lost? They were complaining that the event wasn't fair. They sure didn't act like good sports." If possible, tune into a golf, basketball, or tennis match and point out some of the best losers (and winners) in the sports, such as Michele Wei, Michael Jordan, Tiger Woods, and Roger Federer. Then insist that your child replace his "blame game"

Pay Attention to This!

The National Association of Sports Officials says that it receives two to three calls a week from an umpire or referee who has been verbally abused or assaulted by a parent or spectator.[73] Youth sports programs in at least 163 cities are so concerned about the trend of poor parent sportsmanship that they now require parents to sign a pledge of proper conduct while attending their kids' games. How are you and the other parents in your community behaving at sporting events?

antics with a new way to lose gracefully and display good sportsmanship, or he will not be allowed to play a game. (And if it comes to that, follow through on your word so that he learns his lesson.)

Why Change?

"The referee sucks." "The coach should have given me another chance." "Why should I shake their hands? They're losers!" Sound familiar? One of the most humiliating parenting moments is watching your kid act like a poor sport. Oh, she may be the best player on the field, the best swimmer in the pool, or the faster runner on the track, but as soon as she starts arguing, cheating, changing the rules to suit herself, or booing, her abilities are no longer the issue. Now her character is at stake.

Playing games and sports is an important part of any child's educational and social development. Sport is like a warm-up for real life, or a metaphor for the vicissitudes of our life's journey, or . . . it really is real life. We have to form temporary alliances to cooperate and compete. We try to do our best and must occasionally make sacrifices in order to make the team, whether we win or not. We have to learn what works for us and what doesn't. We try to do better at working with others. We experience a tremendous range of emotions, including happiness and humiliation, success and failure, victory and defeat. So it's normal for kids to have problems coming to term with sports, and it's perfectly normal, not at all uncommon, for them to be poor sports—some from time to time, others continually, to the point where it gets to be a big problem for them, their parents, their peers, and everyone else around them. Transforming poor sports and tuning up good sportsmanship are about helping our kids play the game called life—and play it well.

Signs and Symptoms

- Gloats when she wins
- Makes excuses or blames others for a poor game
- Cheats, or wins at any cost
- Quits or gives up before the game is over
- Displays a negative attitude: sulks, pouts
- Changes rules midstream
- Hoards equipment; doesn't share
- Criticizes, calls people names, or boos other players
- Brags or shows off
- Argues with the coach, ump, teammates, or other team
- Fails to congratulate the other players or does so insincerely

THE SOLUTION

Step 1. Early Intervention

- *Identify the reason your child is a poor sport.* There can be many reasons for a child's being a poor sport. The checklist has a few preliminary possible reasons. What is your best guess as to why your child is a poor sport? Check those that apply to your child and situation. Once you know the answer, you can begin implementing simple solutions and parent for this change.

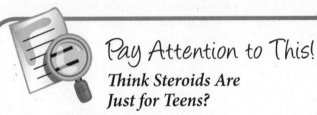

Pay Attention to This!
Think Steroids Are Just for Teens?

A survey found that kids as young as ten (fifth graders!) are taking illegal steroids to do better in sports. And it isn't just boys who are partaking: use among tween girls is almost as prevalent as it is among boys (2.8 percent of boys and 2.6 percent of girls).[74] Steroids can harm the liver, stunt growth, and cause a host of other long-term ailments. Young bodies are particularly vulnerable. Talk to your kids about the dangers of steroids. The main reason kids say they are abusing is to *please their parents* (who hope their kids get an athletic scholarship). Curb that tongue! (See *Steroids,* p. 407.)

- ☐ Poor role models
- ☐ No enjoyment of the game
- ☐ Lack of the necessary athletic skills or ability
- ☐ Attempt to live up to unrealistic expectations
- ☐ Overemphasis on winning and individual performance
- ☐ Negative or competitive coach
- ☐ Highly competitive, status-oriented teammates
- ☐ Low self-esteem: needs acceptance and approval
- ☐ Fear of peer humiliation and rejection
- ☐ Attempt to impress others
- ☐ Fear of losing or of making a mistake
- ☐ Lack of maturity

- *Confront your own behavior.* Do you make excuses for your bad playing? Blame your teammates if something goes wrong? Yell at your kid's coach? Criticize her teammates? Cheer when the opponent gets hurt? Could your kid be picking this up from you? Tune up your sportsmanship so that your kid has a healthy model of fair play to copy.

- *Challenge your expectations.* Is your child developmentally mature enough for the sport? Does she have the skills to play this game or activity? Is this activity

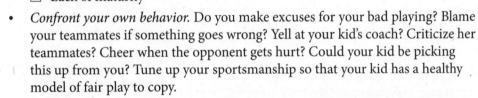

something your child *really* wants to do, or is it what you want for your child? Will this activity boost your child's self-esteem and love for this game? If not, find an activity or sport more in line with your child's talents, abilities, and interests.

- *Watch out for crazy coaches.* Your influence on your kid is great, but teachers, coaches, and mentors also can have a lot of impact. A coach can make a big difference in your child's attitude toward playing sports and sportsmanship. So if you're ever in a position to choose your kid's instructor, be picky. A recent study on youth sports finds that at least 10 percent of athletes admit to cheating, often because their coaches encourage it.[75] If you can't choose, talk to the coach about his or her competitive approach. The last thing an overly competitive kid needs is an overly competitive coach with a win-at-all-cost philosophy.

- *Reduce excessive competitiveness.* Does your family emphasize "Win-win-win"? Does the coach tell your kid, "Win at any cost"? Then bring out the fun, cooperative oldies but goodies, games like musical socks, monkeyshines, soggy-Susan, and bucket-head (really). Get a copy of *Unplugged Play,* by Bobbi Conner, or *The Cooperative Sports and Game Book,* by Terry Orlick, to find ways just to have pure fun with kids without emphasizing competition and winning.

ONE SIMPLE SOLUTION

How to Lose Gracefully

Kids must learn to accept victory and defeat *gracefully.* These steps teach how to lose with poise:

1. *Look cool and poised.* Turn off your upset look and put on a "good-sport" look. A poised loser is cool, calm, and collected.

2. *Congratulate the victor.* Hold your head high, put on a smile, and walk toward the victor. In a sincere tone say, "Good game!" or "Congratulations!" or "That was impressive!"

3. *Shake hands.* Offer your hand and shake each opponent's hand firmly. Give a high five or a pat on the back to your team members.

4. *Walk off the field with your head still high.* Do *not* make any negative comments under your breath or out loud. No crying, whining, or pouting.

Step 2. Rapid Response

- *Define sportsmanship.* Explain what you mean by "being a good sport" so that your kid understands your expectations. For example, discuss having a good attitude, being a good loser and gracious winner, respecting the final decision of any referee or umpire, and giving your maximum effort. Stress that there are different ways to show good sportsmanship, from shaking hands with an opponent or encouraging your teammate with a high five to passing the ball to someone else who has a better chance of scoring. It isn't always easy to congratulate the other team after you lose a close game, but this is exactly the kind of behavior you should explain is required.

- *Don't always let your kid win.* Make sure your child has the "opportunity" to lose (translation: don't always stack the deck in her favor) so that she'll be able to practice how to do so gracefully whenever she does lose (or win).

- *Challenge the poor-sport view.* If your child typically blames other people, criticizes her peers, or make excuses for her mistakes, challenge her view of the facts and help her understand why (in some cases) the loss was nobody's fault but her own. Then help her do an instant replay of the scenario in a responsible and more mature way.

- *Emphasize personal best, not results.* Don't ask "Did you win?" or "How many points did you make?" Your child quickly learns that you value the result of the contest far more than how she played or what she learned. Instead guide your child to think about her progress and her personal performance by asking such questions as

  "How did you play?"

  "How was that for you?"

  "Did you do the best you could?"

  "How did you feel doing that?"

  "What's the most important thing you learned today?"

  "Is there anything you wish you could have done differently?"

  "What will you do differently next time?"

  "Don't worry about the other kids. You can't change their performance, only yours."

- *Penalize any uncivil, aggressive behavior.* If your child does display any aggressive, insulting, or rude behavior that goes over your line—such as booing, hitting, or cheating—follow through on your word and remove her ASAP from the activity. If your child's unsportsmanlike behavior is particularly egregious, let the coach know your intentions of removing her from the game. Ask the coach for support, and encourage him to "red card" your child as well.

- *Call "foul" at the first hint of poor sportsmanship.* Each and *every* time your kid displays poor sportsmanship, take her aside to correct the action immediately (or as soon as convenient). Point out the exact behavior that concerns you: *"I heard you blaming others for your mistake." "You're fighting with the referee." "You're not letting anyone else take a turn."* Then make sure she understands how to correct her behavior.

One Parent's Answer

A mom from Houston shares:

My son always used to quit games before the end. Candyland, soccer, bowling—any game—he'd quit. He has a short attention span, but even so, he was getting the reputation of a bad sport. So I'd set an oven timer before any game for a specific play time (not too long), and I only gradually increased the time length. I told him he had to play until the buzzer went off. It worked like a charm! No more quitting midstream and a major turnaround in his sportsmanship.

Step 3. Develop Habits for Change

- *Play and lose together gracefully.* Dust off the Monopoly or Clue games and hold Family Game Nights. Or set up a volleyball net or chalk up a basketball court on the driveway. Playing games together is a great way to help kids learn the rules of good sportsmanship. Model the rules of good sports as you play together: stick to the rules, make no excuses or criticism, play to the end, congratulate the winner. And if you do lose, show *how to do so gracefully.*

- *Identify a poor losing response.* What is the typical way your child displays poor sportsmanship? For instance, does she lose her temper? Insult the other players? Argue with the coach? Change rules midstream for her advantage? Cry or complain? Quit midstream? Once you identify the exact behavior, point it out to your child and tell her what to do instead. *"If you start the game, you must finish." "You must stick to the rules you agreed to." "You may not argue with the referee."* Then focus on correcting that one poor-loser response.

- *Evaluate sports manners that need a tune-up.* Your next step to boosting good sportsmanship is to evaluate which sports manners need a tune-up. Here are a few of the core principles of good sportsmanship to help in your assessment. How many sportsmanlike habits does your child display? Check those that apply to your child:

  ☐ Takes the game seriously; no clowning

  ☐ Shares materials; doesn't hoard

  ☐ Waits her turn

  ☐ Accepts criticism

  ☐ Encourages peers; doesn't criticize their errors or abilities

  ☐ Is humble: doesn't brag or show off

  ☐ Stays positive; doesn't cheer others' mistakes or boo

☐ Avoids arguments with referee, ump, coach, or other players

☐ Congratulates opponents

☐ Sticks to the rules; doesn't change them midstream or cheat

☐ Doesn't quit midgame or leave when bored or tired or upset

☐ Accepts defeat gracefully; doesn't cry, complain, or make excuses

☐ Works to improve performance

Choose one of the principles of good sportsmanship from the list. Begin teaching it by asking your child to explain how she would use it. Rehearse the principle a few times at home and then find opportunities for your kid to use it at a scheduled sport activity. Later that day, review how things went: *"How did the other kids react? What will you do next time?"* Continue teaching new principles as instances come up.

- *Create consequences.* Let your child know plain and simple that poor sportsmanship isn't going to be tolerated anymore. Also be clear that if she displays unsportsmanlike behavior again, she will apologize immediately (to the playgroup, scout meeting, or whatever) or leave the game. If the behavior is repeated, she should be suspended from playing for a week, month, or—if it continues—for the entire season. Your child has to recognize that she *must* be cooperative, respectful, openhearted, and considerate of other people's feelings, and if she is not, she simply may not participate.

WHAT TO EXPECT BY STAGES AND AGES

Preschooler Because these little folks are so self-centered, they perceive fairness as what meets their needs. It is also why three- and four-year-olds are generally poor losers. Four- and five-year-olds play fair because adults tell them they should. *"I'll throw Ken the ball because my coach says so."* At this point, actual winning isn't important (unless the adults make it so); it's all about fun and getting your share of turns.

School Age Kids at this age see sportsmanship as something that should be returned. *"If he's a good sport, I'll be*

More Helpful Advice

How to Win at Sports Parenting: Maximizing the Sports Experience for You and Your Child, by Jim and Janet Sundberg

Learning to Play, Playing to Learn: Games and Activities to Teach Sharing, Caring, and Compromise, by Charlie Steffens and Spencer Gorin

Parenting Young Athletes the Ripken Way: Ensuring the Best Experience for Your Kids in Any Sport, by Cal Ripken Jr. and Rick Wolff

The Cheers and the Tears: A Healthy Alternative to the Dark Side of Youth Sports Today, by Shane Murphy

one." Early school agers are passionate about equality and ensuring that everything is "even Steven." Eight- and nine-year-olds begin to consider the needs and feelings of their teammates and even their opponents. As competitive sports increase, kids become more focused on winning. Before age nine, most kids don't make the distinction between effort and ability. Beware: competition can be quite stressful to kids this age. Losing in front of peers can be humiliating and stressful.

Tween   A true sense of justice begins to emerge, but competition can be fierce. Stress and peer pressure mount, and tweens can be quite upset with bad calls or unfair referees. They can also extend favors to teammates without expecting anything in return. Beware: by age thirteen, 70 percent of kids who play league sports never play again because it is no longer fun.[76]

Selfish and Spoiled

SEE ALSO: *Bossy, Depressed, Insensitive, Materialistic, Money, Sharing, Ungrateful*

THE PROBLEM

Red Flags

Can't take no; wants things ASAP; feels entitled to receive special privileges; always wants to be entertained; is unappreciative, never satisfied, selfish, greedy

The Change to Parent For

Your child learns to consider other people's needs and feelings and recognize that who you are is more important than what you own.

Question: "I focused so much attention on my son that he sees the world as one big catering service just for him. What can I do so he's less selfish and thinks of someone besides himself? Help!"

Answer: The way to bring selfish kids "back to the civilized world" is to stop indulging their every whim and to show them how to consider other people's needs and feelings. It will take patience, energy, and fortitude, but research shows it's actually what makes kids happier *and* more fulfilled.

Why Change?

Do you have a little princess or prince in your house who feels entitled to luxury and privilege? Does she think only of herself? Does he expect the world to revolve around him? If so, you're not alone. In fact, national surveys show that two-thirds of parents say their kids measure their self-worth by possessions and are spoiled.[77] Eighty percent of respondents in a recent AOL/Time Warner poll said kids in America are more spoiled than kids of ten or fifteen years ago, and two-thirds of parents admit their kids are spoiled.[78] One thing is for sure: selfish kids are no joy to have around. These critters always want things *their* way, put *their* needs and concerns ahead of other people's, and rarely stop to consider others' feelings. And that's because they want you to believe that *their* feelings are actually more important than the feelings and needs of others.

The truth is, kids don't arrive in this world selfish. Research shows that our children are born with the marvelous gift to care and be concerned about others. But unless we nurture those virtues, they will lie dormant. Research also proves that you're not doing your kid any favors if you allow that selfish streak to continue. Selfish, spoiled kids are found to be less happy and satisfied about life, to have more troubles with relationships, and to have difficulty handling adversity.[79] They are also less popular and more likely to be depressed and anxious.[80] And they argue more with their parents. Without intervention, spoiled kids are *more* likely to become *less* happy adults. So let's roll up our sleeves to squelch this bad attitude and pronto.

Signs and Symptoms

Four words (*No, Gimme, Me, Now*) best describe selfish and spoiled kids. That's because they all are about putting their needs first and not considering others. So think of your child's usual daily behaviors, then read the following descriptions. The presence of any one of these kinds of behaviors can mean your child is slipping into the "spoiled" category.

1. *"No!"* The child can't take no for an answer. He expects to get his way and usually does.

2. *"Gimme!"* The child is more into getting than receiving. He is usually unappreciative and a bit greedy.

3. *"Me!"* The child thinks more of himself than of others. He expects (and receives) special favors and privileges.

4. *"Now!"* The child has the ability to wait, but won't. He wants his way ASAP, and it's usually easier to give in than to delay his request. He doesn't stop to consider that others may be inconvenienced as well.

LATE-BREAKING NEWS

Use Discipline That Sensitizes Kids to Others' Feelings

University of Michigan: Martin Hoffman, a world-renowned authority on empathy, aimed one of his most influential studies on selfless kids.[81] He wanted to determine the type of discipline their parents most frequently used with their children, and the finding was clear. The most common discipline technique parents of highly considerate children use is reasoning with them about their uncaring, selfish behavior. Their reasoning lessons helped sensitize their children to the feelings of others and realize how their actions may affect others. It's an important parenting point to keep in mind in those moments when we confront our own kids for any uncaring, selfish deed.

Pay Attention to This!

There are two legitimate reasons kids may appear to be selfish or spoiled but are not.

Developmental lags. Young children are self-centered because they are egocentric. They will have trouble waiting and do want their needs met ASAP. As they mature, they will be able to think of others. Also, any child diagnosed with attention or impulsivity deficits will have difficulty "waiting." *Solution: tailor your expectations to your child's capabilities.*

Emotional lags. Children who suffer trauma, who are depressed or overly stressed, or who have low self-esteem will appear selfish. Their emotional pain hinders them from reaching out to others. Children with Asperger's, attachment disorders, and dyssemia (a term coined by psychologists Marshall Duke and Stephen Nowicki to describe difficulties with nonverbal communication[82]) will also have trouble reading emotional cues and may seem inconsiderate. *Solution: please seek professional help.*

THE SOLUTION

Step 1. Early Intervention

- *Identify the reason.* Your first step to changing your child's selfish and spoiled ways is to figure out why your kid has this attitude. Once you figure out where his selfish ways are coming from, you'll be in a better place to turn them around. Here are a few of the most common reasons. Check those that may apply to your child or situation:

    ☐ You are spoiling your child out of guilt. (You feel that you are not patient, that you need to make amends for your past mistakes, or that you don't spend enough time with him.)

    ☐ You want your child to have a "better" childhood than your own.

    ☐ You are living in a "competitive" community where what you have matters.

    ☐ You've always treated him as if the world revolved around him.

    ☐ You or another adult member of your family is modeling selfishness.

    ☐ Your kid is jealous of your partner or a sibling, or is craving your love and approval.

    ☐ Your child has never been taught the value of selflessness.

☐ Your child has poor emotional intelligence and has difficulty identifying or understanding other people's emotions.

☐ Your child has had a past (or present) trauma, illness, preexisting condition, learning disability, or something else that caused pain in his life, and you feel you need to make it up to him with "stuff."

☐ Your child is angry, anxious, or depressed or having some other problem that makes it difficult for him to think of others.

☐ You don't treat discipline and setting limits as a high priority in your parenting, and your child has learned that he is going to get his way if he keeps at you long enough.

☐ You (or other family members) have the money, so your thinking is "Why not raise our child with privilege?"

Once you figure out what is causing your child's selfish, spoiled ways, create one simple solution you can implement to prevent it from escalating further.

- *Use the right parenting formula.* Research shows that the best formula for raising less selfish, more considerate kids has two equal parts: unconditional love *and* firm limits. Is your parenting evenly balanced between the two parts? Or are you providing too much nurturance and not enough structure? If your present parenting formula isn't balanced, then realign your response so you are more likely to get the right results.

- *Model selflessness.* The simplest and most powerful way kids learn kindness, consideration, and thoughtfulness is by seeing it in action. Make sure you are the model you want your child to copy. And when you do those simple, selfless acts—such as watching your friend's child, phoning a friend who is down, picking up trash, giving directions, asking someone how she is, baking cookies for your family—make sure you convey to your child how much pleasure you get from giving to others. By seeing consideration in your daily words and deeds and hearing you emphasize how being kind and caring makes you feel good, your child will be much more likely to follow your example. The old saying about children learning what they live has a lot of truth to it.

- *Nurture empathy.* Kids who are empathic can understand where other people are coming from because they can put themselves in others' shoes and feel how they feel. And because they can "feel with" someone else, they are more unselfish. So nurture your child's empathy to help him see beyond himself and into the views of others. You might help him imagine how the other person feels about a special situation. *"Imagine you're a new student and you're walking into a brand-new school and don't know anyone. How would you feel?"* Ask such questions often, because they help kids understand the feelings and needs of other people.

- *Boost character.* Selfish kids see what they have as more important than who they are. So watch out for comparisons ("Did you see what Sally is wearing?") and comments about appearance ("I love Jen's new haircut—you should get your hair cut just like hers"). Emphasize in your child the things you *can't see or buy*: perseverance, compassion, honesty, respect, responsibility. And do stress why you value them. Your child will be more likely to adopt those values.

- *Don't let your kid always be the center of attention.* Receiving constant praise and rewards can make your kid think life revolves around him, and increases self-centeredness. Praise only when your child earns and deserves the praise. Also teach your child to deal with boredom and enjoy his own company so that he doesn't feel the need to be entertained at all times.

- *Watch those TV commercials.* Admit it! We're all susceptible to being seduced by advertising, and so are our kids. Need proof? Since the 1970s, the average number of commercials a kid sees in a year has doubled, and marketers now spend more than $3 billion annually on advertising directed at kids.[83] And kids are not only spending more but also becoming more consumption driven and spoiled. A study by Penn State concluded that today's kids are also launching their big-time shopping careers at much younger ages.[84] One reason is that they are seeing those TV commercials, which fuel their spending desires. The second reason: we're giving into their whims. Although the recession is causing a downturn in kids' spending, it hasn't seemed to have made a dent in curbing their selfish notions. There are two simple solutions: limit television viewing *and* just say no.

Step 2: Rapid Response

Your second step to deprogramming a spoiled kid is to change *your* current response so that your parenting is aligned with proven practices that raise less selfish and more considerate kids.

- *Decide to change* your *ways.* Turning around your kid's spoiled habits isn't going to be easy or pretty. Expect big-time resistance from your child, and so be it. Keep a mantra going inside

ONE SIMPLE SOLUTION

Play the "Step into My Shoes" Game

Research proves that a great way to stretch your child from always thinking "me-me-me" is to have him actually stand in another person's shoes. You can start with your own shoes or that of an older or younger sibling. Your child literally acts out the situation from the other perspective. *"How do I feel? What would I say? What would I want to have happen instead of what did?"* The trick is to help your kid switch roles so that he starts thinking about others instead of always himself.

your head: "I'm doing what is best for my child." You *must* be consistent and determined. You *will* prevail. Be strong!

- *Take back control and set limits.* How many times do you have to say no to your child before he understands you *really* mean it? Selfish, spoiled kids have learned to get what they desire. And the more often they do, the less likely they will think about others. Decide what issues and things you will *not—under any circumstances*—give in to (such as spending extra money on a particular video game, seeing a PG-13 or R-rated movie, staying out late on a weeknight). If you think through your priorities, you'll be more likely not to back down or let your kid wear you down. And if you need a little reinforcement, do know that hundreds of child development studies conclude that parents who set clear behavior expectations and stick to them turn out less selfish kids. (P.S. Research shows that the average kid nags nine times to get parents to give in to his whims.[85] Keep saying no until your kid learns you *won't give in!*)

- *Censor selfishness.* If you really are serious about changing your child's selfish ways, you must stand firm and be consistent. Start by clearly laying down your new expectations: *"In this house you are always to be considerate of others."* Then clearly state your disapproval each and every time your child acts selfishly. It won't be easy, especially if your kid is accustomed to having his every whim catered to. But a major step in squelching your child's selfishness is simply not to tolerate it.

- *Maintain your rights.* You should be allowed to talk on the phone without being interrupted. You should be able to sleep in your bed without another warm body less than three feet tall curled up beside you. You should be able to say no to your kid without feeling guilty. You are the parent. Don't feel as if you always have to put your kid up on that pedestal and shove your own needs aside. If you do, you're liable to end up with a spoiled child who feels entitled to get his way.

- *Call out selfish deeds.* Whenever your child does anything even remotely inconsiderate, always express your objections to the self-centered behavior. Allowing the selfish action sends a message that you tolerate it. So call it for what it is: *"That was selfish"* (or inconsiderate or unkind). Then help your child consider the needs of the other person. *"How would you feel if that happened to you?" "How do you think your friend felt?" "What can you do next time so you consider your friend's feelings?"* That simple reasoning process helps kid become less selfish and more sensitized to the feelings of others.

- *Get other caregivers on board.* You'll be more successful at changing your child's spoiled ways if you get at least one other person who cares about your kid to support your deprogramming plan. You may have to have a serious talk with other caregivers in your kid's life (such as grandparents) who are guilty of overindulging or always making this kid the center of attention. Let those folks know in no uncertain terms that you are serious about curbing your kid's selfish attitude and need their cooperation to do so.

Step 3. Develop Habits for Change

The third step to deprogramming selfish, spoiled kids is to stretch them away from assuming the world revolves around them, so that they start thinking about others. Here are simple, proven ways:

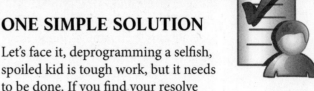

ONE SIMPLE SOLUTION

Let's face it, deprogramming a selfish, spoiled kid is tough work, but it needs to be done. If you find your resolve waning a bit, answer this simple question: *"How would you or others honestly describe your child's typical behavior?"* If most terms are derogatory (such as rude, demanding, self-centered, obnoxious, impulsive, bossy, materialistic, selfish, only thinks of himself), reenergize your commitment to change your kid's current ways.

- *Focus on others.* Selfish kids put themselves first. So gently start helping your kid step to the side and think of others. *"No, let Rob have a turn. He's been waiting just as long as you." "I know you wanted to use the Wii, but let's think of your brother also."* Also help your child recognize the strengths of others. *"Kira is a good artist. Let's ask her to help draw the poster."*

- *Teach your child to wait.* Selfish kids want their way N-O-W. They rarely stop to consider whether you or anyone else is being inconvenienced. You need to stretch your child's waiting quotient so that he doesn't put his own needs in front of others'. If you're on the phone, put up your finger and signal that you'll talk to him in a certain number of minutes. If you're at the mall, tell him you won't stop what you're doing to go to the bank for more cash. He'll have to make the purchase when he remembers to bring his allowance. If he wants to get on the computer, don't let him push his sister's time aside to suit his own convenience. It will take patience and fortitude on your part, but a less selfish attitude will be the outcome.

- *Reinforce selfless acts.* One of the fastest ways to increase selflessness is by "catching" your kid doing considerate and unselfish acts. So look for selfless behaviors in your child and acknowledge them. Describe the deed so that he clearly understands the virtue and point out the impact it had on the recipient. Doing so will also help your child be more likely to repeat the same act another time. *"Did you see Kelly's smile when you shared your toys? You made her happy." "Thanks for giving your CDs to your brother. I know you don't listen to rap anymore, but he just loves it."*

- *Require giving back.* Dr. Ervin Staub, a world-renowned researcher at the University of Massachusetts, has extensively studied the development of selfless, considerate kids.[86] His studies found that children who are given the opportunity to help others tend to become more helpful (and less selfish) in their everyday lives. Require your child to do for others on a regular basis, every day: do his chores; give part of his weekly allowance to charity; bring cookies to the shut-in neighbor; take the dog for a walk; call Grandma every Sunday to see how she's doing. Just plain expect that he think of someone besides himself and contribute to your family. If you don't expect him to give to others, he will feel entitled.

- *Help kids realize the impact of giving.* Research also finds that it is important not only for kids to help others but also to understand the effect of their kind-hearted action on the people they helped.[87] Posing the right questions to a child after he performs any selfless, considerate act helps a child recognize the impact his behavior can have on others as well as on himself. So use giving actions to stretch your child from "me" to "we" by posing such questions as these:

"What did the person do when you were considerate?"

"How do you think she felt?"

"How would you feel if you were the person?"

"How did you feel when you were being kind to her?"

"How did you feel when you saw her reaction to your gesture?"

Even better, decide to give back as a family. Find a cause you support and then bring your kids along to experience the miracle of giving. It could be taking extra toys to a children's ward in a hospital, helping at an animal shelter, reading to the elderly. There is no better way to stretch your child than having him experience the joy of giving.

One Parent's Answer

A mom from Toronto shares:

My husband and I always volunteered in our community, but my son was always too busy. It was when I saw a selfish side of him that I decided to drop his violin lessons so he could work with me at the homeless shelter each week. He hated it at first, but I insisted that he had to start giving back. When he began playing games with the kids, within weeks his selfishness was gone—all because he was required to think of somebody besides himself.

WHAT TO EXPECT BY STAGES AND AGES

Preschooler   Kids this age will be a bit self-centered and egocentric. They need reminders to wait their turn, share their toys, and think about others. Your goal is to stretch them to consider others' needs and feelings.

School Age   Competitiveness gears up, which can make kids more one sided in their thinking and inconsiderate of their class- or teammates' feelings. Use competitions and team activities as opportunities to help your child be less selfish. Watch for a materialistic need always to be "one up" on another friend.

Tween   Self-centeredness and the need to "fit in" peaks during these ages. Watch out for put-downs, vicious gossip, and verbal bullying (especially among girls), which are usually rampant with tweens. Call your kid on any callous actions so that she considers the other girls' feelings.

More Helpful Advice

Don't Give Me That Attitude! 24 Rude, Selfish, Insensitive Things Kids Do and How to Stop Them, by Michele Borba

The Epidemic: The Rot of American Culture, Absentee and Permissive Parenting, and the Resultant Plague of Joyless, Selfish Children, by Robert Shaw

Too Much of a Good Thing: Raising Children of Character in an Indulgent Age, by Dan Kindlon

CHARACTER

Steals

SEE ALSO: *Attention Deficit, Communicating, Lying, Not Knowing Right from Wrong, Peer Pressure*

THE PROBLEM

Red Flags

Takes things from peers or family members without asking and knows it to be wrong; shoplifts or steals

The Change to Parent For

Your child understands the value of honesty and realizes that stealing is wrong, and her actions match her conscience and your family values.

Why Change?

You see your child take a candy bar from the store and put it in her pocket. You notice your daughter put her friend's Barbie under her jacket as she leaves the playgroup. You find a video game in your son's closet, and know it doesn't belong to him. Your child has everything he could possible want, so why would he steal? Do you have the makings of a kleptomaniac on your hands? Now what is a parent to do?

Discovering that your kid has stolen something is guaranteed to shake even the calmest parent. Be assured that stealing is far more common than you might realize—especially among the younger set, who still have a flimsy grasp of ownership and an under-developed conscience. It's not until between five and seven that kids usually understand the hurtful effects of stealing. But once they grasp that stealing violates someone's rights and can result in serious legal action against them, the problem becomes much more serious. And stealing has become a troubling new youth trend.

Store owners tell me shoplifting is so common that they are forced to install pricey security cameras and hire guards—youths are always the biggest offenders. In an attempt to curtail the problem, malls across America now demand that parents accompany their kids. School libraries are installing security systems to detect book theft. Principals complain that one of the biggest discipline issues is having to deal with students stealing from one another. (Hint on this one: tell your child to leave those expensive electronic gadgets at home!) Research also finds that most kids don't steal out of financial need or

Pay Attention to This!

Although stealing is highly inappropriate and should never be allowed, it is a typical part of growing up and does not necessarily connote a more serious problem. However, seek the help of a trained mental health professional if you notice your older child exhibiting these warning signs:

- Your child's stealing episodes are increasing in frequency, or the stolen items are much more expensive.

- Your child displays other worrisome behavior problems (such as truancy, impulsivity, defiance, setting fires, cruelty to animals, and signs of depression)

- Your child has no sense of shame, regret, or guilt about stealing. He doesn't think stealing is wrong.

- Your instinct says something is not right, and your worry has lasted too long. *Get help!*

greed: they typically have more than they could ever need or want. Although stealing is a common childhood problem, it should *never* be allowed. The impact on your child's conscience, reputation, and honesty quotient is just too great. One thing is certain: how you react can be either destructive or productive in helping your child learn right from wrong and stop or repeat this troublesome behavior. Here are six solutions to nip this troublesome behavior in the bud ASAP.

THE SOLUTION

Six Strategies for Change

1. *Model honesty.* Start by assessing your daily honesty example. For instance, do you ever eat a small "sample" from the grocery store's candy bin without paying, take from a restaurant or hotel a small "souvenir" that was not meant to be taken, or bring a few supplies home from your office? If so, think about the message it's sending to your kid. Then commit yourself to improving your example. The best way our kids learn honesty is by observing our own behavior and expectations.

2. *Calmly confront and assess your child's intention.* The first step is to try to determine answers to the five essential "W" questions: *what* happened, *where* and *when* did the incident take place, *who* was your child with, and *why* did your child steal.

(Hint: do keep in mind your child's age and stage of moral development. Young children often have problems separating "real" from "make-believe," so they often fabricate stories and do not intentionally lie or steal.) Unfortunately, asking straight out "Why did you steal?" usually gets you nowhere. A better approach is to begin by simply describing what you believe happened and how you feel about it. Try to stay calm and not overreact. You'll be more successful in getting your kid to open up. Here is an example: *"Tim, I was upset to find a video game that doesn't belong to you in your closet. So what are we going to do about this shoplifting?"* Don't accuse your child of stealing or label her a thief. Accusations never solve anything, and your child may lie to avoid punishment or your disapproval. Just take it for granted that you have a problem and deal with it together.

3. *Boost honesty and review why stealing is wrong.* Make sure your child understands why stealing is not right and why it defies your family's moral standards. Be brief and stick to explaining why stealing is wrong. For example: *"Taking something that doesn't belong to you without asking is very wrong. We do not take things that don't belong to us. We need to be able to trust each other. I expect you to respect other people's property and always ask permission before you borrow something that is not yours."* Young kids often have difficulty grasping the difference between "borrowing" and "taking," so you might need to explain the concepts of ownership and respect for property. For an older kid, discuss possible consequences, such as losing friends, developing a bad reputation, losing people's trust, and getting into trouble with the law. Mention that some stores have a zero-tolerance policy and will call the police. Plan to review honesty frequently over the next few weeks with your child, so that she not only understands your expectations but also incorporates the virtue into her daily actions. A one-time honesty talk will never be enough to create long-lasting behavior change.

4. *Reprimand and reflect on impact.* Most kids don't usually stop to think about the hurtful effects of stealing, but need to learn the full impact of its consequences. The trick is to try getting your child into her victims' shoes so that she realizes it's upsetting to have your personal possessions or retail assets taken away. With a younger child, try play-acting the scene by using a favorite toy. After "stealing" her toy ask, *"How would you feel if somebody stole your toy? Would it be fair?"* With an older kid you might ask, *"Pretend you're the victim, and you found out all the money in your wallet has been stolen. How would you feel? What would you want to say to the person?"* Kids will always be torn between what they *want* to do and what they *should* do. But posing the right questions can help activate your child's conscience so that she recognizes why stealing is wrong, the impact it has on others, and that you expect honesty.

5. *Require a restitution to right the wrong.* Make sure that your child realizes not only *why* stealing is wrong but also *how to make it right.* The best punishment is generally to require the offender to apologize to the victim and return the stolen item. It

makes no difference if the stolen item is a ten-cent pack of gum or a pricey video game: it *must* be returned. (It's usually best if you accompany your child.) If the theft occurred at a store, brief the store owners so that a sympathetic clerk doesn't excuse your kid from the deed. And then have your kid—not you—do the apologizing to the clerk. "I'm sorry I took [name the item]. I know it's wrong, so I'm bringing it back." If the clerk speaks to you (and most times they do), redirect the focus back to your child. The key here is for your child to learn that she is accountable for her actions and will be the one who is doing the restitution. If the item is now damaged or no longer returnable, your child should pay the cost. You may have to cover her expenses at the time, but then make her responsible for paying you back through her allowance or additional assigned chores. Usually bringing the item back to the store, friend, or school is a strong enough lesson, and no further punishment is required. Beware: find out in advance if the store requires police intervention for any theft. Some stores are required to call the police, and you may have a legal issue on your hands.

6. *Be vigilant and dig deeper.* If you suspect that your kid is continuing to steal, then monitor her behavior more closely. You may need to accompany her into a store if you feel she can't be trusted; you may even need to lock away certain items in your home. Most important, you need to figure out what is prompting your child to steal. Although kids often steal just to see if they can get away with it, the behavior may be signaling a more deep-seated need that is not being met. Talk with adults whose opinions you trust for new insight. Here are a few of the most common reasons. Check those that apply to your child or situation:

☐ Traumatic change in the family, such as a divorce, a remarriage, or a move, that makes your child crave attention or need to vent unresolved feelings of fear or anger

☐ Attention deficit, impulsivity, or insufficient self-control (though don't use those to excuse stealing)

☐ Insensitivity, lack of empathy, and failure to realize (or care about) the victim's hurt

☐ Failure to grasp the concept of honesty and ownership, weak or lacking conscience

☐ Lax rules about ownership in your home

☐ Peer pressure and the need to "fit in" and gain group access, a dare from a peer

☐ Attempt to seek revenge or to get back at someone who has hurt her (could be a parent as well as a peer)

☐ Thrill-seeking, risk-taking behavior; seeing if she can get away with it

☐ Naïveté—thinks she won't get caught or that stores can afford their losses

☐ Substance abuse habit (alcohol, smoking, drugs, steroids, or gambling)

One Parent's Answer

A mom from Columbus shares:

Our son was caught stealing CDs at a music store, and we were mortified as well as baffled because he had more than enough money to buy them. We told him how disappointed we were and insisted he take the CDs to the store and apologize to the owner. The man was great and told my son how much money he loses each month in shoplifters. I could see my son had never considered the owner's perspective. That owner's talk with my son stirred his conscience better than any lecture I could ever give. I'm so glad I made him go back to that store.

Once you discover why your kid is stealing, it's time to develop a well thought out solution. For instance, if you think your kid is shoplifting as a means of gaining favor with peers, then you'll need to help her both find friends who will nurture her character and learn to stand up to her peers. Identify one solution you can use to remedy the problem, and commit to doing that with your kid. If the stealing does not stop or increases, then it is time to seek the advice of a trained mental health professional. Please don't wait any longer.

WHAT TO EXPECT BY STAGES AND AGES

Preschooler   Kids at this age begin to respect things that belong to others, but still have a weak sense of ownership and will trade property. This is the age of imaginary playmates and make-believe, so expect for them to use wishful thinking ("The truck is mine" really means "I wish the truck were mine") and to fabricate stories in their favor. Taking something is more a matter of seeing the object they want at the moment and is *not* intentional. Their inability to control their impulses and "stop and think" makes shoplifting common at this age. Don't treat an incident of stealing as a crime, but instead as the opportunity to teach a strong moral lesson.

School Age   Although respect for property is still developing, children at this age understand that stealing is wrong, and a truer understanding of the hurtful nature of stealing begins to develop. Although younger children steal items for immediate use, school-age kids now steal "for keeps." The most common reasons for stealing are low self-esteem or lack of friends, and taking things is done to try to "buy" or impress a buddy with the stolen item. Stealing and lying are more common in boys and occur most often in kids ages five to eight.[88] Fear of parental disapproval is the strongest deterrent to stealing.

Tween   Internal motivations of conscience and guilt begin to develop, so children now fully understand that stealing is wrong, and it becomes an intentional act.[89] Peer pressure and "fitting in" play a big part in shoplifting. A survey of almost a thousand nine- to fourteen-year-olds found that 36 percent feel pressure to shoplift.[90] Beware: kids this age can become highly skilled at stealing and even proud of their accomplishment.

LATE-BREAKING NEWS

Parent Alert: Could Your Child Be Shoplifting?

In a survey of over twenty thousand middle school and high school students, 47 percent of all respondents admitted having stolen something from a store in the previous twelve-month period.[91] More than a quarter of high school students said they had committed store theft at least two times. Take shoplifting behavior seriously! Many states arrest juvenile offenders. One in four kids shoplift, and your best defense is to catch this behavior *now*. Here are warning signs from the San Diego Police Department and Burbank Police Department in Illinois that your child may be shoplifting:[92]

1. Price tags or package wrapping is hidden in the trash.

2. Goods show up in your house that you do not remember purchasing, or your child is wearing new clothes or carrying electronic items that you know she didn't have the money to buy.

3. Your child gives pricey gifts to friends or you and is secretive about extra income she gets.

4. Your child leaves the house with an empty backpack or wears baggy clothes or puts on a jacket when it's warm outside (which could be indicative of another problem).

5. Money or property begins disappearing from family members.

Ungrateful

SEE ALSO: *Materialistic, Money, Selfish and Spoiled, Sharing*

THE PROBLEM
Red Flags

Is unaware of or insensitive to simple gestures of generosity, financial support, or kindness; is unappreciative of what he has; needs constant reminders to say thank you; is oblivious of simple everyday joys

The Change to Parent For

Your child learns habits that nurture gratitude, appreciation, and charity, and becomes more appreciative of his everyday blessings that surround him.

Question: "I try to give our son everything he needs, but instead of being grateful, he only seems to want more. Is there something I can do to help him be more appreciative?"

Answer: Kids' spirits of gratitude are developed through real experiences that help them see how appreciative others are for his kind gestures. So put away that wallet and find opportunities for your child to give to others so that he can feel and appreciate the recipient's gratitude. He might take homemade cookies to a nursing home, rake leaves for an elderly neighbor, deliver children's books to a pediatric ward, visit a lonely relative or friend. Insist that at least one day a week, your child is the giver instead of the getter. That one little switch may do wonders for raising his gratitude quotient.

Why Change?

Of course we want our kids to be happy, and we like being able to give them what they want. But have you noticed that sometimes our best intentions backfire? Instead of our kids being grateful for what they are given, they are disappointed, or always seem to want "more"? In all fairness, there are a number of factors that work against our kids' being appreciative of the good things in life. For starters: relentless consumption-driven media that push kid to think they need more; a fast-paced lifestyle that leaves little time to help kids count their blessings; and the sometimes overwhelming impact of troubling news that focuses on the bad parts of life instead of helping kids appreciate the good. Or sometimes it's

LATE-BREAKING NEWS

University of California at Davis and University of Miami:
Researchers find that being thankful may be the key to
increasing your child's happiness and well-being.[93] You read that correctly. For the
past ten years, two professors, Robert Emmons and Michael McCullough, studied
several hundred people who were involved in their simple gratitude experiments.
One ten-week study asked the participants to use a journal four days a week to
write down five things they were grateful for that had happened in the previous
week. A second group of participants was asked to list ways they were better off
than others as a way to appreciate their blessings. The psychologists then looked
at medical and psychological tests of each participant prior to the study and then
again ten weeks later. Those simple gratitude exercises made those participants
feel 25 percent happier. But that's not all: they felt better about their lives, slept
better, and felt healthier and less stressed; they were also more optimistic about
the future, less materialistic, and more likely to help others. Those results were
not hard to achieve. Better yet, you can help your child reap similar benefits just
by encouraging him to use some of the gratitude rituals listed later in this entry.

our guilt for not being home enough or our competitive instincts that compel us to keep
up with the Joneses that drive us to lavish our kids with the latest and best of everything.

Whatever the cause, there is one crucial reason we must change for our kids'
sake. Compelling research now proves that the happiest children are the ones who feel a
sense of appreciation for life—and that's regardless of their wealth or personal circumstances. Those studies show that because kids feel grateful, they are actually more joyful,
determined, optimistic, and resilient; less stressed; and even healthier. So if you hope
your child can achieve these traits (and what parent doesn't), then you must replace any
hint of an ungrateful attitude with gratitude. The good news is that there are also simple
proven strategies to make that change happen for your child.

Signs and Symptoms

Here are the top nine symptoms of ingratitude in kids. Every kid slips every now and
then, but how many signs are typical of your child's daily behavior?

- *Bad manners:* needs constant reminders to say thank you or show his
  appreciation
- *Envy:* wants what others have, envies others' possessions

- *Lack of appreciation:* takes for granted your daily kind and thoughtful gestures
- *Huge sense of entitlement:* feels he deserves to have luxuries or privileges
- *Dissatisfaction:* always seems to want "more," "better," or "newer"
- *Materialism:* values only material things, brand names, or the "latest"
- *Self-centeredness:* is unwilling to reciprocate with gifts or kind acts to others
- *Ungraciousness:* acts disappointed with presents, blurts out "I didn't want this"
- *Thoughtlessness:* doesn't consider other person's feelings or the thought or effort that went into her gesture

THE SOLUTION

Step 1. Early Intervention

- *Model gratitude.* Kids learn gratitude by seeing others display appreciation in everyday, unplanned moments. How often do your kids see you convey your appreciation with hugs, words, or small notes to others? How often do you tell your kids how much you appreciate them? Tune up your attitude of gratitude so that your kids are more likely to copy your example.
- *Set limits.* Having too much "stuff" squelches appreciation. So fight the tendency to overindulge your child with too many things. Always giving kids what they want does not help them learn to be grateful and appreciative of what they have.
- *Thank your kids.* Don't overlook your kids' daily thoughtful deeds. Just be sure to tell them *what* they did that you appreciate so that they are more likely to copy your example and send their own "appreciation messages" to others.
  "Josh, thanks for remembering to take out the trash. I appreciate your helpfulness."
  "Thanks for giving me a moment alone, Hannah. I had a hard day, and I appreciate your thoughtfulness."
- *Teach gratitude with books.* Here are a few great books to start that discussion:
  For younger kids: *Yes, Please! No, Thank You!* by Valerie Wheeler and Glin Dibley; *Emily's Magic Words: Please, Thank You, and More,* by Cindy Post Senning, Peggy Post, and Leo Landry

  For older kids: *Giving Thanks: A Native American Good Morning Message,* by Jake Swamp; *Lady in the Box,* by Ann McGovern; *The Giving Tree,* by Shel Silverstein; *Focus on the Good Stuff: The Power of Appreciation,* by Mike Robbins; *Gratefully Yours,* by Jane Buchanan
- *Expose your kids to the less fortunate.* Face-to-face experiences can go a long way in helping kids appreciate their blessings. So find ways for you and your child to do charitable work (playing with kids in a homeless shelter, reading to the blind, building low-cost housing, or delivering meals for the bedridden).

Step 2. Rapid Response

- *Use gratitude reminders.* Have your kids make notes, pictures, or posters or just leave Post-its in visible places around your home to remind everyone to pause and be grateful. There is truth to that old adage, "The more you see it, the more you do it."

- *Make them say thank you.* Parents who raise grateful kids don't do so by accident. They expect their kids to be appreciative, and require

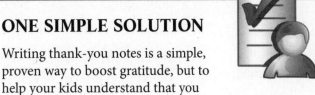

ONE SIMPLE SOLUTION

Writing thank-you notes is a simple, proven way to boost gratitude, but to help your kids understand that you expect them to use that practice, enforce one simple family rule: *"You must write the thank-you note first, and then you may use the gift."* A young child can dictate his comments and only needs to sign his name. School-age kids should use this rule from the Etiquette and Leadership Institute in Athens, Georgia: the total number of sentences in a thank-you note should be half the child's age.[94] So a ten-year-old should be expected to write a minimum of five complete sentences.

their children to say thank you from the time the kids learn to talk. Keep in mind that kids may need constant reminders: *"Did you remember to thank Jeff's mom?"* And don't overlook their slips: *"You can call to thank her when you get home."*

- *Help imagine the recipient's feelings.* One way to help stretch your child from "me" to "you" is through role playing. Suppose your child just sent a thank-you card to his aunt for the birthday present he received. Use it as an opportunity to help him recognize his aunt's feelings when she receives the card by having him pretend to be the recipient. *"Pretend you're Aunt Jo opening up her mailbox and finding this card. How will you feel when you read what your nephew wrote?"*

- *Understand the emotion behind the gesture.* A hard lesson for kids to learn is that they're really thanking the person not for the gift but the thoughtfulness behind it. *"Grandma thought a lot about what to give you this year." "Mark went to five stores to try to find what would make you happiest."* Keep reinforcing the thought that went into the purchase.

Step 3. Develop Habits for Change

The best way to boost gratitude is by establishing rituals in which your family takes times to count their everyday blessings. To reap the benefits, you must be committed and do the ritual a few minutes each day for at least three weeks until it becomes a habit. Here are a few ideas:

Thank-you ABCs. This one is great for younger kids to do at the dinner table. You and your kids say the alphabet together, but for each letter include something you are grateful for: *A, Aunt Helen; B, my brother; C, my cat,* and so on. Take it

ONE SIMPLE SOLUTION

Teach Your Child How to Be Appreciative—Even If He's Disappointed

It's easy for kids to look grateful about receiving gifts they like, but it's much harder for kids to learn to accept an unappealing gift with grace. So teach your child how to accept gifts graciously by rehearsing polite comebacks *prior* to the event. A few gracious responses might be "Thank you for this. I really appreciate it" or "Thanks. That was nice of you." Sometimes "Thank you so much!" might be best. Stress that your child doesn't have to like a gift, but he must show his appreciation for the thought that went behind the effort.

up a notch by having the person explain why he is grateful. Families with small kids rarely get beyond *H*, but the point is that you're having fun together, and your kids are also learning to be appreciative. Older kids can reveal one thing they are grateful for that happened to them during the day and why.

Prayers of thanksgiving. Say a prayer of thanks together before meals. Some families take turns so that each night a different member leads the prayer.

Bedtime family blessings. Each child exchanges messages of appreciation for one another, followed by a good-night hug and kiss.

Gratitude letters. Your child writes a letter to someone who has made a positive difference in his life but whom he has probably not thanked properly in the past (such as his teacher, coach, scoutmaster, or grandparent). Research shows that to maximize the impact, your child should read the letter to the person face-to-face. If the person lives far away, videotape your child reading the note and send it to recipient, or have the child read his note over the phone. And if you happen to have a video conferencing feature on your computer, use it so the recipient and your child can see each other and share the moment.

Gratitude journals. Younger kids can draw or dictate things they are most grateful for; older kids can write in a diary or in a computer. Just remember to start one for yourself or for your family. Research shows that your kids should write something they feel grateful for four times a week and continue for at least three weeks.

Focusing on giving, not getting. Involve your child more in the process of choosing, making, and wrapping gifts. Give your kid the honor of handing out presents to relatives during the holidays and giving a thank-you gift to the hostess, teacher, or coach. Switching the emphasis from the role of getter to that of giver may help your child recognize the effort and thoughtfulness that goes into selecting those gifts.

WHAT TO EXPECT BY STAGES AND AGES

Preschooler   Kids can learn to say thank you and please as soon as they can talk, but will need constant reminders. Expect kids' focus to center on themselves and what "I got" instead of the giver. Although they are egocentric, they can be gently stretched to think of others. Children at this age start to understand that giving and getting are connected.

School Age   Children begin to move out of the egocentric stage and understand gratitude. There is a noticeable increase in efforts to support those in need and appreciate the kind gestures of others. Sports and contests fuel a competitive spirit, so watch for your child starting to compare his possessions to others'.

Tween   Tweens can take others' perspective into consideration, so they are better able to appreciate the thought that went into a gift. They finally comprehend the full rewards of give-and-take, though they still need reminders to send out those thank-you notes. Peer pressure and the need to fit in are huge; appreciation for what he has is frequently not as important as his interest in what the other kids have.

One Parent's Answer

A mom from Portland, Oregon, writes:

My kids were not as appreciative as I'd hoped and were taking things for granted. Then it dawned on me that I wasn't necessarily the greatest model of gratefulness. I made a pledge to share little things I was thankful for with my kids every day—like my health, job, kids, and friends. They were skeptical at first, but they're now sharing things they're grateful for. My son calls it our "Count Your Blessings" talk.

CHARACTER

More Helpful Advice

Simple Abundance Journal of Gratitude, by Sarah Ban Breathnach

Thank You Power: Making the Science of Gratitude Work for You, by Deborah Norville

Thanks! How the New Science of Gratitude Can Make You Happier, by Robert Emmons

The How of Happiness: A Scientific Approach to Getting the Life You Want, by Sonja Lyubomirsky

Why Good Things Happen to Good People: The Exciting New Research That Proves the Link Between Doing Good and Living a Longer, Healthier, Happier Life, by Stephen Post

Part 4
Emotions

OUT OF THE MOUTHS OF BABES
WHY GOD MADE MOMS

Answers given by second-grade schoolchildren to the following question:

What did Mom need to know about Dad before she married him?

1. His last name.

2. She had to know his background. Like is he a crook?
Does he get drunk on beer?

3. Does he make at least $800 a year?
Did he say NO to drugs and YES to chores?

Angry

SEE ALSO: *Argues, Bites, Defiant, Depressed, Stressed, Swears, Tantrums, Time-Out*

THE PROBLEM

Red Flags

Loses control, shouts, and screams; becomes ticked off at the littlest things; is quick to anger; has low frustration threshold

The Change to Parent For

Your child learns to control his anger and finds healthier ways to express his strong needs and feelings.

Question: "My son has such a good heart, but what a temper! He has all this excess energy, and whenever he's upset, he kicks and punches anyone or anything in sight. We've tried time-outs, withholding privileges, and even spanking, but it's not working. How can I help him handle his anger?"

Answer: If you want your kid to handle anger more appropriately, then he must learn substitute behaviors to relieve that pent-up energy. The trick is to find what works for your child so that he can learn how to take control of his temper. Some possibilities: jumping on a trampoline, using a punching bag, taking karate, or shooting baskets. Some parents swear that learning deep-breathing yoga techniques helped their kids manage their anger.

Why Change?

Yelling. Fighting. Hitting. Tantrums. Biting. Sound familiar? They are typical behaviors of quick-to-anger children. But don't forget that anger isn't always displayed as an outburst; some kids hold their intense feelings inside. Unreleased anger and pent-up frustrations can lead to anxiety and even depression. Teaching kids a new way to cope with their intense feelings is not easy—especially if they have been in the habit of using a quick temper to deal with their frustrations.

LATE-BREAKING NEWS

After a thorough review of research, the American Academy of Pediatrics and five other prominent medical groups conclude that "viewing entertainment violence can lead to increases in aggressive attitudes, values, and behavior, particularly in children."[1] So monitor what your children watch, and listen to what they consume.

Calming a hot temper is not only teachable but also essential for growing up in a sometimes violent, unpredictable world. Besides, eliminating this behavior will do absolute wonders in creating both a child who is far more enjoyable to be with and a more peaceful family. So don't wait and don't give up! If you're consistent, you'll be able to help your child learn a healthier way to handle his anger. You may also be able to help him discover the source of his anger.

Signs and Symptoms

Here are a few common behaviors that may indicate a child has anger management issues:

- Has frequent angry outbursts, even over minor issues
- Is unable to explain feelings when upset
- Has trouble calming down when frustrated or upset, even to the point of hyperventilating
- Resorts to using physical aggression, such as hitting, fighting, kicking, shouting, spitting, swearing, tantrums
- Doesn't seem to care about animals' or people's feelings
- Doesn't accept responsibility for his aggression; blames others
- Needs reminders, coaxing, or reprimands to control temper
- Has trouble bouncing back from frustrations
- Acts without thinking
- Behaves recklessly
- Is super sullen and silent; holds in feelings
- Talks, writes, or draws pictures about violence

If your child only displays angry outbursts when interacting with you or other family members, this may be a relationship issue and not a problem with anger. Maybe it's *your* discipline style, interaction with your child, or communication skills that need changing and not your child.

EMOTIONS

Pay Attention to This!

Remember: anger is normal, but when the outbursts become more intense, last longer, or start crippling your child's relationships in your family or with others, and when those changes aren't due to illness or medication, it's time to seek the help of a trained mental health professional.

THE SOLUTION

Step 1. Early Intervention

- *Identify the underlying reason.* Every child has certain issues that trigger deeper frustrations that may result in angry outbursts. If you can identify *why* your child is short fused, you may be able to prevent those outbursts. Here are typical reasons kids display inappropriate anger. Check any that apply to your child:

  ☐ Has a naturally more tightly wound temperament; always more quick tempered

  ☐ Is bullied, harassed, threatened, or picked on by peers

  ☐ Is frequently punished, yelled at, or spanked

  ☐ Has a physical problem—for example, lack of sleep, an illness, a certain medication

  ☐ Has a biochemical or neurological impairment, such as Tourette Syndrome, Bipolar Disorder, attention deficit, or depression

  ☐ Holds excessive or unrealistic expectations that cause discouragement and fear of failure

  ☐ Doesn't know more acceptable ways to calm down and express his needs

  ☐ Has never been held accountable; is allowed to get away with angry acting out

  ☐ Copies the aggressive behavior of others (adult or kids)

  ☐ Is repeatedly exposed to violent media and entertainment

  ☐ Feels unappreciated; is trying to "hold his own"; nobody listens to him

  ☐ Has experienced a stressful event—for example, trauma, a divorce, family friction, an illness, a recent move

- *Change what you can to reduce the number of anger triggers.* For instance, what about finding a less crowded day-care facility where your child would be less wound up? Is his overly competitive classroom the best placement for your child who is constantly struggling to catch up? Can you agree with your spouse that if you must argue, you won't do so in front of the kids? Some things you can't change, but alter what you can so as to reduce your child's anger load.

- *Track your child's anger pattern.* If you still are having problems identifying the reason for your child's consistent outbursts, then consider tracking your child's anger incidents on a chart, a calendar, or in a journal. You may discover that your child is having a more difficult time coping at a particular time, such as right before bed, on his way to day care, or before a test. Most important, it'll help you tune in to what may be triggering your child's outbursts—which is always the first step to turning things around.

- *Model calmness.* Your behavior is a living textbook that your child copies, so seriously reflect on how you deal with anger. For instance, how do you act in front of your kids after a hard, stressful day? When you're driving with your kids and another car cuts in front of you? When the bank calls to say you're overdrawn? What about other members of your family? How do you typically respond to your child's anger? What lessons might your kid be learning from your actions? Tune up how you express your own anger to make sure your behavior is what you want your child to learn.

- *Set new expectations.* Explain to your child that everyone gets angry—you, Grandma, the postman, the president—but also emphasize that people have choices in how they display their anger. Hitting, punching, screaming, kicking, biting, and fighting are all inappropriate and unhealthy ways to show anger. If your child chooses to show his anger in such a manner, there *will* be a consequence for the outburst—anytime and anyplace. (Time-out or loss of a privilege is generally the most appropriate consequence for aggressive behaviors.) Then explain that you will teach him healthier ways to express his anger. (See *Time-Out*, p. 118.)

- *Refuse to engage with an angry kid.* If your child starts to lose his temper, *stay calm* and don't overreact. Doing so will only escalate your child's outburst. If you need to, walk away and go about your business until your child is calm. Be consistent with your calm response so your child understands that he needs to control his temper if he wants your attention. If he is in danger of hurting himself or someone else, do move him to a "safe zone."

- *Stress the importance of calmness.* Use a balloon to help your child understand the importance of staying calm. *"We all get angry with friends sometimes, especially when things aren't going the way we plan."* Hold up the balloon and slowly blow it up halfway and pinch the tip to keep the air in. *"When we're upset, anger inside us can blow up very quickly. Watch what happens."* Continue blowing the balloon to full size, then pinch the balloon to hold the air. *"When there's so much anger in you, it's hard to think. Your heart is pounding, and you are breathing faster. This is when you can make poor choices and say things to friends you may regret later."* Quickly let go of the balloon so that it flies around the room. *"See how it spins out of control all over? That's what happens when you don't stay calm."*

ONE SIMPLE SOLUTION

A Quick Lesson on the Bad Effects of Anger

Print out the word **ANGER** in large bold letters on a big piece of paper, and then add a large **D** so that it spells **DANGER**. Now talk with your child about the negative effects of using inappropriate anger. For instance: he could lose friends, get a bad reputation, lose a job, be suspended, or get hurt. Once your child recognizes the "dangers" of anger, stress that you will help him find more appropriate ways to express his needs and keep his anger in check.

Step 2. Rapid Response

- *Recognize potential temper triggers.* Start paying closer attention to the issues and situations that are more prone to trigger an outburst in your child (Dad's certain look, his teacher's critical tone, or when he's rushed). Then share your observations privately with your child so that he works harder in controlling his temper in those situations. *"I noticed that whenever George starts exaggerating, you hit the roof." "Have you noticed that whenever Dad criticizes your batting form, you start breathing harder and clench your teeth?"*

- *Identify body temper alarms.* Explain to your older child that we all have our own little signs that warn us we're getting angry, and that we should listen to them because they can help us stay out of trouble. Next, help your child recognize what specific warning signs he may have that tell him he's starting to get upset. For example: *"Looks like you're tense. Your hands are in a fist. Do you feel yourself starting to get angry?"* Hint: each of us has our own physiological signs. They materialize whenever we're under stress and have a fight-or-flight response. The trick is to help your child identify his unique signs *before* he loses his temper. Don't expect instant recognition: it may take some time before children can identify their signs. Younger children will need to rely on you to point them out.

- *Develop a feeling vocabulary.* Many kids display aggression (kicking, screaming, hitting, biting) because they simply don't know how to express their frustrations any other way. They need an emotional vocabulary to express how they feel, and you can help your kid develop one. Here are a few words to start with: *angry, upset, mad, frustrated, agitated, furious, apprehensive, tense, nervous, anxious, irritated, furious, ticked off, irate.* When your child is angry, use emotion words so that he has a model to copy: *"Looks like you're really ticked off. Want to talk about it?" "You seem really irritated. Do you need to walk it off?"*

- *Reinforce "talking anger out."* Once your child learns emotion words, encourage him to "talk out his anger." Beware: your child might yell, "I'm really angry!" or blurt out "You make me so mad." Do *not* discipline him. It's exactly what you want him to do so that he learns to express his anger instead of lashing out or holding the anger in.

Step 3. Develop Habits for Change

Each child is different, so it's best to use the trial-and-error approach: teach a strategy and then watch to see how your child responds. If the strategy and your child seem to "click," then focus on that one technique by practicing it again and again until your child can use it alone.

- *Use self-talk.* Teach a simple, positive message your child can say to himself in stressful situations. For example: "Stop and calm down," "Stay in control," "I can handle this."

- *Pound it out.* Help your child find the most effective way to calm his temper, and then encourage him to use the technique. He can pound clay, hit a pillow, shoot baskets, punch a punching bag, throw rocks at a wall (away from people), hit a wall with a foam bat.

- *Go to a calm spot.* Ask your child to help you set up a place where he can go to gain control. Put a few soothing things there, such as books, music, pens, and paper, and then encourage him to use the spot to cool down.

- *Tear your anger into little pieces.* Tell your child to draw or write what is upsetting him on a piece of paper, then tear it into little

ONE SIMPLE SOLUTION

Once your child can recognize his anger triggers and signs, teach him this simple four-step skill to control a hot temper. Teach one step at a time until he can use all four parts on his own.

1. *Listen.* Pay attention to your body signs—rapid breathing, flushed cheeks, clenched fists, pounding heart—that warn you that you're starting to lose control.

2. *Stop.* Find what works to put the brakes on your anger even for a few seconds. You might pretend to pull a stop sign in front of your eyes or yell "Stop!" or "Chill!" inside your head.

3. *Breathe.* Take a few slow, deep breaths to get yourself back in control.

4. *Separate.* Count to ten (or backwards from twenty, or to one hundred); hum a few bars of "Happy Birthday," think of a cheese pizza, or do whatever it takes to back away from what upsets you and to cool down.

pieces and "throw the anger away." He can also use the concept by imagining that his anger is slowly leaving him in little pieces.

- *Stop and breathe.* Show your child how to inhale slowly to a count of five, pause for two counts, then slowly breathe out the same way, again counting to five. Repeating the sequence creates maximum relaxation and reduces stress that could turn into anger.

- *Use "1 + 3 + 10."* Explain the formula: "As soon as you feel your body sending you a warning sign that says you're losing control, do three things. First, stop and say, 'Be calm.' That's 1. Now take three deep, slow breaths from your tummy. That's 3. Finally, count slowly to ten inside your head. That's 10. Put them all together and you have 1 + 3 + 10, and doing it helps you calm down and get back in control."

- *Imagine a calm place.* Have your child think of a place that feels calm, relaxing, and safe (the beach, his bed, Grandpa's backyard, a tree house). Tell him that the second he feels his body's warning signs kick in, he should close his eyes and imagine the spot, while breathing slowly.

WHAT TO EXPECT BY STAGES AND AGES

Preschooler   Cognitive ability and vocabulary hinder kids this age from expressing angry feelings in words, so aggressive behaviors such as biting and hitting are at a peak. Once kids learn to express their needs and recognize that aggression won't be tolerated, such behaviors begin to wane. They often talk out loud as a means of controlling behavior: *"I better not kick Johnny because Mommy will be mad."*

One Parent's Answer

A mom from Topeka writes:

My son came up with the idea of a "Temper Thermometer" that helps him keep his anger in control. The imaginary device measures his anger on a scale of one to ten (one is relaxed enough to be asleep; ten is ready to erupt like a volcano). Now when David is upset he tells us his "anger temperature." A high number warns him to calm down and make his temper drop. We all pitch in to find the best way to get there, from a time-out to a cup of hot milk.

School Age   At this age, kids are now using inner thoughts to manage their impulses, though adult reminders are often necessary. They can also learn beginning problem-solving skills and anger management techniques so that they can learn to control their anger; they will need a lot of practice in order to internalize the new habits. Boys at this age are prone to using more aggression in acting out their anger than are girls.

Tween Tweens are much more aware of their own behavioral urges and triggers, so they can control their anger in more healthy ways. Watch out for mounting stress and peer pressure, which exacerbate anger. Also know that many adolescents resort to hitting when their anger flares and that your tween may be witnessing such behavior. A national survey by the Josephson Institute found that almost one in every four middle school and high school males said they had hit a person in the past twelve months "because they were angry."[2]

More Helpful Advice

Angry Kids: Understanding and Managing the Emotions That Control Them, by Richard L. Berry

The Angry Child: Regaining Control When Your Child Is Out of Control, by Dr. Tim Murphy and Loriann Hoff Oberlin

The Explosive Child: A New Approach for Understanding and Parenting Easily Frustrated, "Chronically Inflexible" Children, by Ross W. Greene

When Anger Hurts Your Kids: A Parent's Guide, by Patrick McKay

Dependent

SEE ALSO: *Bullied, Indecisive, Peer Pressure, Shy, Teased*

THE PROBLEM
Red Flags

Expects to be rescued, can't thrive without you, lacks initiative, is clingy

The Change to Parent For

Your child learns habits that cultivate confidence and resourcefulness to help her become more self-reliant and better prepared to face life on her own.

Question: "My ten-year-old depends on me to be her problem solver and help her out of jams. I wanted to save her from being discouraged, so I'd help her, but now she just expects me to rescue her. How do I change things?"

Answer: One of the simplest ways to help your daughter be less dependent is to just stop rescuing! Do not write one more cover-up note to her teacher. Do not put out the garbage when she conveniently disappears. Do not take her overdue library book back and pay the fine. Your actions will help her know you expect her to be responsible and resourceful and that you believe she is capable of being so. And she may just learn to recognize that she doesn't need your rescue.

Why Change?

Of course we love our kids to death and hate to see them fail. We want them to come to us for advice. We hate the thought (at least *most* of the time) that they'll leave us someday and be out on their own. But the truth is, one of our most important parenting roles is to prepare our kids for the future so that they can survive and thrive someday without us. That also means that if our kids are *too* dependent and rely on us to be their problem solver, make the hard calls, and be their bodyguards, they are probably going to have a tougher time out there on their own. That means we need to start slowly cutting that umbilical cord so that our kids aren't so dependent on us.

LATE-BREAKING NEWS

Are We Raising a Generation of Dependent Kids?

According to the 2002 census, there is a clear trend among today's twenty-something kids: a large number are moving back home after college. In fact, 60 percent say they plan to live at home after graduation, and 21 percent say they plan to remain there for more than a year.[3] It may be time to do some serious thinking as to how we raise our kids so they are less dependent on the comforts of home. Otherwise, hold off on the new house designs!

The first step is to change our parenting response and start helping our kids learn the habits they need in order to be able to stand on their own two feet without our holding them. It's the best way to help our children become more self-sufficient, resourceful, and independent—so that they can succeed in life *without us*. There's a wonderful Navaho proverb that sums up what parenting for this change is all about: "We raise our children to leave us." Keep those words in mind—they'll help you find dozens of daily opportunities to help your kids learn to be more resourceful and less dependent.

Signs and Symptoms

Here are a few common behaviors that may indicate that your child is too dependent in areas that she is capable of handling alone. Any one behavior can be a sign that your child is too dependent.

- Is unassertive, more a pushover or follower
- Is wary, hesitant, or anxious by nature; has a more reserved temperament
- Is fearful of venturing too far away or leaving you out of sight; clingy
- Lacks drive and motivation; needs to be "jump-started"
- Falls back on her safe but limited repertoire; does not take chances or explore
- May seek help by acting younger
- Acts helpless: may avoid new tasks or old responsibilities by using an "I can't do it" manner
- Often regards new people and situations "too cautiously" or "too skeptically"
- Doesn't take responsibility; waits for someone else to do the job or start the task

If your child only displays dependent, clingy behaviors when interacting with you or other family members, this may be a relationship issue and not a real dependency problem. So watch how she responds in other settings and with other people. If she acts noticeably more resourceful and independent in other situations, maybe it's *your* interaction with your child that needs changing and not your child.

THE SOLUTION

Step 1. Early Intervention

- *Identify the underlying reason.* Your first step to solving this problem is to figure out *why* your child is so dependent. Here are common reasons kids are too dependent. Check ones that apply to your child:

  ☐ Is developmentally or mentally delayed; incapable of achieving at the level of her peers

  ☐ Fears failing a task or letting you down; is a perfectionist

  ☐ Feels insecure or unsafe due to a traumatizing event, such as a divorce, a death, moving, a new illness, an accident

  ☐ Has separation anxiety: is fearful she will "lose" you either physically or emotionally

  ☐ Is never given responsibilities; expectations are set too low for her capabilities

  ☐ Is too impulsive, easily frustrated, or quick tempered to stick with a task

  ☐ Is always rescued; somebody is always there to pick up the pieces or do the task

  ☐ Has "youngest kid syndrome": everyone does everything for her

  Another possibility is that it's your problem, not your child's. You're the one who is afraid to let go. If so, see the next tip.

- *Identify your current parenting response.* Would any of these traits describe your parenting mode? And would the rest of your family agree with your verdict?

  Enabler: "I know how hard that is. Let me help."

  Rescuer: "You're going to be in trouble if you can't find your book. I'll tell your teacher I lost it."

  Impatient: "We're late. I'll tie your shoes."

  Protector: "I'll call Brian's mom and tell her how sorry you are."

  Guilt-ridden: "Don't worry about your chores. I've been gone so much this week, I'll do them."

  Competitive: "You know Ryan's project is going to be really good. Let's add more pictures."

  Paranoid: "Call me every fifteen minutes so I know you're safe."

  Egocentric: "Not now. I don't have time."

Perfectionist: "You run along and I'll redo your science project. Those letters you pasted on just don't look right."

Now that you've thought about how you typically respond, would you say that your behavior usually strengthens your child's independence muscle or weakens it? Is there one thing you're currently doing that might be robbing your child of the chance to figure things out for herself? Is there one thing you might change? So what are you waiting for? Get started!

- *Set a "No More Excuses" policy.* Have you found yourself making excuses for your kids or taking on their responsibilities? "My son is so tired; I'll do his homework tonight." "My daughter is too busy; I'll do her chores this time." It's an easy habit to get into, but if you want to raise a resourceful kid who doesn't always depend on you, these are major parenting no-nos. So set a new house rule: *"We have a new policy: no more excuses. You need to take responsibility."* Then stick to that rule!

- *Reinforce assertiveness.* If you want your child to untie herself from your apron strings (when she's ready, of course) and be able to stand up for herself, then encourage her to speak for herself. And bite your tongue whenever you feel the urge to be your kid's translator ("What she really means is . . .") or ventriloquist ("She's shy, so let me tell you what she wants to say"). Kids learn habits young, so the sooner you let your child speak for herself and not become dependent on you, the better.

ONE SIMPLE SOLUTION

Four Steps to Help Kids Master Any New Skill or Habit

Pick one age-appropriate and doable job that you can teach your child. Use these four steps whenever you feel your child is mature enough to master this or any new skill and move toward independence.[4] For example, suppose you want to teach your child to load the dishwasher:

1. *Show.* First, load the dishwasher while your child watches. Explain each step in the process.

2. *Guide.* After she watches, your child helps you do the task. Keep explaining each step until you are sure she can do the task independently.

3. *Check.* Don't leave just yet! Watch her do the task a few times until you are sure she can do it alone. Offer her feedback, correct any wrong steps, and encourage her efforts.

4. *Step away.* Once she masters the skill, expect her to do it alone. No more help or rescue!

The key is always to choose a task set at your child's level and then break it into smaller, achievable parts so that your child is capable of success and can do it alone.

- *Talk about their future.* Encourage your kids to think beyond the here and now: going away to camp, changing schools, going to college, living in an apartment, making career choices. Discussing your children's lives in the future can be part of your dinner table conversations. Sure they can change their minds (and majors), but the goal is to help your child think toward the future and realize that someday she really won't be living with you. (If you're a parent of a tween, that day may arrive much sooner than you think. Get moving!)

Step 2. Rapid Response

- *Create a new parenting mantra.* Instead of "Always give a child what she wants" or "Do anything you can for a child," change your mantra to *"Never do for your child what your child can do for herself."*
- *Back off with small steps.* What tasks might your child be capable of doing herself instead of relying on you? Maybe it's time for her to learn to make her own lunch, do laundry, make her bed, or call to make her dentist appointments? Of course, this will depend on your child's age, maturation, and current capabilities. The goal here isn't to overwhelm her by piling on your new expectations, but to gradually introduce one new task at a time beginning at the level your child can easily control, so the task is not daunting but achievable.
- *Track your child's progress.* Suppose your daughter cries and wants you to stay when you leave her at school. Of course your goal is to help her feel more secure so she can walk alone, but that change may take a while. So stick to your goal, but also take brief daily notes to help you track any progress. Without jotting down your notes, you may not realize that your child's behavior is changing or know that maybe you need to change your parenting response. For instance: "First day: cried 30 minutes. Holds on for dear life." "Tues: cried 29 minutes." "Wed: cried 27 minutes but less clingy." Just remember: new habits generally take around twenty-one days to change. So stay the course! "Day 30: Sara walked into class by herself with no tears!"
- *Be patient.* Nurturing independence in an overly dependent child will take time, so be realistic. Forget what the other kids can do or are doing. Your expectations should be aimed at gently stretching your child, moving her from where she is now to what you think she is capable of achieving. Just do remember to acknowledge any effort—big or little—your child makes to be more self-reliant.

ONE SIMPLE SOLUTION

The Five Questions That Tell You If Your Kid Is Ready for Independence

There is no set age when kids are "old enough" to do a specific activity or task alone (going on a sleepover, staying home, crossing the street), but there are developmental and safety issues to consider. Here are questions to help you gauge if your child is ready for more freedom or if you're pushing her toward independence too quickly. Answer yes to each item before you untie those apron strings!

1. Your child has the necessary skills and maturity to handle the specific task or situation alone.

2. Your child can answer your "What if?" questions about safety and a possible emergency. In our dishwasher example, you might ask, "What do you do if you see water and suds overflowing the dishwasher and running all over the floor?"

3. Your child is trustworthy and can be counted on to keep her word.

4. You have watched her do the task a few times, and she has proven she can do it without you.

5. Your instinct says, "She's ready!" Rely on your gut reaction.

Step 3. Develop Habits for Change

Your parenting goal is to help your child develop habits tailored to her level that will help her become more self-reliant and independent. Here are skills every child needs in order to be more resourceful and less dependent. (See *Indecisive*, p. 100.)

- *Teach brainstorming so that your child can solve problems without you.* The next time your child has a problem, don't be so quick to offer a solution. Instead, teach her how to brainstorm options. First, say to your child: *"Tell me what's bothering you."* (You might need to help her find the words: "I can't think of anything to bring for sharing.") Express your faith that she can work things out: *"I know you'll come up with a solution for your sharing."* Then encourage her to brainstorm ideas. *"Don't worry how silly your idea sounds. Just say it, because it may help your think of things to share."* You might even call it "The Solution Game"; just remind your child to use it whenever she encounters a problem.

With enough practice, your child will be able to use brainstorming to solve many troubling issues that creep up during the day.

- *Boost organizational skills.* Is your child misplacing library books? Unable to find his sports gear? Losing teacher notes? Chances are your child's lack of organization is a big reason why she depends on you. Learning how to be organized is a skill your child will need for managing her own life; the goal is for her to rely less and less on you as time goes by. Here are a few common "dependency" problems with simple solutions that enable your child to start assuming more personal responsibility. And once you teach the brainstorming habits in the previous tip, your child can generate the solutions.

Problem: You are her personal calendar, Palm Pilot, job and event reminder. **Solution:** Your child hangs a calendar in her room and marks her library due date on it: "Return library books every Wednesday." Your child uses a white board and grease pen to mark her weekly music lessons, soccer practice, field trips, sharing days, and spelling tests. Little kids can draw picture reminders.

Problem: You constantly play search and rescue for her lost items. **Solution:** Your child places the repeatedly lost item (backpack, sports gears, coats, mittens) at a designated spot—at the front door, in an ample desktop basket, or on a hook—*before* going to bed.

Problem: You are her wardrobe consultant in the morning rush hour. **Solution:** Your child lays her clothes out at night.

Problem: You're always "Big Ben." **Solution:** Your child learns to set a simple-to-use alarm clock each night so that you're not screaming "Wake up!" fifty times every morning.

One Parent's Answer

A mom from Sacramento shares:

My child was always hesitant to try things without me standing by her side. I found that role-playing situations first with me made her feel less needy. Before she went to her first sleepover, for example, we had several practice ones at home. And she finally got a classmate to stop teasing her by first acting out ways to tell the girl to leave her alone. The role-plays helped her learn to be more resourceful and less dependent on me.

WHAT TO EXPECT BY STAGES AND AGES

Preschooler Preschoolers are too distractible and impulsive to do some things alone, such as crossing the street or wandering alone in the grocery store, but they can do simple tasks. They start venturing off, but still come back to ensure you're there. At three to four years of age, they can dress themselves (though buttons, zippers, and shoe tying are still difficult), make simple decisions regarding two or three choices (the red or green dress), and do easy chores (water plants, empty wastebaskets, clean a counter).

School Age   Attention span, confidence, and coordination are increasing, and school-age kids have learned that rules and authority figures must be obeyed. They should be able to follow basic instructions, complete simple chores, care for personal belongings, and work independently. At age six, a child can brush her teeth[5] and shower without help (though she may need help with hot and cold knobs) and can answer the phone saying "Who's calling please?" At age seven, a kid is ready for her first sleepover, but only to the home of a good friend (it may take longer to spend the whole night without being homesick). At age eight, a child can write down phone messages with some accuracy; she is coordinated enough to pack her own lunch and do various chores around the house to help out. (See also *Chores,* p. 538.)

Tween   Fine motor skills are fully developed, and tweens can understand the reasons and consequences behind certain safety issues. At age twelve, a child can use a sharp knife or tool and "watch" a younger school-age sibling, though she should never be responsible for minding a baby or toddler unassisted. Most experts agree that children of thirteen are responsible enough to babysit.

More Helpful Advice

Raising a Thinking Child (also *Raising a Thinking Tween*), both by Myrna Shure

"I Think I Can, I Know I Can!" by Susan Isaacs and Wendy Ritchey

Raising Resilient Children: Fostering Strength, Hope, and Optimism in Your Child, by Robert Brooks and Sam Goldstein

Ready or Not, Here Life Comes! by Mel Levine

The Myth of Maturity: What Teenagers Need from Parents to Become Adults, by Terri Apter

Fearful

SEE ALSO: *Bullied, Grief, Sensitive, Shy, Stressed*

THE PROBLEM

Red Flags

Avoids or withdraws from many encounters or situations with peers, with friends and family, in school, or in life in general due to fear or excessive worrying

The Change to Parent For

Your child learns habits that help him reduce anxieties and handle normal childhood fears with skills, techniques, and habits—such as sharing worries, normalizing expectations, practicing relaxation, and others—that he can use the rest of his life.

Question: "My son gets so fearful and anxious that he literally shakes. The kids are calling him "Scaredy Cat." What can I do to help him relax so his fears don't hinder him from enjoying life?"

Answer: Here are two simple strategies that can start to produce calming effects when kids are worried. Tell him to picture a relaxing place in his mind and then slowly count backwards from ten. Or if he's at the doctor's office worried about getting a shot, get his mind off fear by guessing how many tiles are on the floor, then slowly counting to see if his guess was correct. Whatever distracting technique to reduce fearfulness he tries, your son must practice until the strategy becomes a habit to help him relax.

Why Change?

Fears are a normal part of child development, but some kids are a lot more fearful and anxious than others. Data show that between 8 and 10 percent of American children are seriously troubled by anxiety.[6] What's more, such anxious kids are two to four times more likely to develop depression, and as teens they are much more likely to become involved with substance abuse. But the good news is that research also proves that even kids who are more anxious can learn skills to help manage and ease their fears so that they can participate in life and not be held back by their anxious feelings. In fact, studies have shown that about 90 percent of more anxious children can be greatly helped by learning coping skills.[7]

It's up to us to teach our kids coping strategies that they can use to help them deal with whatever troubling event they encounter. Best yet, if we help our kids practice those strategies enough that they become habits, our kids will be able to use them the rest of their lives. This entry offers proven ways you can parent for change—modeling courage, monitoring media input, and teaching step-by-step acclimation—that will boost kids' resilience, help them cope with everyday fears in healthier ways, and prevent anxiety from shortchanging their lives.

Signs and Symptoms

Keep in mind that your child may or may not tell you what worries him, so look for signs. Here are a few common symptoms of childhood anxiety:

- *Sleep disturbances:* difficulty going to sleep and staying asleep; afraid to be alone in the dark

- *Avoidance:* withdrawing, resisting certain situations, or refusing to move

- *Acting out:* may resort to tantrums or acting out when forced to face a specific fear, such as leaving the home or speaking in class

- *Clinginess:* won't let you out of his sight; shadows another person for safety

- *Physical stress:* accelerated heart rate, perspiration, rapid breathing, sweaty hands, nausea

- *Terror:* trembling, crying, or whimpering

- *Regression:* may start sucking thumb, bedwetting, or using his security blanket again

Pay Attention to This!
Could Your Child Be Having a Panic Attack?

Most childhood fears are normal and eventually fade, but when a child experiences reoccurring intense episodes of unexpected terror, he might be having panic attacks. They are rare in young kids, but are more common in older children and adolescents. For an episode to be considered a panic attack, four or more of these symptoms must develop unexpectedly and last about ten minutes:[8]

- Pounding heart, increased heart rate
- Sweating
- Trembling or shaking
- Shortness of breath
- Choking sensation
- Chest pain or discomfort
- Feeling dizzy, lightheaded, or faint
- Fear of losing control or going crazy
- Feeling of unreality or detachment from self
- Fear of dying
- Numbness or tingling

If a child is in the middle of the attack, he usually is unable to name what is causing the anxiety. Seek the help of a mental health professional.

- *Nervousness:* nail biting, chattering teeth, clenched fists; "butterflies" in stomach, temporary twitches

THE SOLUTION

Step 1. Early Intervention

- *Pay attention to hidden fears.* What are the two things your child worries about most? If you don't know, then watch for them a bit more closely for the next week. Listen to what he says and tune in to what he draws and plays, which often gives insight into his worries that he may not openly discuss. Once you identify his fears, you can find positive ways to help him cope.

- *Watch for specific triggers.* Certain situations are more likely to exacerbate fears, so whenever you see your child becoming anxious (see Signs and Symptoms), think in reverse. What happened that might have triggered the reaction? If you make that connection, you might be able to create a solution to reduce the fear. For example, suppose you identify the problem: Emma had a bad nightmare. The trigger? She watched *Sleeping Beauty* that night. The solution: Don't let her watch scary movies—especially at bedtime! Substitute something less scary, like *Mary Poppins* or an old *Sesame Street* show.

- *Expect fearfulness after traumatic life events.* Whenever your child faces a stressful life event (such as moving, an accident, bullying, changing schools, a divorce, losing a loved one, a natural disaster), tune in more closely to how he is coping. Traumatic events can cause anxiety, and research finds that repeated exposure to overwhelming real-life stress (such as a chaotic family life) may lead to depression or even anxiety disorders in later life. So watch your child!

- *Model courage.* Fears can be caught, so beware that you don't pass them on. For instance, if you run and hide when lightning strikes, don't be surprised if your child trembles with you. If you describe your childhood terror of snakes, don't be taken aback if your kid becomes terrified of snakes as well. Your child is watching and may well adopt your fears.

- *Monitor scary media consumption.* Images from movies, video games, music videos, Internet sites, and television news stories can trigger fears or make them even worse. So monitor your child's media exposure and be especially particular about what your child watches closer to bedtime. Hint: one sign that a movie is too overwhelming for a child (regardless of age) is how long he takes to recover. If your tween is still shaking or putting chairs in front of doors for the next few days after watching that scary Halloween flick he "just had to see," maybe it's time to tone down the horror factor.

LATE-BREAKING NEWS

Researchers Conclude That Overprotecting Kids from Fears Can Backfire

Columbia and Harvard University: Studies of hundreds of infants found that those whose parents tried to shield them from stressful events wound up *more* fearful. What's more, those adults who had unusually high numbers of panic attacks had been overprotected in their childhoods.[9] It appears that allowing kids to deal with typical daily troubles actually helps them develop more resilience and better coping strategies. So don't be so quick to shield your child from stressful events. You just may be doing more harm than good.

- *Encourage your child to share his worries.* Encourage your child to talk about his fears. Putting a worry into words makes it more manageable. Your goal is to "catch" his worries early before they blow out of proportion and become full-fledged fears, so be sure he knows you will listen. You can then not only reassure your child but also clarify any misconceptions and answer questions.

Step 2. Rapid Response

- *Recognize that the fear is real.* As trivial or unfounded as a worry may seem, the feeling is real to your child, and it's causing anxiety. Ridiculing, lecturing, ignoring, or trying to use logic with your child will not help.

- *Don't belittle the fear.* Telling him "Don't be silly! There are no ghosts under your bed!" may get your child to go to bed, but it won't make the fear go away. Think back to your own childhood. Such statements as "There's no such thing as a monster" or "Don't be such a baby" probably didn't make you feel any better. So don't use them with your child.

- *Refrain from adopting the "protector" role.* As tempting as it may be to tell your child "Mommy is here and will defend you," don't do it. Your child may just end up running to you each time he is scared. Research also shows that shielding your child from stressful situations is not the answer. The child won't learn to extinguish the fear response on his own.

- *Do provide support.* Help your child feel safe. And don't undermine the power of your words. When your child does confront a fear and hears your comforting "It will be okay" (or gets the same message from Daddy holding his hand), he will feel more secure, and remember and apply those comforting moments to other trying times.

One Parent's Answer

A mom from Bangor writes:

My daughter was so scared of monsters she was afraid to sleep. So we encouraged her to use her vivid imagination to turn the scary monster into a funny one. She would walk into her bedroom, squeeze her eyes shut, and transform her terrifying image into a friendly "monster buddy" who protected her all night from any "bad monsters." It worked!

- *Help your child know what to expect.* There are some fears that we can't protect our kids from and that just must be endured. Educating your child about the event can clear up misperceptions as well as boost security. For example, here is how you might ease your child's anxieties about an upcoming hospital stay: arrange a hospital tour, read a book such as *Franklin Goes to the Hospital* to help him talk about his worries, buy a toy doctor's kit to play with, and suggest he tuck his teddy bear and blanket in his backpack before he leaves.

- *Read books that deal with the fear.* Telling stories, acting out situations, or reading books about a particular scary situation can help kids overcome fears. A few favorite books include *Wemberly Worried*, by Kevin Henkes; *Fears, Doubts, Blues and Pouts*, by Norman Wright, Gary J. Olver, and Sharon Dahl; *What to Do When You Worry Too Much*, by Dawn Huebner; *What to Do When You're Scared and Worried*, by James J. Christ.

Step 3. Develop Habits for Change

Here are a few ways to help your child cope with scary events and normal childhood fears:

- *Handle the fear in baby steps.* Studies show we can help kids cope by exposing them to the threat or stress at levels they can manage.[10] The trick is to introduce the stress in small amounts and then gradually increase the dose until the fear is reduced. Here are problems with solutions to two typical kid fears using the "baby step" model:

  Problem: Terrified of the neighbor's large dog. **Solution:** He first looks at pictures of dogs, then plays with a small puppy and then a medium-size dog, until he can face the neighbor's standard poodle.

  Problem: Afraid to take swim lessons in the community pool. **Solution:** First he paddles in a wading pool; next he dips into the shallow end; finally he graduates to the middle and ultimately the deep end of the pool.

- *Watch your child's reactions closely so that you don't push too quickly.* Wait until your child is ready and then allow him to work through his anxiety at his pace as you gently encourage him.

- *Say fear-reducing self-statements.* Teach your child to face the fear by helping him learn to say a positive phrase. It's best to have your child choose only one phrase and to help him practice saying the same one several times a day until he can say it to himself when feeling anxious. A few fear reducers include "I can do this," "I can handle this," "I will be OK," or "It's not a big deal."

- *Practice relaxation strategies.* If the fear makes your child tense, having him learn relaxation strategies could help. Tell him that the moment he starts to feel tense, he should imagine he is floating peacefully on a cloud or lying quietly on a beach. Taking slow, deep breaths also reduces anxiety. Teach your child to pretend that his lungs are balloons filled to the brim and to slowly let the air out of them as his fears go away.

- *Put your kid in the driver seat.* Research shows that feeling as if you have some control over a situation helps reduce the worry. So empower your child by helping him develop his own fear-reducing plan. Start by identifying one fear. For example: "The weird shadows on my wall make me scared to sleep in the dark." Next ask: "What might help you feel safer?" Then brainstorm reasonable options until your child can find at least one thing that might help him feel more in control, and then carry it out. Kid-generated solutions: "Tuck a flashlight under my pillow" and "Move my bed away from the bookcase so I don't see the shadows on the wall."

Pay Attention to This!

A Quick Quiz to Help You Know When to Worry About Your Child's Fears

If you answer "True" to at least two of these statements because they apply to your child's inability to cope with an ongoing fear, consider seeking the advice of a mental health professional.

1. The fear and your child's response are *not* typical for a child his age.
2. The fear is becoming more severe and continuing over several weeks.
3. The fear is upsetting your child's personal, social, and school life.
4. The fear seems unreasonable or a possible sign of a more serious problem. You're seeing other behavior or symptoms that concern you as well.

WHAT TO EXPECT BY STAGES AND AGES

Childhood fears are a normal part of development, and they differ depending on the child's age. Here is a brief guide to help you understand what is typical for each stage:[11]

Preschooler   Children at this age can't yet distinguish make-believe from reality, so their active imaginations help fuel their fears. At the ages of three and four, kids are frightened by loud noises (such as thunder and lightning), dogs, darkness, separation from parents, monsters, and people with unusual appearances. At age five, they fear bodily harm, falling, death, loss of a parent, bedtime, strangers, and ghosts.

School Age   School-age kids can distinguish between real and make-believe and begin realizing that they can handle their fears by working through them. From five to seven, kids typically fear animals, getting lost, loss of a parent, death, and divorce. When they are seven and eight, common fears include real-life catastrophes, such as storms, fires, or personal injury; not being liked; being late for school or left out of school or family events. At the ages of eight and nine, kids often fear personal humiliation; failure in school or problems with peers; their parents fighting, separating, or being hurt; or being the victim of physical violence—71 percent are afraid of being shot or stabbed at school or at home.[12]

Tween   Most tweens recognize that fears don't have to be debilitating, because they have learned ways to cope. Typical fears for kids ages nine to eleven include failure in school or sports, becoming sick, specific animals, sinister people (killers and molesters), and heights. From eleven to thirteen, kids may fear failure in school or sports, loss of social popularity, looking and acting "strange," death or life-threatening illness, divorce, personal danger, gossip, such real-world events as war, and personal danger (such as kidnapping).

More Helpful Advice

Freeing Your Child from Anxiety: Powerful, Practical Solutions to Overcome Your Child's Fears, Worries and Phobias, by Tamar E. Chansky

Helping Your Anxious Child: A Step-by-Step Guide for Parents, by Sue Spence, Vanessa Cobham, Ann Wignall, and Ronald M. Rapee

Monsters Under the Bed and Other Childhood Fears: Helping Your Child Overcome Anxieties, Fears, and Phobias, by Stephen W. Garber, Robyn Freedman Spizman, and Marianne Daniels Garber

The Anxiety Cure for Kids: A Guide for Parents, by Elizabeth DuPont Spencer

Your Anxious Child: How Parents and Teachers Can Relieve Anxiety in Children, by John S. Dacey and Lisa B. Fiore

Grief

SEE ALSO: *Dependent, Depressed, Divorce, Fearful, Sleepless, Stressed*

THE PROBLEM

Red Flags

Sorrow and grief from experiencing the loss of a loved one, extreme emotions, difficulty returning back to "normal" everyday life

The Change to Parent For

Your child learns healthy ways to cope with grief, regain a feeling of security in the coming days, and restore a positive sense of hope for the future.

Question: "My mother just had a stroke and isn't expected to live through the week. This will be the first time my seven-year-old daughter, Mabel, has dealt with the death of a family member, and I don't have a clue how she will respond. In the past, Mabel was crushed and stayed home from school for a week when her cat died. What should I expect now?"

Answer: A child's level of maturity, her temperament, and her previous experiences with death (such as losing a pet) are often better predictors of how she will grieve than her chronological age. Because in this case you know how upsetting the cat's death was, you might assume this will be even worse. But the truth is that you just never know how a child will handle death or how she will grieve. This is one of those times when your best response is to follow your child's lead and provide all the assurance and guidance she will need to get through these times.

Why Change?

The death of a loved one is one of the most stressful events that a youngster can ever face. When the unthinkable happens and that death involves our child's parent or sibling, how we respond is critical, as it can have a powerful impact on our child's emotional health and life outlook. When the deceased is significant to the parent as well, the problem becomes even more complicated. After all, grief is one of the most intense emotions we can experience, and somehow we must deal with our own sorrow as well as help our child.

EMOTIONS

LATE-BREAKING NEWS
Don't Lie to Your Child About Death

University of Santa Barbara: Researchers discovered that when adults were asked to recall the worst lie they were ever told, it was usually from their parent concerning the death of a loved one.[13] They never got over the feeling of being deceived as a child and have resented it ever since. But when their parent was asked about his or her deception, the parent thought that lying to protect his or her child was the right thing to do, even calling it an act of love. So a word to the wise: don't underestimate what your child knows. And *never* cover up or deceive your child, who may be picking up on your tension or who might hear the troubling news from others. Better that your child hears the truth from you than from someone else.

Late-breaking research reveals parenting techniques that will help youngsters deal with profound loss as well as regain hope for their future. These techniques include always telling the truth, allowing the child to ask questions and express herself, suggesting a positive outlet (such as starting a fund or social activity to honor the loved one), and including the child in family or religious rituals. Understanding the new research and a few of those strategies may help you and your family cope in a difficult time.

Signs and Symptoms

The American Academy of Pediatrics reports the common signs of grief in children and the symptoms of a bigger problem that requires professional help:[14]

Normal Signs of Grief	Signs Requiring Professional Help
Duration of several days or weeks	Duration of weeks or months
Shock or numbness	Long-term denial and avoidance of feelings
Sadness	Debilitating depression; suicidal thoughts
Unhappiness	Persistent unhappiness
Anger	Persistent anger
Guilty feelings	Believes she's guilty or is to blame
Loss of appetite	Eating disorder
Concerns kept to self	Social withdrawal
Temporary troubles sleeping	Persistent sleep problems; nightmares

Temporary regression	Disabling or persistent regression
Increased clinging	Separation anxiety
Crying	Repeated crying spells
Disobedience	Oppositional or conduct disorder
Belief that deceased is still alive	Persistent belief that deceased is still alive

THE SOLUTION

Here are parenting solutions that help children cope with the death of a loved one and help you parent for this difficult change in your child's life.

Step 1. Early Intervention

- *Watch how your child reacts.* Every child reacts differently to the death of a loved one. Your job is to watch and listen to how *your* child reacts so that you can change your response to best help her deal with grief. Here are common and normal children's reactions and comments about the death of a loved one. Check those issues that may apply to your child's situation:[15]

  - ☐ *Denial:* "I don't believe it." "Grandpa's not dead."
  - ☐ *Physical distress:* "I can't breathe." "I can't sleep."
  - ☐ *Hostility:* "Didn't she love me enough to stay alive?"
  - ☐ *Guilt:* "She got sick because I never listened." "I killed her because I made her so sad!"
  - ☐ *Blame:* "It is the doctor's fault. He didn't give Dad the right treatment."
  - ☐ *Replacement:* "Uncle Ben, do you love me, really love me?"
  - ☐ *Adopting mannerisms of the deceased:* "Do I look like Daddy?" "I'm a good dancer like Mommy."
  - ☐ *Idealization:* "Don't say anything against Mommy! She was perfect."
  - ☐ *Anxiety:* "I have a pain in my chest just like Mommy when she died."
  - ☐ *Panic:* "Who will take care of me now?" "Who will take me to the father-daughter banquet?"
  - ☐ *Regression:* "I just need my security blanket again." "I have to suck my thumb."
  - ☐ *Aggression:* "I didn't mean to hit him." "I can't stop and calm down."
  - ☐ *Disrupted relationships:* "I want new friends." "I don't want to go to school."

- *Think about what you want to say.* Talking about death to a child is difficult. It's a subject we are usually least prepared for. So take time to plan what you'd like to tell your child. It will help to know where she is coming from, so watch for the ways she is responding (as noted in the previous tip). You will want to be honest and meet your child's needs. If you don't feel comfortable talking to your child by yourself, then ask your religious leader, a close relative, or a friend to be with you for support.

- *Don't hide your feelings.* It's okay to show sadness, shock, and anger and to express how you feel. Shed your tears, but remember that your child is also looking to you to help guide her through the process. You might also share your memories with pictures and stories about the loved one.[16] Research shows that doing so can help reduce your child's sense of isolation.

- *Inform those needing to know.* Get word to your child's school (especially her teacher), coach, and any other adults who should know about the death. Ask your child if she would like you to tell her friends (or parents of the friends).

- *Take care of yourself.* Your child needs you or some other adult to help guide her through the process. If the deceased was close to you, such as your spouse, child, or parent, you may wish to consider seeking counseling for yourself. You don't want your child to worry about you as well.

ONE SIMPLE SOLUTION

Give Your Child Books Dealing with Death

Counselors often recommend reading a book about death to help children open up about the subject. Here are a few perennial favorites that might be helpful:

For younger children: *Accident,* by Carol Carrick; *Help Me Say Goodbye: Activities for Helping Kids Cope When a Special Person Dies,* by Janis Silverman; *I Miss You: A First Look at Death,* by Pat Thomas and Leslie Harker; *Lifetimes: The Beautiful Way to Explain Death to Children,* by Bryan Mellonie and Robert Ingpen; *The Dead Bird,* by Margaret Wise Brown; *When Someone Very Special Dies: Children Can Learn to Cope with Grief,* by Marge Heegaard; *When Dinosaurs Die: A Guide to Understanding Death,* by Laurie Krasny Brown

For older children and tweens: *A Taste of Blackberries,* by Doris B. Smith; *Beat the Turtle Drum,* by Constance C. Greene; *Bridge to Terabithia,* by Katherine Paterson; *Straight Talk About Death for Teenagers,* by Earl A. Grollman; *What on Earth Do You Do When Someone Dies?* by Trevor Romain; *The Magic Moth,* by Virginia Lee

Step 2. Rapid Response

- *Talk in terms your child understands.* Explain what has happened, giving specific explanations about the physical reality of death. Clarify that death means that life stops, the deceased cannot return, and the body is buried or cremated. The person stopped breathing, eating, and walking and is no longer feeling pain, worry, or hunger. *"Grandpa died because his heart stopped beating." "Tara died because her seat belt was not used and her body was badly hurt in the car accident."* Anything less simple and explicit can cause confusion and be misinterpreted by the child. Children's understanding of death differs vastly from adults, so refer to What to Expect by Stages and Ages (p. 262) before holding any discussion.

- *Be honest, open, and direct.* Do not generalize that old people just die. Explain that there are some things you (or anyone else, for that matter) don't understand. Clear up any misunderstandings about death your child may have. Give the details your child needs to know. Withhold those facts that are not in your child's best interests. If you don't have an answer, just admit you don't know.

- *Encourage questions.* Don't be put off by your child's candid comments. Be prepared to answer the same question again and again. It's how children process information they don't understand. Let your child know you are available anytime to talk. Here are the five questions the American Academy of Pediatrics says kids are most likely to ask and that deserve honest, open, and simple explanations:[17]

  "What is death?"

  "What made the person die?"

  "Where is the person now?"

  "Can it happen to me?"

  "Who will take care of me?"

- *Avoid euphemisms.* Keep in mind that your child may not grasp the concept of death and therefore take your comments literally. So refrain from such statements as *"Grandma is in a deep sleep," "Daddy was laid to rest." "She slipped away." "Mommy is resting peacefully," "Aunt Harriet was very sick, and the illness made her die,"* or *"God took her away."* Such comments are often confusing and can cause children to worry that the same thing may happen to them as well: (*"If I'm sick, I may die, too." "If I go to sleep, I will go to heaven."*)

- *Don't trivialize the loss.* Avoid such statements as *"At least you have another grandparent," "You can always get a new dog," "Some children don't have another brother like you do,"* or *"Don't worry, things will be OK."*

- *Be prepared for tough questions.* As children begin to understand that death is final, death will become more personal. Your child may ask, "Will you die?" Usually the questions are more to alleviate their own fears of losing another loved one. Although you can't make false promises to your child, you can provide comfort and alleviate their fears. You might say, *"My doctor says I'm in good health." "I hope to be around for a very long time." "I hope I'm here until you grow very old."*

- *Avoid clichés.* Don't say, *"You're such a strong girl," "You must be strong so I don't have to worry about you," "Big boys don't cry," "You've got to be tough to help your mother,"* or *"Now you're the man of the house."* Relieve your child from attempts she may make to assume adult responsibilities.

- *Give permission to grieve.* Let your child know that her emotions are normal. Accept her regressions or emotional outbursts. Agree that losing a loved one is not fair. Affirm that crying and sadness or any other emotion are all part of grieving and that it may take some time for her to feel happy or like her old self again.

- *Be supportive.* The trick is to be supportive without pushing. Don't assume your child can handle dealing with grief without help and support. Be lavish with your hugs and your love. This is a tough time for both of you. Let your child know in no uncertain terms that you are available for anything she needs.

- *Seek the help of a counselor.* If you're concerned about how your child is coping with this trauma, consider asking a mental health counselor for advice. Grief counselors are specially trained in helping children deal with death and may be able to alleviate your concerns and help you cope with the loss.

- *Decide whether to bring your child to the funeral or other memorials.* Most grief counselors encourage children to attend a service because it provides closure: a way for the child to "let go" or say good-bye, celebrate the memory of the deceased, and be part of a community grieving process. Consider your child's age and maturity, the length of the service, her receptivity to the idea of attending, and whether it is to be an open or closed casket. If you decide that your child can go to the funeral, simply state that you are going to say good-bye. Inform the child that many people will be sad and will be missing the person, so people may be crying and that's okay. A child under age five should not be expected to understand funerals or to behave appropriately at one. If the deceased is a loved

One Parent's Answer

A mom from Austin shares:

When my husband died, I put together a Memory Box for each of my children about their dad. I gathered photographs of him with the child, his letters, and special mementos (like his fishing tackle, shaving lotion, and a necktie) that they would remember, and put them into each box. Then I encouraged them to gather their own "memories" and add them to their box. It helped my children not only work through their grief but also recognize that though their father was gone, his memories would never leave them.

one for you as well, it may help to ask another adult with whom your child is close to stay with your child. Whatever your decision, do know that many grief counselors say that children are more upset if they are not allowed to attend and regret not going to say their good-byes.

Step 3. Develop Habits for Change

Children vary greatly in terms of how long they will grieve, but here are coping strategies that may help them deal with their intense sorrow. (See also *Fearful*, p. 248, and *Stressed*, p. 303.)

- *Encourage expressive experiences.* Grief counselors point out that many children have trouble verbalizing their feelings about death and loss. So consider providing an outlet for your child that helps her express her grief. Younger children might draw or paint their intense feelings; older children may wish to write their feelings in a diary, journal, or notebook or even to compose a letter to the deceased expressing things she never got to say. Do let your child know she can always talk to you, a close relative, or a counselor.

- *Suggest positive outlets for the grief.* Some families have helped their child start a memorial fund or activity to honor a loved one who has died. Others find some kind of healthy physical activity that their child can do to work off tension and sadness: work out at the gym, ride a bike, jog, do yoga, shoot baskets, visit a friend, or have a friend over. If the mood around your house becomes too morose or tense, find a supportive adult who can take your child on an outing. Allow her also to laugh or be happy if that moment comes.

- *Find ways to involve your child in the grieving process.* She could choose a musical selection or prayer for the ceremony, pick out the dessert for the wake, create a photo album or video presentation about the life of the deceased, write a note, make a floral bouquet, or draw a picture to give to the bereaved. Helping your child find a way to contribute might help her release her grief in a proactive way. You might also encourage your child to commemorate the loss in some concrete way, such as by planting a tree. Research shows that such acts help children feel more included in the grieving process as well as create positive memories.

- *Monitor your child closely.* It is hard to predict how a child will respond to grief, so keep a closer eye on your child during these times to continually assess how she is coping with the loss. Be tolerant of regressive behaviors (wanting to suck her thumb, not let you out of her sight, keep the light on, or even sleep with someone). Bedtime is particularly difficult for kids who have just lost a loved one. Also identify any specific fears or worries your child may have (see *Fearful*, p. 248) so that you can alleviate any misconceptions, and listen if your child wants to share any bad dreams.

- *Keep to normal routines whenever possible.* Routines and rituals create security for children, especially during times of trauma. Whenever possible, keep some semblance of the child's normal schedule intact (bedtime rituals, evening meals, special family practices).

- *Pass on your religious or cultural customs.* Sharing your religious rituals for the deceased can help a child learn how to grieve. So whether your custom is to light a candle, say a rosary, sit on a hard stool to receive mourning visitors' condolences, offer special prayers, or go to a religious service, teach them to your child and do them together. Doing so is often not only comforting but also a way to help your child learn a lifelong coping strategy.

WHAT TO EXPECT BY STAGES AND AGES

The understanding of death evolves gradually; here is what you can expect by stage and age:[18]

Pay Attention to This!

Monitor your child closely to ensure that there is a *gradual* diminishment of grief. Not appearing to have any grief at all after only a short time probably isn't authentic or healthy. And if some form of the grief continues to affect her daily life; if the child has trouble eating, concentrating, or sleeping; or if she appears depressed, please seek the help of a mental health professional. (See *Depressed*, p. 488.) Pay close attention to children who have faced previous significant losses, or when the death involved a parent or sibling; involved a lingering illness; was unexpected, sudden, or violent; or was caused by a disaster or involved multiple deaths.[19] Also note that some symptoms of grief can continue or reemerge after many weeks and even months.[20] Beware that the most difficult times for a child are often the anniversary of the death, during holidays, during a school event (when the deceased would have been included), or at times of other losses.

Preschooler   Children at this age think that death is only temporary, like going to sleep. (The dead might or might not wake up after a while.) They have difficulty separating reality from fantasy, so they often believe that their thoughts or actions may have caused the death (especially if they were "bad"). "Wishing hard enough" or "acting right" might bring the deceased back. Abstract concepts such as heaven are difficult to grasp. Most assume they personally will not die; it happens only to others.

School Age   At this age, children gradually begin to understand that death is final (the dead stay dead and aren't just sleeping), but they still need perspective. They may think of death as a person or ghostly figure, such as a clown, shadowy death-man, or skeletal figure. They believe that thoughts can make things happen, so some see the possibility of escaping from death if they are clever or lucky enough. Children at this age may fear that death is contagious and that other loved ones (themselves included) will "catch it" and die as well. Abstract concepts (heaven, an afterlife, spirituality) are still difficult to comprehend.

Tween By the age of ten or so, most understand that death is an irreversible and inescapable part of life and are now aware of the possibility of their own death. They are more aware of how their world will change with someone's death and of the impact that losing a loved one has on their future (*"Who will go with me to the football banquet?"* *"Who will walk me down the aisle at my wedding?"*) Curiosity about the process of death develops, and children may ask for more specific details, such as *"Is the body cold?"* *"Where does the body go?"*

More Helpful Advice

35 Ways to Help a Grieving Child, by Dougy Center for Grieving Children

Children and Grief: When a Parent Dies, by J. William Worden

Helping Children Cope with the Loss of a Loved One: A Guide for Grownups, by William C. Kroen and Pamela Espeland

Helping Children Cope with Death, by Dougy Center for Grieving Children

Keys to Helping Children Deal with Death and Grief, by Joy Johnson

Talking About Death: A Dialogue Between Parent and Child, by Earl A. Grollman

Homesick

SEE ALSO: *Dependent, Depressed, Fearful, Grief, Rejected, Separation Anxiety, Stressed*

THE PROBLEM

Red Flags

Is afraid to leave home, misses the comforts of home and always wants to come back

The Change to Parent For

Your child learns skills and techniques that will help him feel more secure when he's away from home, reduce his chances of being homesick, and enable him to enjoy the experience of being away from house and family.

Question: "My child just went away to camp for the first time, and now he's calling me and asking to come home. Is this normal, and is there some way of knowing how bad he really feels?"

Answer: Up to 95 percent of kids who go to sleep-away camp miss something about home, but the good news is that the majority of those pangs begin to ease over the next two or three days.[21] The best way to gauge how well your child is doing is to ask a simple question: "How homesick have you been feeling?"[22] Most parents assume that asking will worsen the symptoms, when on the contrary researchers find it actually puts you in a better position to hear where your child is coming from and to check in on his emotional state. Then you can decide if he can make it a bit longer or does need to be rescued.

Why Change?

Sleepovers. Slumber parties. Weekend or summer camp. Boarding school. Hospitalization. Moving. There are a number of reasons kids go away from home. Going away may seem like a great experience, but for many kids the idea of spending time away from you, where you live, and everything that's familiar is scary—especially for the first few times. And then there are doubts in our own minds as well: Should I let him go? Is he old enough? Will he make it through the night? Why doesn't he want to go—should I insist? If your kid is older, there's a whole different set of worries: Will he be supervised? Will he

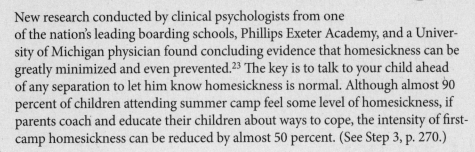

LATE-BREAKING NEWS

Research Finds That Homesickness Is Preventable

New research conducted by clinical psychologists from one of the nation's leading boarding schools, Phillips Exeter Academy, and a University of Michigan physician found concluding evidence that homesickness can be greatly minimized and even prevented.[23] The key is to talk to your child ahead of any separation to let him know homesickness is normal. Although almost 90 percent of children attending summer camp feel some level of homesickness, if parents coach and educate their children about ways to cope, the intensity of first-camp homesickness can be reduced by almost 50 percent. (See Step 3, p. 270.)

get any sleep? Will there be any drugs or alcohol? Are he and his buddy *really* going to stay in the house all night? Ah, the joys of parenting! But then there's another worry that can be even more upsetting—homesickness!

Although the longing for the comforts of home is normal for *any* age, those pangs can range from mild to almost debilitating. But now groundbreaking research finds that parents really can make a difference in minimizing—even preventing—homesickness and help their kids enjoy those away-from-home experiences far more. This entry shows you how to parent for change based on proven research that will help your preschooler, school ager, tween, or even teen prepare to venture off on his own.

Signs and Symptoms

Almost everyone—young and old—experiences homesickness to some degree, and there seems to be no difference among boys and girls. Symptoms can range from mild to severe. Here are some of the most common signs of homesickness:

- Calls, writes, or e-mails far more than usual; looks for reasons to connect
- Stops participating in activities, withdraws
- Experiences physical ailments, such as headaches, nausea, lack of appetite, sleeplessness, anxiety
- Exhibits depression-like symptoms, such as excessive crying, marked sadness, lethargy, fatigue
- Acts out with anger or belligerence
- Can't enjoy the experience or time with his friends because he longs to be back home

Although it's hard to predict just how a child will respond to being away from home, these factors put a child at greater risk for homesickness:

- Is younger, more immature, or anxious
- Has little experience being away from home
- Has low expectations for the experience; doesn't want to go to the sleepover or camp
- Feels forced to go to the sleepover, boarding school, or camp
- Is unsure whether adults will help him if he needs help
- Has had limited practice handling negative emotions or lacks coping skills
- Has parents who express a lot of anxiety or concern about his going away

THE SOLUTION

Step 1. Early Intervention

- *Be sure your kid is ready.* There is no magic age when your child is emotionally ready to be away from home—even if he begs to spend a few hours or the night away, he may not be ready. Here are some basic questions to ask so as to gauge whether he is ready to venture forth without you:

  Is your child sleeping in his own bed through the night, or is he climbing in with you at two o'clock in the morning?

  Does he have any problems separating from you when he goes to day care, the babysitter's, or school?

  Does your child get along with this kid well enough to spend a whole night together?

  Does he feel comfortable with the child's parents?

  Does he get along well enough with the other kids or feel secure enough with the parent to make it through what would be considered a twelve-hour playdate?

  Is this something he wants to do (or only what you hope he will do)? Just ask yourself that key question one more time and search for the honest answer.

Pay Attention to This!
When to Know Your Child Is Too Homesick

Research finds that about 90 percent of children attending summer camp feel *some* level of homesickness. Of those cases, 20 percent are severe, and about 7 percent—if untreated—will worsen over time and could lead to depression.[24] If you are concerned that your child sounds overly distressed or angry and belligerent, or if he is not eating or sleeping due to anxiety or depression, it is time to go home. Do talk to the counselor and get his perspective, but in the end rely on your own instinct. Nobody knows your child better than you do.

- *Create solutions for any concerns.* Research shows that if children have some control in preparing for the event, they feel more comfortable about going away.[25] So identify any questions or concerns your child may have and then encourage him to brainstorm a solution (with your help). Here are a few common problems and simple kid-generated solutions:

  Problem: Afraid of the dark. **Solution:** Pack a flashlight in his backpack.

  Problem: Won't like the food. **Solution:** Pack food you know he likes.

  Problem: Afraid of wetting the bed. **Solution:** Bring a sleeping bag with a rubber sheet tucked inside just in case he has an accident.

  Problem: Worried he can't reach you. **Solution:** Lend him a cell phone with your number plugged in on speed dial (or a calling card for camp for reassurance that he can call you anytime if really needed).

  A few packed items can make even the most anxious kid more comfortable. Think of what might make your child feel safer.

- *Show him where he's going.* For a sleepover, ideally the child should first have gone to the house on a playdate so he can "get the lay of the land" and feels comfortable with the parents. To prepare for a camp experience, give your child an online tour of the camp, show him the brochures, and talk up the cool features and things he'll get to do.

- *Keep any concerns to yourself.* Beware of sending any negative vibes to your child. If he hears you expressing some concern about whether this will work out, he will lose confidence. And don't ever bribe your child to stay. It only sends the wrong message.

- *Choose the camp or activity based on your child's strengths and temperament.* Forget what the neighbor's kid is going. Don't base your decisions on that glossy brochure that came through the mail. The best way to choose a camp is to match it to your child. Solicit his input. What are his interests? Can he spend that much time away from home? Does he need structure? What do you want him to gain from his camp experience? When in doubt, ask your child's teacher for her opinion. A teacher is well equipped to assess the fit between your child and the camp's program. Remember, the bottom line is that you want your child's camp experience to be fun and positive.

- *Meet the parents or camp leader.* No matter how old your child is, do meet the parents or camp counselor face-to-face. You want to be sure that parents will be supervising the whole night; be clear that if there are any problems you want to be called, and make sure they have your phone number handy.

- *Don't forgo medications.* If your child is on any medication—whether it be for asthma, hay fever, bedwetting, or ADHD—don't omit the dosage. Time away is not the time to alter his medication. Talk to the camp nurse or the parent; if your child doesn't want the other kids to know, then find a way to make a quick stop at the house to deliver the dosage.

- *Do a practice run.* Try a rehearsal away from home, such as an overnight a few times at a good friend's or a relative's. If you are sending your child to camp for an extended time, then the practice run should be at least two or three days with no telephone calls but only the opportunity to write a letter or e-mail home (just don't be instant messaging your kid back).

Step 2. Rapid Response

- *Have a positive send-off.* Be cheerful and optimistic as you pack and get ready to go. Go to the door, meet the parents, and wait until your child looks settled. Give him a big hug and kiss. Then leave. Don't linger.

- *Set a definite pickup time.* "I'll be at the door at ten o'clock sharp to pick you up tomorrow morning." "I'll be back in two weeks and waiting for you right here at eleven o'clock."

ONE SIMPLE SOLUTION

Six Questions to Help Your Kid Feel More Secure

Finding out the answers to these questions may help your child feel more comfortable, whether he's spending the night at someone's house or a few weeks away at camp. Knowing what to expect always boosts security and lowers the risk of homesickness.

1. *Time frame.* What date or time will I arrive, and when will I be leaving?
2. *Supplies.* What should I bring? Do I need any special clothing or my backpack?
3. *Other kids.* Who will be staying over with me? What adults will be there?
4. *Activities.* What will we be doing? Is there a plan?
5. *Eating.* What and when will we eat? Should I eat before I come?
6. *Special concerns.* Do you have any pets? Where does the dog sleep? Where will I sleep? Is anyone else a vegetarian? Do you say prayers before you eat? Is it okay if I don't shower?

- *Show him the activities.* Other than finding one buddy to "hang with," the next thing researchers say will alleviate homesickness is *involvement* in an activity (tennis, crafts, kayaking, swimming, beading—anything). If you can get your child excited about one activity, he will be more likely to feel a little more comfortable. And he'll have something to look forward to doing. If there is an upcoming swimming party—and your child can't swim—then this is the ideal time to tune up that skill a few weeks before the event.

- *Don't make a deal.* Beware: promising your child that if he "hates it" you'll be right there to pick him up actually decreases the likelihood that he will succeed in that time-away situation.[26] Doing so gives your child the impression that you don't have confidence in his ability to make it through the day (or week or month) and sets an initial mind-set that you'll bail him out.

- *Affirm the possibility of homesickness.* If your child says, "What if I want to come home?" or "Suppose I get homesick?" just simply acknowledge that that may be the case, and let him know that it's normal to feel homesick. A matter-of-fact statement is best: *"You probably will feel a little homesick, but those times you practiced have helped you know what to do in case any homesickness bothers you. Besides, the camp leaders (or parent or scout leader) will be there to talk to you and help you make it through."*

- *Beware of calling too often.* Studies show that always calling and even instant messaging your kid can increase homesickness during short camp stays away from home.[27] Old-fashioned letters and packages seem to be better ways to communicate.

- *Hold off making a quick decision.* If your child does call begging to come home, keep calm and listen. Avoid the temptation to take your kid home early. For a younger child, tell him you'll call back in an hour (give a specific length of time) to check in, then do keep your word. Talk to him privately to determine what he wants to do. You never know—he may have changed his mind. Then call the parent or the camp director (without your kid knowing) to get that person's take on things. If it sounds as though your child can pull through, don't feel guilty about making him stay. If your child is at camp, usually most incidents of homesickness will pass in a day or two.

- *Pick him up with a cheerful attitude.* So what if your kid doesn't make it all through the night or the whole camp period? If you want this to work in the long run, emphasize the positive accomplishment. *"You stayed there two hours past your bedtime. That was much longer than last time." "It's not a big deal. You'll have lots of opportunities to spend the night at friends' houses again."* Whatever you do, don't make a big deal out of the "spoiled evening" or "money down the drain." And don't plead for him to stay. Instead, just reassure him (and yourself) that there will be other times.

One Parent's Answer

A mom from Macon writes:

My child wanted so to go away to camp, but worried that he wouldn't have any friends. So I called the camp director and asked her to give me the name of a same-age child and contact information. The two boys started e-mailing and then phoning one another. By the time camp started, they already were best friends.

Step 3. Develop Habits for Change

Here are a few research-proven skills parents can teach their children *before* they leave that will better prepare them to cope with their time away, as well as reduce homesickness:[28]

- *Learn to occupy time alone.* Help him find ways to entertain himself (for example, reading, drawing, doing a jigsaw or crossword puzzle, playing Solitaire) so that he can fill up "alone time." Then suggest he tuck that activity away in a backpack just in case homesick feelings crop up.

- *Think positively.* Encourage him to "always look at the bright side of life" (such as his friends, activities, or upcoming events) to help him feel better.

- *Mark off time.* Teach your child to use a wall calendar to mark off the days or to tell time so he can see that the hours until he sees you are clicking away. Doing so helps kids keep the perspective that the separation isn't an eternity.

- *Teach conversation openers.* Help your child rehearse a few icebreakers, such as "I have some CDs you might like" or "Do you want to go swimming later?" Research finds that if kids feel alienated, they are more liked to get homesick.

- *Practice correspondence skills.* Teach your child how to dial your phone number or make a collect call through the operator or on a calling card, use the Internet to send an e-mail home, or write and address a letter.

- *Learn positive self-talk.* Teach your child one comment he can learn to say inside his head to help him "talk away" any feelings of homesickness: *"I can get through this." "It's only a few more days!" "I can do this."*

WHAT TO EXPECT BY STAGES AND AGES

Preschooler   These are the ages when kids are most at risk for homesickness. Separation or losing a parent as well as fear of darkness are prime fears, so most experts agree that preschoolers are not ready to spend even a night away from home unless it's at Grandma's.

School Age Six is the earliest age for spending the night (but only if the child knows the other kid very well). Seven is the age when most mothers feel kids are ready.[29] Eight years of age is the usual time for first sleepover invites and when camp directors feel that children are ready for overnight camp. A top reason for severe homesickness at camp for kids this age is "not knowing or liking the other kids."[30] Bedwetting, fear of darkness, a dog, or a yelling parent can cause kids to beg to come home even after all the pleading to go away. Be clear about your policy on movie ratings, violent video games, and guns in the home.

Tween Don't assume tweens are "too old" to be homesick—even college kids and adults can have severe bouts of homesickness. Slumber parties become common, so be clear about your rules, especially those regarding moving ratings, unsupervised time on the computer, and "sneaking out" at night. Peer pressure peaks, and dares to experiment are common (especially with alcohol and cigarettes). Beware: a child's first alcoholic drink is usually taken in his home or at the home of a friend!

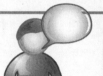

More Helpful Advice

Slumber Parties: What Do I Do? by Wilhelminia Ripple, Kathryn Totten, Heather Anderson, and Dianne Lorang

Homesick Blues, Here's What to Do (American Girl Backpack Books), by Pleasant Company

Homesick (We Can Read!), by Jacqueline Sweeney

Ira Sleeps Over, by Bernard Waber (ages 4 to 7)

Slumber Parties, by Penny Warner (ages 9 to 12)

The Summer Camp Handbook: Everything You Need to Find, Choose and Get Ready for Overnight Camp—and Skip the Homesickness, by Christopher A. Thurber and Jon C. Malinowski

Super Slumber Parties (American Girl Library), by Brooks Whitney and Nadine Bernard (ages 9 to 12)

The Sleepover Book, by Margot Griffin and Jane Kurisu (ages 9 to 12)

Perfectionist

SEE ALSO: *Angry, Depressed, Eating Disorders, Gives Up, Homework, Oldest Child, Perseverance, Procrastinates, Stressed, Test Anxiety*

THE PROBLEM

Red Flags

Never seems to feel "good enough" about his work, appearance, or performance; can't stand accepting second place; is intensely competitive to the point of its being unhealthy; self-esteem tied to grades, scores, and achievement

The Change to Parent For

Your child learns to cope with adversity, is less afraid to try new endeavors, and develops a healthier view of achievement.

Question: "My ten-year-old is second in her class, and it makes her nuts. She stayed up until one in the morning last night memorizing state capitals. I worry that if she keeps up this pace she'll have a nervous breakdown. What should I do?"

Answer: First applaud her effort for trying to do her best. But set a limit on how late she can work. Explain that nothing horrid will happen if she isn't always the best at everything. Most important, tell her again that you love her for who she is.

Why Change?

Of course we want our children to reach their potential and to excel. But often a child feels so much pressure that she becomes obsessed to an unhealthy degree with doing everything perfectly, leaving her feeling anxious, frustrated, and worried most of the time. "Will it be enough?" "What will others think?" And because these kids are never satisfied and always pushing themselves, frustration and heightened stress put them at serious risk for anxiety, depression, eating disorders, migraines, and even suicide. Perfectionists are more at risk for emotional, physical, and relational problems.[31] This isn't just a big-kid problem. Even preschoolers are beginning to exhibit perfectionist behavior.

ONE SIMPLE SOLUTION

Of course always taking the quest for perfection to an extreme can take a toll on a child's emotional health as well as disrupt her life. So pay closer attention and seek the help of a mental health professional if you notice any of these reoccurring and debilitating behaviors:

Eating disorder: The child's concern about having the "perfect" body leads to an unhealthy preoccupation with food and eating, including self-induced starvation (anorexia nervosa), obsessive-compulsive eating, bulimia, and restrictive eating.[32]

Depression: The child's concern about achieving and being perfect are so extreme that she has difficulty eating, sleeping, and concentrating, and may begin to withdraw; the child appears apathetic, is excessively irritable and sad, and may have suicidal thoughts.[33]

Signs and Symptoms

Here are a few common signs of children who are perfectionists:

- *Is intensely competitive:* is always comparing herself to others; can't stand coming in second place or doing worse than others; wants to be the best, and anything less is not good enough

- *Suffers physical stress ailments:* experiences migraines or headaches, stomachaches, trouble sleeping, or other physical ailments before, after, or during a performance

- *Is unwilling to risk:* is too cautious about trying something new that may be outside her area of expertise and that may mean she won't excel

- *Is quick to anger:* has tantrums, is easily frustrated, becomes angry when she errs or falls short of expectations

- *May put others down:* is motivated by the effort to be her best and make the other person feel less perfect—or inadequate

- *May expect perfection from others:* may put the same high standards on others

- *May avoid or procrastinate:* worries that what she's done won't be good enough, or fears failure; avoids difficult or stressful tasks; leaves work unfinished out of fear it won't be perfect

- *Focuses on mistakes:* concentrates on the mistake instead of the overall job or how well she performed

- *Takes life too seriously:* is way too hard on herself; can't laugh at herself or her own mistakes

- *Is inflexible:* approaches tasks with an "all-or-nothing" attitude; there is only one right way

- *Is afraid to ask for help:* doesn't want to admit she doesn't understand; feels that asking for help will be perceived by others as weakness or failure

THE SOLUTION

Step 1. Early Intervention

- *Figure out the reason.* The more you can get into your child's shoes and figure out what's fueling her quest for perfection, the better you can head off the problem before it becomes overwhelming. Here are common reasons kids push themselves to be perfect. Check those that may apply to your child:

  ☐ *Temperament:* has inborn tendency and temperament you've recognized from your child's toddler days

  ☐ *Insecurity:* lacks confidence; has strong feelings of inadequacy

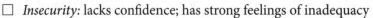

LATE-BREAKING NEWS

University of British Columbia: Professor Paul Hewitt found that although all perfectionists hold unrealistically high standards for themselves and others, they differ in how they show their perfectionism.[34] Here are the three kinds of perfectionists:

1. *The self-promoter.* Always attempts to impress others by bragging or showing off her perfection. This one is easy to spot because a self-promoter can annoy others and be a real turnoff.

2. *The shunner.* This child fears failing (and being less than perfect), so she avoids situations or events in which she may be less than perfect. (She doesn't feel she could be the star soccer player, so she avoids the sport; she worries she could never be as perfect a violin player as her friend, so she takes up cello.) This is common with younger children.

3. *The quiet sufferer.* This child keeps her problems to herself. She can't admit failure to others. She would never ask for help because it means she may not be good enough.

- ☐ *Fear of humiliation:* is afraid of being laughed at or made fun of by others; is easily embarrassed
- ☐ *Poor modeling:* copies the perfectionist behaviors of a sibling or parent
- ☐ *Overemphasis on performance:* experiences excessive demands for achievement from teacher or parent; has unrealistic goals
- ☐ *Fear of losing approval or respect.*
- ☐ *Status as a trophy child:* achievements and talents always on display

- *Help her get a reality check.* Show your child the advantages and disadvantages of being a perfectionist. Specify things your child can and cannot control. Redefine success not as perfection but as excellence.

- *Look within.* Are you a perfectionist? Go back over the list of perfectionist symptoms. How many of those apply to you? Beware: research shows that moms who are perfectionists or who base their self-esteem on their kids' achievement are more likely to have perfectionist kids.[35]

- *Get real about her abilities.* Don't try to turn your child into the "Superkid Perfect-in-Everything." Instead, be more practical about your child abilities and be honest with her. Start assessing and refining her natural strengths—her singing ability, artistic flair, or creative nature. Then monitor, encourage, and strengthen those traits and skills so that she doesn't try to push herself so hard in too many areas but instead narrows her focus and has a more realistic assessment of her talents.

Step 2. Rapid Response

- *Lighten your child's load.* Check her schedule: Is there any time for just downtime or play? Are there any activities that can be eliminated or reduced?

- *Teach her to be her own "timekeeper."* If she works hours on her writing but actually does a great job the first time through, set a time limit on how long she can work on a particular activity.

ONE SIMPLE SOLUTION

Stress Effort Rather Than Outcome

- Switch from praising the end product (the grade or goal) to acknowledging your child's effort along the way. "You put a lot of work into this."

- Acknowledge courage. "That was brave of you to try something you weren't sure of. Good for you."

- Praise attributes other than achievement. "Good for you. You took turns with your playmates."

- *Make sure there's time for fun.* Encourage laughter and just sitting outside every once in a while and watching the clouds drift by. Teach your child she can always go back and finish up an activity, but give her permission to just plain enjoy life.

- *Teach stress busters.* Show your child a few simple relaxation strategies, such as taking slow, deep breaths; listening to soothing music; walking; or just taking ten and lying on the couch, to help improve her frame of mind and reduce a bit of that intensity—at least for a few minutes.

- *Halt the "parading."* I know you're proud, but stop putting your kid on center stage to always perform. It's all right on the soccer field or in a musical concert, but lower the curtains in your home. Do you reinforce her professions of greatness by agreeing with her? Do you encourage her by reminding her of other talents she's overlooked? Are you cheering her "know-it-all" attitude because you feel it is the sign of high self-esteem?

- *Help your child handle disappointment.* The inner dialogue of a perfectionist is self-defeating: "I'm never good enough." "I knew I'd blow it." So help your child reframe her self-talk by teaching her to say a more positive phrase that's less critical and judgmental and more based in reality, such as "Nobody is perfect." "All I can do is try my best." "I'll try again next time." "Believing in myself will help me relax."

One Parent's Answer

A mom from Kansas City writes:

My eldest daughter is such a perfectionist. She'd spend hours working on schoolwork or anything else to ensure it was absolutely flawless. I couldn't figure out why she felt the need to do everything to such an extreme when she pointed out to me that I do the exact same thing. And she was right! At that moment I realized what a poor example I was, always doing everything over and correcting her and basically sending the message, "You're not good enough." It was at that moment I vowed to lighten things up in our household and take time to have more fun. It's been a much harder task than I ever thought, and I know my daughter and I will always be overachiever, type-A personalities, but at least my daughter and I are learning to laugh more and not take things so hard—and the two of us get along better as well.

Step 3. Develop Habits for Change

- *Use children's literature.* There are wonderful children's books you can use as conversation starters about the dangers of perfectionism, such as *I'm Perfick!* by Bernard Waber; *Persnickity,* by Steven Cosgrove, *Will the Real Gertrude Hollings Please Stand Up?* by S. Greenwalk; *Be a Perfect Person in Just Three Days,* by Stephen Manes; *Dreams and Drummers,* by D. B. Smith; *What to Do When Good Isn't Good Enough: The Real Deal on Perfectionism: A Guide for Kids,* by Thomas S. Greenspon.

- *Use a family mantra.* One way to help your child realize that mistakes don't have to be seen as failures is to come up with a phrase to use as your family mantra. Here are a few favorites: "A mistake is a chance to start again." "Whether you think you can or think you can't, you're right" (Henry Ford). "You'll never make it unless you try." Then pick one phrase and say it again and again. You might even print out a computer-made sign and hang it on your refrigerator.

- *Teach taking a reality check.* Perfectionistic kids imagine something horrid will happen if they hit the wrong note, don't stick the gymnastics move, don't make the standard they've set for themselves. Your role is to challenge their views so that they don't think in such all-or-nothing, black-or-white terms. Help them dispute their belief.

  Kid: "Nobody who ever got a B got into college." You: "What about your cousin Kevin, who even had a few C's?"

  Kid: "I'll lose cleanup spot in the batting order if I strike out." You: "What about Babe Ruth? The year he hit the most home runs was the same year he made the most strikeouts."

  Kid: "I know the moment I pick up my pencil I'm going to forget everything I studied all year." You: "That's never happened in your entire life. Why now?"

WHAT TO EXPECT BY STAGES AND AGES

Preschooler   Children as young as four and five are sometimes perfectionists, most noticeably when they first enter kindergarten, as they take on more responsibilities and worry about meeting the challenges.

School Age   Intellectual and emotional skills expand, so kids are more aware of their shortcomings and can be very hard on themselves. Watch out for their setting unattainable goals. School-age kids can be hesitant to try new skills or games, fearing they won't

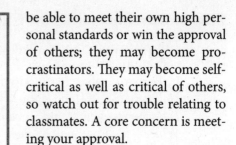

More Helpful Advice

Being Perfect, by Anna Quindlin

Freeing Our Families from Perfectionism, by Thomas S. Greenspon

Perfectionism: What's Bad About Being Too Good? by Miriam Adderholdt and Jan Goldberg

When Perfect Isn't Good Enough: Strategies for Coping with Perfectionism, by Martin M. Antony and Richard P. Swinson

For Kids

Picture Perfect: What You Need to Feel Better About Your Body, by Jill S. Zimmerman Rutledge

Too Perfect, by Trudy Ludwig (the "perfect" read-aloud for your school-age daughter)

What to Do When Good Enough Isn't Good Enough: A Guide for Kids, by Thomas S. Greenspon

be able to meet their own high personal standards or win the approval of others; they may become procrastinators. They may become self-critical as well as critical of others, so watch out for trouble relating to classmates. A core concern is meeting your approval.

Tween   Tweens become more concerned about fitting in and about their appearance and weight. Watch out for anorexia and bulimia. (See *Eating Disorders,* p. 498.) Girls very often are perfectionistic about their body image. Stress builds as homework dramatically increases.

Pessimistic

SEE ALSO: *Depressed, Fearful, Perfectionist, Stressed, Worried About the World*

THE PROBLEM

Red Flags

Sees only the negative side, expects the worst to happen in most events, looks for the bad in a bleak situation, has a "Why bother?" attitude, assumes failure without proof

The Change to Parent For

Your child learns to tune in to his pessimistic views, counter them with a more positive outlook, and cope with everyday events with more optimistic beliefs.

Why Change?

"What's the point of trying? I'll never make the team." "It isn't worth the effort, I'm just going to flunk the test." "Why should I bother?" Heard any of these from your offspring lately? If so, you may be dealing with a pessimistic kid, and beware. Pessimistic children can be

LATE-BREAKING NEWS

Penn State University: Research by Martin Seligman, former president of the American Psychological Association, found that helping kids become more optimistic and less cynical not only helps protect them from depression but also helps them to be less frequently depressed, more successful at school and on the job, better able to bounce back from adversity, and even physically healthier.[36] Seligman's work also found that optimism can be nurtured and pessimism can be reduced. And there is a critical reason to do so: a child born today is ten times more likely to be seriously depressed compared to a child born in the first third of this century. So how are you squelching pessimism in your kid? For more information, read Martin Seligman's wonderful book *The Optimistic Child: A Revolutionary Program That Safeguards Children Against Depression and Builds Lifelong Resilience.*

One Parent's Answer

A mom from Scottsdale shares:

My daughter was always positive, so when she suddenly became so negative about the world we were floored. We couldn't figure out where she was getting such a dismal view until one day we noticed her glued to the cable news stations. We'd encouraged her to watch the news to boost her knowledge of current events, but instead all those reports about war, global warming, and financial hard times were bumming her out. Once we prohibited her from watching, her sunnier disposition came back.

a frustrating breed. No matter what the experience, they have a preset "What's the point?" attitude. But the bigger problem is that their negative outlook can dramatically influence every arena in their world. They can give up easily, believe that nothing they do will make a difference, and assume they won't succeed. Then when they do achieve or do something well, they discount the accomplishment: "It wasn't that great." "It was just luck." Sadly, they rarely see the wonderful parts of life but dwell instead on the negative or bad, often including themselves. They are also often quick to find their own inadequacies: "I'm so dumb; why study?" "Nobody's going to like me; why bother?" "I'm not trying out. Who would pick me for their team?" If left unchecked, a pessimistic attitude can spiral into cynicism and criticism, and plant the seeds of underachievement and even depression.

Take heart: longitudinal studies at Penn State University find that parents can enhance their children's life outlook and even change their pessimistic views.[37] Helping your child make this change can have a huge impact on his potential for happiness. This entry offers proven solutions that help your child become more optimistic and hopeful about life.

THE SOLUTION

Seven Strategies for Change

1. *Check your attitude!* Kids aren't born pessimistic, so where is your kid acquiring this attitude? From siblings? Friends? Neighbors? Relatives? Here are a few questions to help you consider if you are more optimistic or pessimistic in the way you handle those everyday events and if perhaps *you* just might be the source:

   A tragic world event is flashed on TV: Do you say that there may well be a catastrophic outcome, or express your view that world leaders will be able to solve it?

   You're dealt a big financial setback: Do you express your concerns that you will suffer severe losses that you might never recoup, or offer encouragement that you'll be able to make ends meet?

   You and your best friend have a tiff: Do you blame your friend for causing the friction, or convey that the two of you will work things through and remain friends?

Your kid has a bad report card: Do you tell her not to worry because women in your family were never good in math, or brainstorm a plan to help improve her grade because you know she's capable?

An elderly friend is seriously ill: Do you express your concern that your friend may never recover, or state your belief that she'll improve because of her tough spirit and the excellent medical care she is receiving?

Make sure your responses to life events are ones you want your child to copy. Try to help your kids associate with people with more optimistic outlooks. Kids do pick up our attitudes.

2. *Look for the positive.* Start emphasizing a more optimistic outlook in your home so that your kid sees the good parts of life instead of the downside. Here are a few ways to look for the positive as a family:

   - *Monitor what your kid watches and reads.* A constant onslaught of gloomy news can have an impact on a kid's outlook. Tune in to those uplifting documentaries and inspiring movies. Focus on the good news happening in the world and share it with your kids.

   - *Start "Good News" reports.* Consider starting your dinner with a Good News Report in which each family member reports something positive that happened during the day. Cut out actual news stories from the paper and share them with your kids. Or institute a nighttime tradition of reviewing with your child the good parts about his day, sharing your highlights as well. Doing so is a precious way to spend the last waking hours with your kid, as well as to instill the habit of looking for the good in life.

   - *Share optimistic stories.* Look for examples of individuals who suffered enormous obstacles but didn't cave into pessimistic thinking and kept at their dreams. Share them with your kids. Here are a few: Beethoven's music teacher told him he was hopeless as a composer; Michael Jordan was cut from his high school basketball team; Walt Disney went bankrupt and had nervous breakdowns; Louisa May Alcott was rejected by countless publishers who told her no one would ever read *Little Women*.

3. *Confront pessimistic thinking.* Many kids don't change their pessimistic ways because they are unaware of how often they are pessimistic. Psychologists teach clients to track their cynical thoughts using tokens, such as marbles or poker chips. They instruct them to put the tokens in their left pocket and then transfer a token to the right pocket for each negative comment stated either inside or outside their heads. That way the clients now have evidence of how often they are pessimistic and are more receptive to changing. Here are ways to help your kid tune in to his more pessimistic, cynical thoughts and learn to confront them.

- *Point out cynicism.* Create a code—such as pulling on your ear or touching your elbow—that only you and your kid know. The code means he's uttered a cynical comment.

- *Confront "stinkin' thinking."* Teach your kid to "talk back to the pessimistic voice" so that he learns not to listen to it. One way to do so is to use yourself as an example (and feel free to fictionalize, just as long as your child gets the point). "I remember when I was your age. Right before I'd take a test, a voice inside me would say, 'You're not going to do well.' I learned to talk back to it. I'd tell it: 'I'm going to try my best. If I try my best, I'll do okay.' Pretty soon the voice faded away because I refused to listen to it. When you hear that voice, talk to it and say it's wrong." Tamar Chansky's book *Freeing Your Child from Negative Thinking* is a must-read for parents and offers a wealth of strategies to build children's resilience.

4. *Balance their pessimistic view.* Cynical kids can get trapped in pessimistic thinking patterns, seeing only the downside and blowing things way out of proportion so that they miss the upside. So provide your kid with a more balanced perspective to help him learn to counter his own inner pessimistic talk. Suppose your son won't go to a friend's birthday because he thinks no one likes him. *Offer a more balanced view:* "If Sunny didn't like you, you'd never have been invited." Suppose your oldest blows his math exam and says he can never do anything right. *Counter his comment:* "I see how upset you are, but nobody can be good at everything. You're good in history and art. Meanwhile, let's figure out a way to help improve your math."

5. *Encourage positive speculation.* Pessimistic kids often think of the gloomy outcome and "bad possibilities" in any situation such that they can greatly shortchange their potential for success. Try these ways to help your kid think through the possible outcomes so that he's more likely to have a realistic appraisal before making a decision. Ask "What if?" questions. "What might happen if you tried that?" "What might happen if you didn't try?"

   - *Weigh the pros and cons.* "What are all the good things that might happen if you choose that? What are the bad things? Now weigh the good with the bad." "Are there more good or bad outcomes?"

   - *Name the worst thing.* Ask, "What is the absolute worst thing that could happen?" Then help him determine if the outcome really is all that bad, as well as come up with ways to deal with it.

6. *Acknowledge optimistic thinking.* Change is always difficult—especially when you are trying to alter an attitude that is an engrained habit. So be on the alert for those times when your child does utter optimistic statements. If you're not looking for the behavior, you may well miss those moments when your child is trying a new approach. So whenever you do hear optimism, acknowledge it. Just be sure to remind your child of what he said that was optimistic and why you appreciate the comment: "*I know how difficult your math tests have been. But saying you think*

Pay Attention to This!

If your child's pessimistic outlook is a sudden change from his otherwise more optimistic nature, then take a closer look at what could be the cause. The following are some possibilities:

- **Medication.** Certain medications—both over-the-counter and prescription drugs—can bring on depression-like symptoms. Review with your pharmacist and doctor the side effects of any medication your child may be currently taking. Also check to make sure your prescriptions aren't being "borrowed" by your child or his friends.

- **Substance abuse.** For your older child, substance abuse, cold and cough syrup addiction, or steroids can also contribute to pessimism. Don't overlook this as a possibility.

- **Traumatic event.** Did a particular traumatic event (such as an accident, death of a loved one, fire, flood, parent's military deployment) beget this new life view? If so, seek the help of a counselor to ensure that your child's pessimism is not caused by posttraumatic stress or grief.

- **Health or emotional issue.** Pessimism can be a sign of more serious issues, such as physical health problems, anxiety, low self-esteem, trauma, or depression. If you think any of these more deeply engrained issues could be the cause, seek help from a trained professional.

Hint: if there is a recurring pattern in your child's pessimism, play detective. For instance, is he always gloomier on the first weekend of the month when he visits his elderly grandparents? Or on Mondays when he has a history test?

you'll do better was being so optimistic. I'm sure you'll do better because you've been studying so hard." "Son, it pleases me that you said you'll try your best to tie your shoes by yourself. Way to be positive!"

7. *Take a reality check.* If you've tried all these techniques and your child's pessimism continues, then there are two more options to consider. First, could your child's negative complaints be legitimate? For instance, is he really doomed to flunk that test because the class is too accelerated? Will he strike out because he really doesn't have the abilities or coordination for Little League? Do the other kids make fun of him because he really does act weird or dress too "geeky"? If so, it's time to check your expectations and make sure they are realistic for your child. Put him in a less advanced math class and get him a tutor, drop Little League so that he can take the karate class he really wanted to take, enroll him in a class that builds social skills. Second, please make sure that your child's pessimism is not really depression or deep-seated anger. If it is, please get him the help he needs with a trained mental health professional.

Sensitive

SEE ALSO: *Bullied, Cyberbullying, Fearful, Rejected, Shy, Stressed, Teased*

THE PROBLEM

Red Flags

Is thin skinned, overreactive, easily frustrated, prone to outbursts and tantrums; misinterprets other people's words and reactions; cries easily; has difficulty making needs known; experiences quickly changing moods

The Change to Parent For

Your child develops ways to control her strong feelings so that she is not so quick to react.

Question: "The other kids call my son 'Crybaby' because any little thing sets him off. Is there anything I can do to help him so he isn't quite so thin skinned?"

Answer: The most important things you can do for an overly sensitive child is first to accept his natural temperament and then help him learn *how* to control his reactions. One way to do so is by capitalizing on your child's strength: the ability to be highly tuned to other people's feelings. So teach him a skill that utilizes his natural gift of empathy. "As soon as you start to feel upset or think you're going to cry, ask yourself what you think the other person is feeling. Think so hard that you can almost feel where they're coming from." That simple "think of the other person" replacement technique helps kids channel their strong feelings more constructively and even recognize that they may have overreacted or misinterpreted where the other person is coming from. The technique may take a lot of practice to become a habit, but often helps overly sensitive kids use those emotions to their benefit.

Why Change?

Does your child worry endlessly about what her friends think of her, and take friendly teasing far too hard? Does watching a sad movie or reading a distressing book cause your kid anguish? Are you finding yourself thinking carefully before you speak to your kid because one wrong comment can cause an all-night tirade? Does your child appear "fine" one minute and then moody and irritable the next? Would you label your kid "high maintenance": fussy, picky, with a lot of highs and lows? If so, you have a sensitive critter on your hands, and you're not alone. Research says that about 15 to 20 percent of kids are highly sensitive.[38]

Most parents would tell you that sensitive kids usually arrive that way. By nature these children seem more "touchy" from birth: they're more sensitive to sound and change, become teary-eyed easily, and take criticism far too seriously. Although those traits can be highly desirable (after all, the world certainly needs more compassionate people), being overly sensitive can cause problems at home, in school, and in life. And the biggest reason is that sensitive kids don't know how to respond to put-downs, teasing, and critical comments. Instead of shrugging them off, they take the jabs with too much emotion and drama. That turns the other kids off big-time, so oversensitivity is a frequent cause of peer problems.

Sure, you can't change your naturally sensitive child into a little thick-skinned toughie. And you shouldn't: your kid's sensitive nature is an asset, so you'll want to help her see it positively. Besides, your role isn't to change your child's natural personality, but to help her cope more successfully and learn to control *how* she responds. Doing so can make a huge difference in helping your tenderhearted child survive in a not-so-sensitive world.

Signs and Symptoms

Here are signs of oversensitivity derived from Dr. Elaine N. Aron's research.[39] Check ones that apply to your child:

- ☐ Startles easily
- ☐ Notices the slightest unusual odor
- ☐ Seems very intuitive
- ☐ Doesn't do well with big changes
- ☐ Notices and is upset by the distress of others
- ☐ Prefers quiet play
- ☐ Asks deep, thought-provoking questions
- ☐ Notices subtleties (something that's been moved, a change in a person's appearance, and so on)
- ☐ Feels things deeply

If you checked off several of the signs, your child is probably highly sensitive. If only one or two questions are true of your child, but they are "extremely" true, you might also be justified in calling your child highly sensitive.

THE SOLUTION

Step 1. Early Intervention

- *Respect your child's nature.* Your child's natural temperament is probably more high strung and intuitive. This isn't about changing her nature (you can't), but it is about helping your child recognize her personality and letting her know you're not trying to change that side of her. *"You are a sensitive and caring kid. You'll always be a wonderful friend and make the world a better place. Sometimes your strong feelings can get in the way with your relationships. So let's help you learn to turn down those feelings so kids won't be as likely to pick on you."*

- *Identify other possibilities.* Yes, a naturally more emotional temperament is usually the reason kids are highly sensitive. But there are other reasons for kids to be overly sensitive. Would any of these reasons be causing your child to be overly sensitive? Check those that apply to your child:

  - ☐ Lacks self-esteem or self-confidence
  - ☐ Is experiencing home-front issues (recent move, family friction, a potential divorce, military deployment, financial stress, family's reputation)
  - ☐ Was raised to be "so nice," and now has trouble dealing with the cruel world
  - ☐ Is overtired, physically ill, depressed, or under a lot of stress
  - ☐ Has a disability or is "different" (speech impediment, physical illness, learning disability)
  - ☐ Has new braces, glasses, freckles, large ears, acne, weight issues, unusual height, unusual dress style
  - ☐ Is made the butt of kids' jokes because she doesn't "fit in"
  - ☐ Has been rescued or babied; depends on you for rescue
  - ☐ Is experiencing mood swings brought on by puberty and hormones

☐ Has had limited social experiences; not used to "normal" teasing

☐ Is encountering repeated verbal abuse, bullying, or physical abuse

- *Identify the "right fit."* What works best to help your child so that she's not quite so sensitive or moody? Playing in a smaller group? Limiting stimulation, such as noise or lights? Talking in a lower voice? Sticking to a routine? Giving transition time? Explaining your emotions? Watch your child carefully over the next week and log what helps your child handle life more successfully. Then stick to those parameters whenever possible.

- *Empower your child.* Stress to your child that she has control over how she chooses to react to another child. *"You can't control what another person says or does, but you can control how you respond." "You may not be able to stop that kid from being so mean, but if you practice, you can learn not to cry when he calls you names."* Be mindful that you're not allowing your child to depend on you to bail her out or stick up for her. It's important for her to recognize that she has control over situations and can't always rely on you.

- *"Turn down" strong feelings.* If your child doesn't learn to "turn down" or "switch off" her always-on upset facial gestures, she'll never convince the other kids that she's not headed for a meltdown. So help her learn ways to turn down those emotions and switch to a more neutral expression. Try modeling or discovering together a different expression to substitute whenever appropriate, such as smiling or looking surprised or puzzled, so it's harder for her friends to tell what she's feeling.

- *Watch labels.* Highly sensitive kids are often stereotyped as problem children or as overly inhibited, fearful, or fussy. So don't let teachers, family, or friends label your child and don't do so yourself.

Pay Attention to This!
Could Your Child Have a Sensory Processing Disorder?

Some children have difficulties in the area of sensory integration and may be highly sensitized to any sort of sensory stimulation. It can lead to behavioral problems and other issues. If you think this may be your child, check out the list of symptoms of Sensory Processing Disorder at http://www.sensory-processing-disorder.com/sensory-processing-disorder-checklist.html, or read *Sensational Kids: Hope and Help for Children with Sensory Processing Disorder,* by Lucy Jane Miller; *The Out-of-Sync Child,* by Carol Stock Kranowit, or *Raising a Sensory Smart Child: The Definitive Handbook for Helping Your Child with Sensory Integration Issues,* by Lindsey Biel.

Step 2. Rapid Response

- *Don't say "Toughen up."* Overly sensitive kids can't toughen up. They really don't want to get so teary-eyed and to be so hypersensitive: it's usually part of their personality. So refrain from saying such things as "Don't be such a baby," "Cut it out; the kids are going to call you a sissy," "Boys don't cry," or "You're too old to act like that."

- *Turn it into an advantage.* Yes, your child is oversensitive, but the flip side is that she is also highly in tune with people's feelings. Stress the value of her temperament so that she recognizes the power of her highly tuned emotional nature and how it can become a valuable tool. Sensitive children can develop a deep sense of compassion, empathy, and emotional intelligence. *"I don't want you ever to stop being such a caring person. That's one of the your greatest gifts. But you can learn how to make your face not look so upset."*

- *Don't overprotect!* It's tough when our children are upset, but be careful so as not to always rescue your child from those emotional hardships. Doing so will only make her depend on you, and she'll be less likely to make it on her own.

- *Teach how to use a firm voice.* Whimpering, crying, whining, sniveling, sobbing, whispering, and quivering voice tones are kid turnoffs. So tell your child before she talks to clear her throat and think "firm and strong" (more Rambo, less Tinkerbell). She'll probably need help distinguishing between firm and whiny voice tones, so role-play various tones and have her practice different voices until she can speak with a stronger, more confident voice.

Step 3. Develop Habits for Change

- *Keep to a routine.* A sensitive kid has trouble with change and transition, so planning ahead, preparing your child for what to expect, and keeping things on a regular and calmer schedule are often helpful.

One Parent's Answer

A mom from Carson City writes:

Any little tease or criticism and my son would tear up, and then we happened to watch a super hero cartoon. Jacob came up with the idea that if he wore a make believe armored vest like the cartoon character it might help. Any tease would bounce right off and never get to him. And the strategy seemed to work. When the kids teased him he just pulled out his magic vest in his mind, wrapped himself in it, and those "mean words" just bounced right off of him.

LATE-BREAKING NEWS

San Diego State University: A study by Robert McGivern shows that tweens eleven to twelve years of age have a difficult time reading emotions correctly and may think you are upset when you are not.[40] At this age, there is a normal and natural increase in nerve activity in the brain's prefrontal cortex (where experience and perceptions are weighed). So it may be helpful if you state your emotion to your child: "You may think I'm ticked off, but I'm really tired." "I know you think I'm angry with you, but I just had a tough day at work, and that's why my face looks stressed."

- *Watch out for overstimulation.* Big groups, lack of sleep, stressful schedules, crowded carpools, noisy classrooms, and hyped-up parties can be tough for a sensitive kid. Tone down what you can and keep things on a more even keel.

- *Do a "Feeling Watch."* At the mall, park, grocery store, or parking lot point out "upset" and "calm" facial expressions of others. "Do you see that little girl over there? Do you think she looks upset or calm? How can you tell?" Use photographs from newspapers, picture books, or magazines to help your child recognize different facial expressions. You might also take photos of your child with different expressions (calm and upset) so she can see the difference in the look on herself.

- *Help her adopt a "relaxed" neutral expression.* In their book *Teaching Your Child the Language of Social Success,* Marshall Duke, Elisabeth Martin, and Stephen Nowicki suggest taking a photograph of your child using facial expression that conveys little emotion.[41] (You may have to catch her unaware while she's watching television or reading a book.) Then take a photo of her when she's in the throes of some heightened emotion. Put the two photos together and help her study the expressions, then ask: "Which face would make your friends less likely to pick on you?" "Which one will make them more apt to tease you?" Once your child identifies that the "right" expression looks less sensitive, help her practice achieving that more neutral look.

- *Suggest replacers.* If your child becomes teary easily, she'll need to learn what to do instead of crying. Talk about possible suggestions and then have your child choose the one she likes best. *"Think of a really fun place inside your head, and make your mind go there." "Walk away really quickly." "Clear your throat and bite your tongue." "Count to 10 inside your head." "Hum a song (only inside your head)." "Take a long, slow breath."* In order for the "crying replacement" to become a habit, she'll have to practice it again and again.

More Helpful Advice

Raising Your Spirited Child: A Guide for Parents Whose Child Is More Intense, Sensitive, Perceptive, Persistent, Energetic, by Mary Sheedy Kurchinka

The Challenging Child: Understanding, Raising, and Enjoying the Five "Difficult" Types of Children, by Stanley I. Greenspan

The Highly Sensitive Child: Helping Our Children Thrive When the World Overwhelms Them, by Elaine Aron

The Sensory-Sensitive Child: Practical Solutions for Out-of-Bounds Behavior, by Lucy Jane Miller and Sharon A. Cermak

Too Loud, Too Bright, Too Fast, Too Tight: What to Do If You Are Sensory Defensive in an Overstimulating World, by Sharon Heller

The Out-of-Sync Child: Recognizing and Coping with Sensory Integration Dysfunction, by Carol Stock Krantrowitz and Larry B. Silver

WHAT TO EXPECT BY STAGES AND AGES

Preschooler   Shyer, more anxious children as well as those who have not had many social experiences can be particularly sensitive to criticism and peer rejection.

School Age   Kids compare their appearance and athletic and intellectual abilities to those of their friends and are most sensitive to peer reactions in the fourth and fifth grades.[42] Surveys of six- to eleven-year-olds in six countries showed that the number one concern to kids (next to losing the security of their family) is losing face among friends. Rejection and losing publicly can cause overreaction and emotional distress.

Tween   Hormones are starting to kick in, so your moody kid may just get moodier. Being the butt of gossip and rejection and being laughed at cause big-time distress and are guaranteed to bring on heightened feelings of sensitivity.[43] (See also the Late Breaking News box for this entry.)

Shy

SEE ALSO: *Rejected, Sensitive, Stressed, Teased*

THE PROBLEM

Red Flags

Avoids other kids; is clingy and dependent, uncomfortable or nervous, anxious away from home; refuses to participate

The Change to Parent For

Your child learns to recognize his anxiety signs and develops coping strategies that help him learn to feel more comfortable and confident in social settings.

Question: "My daughter is shy and has been so since she was a toddler. I know I can't change her temperament, but is there something I can do to help her feel more comfortable around other kids so she doesn't miss out on so much fun?"

Answer: Shyer children are by nature more hesitant and anxious. Although you can't change your child's natural temperament, studies show that about 90 percent of anxious kids can be greatly helped if they are taught specific coping skills. A few of those teachable skills include calming down, using eye contact, using a stronger voice and more confident body language, introducing themselves and making new friends, and starting and ending a conversation. And the best news is that parents can teach those skills to their children so that they not only appear less timid but also are more confident in social settings. Those same skills will be ones your child can use in that sometimes tense social jungle for the rest of their lives and will help them gain social competence.

Why Change?

"You go ahead without me." "I'm afraid to raise my hand." "I'd rather be by myself."

Kids who hang back and are shy are often handicapped from experiencing life to its fullest. Shy children often curtail their experiences and don't take the necessary social risks, and as a result don't gain confidence in social situations. Not being able to join a group and make new friends will haunt them the rest of their lives. Finally, the pain of social rejection will set in.

EMOTIONS

LATE-BREAKING NEWS

Shyness Is Not Uncommon

Reassure your child that shyness is a universal and widespread feeling that millions of people cope with every day. In his twenty years of research at Harvard University, Jerome Kagan found that 10 to 15 percent of kindergartners through eighth graders are very shy, 25 percent are outgoing and sociable, and the rest fall in between. Of the children who start off with shy tendencies, two-thirds remain that way when they become young adults, but the other one-third overcome their inhibitions. Kagan explains, "If you're born shy, it may be hard for you to become a Bill Clinton, but you can move toward the middle."[44]

Keep in mind that in all likelihood, your parenting did not cause your child to be tense or more hesitant or even fearful in social settings. Chances are your child was born with a more hesitant temperament. His genetic code causes him to be more tense and anxious in certain situations. And the fear your child shows is real. Those unfamiliar or more threatening social situations actually arouse your child's nervous system and causes symptoms of inner turmoil, from rapid heartbeat to sweaty palms to paler skin tone.[45] It's not that a shyer child's brain is any different in structure from anyone else's; just certain *parts* are more sensitive. And those brain differences will persist from infancy to adulthood.[46] The good news is that research shows we can help kids feel more comfortable in groups and reduce their fears through how we respond and the skills we teach. This entry describes some of the proven ways to help your shyer child feel less tense and more comfortable in social settings so that he enjoys life more fully.

Signs and Symptoms

- Refuses to go places or participate, or begs to leave
- Warms up slowly, stays on fringe
- Is clingy; won't let you out of his sight
- Is irritable, agitated; bites nails
- Freezes or retreats from group
- Needs excessive and repeated reassurance
- Regresses to babylike behavior: whines, sucks thumb
- Throws a tantrum or cries
- Is anxious, shaky, tense, or fearful

- Complains of physical ailments (headaches, stomachaches)
- Is negative about scene or self ("I'll hate it," "The kids will hate me")

THE SOLUTION

Step 1. Early Intervention

- *Know your child's tension signs.* Your child isn't likely to come out and say, "I'm feeling really anxious here today," but his body language and behavior can alert you. It helps to observe how he usually reacts in those situations that cause him the most stress. Once you know your child's unique body signs, you can watch

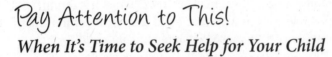

Pay Attention to This!

When It's Time to Seek Help for Your Child

Although shyness is a normal childhood trait, some kids are on a level far beyond "normal shyness." Thirteen percent of youth ages nine to seventeen suffer from anxiety disorders,[47] and children with more severe shyness are more prone to develop depression and anxiety later in life and are also at greater risk for developing full-blown social phobia.[48] If the following traits describe your child, seek the help of a trained medical professional.[49]

- The child experiences significant and persistent fear of social situations in which embarrassment or rejection may occur and often tries to avoid the feared situation at any cost.

- The child experiences physical reactions to feared social situations, such as shortness of breath, inability to speak, nausea and vomiting, uncontrollable sobbing; a younger child responds with crying, tantrums, or withdrawal.

- The child realizes that his fears are exaggerated, but he feels powerless to do anything about them. A younger child typically does not realize that his fears are unreasonable or abnormal, so you will have to decide if his worries are unfounded.

When shyness has an impact on your child's social life and his fears become debilitating, it's time to seek help. Children with social phobia are at a greater risk of developing depression, panic attacks, and substance abuse problems.[50] Social phobia is also highly treatable if caught early.

for them and then suggest strategies to help reduce his tension *before* it increases. For instance, when he is in a crowd, does he start to bite his nails, fiddle with his hair, clench his fists, or retreat behind you? The moment you recognize your child's signs is the best time to quietly point them out to prevent his tension buildup: *"Jon, you're biting your nails. Take slow, deep breaths to help you feel less tense." "You're twirling your hair. Tell yourself your 'happy thought' to help your body be less tense."*

- *Accept your child's natural temperament.* This isn't about changing your introvert into a social butterfly. Don't even try. Shyer children generally need structure; less pushy parents; time to warm up; understanding and sensitivity; calm, less intense adults; and quiet discipline that preserves their dignity. What are you doing to tailor your parenting to your child's natural shy tendencies?

- *Identify anxiety contributors.* Although your child may have a more introverted temperament, there may be other factors triggering his shyness. Here are some possible reasons why your child feels so uncomfortable, particularly in certain settings. Check those that apply to your child:

  ☐ Fears failure or humiliation (recitals, sports events, public speaking)

  ☐ Is labeled "shy," so acts shy

  ☐ Relies on an adult to rescue him from tough situations

  ☐ Has experienced trauma: an accident, divorce, an embarrassing family event, a death

  ☐ Is uncomfortable with adults in charge; feels humiliated, yelled at, unaccepted

  ☐ Has had limited quality social experiences; is isolated due to familial, cultural, or financial reasons

  ☐ Is "new" to the group (neighborhood, class, school, club, or team)

  ☐ Lacks the social skills to "fit in"

  ☐ Is uncomfortable with a physical change: hormone fluctuations, acne, weight gain, braces

  ☐ Is "different" from peers physically, or in terms of intellect, appearance, socioeconomic status, or cultural, racial, or religious background

  ☐ Runs with the wrong crowd: kids are too advanced, mature, or "smart," or the opposite

  ☐ Exposed to peer pressure: kids dressing, acting, or doing things your child is not comfortable participating in

  ☐ Labors under unrealistic parental expectations in relation to his developmental level or abilities; feels inadequate

  ☐ Has trouble reading emotional cues

LATE-BREAKING NEWS

Shyer Children Have Difficulty Identifying Facial Expressions

San Raffaele University, Milan, Italy: Researcher Marco Battaglia ranked a group of third and fourth graders on a shyness scale and then showed all the students pictures of faces depicting joy, anger, or no emotion and asked them to name the expressions.[51] He found that those who scored higher on the shyness scale had a consistently harder time identifying the neutral and angry faces. Battaglia concluded that shyer kids are less capable of reading facial signs that other kids use to rely on for social cues. Their inability causes them to feel more anxious about any facial expression they can't make out. Here is the parenting lesson from this important research: recognize that your shy child may have difficulty interpreting social cues and that this inability makes him feel tenser in social settings. Pointing out subtle facial cues can help him not only feel less tense but also learn to read facial expressions: "Sally looks angry. See how her brow is furrowed?" "Do you think Shoshana is mad? She is breathing quickly."

- *Check your expectations.* Although shyness is largely genetic, your parenting style can help your child "outgrow" his more hesitant, anxious social tendencies. The renowned Harvard child psychologist Jerome Kagan conducted a twenty-year study and found that one in three shy children did climb out of his shell.[52] Those who did usually had a parent who refused to overprotect her shy child, served as a role model for social skills, and coached her child on how to interact with peers. Here are kinds of adult behaviors that can exacerbate shyness. Do any apply to you or your parenting partner? Do you . . .

  ☐ Force your kid to perform in public?

  ☐ Push him too quickly to join a group without "warm-up" time?

  ☐ Push him to do things that might be important to you but not to him?

  ☐ Compare his performance and personality to those of his siblings, and negatively?

  ☐ Tend to "rescue" your child in social settings by doing tasks for him?

  ☐ Make excuses for him so that he is relieved from social encounters?

  ☐ Speak for your child when he's timid so that he learns to depend on you?

- *Don't use the "shy" label.* Experts agree that one of the biggest reasons kids act shy is that they are labeled shy. *Never* let anyone—teacher, friend, relative, sibling, stranger, you—call your child *shy*. "He's not shy. He just likes watching first and sizing things up." "You just take time to warm up. That's fine. Lots of people do the same thing." Research at Stanford University shows that although our children may be born with the tendency toward shyness, whether or not they become shy is largely due to whether or not we label them shy.

Step 2. Rapid Response

- *Empathize and acknowledge anxiety.* Empathize with your child's tension. Let him know you are aware that he feels uncomfortable with other kids and that joining in is hard for him. Emphasize that his tension is *not* something he causes and that it has nothing to do with being "bad."[53] Stress that he's not alone: 50 percent of people are shy. *"I'm going to help you deal with it. You're not being a baby." "I saw you biting your nails at Jim's house. I get a little anxious when I'm with people I don't know, too." "You didn't say anything at scouts. What would it take to make you feel more comfortable at these meetings?"*

- *Create a tension scale.* Shyer children have a hard time verbalizing their concerns. Create a tension scale from one to ten (younger kids can call it a "Fear Thermometer"), then teach it to your child. Explain: *"One is no tension. You feel calm and confident. Ten is a 'high fear factor' when you feel extremely tense about the situation, your heart palpitates, or you're afraid to move."* When you see your child's shy signs flare up, and you know that he feels uncomfortable and tense, ask: *"How bad is your fear on a scale of one to ten?"* Once you know the extent of his anxiety you can help him find the best way to cope. For instance, you could say, *"If it's a one, then maybe just finding one person you feel comfortable with might help." "If it's a six, you may need to leave the scene and take a number of slow, deep breaths and talk back to your fears."*

- *Use books addressing shyness.* One way to help a shyer child open up and talk about his feelings is by reading a book that addresses shyness. Here are a few favorites to try. For preschoolers: *Shy Charles,* by Rosemary Wells; *Little Miss Shy,* by Roger Hargreaves. For school agers: *I Don't Know Why . . . I Guess I'm Shy: A Story About Taming Imaginary Fears,* by Barbara S. Cain. For tweens: *Painfully Shy: How to Overcome Social Anxiety and Reclaim Your Life,* by Barbara G. Markway and Gregory P. Markway.

- *Emphasize prior success.* It's natural for a shy child to focus on past failures. So help him recall previous experiences when things went really well. *"Remember last year's swimming lessons? You begged not to go, but did and met a new friend." "Before you went to Sara's party you wanted to stay home also. But you agreed to stay at least a half an hour, and you ended up one of the last ones to leave."*

- *Teach anxiety reducers.* Find one way for your child to reduce the tension. Taking a deep, slow breath is one of the best ways to relax. So teach your child to "Take Ten": *"Take a deep breath while counting slowly to five; now slowly let your breath (and tension) out through your nose while you count to five."* (See also *Stressed*, p. 303.)

- *Schedule warm-up time.* Some kids take longer to warm up in a social set-ting, so give your child time to settle in. Go early when there might not be such a noisy crowd. Be patient and don't push too quickly. Research finds that parents who tend to gently encourage and loosely supervise their kid's social activities are more successful in helping shyer kids than parents who micromanage and supervise too closely. So fight the temptation to play "cruise director" and arrange your child's social world. Instead, let him watch a bit and figure out what's up; offer a suggestion or two as to how he could get started, but let him set his own time frame for joining in.

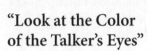

ONE SIMPLE SOLUTION

"Look at the Color of the Talker's Eyes"

Shyer kids usually look down when someone is talking, which makes them seem uninterested—a huge kid turn-off. So teach your child an easy confidence builder: "Always look at the color of the talker's eyes." Doing so makes your child appear more interested and confident (though he may not feel so) just because his head is raised. And you're also reinforcing eye contact—a critical skill of social success. If eye contact is too threatening, then teach this approach: "Look at the spot in the middle of your friend's eyes on the bridge of his nose. He won't know you're not looking in his eyes." With practice, your child may feel less anxious and learn eye contact.

- *Reinforce any social efforts.* Any and every effort your child makes to be even a tad more social deserves a pat on the back: *"I saw how you walked up to that new boy today. Good for you!"* *"I noticed that you really made an effort to say hello to Sheila's mom. She looked so pleased!"*

Step 3. Develop Habits for Change

- *Rehearse social situations.* Prepare your kid for an upcoming social event by describing the setting, expectations, and other kids who will be there. Then help him practice how to meet others, make small talk, and even say good-bye; make sure he knows basic table manners. Practicing conversation skills on the telephone with a supportive listener on the other end is always less threatening for shyer kids than doing so face-to-face. Such practice will decrease some of the anxiety he's bound to have from being in a new setting.

- *Practice skills with younger peers.* Research at Stanford University finds that pairing older kids with younger children for brief periods is a proven way to help the older child try out new social skills that he may feel uncomfortable about with friends his own age. So create opportunities for your kid to play with one other child who is younger: a younger sibling, cousin, neighbor, or one of your friend's younger kids. For teens, try babysitting: it's a great way for a shy kid to earn money as well as practice social skills—such as starting a conversation and using eye contact—that she is reticent about trying with kids her age.

- *Reinforce smiling!* One of the most common characteristics of confident, well-liked kids is that they smile and smile. So whenever your child displays a smile, reinforce it: *"What a great smile!"* or *"That smile of yours always wins people over."* Also point out how your child's smile affects others: *"Do see how kids smile back when you smile?" "That little boy saw your smile and came over to play. Your smile let him know you were friendly."*

- *Make one-to-one playdates.* Research finds that one of the best ways to help shyer kids gain social confidence is with one-on-one playdates. So provide those opportunities for your child to connect with other children he feels comfortable with. Many kids can be overwhelmed in groups, so limit the number of friends to one at a time. Then gradually increase the number as your child gains confidence.

- *Teach your child to defeat bad "self-talk."* Shyer children generally use destructive "self-talk," which psyches them out when other kids are around. For instance, they put a negative spin on things and imagine that other kids are far more concerned about them than they really are: "Everyone is going to be looking at my hair and saying it looks dumb." "Everyone is going to look at me when I go on the bus." You can help your shy child counter that talk by teaching positive statement replacements. For instance, have your child envision a child he and others admire (a more popular, confident child). *You:* "What do you think Mary would say to herself when she gets on the bus?" *Child:* "Mary probably wouldn't worry and would just say hello to her best friends." *You:* "Then tell yourself not to worry like Mary." This cognitive therapy technique was developed by Temple University and is proven to help shy kids. (See www.childanxiety.org for more details.)

- *Expose your child to the fear in small doses.* Shyer, more hesitant kids fear the worst possible scenario before they even get to the event. "I'll forget my speech." "Nobody will like me." "I'll wet my pants." Telling your child that his fear is unfounded will get you nowhere—remember, the fear is real! But if your child can experience the event and realize that the worst thing didn't happen, he will begin to lose the fear. The trick is to expose your child to the dreaded situation, slowly and in small doses at a level he can handle, then gradually increase the "scariness factor." For instance: if he absolutely refuses to go to the birthday party, then encourage him to drop by just to deliver his present. If he is terrified of going to playgroup with all the kids, then suggest he go thirty minutes early when only the host is there. Beware: pushing your child too quickly into a fear-inducing situation can backfire and could even increase his hesitancy, but avoiding life will become debilitating. Watch your child's stress signs carefully and always follow his lead. When in doubt, seek the counsel of a trained mental health professional.

One Parent's Answer

A mom from Lansing shares:

My daughter was so uncomfortable about going to birthday parties, and begged me to take her home. I finally found that when we practiced the "very first thing" to do when she arrived, her anxiety went down. It could be: smile at the mom, give the birthday kid the gift, walk to your friend, have something to eat or drink. Once she had rehearsed and knew exactly what she was going to do when she first got there, Hanna felt more comfortable.

- *Debrief a stressful event.* If your kid has had a really embarrassing attack of shyness, find a time to discuss what happened and how he might handle it better next time. *"Let's think of one thing we can do next time so you won't be so uncomfortable at Jonah's house." "It sounds like you really didn't like being with so many kids. What if you invite only one friend at a time?" "If you don't want to ask Nick face-to-face, why not ask him on the phone?"*

WHAT TO EXPECT BY STAGES AND AGES

Although each child is unique, here are situations that intensify shyness at different ages.

Preschooler   Strangers, new situations (playgroups, day care, preschool), being the focus of attention, and leaving Mom or Dad can all bring on feelings of shyness.

School Age   Performing in front of a group, peer intimidation, being singled out, public criticism, exclusion, and fear of failure (especially in front of peers) are shyness intensifiers for school-age kids.

Tween   Tweens can feel shy about physical appearance, acne, braces, puberty, the opposite sex, rejection, and all the issues that plague school-age kids as well. This is the age of heightened self-consciousness, so shy tendencies that seem out of character for the child may suddenly materialize.

More Helpful Advice

The Shy Child: Helping Children Triumph over Shyness, by Ward Kent Swallow with Laurie Halse Anderson

The Shy Child: A Parent's Guide to Preventing and Overcoming Shyness from Infancy to Adulthood (2nd ed.), by Philip G. Zimbardo and Shirley Radl

The Shyness Breakthrough: A No-Stress Plan to Help Your Shy Child Warm Up, Open Up, and Join the Fun, by Bernardo J. Carducci

Nurturing the Shy Child, by Barbara G. and Gregory P. Markway

Separation Anxiety

SEE ALSO: *Dependent, Fearful, Shy*

THE QUESTION

"My daughter is starting school in a few weeks, and she's always been more of a clinger. Do you have suggestions on how to make the send-off more positive and help her feel more secure?"

THE ANSWER

Having our kids leave us for the first time—whether it be to school, day care, a sleepover, or camp—can be a tough parenting moment. We realize that the umbilical cord has really been severed and our babies are growing up. But saying good-bye can be a frightening experience for some kids as well. There are big adjustments to make: learning someone else's rules and dealing with such worries as where the bathroom is and getting along with other kids. It's only natural for children to feel a little anxious. So here are tips to help make that good-bye smoother and less stressful for the two of you:

- *Prepare to separate.* For a few weeks *prior* to the big send-off, have your child stay a bit longer than usual with a babysitter, grandparent, or friend. Also create and then practice a special private good-bye between the two of you, such as a secret handshake or special kiss, to help her start to pull away. Rehearsing a good-bye can help a child feel more secure when the big moment really comes. Or try putting a special pebble or keychain with your photo in her pocket and explain that whenever she touches it, it means you're thinking of her wherever you are. (This is a great tip if you have to be away on more extended business trips or longer meetings.)

- *Check out the new surroundings.* A week or so before the big day, take her for a visit to the school so she can view her new surroundings and find those key places, such as her classroom, the water fountain, and the restroom, but don't overhype it! You don't want to build up expectations so much that she will be disappointed if things fall short. Ideally, help her meet at least one child who will be in that classroom. Kids often play at playgrounds and parks near the school, so congregate there with your kid and start asking if anyone will be in that classroom. If possible, ask your child's teacher and see if she can give you the name of just one child to contact.

- *Don't linger.* On the actual send-off day, stay positive and calm. Your child picks up on your cues and reacts. Look for an activity she may enjoy—such as a puzzle or blocks—or help her find that familiar face, and then guide her in that direction so that she will have something to do. Keep good-byes short and use that secret good-bye ritual, but don't linger! It only increases anxiety. It sometimes helps to give an anxious child a watch to wear that's marked with a marking pen to show the exact time you'll pick her up.

- *Pick up on schedule.* Be sure that you or your designated caregiver picks your child up when you said and at the exact spot you prearranged. If she cries when you pick her up, take it as a compliment! It usually means she's delighted to see you—not that she hates school.

If separation anxiety still continues, check in with the teacher to see if she has suggestions. Adjustment may take from a day to several weeks, so be patient. Learning to say good-bye is just one more part of growing up and helping your child learn to separate and handle life confidently without you.

Stressed

SEE ALSO: *Angry, Argues, Defiant, Depressed, Fearful, Grief, Moving, Peer Pressure, Pessimistic, Sleepless*

THE PROBLEM

Red Flags

Physiological signs: bedwetting, nausea and diarrhea, stuttering, colds and fatigue, nail biting or hair twirling, restlessness and irritability. Psychological signs: big mood swings, short-temperedness, withdrawal, inability to concentrate, arguing, excessive whining or crying, increased clinginess and dependency.

The Change to Parent For

Your child learns to recognize how his body responds to stress and situations that increase it and develops ways to reduce tension as well as cope.

Question: "My eight-year-old is so tense lately. She can't sleep, is moody, and is having a tough time focusing on her schoolwork. Could this be stress-related? I don't know how to help her."

Answer: Stress isn't just for adults. Studies show that today's kids are feeling a lot more pressure than we think they are, and stress symptoms are showing up in kids as young as three. Ask yourself these three critical questions: How does *my* child handle stress? What could be triggering it? and Does my child know healthy ways to reduce the stress?

Why Change?

Think stress is just for adults? Not these days. In fact, a recent iVillage poll found that almost 90 percent of mothers think kids these days are far more stressed than when they themselves were growing up.[54] Research finds that between 8 and 10 percent of American children are seriously troubled by stress and symptoms;[55] if left untreated, stress can not only affect your child's friendships and school success but also his physical and emotional well-being. Overscheduled days, competition, school, treadmill-paced lives, home problems, scary nightly news, and stressed-out parents are just a few contributors.

One thing is certain: stress is part of life, and some kids actually do seem to thrive on it. But one in three kids suffers from chronic stress symptoms that can not only break down his immune system[56] but also increase his likelihood for depression.[57] Your critical parenting question is this: Does the stress stimulate my kid or paralyze him? In order to know that answer, you need to recognize how your child handles normal stress and what unique signs he exhibits when on overload. When he gets to that level and stress is having too negative an effect, it is critical that you intervene for your child's physical as well as psychological health. This entry describes proven solutions to help you determine just how well your child is coping, and ways to reduce your child's stress.

Signs and Symptoms

Each kid responds differently, but the key is to identify *your* child's physical behavioral or emotions signs *before* he is on overload. A clue is to look for behaviors that are *not* typical for your child.

Physical Stress Signs

- Headache, neck aches, and backaches
- Nausea, diarrhea, constipation, stomachache, vomiting
- Shaky hands, sweaty palms, feeling shaky, lightheadedness
- Bedwetting
- Trouble sleeping, nightmares
- Change in appetite
- Stuttering
- Frequent colds, fatigue

LATE-BREAKING NEWS

Kids Under Stress Develop More Fevers and Colds

University of Rochester Medical Center: A three-year study of five- to ten-year-olds found that those kids with parents and families under ongoing stress have more fevers accompanying illnesses than other children.[58] Chronic stress also breaks down immune systems, making kids more vulnerable to colds and flu, and can set off asthma, diabetes, and other illnesses. So if you're noticing that your child has frequent colds or headaches or complains he doesn't feel well, consider whether stress may be the cause.

**Emotional or Behavioral
Stress Signs**

- New or reoccurring fears; anxiety and worries

- Trouble concentrating; frequent daydreaming

- Restlessness or irritability

- Social withdrawal, unwillingness to participate in school or family activities

- Moodiness, sulking, or inability to control emotions

- Nail biting, hair twirling, thumb sucking, fist clenching, foot tapping

- Acting out, anger, aggressive behaviors such as tantrums, disorderly conduct

- Regression or babylike behaviors

- Excessive whining or crying

- Clinginess, more dependency, withdrawal; won't let you out of sight

Pay Attention to This!
When Should You Worry?

All kids will display signs of stress every now and then. Be concerned when you see a *marked change* in what is "normal" for *your* child's behavior that lasts longer than two weeks.[59] When you see your child struggling and feeling overwhelmed, it's time to seek help from a mental health professional. And don't wait: stressed-out kids are two to four times more likely to develop depression, and as teens they are much more likely to become involved with substance abuse.[60]

THE SOLUTION

Step 1. Early Intervention

- *Identify the reasons.* Stress is an unavoidable part of life, but *too* much stress is unhealthy. Your first step is to identify *why* your child is experiencing stress overload so that you can develop a realistic plan to reduce it. Here are common causes of unhealthy kid stress. Check those that apply to your child:

  ☐ *Genetics:* predisposition to stress out

  ☐ *Overload:* too many after-school activities with no time to relax; overscheduled

  ☐ *Real-world events:* scary nightly news or world events

  ☐ *Trauma:* fire, divorce, flood, accident, death of parent

  ☐ *Peer problems:* peer pressure, bullying, rejection; racial differences

  ☐ *Appearance:* concern with clothes, weight, appearance, fitting in

  ☐ *School:* grades, homework, overemphasis on performance

EMOTIONS

☐ *Unrealistic expectations:* too pressured; too high of standards in relation to abilities

☐ *Home problems:* divorce, illness, a move, financial strains, stressed parents, sibling rivalry

- *Get enough Z's.* Heavy workloads and overscheduling can wreak havoc on kids' sleep patterns. And without a good night's sleep, stress can build. Make sure your child is getting enough sleep. (See *Sleepless,* p. 585.) Also check to make sure she is not using the computer within thirty minutes of going to bed (flickering lights on the screen can inhibit sleep) and not drinking caffeinated sodas or energy drinks.

- *Identify potential stressors.* Frightening nightly news on the TV? A bully on the bus? Too much yelling at home? You can't (and shouldn't) protect kids from all stress, but is there one thing that is causing unhealthy stress that you can eliminate? For instance, hire a tutor to help with his science homework. Stop yelling in front of the kids. Turn off that scary nightly news. Minimize those stressors you do have control over.

- *Cut one thing.* Many parents admit that a major kid stress culprit these days is overscheduling. Could this be your kid's problem? Spend a week evaluating your child's daily schedule of school, home, and all extracurricular activities. How much free time does your child have left? If you can cut out just one thing in your child's weekly activity, it may make a tremendous difference in reducing the stress.

- *Keep to family routines.* Sticking to a routine helps reduce stress because it boosts predictability for a child. Those family meals, bedtime rituals, nighttime stories, hot baths, hugs, and backrubs not only create great family memories but also bust stress.

- *Monitor TV viewing.* Tweens say one a big stressor is watching late-breaking news without an adult to explain the event. So monitor what your child views, limit viewing of those stressful real-world news events (terrorism, war, kidnappings, storms), or at least be there to reassure your child about that sometimes scary news.

- *Help your child learn stress signs.* Point out your child's stress signs so that he will learn to recognize them. *"When you get tense you clench your fists." "Have you noticed that whenever you worry you get a headache?"*

- *Don't overprotect!* Of course it's tough to watch our children deal with tense situations and feel stressed. Our parental instinct is to swoop in and rescue them, but fight that urge. Researchers from Johns Hopkins University School of Medicine analyzed over twenty studies and found that too much parental control and overprotection actually increase kids' anxiety.[61] Stress is a part of life, so your child will have to learn how to cope. And the only way he will learn how to handle stress is by experiencing it. The parenting secret is knowing when your child is on overload and dealing with *too much stress* or doesn't know how to cut back to reduce it.

ONE SIMPLE SOLUTION

Taking Deep Breaths to Blow Your Worries Away

An instant way to relax (and get oxygen to your brain) is to take a slow, deep breath from your diaphragm. A quick way to teach the skill is to tell your child to pretend he's blowing up a balloon in his tummy (as you count "one, two, three" slowly). Then he lets the air out with an exaggerated "Ah-h-h-h" sound (like when the doctor looks in his throat). Explain that taking slow breaths from deep in his tummy will help blow his worries away. Encourage him to practice taking slow, steady breaths by blowing soap bubbles or using a pinwheel.

Step 2. Rapid Response

- *Stay calm.* If you're frazzled, your child's stress level will only increase. So whenever you're tense or upset, take a few deep breaths to calm down. Doing so will reduce your child's stress faster and help him stay calm.

- *Melt the tension.* Tell your child to make his body feel stiff and straight like a wooden soldier. Every bone from head to toe is "tense" (or "stressed"). Now tell him to make his body limp (or "relaxed") like a rag doll or windsock. Once he realizes he can make himself relax, he can find the spot in his body where he feels the most tension—perhaps his neck, shoulder muscles, or jaw. He then closes his eyes, concentrates on the spot, tenses it up for three or four seconds, and lets it go. Tell him that while doing so, he should imagine the stress slowly melting away from the top of his head and out his toes until he feels relaxed or calmer.

- *Use a positive phrase.* Teach your child to say a comment inside his head to help him handle stress. Here are a few: "Calm down." "I can do this." "Stay calm and breathe slowly." "It's nothing I can't handle."

- *Teach elevator breathing.* Tell your child to close his eyes and take a slow, deep breath, then imagine he's in an elevator on the twentieth floor of a tall building. He presses the button for the first floor and watches the buttons for each level slowly light up as the elevator goes down. Tell him to take a slow, deep breath and visualize each button lighting as the elevator descends from the twentieth to the ground level and his stress gradually fades away.

One Parent's Answer

A mom from Topeka writes:

My husband lost his job and there was a lot of tension at home. Jen picked up our stress. She couldn't sleep and had a hard time with schoolwork. When she got tense she would hum and cover her ears. Her Granny bought her an iPod. Now she plops on the coach wearing the earphones and zones out listening to the music. It has helped her cope.

- *Visualize a calm place.* Ask your child to think of an actual place he's been to, one where he feels peaceful. For instance, the beach, his bed, Grandpa's backyard, a tree house. When stress kicks in, tell him to close his eyes and imagine that spot, while breathing slowly.

Step 3. Develop Habits for Change

- *Reduce stress as a family.* Meditate with your kids, do yoga with your daughter, go to a gym with your son, ride bikes with your preschooler, listen to relaxation tapes with your kids. You'll not only help your kids learn healthy ways to minimize their stress but also reduce your own. And after all, less stressed parents make less stressed kids!

- *Label emotions.* Help your child name his feelings so that he begins to know when he's starting to feel tense. Your child will also have the words to tell you how he feels so that you can help him reduce that stress. *"I see you're gritting your teeth. Is your math frustrating you and making you feel tense? Need some help?" "You look mad because you really wanted your friend to play with you. Do you want to come sit by me so we can talk about it?"*

- *Find a relaxer.* Every child is different, so find what helps your kid relax, and then encourage him to use it on a regular basis. Some kids respond to drawing pictures or writing about their stress in a journal. Other kids say that imagining what "relaxing" or "calm" feels like helps. (Show him how to make his body feel like a slowly moving fluffy white cloud or a rag doll.) Or allocate a cozy place in your home where your kid can chill out when he needs to ease the tension. In a survey of almost nine hundred tweens, the kids said their best stress reducers are doing something active, listening to music, watching TV or playing a video game, exercising, talking to a friend, being alone or with friends, or talking to a parent.[62]

- *Open up the communication.* Your stressed child may not seek you out, so go to your child. In the same survey, 75 percent of tweens said they need their parents' help to reduce their stress and *like* having their parents talk with them, help them solve their worries, try to cheer them up, or just spend time with them.

- *Model how to cope.* Don't cover up your stress about your overdrawn checkbook or the new boss. Instead admit your worries, then model healthy ways you deal with it. Whether you're taking a walk around the block, soaking in a hot tub, writing in your journal, or heading for the gym, your child needs to know not only that stress is normal but also that there are ways to reduce it.

WHAT TO EXPECT BY STAGES AND AGES

Preschooler   Kids as young as three years of age experience stress, but it can go unnoticed because preschoolers can't put their feelings into words. Pay closer attention to your child's stress symptoms. Stressors include new things, dogs, monsters, spiders, being sucked down a drain, and abandonment of any kind: being away from home, separation from parents or loved ones, being kidnapped.

School Age   Stressors include performing in front of others (for example, a speech, recital, or sporting event); tests, grades, and school; bedwetting; being chosen last on any team; getting along with peers; disappointing their parents; and real-world dangers: fires, burglars, illness, storms. Kids younger than ten are especially vulnerable to repeated stress.

Tween   Stressors include grades, school, and homework; taking on too many activities; negative thoughts and feelings about themselves; moving or changing schools; family pressure, arguing, financial problems, and tension; friends and peer acceptance; peer humiliation and pressure; gossip and teasing; worry about their changing bodies and being different from others; and letting their parents down.

More Helpful Advice

Don't Pop Your Cork on Mondays: The Children's Anti-Stress Book, by Adolph J. Moser

KidStress, by Georgia Witkin

Freeing Your Child from Anxiety, by Tamar E. Chansky

Stress and Your Child: Helping Kids Cope with the Strains and Pressures of Life, by Bettie B. Youngs

Your Anxious Child: How Parents and Teachers Can Relieve Anxiety in Children, by John S. Dacey and Lisa B. Fiore

EMOTIONS

Worried About the World

SEE ALSO: *Angry, Depressed, Fearful, Perfectionist, Pessimistic, Sensitive, Stressed*

THE QUESTION

"My child is so worried about what's happening in the world. She's only ten but she just talks about the 'gloom and doom' grown-up issues like terrorism, AIDS, war, and global warming. How do I temper her fears so she realizes there is still goodness left in the world?"

THE ANSWER

It can be a scary world for kids, and a big reason is that they are constantly exposed in the media to such tragic and frightening images—terrorism, school shootings, crime, financial meltdowns, war, and AIDS. The sad thing is that those horrific scenarios seem to be affecting our kids. One survey showed that only about 25 percent of American children feel safe from a terror attack or when they travel.[63] Only about 29 percent are optimistic about the future of the United States over the next ten years.[64] The fact is, many of our kids see their world as a mean and dangerous place. Here are a few ways to reduce your child's worries and reassure her that all is well:

- *Watch your tongue.* Watch how you react, and listen to your views—particularly during a crisis. "That virus is going to spread like wildfire." "They'll never stop those terrorists." "We're all going to blow up." Our kids do imitate what they see and hear, and they pick up on our fears. Could your child be picking up such catastrophic beliefs from anyone else, such as friend or relative? A worrywart needs to be surrounded by people who offer a realistic and hopeful perspective, so find folks who tout more optimistic views.

- *Don't over protect, but assure safety.* Whenever there is a scary real-world event in our neighborhood or country or on another continent, our gut reflex is to shield our kids from these more worrisome parts of life. Don't be so quick to do so. Children know when something is up, or they will hear about it elsewhere. If kids feel we are trying to withhold information, it only fuels their worries. It's better to calmly address the issue: "Did you hear the news about the financial meltdown?" "What are your friends saying about the smallpox epidemic?" Then reassure your child that the folks in charge (police, government, doctors, firefighters) are doing what they can to take care of the situation. Give only as much information as your child needs to know, and make sure that the facts are developmentally appropriate for your child's level of understanding. Young kids often feel as though the problem is right next door: *"The war is in a country that is across a huge ocean. The bombs can't get to us."* The key is to use a calm and confident voice so that your child senses that you feel safe and sure that all will be well.

- *Monitor news consumption.* One poll of young people surveyed by Children Now found that half of those kids polled said they felt "angry, afraid, sad, or depressed after watching the news."[65] So carefully monitor the news that your child sees or hears and turn the TV off whenever there is a traumatic event. Avoid tabloid-type stations that sensationalize news and hype the fear factor. Actual images or news feeds are far more frightening to a child than newspaper pictures. And above all, talk to your child about a "scary" event. Research at the University of Pennsylvania found that adolescents who talk with their parents about what they see on the TV (or read in the newspaper) tend to have a more accurate view of reality than those who don't, so talk to your child.[66] Meanwhile, offer your child less worrisome news alternatives, such as programs on cable and educational channels or a subscription to a kids' news magazine, or bookmark appropriate kids' Web sites.

- *Offer a more balanced view.* Although we can't prevent tragedies from occurring, we can help our children see the good aspects of the world. So expose your child to those good parts. Clip out those articles about the wonderful, caring things people do. They're usually tucked away in the back pages of the paper. Share them as "Good News Reports" with your kids. Then ask them to be on the lookout for other good aspects of life.

- *Tune in more closely.* It's one thing for your child to worry occasionally, but when your child's fears become excessive and have an impact on her day-to-day living, it's time to get help. Watch in particular for these signs: excessive distress, crying, irritability, hopelessness, frustration; ready agitation, fear of leaving home; worrying hours, days, or weeks ahead; avoidance of social activities or resistance to going to school. Watch too for physical ailments, such as headaches and stomachaches. Be concerned when there is an intense change in your child's normal temperament that lasts at least two weeks. Call the guidance counselor, school psychologist, or your child's doctor for advice.

EMOTIONS

Part 5
Social Scene

**OUT OF THE MOUTHS OF BABES
WHY GOD MADE MOMS**

Answers given by second-grade schoolchildren to the following question:

Why did your mom marry your dad?

1. My dad makes the best spaghetti in the world. And my mom eats a lot.

2. She got too old to do anything else with him.

3. My grandma says that Mom didn't have her thinking cap on.

Bad Friends

SEE ALSO: *Cliques, Drinking, Peer Pressure, Sex, Swears*

THE PROBLEM

Red Flags

Chooses pals with different values or inappropriate behaviors who influence your child's behavior in negative ways

The Change to Parent For

Your child understands the characteristics of a good friend, chooses friends based on those characteristics, and learns exit strategies or habits to say no to negative influences if he faces them from peers.

Question: "My daughter's new 'friend' is twelve going on twenty-five. She wears makeup, jeans that fit way too tightly, and has a pierced navel. I'm worried that this girl will be a negative influence. Should I worry?"

Answer: Ask yourself: "Why does my daughter want to be friends with this girl?" If it's just to be included, then help her think through if this group of girls really matches her values and interests. Help her find better friendship choices. But halt any relationship that could damage her character, reputation, or health.

Why Change?

"Why don't you like my friend's piercings?" "So what if Zach wears a black trench coat? It doesn't mean he's a bad kid." "Why don't you trust me? Sam isn't a bad kid." "Chill out! It's not like she's selling drugs!"

Bad friends. They're every parent's nightmare. We imagine only the worst: drugs, smoking, sex, trouble with the law. But what should parents do if they notice that their daughter is hanging out more with a kid whose values don't seem in sync with their own? Is there ever a time when you should forbid your son from being with a particular friend? Yes, there is, but don't jump to this conclusion too quickly. It's okay for your kid to have different kinds of friends. In fact, we should encourage those relationships. Exposing our kids to diversity is a big part of helping them broaden their horizons, develop tolerance

---

LATE-BREAKING NEWS

Ohio State University: Research confirms that although children are influenced by peers, parents are still the most influential factor in their kids' lives. Chris Knoester, lead author of the study and assistant professor of sociology at Ohio State University, studied data from 11,483 students and their parents.[1] His team found clear evidence that parents can act as architects of the friendship choices their kids make even after they reach adolescence. In fact, kids are more likely to have good friends (ones who don't fight and who have future college plans) if they have a warm, positive relationship with their parents. The study also found that parents can indirectly influence their kids' friendship choices by monitoring and supervising their kids, being familiar with their children's friends, and having low conflict with their kid. So don't undermine your power. These findings show that parents can indirectly influence their children's behaviors by shaping their choice of friends.

---

and empathy, learn new habits, develop new perspectives, and get along with others. The trick here is to figure out when the other kid's values or lifestyle is really reckless, self-destructive, or totally inappropriate.

Consider this: Could hanging around this kid damage your child's character, reputation, or health? Keep in mind that our kids are rarely "made bad" by another kid, but the friends our kids choose to hang around with sure can increase the odds that they may—or may not—get into trouble.

Signs and Symptoms

Here are a few warning signs that may indicate that the pal is becoming a negative influence:

- *Secretiveness.* Your child becomes very secretive, locks his room, and covers up what he's doing.

- *Changes in appearance.* Your child starts wearing "provocative" attire, wants only pricey or name-brand items, has a complete change in hairstyle, or starts wearing gizmos that "just aren't your kid."

- *School problems.* Your child's grades drop; he loses interest in school, gets detentions or tardies, doesn't turn in homework; you have received worried calls or notes from his teacher.

- *Changes in activities.* Your child pulls away from past friends; sees this kid exclusively; is negative about "former" pals; or quits a team or sport or other activities that he has always loved.

316

- *Character changes.* Your child's integrity and your family values, culture, or religious beliefs are affected; he is more withdrawn, moody, or sad.

- *Untrustworthiness.* You can no longer count on your child's word; he lies, doesn't keep his promises, isn't where he says he is, misses his curfew, sneaks out.

- *Decline in reputation.* Your child's image is negatively affected: teachers, coaches, other parents, or kids pull away or say your kid "has changed"—and not for the better.

- *Tense family relations.* You and your child have frequent arguments, and your relationship with your child is strained.

- *Violence.* Your child is preoccupied with violence in his drawings, writings, vocabulary, or choice of activities.

Of course any kid could show some of these traits, and they may have nothing to do with the friend he is hanging out with. The trick is to keep a closer eye on your child and this new friend: how many of these symptoms showed up *because* this kid came into his life? Also, are you sure the other kid is the negative influence—and not vice versa?

THE SOLUTION

Step 1. Early Intervention

- *Figure out the cause.* If you don't like the friend but haven't seen any negative changes in your child's behavior, your best bet is to stay calm and figure out what really concerns you. Here are some possible reasons kids associate with "bad" friends. Could any of these be what's motivating your child? Check those that apply to your child or situation. (By the way, don't be so quick to blame the "bad" friend. Focus instead on why your child is choosing to hang with this kid.)

ONE SIMPLE SOLUTION

Use "What If?" Questions

A quick way to assess your kid's ability to handle troubling peers is to pose "What if?" questions. You make up the scenario, then listen to how your child responds. "What if . . . *you go to a party and there aren't any parents? the kids want to sneak out of the slumber party to meet boys? your friend dares you to go through those abandoned houses?*" Your child's answers will be a springboard to talk about possible peer problems and solutions as well as clue you in to your kid's reasoning and skill levels.

☐ *Emotional need.* Your child has low self-esteem; there is a conflict at home.

☐ *Friendship.* The kid offers a place to hang out and have a good time.

☐ *Protection.* Your kid is bullied or harassed, or otherwise doesn't feel safe; this kid offers protection.

☐ *Excitement.* The pal "pushes the envelope" and is exciting to be around.

☐ *Peer approval.* Your child has trouble fitting in with a clique or group.

☐ *Similar interests.* This kid shares similar interests, such as music, sports, or academics.

☐ *Support.* Your child needs help with homework or with athletics; this pal can help.

- *Look for simple solutions.* Think through all the possible reasons your child may be hanging around this kid. The key question is, "Why is your child attracted to this kid?" Once you have that answer, you may be able to create simple solutions to deal with this problem pal. Here are a few:

  Problem: Needs protection from the bully. **Solution:** Hold a conference with school personnel to create a safety plan, identify other adults and kids he can turn to, locate where the bullying usually happens so that your child avoids those spots and doesn't have to rely on this kid, enroll him in a martial arts class to help him gain confidence.

  Problem: Recently moved, so problem pal is your kid's only friend. **Solution:** Enroll him in scouts or an after-school activity to make new friends, ask teacher for "pal ideas," join the PTA so you can befriend parents and build a social network, teach him how to make new friends.

- *Find the attraction.* If you're really struggling with why your kid likes this pal, then simply ask him: *"What do you enjoy about Jimmy?" "You seem to really like his company. Why?" "What do you two like doing together?" "What do you like about him compared to your other friends?"*

- *Spell out expectations.* Sit down with your kid and review your family rules and behavior expectations. Be clear as to what your child can and can't do and what the consequences will be if he crosses that line. Post those rules in a visible spot so that there are no questions.

- *Get to know the "enemy."* Appearances can be deceiving, so give the pal the benefit of the doubt. Make your home a kid-friendly hangout so that you can get to know this kid on your turf. You will be not only more comfortable knowing where your kid is but also able to keep your eyes open to see if your concerns are grounded. Also volunteer to chauffer your kid and this pal to events and gatherings. A great time to find out about this kid is when he and your child are locked in your car together. Use that rearview mirror and watch closely!

- *Talk about what makes a good friendship.* Kids generally turn off if parents criticize their friends (you also run the risk that your child just may spend more time with him to spite you). A better approach is to help your kid analyze what he is getting from this relationship and help him talk through what makes a good friendship so that he can reach his own conclusions. *"How do you see yourself when you are with this friend?" "How do you want to be described by others? Will being with this kid help or hinder that image?"* Here is a "quiz" to help your child assess his current relationships. Although no friendship is perfect, if your child can't say yes to most of these comments, it may be time for him to "move on."

  My friend sticks up for me if other kids talk about me.

  My friend and I have fun being together.

  When something good (or bad) happens, I want to share it with my friend.

  My friend and I may disagree, but we talk things through.

  My friend and I look out for one another.

  My friend and I can share secrets with one another.

  My friend and I know all about one other and like each other just the same.

  My friend makes me feel better if I'm sad.

  My friend encourages me to do what's right.

  My friend makes me feel good about myself.

- *Look in the mirror.* Is your concern really legitimate, or is it that this friend doesn't measure up to *your* expectations? Not all our kids' friends can be the "Little Miss Sunshine" type or whatever is your favorite type of friend for yourself, so don't expect to like all your kid's friends.

Pay Attention to This!
When to Monitor Your Kid and That Pal Even More Closely

The after-school hours between three and six o'clock are the prime time for riskier kid behaviors. Keep closer tabs on your kid after school, get him involved in supervised after-school programs or sports, or enlist the help of other parents to open their homes so that your kids have safe hangouts. Insist that he call as soon as school is over so that you know where he is at all times. Set clear parameters as to where he may or may not go after school, and enforce your rules.

Step 2. Rapid Response

If you notice negative behaviors emerging (such as slipping grades, missing curfews, the desire for "provocative" new attire, a surly attitude), *and* the change corresponds to when this pal came into your kid's world, it's time to be more proactive.

- *Tune up your radar.* Dig deeper and confirm that this kid really is an unhealthy match for your child and becoming a negative influence you suspect and fear. Watch your child in the company of this kid. In particular, do you see a change in your child? Does he act different when this kid is around (disruptive or aggressive, and breaking your rules)? Does he put on a new (and unflattering) demeanor (ruder, meaner, surlier)? Confirm your suspicions.

- *Talk to other adults.* Ask teachers, coaches, counselors, or parents who know this child. They often can offer a fresh perspective. Do they share your worries or have advice? Use them to help you get perspective and evidence.

- *Share your concerns with your child.* Instead of criticizing your kid's companion (guaranteed to halt a conversation), cite specific concerns: *"Your grades are way down," "You're swearing," "You've treated your old friends meanly."* The right questions can help your child think through if this pal really is a good friend. His answers will help you assess your concern.

- *Meet the parents.* Find a way to meet this kid's parents or just pick up the phone and introduce yourself: *"Our boys have being seeing a lot of each other, and I just wanted to introduce myself."* You can use it as a pretext of exchanging phone numbers, but it may also help you get a sense of whether your concerns are grounded. And if your kid has a fit, so be it. Make a house rule that whenever your kid starts hanging around with a new pal, you will connect with that parent and introduce yourself.

- *Limit time with this friend.* Once you are certain this pal is a negative influence on your child, then it's time to cut back on the relationship and find ways for your kid to develop new, healthier relationships. If this kid is a safety risk, then go to Code Red and cut all contact with him ASAP.

  - *Occupy your kid's time.* The best way to limit your kid's time with an undesirable pal is to find healthier alternatives. Arrange activities your child enjoys. Fill his social calendar during the times he'd be hanging out with this kid.

  - *Monitor closely.* Know where your child is at all times. Arrange for someone to pick your child up after school and for adult supervision when you're not around. Be clear that you expect your child to be where you specify. No excuses, or there will be sanctions. Don't be shy about calling the other house or driving by to make sure that your child is where he's supposed to be. And don't be afraid to say no.

- *Limit privileges.* Establish clear rules and review them again and again. Halt *all* contact with this friend: cell phone, text messages, and e-mail correspondence should also be forbidden. Pull the plug from the computer or take control of that cell phone for any infraction. Remember, you pay those phone and electricity bills.

- *Change activities or classes.* Pull your kid from any after-school activity with this pal. Ask the teacher to rearrange their seating so they don't sit near one another. A school counselor might switch activity periods or class schedules so they are separated.

- *Change schools.* In the most extreme cases, you may need to switch schools, send your child away for the summer, or even move. Yes, these measures are severe, but your job is to prevent a tragedy from happening.

Step 3. Develop Habits for Change

Once you know that this "friend" is not only a bad influence but also a danger to your child's safety or values if the relationship continues, it's time to halt the friendship and teach habits that help your child move on and make new friends.

ONE SIMPLE SOLUTION

How Well Do You Know Your Kid's Pals?

Research proves that the more you know your kid's friends—and they you—the less likely it is that your child will choose problem pals and engage in risky behaviors.[2] How many of these can you answer?

1. The name of your child's best friend and the next five or six closest pals

2. The favorite pastime of each pal

3. The first names of the parents of each pal

4. The kind of relationship each pal has with his or her parent

If you aren't able to answer at least two of those questions, then it's time to get more involved in your child's social life so that you can boost your influence on his friendship choices.

- *Boost friendship skills.* Does your kid keep hanging around this child because he doesn't know how to make new friends? If so, teach your child how to introduce himself to a new kid, make simple conversation, and listen attentively. Friendship skills are teachable, and the easiest way to teach the skill is to model it for your child and then let him practice and practice it. If you need specific tips on teaching social skills, my book *Nobody Likes Me, Everybody Hates Me* shows how to teach twenty-five crucial social skills, or you can talk to your school counselor or psychologist for more advice.

- *Teach how to say no.* Whether he has a problem pal or not, your kid needs to learn exit strategies to help him get out of awkward or risky social situations. Here are a few skills to teach your child to help him stand up to a troublesome pal. It's best to let your kid choose the ones he feels most comfortable with and then practice them over and over until he can finally use them in the real world.

  - *Blame you.* Tell your kid he can *always* pin the blame on you: "My parents won't let me." "My dad will ground me for life." "It's their stupid rule."

  - *Give an alternative.* "Why don't we go to Jimmy's?" "Let's do this instead . . ."

  - *Phone home.* Set up a secret code that your child uses only when he needs help in a tough situation: "Mom, I think I'm getting the flu." If he calls with the code, drop everything and go pick him up. And don't let your kid out of the house without change, a calling card, or a cell phone so he can call home if needed.

  - *Find another kid.* There is sometimes safety in numbers, so tell your child to move toward other kids, walk toward an adult, or find another kid to join up with.

  - *Stay firm.* Stress to your kid that it may be hard, but he should continue to repeat "No" like a broken record until the kid gets the hint. Emphasize that his goal is not to change his friend's mind or alter his behavior, but instead to stick to what he himself knows is the right thing to do. And stress this idea: *"If it feels wrong, it probably is."*

WHAT TO EXPECT BY STAGES AND AGES

Preschooler Friends are chosen out of convenience: "He lives close and has good toys." Arrange playdates. Find playmates your child would enjoy. Talk about the traits of good friends. Friendship-making skills and values learned now play a big role in friendship choices later.

School Age Friends are selected because of certain traits and shared interests. Enroll your kid in activities that match his passions (sports, art, music) so that he can meet other kids with similar interests. Teach problem-solving tactics so that he knows what to do in troubling situations.

One Parent's Answer

A dad from Tempe writes:

My twelve-year-old befriended a kid who should have had "Trouble" tattooed on his forehead. I was sure I'd be mortgaging my home for bail if they kept paling around. Josh always wanted a guitar, and I figured what better time. I bought a used one and signed him up for after-school lessons. He found two boys who shared his music passion, and they started a band. By that time the other kid faded from his life.

Tween   The need for peer acceptance is huge, generally peaking in the seventh to ninth grade. Cliques, peer pressure, and social rejection are the hot-button topics, so teach ways to resist peer pressure. Find ways he can be involved with kids outside of school to reduce the negative impact of cliques. Network with the other parents. Make your house kid friendly. Kids begin to pull away from parents in the quest for independence, so stay involved in his world. Know where your kid is. Period.

More Helpful Advice

Best Friends, Worst Enemies: Understanding the Social Lives of Children, by Michael Thompson and Catherine O'Neill Grace

Nobody Likes Me, Everybody Hates Me: The Top 25 Friendship Problems and How to Solve Them, by Michele Borba

The Behavior Survival Guide for Kids: How to Make Good Choices and Stay out of Trouble, by Tom McIntyre

The Friendship Factor: Helping Our Children Navigate Their Social World—and Why It Matters for Their Success and Happiness, by Kenneth H. Rubin

Bullied

SEE ALSO: *Bad Friends, Cyberbullying, Dependent, Depressed, Fearful, Internet Safety, Peer Pressure, Rejected, Shy, Stressed, Teased*

THE PROBLEM

Red Flags

Verbally or physically abused, repeatedly harassed in a mean-spirited manner, unable to defend or stick up for himself

The Change to Parent For

Your child learns to defend himself, feels safer and more confident, and is less likely to be targeted by a bully.

Question: "There is a neighborhood boy who constantly bullies my son. Is there anything I can do so my child isn't always victimized?"

Answer: Although we can't protect our kids against cruel-hearted kids, we can lessen the likelihood that they will be victimized. The first step is to teach your son an important secret: bullies want power, and they are looking for a reaction. If you look upset, the bully wins—and once he does, he is also more likely to repeat his cruel tactics. Once your child knows that secret, help him practice giving a "cool, unfazed" look he can use with his tormentor.

Why Change?

If your child is bullied, it means that peers are *intentionally* causing him pain. Reports confirm that bullying is starting at younger ages and is more frequent and aggressive than ever before. What's more, one study showed that those who bullied *or were bullied* were more likely to be involved in violent behavior.[3] Bottom line: bullying behavior must be taken very seriously whether your child is the victim or the perpetrator. (See also *Bullying*, p. 332.)

A bully can "attack" his victim verbally (spreading rumors, saying prejudicial comments, delivering cruel remarks, making sexual comments or gestures); physically (hitting,

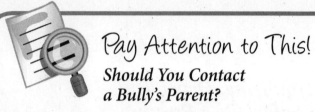

Pay Attention to This!
Should You Contact a Bully's Parent?

A national PTA survey found that only one-fourth of parents support contacting other parents to deal with bullying.[4] A bully's parent usually denies that her kid is guilty and may blame your child, as well as feel that you are criticizing her parenting. You may need to get an objective outsider, such as a principal or day-care supervisor, to mediate. A diplomatic *"I'm concerned about the relationship between our kids"* may be your best opener. And if *you* get a call accusing your kid, listen. He just may be less innocent than you think.

slamming); emotionally (excluding, humiliating, threatening, extorting, hazing); and electronically (through cell phone, text messaging, e-mail, or Web site). Actual bullying rates differ according to the study or source. One study estimates that almost one in three American schoolchildren is either a bully or a victim;[5] Another study found that one out of every four children will be bullied by another youth in school this month.[6] Research has found that 160,000 children a day skip school because they fear being attacked or intimidated by other students.[7] One fact is clear: bullying is an ongoing problem, and chances are that your child *will be bullied.*

Make no mistake: those cruel, aggressive habits are learned and should *never* be tolerated. What's more, a new report finds that bullying tops the list of school troubles and that many students say talking with their parents does little to ease the stress.[8] Although you can't always be there to step in and protect your child, there are ways to help your son or daughter be less likely to be victimized in the first place. This entry provides solutions to offer your child.

Signs and Symptoms

Here are a warning signs that a child may be bullied and needs your support. If your child complains of being taunted, picked on, or threatened by peers, please take him seriously. Unfortunately, however, chances are that if your child is bullied, he won't tell you, so watch for changes in your child's typical behavior.

- Can't explain physical marks, cuts, bruises and scrapes, or torn clothing
- Can't explain loss of toys, school supplies, clothing, lunches, or money
- Fears being left alone; doesn't want to go to school; is afraid of riding the school bus; wants you there at dismissal; is suddenly clingy
- Is suddenly sullen, withdrawn, evasive; remarks about feeling lonely
- Undergoes marked change in typical behavior or personality

- Has physical complaints: headaches, stomachaches, frequent visits to the school nurse's office
- Has difficulty sleeping, nightmares; cries self to sleep; wets the bed
- Begins bullying siblings or younger kids
- Waits to get home to use the bathroom
- Eats ravenously when he comes home (lunch money or lunch may be stolen)
- Experiences sudden and significant drop in grades; has difficulty focusing and concentrating

THE SOLUTION

Step 1. Early Intervention

- *Start the talk now!* Children who are embarrassed or humiliated about being bullied are unlikely to discuss it with their parents or teachers and generally suffer in silence, withdraw, and try to stay away from school.[9] So start talking to your child about bullying before it ever happens. Tell your child you are always available and that you recognize that it's a growing problem. Notice when other children are reported to be bullied in your child's circle of friends and acquaintances or when there's an example in the media or on TV, and use it as an occasion to bring up the subject.

LATE-BREAKING NEWS

University of Minnesota: Tune in more closely to your child. Please. Repeated bullying causes severe emotional harm and erodes your child's fragile self-esteem.[10] Boys and girls are bullied differently: girls are more likely to be victims of emotional and verbal bullying; boys are usually bullied with physical harm or threat. But whether the bullying is verbal, physical, or relational, the long-term effects are equally harmful. Both boys and girls have reported high levels of emotional distress and loneliness as well as lower self-esteem, anxiety, and depression.[11]

University of Warwick: Late-breaking research also finds that girls victimized by bullies (including being beaten and suffering physical or verbal threats) at six years of age are significantly more likely to remain victims at age ten.[12]

Both studies caution parents to keep a watchful eye on their children and take bullying seriously.

- *Stop rescuing.* If you want your child to stick up for himself, then don't be so quick to step in and solve his problems or speak for him. Children need practice to speak up and be assertive so that when the moment comes that they do need to stand up to a bully, they can. Always rescuing can create the conditions under which a child can become a victim of bullying.

- *Have him avoid areas where bullies prey.* Bullying usually happens in unsupervised areas, such as hallways, stairwells, playgrounds (under trees and equipment, in far corners), lockers, parks, and bathrooms (in malls, schools, parks, and even libraries). In fact, a nationwide survey found that 43 percent of children said they were afraid to use the school bathroom for fear of being harassed.[13] Familiarize your child with "hot spots" (places most likely to be frequently by bullies) and tell him to avoid those areas.

- *Encourage him to find a supportive companion.* Tell your child there is sometimes safety in numbers. Kids who have even one friend to confide in can deal with bullying better than those on their own. Is there one kid your child can pair up with?

ONE SIMPLE SOLUTION

Help Your Child Create a PLAN to Be Less Likely to Be Bullied

Teach your child the acronym PLAN and its four parts to keep him safer from bullies or injury.

P – **Pal up.** Hang out with a large group; stay with one companion or find someone who is older or bigger who can help look out for you.

L – **Let an adult know.** Talk to someone you trust and seek that person out if you don't feel safe.

A – **Avoid "hot spots."** Stay away from areas where bullying is more likely to happen (bathrooms, the back of the bus, far corners of a playground, under stairwells).

N – **Notice your surroundings.** If you think there could be trouble, leave that spot. Take a different route, but don't go off alone.

Step 2. Rapid Response

- *Take your child seriously.* One of the biggest parenting mistakes is to not take our kids seriously when they report bullying episodes. So reassure your child that you believe him, thank him for coming to you, and stress that you will find a way to keep him safe. Research finds that 49 percent of kids say they've been bullied at least once or twice during the school term, but only 32 percent of their parents believed them.[14] In one survey, eight- to eleven-year-olds whose parents said they discussed their bullying troubles reported that those talks were infrequent and not very memorable; half the kids didn't remember the talk at all (that's despite 74 percent saying teasing and bullying occur at their school).[15]

- *Determine if it's bullying.* Bullying is always intentional and mean-spirited; it rarely happens only once, and there is always a power imbalance. The victim cannot hold his own. It is *not* the same as teasing: bullying involves a higher level of threat and abuse. First establish that this is indeed bullying so that you can respond in the appropriate way. You might ask:

"Was it an accident, or did he hurt you on purpose?"

"Did you do or say anything first to upset him?"

"Did she mean to be mean?"

"Did he do it more than once?"

"Did he know that he was hurting you?"

"Did she care that you were sad or angry?"

"Did you tell her to stop?"

"Did he listen?"

If your child is unsure if this is really bullying, encourage him to talk with witnesses to get their take.

- *Get to the bottom of anything suspicious.* Kids often don't tell adults they're bullied; you may have to voice your concerns. Review the signs of bullying listed earlier and then ask direct questions. *"You're always hungry: have you been eating your lunch?" "Your CDs are missing. Did someone take them?" "Your jacket is ripped. Did someone do that to you?"*

- *Gather facts.* Next, you need all the facts so you can help your kid create a plan to stop the bullying:

"What happened?"

"Who did this?"

"Where were you?"

"Who was there?"

"Were you alone?"

"Has it happened before? How often?"

"How does it start?"

"What did you do?"

"Do you think he'll do it again?"

"Did anyone help you?"

"Did an adult see this? Did the adult help?"

- *Offer specific tips for a plan of action.* Most kids can't handle bullying on their own; they need your help, so provide a specific plan. For instance, if bullying is happening on the bus, tell your child to sit behind the bus driver on the left side of the bus (the worst place to sit is near the back on the right-hand side where the driver can't see the passengers in the mirror). You could ask an older kid to "watch out" for your child, or offer to pick your child up from school.

- *Identify a trusting adult.* Find an adult who can help your child when you're not around. It must be someone who'll take this seriously, protect your child, and, if necessary, keep this confidential. It could be a secretary, teacher, neighbor, school nurse, bus driver, or even the custodian—anyone your child trusts. Tweens are far less likely to seek help. This is also the time bullying can be most intense, and the victim feels trapped and isolated.

- *Don't make promises.* You may have to protect your child, so make *no* promises to keep things confidential. "I want to make sure you don't get hurt, so I can't guarantee I won't tell. Let's see what we can do so that this doesn't happen again."

One Parent's Answer

A mom from Nashville writes:

Once I knew my son was being bullied, I started talking to other parents and found out bullying was prevalent not only in the school but also in our town. A few of us started a "Neighborhood Watch" group and designated "safe houses" for our kids to go to after school. Then we created a parent group to discuss our concerns with educators and enlisted the help of the PTA. It took a group of us to stand together to get bullying under control, but we did it.

Step 3. Develop Habits for Change

The final step is to teach your child new habits so that he learns to assert himself safely and make it less likely that he'll be targeted in the future. Here are bullyproofing strategies every child should know:

- *Don't look like a victim.* Kids with an assertive posture are less likely to be picked on. Stress to your child that he should stand tall and hold his head up to appear more confident and less vulnerable.

- *Stay calm and do not react.* Bullies love power and knowing they can push other kids' buttons, so tell your child to stay calm and try not to let his tormentor know he upset him. Stress to your child never to cry or to insult or threaten a bully—the bully will only escalate things. It sometimes helps a younger child to pretend to wear a special bullyproof vest that bounces the taunts off and helps him not look afraid.

- *Say no using a firm voice.* Stress to your child that if he needs to respond, simple direct commands work best, delivered in a strong, determined voice: "No." "Cut it out." "No way." "Stop." "Back off." Then he should walk away with shoulders held back. Pleading ("Please stop that") or feeling-laden messages ("It really makes feel mad when you do that") rarely work. Once your child agrees on a strategy, you *must* rehearse it with him until he feels confident enough to use it alone. A big part of success is the ability to deliver comebacks assertively with the right tone. (See *Teased,* p. 415, for more comebacks for verbal bullying.)

- *Use a stone-faced glare.* Have your child practice using a mean stare that goes straight through the bully so that he seems in control and not bothered.

- *Leave the scene.* Stress that your child should leave the scene as soon as possible. Ideally he should walk toward other kids or an adult. Tell him not to look back, get help if he needs to, and fight only as a very last resort if he must defend yourself.

- *Boost self-confidence.* Research finds that arming your child with confidence is one of the best defenses against bullying.[16] Kids who lack confidence are more likely to be victimized. A few self-confidence boosters include learning martial arts, boxing, or weightlifting; finding an avenue—such as a hobby, interest, sport, or talent—that he enjoys and in which he can excel; and giving him opportunities to solve his problems and speak up for himself.

Pay Attention to This!

Eight Things to Do If Bullying Escalates and Becomes More Serious

Research shows that bullying is escalating[17] and that bullies are more likely these days to be aggressive and possibly carrying a weapon. Here are things to do if your previous efforts fail and bullying intensifies.

1. *Be ready to advocate.* If there's ever the possibility your child could be injured—step in.

2. *Notify authorities and gather support.* Tell those directly responsible for your child (his teacher, coach, pediatrician, day-care worker). A multidisciplinary approach in which all the adults in your child's life are involved in finding a solution is best. Do talk to the school nurse: victims often go to the nurse's office complaining of physical problems as an escape.

3. *Keep records.* You may need proof, so keep such evidence as torn clothing; threatening e-mails; and witnesses' names, phone numbers, and details.

4. *Demand confidentiality.* You don't want retaliation, so limit the number of people you tell wherever possible.

5. *Expect protection.* Get specifics: "What will you do to ensure my child's safety?" If you do not get support, go up a level: call the principal, superintendent, school board, or the police.

6. *Ensure there is no face-to-face contact.* Distance your child from the bully: class, lunch, bus, team. Ideally the bully should not come within a certain number of feet of your child.

7. *Be prepared for resistance.* Don't be surprised if you are told to "toughen your kid up."

8. *Be vigilant.* You may need to change classes, teams, or even schools to protect your kid.

WHAT TO EXPECT BY STAGES AND AGES

Preschooler   This is the age bullying behaviors are first adopted because kids learn that the behaviors work as a means of getting their way. Bullying is mostly physical (biting, pinching, kicking, or shoving) and usually not intentional (the true definition of bullying). Aggression is mostly due to impulsivity and the inability to regulate emotions. Do not allow aggressive behavior or cruelty.

School Age   Direct bullying seems to increase through the elementary school years.[18] Verbal bullying (saying mean comments, put-downs, and taunts) is prevalent. Physical bullying continues with younger kids. Around fourth grade, social exclusion (leaving kids out and knowingly hurting their feelings) begins. New research shows that more cross-gender bullying (in particular, unpopular boys bullying popular girls) happens in the fourth to sixth grades than previously thought.[19]

Tween   Bullying peaks during these years and is also the most prevalent among sixth to eighth graders.[20] The average middle school student experiences at least one verbal harassment per day.[21] Relational aggression, rumor spreading, and emotional bullying are common among girls. Electronic bullying (via text, instant messaging, pagers, cell phones, Web sites, social networking sites, and e-mails) also begins, as well as sexual harassment. Forty percent of fifth through eighth graders say they've been sexually harassed by peers (mostly boys).[22]

More Helpful Advice

Bullies and Victims: Helping Your Child Through the Schoolyard Battlefield, by SuEllen and Paula Fried

Facing the Schoolyard Bully: How to Raise an Assertive Child in an Aggressive World, by Kim Zarzour

Girl War: 12 Strategies That Will End Female Bullying, by Cheryl Dellasega and Charisse Nixon

The Bully, the Bullied, and the Bystander, by Barbara Coloroso

Your Child: Bully or Victim? Understanding and Ending Schoolyard Tyranny, by Peter Sheras

SOCIAL SCENE

Bullying

SEE ALSO: *Angry, Biting, Bullied, Cyberbullying, Insensitive, Internet Safety, Intolerant, Not Knowing Right from Wrong, Tantrums*

THE PROBLEM

Red Flags

Doesn't show empathy or consider other people's feelings, sees things only from his view, bullies or displays aggressive behaviors and often fails to see the impact or take responsibility for cruel actions

The Change to Parent For

Your child learns to be more sensitive to another's feelings, recognizes that aggression is not the way to resolve problems, takes responsibility for hurting others, and tries to make amends.

Question: "My son's teacher says he bullies a classmate by saying cruel things, deliberately slamming or tripping him. He denies being mean, and says the other kid is just a 'wimp' and deserves it. My husband says this is just a phase and a 'boy thing.' Do I believe my husband or the teacher?"

Answer: Bullying is cruelty and always contains these four elements:

1. It is an aggressive act that is usually repeated.
2. The bully has more power (strength, status, size) than the victim, who cannot hold his own.
3. The hurtful behavior is not an accident, but intentional. The bully usually seems to enjoy seeing the victim in distress.
4. The bully rarely accepts responsibility and often says the victim "deserved" the hurtful treatment.

Take the teacher's word and work with her to develop a full-blown plan to stop your child's bullying ASAP. Bullying should never be considered "just a phase" or a "boy thing." There is *never* an excuse for cruelty.

Why Change?

Bullying is a learned behavior that is on the rise. What's more, it is far more intense and occurs more frequently and at younger ages than in years past. The U.S. National School Safety Center warns that bullying has become the most enduring and underrated problem in American schools."[23] One recent study prepared for the American Psychological Association showed that 80 percent of middle school students admitted to bullying behavior in the prior thirty days.[24] Another survey found that 40 percent of nine- to thirteen-year-olds admitted to bullying.[25] Bullying has become so serious that some school-age victims have died from the savage beatings or committed suicide (called *bullycide* as a result of bullying and depression).

Today's bully is far from the stereotyped image of the "bad kid down the block." A bully may be male or female, a preschooler or teen, rich or poor, urban or rural. One study of 452 fourth- through sixth-grade boys from a variety of backgrounds found that bullies are often self-assured kids who are surprisingly intelligent and sociable, and are frequently rated "most popular" by classmates (or are just as likely to be disruptive and hyperactive).[26]

No matter the age, gender, religion, or ethnicity, any child resorting to bullying needs an immediate behavior intervention. Do not make the mistake of thinking this is just "a phase" or a boys' rite of passage. One study found that nearly 60 percent of males who were identified as chronic bullies in middle school had at least one criminal conviction by the age of twenty-four.[27] The consequences of letting this go unheeded are disastrous to your child's character and conscience. The good news is that because bullying is a learned behavior, it can also be unlearned.

Signs and Symptoms

Look for *repeated* and *intentional* patterns of verbal, emotional, or physical aggression:

- Excludes or shuns another child
- Taunts, intimidates, or harasses
- Spreads vicious rumors verbally or electronically that hurt or ruin another's reputation
- Is physically aggressive (hits, punches, kicks, slams, chokes) or threatens with force or fear
- Damages another child's property or clothing
- Takes pleasure in seeing a child (or animal) in distress; is unconcerned if someone is upset
- Finds it difficult to see a situation from the other person's point of view
- Refuses to accept responsibility or denies wrongdoing when evidence shows guilt
- Blames the victim or says the child "deserved what he got"
- Targets those who are weaker or younger, or animals

LATE-BREAKING NEWS

Types of Parenting That Encourage Bullying

University of Norway: Dan Olweus, a foremost authority on bullying, identified four factors most likely to encourage bullying behavior.[28] Could any of these be an issue in your home?

- Lack of parental warmth and involvement
- Permissive or "tolerant" attitude toward the child's abusive behavior; no clear limits set on the child's bullying
- Use of physical punishment or emotional outbursts when disciplining the child
- Parenting style that does not match the child's natural temperament (which may be more aggressive, impulsive, and quick to anger)

THE SOLUTION

Step 1. Early Intervention

- *Identify the reason.* Your first step is to determine why your child is using this behavior. One survey of over twenty thousand kids found that the top reasons eight- to twelve-year-olds give for bullying are "They annoyed me" or "To get even."[29] Here are other possibilities. Please check those that apply to your child or situation:

  - ☐ *Permissive caregivers.* Bullying is excused as a "boys will be boys" rite of passage; the child recognizes that there are few or no behavior limits and that he can get away with it; adults turn a blind eye to the behavior.

  - ☐ *Authoritarian caregivers.* The child has been exposed to overly harsh discipline; upbringing has been too rigid or strict; parents give only "conditional" love.

  - ☐ *Lack of self-esteem.* The child has an exaggerated need for attention or respect.

  - ☐ *Feelings of powerlessness.* Aggression is used to gain rank, attention, or power, or to show "toughness."

  - ☐ *Underdeveloped empathy.* Empathy is not encouraged or nurtured at home; the child has experienced early trauma or depression that may inhibit the development of empathy.

☐ *For fun.* The child sees bullying as a "game," is bored, and enjoys seeing another upset.

☐ *Aggressive pals.* The child hangs with a group who believes it's cool to be cruel.

☐ *Desire for friends.* The child lacks social skills, feels rejected or isolated by peers, and is trying to fit in.

☐ *Poor coping skills.* The child is impulsive, unable to control anger; he tends to "act out."

☐ *Revenge.* The child is getting back or getting even, is picked on or bullied by others.

☐ *Media overexposure.* The child watches television shows, movies, and video or computer games that glamorize aggression and cruelty, and the exposure affects his behavior and attitude.

What do you think is triggering this behavior? What action can you take right now to turn this problem around?

- *Take reports seriously.* It's not easy to hear negative things about your child, but don't dismiss or excuse any report that your child is bullying. ("He has friends." "She's a model student.") One study shows that some of the most popular kids in school and even those in leadership roles display antisocial behaviors.[30] Catching an aggressive behavior early is the best way to stop it. So ask the source for further details. Monitor your child a bit more closely. Watch for signs of bullying and then respond ASAP if you suspect that those reports have validity. University of Michigan psychologist Leonard Eron tracked more than eight hundred eight-year-olds over four decades and singled out the 25 percent who often showed bullying behavior. By age thirty, one in four had an arrest record, whereas only 5 percent of the nonaggressive children did.[31]

- *Monitor media consumption.* The American Academy of Pediatrics and five other prominent medical groups have stated that "viewing entertainment violence can lead to increases in aggressive attitudes, values, and behavior, particularly in children."[32] The American Psychological Association warns that "more than four decades of research have revealed that TV violence has a strong influence on the aggressive behavior of children and adults. Exposure to violent media increases feelings of hostility, thoughts about aggression, suspicions about the motives of others and demonstrates violence as a method to deal with conflict."[33] So watch your child's behavior. Does he become more aggressive after playing certain video games or watching particular movies or television shows espousing the view that aggression is acceptable? If so, set clear limits on your child's viewing habits and then enforce those limits.

- *Model empathy.* Consciously model kinder, gentler behaviors for your child to copy. And make sure the kids and adults your child hangs around are those who are appropriate models as well. Studies conclusively reveal that kids learn aggressive behaviors by watching others. Research also shows that when parents are empathic, their kids are more likely to become empathic themselves, just because those behaviors have been modeled for them.[34]

- *Get dad involved.* Kids whose dads were positively involved in their care when they were age five were found thirty years later to be more empathic, sensitive adults than those whose fathers were absent.[35] Involved dads can make a major contribution to raising sensitive kids, so get those males involved! And research shows that many bullies come from homes where dads are aggressive or uninvolved. If this describes your child, seek out strong male role models who can connect with and care about your son, including an uncle, cousin, stepdad, or even Big Brother.

Step 2. Rapid Response

Responses for a First-Time Bullying Offense

- *Step in ASAP.* The minute you see or hear that your child is involved in bully-like behavior, step in. Stay calm so as not to escalate the situation. Remove your child immediately from the situation (or as soon as convenient). Then sit down with your child and in a serious and firm tone call the behavior for what it is (bullying), describe the action, and explain why it is wrong.

- *Review your expectations.* Voice your strong objections to your child's behavior. One survey of 5,548 students asked "What stops children from bullying?" The

One Parent's Answer

A mom from Reno shares:

It took a while for me to acknowledge that my child was a bully. But when I realized Jacob never owned up to the hurt he caused, it was my "Enough!" moment. I started demanding that he apologize to anyone he had bullied—and sincerely. I insisted that he apologize face-to-face, call and say he was sorry, or offer to do something to try and make up for the cruel act. Once he knew I wasn't going to allow him to get away with his meanness, he started turning the corner and taking responsibility for his actions.

top answer: "If the child knew their parents disapproved and how their mom and dad would think about them if they bullied someone."[36] On average, the kids said they cared as much about their parents' judgments as they did about those of their peers. That feeling of shame can be a strong motivational force. So clearly lay down your rules: *"In this house you are always to be kind to others." "You will not treat another person cruelly."*

- *Listen carefully to your child.* Now get your child's take on the situation. Your role is to try to discover what might be bothering your child or triggering this behavior so that you can help. So listen carefully and try to gather facts. For instance: Was he falsely accused, or could he be the victim of bullying himself? Was he trying to protect himself? Is this the only way he can figure out how to find a friend? Then dig deeper. Where and when did this happen? What started it? Which kids were involved? How frequently does this happen? Were there any adult witnesses? Those details will help you piece together what is going on to help prevent a reoccurrence. Also keep in mind that bullies often deny their actions or blame the other kid. You may need to call witnesses to help you get the most accurate picture.

- *Create a positive solution.* Once you determine what prompted the offense (he uses aggression to make friends, protect himself, for revenge, to try to look cool), your next step is to work together to try to create a solution. The objective isn't to let your child off the hook, but to develop alternatives so the bullying won't happen again. Here are two examples:

Problem: He bullies to seek power and find friends. **Solution:** Find other social avenues where your child can make a new friend; teach him friendship-making skills to boost his social competence. (See *Nobody Likes Me, Everybody Hates Me,* by yours truly.)

Problem: He bullies due to inability to control anger. **Solution:** Teach specific anger management strategies. (See *Angry,* p. 232.)

- *Enforce a consequence.* Even as you respond supportively to your child, you also can't let him think he can get away with abusive behavior. Insist that your child be held responsible for any aggressive or hurtful action. If he doesn't have a suggestion for a reasonable consequence, then you can state one that "fits the crime." If your daughter sends a cruel text message to a friend, she loses her cell phone privilege. If your son gets other kids to gang up on a classmate, he forgoes the next playdate. If your daughter spread vicious rumors about a peer, she is prohibited from the upcoming sleepover. If your child has taunted another child, insist that he do some kind of charitable deed, such as spend a Saturday afternoon helping out at a soup kitchen. Whatever the consequence, don't let him off the hook. Warning: do not use physical punishment for a bullying offense. It only reinforces the idea that aggression is the way to get others to respond.

- *Require restitution.* Your child should also be required to make amends for the hurt he caused. Doing so will help him realize that even though he can't take away the victim's pain, he will be required to do something to make amends. He could offer a sincere apology, pay for any physical loss he may have inflicted, or repair or replace any broken property. You might start by asking your child what *he* plans to do to make amends to the victim. You should speak to the victim's parents and explain the situation and that your child would like to apologize. If you go to the victim's home to do so, it is best that you accompany your child. Bullying can make a victim emotionally distraught and fearful, and face-to-face contact with a bully (even if it is your child) can be intimidating. Remember, this is not a simple "argument" between two kids, nor is this the "victim's problem." Bullying always involves a power imbalance in which the victim cannot hold his own. In a particularly egregious bullying offense, know that an interaction with all parties could get tense. So determine whether the apology is best made face-to-face, on the phone, via letter, or even with a mediator present.

- *Review your expectations repeatedly.* Don't expect your one-time lecture to make a lasting change in your child's behavior. Be vigilant and continue to review your expectations with your child that bullying is not acceptable in your family or in society. It may help to remind your child prior to a social encounter: *"Jason is coming over. I expect you to be kind, or I will have to tell him that you can't play." "I expect you to be nice and to include all the girls when you go to Haley's house."*

Responses for More Severe or Repeated Bullying

- *Monitor your child more closely.* Let your child know you will supervise him with other kids when you're around or check on his actions outside your home. If he is bullying a particular child, set an "Off-Limits" Policy: your child is not to be within twenty-five feet of that child. (For a younger child, use a visual reference, such as the length of a room.) No excuses allowed. For example, forbid your child from playing with a friend until he understands he *must* treat others kindly. If you need to have another adult supervise your child, do so.

- *Have a conference with caregivers.* Explain to your child that you will talk with all relevant caregivers (teacher, coach, babysitter) to ensure that everyone is on the same behavior plan. Then set up an appointment within the next few days. You and your child should attend the conference together so that everyone is on the same page. At that meeting, listen carefully to the teacher's take on the situation, as well as your child's perspective. Then develop a plan to help defuse the aggressive behavior and find positive alternatives.

- *Seek professional help.* If your child's bullying does not gradually improve or if it increases, request a meeting with the school psychologist for a more thorough behavioral and psychological evaluation of your child. If you can't find this kind of help at your school, seek a trained mental health professional in the community. Your child's pediatrician should have a list of references. Your goal is to find someone who can create a behavior plan to stop the aggressive behaviors as well as help your child develop new habits for change.

Step 3. Develop Habits for Change

One big part of your helping your child change is to figure out why your child is resorting to bullying behavior, and then teach new habits to replace inappropriate ones. Here are a few habits to teach, but choose ones that apply to your child and situation:

- *Teach friendship skills.* If you suspect your child is bullying because he doesn't know how to make or keep friends, then watch him a bit more closely (without his knowing you are doing so) to identify the particular friendship skills he needs to learn. For instance: how to start a conversation, lose gracefully, ask permission, or solve problems peacefully. (See *Argues,* p. 46.) Then target and teach one new skill at a time by showing your child the new strategy and then practicing it with him until your child can use it alone. (See *Rejected,* p. 381.)

- *Check for aggressive "friends."* Is your child picking up on this behavior by mimicking other children? Bullying is a learned behavior, so watch to see who your kid pals around with. Also, check out the day-care center, sports teams, or other after-school programs your child is enrolled in. Ask teachers and coaches. If your child is involved with other kids who enjoy exerting their physical or emotional power, then wean your child away from them and help find him a new set of friends. Forbid your child from communicating via phone or computer. (Your carrier can block the child's phone number and e-mail address.) In some cases you may have to change your child's schedule, ask the teacher to move your child's desk, pick him up from school, change his class, or, in a worst-case scenario, change schools or even move. But don't let him associate with kids who abuse others. In the meantime, pursue other social avenues that enable your child to find and make new friends, such as a church group, Boys and Girls Club, scouting, or a sports team. (See *Bad Friends,* p. 314.)

- *Nurture empathy.* If your child doesn't recognize or even care that his behavior is causing his victim distress, boost his empathy. (See *Insensitive,* p. 159.) Here are a few ways to do so:
    - *Role-play.* Ask him to "switch places" and pretend to be the victim. Then ask, *"How would you feel if someone said that about you?"* Younger kids can use stuffed animals or puppets to role-play different roles and perspectives.

- *Use stories.* Tell or read a story about a child who is victimized. Make it up or look for real examples in the news. *"Who do you think is most like you in this story?" "How do you think Sara felt when Jake told his friends those lies about her?"*

- *Have him tutor a younger child.* Have your child teach a younger child (a cousin, next-door neighbor, your friend's child) a skill or subject he excels in.

- *Use children's literature or movies.* Read books or watch movies laced with compassion, such as *Dumbo, The Velveteen Rabbit, Stone Fox, Charlotte's Web, The Hundred Dresses, The Secret Garden,* or *The Diary of Anne Frank.*

- *Label emotions.* Talk about feelings and point out the emotions of people in distress.

- *Reinforce caring acts.* Acknowledge your child's kind acts so that he'll be more likely to repeat the action: *"Jack, that was so kind of you to tell Peter you're sorry his grandpa is ill. It really made him feel better."*

- *Find ways to "do good."* Consider doing community service as a family. Food drives, picking up trash in the park, painting shelters for battered women, serving meals at homeless shelters, or delivering meals to sick and elderly folks who are housebound are just a few options.

- *Find healthy ways to reroute aggression.* Does your child have a surplus of energy that often is acted out? Then offer a positive alternative to channel his aggression, such as karate, boxing, swimming, Jazzercise, weightlifting, soccer, football, or the marching band. The goal is to find a physical outlet for your kid to direct his strength and also be praised for his effort. Also make sure you teach strategies to help control his anger. (See *Angry,* p. 232.)

More Helpful Advice

Building Moral Intelligence: The Seven Essential Virtues That Teach Kids to Do the Right Thing, by Michele Borba

Bullying at School: What We Know and What We Can Do (Understanding Children's Worlds), by Dan Olweus

Girl Wars: 12 Strategies That Will End Female Bullying, by Cheryl Dellasega and Charisse Nixon

The Bully, the Bullied, and the Bystander, by Barbara Coloroso

Your Child: Bully or Victim? Understanding and Ending Schoolyard Tyranny, by Peter Sheras

WHAT TO EXPECT BY STAGES AND AGES

Preschooler   At this age, bullying is more likely to be physical, such hitting, biting, pinching, poking, and tripping. Although bullying at this age is usually not intentional, it can become a habit if it is allowed to continue. Preschoolers are egocentric by nature, so expect difficulty getting them to consider the feelings and needs of others.

School Age   Bullying increases during the school-age years; verbal insults and put-downs become prevalent. Social exclusion and leaving other kids out become issues around fourth grade.

Tween   Bullying peaks in eleven- to-twelve-year olds, and it becomes more covert; these are the ages when kids tend to blame the victim.[37] Girls are more prone to use "relational cruelty": deliberately excluding, shunning another girl, or spreading vicious rumors.

Cliques

SEE ALSO: *Bullied, Peer Pressure, Rejected, Sensitive, Teased*

THE PROBLEM
Red Flags

Is always the outsider, on the fringe; is never included or not quite "in" with the group; feels excluded or ostracized; is the victim of gossip or jealousy

The Change to Parent For

Your child learns ways to navigate the social jungle by identifying groups she would like to associate with because of similar values and interests, not just popularity, and learns ways to handle group rejection.

Question: "My daughter is always in tears because there's always one girl or another who is threatening to exclude her from the clique she belongs to. I'd love to call these girls' mothers and give them a piece of my mind. Should I?"

Answer: I would not recommend picking up the phone and blasting the parents. It could definitely backfire. A better response is to help your daughter learn from the experience, and the first lesson is to figure out whether this really is the right group for her. Talk about your own friends. Watch movies like *Bring It On, Mystic Pizza,* and *Pretty in Pink.* Expose her to other girls with whom she'd have more in common. It may take some time for her to recognize that true friends are loyal and fun to be with, but once she does, she'll be happier. Unfortunately, she can only learn the lesson herself.

Why Change?

A clique is a tightly bound group of friends who hang out almost exclusively together. Don't get me wrong: they're not always bad. They can be your child's safety net: the kids share secrets, hang out, enjoy each other's company. The danger is when they become extremely exclusive, and the ringleader's mentality borders on cruelty through rejection. (In the world of girl social research, it's called *relational aggression*.)

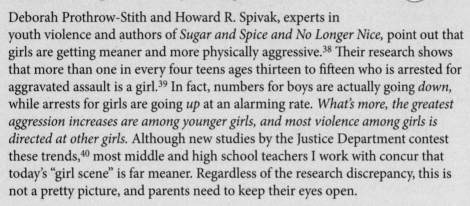

LATE-BREAKING NEWS

Mean Girl Cliques Are Only Getting Meaner!

Deborah Prothrow-Stith and Howard R. Spivak, experts in youth violence and authors of *Sugar and Spice and No Longer Nice,* point out that girls are getting meaner and more physically aggressive.[38] Their research shows that more than one in every four teens ages thirteen to fifteen who is arrested for aggravated assault is a girl.[39] In fact, numbers for boys are actually going *down,* while arrests for girls are going *up* at an alarming rate. *What's more, the greatest aggression increases are among younger girls, and most violence among girls is directed at other girls.* Although new studies by the Justice Department contest these trends,[40] most middle and high school teachers I work with concur that today's "girl scene" is far meaner. Regardless of the research discrepancy, this is not a pretty picture, and parents need to keep their eyes open.

Research shows that cliques are not only starting up at younger ages but also becoming meaner and more vicious. The pain from being ostracized, repeatedly rejected, or having vicious rumors spread about you can be almost unbearable. Luckily, new studies also show that there are things parents can do to help kids deal with a painful social scene as well as figure out whether it's worth getting into this particular group or moving on to another. Our children need to learn these lessons both for their school years and for their future. Cliques don't stop at graduation but continue throughout life, so learning new habits today only makes things easier later on.

Signs and Symptoms

Almost every child has troubles with a clique, but when you notice these signs increasing or lasting more than a few weeks, and your child's demeanor is changing, it's time to look further. Here's what to watch out for:

- Your child seems upset or defensive whenever you bring up certain friends' names.
- You hear or your child shares unfounded rumors or nasty gossip about her.
- Phone calls or invitations from pals stop; friends who used to drop by no longer do so.
- Your child is repeatedly left out of events where she had previously been included.
- Your child wants to avoid places she frequented with pals; resists going to school; wants to drop being on a team, scouts, or a club she once enjoyed.

- Your child badmouths those who were her friends; she doesn't want to talk about certain kids.

- Your outgoing kid suddenly becomes withdrawn, defiant, or moody; she loses her appetite, cries easily, loses interest in school, or has trouble sleeping—all around the same time that those friends stop calling. She comes home frequently from school or a social gathering noticeably more upset, angry, or sullen than when she left.

THE SOLUTION

Step 1. Early Intervention

- *Be a good role model.* Do you gossip about your girlfriends? Do you put your friend down behind her back? Do you exclude other women from your group of friends? Watch out. Your daughter is watching! Be the strong role model you want your child to become.

- *Get savvy.* Although cliques have always been around, they are different nowadays. Kids are meaner and more physically aggressive. You can help your child navigate that social jungle better if you educate yourself about the social scene. See the More Helpful Advice box for a list of books about cliques.

- *Stay involved in your child's life.* It's almost impossible for parents to prevent their kid's involvement with cliques. So don't try. But even though your child may be pulling away from your family physically, she still needs you emotionally. Find ways to stay connected; one way may be by involving the moms of your child's friends. Try forming a mother-daughter book club with clique members and their moms (or find a new group to help her separate from the

Pay Attention to This!

Dr. L. Kris Gowen studied 157 girls between the ages of ten and thirteen.[41] Those girls who were socially ridiculed or left out by cliques were particularly vulnerable to developing a negative body image and low self-esteem. The research also found that the girls mistakenly believed that if they were just prettier or thinner, they wouldn't be teased and would be more likely to be included. But the only thing they did develop was a dangerous eating disorder. Tune in to your daughter's feelings about her body and weight, especially during the tween years.

existing one); take up yoga with her (or with a few of her friends). Or just find ways to hang out together and watch her favorite reality TV show (and pretend to enjoy it).

Step 2. Rapid Response

- *Figure out what is going on.* If your child is being permanently or even temporarily excluded by a group she *really wants* to belong to, there are many questions you need to ask to figure out why this is happening. The tricky part is that kids usually don't tell us why they are rejected, and they often don't know the answer themselves. Once you get at least an indication, you may—or may not—be able to help or at least advise your kid that it's time to move on and find another group. Here are possibilities to consider. Check those that might apply to your child or situation:

One Parent's Answer

A mom from Spokane shares:

Sixth grade was a nightmare for my daughter. She'd come home in tears almost every day, saying the girls were leaving her out. I'd just always tell her to go stand up for herself. Finally I realized she didn't know how, so we started role-playing the situations she faced and then coming up with solutions. It helped Dana gain the confidence she needed to face those mean girls until she finally found a nicer group of friends.

- ☐ Your child stands apart because she is of a different race, religion, culture, or social stratum; she is identified as "gifted" or "learning disabled"; she looks, talks, or acts "different." (The top reason for rejection is because the kid is "different.")
- ☐ Your child does something to turn the kids off: too pushy, too meek, too loud, too flamboyant, too boring, has poor hygiene or unfashionable clothes.
- ☐ She is brand new to the scene or trying to join a well-established group.
- ☐ She or your family has a bad reputation.
- ☐ Your child has other friends whom the clique doesn't approve of.
- ☐ The group shares a common bond your child doesn't possess, such as sports, boyfriends, cognitive ability, ethnicity, or past history.
- ☐ The group is too high up the popularity ladder for your child to aspire to, or they are mean-spirited kids who happen to be the "in group" that your kid shouldn't be part of.
- ☐ She lacks the social skills that would help her fit in better; she has never been a member of any group.
- ☐ You want or are pushing your child to belong to a group that she really doesn't want to join.

- *Validate feelings.* Being ostracized is awful. Don't minimize your child's worries. Doing so is a blow to her self-esteem. Don't press too hard for her to give you all the details. It's often humiliating for your child to confess her rejection. She may open up later, but for now be available and acknowledge the seriousness of your child's concern. She needs your support.

- *Don't tolerate cruelty.* If you find out that your daughter is the "Mean Girl" in her clique, step in ASAP. Demand that she apply the Golden Rule both inside and outside your home. Prioritize your daughter's character over clique membership.

- *Don't belittle the other kids.* They may be excluding your kid, but criticizing them won't help. Your child wants their friendship, so don't say "Why would you want to be friends with them anyway?" Do say "*They have their way of doing things. We just have to find a way for you to fit in.*"

- *Provide perspective.* The fact is that everyone is rejected or left out sometimes, so let your child know that she is not alone in her misery. Let her know that cliques are most severe during the middle school years and that things will improve. Share your own ordeals when you were growing up. Find a movie about clique angst, such as *Mean Girls, Angus, The Breakfast Club,* and *Clueless,* or a book for her to read, such as *Queen Bees and Wannabes,* by Rosalind Wiseman, or *Please Stop Laughing at Me,* by Jodee Blanco.

- *Help her find the right fit.* A clique can be a means of belonging, but it has to be the right fit for your kid. Ask questions that help her recognize the clique dynamics and assess if the group is the right for her. Here are a few to get you started:

  "Why do you want to be a part of that group?"

  "How do they treat others?"

  "What compromises do you have to make to belong?"

  "Do you feel comfortable with all the kids?"

  "Do they talk about things you're interested in?"

  "Who is included? Who is not?"

  "Who calls the shots?"

  "What if the leader pushed you to do something you didn't want to do?

  The right questions may help her decide if she really wants to maintain a relationship with this group. Hint: the word "clique" is a big turnoff with kids. You're better off not using the term and just using the word "group." Otherwise your kid might shut down.

Step 3. Develop Habits for Change

- *Find one ally.* One friend can be your child's social entry card into a clique. Tell your child not to aim at first for the whole group but to start with just a one-to-one relationship with someone already there. Suggest that she invite that person to do something with her—go to the movies, stay over, or just spend time together. Do prepare your kid for disappointment. Even if they become a twosome outside school, chances are that the pal may slip back into the clique at school.

- *Nurture out-of-school friendships.* If your child can't find healthy relationships in school, then help her look elsewhere: an art class, martial arts, guitar, hockey—any group activity she can take part in that gives her an opportunity to connect with other kids and fit in to a social group.

- *Help her learn to discuss the "hot topic."* If your child wants to break into a specific clique, she needs to be knowledgeable about the hot conversation topic of *that* group (fashion, celebrities, baseball). Hint: girls are more prone to talk about school, boys about sports. Research shows that kids are more likely to be rejected if they have quirky interests that the other kids don't care about (for example: Civil War battles, 1940s music).[43] They are more likely to gain friends by expressing interests in *the other kids'* passions instead of trying to promote their own. Teach that tip. Or encourage your child to find a different group that is interested in her special passion.

- *Discuss peer pressure and group dynamics.* Your child needs to understand how a group of individuals can push kids to do things they may not want to do. Most important, your child needs to learn a few strategies to stand up to peers—

ONE SIMPLE SOLUTION

Identify a Solution for "the Worst Place for Cliques"

School cafeterias during lunch are the place where kids are most likely to be excluded. Other "hot spots" are the playground, bus, assembly hall, and bathroom. Charlene Giannetti and Margaret Sagarese, authors of *Cliques: 8 Steps to Help Your Child Survive the Social Jungle,* suggest that one way to assess if this is happening is to have your child draw a map showing where everyone sits.[42] Ask "Where do you sit?" "Does anybody sit next to you?" "Is there anybody sitting alone?" "Where do the other kids sit?" If your child doesn't have an ally during these times, the pain can be severe. So help her create a plan for the time and place she feels most alone. For instance, in the cafeteria: find another kid to join; make one new friend; join a club that meets during lunchtime. If the situation is severe, find a counselor's room to go to during that period or ask for a hall pass to go to the library.

especially that ringleader. One way to do so is by giving your child "What if she told you to . . ." scenarios and then helping her learn effective responses. Here are a few to get started. "What if she told you to . . . *do something you weren't comfortable with? spread untrue gossip about another girl? cut your hair to stay in the group? supply liquor at a sleepover?*" Stress that you expect your child to speak out if she doesn't approve of the members' behavior. Then help her create comebacks she can use to stand up to these girls: "I don't want to." "No thanks; that's not my style." "I'd like to, but not today." "Get real, would ya?"

- *Talk to other adults.* Assess the prevalence of cliques in your child's school by talking to teachers, coaches, or counselors who are with the kids every day. It will help you gain perspective on the severity of the problem. And if the clique scene is severe, then think of ways to change the school culture. Some schools have "Mix-Up Days" in which teachers "mix up" students so that they eat lunch with new classmates and discover new friends.

ONE SIMPLE SOLUTION

Help your child develop options for what to do when things get really tough with the clique and she is left out. The more strategies she has to handle those "bad, painful days," the better she can cope. Here are suggestions you can give her:

- Change your schedule. Talk to the counselor and see if you can switch one class.

- Find an adult to talk to, such as a counselor, librarian, teacher, or coach.

- Find a safe place to go, such as the library, a friend's house, or the Boys and Girls Club.

- Develop a new circle of friends. You might join a team, scouts, a school club, the gym, or a book club, or start a band. Look in your neighborhood and find one new kid.

- Do something to make yourself feel better. Mentor a child after school, do a service project, stop off at your church and do a community project.

- Start a new hobby. Ask your grandmother to teach you knitting. Take a computer class.

- Read *GirlWise: How to Be Confident, Capable, Cool, and in Control,* by Julia Devillers; *Cliques, Phonies and Other Baloney,* by Trevor Romain; or *Stick Up for Yourself: Every Kid's Guide to Personal Power and Positive Self-Esteem,* by Gershen Kaufman.

WHAT TO EXPECT BY STAGES AND AGES

Preschooler   Kids begin to pair off and start to exclude others. Five-year-olds can pick out the popular and unpopular peers. Cliques can form this early, but usually only because adults tolerate it, are cliquish themselves, or create situations in which kids are excluded.

School Age   When kids are around eight years of age, group distinctions begin forming; kids start associating with those who are similar and who share their interests. Cliques become more often of the same gender, and the larger the school, the greater the number and diversity of cliques.

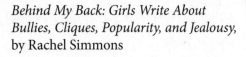

More Helpful Advice

Behind My Back: Girls Write About Bullies, Cliques, Popularity, and Jealousy, by Rachel Simmons

Cliques: 8 Steps to Help Your Child Survive the Social Jungle, by Charlene C. Giannetti and Margaret Sagarese

Girl Wars: 12 Strategies That Will End Female Bullying, by Cheryl Dellasega and Charisse Nixon

Odd Girl Out: The Hidden Culture of Aggression in Girls, by Rachel Simmons

Queen Bees and Wannabes: Helping Your Daughter Survive Cliques, Gossip, Boyfriends and Other Realities of Adolescence, by Rosalind Wiseman

Reviving Ophelia: Saving the Selves of Adolescent Girls, by Mary Pipher

Tween   Cliques hit their peak between sixth and eighth grades, then decline during high school. The urgency for kids to know where they stand in the group is a huge concern; tweens are strongly affected by clique rejection and exclusion. Although both genders form cliques, girls are more covert in how they treat others outside their group and tend to be more concerned about being liked than boys are. Boys establish themselves socially more by being athletic, tough, risk taking, and funny.

Clothes and Appearance

SEE ALSO: *Eating Disorders, Materialism, Peer Pressure, Role Models*

THE QUESTION

"My kids are obsessed with what they wear and their appearance. 'I have to have a Coach bag. All the girls have one!' 'The shirt *has* to have an alligator on it, Dad. That's what the other guys wear.' But I'm more concerned about the image that wearing those clothes can portray. Is there a happy medium?"

THE ANSWER

Don't get hung up arguing with your kid about "style." If you need a reality check, take a look at your old school photos to help you realize that fashions have never been the most flattering, but just part of the culture children are trying to fit into. Instead, hold the line on bigger issues that can have a real impact on your child's reputation and attitude. Kids have always wanted to fit in; what they wear is a big part of how they form identity and let others know which group they hang with. This is why you see them in groups wearing almost the identical "look"—from backpacks to shoes to clothing styles.

The problem is that achieving that desired "look" these days comes with a price. First, these name brands that are all the rage can be ridiculously expensive. Second, clothing styles these days are often sexually provocative even for the preschool set. Messages printed on kids' apparel are often in poor taste (and that's putting it mildly). Here are six ways to help you navigate today's pricey, sexy kid fashion industry:

1. *Make sure your child adheres to the school dress code.* Each school district sets clear rules as to acceptable and unacceptable attire; these are usually published in the school handbook. The general belief of educators is that a child's appearance—including gadgets, attire, and makeup—should not distract from learning, and I'm a firm supporter of that philosophy. Many schools require uniforms to avoid those clothing hassles. Get a copy of your child's school handbook (check the school Web site), review those rules with your child, and then set a clear rule that anything worn on school grounds or to a school affair (games, field trips, dances, competitions) must follow those standards. If you have *any* hesitation about the acceptability of your child's attire, it's better to be on the safe side and have her change so that she is not disciplined (or sent home). Beware: wearing certain colors may be prohibited as a safety issue because they represent gangs in a nearby area.

2. *Hold a firm line on sexy attire.* These days some kid's clothing is so provocative that it's been aptly named the "come-hither look." And designs are sized for even the preschool set. "The sleaze look" appears to be catching on: in just one year, seven- to twelve-year-olds spent $1.6 million on thong underwear alone.[44] Beware: most adults frown upon such attire, and wearing such a sexy look could well affect your child's reputation. It also sends a message to your child that you approve of sexual apparel, which could influence your child's attitudes and behavior. One rule to consider adopting in your family that sets clears parameters on provocative attire is my "Three B Rule." It simply means that apparel revealing any anatomy beginning with the letter *B*—bottom, boobs, or belly button—may not be worn. You might extend the rule to include that no underwear or bra straps may be shown either.

3. *Beware of distasteful messages.* T-shirts, hats, backpacks, sweatshirts, and the like are laced with "attitude" and distasteful wording, logos, or drawings. Those messages range from mild ("Cute But Psycho," "#1 Brat," and "Math Never Spells Fun") to outright distasteful ("You can look but you can't touch" or "FCUK"). Be clear that you will not tolerate any apparel that is offensive or provocative or that shows your child in a poor light. Such slogans as "Professional Drama Queen" may seem cute and harmless, but those images can stick and become self-fulfilling prophecies, especially as others comment about them, and they could influence your child's reputation or her attitude. Set a rule that your child must receive your permission to purchase or wear apparel with writing on it (other than a nationally known sports teams or logo). Even then, you might want to get a second interpretation of the message. One tween bought a shirt touting "I like boys who vote" with her mom's blessing. Both mother and daughter assumed the message was patriotic. The mom was mortified when a father explained to her that wearing the shirt meant the ten-year-old preferred men eighteen and older, and encouraged her not to let her daughter wear it. So when in doubt, ask for a second opinion.

4. *Set a clothing budget and stick to it.* Designer labels are no longer just for adults, but are now aimed even at infants. Studies also show that our kids are more materialistic than ever. So don't be afraid to set a realistic clothing budget for your child and stick to it. And don't give out loans. Teach your child to be a comparison shopper, prioritize her shopping needs, and shop for sales. Also set clothing limits. For instance, you will buy one pair of "have to have" shoes, but your kid has to earn money to buy the second. Or just feel free to say no to brand-name items altogether. (Just make sure you're not drooling over those hot name-brand items yourself and sending a mixed message to your daughter.)

5. *Help your child make a good first impression.* First impressions *do* make a difference, so take a serious look at the way your kid presents herself. Kids do need to learn that how they choose to dress and behave does create an image that can turn folks off or on. Don't assume that your child knows what image her attire is sending or

even what the message implies. Rosalind Wiseman, author of *Queen Bees and Wannabes,* finds that girls respond much better to the word "image" than "reputation." So your daughter may be more receptive if you say, "You know, I'm afraid you'll project the wrong image if you wear those jeans so low."

6. *Get on board with other parents.* Is your child is pushing you to let her wear make-up? Does your son say you're the world's meanest parent because you won't let him wear shirts covered with those "in your face" messages? Consider talking with parents of your child's friends and hear their views. Chances are they share your dress standards, and standing together as to what is acceptable attire will reduce those "You're the only parent who feels that way" guilt trips.

Any child can be well groomed, have good hygiene, and dress in a style that allows her to fit in with the rest. Just remember that first impressions do count. So every once in a while, take a more objective look at your child and ask yourself what kind of image she is projecting. If there is just *one* thing you can tune up—a more conservative haircut, less tightly fitting jeans, a slightly less baggy look—consider making that adjustment. Remember that regardless of the peer and consumer push, tweens do seek guidance from their parents.[45] So use your influence!

Crushes

SEE ALSO: *Cliques, Growing Up Too Fast, Peer Pressure, Rejected, Sex*

THE QUESTION

"My daughter is only in middle school, but started 'seeing' a boy in her class. Now he's decided that things were too serious and went off to play football. Meanwhile my daughter is devastated and says she loves him. Can kids this young really be in love? And now what do I do to mend my daughter's heart?"

THE ANSWER

Kids usually have those first crushes and start "pairing off" and being involved in more intense relationships around twelve and thirteen, though sometimes as early as fifth grade. First crushes also typically coincide with the onset of hormonal changes and puberty.[46] Those first big crushes can be nerve racking as all get-out to parents as we envision only the worst (translation: S-E-X). But for the most part, these relationship are platonic. Research finds that it usually isn't until late adolescence that more serious and lasting romances develop.[47] Seven- to twelve-year-old boys are the ones testing the limits (and hoping for the best), but it's our daughters who remain more focused on the romance.

Regardless of whether or not those early relationships hold together (and the vast majority don't)—those deep first feelings are real, so a breakup can be quite painful to both girls and boys. This is emotionally distressing stuff, and a new study shows that getting dumped at age twelve may feel even more emotionally devastating than at age forty.[48] That's because kids don't yet have the inner stamina or coping skills to help them get through heartbreak. It's never happened to them before.

But don't shortchange those first love interests. They are actual dress rehearsals for later intimacy and help preadolescents learn crucial life skills like empathy, respect, communication, compromise, sensitivity, and sharing, in addition to undergoing emotional growth. Of course a lot more dating and maturing is needed before kids have those traits under their belt. Meanwhile, here are a few parenting strategies to help your child (and you) get through this troubling time:

- *Don't dismiss your child's pain.* The heartbreak is real, and your child does hurt despite her young age. It's far better to show a little empathy: *"I'm so sorry. You must hurt."*

- *Refrain from being Dear Abby.* Ask questions and offer advice *only* if asked. Your lectures on why this one wasn't Mr. Right can be held back for a later time. In fact, it's best not to badmouth the old boyfriend. You never know if they'll get back together. While you're at it, hold the "You'll get over it" comment as well. You know she'll find another love and move on, but your kid doesn't want or need to hear that right now.

- *Be available.* Right now just sympathize and show support. Offer to take her for ice cream or invite friends over for a sleepover. But try to help reconnect her with her old cadre of friends so she has a support system.

Expect your daughter to cry and perhaps even have trouble sleeping. (Do keep an eye on her to make sure that she gradually does start bouncing back to her regular self.) This is a loss, and many kids respond to a more intense breakup with grieflike symptoms. Your daughter may be young, but she still has those grown-up feelings, and that's exactly why you need to have talks about sex with your child. If you haven't done so before, there is no time better than the present. (See *Sex,* p. 394.)

Disciplining Other Kids

SEE ALSO: *Argues, Bad Friends, Bossy, Bullied, Conscience, Time-Out*

THE QUESTION

"I'm in a big debate with my girlfriends, who believe that only a parent should be allowed to discipline her own child. What if your child's friend misbehaves at your house? There have to be instances when parents should discipline the 'other' kids, but please clarify those instances."

THE ANSWER

Oh, how parenting has changed. When I was growing up, if I misbehaved, I was set straight by the parent in charge, and if my friends misbehaved at my house, they were held accountable by my mom and dad. But these days parents are much more cautious about disciplining kids who are not theirs. The biggest reason for that policy switch is probably that our society has become so litigious. Parents are afraid of being sued if they touch or discipline someone else's child in any way. So parents are concerned about stepping over the line.

But there are times when I believe that a parent can't allow certain bad behaviors to slide and must hold the kid accountable. Not to do so sends the wrong message to your child ("Your friend can get away with that behavior, but you can't") and to the other kid ("This mom doesn't care what I do"). Allowing certain misbehaviors to go unheeded could be dangerous as well.

Here are solutions to navigating tricky issues of disciplining the "other" kid when the child is in your care and *you are in charge.*

- *Get on board with the other parent.* Anytime you are responsible for the care of another child (such as carpooling, playdates, or sleepovers), always introduce yourself to the other kid's parent. You can exchange emergency and contact information, but also bring up discipline. Here is a tactful beginning: *"I'm so glad our kids are spending time together. Are there any special rules you'd like your child to follow?"* (You can also exchange your rules.) *"Kids will be kids, you know, so if mine ever misbehaves, please let me know and feel free to tell him your expectations. What would you like me to do if they act up when they're with me?"* A brief discussion will clue you in to the parent's discipline views and whether there are any "red flags"; it will also make things a lot easier in case there is a problem. Also find out if that parent has any rules about special diets (no desserts, for example) and any values about entertainment, such as media ratings (only PG-13, or television is prohibited).

- *Review ground rules.* Lay down the law with your child *before* the friend arrives, such as no eating in the living room, running in the house, leaving your property without permission, playing ball in the house, using the computer, and so on. Consider posting your house rules on your refrigerator so they are clearly visible. Let your child know that your rules don't change just because he has a guest and that you expect the guest to obey those rules as well. Ask your child to review the rules with his guest or feel free to *briefly* explain them to any first-time guest. Your child needs to remember that the guest may have different rules at home, so it's only fair that he know what you expect at your home.

- *Know your discipline limits.* Think of discipline as a teaching tool to help the child learn right from wrong. *"Remember, we walk in the house." "Let's share the toys." "Please stop yelling." "Mom and Dad's room is off-limits."* Most parents have no issue if you remind their kids of your house rules or enforce them. The problem is when you use certain types of *punishment.* Here are some general no-no's of punishing other kids:

  - Don't spank or hit another child. Ever.

  - Don't yell at another child. The only exception is for safety issues.

  - Don't punish. You may not use time-out, take away the other child's personal possessions, or ground a guest from any future event.

  - Don't be too harsh or judgmental. "You're naughty." "Why are you mean?"

  - Don't discipline the child if his parent is present. Whatever the kid does, the parent is in charge. You may take the child by the hand and "return" him to the parent. You may tell the child, "We don't throw balls in my house," but you may not discipline.

- *Make "safety" your core policy.* Whenever you are responsible for another child, your primary concern is for his safety. You would expect no less of the parent who is overseeing your child. In fact, not to enforce safety makes you liable both legally and morally. So always step in for these safety issues:

  Safety gear. Insist that the child wear a seatbelt, bike helmet, and any special safety gear for sports that he is engaged in. If he refuses, you may prohibit the child from engaging in the activity.

  Aggression or cruelty. Step in immediately if there is any hitting, biting, fighting, slapping, or punching as well as any egregious cruel act (locking one child out of the bedroom while the other kids play).

Risky behaviors. Running into the street, climbing a tall tree or sharp fence, jumping off the roof, running with a sharp object, experimenting with alcohol, and playing near a pool are potentially dangerous activities that require you to step in ASAP.

Leaving your property. The parent entrusted you with the care of her child and expects the child to stay on your property, where the parent assumes you are supervising. Always get the parent's permission before her child leaves your house to go to another friend's, to the mall, or even to walk home.

Using technology with Internet access. Any computer or cell phone that has Internet access should be prohibited so that your child or guest cannot access adult-content sites.

- *Use "cool" discipline.* You certainly do not have to tolerate any guest's acting inappropriately. Just remember that the child may later share with his parent how you discipline, and kid's stories are often embellished. So stay as calm as you can, use a cool voice, and watch your terms. (Hint: if you need to separate two kids so they have time away from each other to cool down, it's best not to use the term "time-out" or to single out one kid.) *"Looks like you both need time to cool down. Why not sit here a little bit and do something quiet until you're ready to play again."* Of course, you can always discipline your own child. It's just best to do so privately to preserve his dignity.

- *Call the parent for severe infractions.* If you've tried all the cooler discipline approaches and the guest continues to misbehave, here are your options.

  - *Issue a warning.* Tell the guest that if he continues not to follow your rules, you'll have to call his parent. And if he misbehaves again, follow through on your word.

  - *Separate the kids.* Put your child in another room for the remainder of the playdate, but keep the guest in a central spot you can still supervise. It may be time to pop in that *Cinderella* or *Old Yeller* movie until the parent can pick up her child.

  - *Take the child home.* If you picked the child up (or know the parent is at home), call the parent and explain that the two kids seem to need a break from each other. Then ask if it would be acceptable to drive the child home. (Don't do so without that permission and never tell a child to go home without calling the parent to make sure she is there.)

  - *Tell the parent.* Decide if the parent needs to be told of the child's misbehavior (so that perhaps the parent can do the disciplining). Do realize that the child may give his own explanation, putting you in a bad light. A tactful, gentler approach is to use the "our problem" strategy: *"This is a little problem we had today and last week. Since I'm sure you would want to know, I just wanted to tell you what the kids were up to."*

Remember, every kid (even yours) has a bad day now and then and deserves a second chance. Talk to your child about the incident when the guest goes home. Get his take on just how important this friendship is and whether he wants to continue to play with the child. But if the guest's behavior continues to be a problem at your home despite your best efforts, it may be time to tell the child that he may not come over until his behavior improves. Just be prepared to tell his parents the same.

Drinking

SEE ALSO: *Growing Up Too Fast, Peer Pressure, Safety*

THE QUESTION

"I'm concerned about some of the older kids my son knows who are into drinking beer and hard liquor after school. When should I talk to my child about this? He isn't even a teenager."

THE ANSWER

Now is exactly when you should talk to your kid about alcohol. In fact, the earlier the better. And here's why. Kids are having their first drink three-and-a-half years *earlier* than kids from the baby-boomer generation.[49] Seven percent of fourth graders and more than 8 percent of fifth graders have drunk beer, liquor, or wine coolers in the past year; and 27 percent of sixth graders have used alcohol *at least once* this past year.[50] One out of six eighth graders are current drinkers.[51] Some reports say that girls are binge drinking as frequently (or even more) as boys.[52] Kids form beliefs about alcohol very early in life, even before they start elementary school.[53] Parents also have far more influence on their children's attitudes when the kids are young. Children nine or under generally perceive drinking as negative, but around thirteen their views change and become more positive.[54] These statistics give you all the reason you need to start those "drinking talks" by the fourth grade at the very latest.

There is one additional irrefutable research-based finding you can't ignore: *the earlier kids start to drink, the more likely they are to have alcohol problems later in life.*[55] Children who start to drink before the age of fifteen are *four times more likely* to report the criteria for alcohol dependence.[56] Research shows that thirteen thousand kids will take their first drink today.[57] Underage drinking is clearly a problem.

Here are solutions to prepare you for that critical must-have ongoing parenting talk with your child about drinking:

- *Take a reality check.* Please don't hold on to a "not my kid" attitude. Underage drinking is a growing problem that we simply can't ignore. Here are signs that your child may be drinking:
  - Slurred or slowed speech, lack of coordination, difficulty carrying on a conversation
  - Efforts to mask his breath (such as using mouthwash, gum, or mints)

- Hanging around a group of much older kids, sneaking out or not telling you where he was or going
- Mysteriously dwindling home liquor supply; hidden liquor bottles
- Unaccounted charges on your credit card from Web sites, pharmacies, or grocery or liquor stores
- Bloodshot eyes, sleeping in, or trouble waking
- Use of names of drinking games, such as Century Club, Power Hour, Quarters, Flippy Cup

- *Be a good model.* Kids get their views about alcohol from watching your behavior and listening to your comments. So watch your own party scene. Forget trying to tell your teen to be a responsible driver later on if you're not one now. Don't glamorize alcohol or say you're using it as a way to unwind; for example, never say "I sure could use a drink!" Instead, show kids other ways you relax. If you're not an example of responsible behavior, don't expect your kid to act responsibly. Your actions speak louder than your words.

- *Set clear rules against drinking.* Feel free to be puritanical and strict. Consistently enforcing those rules and monitoring your kid's behavior will help reduce the likelihood of underage drinking. A study of over a thousand teens found that kids with "hands-on" parents who establish clear behavior expectations, monitor their comings and goings, and aren't afraid to say no *are four times less likely to engage in risky behaviors like drinking.*[58] Be a parent, not a pal. (By the way, don't believe the myth that you should let your underage kid learn to drink in the comforts of home because "youngsters in countries with a lower legal age drink more moderately." There is *no* scientific proof of this claim.[59])

- *Start early and talk often.* This point cannot be overstated: you must talk to your child about drinking, and the earlier the better. Before age nine, kids usually perceive alcohol negatively and see drinking as "bad" with negative consequences. By around the age of thirteen, kids' views of alcohol shift toward the positive and become harder to change.[60] Some kids are experimenting with drinking as young as ten or eleven. It's never too early to start this talk, so don't put it off.

- *Look for teachable moments.* Lectures and stern warnings are kid turnoffs, but you still need to share information about alcohol and its potential dangers. So look for ways to weave the topic naturally into everyday moments. Here are a few ways:
  - *Talk about popular song lyrics.* You may not have to look too far—pull those earphones out of your kid's ear and listen to the lyrics. One out of every three popular songs has a reference to substance abuse—and alcohol is the substance most frequently mentioned.[61]

- *Show them news clippings.* If you read about an accident caused by a teen drunk driver, cut it out and use it to discuss how drinking not only affects judgment and the ability to perform everyday tasks but also destroys lives—including your kid's, if he were that driver.

- *Emphasize the short-term downside.* Kids live in the here and now, so it's often a hard sell to try to convince them of the long-term risks: "You'll get cirrhosis of the liver thirty years from now!" You may have better luck stressing the short term: *"Your brain is still developing and is more susceptible to damage than adult brains,"*[62] or *"Alcohol affects your central nervous system faster because of your smaller body size, so you are more likely to make serious judgment errors and sustain injuries that could even be life threatening."* If that doesn't work, try *"You'll be grounded and miss most of your seventh-grade year."*

- *Avoid or utilize alcohol advertising.* Long-term studies show that kids who see, hear, and read more alcohol ads are more likely to drink and to drink more heavily than their peers.[63] A study with third, sixth, and ninth graders found those kids who thought alcohol ads were desirable are also more likely to view drinking more positively.[64] Use those frequently aired beer and vodka commercials during those ball games you're watching together as opportunities to discuss your values, concerns, and rules about drinking.

- *Forbid drinking and driving.* It makes no difference that your child does not have a driver's license, let alone a car. Now is the time to stress one emphatic rule: *"Never, ever drink and drive."*

- *Get on board with other parents.* Know your kid's friends *and* their parents. Call any parent hosting a party to ensure that they are really supervising those sleepovers or birthday parties. Most kids take their first drink in their own home or at the home of their friends. In fact, 60 percent of eighth graders say it is fairly or very easy to obtain alcohol—and the easiest place is in their own home.[65] Count those bottles in your liquor cabinets. Lock up your liquor supply (and don't tell your kids where the key is). And watch your credit card: the hottest new place kids buy alcohol is on the Internet. Just a word to the wise: 99 percent of parents say they would not be willing to serve alcohol at their kid's party, but 28 percent of teens say they have been at *supervised* parties where alcohol is available.[66] In the same survey, 98 percent of parents say they are present at teen parties at their home, but 33 percent of teens say parents are rarely or never at teen parties. Although the teen party scene may be several years away for you, get to know those parents now. They will be hosting those parties your child may be attending in just a few short years.

- *Give strategies for avoiding trouble.* Forty percent of tweens say they feel pressure from peers to smoke, drink, or take drugs, starting around the age of nine.[67] So teach your child how to buck peer pressure. For example, help your kid come up with reasons that he feels comfortable saying to a peer: "My mom would kill me if she found out—and she always finds out." "I have a big test on Monday, and I need to study." "I promised my parents I wouldn't drink until I graduate." Let your kids know it's always okay to use you as an excuse ("My mom will ground me for life"). Then be sure to role-play different situations so he's ready to use that line with buddies. Emphasize that anytime he is in a situation where there is alcohol, he should call you and you'll come pick him up—no questions asked. (See also *Peer Pressure,* p. 373.)

Drinking is a serious health problem with devastating consequences for tweens. Research shows that today's kids are drinking at younger ages. The reason most frequently cited by kids for *not* drinking is their desire not to harm the relationship they have with their parents.[68] A parent's caring, involved relationship with their child is the best way to prevent to underage drinking. Stay involved! You do make a difference!

Friendship Breakups

SEE ALSO: *Argues, Cliques, Rejected, Sensitive, Teased*

THE PROBLEM
Red Flags

Can't resolve an argument with a good friend; is overly possessive, easily hurt, always arguing with a close pal; doesn't know when to let go

The Change to Parent For

Your child bounces back from a friendship tiff and learns skills to handle disagreements, decide if the friendship is worth saving, or move on.

Why Change?

"But she was my best friend! How could she say those things about me?" "Don't you ever let Sean in our house again! I hate him!" Let's face it: it's hard to see our kids upset, but bumps in the road with close relationships and friendship breakups are normal and inevitable parts of growing up. How quickly your child gets over a friendship falling out depends on the closeness of the relationship, whether there is another friend to turn to, her temperament, and her age. Much as we'd like to try to patch things up and wipe their tears away, too many of us make the mistake of rushing in to try to solve our kids' friendship crises. The fact is, though the disagreement or loss may be hard, the experience may actually help your child learn critical life lessons in how to handle disagreements, choose friends a bit more selectively, and recognize when it's time to sever ties and find new friends.

Pay Attention to This!

Harvard University: Research finds that parents often underestimate the impact of best-friend breakups, so don't take your child's anguish lightly.[69] If you notice that your child's distress (too sad, has difficulty sleeping or concentrating, is easy to anger, withdraws from interests once enjoyed) lasts more than two weeks, and she can't seem to bounce back, continually loses friends, or rejects companions, seek the advice of a mental health professional. It may indicate deeper problems.

THE SOLUTION

Six Strategies for Change

Although you can't usually mend your child's friendship (nor should you), there are six things you can say and do to help your child handle the rift.

1. *Be sympathetic and low key.* Tiffs are painful, especially when they involve a close or long-term friend. Don't rush to say "You'll find another friend." Instead acknowledge your child's hurt and convey optimism that she will make up or find more friends. Also bite your tongue and don't say anything bad about the old friend. There's always a chance the friendship could heal.

2. *Don't play matchmaker!* Promising that you're going to solve this problem or find a new friend for her right away does your child no good. This kind of parental intervention will only make it more difficult for her to learn to move on and find new buddies. Remember, this is your child's problem—not yours—and she needs to learn how to deal with the good as well as the bad parts of friendships. If necessary help your child realize that she'll find other friends, but be careful not to have her feel she must rush out and replace a former one right away.[70]

3. *Have problem-solving talks.* You can help your child think through her situation by asking such questions as

   "What went on between you two?"

   "How did it start?"

   "And what did you say?"

   "What did he want to do?"

   "How did things end up?"

   "Is there anything you could have said or done differently?"

   "Is there anything you could do now to patch things up between you two?"

   Although your role is not to solve your kid's tiffs, you can be instrumental in offering ways to resolve this dispute or help her learn what to do next time so things might not have to go sour again.

4. *Discuss the qualities of good friends.* A University of Maryland survey of six hundred kids found that they consider five traits critical to close friendships.[71] Use the following questions based on those traits to help your child assess whether this friendship is really worth pursuing or whether it's time to let go. Do both friends . . .

   Have the same power?

   Want to be part of this friendship?

   Like each other?

Have fun and enjoy spending time together?

Trust each other to share secrets and personal information?

If the other kid makes a habit of neglecting your child, can't be trusted, is not an "equal partner," or is not loyal, it's time to suggest to your child to move on.

5. *Fill up your child's schedule.* Your child may have relied on the comfort and pleasure of her time together with her friend and may be at a loss as to what to do instead. So find positive ways to occupy your child's time for a while, such as a movie, an after-school activity, a new hobby, or even a weekend getaway.

6. *Help your child make new friends.* Watch your child a little more closely when she's around friends and choose one friendship skill your child lacks. Here are a few:

Taking turns

Shaking hands

Introducing herself

Initiating a conversation

Losing gracefully

Using eye contact

Saying good-bye

Asking to join into a group

Listening without interrupting

Find a private moment to model the new skill to your child, tell her why it is important, and then be sure she can show you how to perform the skill correctly. You might go to a public place, such as a playground or park, so she can observe other kids actually using the skill. Seeing the skill in action helps more than talking about it. Now she needs to try out the skill. It's best that she practice with family members or younger or less skilled kids. When she's confident and can perform the skill without your guidance, suggest she try using it with her own peers. As soon as you can, discuss how the practice session went, asking such questions as *"How did it go? What did you say? How do you think you did? What would you do differently next time?"* Don't criticize what your child didn't do; instead praise what your child did right. If your child wasn't successful, talk through what didn't go well so that she can try it differently the next time. As soon as your child feels comfortable with the skill, you're ready to teach another one. Gradually your child's social competence will grow, and so will her ability to make new friends.

SOCIAL SCENE

WHAT TO EXPECT BY STAGES AND AGES

Preschooler   Unless the pals have been together regularly and rely on one another's companionship, tiffs are not a big issue. Expect some moping, but kids typically bounce back and find new pals. They choose friends more on the basis of proximity, so you can influence new friendships by arranging playdates or providing friendship-making opportunities.

School Age   Best friends are now important, especially as the child's person to hang with at school; it's also normal to switch best pals regularly. Kids this age lack problem-solving skills and have a lot to learn about handling disagreements and making amends.

Tween   Tweens slip in and out of "best friendships" without recognizing that feelings can be hurt, due to an inability to analyze consequences. Friends are a big part of self-esteem, so breakups with close friends can hurt. Girls are prone to backstabbing and gossip, so encourage your daughter *not* to seek revenge.

One Parent's Answer

A mom from San Francisco shares:

My daughter had a big falling out with her best friend, and I assumed it was the other girl's fault. It was a rude awakening to discover my kid was responsible and was spreading vicious rumors. I let her know that I wasn't happy with the way she handled things and that I expected her to treat people nicely, and made her apologize. My daughter learned her lesson, and I learned never to make assumptions about my kids.

Growing Up Too Fast

SEE ALSO: *Clothes and Appearance, Communicating, Crushes, Cyberbullying, Drinking, Eating Disorders, Internet Safety, Peer Pressure, Role Models, Sex, Steroids, Video Games*

THE PROBLEM

Red Flags

Wears or wants attire or gadgets unsuitable for age, hangs around kids or engages in activities inappropriate for internal timetable, is growing up faster than makes good sense or is safe developmentally

The Change to Parent For

Your child chooses and engages in activities that are developmentally appropriate and emotionally and cognitively suitable for her internal timetable.

Why Change?

One thing's for sure, it certainly is a different world than the one we grew up in, and our kids' lives are on a fast track. It's almost as though they are living in an X-rated world, bombarded by sexually explicit movies, clothing touting "adult-only" messages, sexually charged pop music, mature-rated video games, and provocative, "way before their years" fashions—when they've barely made it out of the G-rating age group. What's more, not only do our kids idolize those age-advanced lifestyles and products, but corporations, manufacturers, and retail stores are developing and marketing products aimed to encourage them to do so.

The problem is that adopting that fast-forward world could also affect our children's well-being. First, it "decompresses" their childhood, so they miss out on activities, rituals, and games that are essential to normal development; second, it exposes them to serious issues that they can't fully comprehend, let alone handle. That's why child experts, the medical profession, and parents alike are concerned that the relentless exposure to adult-type subject matter is so harmful and wrong. A recent *Parents* magazine poll found that almost 80 percent of moms and dads worry that their kids are growing up too fast and are exposed to "too much and way too soon."[74] In a *Newsweek* poll, 77 percent of adults feel that those oversexed, underdressed celebrities like Britney, Paris, and Lindsay have too much influence on girls and are pushing them to copy a far too advanced lifestyle way too early.[75]

Although we parents can't put blinders on our kids or change that outside racy world, we sure can put the brakes on what comes into our kids' lives. Here are solutions to help your child develop at a pace geared more appropriately to her chronological age so she won't grow up too fast and can experience those glorious days of childhood that every kids needs and deserves.

Pay Attention to This!
Monitor Your Child's Media Consumption

Our kids are bombarded with sexual imagery and confusing lessons from TV, movies, music lyrics, and newsstand magazines. In fact, *each year* our kids are exposed to more than fourteen thousand sexual references, innuendoes, and jokes on television alone.[76] Seventy-seven percent of prime-time shows on major broadcast networks include sexual material and provocatively attired actors,[77] and 10 percent of TV characters who engage in sexual intercourse are teens.[78] Research now proves that those sexualized media images *do affect our children's childhoods* and are pushing them to grow up too fast, too soon.

- In surveys, over a quarter of adolescents admit that televised sexual content affects their behavior and pushes them to act older and grow up faster.[79]

- The American Academy of Pediatrics found that repeated exposure to sexual content in television, movies, and music increases the likelihood that kids will become sexually active at earlier ages.[80]

- The American Psychological Association concluded that proliferation of sexualized images of young women in advertising, merchandising, and media is harmful to girls' self-image and their healthy development and increases the likelihood of eating disorders and depression.[81]

The lesson: know what media your kids are reading, listening to, and watching, and set clear limits.

THE SOLUTION

Seven Strategies for Change

1. *Stay tuned to what's happening around us.* Take a careful look at a few TV programs that your child's peers watch. Catch the latest reality TV show; flip on MTV and notice those grinding dance numbers and provocative outfits. Listen to the latest pop lyrics. Flip through *CosmoGirl, Teen Vogue,* or *Teen People* and peruse the mall a little more closely to check out the latest tween fashions. Doing so will help you recognize the pressures today's kids are under and help you decide what limits you want to set for your child. It's unrealistic to say no to *everything,* so where will you draw the line? Be clear about where you stand so that you can clarify your reasons to your child.

2. *Take a crash course in child development.* You might have devoured those baby books, but don't overlook learning about your child's current stage of development. Review a few respected sources so you can understand what is age appropriate for your kid. Recommendations include *The Preschool Years,* by Ellen Galinsky; *The Complete and Authoritative Guide to Caring for Your School-Age Child: Ages 5 to 12,* by the American Academy of Pediatrics; or, for tweens, *The Roller-Coaster Years,* by Charlene C. Giannetti and Margaret Sagarese. Ask your health care professional for developmental milestone charts for your child's age. Talk to experts—such as teachers, pediatricians, and yes, even grandparents—who usually understand normal childhood development. Your commitment to slowing the accelerated pace of your kid's childhood will be reinforced by understanding how destructive a fast-forward world is to your child's emotional and social development.

3. *Let your kid be a kid.* According to a University of Michigan study on how kids ages three to twelve spend their time, over the past twenty years there has been a drop of twelve hours a week of free time overall, with unstructured activities like walking or camping falling by 50 percent—while high-pressure structured sports went up by 50 percent.[82] Take a serious look at your child's schedule and scan her list of daily activities. Is there any time left for those cherished childhood traditions like play, make-believe, forts, unscheduled time, and sand castles? Don't buy into that modern-day American parenting myth that "push-push-push" is "better-better-better" for your child. There is *no* proven scientific support of the consumer-driven nonsense that parents should accelerate their kids' performance (from kicking a soccer ball to reading).[83] So what's the rush? Make sure that your child has time just to be a kid.

4. *Insist on developmentally appropriate material.* Let's face it, the culture *is* pushing our kids to grow up faster, and they *do* act older than their actual age. Puberty *is* starting earlier and kids do look more mature. But "looking and acting" like a

grown-up doesn't mean your child is developmentally ready to handle that fast-forward world. Here are actions to take:

- Set your rules and expectations based on your child's actual chronological age.

- Tailor your decisions to what is developmentally appropriate to your child's current emotional, cognitive, and physical stage. (Check child development guides.)

- Lay down certain "rites of passage" or ages your child can go to her first sleep-over, use the Internet alone, obtain a cell phone, see a PG movie, shave her legs, wear makeup, or pierce her ears so that she has something to look forward to.

- Utilize the suggested age guidelines for games, toys, sports equipment, and books.

- Use the age rating system for video games, movies, CDs, and television shows. Recognize that panels of credentialed child development experts spend hours reviewing each product before providing posted guidelines.

- Lead your child toward age-appropriate hobbies and interests. Think swimming, horseback riding, theatre, soccer, knitting, band, scouting, 4-H, and church groups that focus on healthy outlets that are developmentally suitable.

5. *Forbid the "sexy look."* These days, fashions aimed at kids are outright provocative and clearly push the limits of age appropriateness. Makeup. Short skirts. Halter tops. Press-on nails. Lip gloss. Thong underwear. See-through blouses. "Come-hither look" attire clearly is selling sexualization and luring our kids into a far too early and unhealthy focus on appearance with an R-rated twist. Pick your battles when it comes to fashion, go ahead and allow choices, and don't worry so much about "style," but hold a clear line when it comes to fashion with a sexualized look. Regardless of the onset of puberty, your nine-year-old is still nine. Set your standards to your children's chronological age, not their physical appearance. (See also *Clothes and Appearance,* p. 350.)

6. *Start those "grown-up talks" earlier.* Let's face it: kids nowadays are exposed to more grown-up issues at far younger ages. Studies show that drinking, sexual promiscuity, oral sex, depression, eating disorders, stress, peer pressure, puberty, and even acne are all hitting our kids three to four years earlier than when we were growing up. So don't deny your child's fast-forward culture and wait to discuss those "grown-up" subjects you had planned for the teen years. Even if you're not talking about these tougher issues, believe me your child's friends most likely are. Be the one who provides accurate facts that are laced with your moral beliefs and values. Also make sure that your child's doctor is someone your child feels comfortable speaking to. Beware: puberty is striking kids at younger ages, and your child does needs to feel comfortable speaking to someone—if not you—about menstruation or wet dreams.

7. *Stay connected.* The closer your relationship with your child, the better able she will be to navigate that sometimes raunchy, racy culture; find alternatives to those sexual messages; and realize it's okay to be a kid. That's because your child will seek your guidance and use you as a filter. And you do make a difference: a 2007 MTV/Associated Press poll found that the majority of young people listed their parents as their heroes.[85] Find more time for your child to connect with you, her grandparents, and relatives, who can help keep her centered, preserve some ounce of her childhood, and value her for who she really is and not how popular or sexy she looks. Above all, stay connected! A thirteen-year-old typically spends half the amount of time with her parents that she did when she was ten.[86]

LATE-BREAKING NEWS

Puberty Is Hitting Kids Earlier

American Academy of Pediatrics: Over a decade ago, Marcia Herman-Giddens,[84] a pediatrician and now professor at the University of North Carolina School of Public Health, noticed that many young girls in grades 1 to 5 were showing pubic hair and breast development. In her words, "It seemed like there were too many too young," and she launched a major national study involving 225 clinicians and over seventeen thousand girls to prove her hypothesis. As she reported in her famous paper, published in *Pediatrics,* she found that our kids are definitely and absolutely growing up faster.

The average age of the onset of menstruation is four years earlier than currently used norms and 15 percent of seven-years-olds and almost half of eight-year-olds are now developing breasts or pubic hair. Comprehensive data are still not in for boys, but studies show that they are reaching their adult heights at younger ages, suggesting that they too are maturing earlier.

WHAT TO EXPECT BY STAGES AND AGES

Preschooler   Kids at this age are most likely to wear what their parents suggest and choose for them. You will see "sexy" clothing aimed at the preschooler set. Watch out for gender-demeaning slogans, such as "Born to Shop," "Little Princess," and "Professional Drama Queen"; though seemingly harmless, these messages can begin a self-fulfilling prophecy; they can stick, especially as others comment about them. ("You're a little beauty queen, eh?") Attraction to particular clothing labels begins, based on what kids' friends like or what is advertised on their favorite television show. Fashions and accessories worn by kids' favorite Barbie or Bratz dolls also begin to influence attitudes.

School Age   Six- and seven-year-olds are still more influenced by parents than are kids in the tween years, so use your influence. Marketers start to push "pre-makeup," such as glitters, lip glosses, manicures, and spa-like kits. The elementary school set is now the fastest-growing market for digital media players; 31 percent of kids ages six to ten have some form of music player.[87] Puberty signs may begin in girls as young as seven or eight, including pubic or underarm hair and acne.

Tween   Marketers of electronics, fashion, accessories, and makeup (among other things) start intense marketing campaigns aimed at tweens. Tweens feel physically and emotionally awkward at the onset of their puberty.

Peer Pressure

SEE ALSO: *Bad Friends, Bullied, Cliques, Drinking, Indecisive, Materialistic, Not Knowing Right from Wrong, Sensitive, Sex, Shy, Steroids*

THE PROBLEM

Red Flags

Follows the crowd, is submissive and easily swayed, engages in risky behaviors at a friend's urging, doesn't stand up to peers, has difficulty speaking up and letting his opinions be known when with peers

The Change to Parent For

Your child learns to say no and develop assertiveness so that he can stand up to peer pressure, make positive choices, and refrain from engaging in risky behaviors.

Question: "My daughter is such a follower, and I know it's because I always intervene on her behalf. How can I help her be more assertive and less likely to do what other kids tell her to do?"

Answer: If you want to help your daughter stand up for her beliefs, then switch your response. If your role has been apologizing, explaining, or basically "doing" for your child, then stop. No more rescuing and no more speaking for her. Your child will never learn how to stand up for herself; instead, she'll forever be relying on you. Then start reinforcing any efforts she makes to be assertive. *"I know that was tough telling Kara you had to leave early to make your curfew." "I'm proud you*

ONE SIMPLE SOLUTION

If You Want an Assertive Kid, Don't Hover!

Researchers find that parents who encourage their children's social endeavors at a distance are more successful in raising assertive kids. In fact, those parents who tend to intervene in their kids' social lives actually hinder their children's peer relations. Better to stand back and supervise your child informally whenever he's with friends. It will boost his confidence and his ability to stand up to them on his own.

were able to tell Leslie that you didn't want to go to that movie." The sooner you nurture assertiveness, the sooner your child will resist that peer pressure.

Why Change?

Let's face it: it's not always easy to buck the crowd. But for your child's own self-confidence, independence, and future success in life, it's important he learn to stand up to his peers and not be a pushover. Studies show that today's kids are engaging in riskier behaviors (drinking alcohol, taking drugs, smoking, shoplifting, engaging in promiscuous sex) at younger ages, and peer pressure is a big contributor. A national survey by Boys and Girls Clubs of America of forty-six thousand teens found that peer pressure was one of their biggest concerns and that *they wished their parents would them teach skills that worked to help them resist those pressures.*[88]

Teaching refusal skills is exactly what we must do to help our kids cope in the real world and stay safer. Research proves not only that this is doable but also that parents can be tremendously influential in helping their kids learn to handle negative peer pressure, deal with uncomfortable choices, and make wiser decisions that will keep them out of trouble. The best news is that by teaching your child these habits, you'll also be nurturing the crucial leadership traits of assertiveness and confidence that he will need in all arenas for the rest of his life.

Signs and Symptoms

Here are a few signs and symptoms that your child may be negatively influenced by peer pressure and that it's time to boost his assertiveness and teach refusal skills:

- Explains that he did things he didn't want to do because the kids "told him to"
- Makes excessive new demands for "stuff" that other kids have

Pay Attention to This!
Peer Pressure Is Stronger Than You May Think!

A Time/Nickelodeon survey of 991 kids ages nine to fourteen revealed that 36 percent feel pressure from peers to smoke marijuana, 40 percent feel pressure to have sex, 36 percent feel pressure to shoplift, and four out of ten feel pressure to drink.[89] And those pressures are felt at younger ages: 7 percent of fourth graders, 8 percent of fifth graders, and 13 percent of sixth graders have drunk beer, liquor, or wine coolers in the past year. Teach your kids refusal skills so that they can stand up to these pressures.

LATE-BREAKING NEWS

If You Want Your Kid to Engage in Less Risky Behavior, Be a Hands-On Parent

If you ever wondered if parents can counter negative peer pressure, wonder no more. A survey of over a thousand American teens found that those who lived with "hands-on" parents were *four times less likely* to engage in risky behaviors like drinking, smoking, and taking drugs.[90] Hands-on parents are ones who have clear household rules and expectations for their teen's behavior and monitor what their teens do, such as the TV shows they watch, the CDs they buy, what they access on the Internet, and where they are on evenings and weekends. So stay involved in your child's life!

- Is easily pushed around or swayed by other kids; is hesitant to speak up to them
- Ignores your rules and values to do what his friends want
- Misleads you or lies about his whereabouts; is secretive about where he is or what he's doing with friends; is unwilling to share or discuss his activities or plans; has new "secret" meeting places
- Engages in risky behaviors: steals or shoplifts, uses alcohol or drugs, has unexplained cold or cough medications or your prescription drugs in his possession
- Dresses or adopts behaviors of other kids that are out of character for him

THE SOLUTION

Step 1. Early Intervention

- *Figure out the reason.* If you want to help your child be less likely to be pushed around or to buckle to peer pressure, it's time to pay closer attention to the problem. Your first task is to identify why your child is so easily swayed and is hesitant to speak up, and then address that issue. The following list offers some things to consider. Check those that apply to your child or situation:

  ☐ Has unassertive role models; is only copying what he sees

  ☐ Has low self-esteem, a self-consciousness; is less mature than other kids

  ☐ Is unsure of social status; wants to be "one of the guys"; fears rejection if he doesn't comply with peer wishes

  ☐ Has a speech impediment of some kind (lisp, stutter, delayed speech, limited vocabulary, or hearing impairment); believes his opinions don't matter

☐ Relies on someone (you, a sibling, or a friend) to speak for him; has been overprotected by adults who solve his problems or intervene on his behalf

☐ Has not been encouraged or reinforced for assertiveness; is told to "stay quiet"

☐ Is shyer or has a more sensitive temperament; harder for him to speak up

☐ Hangs around a faster or tougher crowd

☐ Is bullied or harassed by peers; is fearful of intimidation by a peer or peers

☐ Has poor decision-making abilities; lacks refusal skills

☐ Is unsupervised; has permissive parents; is allowed to engage in risky behaviors

- *Stay connected.* Research shows that those parents who have strong emotional relationships with their children have kids who are less likely to engage in risky behaviors. So build a close bond with your child and focus on developing an open and honest relationship so that he will tell you his concerns when he is in trouble or having problems.

- *Share your beliefs.* If you want your child to say no, make sure he knows what you stand for so that he can share those beliefs with peers. Share your values and state your rules over and over. *"We don't watch violent movies, so tell your friends you can't go." "The next time a friend dares you to smoke, just walk away. You need to stick up for what you know is right."*

- *Set limits and boundaries.* Make your rules clear to your child and set clear consequences if your child breaks those rules. Know where your child is at all times and who he hangs around with. Be clear as to which places are *off-limits*. If your child is not where he said he would be, set a consequence. Your child needs to know you are serious about mandating your rules; this will help him if he's ever in a risky situation: he can use you as an excuse. *"My dad would ground me for life." "My mom checks up on me. She'd know."*

- *Use historical figures and real-life examples.* Share examples of individuals who stood up for their beliefs and didn't follow the crowd. Abraham Lincoln, Gandhi, Rosa Parks, Martin Luther King Jr., and FBI whistle-blowers are a few. Look for examples of courageous folks in your community or on the nightly news. Let your child know that you value individuals who don't follow the crowd and who stand up for what they believe is right even if their opinion is not popular.

- *Know your kid's friends and parents.* Kids are less likely to use risky behaviors if they are well supervised and stick with friends who share similar values. Get to know your kid's friends *and their parents.* Exchange phone numbers. Find out their rules, movie-viewing policies, and curfews, so you can support each other and so your child will know that those parents are watching his behavior as well.

- *Nurture self-esteem.* Kids with higher self-esteem are less likely to be easily swayed by peers because they have confidence in their own worth. So involve your child in activities that capitalize on his strengths, dole out earned compliments that stress his talents and qualities, and provide opportunities that boost your child's self-regard. Your child will rely on that inner confidence when he needs the strength to stand up to a peer.

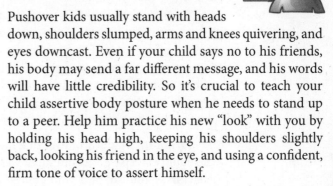

ONE SIMPLE SOLUTION

Teach Assertive Body Language

Pushover kids usually stand with heads down, shoulders slumped, arms and knees quivering, and eyes downcast. Even if your child says no to his friends, his body may send a far different message, and his words will have little credibility. So it's crucial to teach your child assertive body posture when he needs to stand up to a peer. Help him practice his new "look" with you by holding his head high, keeping his shoulders slightly back, looking his friend in the eye, and using a confident, firm tone of voice to assert himself.

Step 2. Rapid Response

It isn't easy to stand up to a peer, but kids who are more assertive are better able to buck peer pressure. Here are ways to help your child learn to be more self-assured so that he can speak up:

- *Model assertiveness.* If you want your child to be confident and assertive and to stand up for his beliefs, make sure you display those behaviors. Kids mimic what they see.

- *Let your child speak up.* The best way for your child to learn to be more self-assured is for him to have the chance to sound off and be heard. So listen more and speak less. Look for opportunities to ask your child what he thinks or feels about an issue. It may take some time, but gradually he will learn that you want to hear his opinion. He'll then be more likely to speak up in front of others.

- *Point out your concerns.* Offer comments that help your child focus on what he should change so that he is more assertive. *"I noticed during playgroup today that Johnny told you to throw sand in the sink, and you did it. You know better. So let's talk about why you went along." "You know Rene's house is off-limits, but you went along with the group anyway. You have to learn to stand up to your friends and do what you know is right."*

- *Hold family debates.* The best way for kids to learn to speak up is right at home, so start weekly "Family Debates." Set these simple rules: everyone is listened to and gets a turn; others may disagree, but must do so respectfully; and no put-downs!

Topics can be the hot-button issues in the world, in school, or right in your home, including house rules, sibling conflicts, allowances, chores, curfews, parent-set movie restrictions, the war in Iraq, or legalizing drugs. Whatever the topic, encourage your hesitant child to speak up and be heard.

- *Find a less bossy playmate.* Is your child always bossed around by a bulldozer-type playmate or sibling? If so, he'll never have the opportunity to speak out or stand up for himself. Invite peers who are a tad on the reserved side or a bit younger or less mature so that your child can assume the "leader" role every once in a while. These new friends don't have to replace his current crop, but they give him the chance to be less led and more assertive. And let a bossier sibling know that everyone in your home has equal billing.

- *Play "What if?"* A study of over one thousand sixth graders found that those who could exercise good judgment were less likely to engage in risky peer behaviors.[91] You can help your child learn to anticipate the outcome of tricky situations by posing "What if?" scenarios. For instance: "What if your friends dare you to . . . *give them your test answers? smoke in the parking lot? take the test off your teacher's desk? ask your brother to buy beer? steal a CD from the music store?*" The trick is to help your kid think through all the consequences and weigh those choices so that he can make the best decision.

- *Don't tolerate excuses.* Suppose you've been working on these skills, but your child is still agreeing to do things he knows are wrong so as to go along with the group. Don't excuse him for going along with the crowd. Set a consequence. Monitor his behavior more closely. Let him know that he needs to earn your trust. Your job is to make sure he is safe and does the right thing. His job is to abide by your house rules.

One Parent's Answer

A mom from Atlanta shares:

I tried teaching my daughter to be assertive, and she still looked like a dish rag. Then it dawned on me that kids learn skills not from lectures but from seeing real examples. We starting searching for people using assertive posture everywhere we went: at the mall, on the playground, in restaurants, even on television. As soon as Ellie was able to spot that "confident look," she got what I meant. Now she's using that look herself.

Step 3. Develop Habits for Change

- *Teach refusal skills and ways to be assertive.* Here are seven refusal strategies to help your child learn ways to buck peer pressure. The key is to identify the one he feels would work best, then help him practice the skill until it becomes a habit he can use with peers. Just teach the acronym ASSERTS to help your child remember the different ways to say no.

  A – **Assert yourself.** Stress that you expect your child to assert himself and not get swayed into doing something he knows is wrong. But he must deliver his views using a strong, determined, firm voice so that he sounds like he means it.

  S – **Say "No!"** Help your child brainstorm ways to refuse. *"NO!" "No, it's not my style." "No, I don't feel like doing that." "No, I don't want to." "No, you can't have my money."* Sometimes a strong *"No thanks"* is all that is needed.

  S – **Sound like a broken record.** Tell your child to repeat the same refusal line like a broken record until the other kid understands he is serious about not complying. The more times you say no, the more confident and convincing you sound. Stress that it's not your child's job to change his friend's mind, but to stay true to his own beliefs.

  E – **Exit the scene or avoid it altogether.** Never follow along if you feel there could be trouble. Sometimes the best choice is to just leave. *"I'm leaving. You can come if you want." "It's a bad idea. I'm going home." "I'm going to hang out with someone else."* Just put one foot in front of the other and start walking.

  R – **Give a reason or an excuse.** A good stalling technique is to give a reason why you don't want to comply: *"I don't want to get in trouble." "No, I studied too hard to give you the answers." "It's a dumb idea." "I have to go home and do my homework." "No. I promised I'd walk the dog."* Tell your child it's always okay to use *you* as an excuse: *"My parents would ground me for life."*

  T – **Talk about something else.** Try changing the subject to give yourself a chance to think. *"That was a great movie." "Can you believe John broke up with Kyla?" "Have you started that report?"*

  S – **Suggest an alternative.** Offer other options. *"I'd rather go to Bob's." "Let's go to my house." "How 'bout we ride bikes instead?" "Instead of . . . , let's go . . . [to my house and watch a movie, get something to eat, to the skate park, to the library, to my house to study]."*

- *Provide role-playing opportunities.* It takes a while to confidently use the refusal skills, so provide role-playing opportunities. Your child could try the skills on younger neighborhood kids or his cousins, in front of his bathroom mirror, with siblings, or with you. The more he practices, the more successful he'll be using them in real life.

More Helpful Advice

Great Books for Kids

Liking Myself, by Pat Palmer

Stick Up for Yourself! Every Kid's Guide to Personal Power and Positive Self-Esteem, by Gershen Kaufman, Lev Raphael, and Pamela Espeland

Coping with Peer Pressure, by Leslie Kaplan

Speak Up and Get Along! Learn the Mighty Might, Thought Chop, and More Tools to Make Friends, Stop Teasing, and Feel Good About Yourself, by Scott Cooper

The Mouse, The Monster and Me! by Pat Palmer

WHAT TO EXPECT BY STAGES AND AGES

Preschooler   Preschoolers comply with adult rules, so peer pressure is not a big issue with this age group. But watch out for aggressive, impulsive peers who can be negative influences on your child's behavior—especially if your child begins copying the peers.

School Age   The time to talk about peer pressure is now. More risky behaviors (especially drinking alcohol and shoplifting) are happening in grade school.

Tween   Eleven to fourteen are the peak ages for succumbing to peer pressure; tweens are more influenced by peers than are older teens. Fitting in and being accepted are paramount; this is also when kids are most likely to follow the crowd even if they don't want to or if the activity is illegal.

Rejected

SEE ALSO: *Angry, Argues, Bad Friends, Bad Manners, Bossy, Bullied, Cliques, Insensitive, Poor Sport, Sensitive, Teased*

THE PROBLEM

Red Flags

Has very few friends; is continually left out, openly snubbed by peers; is constantly made to feel unwelcome by kids his own age

The Change to Parent For

Your child learns skills that boost his social competence so that he is less likely to be rejected and bounces back more quickly and gracefully if he is.

Question: "My child comes home in tears and says the kids won't play with him. My heart just hurts for him. He just gets so upset and cries and carries on whenever someone turns him down. I take him out for a treat to try to make him feel better, but he just comes back the next day sobbing that the other kids rejected him again. What can I do?"

Answer: Knowing that other kids are rejecting our child is heart-wrenching stuff, but if you want to help, you have to play a stronger role than that of supporter. There are things you can do. *First,* you must find out what really happened. He may be doing something to turn the other kids off, so watch him play with other kids (at the park, by volunteering in the classroom, or in the neighborhood). *Next,* identify *one* thing your child does that needs fixing (such as pushing, barging in, whining, being too rough). *Finally,* use that real problem as an opportunity to help him learn *what* he is doing wrong and *how* he can correct that behavior. *"The boys got really mad when you pushed them to get the ball. Let's practice how to ask for something without pushing or grabbing."* Your child needs to understand his own role in the event, whether he is being mean, rough, loud, contrary, and teasing, or sullen, silent, and withdrawn; but he also needs to learn what to do differently to improve his social standing. Then keep practicing that new skill with him until he can use it on his own.

Why Change?

If your kid is nixed from the invite list, turned down by the girl he has a crush on, or made fun of for his new haircut, it can be painful, but it's a normal part of growing up. Believe me, your kid will live. But if his peers continually and consistently exclude your child, then the problem can be more serious. In fact, it can be emotionally debilitating and can greatly diminish your child's happiness. Research shows that kids who are repeatedly rejected are more likely to have lower self-esteem, severe anxiety, depression, and other emotional problems.[92] What's more, rejection is highly correlated with mental health issues further down the road. Studies also find that "rejection" is not a temporary phase: if a child is left out, disliked, or constantly ignored, he in all likelihood will continue to have peer problems unless he learns new social skills.

Always being shunned and left out is downright painful and humiliating. No child should have to endure such suffering. This entry describes proven solutions to help your child learn how to fit in, be less likely to be rejected, and feel more like an insider—and less like an outsider.

Signs and Symptoms

Every child is going to be rejected now and then, but you should worry and seek the advice of a mental health professional if there is a *repeated* pattern of rejection or if your child displays these signs that last more than two weeks and are negatively affecting his daily life:[93]

- Undergoes a change in his typical temperament or personality
- Is more sullen, sad, or angry

LATE-BREAKING NEWS

Macquarie University, Sydney, Australia: Don't be too quick to shrug off your kid's complaints about how much his friends' rejections hurt.[94] Psychology professors in Sydney, Australia, set up brain-imaging tests on volunteers. They then created tasks during which the volunteers were socially snubbed, and the researchers watched their brain images. Participants' brain images lit up when they were rejected, and the researchers discovered that the brain reacts almost the exact way to emotional snubs as it does to physical pain. Being rejected is painful, so acknowledge your child's distress. He really is hurting and needs your support!

- Constantly demeans or insults peers
- Is more clingy; doesn't want you out of his sight
- Loses interest in school, peers, other activities
- Retreats into his own world; is lonely
- Plugs into electronics—computer, TV, video games—as his sole source of companionship
- Has no peer interaction at school or home
- Suddenly chooses the "bad" pals for connection

THE SOLUTION

Step 1. Early Intervention

- *Assess your child's friendship quotient.* Watch your child a bit more closely when he is among peers—for instance, in his playgroup, on the playground, at soccer practice. Try to observe your child in natural situations without his knowing you are watching. Now be honest: Might he be doing something to turn off the other kids? Figuring this out might take a few times, so keep looking for *specific* things your child may be lacking or doing that are causing this rejection. The following is a list of a few of the most common reasons that kids are constantly left out. Check those that typically apply to your child:

  ☐ Lacks friendship-making skills

  ☐ Pushes too hard; can't take no

  ☐ Is too bossy, critical, or domineering; turns kids off

  ☐ Is overly aggressive, impulsive, or disruptive

  ☐ Uses immature, attention-getting behaviors

  ☐ Looks, talks, dresses, or acts "different"

  ☐ Engages in delinquency: is truant, acts out, swears, steals, fights, lies, abuses substances

  ☐ Is unkempt, unclean; has poor personal hygiene

  ☐ Is overly sensitive; cries or whines

  ☐ Can't be trusted, lies, is not loyal

  ☐ Brags, shows off, exaggerates, or fabricates stories

  ☐ Has difficulty reading emotional cues

  ☐ Is not interesting: lacks interests, hobbies, passions

  ☐ Has nothing in common with the group

  ☐ Is arrogant or acts as if he's better than the other kids

Keep a mental note of any traits you can work on to lessen his chances of being left out. For example: if he has poor hygiene, you would insist that he shower each morning and use deodorant; if he's too bossy, you could teach diplomatic phrases for him to use.

- *Empower your kid.* Researchers at Auburn University found that parents can make all the difference in helping kids learn social competence if they talk with their kids about specific peer problems and then coach them with new strategies to try.[95] The research shows that in coaching kids, it is less important that you know exactly what to do than to stimulate your kid to think about what to do. The Pay Attention to This! box lists specific skills rejected kids need that you can help your child learn.

- *Find kids with similar interests.* Keep in mind that kids don't need lots of friends, but just *one* buddy to hang around with. Of course you have more control over kids' friendship choices when they are younger, but you can still be on the lookout for kids whose company your older child might enjoy. As kids grow up, they're more likely to choose friends with similar values or interests. Psychologists call this the "rule of similarity," so think of activities or interests your child enjoys (chess, art, violin, skateboarding) and then find a club, team, or group lessons that support that passion. Help your kid find one pal he enjoys and can hang around with. The experience will be a boost to his self-esteem as well as provide him with the opportunity to practice critical new social skills he'll need to navigate the social jungle and be less likely to be rejected.

Step 2. Rapid Response

- *Show empathy.* Being rejected is painful stuff, so empathize with your child. Hold the "You'll get over it" or "Toughen up" comments as well as "What did you do to turn the kids off?" Most kids who are left out or disliked really do not know what they did to cause the rebuff. Instead, offer soothing comments that acknowledge your child's pain. *"That must have hurt." "I'm so sorry you had a bad day."*

- *Be positive.* When your child comes to you with a recent rejection, reassure him that it may take time to learn a few new skills but that you're confident he'll eventually bounce back and try again. And you'll be there to support him. It might help your kid to appreciate that this kind of rejection by a friend has happened before, and even to you. So share your own stories of peer rejection, but most important, offer hope that things did turn around.

- *Teach nonverbal cues.* Might your child have difficulty picking up other kids' nonverbal social signals, so he's clueless that he is turning kids off? If so, gently point out one thing at a time that needs fixing. That way your child won't feel

Pay Attention to This!

Thirty-One Social Skills Kids Need— Especially Rejected Kids—to Get Along

Children who are always rejected or disliked usually use behaviors that turn other kids off. A big mistake is assuming that the child knows what he is doing wrong or knows the skills he needs. Here are a few of the most crucial social skills your child may need to get along with others. The key is to teach one skill at a time and then provide lots of practice opportunities until he can use the skill on his own. (See also *Poor Sport*, p. 201.)

Cooperation Skills

1. Taking turns and sharing
2. Asking if you can play, have a turn, or join in
3. Keeping secrets
4. Forgiving
5. Apologizing
6. Thinking up fun things to do
7. Giving some attention to the other person

Communication Skills

8. Using eye contact or looking at the other person when talking
9. Listening when the other person talks
10. Offering someone help or suggestions
11. Starting and ending a conversation
12. Making requests or asking for help
13. Introducing yourself or saying good-bye
14. Developing a repertoire of conversation topics
15. Using humor and making an appropriate joke

Validation Skills

16. Giving a smile sometimes
17. Sticking up for a friend
18. Complimenting or cheering when the other person does well
19. Congratulating the victor
20. Encouraging someone when he or she is down
21. Comforting someone
22. Recognizing the feelings of others

Self-Regulation Skills

23. Keeping your cool and managing anger
24. Giving an alternative suggestion if there's a dispute
25. Solving problems
26. Handling teasing
27. Keeping your voice calm and quiet
28. Handling rejection gracefully
29. Leaving quietly
30. Defending yourself
31. Avoiding dangerous situations and refusing to accept a dare

too overwhelmed and will be more encouraged to try tuning up. *"I noticed you always pout if you can't go first. Did you see the looks the boys gave you? Your pouting really turned them off. Let's work on finding a way not to look so upset if you don't get a turn."* Hint: Drs. Stephen Nowicki and Marshall Duke of Emory University use the term *dyssemia* to describe deficits in nonverbal skills that are common with rejected kids. Their book *Helping the Child Who Doesn't Fit In* is an invaluable read.

- *Coach how to enter a group.* If your child begs, whines, or pleads to be included, chances are he will turn the group off. Standing off to the side and waiting to be invited to play won't help either. So show your child *how* to join a group so that he'll be more likely to be included and less likely to be rejected. Here are a few pointers:

  - *Watch the group a few feet back for clues.* Stand close enough for the kids to acknowledge you, but far enough back that you're not "in" the group. Then watch and ask yourself these questions: Do they appear closed or receptive? Is their game just starting or almost over? Do I know the game rules? Do I have the skills to play?

  - *Walk toward the kid or group.* Hold your head high with your shoulders back so you look confident.

  - *Look at one of the kids in the group.* Does the child look friendly? Does the kid acknowledge you? Does the child smile? If the answer is no to any of those questions, walk on. Chances are the kid doesn't want you to join. If yes, go to the next step.

  - *Say hello or give a compliment.* Say "Hello," "Nice shot," or "Looks like fun."

  - *Try to establish eye contact with one member and smile.* If the group appears interested (a good indicator is whether anybody looks at you and smiles back), ask to join. "Can I play?" "Need another player?" "Okay if I join?"

  - *Walk on if they say no.* Don't beg, plead, or cry. Just walk on and try another group.

- *Ask for specifics.* Sometimes a reality check helps us understand the difference between everyday slights and continual rejection. So try to find out how *often* your child is left out. It also helps to find out if just one kid is the offender or if this is a widespread problem and all the kids are rejecting your child. *"Is this the same problem you told me about before?" "How many times a week is this happening?" "Who do you sit with on the bus [or play with on the playground or eat with in the cafeteria]?"* Ask your older kid: *"Can you think of why Leila might not have not invited you to the party?" "What other reasons might there be for Jake to have walked by and snubbed you?"*

- *Get a different perspective.* You might have to ask other adults who see your child in social settings (such as his teacher, school counselor, coach, scout leader) for their take on the situation.

- *Be frank and specific.* A long-term study of four hundred children by the University of Illinois finds that kids who are frequently rejected or disliked by peers often have no idea why other children won't play with them.[96] The researchers' recommendation: use real peer conflicts to help your child focus on what he does that turns kids off. For example: *"I noticed you were whining when you couldn't go first. Did you see the looks the other kids were giving you? Will they want to let you play if you use a voice like that?" "You shoved your way into line. How do you suppose it made the other kids feel? Will they want to play with you if you do stuff like that?"* The researchers found that some kids changed their behavior when they realized the effect they had on the other kids. So be tactful and frank with your child, but also focus on only one thing at a time that needs fixing so that your child won't feel too overwhelmed and will be encouraged to start tuning up.

One Parent's Answer

A mom from Tulsa shares:

My daughter was so pushy and domineering that the other kids frequently rejected her. Telling her to "be nicer" didn't cut it. Then one day we were at a park playing catch when another girl right next to us started throwing so deliberately wide and hard at her friend that her friend finally just walked away in disgust. I was able to show her how kids reacted when another child was too pushy. She got the message. Telling her how to act didn't work. Madeline had to see how bossiness turned kids off. That's what helped her change her behavior.

Step 3. Develop Habits for Change

- *Teach conversation openers.* Child development researchers videotaped accepted and rejected third graders who were told to talk about a topic of their choice.[97] When the researchers watched the tapes, they recognized that accepted kids not only had far greater listening skills but also discussed topics that would engage the other child for a longer time. Help your child build a repertoire of topics that might interest kids his age (school, sports, fashions, movies). Make sure the subjects don't focus only on *his* passions or on narrow things, such as classical pianists or World War I weapons, which can lead to rejection. Then help him practice initiating and maintaining a conversation.

- *Boost identification of emotions.* Researchers at the University of Georgia found that kids who are readily accepted by peers can identify other people's emotions significantly better than kids who are likely to be rejected.[98] So boost your child's emotional IQ. Use words to describe how you see your child feeling. *"You look sad today. I can see your mouth has a huge frown." "What happened? Your eyes are glaring, so it gives your face a mad look."* Point out facial expressions in magazines and books and on the television. Make a game out of watching other kids' expressions and body language at the playground, park, or shopping mall to try to guess their emotional states: *"How does her face look?" "He's standing with his arms crossed; how do you think he's feeling right now?"*

- *Boost one-on-one relationships.* It may be easier for your child to develop a friendship with one child rather than with a group. Breaking into a larger group can be anxiety inducing for kids who are constantly rejected. So suggest he invite individual classmates to play instead.

- *Find outlets outside school that attract peers.* If your child is rejected at school, then help him gain a sense of belonging off campus. Look for opportunities for your child to meet kids elsewhere or anywhere—for example, scouting, park

---

ONE SIMPLE SOLUTION

How to Handle Rejection

A big turnoff is peers who whine, pout, sulk, cry, or tattle when they are rejected. Yes, it hurts, but kids have to learn how to bounce back gracefully. Here are key points to teach your child:

- **Stay poised.** *Poised* means keeping your composure and staying under control. Look at the person who told you "No." Try not to make a face, glare, or grimace.

- **Stay calm.** Having a meltdown turns kids off. So when you are rejected, try to relax. Take a deep breath or think of something else if you start to get upset.

- **Say "Okay" and accept the answer.** Using as firm and strong a voice as you can, reply "Okay, maybe next time." Don't argue or beg. It doesn't work. If you disagree, bring it up at another time. Don't ask "Why not?" every time, or the kids will see you as a moaner.

- **Move on.** Hold your head high and walk away despite the pain.

Help your child practice how to move on gracefully until he can use the skill on his own.

and recreation programs, Boys and Girls Clubs, YMCAs, 4-H, church groups, sports teams, library programs, or after-school programs. Pediatricians' offices and libraries often are good places for picking up schedules of upcoming kid events. Making the friends is his job—your role is to help him find ways to connect with kids.

- *Help your kid blend in.* Take a good look at how the other kids dress and act. Clothes, haircuts, shoe styles, and accessories really do matter in helping kids gain peer approval. Personal hygiene and cleanliness are huge issues with tweens. Take a good look at how the other kids dress and act. If all the other kids wear certain jeans, backpacks, or shoes and you've banned them for your kid's wardrobe, then reconsider your restraint (as long as those items adhere to your values, of course). This is not about making your child conform or squelching his identity. It's more about how your child needs to fit in right now, and the truth is that kids' appearance, behavior, and hygiene do influence peer acceptance.

- *Talk to a professional.* Although only a small portion of children are continually rejected by the majority of their peers, those who are suffer greatly. Studies also show that once kids tag a child to be excluded, a pattern is set.[99] The same child too often continues to be rejected, and it is difficult for the child to overcome the rejection on his own. If this is your child, seek professional help. No kid needs to go through life without friends.

WHAT TO EXPECT BY STAGES AND AGES

Preschooler   Physically aggressive (those who grab objects from others or make threats) or verbally aggressive kids who tease other kids are not welcomed by peers.[100]

School Age   By the time kids are eight, about 3 percent of girls and 8 percent of boys are socially rejected by peers.[101] A common reason for both same-sex and opposite-sex rejection is exhibiting aggressive, impulsive, or disruptive behaviors and violating rules. Using annoying or attention-getting behaviors and being overly sensitive to teasing are also big peer turnoffs.

Tween   Kids most likely to be rejected are those who are troublemakers or are untrustworthy, aggressive, bossy, disruptive, or disrespectful to adults; those who have poor social skills and who consistently exaggerate, lie, or fabricate stories; and those who have poor personal hygiene.[102] Children who appear noticeably "different" from their peers (obese, with speech impediments, or clueless to peer culture) are also likely to be ostracized.

More Helpful Advice

Helping the Child Who Doesn't Fit In, by Stephen Nowicki Jr. and Marshall P. Duke

It's So Much Work to Be Your Friend: Helping the Child with Learning Disabilities Find Social Success, by Richard Lavoie

Nobody Likes Me, Everybody Hates Me: The Top 25 Friendship Skills and How to Teach Them, by Michele Borba

Problem Child or Quirky Kid? A Commonsense Guide, by Rita Sommers-Flanagan and John Sommers-Flanagan

Teaching Your Child the Language of Social Success, by Marshall Duke, Stephen Nowicki Jr., and Elisabeth A. Martin

Role Models

SEE ALSO: *Clothes and Appearance, Communicating, Eating Disorders, Growing Up Too Fast, Materialism, Peer Pressure, Sex, Steroids, TV Addiction*

THE QUESTION

"My son idolizes Roger Clemmons, but I'm concerned about those steroid allegations. My daughter can't get enough of Jamie Lynn Spears, while I can't get past the image of her as an unwed teen mom. How can I help my kids find appropriate role models? How can I persuade them not to behave like these spoiled and morally compromised so-called superstars?"

THE ANSWER

The list of tarnished kid "heroes" these days is seemingly endless: Amy Winehouse, Britney Spears, Barry Bonds, Paris Hilton, and Lindsay Lohan. Our kids may idolize them and adore their fast-paced lifestyles, but we associate them with far more than just being "rich and famous." Try crack, teen pregnancy, mental breakdowns, suicide attempts, steroids, and substance abuse. Is it any wonder that 77 percent of Americans believe that celebrities, hip-hop thugs, scandalous heiresses, and steroid-popping sports stars have far too much influence on our kids?[103]

But now a study by the American Psychological Association confirms what many parents feared: all those raunchy, sexy media messages do have an impact on our kids—particularly our daughters—and are also correlated to the sharp rise in childhood eating disorders, low self-esteem, and depression.[104] Steroid use is rising among our sons. Almost 60 percent of teens said professional athletes they admired who admitted to steroid use influenced their decision to use the drugs themselves.[105]

But don't despair. There are parenting solutions to counter those raunchy icons and help our kids find healthier models to look up to and emulate.

- *Recognize your influence.* If you haven't heard the news, this should make you smile. In a survey of over thirteen hundred young people, the majority of kids listed their parents as their top heroes—and by far.[106] And moms lead the pack. In fact, over three-quarters of adolescents admitted that being with their parents is what brought them even more joy than being with their friends.

- *Watch out for vulnerability factors.* Whether your child is more likely to be influenced by poor role models depends on four factors. The more factors that are present for your child, the more you should tune up your radar and be there!
  1. *Normal developmental issues.* The tween years are when kids are most impressionable to the media blitz, so get educated about tweenagers' emotional and social development.
  2. *Weak identity.* Partying, money, and looks can be appealing to kids with a weak identity. Be sure to downplay popularity, appearance, and fame so that he learns to value himself.
  3. *Fewer hobbies or outside interests.* Kids are more likely to idolize pop culture types if they have fewer interests, so boost your child's unique strengths to build confidence and solid identity and to have healthy outlets.
  4. *Weak parental connection.* Kids with weaker parental relationships are more vulnerable to poor role models. Do whatever it takes to be closer and more connected.

- *Educate your child about heroes.* Don't assume that your child knows the real connotation of a "hero." Help your child hunt for righteous role models by first understanding the term. Look up *hero* and *heroine* in Webster's, discuss the meaning, and then create your own definitions: "Someone you look up to." "A person who's making the world better." Just make sure your child realizes that the person does not have to be rich or famous. Read biographies of real heroes, such as Rosa Parks and Martin Luther King Jr., with your child. Watch videos of Gandhi, the Dalai Lama, and Jackie Robinson and discuss their actions with your child. Or turn on the news and watch real heroes of today, from John McCain to Al Gore.

- *Explain why.* If you're not jumping for joy about the "hero" your child admires, explain your concerns about his American idol: *"That person's done little that contributes to society," "She went to jail [or had numerous DUIs for drunk driving]," "He doesn't seem to care much about his family and is more concerned with publicity."* A 2002 survey by the Search Institute found that only 25 percent of the kids reported that adults talked with them about their personal values.[107] So use your hero talks as an opportunity to clearly state your values and explain why that particular "idol" falls flat. Then let your child know whom you do admire and why. (Hint: the trick is to not sound too judgmental.)

- *Find positive role models.* Steer your child toward positive role models who don't need to rely on drinking, drugs, steroids, breast implants, dieting, and designer labels to feel attractive. And there are some out there! What about J. K. Rowling, Erin Brockovich, Anne Hathaway, Angelina Jolie, Great-Aunt Harriet, or even the neighbor lady next door for your daughter? How about Cal Ripken Jr., Craig Keilburger, Brad Pitt, Bill Gates, Barack Obama, and Grandpa for your son? Expose your child to authentic, confident men and women, and then tell him why you admire them. Also, identify your child's natural interest and steer him toward a positive role model who represents that interest. If she loves golf, then why not Michelle Wei? If he loves hockey, then why not Wayne Gretsky?

- *Stay connected so you can be an influence.* Here's a comforting finding: a survey of over twenty-seven hundred kids conducted by the Girl Scouts of America found that 91 percent of girls ages eight and nine go first to their moms for advice.[108] By ages ten to twelve, girls start pulling away and seek advice from friends almost as much as (and sometimes more) than their mothers. But don't miss the point: mothers are still extremely important confidantes for tweens. The essential point is to find ways to stay connected to your kids—particularly as they reach those tween years—so that you will continue to be a role model. It may take a bit of creativity to stay connected as your child gets older, so here are ideas:

  - *Get other moms on board.* Start a mother-daughter book club or go to yoga, take cooking lessons, go to movies, or walk together. Do things with her friends *and* their moms.

  - *Step into your kid's world.* Watch *Friends* or *Mean Girls* with your daughter. Watch *CSI* or play video games with your son. Read and discuss *Harry Potter* because she loves it. Ask him to teach you to text message because he can. Or do what one mom told me: scan *Teen People* so you can get into his zone and talk his talk.

  - *Find common connectors.* Is there anything—and I do mean anything—you and your kid can enjoy doing together? Yoga, reading, knitting, running, charity work, biking, baseball games, an exercise club. Find one connector, then use it to have those talks, stay connected, and boost your influence!

- *Promote natural passions.* Discover your child's natural passion and talent, whether it be surfing, basketball, art, yoga, or soccer, and then support his involvement. Those positive activities will help you focus more on your child's talents and interests and help him recognize that you value him for his strengths, not his appearance or muscle mass. It will also help your kid develop a stronger identity based on *personal* passions instead of ones borrowed from young, rich celebrities on magazine covers. Promoting your child's own strengths and passions is also the best way to bolster intrinsic power so that your child's hero worship isn't a substitute for self-worth.

There are huge advantages for kids who have positive role models. But research also shows that if the child *personally knows* the role model, he is more like to have higher self-esteem and higher grades.[109] And if that family member, friend, teacher, or coach is someone the child can turn to for help and advice, the child is significantly less likely to engage in risky behaviors, including using drugs, smoking, and early sexual activity. All the more reason to boost your influence with your kid and become the role model he looks up to and seeks out for advice. Remember: the best way to curb negative influences is to become an involved and connected parent. Be there!

Sex

SEE ALSO: *Bad Friends, Communicating, Crushes, Drinking, Growing Up Too Fast, Impulsive, Not Knowing Right from Wrong, Peer Pressure, Role Models*

THE PROBLEM

Red Flags

Is too embarrassed or hesitant to talk to you about sex, gives wrong information or has unhealthy views about sex, hangs around a "fast" crowd, engages in promiscuous behavior

The Change to Parent For

Your child learns that sexuality is a natural, healthy part of life, knows she can come to you with any questions, and understands that promiscuity can result in serious consequences.

Why Change?

You ask, "Why should parents talk to young kids about sex?" I say, "Oh, let me count the ways." And here are my own top reasons:

1. Our children's culture is an MTV-driven, X-rated world, and the latest research shows that repeated exposure to sexual content in music, movies, television, and magazines increases the likelihood that white teens will become sexually active at earlier ages.[110]

2. Sexy content is all too accessible for kids online, with those "not-parent-approved" sites featuring sex, sex, and sex. (And kids do talk, talk, and talk.)

3. Too many of our children's young celebrity "role models" flaunt not only "come-hither" attire but also blatant sexual promiscuity (and then glorify their teen pregnancy as unwed moms).

4. Sexual activity begins at an earlier age than a generation ago. In fact, oral sex is the new craze for thirteen-year-olds.

5. The prevalence of AIDS puts teen promiscuity into the life-threatening category.

6. Unwed pregnancy is on the upswing once again.

Pay Attention to This!

Adolescent sexual activity began to level off around 2001 and for the longest time failed to budge, but suddenly there is the first increase (3 percent) since 1991 in the U.S. teen birth-rate.[111] About one in thirteen teens becomes pregnant every year; 80 percent of those pregnancies are unintended.[112] That's despite $1.5 billion spent since 2000 on abstinence education. In fact, there is no reliable evidence that "abstinence-only" programs work to curtail kids' sexual activity.[113] With the AIDS epidemic and the spread of sexually transmitted diseases, the health stakes for kids are much higher—all the more reason to have repeated talks about the birds and the bees.

So what are you waiting for? Don't you think it's better that your child gets this information from you than from her friends or the media? This entry offers tips to help you discuss this crucial topic with your child. And the sooner you begin, the better!

THE SOLUTION

Six Strategies for Change

1. *Get savvy about today's kid culture.* It's a different world now in many ways, including how our teens view sex. It's far more casual, and they are less likely to have close, personal, high-quality relationships with sex partners. "Hooking up" is the trend. And teens are also engaging in sex acts at far younger ages. The Centers for Disease Control and Prevention found that more than half of teens are having oral sex,[114] and nearly a third believe that oral sex is abstinent behavior.[115] Research published by the American Academy of Pediatrics found that today's adolescents believe oral sex to be safer and less risky than intercourse.[116] So get savvier about your child's too sexy too soon world so that you are "in the know" when you have those talks and can discuss relevant issues that concern her world.

2. *Read up and get prepared!* Today's kids are for the most part more open and ask questions at far younger ages. So be ready. If you're unsure what to say (and don't despair—many parents are), here are references to help you prepare your response:

   But How'd I Get There in the First Place? Talking to Your Young Child About Sex, by Deborah M. Roffman

   Everything You Never Wanted Your Kids to Know About Sex (But Were Afraid They'd Ask), by Justin Richardson

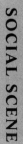

How and When to Tell Your Kids About Sex, by Stanton L. Jones

Talking to Your Kids About Sex: From Toddlers to Tweens, by Lauri Berkenkamp

What's the Big Secret? Talking About Sex with Girls and Boys, by Laurie Krasny Brown

3. *Talk about sex—and the earlier the better.* The earlier your start those talks about the birds and the bees, the more comfortable you'll be discussing the "heavier" topics that come later. That doesn't mean you're going to rattle off explicit details about sex or teach an anatomy lesson to your preschooler. Talks should always be geared to your child's age and stage, so right now just think about your first of many conversations between you and your child about sexuality. Here are few tips to help get you started:

- *Use proper terminology.* Sex education is not a vocabulary lesson, so only use terms as needed. But teach correct anatomical terms as a natural part of the conversation from the time your child learns to talk. It's OK to use the words "penis" and "vagina"; they are not profanity.

- *Follow your child's lead.* You'll know your child is old enough to talk about sex if she's old enough to ask questions. So listen and follow your child's lead.

- *Stay cool.* If you feel you'll be too embarrassed, then rehearse your answers. If her questions leave you stuttering, it's fine to say, "That's a great question. Let me think about it so I can give you the right answer. I'm sure glad you asked." Kids know when we're being evasive; they can sense when we're uncomfortable and may conclude that their question was inappropriate, so they'll stop asking. Your goal is to appear cool and confident so you keep them coming to you.

- *Answer the question.* Don't put your child off or try to avoid questions. But also don't make the mistake of telling too much too soon. Instead listen to your child and then give a simple, direct answers to what was asked. No more, no less. Give little bits of information at a time.

- *Clarify the question.* Make sure you understand what your child is asking so you can give the right answer. You could ask, *"What do you think it means?"* or *"Let me make sure I understand your question. You want to know how babies are made?"* Then ask whether you've cleared up the confusion. Take your cue from your child as to whether she is satisfied with your answer or wants further details.

- *Use teachable moments.* Find ways to talk about sex more in context so that the conversation is more natural. For instance, talk about body parts while she takes a bath; discuss birth when your dog has puppies; use a sexual reference on a television show as your moment for a brief lesson.

- *Keep the discussion going.* Discussing sexuality shouldn't be a one-time lecture, but an ongoing dialogue. Let your child know that you're always available to answer her questions, that you are just fine with her asking you anything, and that you are always available.

4. *Communicate your values.* Your "sex talks" need to be far more than just a lesson about body parts. Be sure to communicate your family's values about sexuality so that your child hears your views about intimacy, commitment, and love. It doesn't mean that your child is necessarily going to adopt your values, but for you to help guide her own behaviors, she certainly needs to hear what you stand for and why. Emphasize that contrary to most kids' beliefs, promiscuity does *not* make you popular. Stress that a reputation for being "easy" is tough to change and stays with you long afterwards. This is the time to discuss birth control and bring up that abstinence is the only 100 percent guaranteed way not to become pregnant or acquire an STD or an HIV infection. Research finds that kids whose parents stressed to them that they should wait to have sex are less likely to engage in early sexual activity.[117] (By the way, you don't ever have to divulge your own sexual history if your child asks. Feel free to take the fifth or say you don't feel comfortable discussing your private life.)

5. *Monitor your child and her friends.* Kids are mostly likely to have their first sexual encounter in your home or their partner's home during the evening hours or when you're away during the weekend.[118] So monitor your kid's comings and goings and get to know her friends. Make a rule starting in those tween years: *"No entertaining the opposite sex in your bedroom. Period."* Also lock up your liquor supply. Studies show that drinking alcohol is a precursor to early sexual activity.[119]

6. *Stay connected.* One of the best deterrents to early sexual activity appears to be the state of your relationship with your child. About 20 percent of both boys and girls whose parents reported a poor relationship with them during the tween years had sex by fifteen, almost double the number of kids who had good parental relationships.[120] So stay closely connected with your child, especially during those tween years when kids naturally start to pull away and seek the advice of their peers. It's the time when they need you most. Studies do show that "kids who feel they can talk with their parents about sex—because their moms and dads speak openly and listen carefully to them—are less likely to engage in high-risk behaviors."[121]

One Parent's Answer

One mom from Raleigh shares:

I waited too late to have the "sex talk," and by the time I got around to doing so I felt so uncomfortable, and I knew my daughter did as well. Then I discovered that sexuality was part of her middle school health curriculum, and suddenly I had an opportunity to talk about sex as she did her homework. If you feel awkward, just look for natural ways to bridge the topic, such as your child's health book or teen magazines, or use another one of those pregnant teen celebrities as an example. There seems to be ample supply these days.

WHAT TO EXPECT BY STAGES AND AGES

Preschooler   Kids at this age begin to recognize physical differences between genders and that having a penis or a vagina is the obvious difference. Sex talks should be simple, light on the details, and developmentally appropriate, and they should use correct terms (such as *penis* and *vagina*). Also discuss "touching" and "private parts" so that your child understands that no one should touch her on "areas covered by a person's bathing suit" and that if anyone does, she should tell you right away.

School Age   Curiosity about sex continues, especially with the subject so prevalent in the movies, media, and among friends. Common questions include "How do you have sex?" and "How does the baby get out of the mother?" By six to eight, the child should know correct biological terms like *vagina, breast, penis,* and *testicles.* If your child is not talking or asking about sex by age seven, it may be a sign that she feels that the subject is taboo, so bring it up yourself.

Tween   Tweens should know the facts about how babies are born and how the reproductive cycle works, as well as the terms *intercourse, semen, ejaculate,* and *sperm.* Peer pressure mounts, and many tweens say they feel pressured to have sex. Discuss ways to say no, healthy "giving" relationships, and love, and that there are no "do-overs." One reason for the increase of oral sex is that teens think it's a low-risk activity. Stress such risk factors as pregnancy, HIV, and the incurability of some sexually transmitted diseases.

LATE-BREAKING NEWS

American Psychological Association: Research shows that one of the best ways to help your daughter abstain from sexual activity is by boosting her self-esteem. In fact, one study found that twelve- and thirteen-year-old girls with low self-esteem are almost twice as likely to have sexual intercourse than peers by age fifteen.[122] What's more, the barrage of sexualized images of girls and young women in advertising, merchandising, and media is harmful to girls' self-image and healthy development, and is also linked to such common mental health problems as eating disorders, low self-esteem, and depression. So find healthy ways to boost your daughter's self-esteem other than how the media suggests: by being pencil thin, exercising nonstop, and looking sexy. Involve her in activities based on her natural interests, be they soccer, piano, cheerleading, guitar, art, or scouting. Find her healthier media outlets in movies, television shows, and magazines.

The study also found that tween boys with higher levels of self-worth were more likely to engage in early sexual activity. So don't forget your sons. Hold serious talks stressing not only that should he wait but also that he should never take advantage of girls, especially those who lack confidence.

Sharing

SEE ALSO: *Bossy, Bullying, Chores, Insensitive, Materialistic, Peer Pressure, Selfish and Spoiled*

THE PROBLEM

Red Flags

Hoards toys and possessions, has trouble taking turns or sharing possessions or time, doesn't consider the needs and feelings of others, is self-centered

The Change to Parent For

Your child learns to consider the needs and feelings of others and is more willing to share, take turns, and make things fair to all those involved.

Question: "I'm embarrassed to admit this, but my five-year-old never wants to share. Is there anything I can do to help her learn to take turns and join the human race?"

Answer: Just telling your child to "play nice" doesn't change behavior: you need to show her how to share and understand why it's important that she do so. Sharing and taking turns are learned behaviors that don't happen by chance. Find everyday moments to demonstrate sharing, taking turns, and compromising—for example, family members taking turns choosing the TV show, the dessert, the evening read-aloud, or the board game—until she realizes that these behaviors are a necessary part of life.

Why Change?

"It's mine!" "I had it first!" "I want a turn!" "You can't use my stuff." "You already had a chance."

If any of those sound familiar, you're not alone. Not sharing is one of the most common kid problems. Tears, squabbles, hurt feelings, and fighting are just a few of the possible results if kids don't learn to make things fair. But learning how to give and take isn't always so easy. Young children have the most difficulty because they're in that developmental "me-me-me" phase. It's tough thinking about others when your own needs are so pressing. But older kids have a hard time as well. Materialistic peers ("My stuff is cooler than yours") and a dog-eat-dog type of competitiveness urging them to put themselves first are just two reasons the spirit of fairness is often lost.

Sharing is an essential habit for kids to learn. It is one of the first and most essential skills that have an impact on our daily interactions, whether we're driving on a freeway, standing in a line, having a conversation, playing a game, ordering in a restaurant, or just waiting. Sharing also lays the foundation for generosity, civility, respect, friendship, solving conflicts, negotiating, and empathy. That's exactly why teaching kids to share and take turns is so critical. These are the habits kids rely on whenever they're in another's company.

Dr. T. Berry Brazelton, Clinical Professor of Pediatrics Emeritus at Harvard Medical School and world-renowned pediatrician, urges parents to help their kids learn to share as soon as possible, at least by age two or three.[123] In this entry we'll look at proven solutions to help your child learn these essential life habits for getting along, being fair, and in some cases joining the human race.

Signs and Symptoms

Although you should expect young children to have trouble sharing due to their egocentric nature, they will need gentle reminders to "take turns." Here are a few symptoms that indicate that your child's inability to share is a problem in need of a parenting solution:

- *Increases selfish behaviors.* Your kid puts his needs above those of other kids; he doesn't consider anyone but himself.
- *Causes arguments.* Squabbles, tiffs, and hurt feelings among friends are the results.
- *One-ups the other kids.* Your child compares his possessions to those of others ("Mine is better").
- *Monopolizes possessions.* He stockpiles possessions so he always has "more."
- *Turns kids off.* Your child's bragging, hoarding, or unfair manner turns off other kids.
- *Plays solo.* Despite the presence of kids, he chooses to play alone.

THE SOLUTION

Step 1. Early Intervention

- *Identify the reason.* The following is a list of a few reasons why your child may not be sharing and taking turns. Check those that routinely apply to your child. Your task is to figure out what could be the cause so that you can create simple solutions.
  - ☐ Is a young child in the normal egocentric phase of development
  - ☐ Is selfish or self-centered; doesn't consider needs of others

☐ Has never been expected to share or to consider the needs of others

☐ Has limited opportunities with other kids to practice sharing and beginning friendship skills

☐ Owns few toys or possessions, so is unwilling to part with them; possessions are too special to share

☐ "Taking care" and "protecting his things" overemphasized by parent, so the child is fearful of outcome

☐ Shares, but peers don't; sharing overtures are unreciprocated

☐ Feels that his possessions are inferior or "not good enough" to share

What is your best guess as to why your child is not sharing? Is there one simple solution you might try?

- *Prioritize sharing.* If you want your children to share, then tune up the whole concept of "fairness" in your home. *"Remember, we listen to everyone's idea." "Everyone gets a turn at the game." "You sat in the front seat last week. Now it's your brother's turn."*

- *Emphasize the value of sharing.* Pointing out the impact of sharing increases the likelihood that your child will repeat the behavior. *"Did you see Jenna's smile when you shared your toys? You made her happy." "Josh enjoyed coming over because you were such a nice host and shared your games." "Did you see how that player passes the ball and doesn't hog it? I bet his teammates appreciate having a turn."*

- *Teach your child how to share.* Research at the University of Kansas found that one of the best ways to teach sharing behaviors is to show children what sharing behaviors look like and then praise them whenever they share and engage in prosocial behaviors.[124] Here are a few ways to teach kids at different ages to share and reciprocate:

  - *Teach by example.* Let your child see you sharing so that he has a model to copy. Offer him the biggest portion of pie, share your funny hat that your kid knows you adore, or just express a bit more how you love to share because you know it makes others happy.

  - *Play "My turn, your turn."* Get on the floor with your young child and gently roll a rubber ball back and forth between you. As you do, say *"My turn . . . now it's your turn. Roll it back to Mommy."* He will begin to get the idea that sharing means taking turns and may even repeat the words of the game.

  - *Set clear expectations before guests arrive.* Once your child knows your rules, then expect him to share. Some kids need sharing reminders prior to a pal's arrival: *"Kim is coming, so set out the toys you think she'll enjoy." "Remember our sharing rule when Sam is here."* Putting away any toys your child does not want to share before his playmate arrives actually promotes sharing. After all, there are certain toys and possessions that may be very special to your child, so putting those items away before a friend arrives reduces potential squabbles. Then prompt him: *"Anything you leave out are things you have to share."* Hint: a child should never have to share his special blanket, stuffed animal, or other objects that give him comfort.

- *Play "Exchange!"* Sit between your preschooler and his playmate and hand each child a toy. Then make a game of exchanging the toys by passing them back and forth. Each time, say *"Now it's your friend's turn. Switch toys please."* Structuring the exchange helps kids learn turn taking.

- *Use board and card games.* Playing games—Candyland, Chutes and Ladders, Fish, Old Maid—is a perfect way to teach turn taking. Just enforce the turn-taking order and then don't deviate from the sequence so kids understand that everyone gets a turn.

- *Tune up taking turns.* Find ways to rotate special family privileges such as choosing the read-aloud, television show, video rental, dessert, chores, or even computer times. Using cards with the names or photos of each family member helps little ones remember the order and be assured that their turn really is coming. Keep the cards stacked in order with a rubber band. Once the person has a turn, his or her photo or name card goes to the bottom of the stack until everyone else has had a turn, and then the order starts over.

Step 2. Rapid Response

- *Set consequences for not sharing.* If despite all your efforts, your child still continues to hoard and refuses to share, it's time to set a natural consequence. Here are a few consequences for children of different ages:

ONE SIMPLE SOLUTION

Buy a Timer!

One of the simplest solutions to ensure that each child has equal time using an item is for kids to use a time-keeping device. The first step is to teach your child how to use the device (an oven timer, sand timer, egg timer, or the minute hand on your watch). Next, the kids agree on a set amount of time—usually only a few minutes—for using an item, and then set the device for that amount. When time is up, the item is passed to the next kid for his turn. Watch those squabbles fade!

- If your child "forgets to share," redo the scene on the spot so that he learns to think of the one deprived of the turn. *"Tell your sister that you'd like a turn without grabbing the toy." "Try that again so your friend has a turn with the bubble blower."*

- If your young child refuses to share an item, the particular toy is given a "time-out" for a brief time. When the time-out is up, the denied friend gets first option with the toy.

- For older kids, use this game rule: *"If you don't share, the other person takes two turns in a row."*

- Ask your child to put himself in the other child's place. *"What do you think he'd like to say to you, watching you play video games all day?"* Or have an older child sit in the friend's spot and talk about what the pal would say and feel: *"You never gave Sue a turn on the computer. How do you think she feels?"* Younger kids can use a doll or stuffed animal to assume the role of the other child. *"What would Teddy like to say?"*

- An older child who continues to refuse to share loses the privilege of playing with the friend. Some parents mandate one rule: *"If you don't share, you don't play."*

One Parent's Answer

A mom from Elmhurst shares:

Playdates were a disaster at my house. My four-year-old just refused to share his things despite all my coaxing and rule setting. Then it hit me that maybe I'd been making too big a deal of "taking care of your things" at our home—probably because the toys were so high-end that I worried they would be broken. I held the next playdate at the park in more "neutral" territory and asked both boys to brings a few toys along. And sure enough, as soon as Josh saw his buddy, he couldn't wait to share what he'd brought. Once I started buying less expensive toys that he could just have fun with, our sharing problems were no more.

Step 3. Develop Habits for Change

Sharing is a skill that doesn't come naturally. It must be taught, and it involves a lot of practice. Here are critical sharing and turn-taking skills to teach your child so that he'll be able to use these them in social settings without your guidance:

- *Use sharing phrases.* Make sure your child knows polite ways to ensure fairness so that he can use them with peers. Here are a few sharing phrases for any social setting that every child should learn: *"Would you like a turn?" "Who wants to go first?" "You choose the first game, then I'll choose the next." "Let's just rotate turns." "It's my turn next." "I'll let you play with this if you promise to return it in the same condition."*

- *Use tiebreakers to reduce squabbles and ensure fairness.* There are a number of great gimmicks to help kids learn to share, take turns, and make things fair among friends. They're also handy for deciding who gets to go first, breaking ties, reducing conflicts, and making sure everyone gets to use a toy or object for the same amount of time. Use the rules with your kids to avoid those everyday squabbles (which family member gets to choose the morning cartoon, the first piece of cake, the comfiest chair, the card game) until they can use them in the real world with friends.

  "Grandma's Rule." Here's the basic rule: *"If you cut the cake, the other person can decide which piece to take."* It can apply to many situations. For example, if one child chooses the game, the other kid gets to go first; if the child pours the juice, the friend gets to choose his glass first.

  Coin toss. This one is great when two kids can't decide on the rules, which kid goes first, or even what to do. The friend who is to toss the coin asks the other to call heads or tails. If the caller correctly chooses the side that is face up, he wins the toss; if not, then the other kid wins and gets to choose.

  Timing device. First, teach kids to agree on a set amount of time—usually only a few minutes—for using an item. Then set a timer (an oven timer, sand timer, or the minute hands of a watch). The child could also count to a hundred *slowly,* say the alphabet, or sing "Happy Birthday" five times. When the time is up, the item is passed to the next kid for his turn.

  Rock, Paper, Scissors. Each kid simultaneously thrusts out a hand forming rock (fist), paper (flat), or scissors (two fingers). Rock breaks scissors; paper covers rocks; scissors cut paper. Whoever survives the round (or "best two out of three") is the winner. Other tiebreakers every kid should learn include picking a number between 1 to 20; drawing straws; and playing Eenie, Meenie, Meinie, Moe.

- *Share what's in sight.* One dad passed on his rule: *"If it belongs to you and it's in sight, then you must share it."* Or *"If you don't want to share it, then put it away before your guest comes."*

- *Don't let toys leave the house.* Some kids hesitate to share out of fear that their favorite toy won't be returned. So assure him that letting go doesn't mean the toy is gone forever. Explain: *"Your friend is going home, but your toys stay here."* And then make sure that the other kids comply with your house rule.

- *Ask before taking.* Teach your child that if he wants to use something that doesn't belong to him, he must ask first. That rule applies at your home as well: *"In our home, you must ask before playing with another person's things." "That's my Dad's. I have to ask him before we can use it."* That also helps enforce the idea that a kid shouldn't be expected to interrupt his play the instant a child swarms in and wants the toy.

LATE-BREAKING NEWS

Southern Illinois University at Carbondale: Researchers discovered a simple way to boost sharing behaviors in preschoolers.[125] First, the researchers read books about characters that share and take turns. Next, the researchers used puppets to reenact the sharing behaviors portrayed by the character in the story. Finally, they encouraged the children to use the puppets themselves to role-play those sharing scenes again. The results showed that the three strategies combined helped increase the children's sharing behaviors. You can use that same strategy with your children.

- *Share only what is yours.* Be clear that your family rule is that you share only what belongs to you; otherwise, you must get permission from the owner. *"That belongs to my brother, so it's not something I can share."*

- *Respect others' property.* Just as your child is possessive of his things, he must learn to respect the other person's possessions. *"Treat your friend's toys just like how you'd like him to treat your things."*

- *Make contributions to the family.* Every child should be required to take a turn in contributing to the family. From setting the table and taking out the trash to helping a younger sibling and walking the dog, list ways kids can do their fair share for one another. And then require that they do.

- *Contribute to the community.* Deliver meals to families through Meals on Wheels. Visit an elderly neighbor. Write letters to soldiers telling them you appreciate what they are doing. Look for real opportunities to help your child give parts of himself to others and recognize that sharing extends beyond his home and to the world. Gradually your child will learn that sharing is caring.

WHAT TO EXPECT BY STAGES AND AGES

Preschooler   By around two-and-a-half years of age, children are able to manage simple social interactions that contain the beginnings of turn taking and responding to others, but will still need frequent adult reminders.[126] Three-year-olds are focused on their own wants and needs, so sharing isn't a priority. Sharing becomes easier at four or five, especially with familiar playmates, but kids will still cling passionately to their possessions. Although they aren't that eager to share, they can be surprisingly generous when encouraged by adults to do so.

School Age Egocentric phase (me-me-me) is now over, so kids should be expected to share without reminders. They begin to consider the needs and feelings of others, though true understanding of another's perspective is still developing and will continue over time.

Tween Tweens are capable of higher-level sharing skills, such as compromising and negotiation. Usually possessive of pricier property and may be unwilling to share clothes, electronics, DVDs, and the like (which is understandable and may be advisable).

More Helpful Advice

Here are a few books about sharing for kids. Be sure to refer to the Late-Breaking News box in this entry that describes a simple and proven way to use books like these to increase your child's sharing behaviors.

For young children: *It's Mine!* by Leo Lionni; *Me First,* by Helen Lester; *Not Like That, Like This!* by Tony Bradman and Joanna Burroughs; *I Am Sharing,* by Mercer Mayer; *Sharing Is Fun,* by Joanna Cole and Maxie Chambliss; *Share and Take Turns* (Learning to Get Along, Book 1), by Cheri J. Meiners and Meredith Johnson

For older kids: *Dad, Share Your Life with Me,* by Kathleen Lashier; *Mom, Share Your Life with Me,* by Kathleen Lashier

For tweens: *The Kids Can Help Book,* by Suzanne Logan; *Whipping Boy,* by Sid Fleischman

Steroids

SEE ALSO: *Cheats, Lying, Peer Pressure, Perfectionist, Poor Loser, Stressed*

THE PROBLEM

Think steroids are for teens? Well, think again. A recent survey found that kids as young as ten (fifth graders!) are taking illegal steroids.[127] And it isn't just boys who are partaking: the American Academy of Pediatrics found that use among middle school girls is almost as prevalent as it is among boys these days (2.6 percent of boys and 2.8 percent of girls).[128] One CNN report found that up to 7 percent of middle school girls—some as young as nine years of age—admit to using anabolic steroids as a way to lose weight.[129] Health professionals and educators alike are alarmed, but so too should be parents. Steroids can harm the liver, permanently stunt growth, and cause a host of other long-term ailments, but young bodies are particularly vulnerable.[130] What's especially troubling is that 40 percent of children say these drugs are easy or *very easy* to get.[131] That's exactly why we should start talking to our kids about the dangers of steroids, and we need to start those conversations when our kids are much younger than we might have thought necessary. Here are a few ways to talk about steroids as well as a few parenting solutions to help you navigate yet another worrisome subject with our kids.

THE SOLUTION

Eight Strategies for Change

1. *Do your homework.* If you want to talk steroids, you'd better be one step ahead of your kid. Keep in mind that your child may know more about this subject than you do, so get savvy. Read up on the dangers so that your facts are accurate. Useful sites include www.steroidabuse.org, www.usantidoping.org, and www.hormone.org/learn/abuse.html. If you still aren't getting through to your child about the serious health risks associated with steroids, enlist the help of your doctor or child's coach.

2. *Open up the dialogue.* You'll probably never hear "Hey Mom, can we talk about steroids?" So don't wait for your kid to come to you about this topic. Open up that conversation with your child, ideally by the time he's in fourth grade. Remember, kids as young as fifth grade are now indulging, so get a one-year head start. Just tailor your talk to your child's age and developmental level. Remember, one talk

isn't going to do it if your kid has a "Steroids are cool" or "Everyone's doing it" attitude. Your talks need to be an ongoing dialogue. (See also *Communicating,* p. 545.)

3. *Use real sport stories.* One teen survey found that 57 percent admitted that professional athletes influenced their decision to use the drugs, and 63 percent of kids said pro athletes influenced their friends' decision to use them.[132] So know that your kid's sport hero may be influencing his decisions. But he also needs to know that even those sports heroes are being held accountable. Cut out an article about Barry Bonds, Marion Jones, or the eighty-some baseball players accused of taking steroids and use the story as your conversation opener: *"Do you think he should make the Hall of Fame if they find out he took steroids?" "Do you think she knew what the long-term damage could be to her body?" "How do you think the other members of her relay team feel about getting their medals stripped for her steroid use?"*

4. *Discuss the health dangers.* There are clear health risks to steroid use that your child needs to know. Risks include severe acne; loss of hair; liver abnormalities (including peliosis, hepatitis, or blood-filled cysts); increase in the harmful kind of cholesterol; rage, angry outbursts, or uncontrolled aggressive behavior; increase in blood clots; and high blood pressure. The results really aren't back yet on the long-term effects of steroid use—especially on young bodies. But 65 percent of steroid users said they were willing to take those risks if steroids guaranteed that they'd reach their athletic dreams, even if they might harm their health; almost 60 percent of users said they would take a pill or powder even if it might shorten their life.[133]

5. *Look for doping signs.* If your child is preoccupied with weights and working out, his athletic performance, or his physique, then keep your radar up for possible doping signs. Possibilities for boys and girls include increased acne, a deeper voice, increased facial or body hair, more aggressive behavior, a marked change in personality, and a fast increase in weight and muscle mass.

6. *Monitor your computer and wallet.* The majority of kids buy anabolic steroids and other so-called performance-enhancement supplements at home, straight off the Internet. Set clear parameters on Internet use, and know which sites your child frequents. Steroids can be pricey—even a few hundred dollars—so check that savings account for any sudden big withdrawals and monitor your credit card statements. Also look to brothers and sisters (and unsuspecting grandparents) as loan sources. Beware: kids often buy steroids from local distributors at private gyms or even from youth coaches. Stay tuned to what is going on in your kid's life.

7. *Downplay appearance and popularity.* Steroids can help enhance muscle definition (which is all the rage in those body-building magazines many of our kids devour), so downplay physical appearance in your home. Find ways to build your kid's self-image from the "inside out" so he doesn't rely on muscle mass as his source of personal pride.

8. *Watch your sports expectations.* It seems that one of the main reasons kids take steroids is to please their parents. If you've been stressing that college scholarship or how proud you are that he's such an athlete ("The Olympics are right around the corner, darling"), then bite your tongue. Eighty-five percent of teen users said they believed that steroids could help them fulfill their athletic dreams.[134] It may be time for you as well as your child to get a grip on reality regarding your expectations for his achievement.

Tell your child why steroids are wrong as well as harmful (think this one through carefully so that you create a strong, powerful case), and clearly state what your family values are (push that this is cheating, lying, and deception). Just as parents are the best antidotes for drugs, they are also the best hope for stopping this dangerous and fast-rising trend. So what are you waiting for?

Tattles

SEE ALSO: *Argues, Friendship Breakups, Sibling Rivalry*

THE PROBLEM

Red Flags

Gossips, complains, or tells about the actions or plans of another with intent to harm, avoid responsibility, get sympathy or attention; doesn't know how to solve problems, so tattles to get someone to be the arbitrator or problem solver

The Change to Parent For

Your child learns when it *is* responsibly appropriate to tell, becomes more selective about what she should tell, and develops skills to solve her own problems.

Why Change?

"Mahhhmmm! Sara just took a cookie!" "Kara pinched me!" "You're going to get in big trouble when I tell Dad." "Wait until I tell the teacher what you just did!"

Let's face it: tattling can be a real friendship stifler. Who wants a friend (or sibling) who just can't wait to snitch to someone in authority about the bad stuff you've done? Tattling is a learned behavior that typically starts when kids are preschoolers and is usually the first step to that other annoying "any age" behavior called malicious gossiping. If your kid keeps telling on her friends, no one is going to want her around. After all, what child wants to play with someone who is always telling on him? And this behavior has no redeeming qualities. It only causes bad feelings between the tattletale and the accused and often leads to resentment and broken friendships. To the other kids, a tattler is someone who can't be trusted or who wants to be a kiss-up Goody Two-Shoes. A tattler can also get a bad reputation among adults. Would you want a kid around who is constantly complaining or bothering you with trivial grievances? The good news is that this annoying behavior can be changed, and this entry offers simple solutions to help you make that change.

ONE SIMPLE SOLUTION

A Five-Finger Problem Solver to Stop Tattling

Some kids—especially young kids—tattle because they don't know how to solve problems. The next time your kid expects you to resolve her problem, teach her how to brainstorm options using her five fingers.

Parent: Hold up your thumb and say your problem.

Child: *(holding up thumb):* Sara took my doll.

Parent: Now name three ways you could fix your problem. Hold up each finger as you say a solution.

Child: *(holding up index finger):* You could buy me a new doll.

Child: *(holding up middle finger):* I could take it from her.

Child: *(holding up ring finger):* We could take turns.

Parent: *(holding up pinkie):* Now there's one finger left, so hold up your pinkie. Which is the best way to fix your problem?

Child: We'll take turns playing with it.

Go through the steps again and again until your child can fix her own problems without tattling or using her hand to remind her of the problem-solving steps. Of course you can use the same problem-solving technique without the fingers with older kids. The trick is to teach them to brainstorm their own solutions.

THE SOLUTION

Five Strategies for Change

1. *Figure out the reason.* Start by asking yourself what might be provoking your child to tattle. Here are a few possibilities. Check those that routinely apply to your child:

   ☐ Could she be craving your attention?

   ☐ Is she seeking control? Think about it: it's pretty powerful knowing you can get a sibling or friend in trouble.

   ☐ Is she trying to get back at a kid who hurt her? Could this be her way of retaliating?

   ☐ Is she stuck in a problem that she doesn't know how to solve, and looking for the adult to step in and fix everything?

☐ Does she not have enough time to be with you and uses tattling as her way of letting you know what's going on with her life?

☐ Does she have poor impulse control and can't keep those thoughts to herself?

☐ Is she trying to align herself with the grown-up population because kids her age aren't letting her into their world?

☐ Does she have an overzealous conscience? An overly strong moral compass can lead to self-righteousness that puts friends off.

☐ Is she lacking assertiveness skills and unable to stick up for herself? Is she resorting to tattling so you can translate her needs to the other kid?

☐ Does she think she's being your "little helper"? Might you have reinforced this? "Thanks for telling me!" "Well, that isn't the kind of friend you should be hanging around." Might you be unintentionally encouraging her tattling by responding positively to her every little complaint?

What is your best guess as to why your kid is tattling? What is one little thing you might do to start changing her ways?

2. *Explain the difference between "tattling" and "telling."* If your child is a repeat tattler, then a little teaching is called for. She needs to understand when tattling is acceptable and when it is not. *"Tattling is when you want to get your friend in trouble. Telling is when you report something that will get your friend out of trouble or help him so he doesn't get hurt."* You *do* want your child to tell you when she (or another child) is scared, touched in an uncomfortable way, feeling unsafe, hurt, in danger, or concerned about something. You *don't* want to hear tattling when the sole purpose is for attention or to get the other person in trouble. So be very clear as to the difference. A few kid books that teach the difference between telling and tattling include *Armadillo Tattletale,* by Helen Ketteman; *A Bad Case of Tattle Tongue,* by Julia Cook and Anita DuFalla; *Telling Isn't Tattling,* by Kathryn M. Hammerseng; *Don't Squeal Unless It's a Big Deal: A Tale of Tattletales,* by Jeanie Franz Ranson and Jackie Urbanovic; *Tattlin' Madeline,* by Carol Cummings; and *The Tattle Tail Tale,* by Tandy Braid.

3. *Announce your new policy.* Once your kid understands the difference between tattling and telling, explain your new rule: *"From now on I will not listen when you tattle about your friends or family members."* Your child needs to know you are serious, so make sure you announce your new rule with a serious tone.

4. *Calmly respond with the new tattling policy.* From this moment on, consistently downplay your child's tattling antics until she realizes they aren't going to work. Of course there are always extenuating circumstances, so here are a few solutions to help you handle the most typical tattling problems:

- If your younger child has problems remembering the rule, just ask this simple question: *"Is that helpful or hurtful?"* Then remind her that you only listen to helpful news.

- If your kids are put off seeing a peer break a house rule that they have had to abide by, acknowledge feelings: *"I know you think it's unfair. Just let your friend know how you feel."*

- If the tattler's information is correct (and you know so because you saw the incident happen), stay cool. Just a simple, *"I'll take care of this"* is all you need to say. Do have a conversation with the little offender, but do so out of earshot of the tattler.

- If your child has depended on you to solve her problems, stop being the arbitrator. Step back so your child knows you want and expect her to solve her own issues.

- If the tattling is affecting a relationship, help your child understand the impact her behavior has on her friend's feelings: *"Every time Maria comes over, you tattle on her. How do you think she feels?"*

- If sibling resentment is a problem because of past tattling, use this rule: *"If I don't see or hear it, I don't punish it."* Of course there may be instances in which you can find evidence and put two and two together, but for the most part stick to that rule and don't punish unobserved acts.

- If your child has an overactive conscience and feels the need to report every rule infraction, use this approach: *"I like how you follow our house rule and put your toys away, but I don't need to know that your friends aren't following our house rules. That's for their parents' to be concerned about."* Also, don't let another kid call your child "a tattle-tale." Other kids can quickly pick up on the term and start the teasing and name-calling game.

5. *Be consistent.* If you want change, you must be consistent with your policy each and every time your kid tattles. Pass your plan on to other caring adults who spend time with your child—Grandma, the teacher, the babysitter, Dad, the playgroup moms—so that they can get on board with you and respond in the same way to your child's tattling. It will take a while

One Parent's Answer

A mom from Sioux Falls shares:

My son tattled constantly, expecting me to solve every little trial and tribulation. So I made up little scenarios like "Your brother fell and can't get up." "Your sister is stuck in the tree." "The ball rolled across the street and Kenny is trying to get it." Then we role-played ways to solve them. He loved acting out the scenes, but it also helped him learn he could resolve his problems without tattling.

SOCIAL SCENE

for your kid to know you mean business, but if you and other adults stick to your new rule, your child will know you really are serious.

WHAT TO EXPECT BY STAGES AND AGES

Preschooler   Expect preschoolers to be a bit more overly conscientious, self-righteous, and concerned about right and wrong because of their stage of moral development. Four- to five-year-olds are especially sensitive to following adult rules and often feel it's their duty to report anything that even remotely breaks them.[135] They can be especially upset if they see another child breaking the same rule they have been required to obey and may have even been punished for. A young child's conscience is all about obeying Mommy and Daddy's rules.

School Age   From five to seven years of age, children become increasingly intolerant of any violation of their rights and privileges (especially by younger siblings). Competitiveness increases, so watch out for tattling as a way of upping a peer.

Tween   Tattling now moves up a notch and turns into malicious gossip, and can be delivered electronically (cell phone, e-mail, text messaging) as well as face-to-face. Rather than tattling to an adult, kids now report peer comings and goings to each other as a means of establishing social rank or status in a clique; this form of "tattling" is more prevalent among girls than boys.

LATE-BREAKING NEWS

When You *Do* Want Kids to "Tattle"

A survey found that 81 percent of American teens have become more willing to break the "code of silence" and report students who pose a threat to school safety or security.[136] Prior to a wave of horrific shootings on school campuses, older kids were leery of reporting threats, considering such reports "tattling" or "snitching." Make sure your child understands that this is *not* tattling or malicious gossip; she should be one of the "willing students." Talk to your child about which adults she would feel safe or comfortable going to if someone were threatened, scared, in danger, or hurt. When it comes to school safety, kids may well be the best metal detector: two-thirds of adolescents who commit homicide, suicide, or a school shooting share their intentions with a peer. Impress on your kids the importance of telling an adult their legitimate concerns with the guarantee that their report will be taken seriously.

Teased

SEE ALSO: *Bullied, Peer Pressure, Rejected, Sensitive, Shy*

THE PROBLEM

Red Flags

Can't handle it when friends poke fun, is overly sensitive to verbal teasing, often over-reacts to playful banter, feels picked on

The Change to Parent For

Your child learns to distinguish between friendly and hurtful teasing and develops habits to handle the teasing, gain confidence, and be less likely to be picked on.

Question: "I know all children are teased, but my son is so sensitive and takes everything to heart. How can I help him handle ribbing a little more gracefully so that he doesn't go all to pieces?"

Answer: The best way to help your child deal with a teaser is by role-playing pretend situations. You say things to him the way a teaser would, and he can try new ways of responding until he finds what works for him. Because your son is sensitive, help him practice hiding his upset look and emphasize that he should maintain eye contact with you. Those two tips will help him look less like a victim and appear more in control. The secret is to keep practicing the new responses until change kicks in and he can use them by himself the next time someone teases him.

Why Change?

Teasing is a fact of life and a big part of growing up. And it's not always harmful to our kids. The playful type of teasing can help kids develop a sense of humor, bounce back and not take themselves so seriously, and even learn social skills they will need in order to deal with life.

But not all teasing is fun and games or useful, especially these days. Research finds that childhood teasing is far harsher and more hurtful than it was, and it's escalating. Every day, 160,000 children skip school because of fear of being harassed, teased, and bullied.[137] During the middle school years, teasing reaches a crescendo and can be cruel and vicious. Those verbal barbs are often slung to ridicule, humiliate, haze, or otherwise deliberately harass the other child.

The plain truth is that certain kids do seem to get more than their fair share of teasing and name-calling. Of course, we tell our children to "shrug it off" and "not take it so seriously," but some kids just can't do that. Those verbal barbs sting! Although we can't protect our kids from those taunts, we can teach them strategies to help them cope with the teasing more effectively as well as be less likely to be targeted. And we must. Children who are taunted repeatedly are more likely to suffer from low self-esteem, anxiety, and depression. It's just further proof that your child needs to learn a repertoire of comeback strategies to use on both friendly and unfriendly teasers.

Signs and Symptoms

Of course all kids will be teased now and then, but researchers have discovered that some children are more likely to be picked on, teased, or called names. Here are the signs that a child is more likely to be the recipient of unfriendly teasing:[138]

- Is physically weaker, smaller in size and stature; appears more vulnerable
- Is quicker to submit to the teaser's (or bully's) demands
- Rewards the teaser by showing signs of distress (cries, whines, looks upset, appears stressed)
- Lacks humor; can't pick up sarcasm
- May have few friends
- May be "different" or socially insecure and awkward
- Lacks social skills or uses inappropriate social skills to try to gain entry into a group

LATE-BREAKING NEWS

University of Warwick: New research dispels the popular myth that "words can never hurt you."[139] The study of adolescents found that contrary to conventional belief, verbal attacks have *more* impact on the victims' sense of self-worth than do physical attacks (such as punching) or attacks on property (such as stealing or the destruction of belongings). Those children who are victims of repeated verbal taunts are much more likely to suffer from lower self-esteem and posttraumatic stress. It's just one more reason to commit to parenting for this change.

THE SOLUTION

Step 1. Early Intervention

- *Identify the underlying reason.* All kids are teased, but some more than others, usually because they are doing some behavior "too much" or to an extreme. Watch your child a bit more closely in social settings to see how he responds or how the other kids tell you he responds when teased. Is there anything he's doing that might be turning the kids off or causing them to target him? The following is a list of possible reasons. Check those that typically apply to your child:

  - [ ] *Too limited in social experiences:* hasn't encountered friendly bantering at home

  - [ ] *Too sensitive and thin skinned:* takes friendly teasing too seriously

  - [ ] *Too reactive:* responds by crying, whining, or threatening "to tell" or tattle to an adult

  - [ ] *Too unassertive:* looks like a victim—is meek, mumbles, shakes, whispers

  - [ ] *Too immature:* acts younger than his peers

  - [ ] *Too different from the other kids:* stands out, whether because of appearance or behavior

  - [ ] *Too irritating:* uses attention-getting behaviors to try to be included

  - [ ] *Too goody-goody:* is the teacher's pet, wins all the awards; kids resent all the attention

  - [ ] *Too marginalized:* is ostracized, targeted because he is alone and has no peer protection

  - [ ] *Too impulsive:* is hyperactive, flies off the handle, makes off-the-cuff remarks, looks almost comical to other kids

- *Explain the two kinds of teasing.* Stress to your child that *all* kids are teased; tell him there are two very different kinds of teasing and that he must learn to distinguish between the two. In *friendly teasing,* kids are *having fun with you* and are just being playful and joking. The intent isn't to hurt your feelings or make you sad. In *unfriendly teasing,* the person is *making fun of you,* be it your accent, weight, skin color, or glasses, and he doesn't care if he makes you feel sad or cry. Your child may need lots of talks to help him learn to distinguish the two

One Parent's Answer

A mom from Pittsburg writes:

My seven-year-old came home in tears almost daily saying the kids were picking on her. We realized we'd protected her so much that she didn't know how to handle teasing. For the next days, my husband and I intentionally started teasing Courtney a bit more. She cried at first, but we let her know that everybody gets teased—even among friends. My husband and I even teased each other so she saw that teasing is okay, and not to make a big deal about it. I knew our ploy was working when a couple of weeks later, two girls greeted Courtney with a friendly barb. She flashed a big smile, and then whispered, "It's okay, Mommy. I know they're just playing."

Pay Attention to This!

Differences in Teasing Between Girls and Boys

Older school-age boys are more likely to tease by aiming comments at the other's area of weakness or by questioning his manhood. Calling someone "gay" and making homophobic comments increase during the tween years. Girls are somewhat more subtle in their teasing and are more likely to spread rumors and make fun of another girl's physical appearance.

teasing types, so plan to discuss the difference frequently. Beware: in one study of older school-age kids, 80 percent of the kids admitted to unfriendly teasing, saying their intent was to make someone else miserable.[140] Only 20 percent claimed to tease with a friendly intent.

Step 2. Rapid Response

- *Bring it up.* Kids rarely come to parents and ask for help with teasing, so turn on your radar. *"You look really mad. Did someone tease you?"* *"Sally told me that you and Tim had a big blow-up because he was making fun of you again. Let's talk about it."* The amount of teasing and kid meanness is steadily increasing. Although it won't ease the pain, it may help your child to know that he's not alone.

- *Gather facts.* You want to find out if this is friendly or hurtful teasing, and whether it could even be sexual harassment or bullying. (If it is, see *Bullied*, p. 323.) Ask your child,

  "What happened?"

  "Has this happened before?"

  "Is it always the same kid who teases?"

  "What's he teasing you about?"

  "What did you say back? Did it work?"

  "Is there anything you might have done differently?"

- *Acknowledge feelings.* Teasing can hurt, so acknowledge your child's feelings. Don't underplay your kid's hurt if he is repeatedly being teased in an unfriendly manner. The latest research using brain scans shows that our brain reacts the same way to teasing or rejection as it does to physical pain.[141] Those verbal snubs really do hurt our kids. *"You seem upset by what Scott said."* *"It sounds like Scarlet really hurt your feelings."* *"You must be really mad. Those were some pretty hurtful things your friend said to you."*

- *Don't play rescuer.* Fight the urge to tell your child not to worry; resist that "I'll take care of it" attitude. And don't focus on what he did wrong, but instead acknowledge him for trying to deal with a tough situation.

- *Talk about why kids tease.* Here are some reasons elementary and middle school students say they tease:[142]

  To get a laugh.

  Because they don't feel good about who they are, so they put the other kid down.

  For attention.

  They say it's just a joke, but it's really because they're mean inside.

  To get even.

  Because the other kids in their clique do it, and they want to be "in."

- *Give your child books to read about teasing.* Counselors say that reading about teasing may help your child share his concerns. Here are a few book suggestions for different ages:

  Preschool: *Let's Talk About Teasing,* by Joy Wilt Berry; *The Berenstain Bears and Too Much Teasing,* by Stan and Jan Berenstain

  School age: *The Meanest Thing to Say,* by Bill Cosby; *Marvin Redpost: Why Pick on Me?* by Louis Sachar; *Simon's Hook: A Story About Teases and Put-Downs,* by Karen Burnett

  Tween: *How to Handle Bullies, Teasers, and Other Meanies,* by Kate Cohen-Posey; *Stick Up for Yourself!* by Gershen Kaufman, Lev Raphael, and Pamela Espeland

---

ONE SIMPLE SOLUTION

Teach Your Child to Look Strong from Head to Toe

Studies find that kids are more likely to be teased when they look like victims—slumped shoulders, lowered head, shaking knees, hands in pockets. So teach your child a simple solution to help him appear more confident just by changing his body language from head to toe:

Head: Stand tall and hold your head up high.

Eyes: Look your tormentor in the eye.

Voice: Speak loud enough and use a firm, strong (not yelling) voice.

Shoulders: Move closer to the teaser as you talk. Don't back away.

Hands: Take your hands out of your pockets.

Feet: Stand with your feet about twelve inches apart.

Step 3. Develop Habits for Change

There are many things kids can do to respond to teasing, but they may not know about them. Here are some of effective comeback responses that kids say have worked for them. Share the strategies with your child, and then have him choose the one he feels most comfortable trying. Then help him practice it over and over until he feels comfortable using it in the real kid world.

- *Question it.* "Why would you say that?" "Why would you want to tell me I am dumb [or fat or whatever] and hurt my feelings?"

- *Send a strong "I want" message.* "I want you to leave me alone" or "I want you to stop teasing me." The trick is to say the message firmly so that it doesn't sound wimpy.

- *Turn it into a compliment.* "Hey, thanks. I appreciate that!" "That was really nice of you to notice." "Thanks for the compliment."

- *Agree.* "You've got that right." "One hundred percent correct!" "Bingo, you win!" "People say that a lot about me."

- *Use sarcasm.* "Like I would care?" "Give me a break." "Oh, that's just great." Your "look" has to match the statement: rolling your eyes and walking away can do the trick. This works usually only for older kids who understand sarcasm.

- *Ignore it.* Walk away without even a look at the teaser, pretend the teaser is invisible, glance at something else and laugh, look completely uninterested, or pretend you don't hear it. This one works best if your child has a tougher time delivering verbal comebacks. It works best in places where your child *can* escape his teasers, such as in a park or at the playground. It *doesn't* work in close quarters, such on a school bus or at a cafeteria table.

- *Be amazed.* "Really? I didn't know that." "Thanks for telling me." Sounding like you really mean it is the trick.

- *Express displeasure.* "It really makes me mad when you tease me like that." Or "I don't like it when you make fun of me in front of the other kids. You may think it's funny, but it's not to me." "If you want us to continue being friends, stop teasing me." If this really is your kid's friend who is causing him such distress, then encourage your child to express his displeasure.

WHAT TO EXPECT BY STAGES AND AGES

Here are typical teasing behaviors you can expect, depending on your child's stage and age.[143]

Preschooler   Teasing and name-calling are common, though they are generally not deliberately hurtful. Kids this age haven't learned to filter comments, so they are likely to say what is on their minds. They're more likely to tease by laughing at others, saying silly things, or sometimes making an innocent comment about something new or different about the child.

School Age   Peer acceptance becomes increasingly important, so kids may partake in teasing to demonstrate their power and connection with peers. Language skills are increasing, so school-age kids learn more subtle and hurtful ways to tease and the best places to deliver their barbs so as not to get caught by overhearing adults. They typically deny any wrongdoing if their behavior is reported by others. Common teasing issues include appearance, weight, behavior, abilities, and clothing.[144]

ONE SIMPLE SOLUTION

The "CALM" Comeback Delivery

Teach your child these four crucial parts to deliver a comeback for maximum effect:

C – **Calm down.** Don't let a teaser know you're upset. Tell yourself to "chill"; take a breath.

A – **Assert yourself.** Choose a comeback you feel comfortable with, then stick up for yourself.

L – **Look the teaser in the eye.** Don't look down. Hold your head high and stand tall.

M – **Mean it.** Say the comeback using a determined voice. Do not insult or tease back.

Tween   Teasing at this age is more hurtful and considered verbal bullying because the intent is usually meant to embarrass, ridicule, and humiliate peers in front of others as a way to gain acceptance from a desired peer group. Tweens can pick up peer vulnerabilities and aim their barbs at those weaknesses. At this age, kids are most likely to be teased about (in descending order): appearance, abilities, identity (gender, race, religion, culture), behavior, family circumstances, possessions, opinions, names, feelings, and friends.[145] Boys often target the physical changes in girls' development and can use sexually explicit language in their barbs.

More Helpful Advice

Easing the Teasing: Helping Your Child Cope with Name-Calling, Ridicule, and Verbal Bullying, by Judy S. Freedman

Mom, They're Teasing Me: Helping Your Child Solve Social Problems, by Michael Thompson and Lawrence J. Cohen, with Catherine O'Neill Grace

Stick and Stones: 7 Ways Your Child Can Deal with Teasing, Conflict, and Other Hard Times, by Scott Cooper

Part 6
School

OUT OF THE MOUTHS OF BABES
WHY GOD MADE MOMS

Answers given by second-grade schoolchildren to the following question:

Who's the boss at your house?

1. Mom doesn't want to be boss, but she has to because Dad's such a goof ball.

2. Mom. You can tell by room inspection. She sees the stuff under the bed.

3. I guess Mom is, but only because she has a lot more to do than Dad.

Day Care

SEE ALSO: *Bad Friends, Biting, Teacher Conference*

THE QUESTION

"I hear so many horror stories about day care. How do I choose the best one for my son?"

THE ANSWER

Here is my strongest recommendation: walk into prospective day-care facilities when kids are there and look around. Ask yourself this key question: *"Is this the place I want my child to spend part of her day?"* The largest and longest-running study on American child care has found both pros and cons.[1] Youngsters who are in high-quality day care have stronger language skills and better short-term memory. However, 17 percent of kids who spend more than thirty hours a week in day care show more aggressive behavior problems (such as hitting, bullying, and interrupting others), and that's regardless of the socioeconomic level of their family. And there is a strong likelihood that those troublesome behaviors persist through sixth grade. You do have to be cautious and choose a day-care facility wisely. Here are ten questions to ask yourself, the staff, and the other parents to help you make your final decision:

1. Are most of the children well behaved, and do they comply with the requests of the staff?

2. Is there a supervised spot where an ill child can be removed from the other children?

3. Is there a consistent daily structure with an established curriculum that can be explained?

4. Is there a large enough ratio of staff to kids to ensure that children are closely watched?

5. Is there a consistent discipline plan that you agree with for handling aggressive kids?

6. Is the program within your budget, and are all costs, such as materials or transportation, spelled out?

7. Are the children enjoying themselves? Do they appear to be happy and active?

8. Is there a variety of age-appropriate activities that your child would enjoy and learn from?

9. Does the staff ensure that children's safety is a primary focus? (For instance, is the facility well gated, are electrical sockets covered, are fire extinguishers available, and is the staff trained in CPR?)

10. Are the staff "kid friendly" and patient? Do they enjoy kids, and do the children enjoy the staff? These people will be sharing their lives with your child, so determine your core beliefs and watch to see if the staff models them. For instance: Are they respectful? Do they require children to be courteous? Are they courteous to children? Are they dressed neatly and appropriately?

Above all, use your instinct. Can you picture your child feeling safe and secure in this setting? If so, chances are that you're right and that it's a good placement. Even then, watch your child closely for any increase in aggressive behaviors for the first weeks after she starts the program. If you notice such sudden changes, talk to the staff ASAP. You may need to change placements if your child's behavior does not improve.

Gives Up

SEE ALSO: *Angry, Depressed, Eating Disorders, Homework, Perfectionist, Stressed*

THE PROBLEM

Red Flags

Quits or gives up when the going gets rough, waits or expects someone to rescue her or bail her out, is easily discouraged, sees mistakes as the sign of personal failure

The Change to Parent For

Your child learns that success is a matter of hard work, recognizes that mistakes are a part of life, and develops skills that help her persevere until she does succeed.

Question: "Math homework is a nightmare! As soon my daughter sees the assignment, she'll do only a few problems at best, and then quits in tears. The teacher stressed that she is capable of doing the work but just stops at the first sign of difficulty because she says she's getting nowhere. What can we do so she doesn't feel so overwhelmed that she gives up?"

Answer: Here are a few things to help your child not give up:

- First, set a new house rule: *"In this family, we finish what we start."* Because the teacher says your daughter is capable, enforce a policy of "No television or phone privilege" until she finishes.

- Second, put an oven timer on her desk and set it for ten minutes (or an appropriate length tailored to her attention span). Explain that she must keep working until the bell goes off, then she can take a quick break and reset the timer.

- Encourage her to tally the number of problems she completes for each time block and make a contest out of seeing how many she can get done before the bell goes off, so that she sees she is succeeding. It may take a few nights for her to get into her new homework routine, but by the end of the week, she should be working the whole ten minutes without help. Then you can increase the time.

- By working shorter periods of time and realizing that she is succeeding in little chunks, she won't feel quite so overwhelmed, and her confidence will grow along with her ability to persevere. Meanwhile, keep encouraging her efforts and hard work!

LATE-BREAKING NEWS

University of Michigan: Harold Stevenson, a professor of psychology, sought to answer a question many Americans ask: "Why do Asian students tend to do better academically than American students?"[2] His research team conducted five intensive cross-national studies analyzing students' achievement in the United States, China, Taiwan, and Japan, and reached a conclusion: a critical key lies in what parents emphasize about their children's learning. Asian parents stress perseverance and effort in the task: "Work as hard as you can, and you will be successful." The researchers found that on the whole, Asian children worked longer and harder than their American counterparts because they had recognized that their success was based on how hard they worked. To the European American parent, the effort a child puts into the process is not nearly as important as the end product—the grade or score.

The crucial parenting lesson: put your emphasis on your child's effort and not on the end product (the grade, score, or points). Research shows that switching your emphasis from "What did you get?" to "How hard are you working?" enhances your child's potential to be more successful—and she probably will stick to that task longer as well.

Why Change?

One of the most critical lessons of success is a simple principle called "stick-to-itiveness." If our children are to survive and succeed in this competitive world, they must learn to hang in there and not quit. Perseverance, or not giving up, often makes the critical difference between success or failure. Does a child have the inner strength and stamina to "keep on keeping on," or will she be plagued by self-defeat, unwilling to give it her best shot—and quite possibly falling just short of success?

The skills of perseverance increase children's potential for success because kids learn to bounce back and not let setbacks get them down. And those are the exact skills today's kids need to handle life's ups and downs for the rest of their lives! This entry offers simple, proven parenting strategies that you can use to stretch your child's stick-to-itiveness.

Signs and Symptoms

- Is unwilling to try new tasks because of overriding concern that she'll fail or make a mistake
- Is easily discouraged when she faces difficulties or setbacks

One Parent's Answer

A mom from Dallas shares:

I had to find a way to help my son stop quitting when the going got tough, so one day I took a ruler and printed "Stick to It Award" across the back with a black marking pen. Then I told everyone to be on alert for family members showing special persistence. Each night at dinner, my husband and I announced who in our house didn't give up, and printed their initials on the stick and told them exactly what they did to deserve the award. Jimmy, because he practiced longer on the piano. Sally, because she hung in there until she learned to tuck the sheet corners in her bed. I couldn't believe how much my kids loved counting how often their initials appeared on the stick! But the best thing is that my son isn't giving up so fast because he wants his initials included on that ruler!

- Needs encouragement or the promise of a reward to complete a challenging task
- Often becomes defensive or blames others when she errs
- Is unwilling to try again if she is not successful with a task
- Doesn't recognize that the way you improve is by working harder; feels that success is more a matter of luck
- Frequently says negative self-comments when she falls short of success
- Is devastated if she isn't successful or doesn't get the highest grade
- Becomes overly frustrated, upset, or quick to anger when something becomes difficult

THE SOLUTION

Step 1. Early Intervention

- *Dig deeper.* Your first step is to identify why your child is quitting. Once you figure that out, you'll be better able to find solutions and increase your kid's stick-to-itiveness. The following is a list of common reasons kids give up. Check those that may apply to your child:

  - ☐ *Fears failure.* Too much emphasis is placed on success, the grade, the trophy, or the reward.

  - ☐ *Holds unrealistic expectations.* The task or placement is too advanced or difficult.

  - ☐ *Fears letting you down.* Your child feels that love your is conditional and based on success.

  - ☐ *Expects rescue.* Someone else always finishes the project, task, chore, or assignment.

  - ☐ *Is a perfectionist.* Quitting is easier than the stress of not measuring up to her standards.

☐ *Has a learning or emotional problem.* A learning, neurological, or emotional problem impedes her ability to follow through and stick to a task.

☐ *Has a short attention span.* Your child has difficulty concentrating, has ADHD or other attention deficit, and is easily distracted.

☐ *Is stressed.* Recent trauma, family discord, or illness makes focusing difficult.

☐ *Fears public humiliation.* Your child doesn't want to lose face among peers or others.

- *Define the word* perseverance. Take time to explain that perseverance means "not giving up" or "hanging in there until you complete what you start." Now find ways to use the word in natural moments to help your kid understand its importance. When your child sticks to a task, point it out: "That's perseverance. You hung in there even though it was hard."

- *Model effort.* Take a pledge to show your kids how you don't give up on a task even when things get difficult. Before starting a new task, make sure your child overhears you say, "I'm going to persevere until I am successful." Modeling a trait is always the number one teaching method, so consciously tune up perseverance in your daily behavior.

- *Start a family "Never Give Up" motto.* If you haven't already, begin using a family motto of "Don't quit until you succeed." A father in Jackson Hole told me that conveying this life message to his children was so important that they spent an afternoon together brainstorming family mottoes about perseverance, such as "Try, try, and try again and then you will win," "In this family, we finish what we start," "You'll never succeed if you give up," and "Quitters never win." They

---

ONE SIMPLE SOLUTION

Emphasize Effort, Not Intelligence

Columbia University: New research shows that the kind of words we say to our children can stretch their perseverance and get them into the habit of completing what they begin, as well as boost their achievement scores and grades.[3] A team of researchers studied hundreds of tweens in middle school math classes and found that those who believed that intelligence could be developed outperformed kids who thought that intelligence was fixed. What's more, the difference in math scores between the two groups widened over two years.

The study found that when kids believe intelligence can be improved by their own hard work and effort, they will work harder and are not as prone to give up. So don't tell your child "You're so smart!" "You're gifted!" or "The teacher says you're so intelligent!" Emphasize instead that achievement and improvement are all a matter of effort and hard work.

wrote them on index cards, and his kids taped them on their bedroom walls. Develop your own family motto as a reminder that your family code of behavior is never to give up.

Step 2. Rapid Response

- *Assess those expectations.* One reason kids quit is that they are burdened by unrealistic expectations. Expectations should always gently stretch your child's capabilities and expand her potential without snapping her confidence. (Use the "Rubber Band Rule": stretch without snapping.) Here are four questions to ask yourself to make sure the expectations you set for your kids are ones that stretch their potential without unintentionally diminishing their self-worth:

    1. *Developmentally appropriate.* Is my child developmentally ready for the tasks I'm requiring, or am I pushing her beyond her internal timetable? Learn what's appropriate for your child's age, but still keep in mind that developmental guidelines are not etched in stone. Start from where your child is.

    2. *Realistic.* Is my expectation fair and reasonable, or am I expecting too much? Realistic expectations stretch kids to aim higher, without pushing them beyond their capabilities. Situations that are too difficult put a child at risk of failing and lowering her feelings of competence.

    3. *Child oriented.* Is what I'm expecting something my child wants or something I want more for myself? We all want our kids to be successful, but we have to be constantly wary of setting goals for our kids that are based on our own dreams and not those of our kids.

    4. *Success oriented.* Am I setting the kind of expectations that tell my child I believe she's responsible, reliable, and worthy? Effective expectations encourage kids to be their best, so that they can develop a solid belief in themselves.

    If you discover that your expectations are unrealistic, then it's time to pull your child from that accelerated class, the soccer league, or that guitar group. Your child's self-esteem matters more, and to continue with unrealistic expectations only sets your kid up for discouragement and a feeling of failure, leading her to want to give up.

- *Stretch work time.* Watch your child a little more closely when she's performing a task she usually gives up on: practicing the cello, going over those math facts, reading her book. Then (without her knowing) clock her to see the usual length of time she works before she quits. Jot down the average amount of time (for instance, "Math fact studying: 5 minutes"). Share your findings and then announce that she must work just "one minute more" (or a reasonable length that is set slightly longer than her current "give up" time). Set the microwave timer or oven timer for that length of time and stress that she must keep working until the timer goes off. Your goal is to keep gently stretching her work time until eventually (translation: however long it takes) it is twice as long. Caution: the stretching process will take a while, so make sure you are realistic with your expectations, and keep reinforcing her efforts.

- *Erase the notion that mistakes are bad.* Children cannot learn to persevere unless they recognize how to deal with failure. In fact, making mistakes is a big part of how kids learn. Succeeding depends on sticking with their efforts and not letting setbacks get them down. Here are four ways to help kids learn that mistakes aren't fatal but instead a chance to start over:

  - *Say "It's okay to make a mistake."* Kids want so much to please us and are under such stress these days to excel. So give your kids "permission to fail." Help them recognize that mistakes can be positive learning experiences.

  - *Admit your own mistakes.* Own up to your errors: doing so helps kids recognize that everyone makes mistakes.

  - *Show acceptance.* The quickest way our kids will learn to erase the idea that mistakes are fatal is for them to feel our accepting response to their errors.

  - *Model how to bounce back.* When you make a mistake, explain to your child not only your error but also what you learned from it. *"I learned I should always read the whole recipe before adding the eggs"* or *"I was late for work because I couldn't find my keys. I learned I need to put my keys in the same place every day."*

ONE SIMPLE SOLUTION

Don't Call It a Mistake!

Studies find a common behavior of high-achieving kids: they are not thrown by errors, so they are less likely to give up. In fact, they often call mistakes by other names (glitch, bug, a "temporary") so that they won't discourage themselves in the middle of their learning. Help your child come up with a word to say inside her head whenever she encounters a mistake. Any word will do—just make sure to help her practice saying it over and over so she'll remember to use it when she really makes a mistake. One teacher taught her students to call mistakes "opportunities." The same day of her lesson, I watched a child make a mistake. Instantly the student next to him leaned over and whispered, "Remember, it's an opportunity!" The smile on the child's face was all the proof I needed that the teacher's lesson had worked!

Step 3. Develop Habits for Change

- *Discuss people who don't give up.* I love to tell children—especially kids who are struggling—brief stories about famous people who succeeded against the odds; their stories offer hope. The world is filled with folks who suffered enormous obstacles and setbacks but didn't cave in or despair. Instead, they looked at their problems as opportunities, and kept at their dreams until they succeeded. Here are a few folks who persevered and are great examples for kids:

  Thomas Edison, the inventor of the light bulb, was told by his teacher that he was too stupid to learn anything.

  Charles Darwin, the famous naturalist and developer of the theory of evolution, did quite poorly in his early grades and even failed a university medical course.

  Woodrow Wilson, a Rhodes scholar and president of the United States, didn't learn the alphabet until he was eight; he didn't read until he was eleven.

  Albert Einstein did not talk until age four or read until age nine. He performed badly in almost all his high school courses and failed his college entrance exams.

  Abraham Lincoln started the Blackhawk War as a captain. By the end of the war he had been demoted to private.

  Beethoven's music teacher told him he was hopeless as a composer.

  Michael Jordan was cut from his high school basketball team.

  Walt Disney was fired by a newspaper editor for lacking great ideas; he went bankrupt, had nervous breakdowns, and was told repeatedly to "get rid of the mouse because there's no potential in it."

- *Teach "bounce back" statements.* An effective way to help your child learn to persevere is to teach her to say a simple statement to help her bounce back from adversity. Saying that statement inside her head can help her hang in there and persevere on a difficult task. The trick is to brainstorm a few statements together, have your child select one she is most comfortable with, and then help her practice saying the same statement out loud several times for a few days until she can remember to use it on her own. Here are a few options: "It doesn't have to be perfect." "I can learn from my mistakes." "It's okay to make a mistake." "Everybody makes mistakes." "It's just a mistake." "I can't get any better unless I try it." "I made a mistake. Now I'll correct it. I can turn it around."

WHAT TO EXPECT BY STAGES AND AGES

Preschooler   The desire to please parents is paramount, so make sure your expectations are reasonable and realistic. Preschoolers (especially boys) have short attention spans, so giving directions and tasks should be tailored to capabilities; to increase success, choose

Pay Attention to This!
When Is It Okay to Let Your Child Quit?

Your child has given the cello her best shot, but says she hates it. Your son says his coach always yells at him, and he wants to quit the team. Your daughter says the math class is too hard and wants to be in the less accelerated class. Here are five factors to help you decide whether you should let your kid quit:

1. *Stressful.* There is a marked, uncharacteristic, and troubling change in your child's behavior (acts stressed, has sleep problems, is irritable, loses appetite, has headaches or stomachaches) that you can correlate to the activity.

2. *Joyless.* Your child derives no satisfaction or enjoyment from a formerly much-loved sport or activity despite the effort.

3. *Beyond abilities.* Despite your child's efforts, the activity is too difficult for her current abilities.

4. *Poor coach.* The coach (or teacher) is not giving your child enough play time, yells way too much, is far too competitive, pushes a win-at-any-cost philosophy, or clearly treats your child unfairly.

5. *Given his best shot.* Your child has tried her hardest, but things aren't improving. Her frustrations and desire to quit continue.

If your child's experience meets any of these criteria, it's probably best to move on, but let your child know you appreciate that she tried her hardest.

the day-care program and preschool aimed at your child's learning style. Watch out for competitive sports teams; put emphasis on fun and learning basic skills, or the outcome will be tears of frustrations and the desire to quit.

School Age   Sports, activities, and contests become competitive, and confidence can tumble if expectations are not appropriate. Watch out for overscheduling: too many activities can lead to stress and wanting to give up. Kids at this age may not have the words or confidence to express frustrations, so they may simply ask to quit the team, class, or activity. Emphasis on grades and test scores mounts. Perfectionism often develops. Your child must know that your love is unconditional and not contingent on those end products. Cheating can become the child's means to achieve if she feels that a task is too difficult.

Tween The urge to fit in and be accepted is paramount. Tweens may quit to avoid peer humiliation from striking out at bat, failing on the spelling bee, or clamming up on the speech. Stress over schoolwork, grades, and test scores mounts and can become overwhelming and debilitating. This is the age that kids are most likely to quit teams because sports are too competitive or are no longer considered enjoyable.

More Helpful Advice

I Think I Can, I Know I Can! by Susan Isaacs and Wendy Ritchey

Mindset: The New Psychology of Success, by Carol Dweck

Parents Do Make a Difference: How to Raise Kids with Solid Character, Strong Minds, and Caring Hearts, by Michele Borba

Positive Self-Talk for Children, by Douglas Blouch

The Learning Gap, by Harold Stevenson and James Stigler

The Myth of Laziness, by Mel Levine

Underachievement Syndrome, by Sylvia Rimm

Homework

SEE ALSO: *Attention Deficit, Gives Up, Sleepless, Stressed*

THE PROBLEM

Red Flags

Arguing, crying, and meltdowns over homework; poor study skills and organization; failure to write down assignments; no independent learning abilities; struggling to complete tasks

The Change to Parent For

Your child learns organization and study skills to become a more successful learner and complete homework assignments independently.

Question: "Seven o'clock is when our kids are supposed to start their homework, but instead it's when all the crying and pleading starts. They expect us to sit there with them and basically do all their assignments for them. Believe me, it's a lot easier than listening to their wailing. What's the secret to getting your kids to do their homework without a world war? My husband and I need a life."

Answer: The single most important parent tip is to recognize that your role with homework is not "doer." The work responsibility rests in your kids' hands, not yours. Sure, you need to make sure they understand the concepts and are capable of doing the assignments, but once they expect you to do it for them, you have to stop. Instead, follow this new parenting mantra: *"Never do for your child what your child can do for himself."* It may take a bit of adjustment, but hang tight until your child achieves the desired change: to become an independent, self-motivated learner. And at that point, your battles will be no more.

Why Change?

"But you helped me last week!" "Can't you write a note and say I'm sick?" "But I did almost all of it." "You didn't tell me I had homework!"

Sound familiar? Well, you're not alone. According to a survey by Public Agenda, a nonprofit research organization, almost half of all parents of school-age students said they have arguments involving tears or yelling at their kids about homework.[4] And one-third of parents admit that those school assignments cause repeated kid meltdowns.

435

There's been some controversy lately about homework; some say it isn't necessary, that it's assigned because of administrative policy that's trying to make the parents feel that the school is serious about education, or to ensure that their attendees pass standardized tests. Nevertheless, research has shown that the right kind of homework assignments helps kids acquire the essential skills for success in school and life: organization, self-pacing, problem solving, internal motivation, concentration, memory, goal setting, good old "stick-to-itiveness"—and, don't forget, they might learn something!

Signs and Symptoms

Let's face it: it's a rare child who enjoys homework. Most would rather be running around and having fun. Can you blame them? But here are signs that the problem is in need of a solution:

- *Constant battles.* There are tears, arguing, tantrums, yelling. Your relationship becomes a painful struggle every night.
- *Manipulation.* Your child tells you there is no homework or that it's finished, and you know otherwise.
- *No challenge.* Assignments are primarily "busywork"; the work is boring or below your child's capability.
- *Struggles in learning.* Assignments are too hard and are beyond your child's abilities; learning is difficult.
- *Dependence.* Someone else generally starts or finishes your child's work; there is no self-pacing or independence.

LATE-BREAKING NEWS

Duke University: Reviewing over sixty studies, Harris Cooper, the director of education at Duke, found that the greatest benefits of homework are seen at the high school level, especially when students do at least five to ten hours per week.[5] Anything less demanding does not result in learning gains. Performance improves at the middle school level if kids do a maximum of ninety minutes of homework nightly. Homework has relatively little effect on academic achievement during the elementary school years, but will enhance qualities that are critical to learning, such as persistence, diligence, and the ability to delay gratification.[6] And those are the very skills that become increasingly necessary for success as your child advances up the levels of schooling.

THE SOLUTION

Step 1. Early Intervention

- *Rule out potential problems.* Your first task is to determine the cause of the problem. The following list includes the usual culprits, so check those that may apply to your child:

  ☐ Are the tasks above or below his abilities?

  ☐ Is the class, curriculum, or program too hard or accelerated?

  ☐ Does he need tutoring to catch up?

  ☐ Is he too easily distracted? Might he have an attention deficit? (See *Attention Deficit,* p. 466.) Does he have the study or organizational skills needed to achieve success?

  ☐ Is your child rubbing his eyes, blinking excessively, or squinting? Does he possibly need an eye exam?

  ☐ Might he have a learning or emotional problem that needs a psychological assessment? (Ask the teacher.)

  ☐ Is stress or an overextended schedule hindering his concentration?

  ☐ Is this problem really about wanting to get out of doing the work, and so far the ploy has succeeded?

  If you suspect a special kind of problem (such as difficulty seeing, concentrating, or recalling information), seek the advice of the appropriate authority, whether that's a pediatrician, neurologist, speech therapist, optometrist, school psychologist, teacher, or counselor, to help you develop a solution. Meanwhile, are there any simple changes you can make to help your child be more successful?

- *Make homework not a choice.* From the beginning, maintain a firm, serious attitude about homework. Your kid needs to know that homework has to be done well and that there are no ifs, ands, or buts about it. Enforce the "work before play" rule. (And by the way, when your kids are doing homework, turn off the television. It's not fair having the noise of that television or video game on when a child is struggling with a homework assignment. Instead, pick up a newspaper or read a book!)

- *Develop a weekly homework reminder.* Help your child plot out a homework schedule so that he has a simple reminder of daily or weekly assignments as well as long-term projects and reports. A white board or chalkboard is preferable because it is reusable. With a permanent marker, list the days of the week or month and then note regular daily or weekly assignments (Monday: sharing; Wednesday: library; Friday: spelling test) as well as practice dates, scout meetings, tutoring, and so on. Use a different color to represent each kid (John is blue; Sally is green). Keep it in a central place in your home for everyone to quickly refer to.

- *Know the teacher's expectations.* The better your relationship with your child's teacher, the more positive your child's school experience. Your goal is to create a collaborative relationship with the teacher. Attend the open house and all conferences. Read those teacher notes. Be very clear about her expectations and homework policy so that you, the teacher, and your child are on the same page. Does she post homework assignments online or via e-mail? How much will the homework affect your child's grade? How often will it be assigned? How will you be informed of your child's progress or any problems? And most important: on average, how long should the homework take per night? Once you know the policy, have a talk with your child so that he knows that you not only are aware of those expectations but will support them. If your child is in middle school, he probably has a number of teachers, so you will have to make the same queries of each teacher.

Step 2. Rapid Response

- *Assess your role.* So what's your current response to these battles? For instance: Are you pleading, arguing, or demanding? Hovering, overcorrecting, or protecting? Excusing, signing, or bribing? Are your expectations realistic and tailored to your child? Are you consistent with those expectations? Is there one thing you might do to change *your* response so that your relationship with your kid isn't hindered—and he completes his homework?

- *Create a special homework spot.* To help your kid gain a sense of the importance of homework, set aside a special place just for him to work. Involve him in the selection of this space. Any place that has good lighting and is reasonably quiet is fine. The general rule is that the younger the child, the closer proximity to you the spot will be (such as the kitchen table, as it's near you when you're preparing dinner). Then have your kid help stock it with necessary supplies, such as pens, pencils, paper, scissors, ruler, calculator, and dictionary. If you don't have a desk, store supplies in a plastic bin or box. It will help your kid get organized and avoid those time wasters: "I can't find a ruler!" "Where's the dictionary?" If you have a computer, do put it in a place where you can carefully view what your child is doing online.

One Parent's Answer

A mom from Salt Lake City writes:

My son was a homework dawdler, and I turned into a nagger. I found the best solution was to set the oven timer and tell Jacob to see how many problems he could do before the buzzer went off. Not only did it help him work faster, but he also loved competing against himself. And I got to stop nagging.

- *Set a routine from the beginning.* Select a time that works best for your kid to do his homework—after school, before dinner, after dinner—then stick to it. Ask your child for his input and do try to accommodate his schedule. If "homework time" is right after school, always first give your child a snack and time to cool down from a packed day. A set and predictable schedule helps reduce the battles and gets your kid into a routine. Drawing a clock face with the set time helps younger kids.

- *Stay positive.* Look for those moments when your kid *is* on task, *does* write down the assignment, *does* begin his work without you. Then praise those efforts! And restrain the urge to correct all his errors or focus on the mistakes.

Step 3. Develop Habits for Change

- *Learn planning skills.* Show your kid how to make a list of what needs to be done each night in order of priority. He can then cross items off as each is done. A young child can draw a different task on individual paper strips, then put them in the order he plans to complete them and staple the packet together. Each time a task is finished, your child tears off a strip until no more remain. A helpful tool for older kids is *The Study Skills Handbook,* by Judith Dodge.

- *Divide the assignment into smaller parts.* Breaking up homework into smaller chunks is often helpful for kids who have difficulty sticking to a task or who seem overwhelmed with an assignment. Just tell your child to do "one chunk at a time." Gradually you can increase the size of the "work chunks" as your child's confidence increases. If your child has trouble focusing, then suggest he work in twenty-minute bouts, then take a quick refresher break. Think smaller chunks or working in shorter amounts of times.

- *Do the hardest first.* Teach your child to do the hardest homework assignment first. It will take the most concentration (which is usually strongest at the beginning of a study session) and the longest amount of time. Also, if there are facts to be memorized or information to be reviewed for a test, don't wait until the last minute. The review should be done early when he is the freshest, and ideally in chunks during the week. And have him review it one more time in the morning before school.

- *Have a parent check the finished product.* Teachers often ask that a parent sign completed homework, so for a younger child, set a routine in which he shows you the finished paper. Be sure to ask an older child to show you any reports—especially if he's used a computer to do his research. Ask specific questions about the material, and if he doesn't know the answers, it's a red flag that he may have cut and pasted content from other sources without citation.

If he has errors, don't show him where they are, but guide him to them. *"I see two mistakes on the first line." "Four of your problems are wrong on the top half. Check your answers."* Establish a routine that once the work is done, your child immediately puts it in his folder or binder, places it in his backpack, and sets the backpack by the door (so he can easily find it the next morning).

- *Know there will be a consequence for incompletion.* If you find out that the homework isn't getting done or isn't done with the quality you expect, then state a consequence. Your child needs to understand that completing homework is not optional. For instance, if work isn't finished by a predetermined time (ideally, the same time each night), your kid knows he will lose a desired privilege either that evening or the following day. Or set up the "Homework first, then play" rule. Also make a rule that a child may do his homework alone in his room only if he has a proven track record of being able to complete it meeting the standards you expect.

Pay Attention to This!
Does Your Child Have Too Much Homework?

The National Education Association and the PTA recommend *a maximum of ten minutes of homework per grade level per night.*[7] But that homework recommendation doesn't seem to be applied in many homes. A University of Michigan study found that many kids are doing three times that amount.[8] If you are concerned that your child is struggling because of an excessive workload, record and add up the total amount of time spent during a typical week. Let the teacher know about tasks that cause struggles or require excessive time: "This took two hours. Did you intend it to take so long?" If the heavy workload continues, set up a teacher conference to voice your concerns. If you think the teacher's expectations are not realistic, talk to other parents. Do they think the tasks are too hard, too easy, or just right? How are their kids doing? If you still feel that the homework is severely excessive (and many other parents agree), then next talk to the principal, the parent-teacher association, and, if necessary, the school board. *The Case Against Homework,* by Nancy Kalish and Sara Bennett, is helpful.

WHAT TO EXPECT BY STAGES AND AGES

Preschooler   The best "homework" is reading to your child on a nightly basis in a fun, relaxed way. Usually the only homework assignment for kids this age is bringing weekly sharing to school; start organization skills by teaching your child to put his backpack and schoolwork in a designated spot each day. It is recommended that all children have their first eye exam by the age of three; 70 percent of parents with kids under six have not had them tested.[9]

School Age   This is the best time to start a regular homework routine where the work is done at the same time and place each night. Teach your child to write tasks in a notebook, put assignments in a backpack, and ask his teacher for clarification *before* coming home if he's uncertain about an assignment. No more than ten minutes of homework per night per grade is the general rule. For kids age five, ten minutes of nightly homework is appropriate; for age seven, thirty minutes. Although nine-year-olds are able to handle about forty-five to sixty minutes a night, most experts suggest no more than forty minutes per night.

Tween Independent work habits and self-pacing skills become more crucial as assignments become lengthier. The number of teachers and subjects increases, so routinely writing down assignments and organizing work are essential for success. Tween girls spend an average of 1.4 hours a day on homework, compared to 1.1 hours for tween boys.[10] Watch out for stress and overload as pressure regarding schoolwork rises sharply.

DOES YOUR CHILD NEED A TUTOR?

There can come a time when those homework struggles become too much, and you wonder if your child needs a tutor. These days, tutoring is a billion-dollar business, and prices can vary from $10 to $250 an hour. The best tutor isn't necessarily the one everyone in town is using or the one who charges the most. Consider a retired teacher, a high school student who is a Spanish whiz, or the twelve-year-old next door whom your kid adores. Here are four solutions to help you hire the best tutor for your child and help your child get the most out of tutoring:

1. *Seek out your child's teacher.* Ask her these questions:

   Do you think my child needs a tutor?

   What specific skills or subjects does he need help in?

   Is there a test schedule so that the tutor can review the material?

   Does the tutor need teaching experience?

   Do you have any tutor recommendations?

   What tutoring schedule would best fit my child's attention span and learning capabilities?

2. *Tailor the tutoring to fit your child's learning style.* Here are three factors to consider:

   Schedule: What would be the best tutoring schedule for your child? Once- or twice-a-week sessions? Thirty-minute or one- or two-hour sessions? Individual or group sessions? How long can he attend to his homework without being distracted?

   Personality: What type of personality is your child most receptive to? The tutor should be someone your child feels comfortable with. Match the tutor's personality to your child.

Learning style: Is your child a visual, auditory, or kinesthetic learner? (If you don't know, ask the teacher.) If your child is struggling, then teaching the concept using the same unsuccessful approach as that of the classroom teacher may not be advisable. Your child may need a more creative tutor who customizes her sessions to your child's learning needs.

Interview the prospective tutor yourself, ask for recommendations, and hire the person who would be best for your kid's temperament, personality, and learning style; who is experienced in the subject matter; and who is affordable.

3. *Create a specific tutoring plan.* Next, sit down and create a tutoring plan (ideally with your child present) that includes the specific steps the tutor plans to take to help your child; how progress will be assessed; how school assignments and tests will be covered in the sessions; and how you will know that progress is being made. Do then check in briefly at least every other week to see how things are going. Be clear from the start as to the tutoring schedule as well as payment.

4. *Prioritize tutoring.* Your child needs to know tutoring is a priority and as important as soccer practice or violin lessons or scouting. In fact, something may have to give so that your child isn't overscheduled. Also arrange the tutoring at the best time in your child's schedule so that he can concentrate at those sessions.

No tutor is a miracle worker, so it may take time to see progress. *A Parent's Guide to Tutors and Tutoring,* by Jim Mendelsohn, offers helpful advice about the tutoring process. Just remember to keep encouraging your child's learning efforts, as this can be a frustrating ordeal for the both of you.

More Helpful Advice

Ending the Homework Hassle, by John K. Rosemond

How to Help Your Child with Homework: The Complete Guide to Encouraging Good Study Habits and Ending the Homework Wars, by Jean Shay Schumm

Seven Steps to Homework Success: A Family Guide for Solving Common Homework Problems, by Sydney Zentall and Sam Goldstein

The Homework Handbook: Practical Advice You Can Use Tonight to Help Your Child Succeed Tomorrow, by Harriett Cholden, John A. Friedman, and Ethel Tiersky

Leadership

SEE ALSO: *Argues, Chores, Dependent, Peer Pressure, Role Models*

THE QUESTION

"Our daughter is too much of a follower, always going along with the pack or doing only what the other kids tell her to do. How can I instill in her some independence of mind, confidence, and leadership?"

THE ANSWER

What parent doesn't want her child to be a leader? After all, that top role—be it football captain, head cheerleader, debate captain, newspaper editor, play director, student body president—is deemed the epitome of success. They are the kids who adults applaud and peers look up to. And make no mistake, assuming those leadership positions now gives kids the confidence to lead a team, head a group, or run for an office. Each leadership success is one more step up a ladder, and each rung up gives kids that needed "edge" to be accepted to their choice of college, win that scholarship, or be hired for that lucrative job. But even more important: those positions are the best ways to build a child's character, integrity, and confidence.

But what if your child has the smarts and the integrity, yet seems to lack the confidence or interest in assuming a leadership role? Well, here's news: there are proven ways to help kids follow less and lead more. Research also shows that positive leadership traits are teachable at any age, though the earlier we begin, the better. The best news is that these same leadership traits will help boost your child's potential for success in every arena of life both now and forever. So here are some answers:

- *Be an example.* Regardless of age, gender, region, or income, kids identify immediate family members and relatives—most particularly their mothers—as the people they most admire.[11] How would your kid describe your leadership style? Do you speak up at home and in public? Help out in causes that concern you? Share your opinions with your family? Stay current with what's going on in the world and talk about it with your children? State your political opinions? Vote? Bring your child along to charitable events you are organizing? Don't undermine your power! Your kids are watching—and copying—your actions as well as those of others.

- *Learn different leadership styles.* Kids need to learn that there are different leadership styles—active, reflective, and supportive. You can provide examples of different types of famous leaders, such as Abraham Lincoln, Winston Churchill, Nancy Pelosi, Norman Schwarzkopf, and Golda Meir in books, magazines, videos, and newspapers. Discuss that leaders can have a positive as well as negative influence (throw in Lenin, Stalin, and Hitler). Point out the quiet, compassionate leadership style of Gandhi, Nelson Mandela, and the Dalai Lama or the supportive, team-building style of Bill Walsh, Vince Lombardi, or Pete Carroll, and then help your child identify her own style. Emphasize that she doesn't have to be strong and pushy to be a leader. The key is always to lead from her own unique strengths and talents—and sometimes it's fine to be a follower as well.

- *Encourage your child's voice.* Kids say that their fear of public speaking is the biggest obstacle (followed by shyness and embarrassment) to assuming leadership roles.[12] If your child has this fear, find ways to build her confidence in speaking up so that she is less likely to be intimidated.

  - *Don't interpret.* If you want your child to speak out, then let her! Don't be her translator ("What she really means is . . .") or allow shyness, a speech impediment, or a young age to be an excuse for her not speaking. Let your child be heard!

  - *Ask your child's opinion.* Even when your child is very young, ask her for her ideas and then listen. You don't have to agree with her opinions, but you do have to let her know you are interested.

  - *Create family forums.* Look for ways your child can practice getting her point across at home so that she will feel comfortable speaking out among friends. Cut out articles about controversial news stories and hold family debates; start family meetings; use family dinners or evenings to discuss politics, global warming, or school events. But talk!

  - *Find confidence builders.* Theatre, debate, drama, choir, or public speaking classes are just a few forums that help kids gain confidence. Find something for your child.

  - *Expose your child to public speakers.* Bring your child to political speeches or plop down in front of the TV together and watch *Meet the Press,* political debates, news conferences, or politicians on C-SPAN and critique their speaking style.

  - *Watch out for your daughter.* Studies repeatedly find that girls feel more threatened speaking out with boys around.[13] So boost your daughter's security by first giving her a protected environment in which to find her voice and build confidence. Then gradually begin inviting the opposite sex to listen to her so that she learns to hold her own comfortably.

- *Put your kid in charge.* Countless studies show that the oldest kid in the family is the most likely to be a CEO, win a Nobel Prize, or become a U.S. president. Studies also show that this tendency for oldest children to be leaders is not due to genetics. It's simply because we give our oldest children more responsibilities at younger ages, and as a result, the older kids learn to take charge.[14] So don't deprive your other kids of their leadership potential. By handing out those household duties and stretching their family obligations, you'll be planting the seeds of leadership. Add chores to her list that not only give more her responsibilities but also prepare her for life. Ask her to help you plan a part of the family meal, do her laundry, plan and organize the outdoor garden, or decide on the schedule for visiting the zoo. Just tailor your expectations to your child's abilities and age, of course. (See also *Chores,* p. 538.)

- *Hold family meetings.* A great way for kids to learn leadership skills, teamwork, speaking up, solving problems, and the workings of democracy is right at home: the family meeting. There are endless possible topics for your meetings, from settling sibling conflicts, negotiating chores or allowances, debating politics, or just enjoying each other's company. Here are a few principles that help kids learn democratic principles and leadership, but do modify them to fit your family's needs:

  - *Make it democratic.* Encourage your children to speak up, while you hold back your judgments. Each member's opinion is considered equal, everyone has a right to be heard, and anyone can bring up any sort of problem or concern.

  - *Determine decision making.* Usually decisions are based on the majority's vote, though some experts feel that agreement should be made by unanimous consensus.

  - *Schedule regular meetings.* Hold meetings at least once a week; they should last twenty to thirty minutes for younger kids, slightly longer for older. Mandate everyone's attendance. If something big is going on in your family—such as moving, or picking a new school—have more frequent meetings.

  - *Rotate meeting roles.* One way to help kids learn leadership roles is to assign different positions that can be rotated weekly. Possibilities might be a chairperson, who starts and stops meetings and keeps everyone to the agenda; a parliamentarian, who makes sure rules are followed; a meeting planner, who posts the meeting date and time; and a secretary, who keeps meeting notes. Younger kids can use a tape recorder to record the meetings.

- *Look for leadership opportunities.* Kids don't learn leadership traits from reading or hearing about leadership but by leading. So it's critical that your child find ways to be in charge so she can gain confidence and practice those crucial leadership skills. Just don't think of leadership roles as only elected positions, such as class president or team captain. *Any* opportunity for your child to lead another is fine. For example: babysitting, tutoring a neighbor child, watching a younger sibling, or teaching a small Sunday school class. The size of the group isn't what matters; the opportunity to lead is. Hint: watch out that you don't enroll your kid in too many adult-supervised, highly structured activities. Children will never be able to practice leading if someone always leads them.

- *Find ways to help your child make a difference.* The fact is, any leader—young or old—can't lead without a cause. Identify your child's passions or concerns (polar bears, cleanliness, fossil fuel, graffiti) and then expand her knowledge about that issue. Cut out news articles, check out library books, or surf the Internet, but increase your child's interest and understanding about that issue. Encourage her to be in charge of the church clothing drive for the women's shelter, raise money for flood victims, volunteer to do community service, plan a garage sale for the homeless, or stop the bullying epidemic at her school. Then encourage her to develop a plan to connect with like-minded kids, voice their concerns, and lead a group—whatever the size—to make a difference in her world through positive leadership.

Almost 70 percent of kids today say that they want to be the kind of leader who helps others, and almost half of kids surveyed say they want to change the world. At the top of their list of leaders they admire most is one committed to fighting against social injustice, helping others, and standing up for his or her beliefs.[15] Our kids are the next generation, so let's prepare them to lead well. And one more thing: take part in the democratic process yourself and vote in each and every election so that your kids copy that tradition in the future.

Organized Sports

SEE ALSO: *Gives Up, Growing Up Too Fast, Overscheduled, Perfectionist, Poor Sport*

THE QUESTION

"I'd love my son to play organized sports, but how do I know if he's ready so I can sign him up?"

THE ANSWER

Although each child grows and matures at different rates, most experts—including the American Academy of Pediatrics—think kids aren't ready for organized team sports until around six years of age or contact sports until age eight.[16] That's because it isn't until at least six that children can follow directions and stick to the rules. Pushing a child into a sport before he is ready can set him up for frustrations and create negative memories. The trick is to figure out whether *your* child is ready to participate in an organized sport, and here are seven issues to help you make that decision:

1. *Interest:* Is this something *your child* wants to do and has expressed an interest in?

2. *Attention span:* Can he follow directions, listen to an adult, and stick to the rules?

3. *Teamwork:* Does he understand the concept of teamwork and getting along with other kids?

4. *Emotional readiness:* Can he handle frustrations and the rigors of competition?

5. *Physical readiness:* Does he have the endurance and physical skills to keep up? Is he about the same height and weight as the other kids? (Make sure your child has a physical.)

6. *Coach:* Is the coach kid-friendly and knowledgeable about the sport so that he can teach your child basic skills and provide a fun and positive experience?

7. *Instinct:* Do you think your child is really ready for organized sports? Will this fit your family's schedule and budget?

If you do decide to sign your child up, make sure you are willing to let your child play the game while you maintain the role of a positive and encouraging spectator. Remember: signing a child up too early can create more tears than smiles and even turn him off to sports.

Procrastinates

SEE ALSO: *Attention Deficit, Depressed, Gives Up, Homework, Perfectionist, Stressed*

THE PROBLEM

Red Flags

Puts things off to the last minute, dawdles, waits for someone to rescue her or get her started, has poor internal sense of time

The Change to Parent For

Your child learns to manage time more effectively, set more realistic deadlines, and start projects and tasks without reminders.

Why Change?

"You never give me enough time!" "I told you I'll finish it tomorrow." "Stop rushing me!"

Do any of these sound familiar? If so, you have a little dawdler. It's almost as though the internal clocks of these kids are set for a different time zone. And as homework, expectations, and activities get tougher at each grade level, procrastinating can be a major handicap for academic as well as social success. Let's face it: no teacher, coach, or even friend appreciates lateness.

Although there is no magical cure for procrastination, there are tips that help your child learn crucial time management and organization skills so that she can start those tasks a whole lot sooner and not put things off. The parenting secret to keep in mind is that procrastination is not a biological malfunction in your kid but a bad habit that needs to be broken. Here are solutions to get you started parenting for this important change.

Pay Attention to This!

St. Lawrence University: Pamela Thacher, an associate professor of psychology, analyzed students' studying habits, and those who procrastinated or crammed their studying into all-nighters had far lower grade-point averages and test scores than those students who didn't.[17] It's just one more reason to change your child's procrastination habits now to improve her study skills. Putting things off until the last minute doesn't work when it comes to raising grades or test scores.

THE SOLUTION

Six Strategies for Change

1. *Identify the reason.* Your first step is to figure out what's causing your child's chronic lateness and putting things off. Once you dig deeper and discover the real reason, you'll be better able to apply solutions. Do take a moment to calmly ask her, for example, *"You put off that science project until the last minute. Why did you wait so long? What would have helped you get started sooner?"* (The answer may be simpler than you think, such as that she was ill the day the assignment was given or that she didn't have the right supplies to get started.) If your kid can't supply the reason, this list includes possibilities to consider. Check those that may apply to your child:

☐ *Is mimicking.* She sees others (you?) not meeting deadlines or waiting until the last minute.

☐ *Is always getting rescued.* Someone gets her started or completes the chore, activity, or homework.

☐ *Has an attention deficit.* Your child has a learning disability, short attention span, difficulty focusing; she's impulsive.

☐ *Has a "slower" temperament.* Your child has a more relaxed, laid-back nature; she "takes her own sweet time."

☐ *Doesn't rely on timing devices.* Your child can't tell time or doesn't have a watch to refer to.

☐ *Engages in power plays.* She uses behavior to provoke you and to avoid the task; your child is exercising newfound independence.

☐ *Is overwhelmed.* She doesn't know when or how to begin, or is stressed, ill, or depressed.

☐ *Has poor study skills.* Your child misplaces items, can't find materials, lacks study skills.

☐ *Works in a chaotic home.* Your child has no place to study; the environment is too distracting; siblings destroy her work or projects.

☐ *Is lazy.* She considers the task "too much work," has no perseverance, or would rather play.

☐ *Isn't held accountable.* Your child has never suffered a consequence or been disciplined for being late.

☐ *Fears failure.* She is perfectionistic and is afraid to do the task because she doesn't want to fail.

☐ *Holds unrealistic expectations.* The task is developmentally inappropriate or too difficult.

2. *Model time management.* On a scale of one to ten, how good of an example are you of jumping right into a task and finishing in a timely manner? For instance, do your kids ever hear you say, "I'll do it tomorrow," "There's always another day," or "I have other things to do"? If you want to change your kid's bad habits, then make sure you mend any flaws in your own habits. If you have an organizational system (Palm Pilot, date book, kitchen calendar, lists—however you keep track of upcoming tasks and activities), share it with your child.

3. *Teach her to break up assignments and date each part.* If your child puts things off because she feels overwhelmed, then teach her to break up her assignments or those bigger tasks into smaller parts. Put away clothes on Tuesday and organize the closet on Wednesday. Read ten pages each night for a week; start the book report on Saturday and finish it on Sunday. The trick is to help your child look at that lengthier task, such as the science project or book report, and figure out how to break it into smaller parts. Then assign a deadline to each small part. Hint: it may help to give your kid a little incentive at the end of each finished project (an extra hour on the computer or a sleepover with a friend). Just be careful not to let your child become overly focused on the reward. (See *Hooked on Rewards,* p. 88.)

4. *Create rules and routines.* Dawdlers operate in an "I'll do it later" mode. They also waste time, are perpetual slowpokes, and have learned prizewinning delay tactics. Here are strategies that curb that tendency to put things off:

   - *Make "first things first" rules.* Identify those hot-button issues that your kid always puts off, set clear "first things first" rules, and consistently enforce them. For example: *"No IM-ing before practicing." "Homework then TV." "Chores then play."*

   - *Set clear schedules.* Procrastinators are more likely to start and finish tasks when they follow established routines. Start by creating a realistic schedule for both you and your child. For instance, homework is from seven to eight o'clock on school nights; chores are on Saturday from ten to eleven before the soccer game. A quick review of the day's events is helpful, so give your kid a play-by-play of what's expected.

   - *Provide an agenda.* Find a simple organizer or notebook, then teach your child how to record her daily events and assignments, dating and timing each upcoming task.

   - *Hang up a calendar.* Each week, assign your child the duty of noting any tasks or assignments on a large monthly calendar. Have her cross off each day so she gets the idea that the project is approaching and that she can't put off the assignment anymore.

   - *Issue reminders.* Encourage her to post notes on her bathroom mirror or computer to remind herself of an upcoming deadline.

5. *Use time management strategies.* A procrastinator lives in the here and now, so she often puts things off until later, so try these tips to give your child a better sense of time.

- *Give a warning.* Your kid can always use a heads-up. *"Start getting ready. Mrs. Jones is picking you up ten minutes." "Your soccer practice is in half an hour. Make sure you give yourself enough time to get ready so you won't miss it this time."*

- *Use timing devices.* Put a sticker next to the hour of a crucial event. Buy her an alarm clock or set that alarm feature on her cell phone. Draw a picture of a clock showing the task and time and set it next to a real clock. Provide her with any kind of timing device, such as a sand, egg, microwave, or oven timer. Your child starts the timer and keeps working until it goes off (then you'll be back).

- *Add time.* If your child takes forever getting started (and it's guaranteed to cause friction or make your family late), then build in extra time.

  Problem: He misses the bus because he takes forever to get ready. **Solution:** Wake him thirty minutes earlier. Lay out clothes night before.

  Problem: She takes forever walking out to the hockey carpool. **Solution:** She walks out to the driveway ten minutes before the driver comes.

- *Play "Beat the Clock."* Turn your directions into a game with a timed challenge: "How fast you can pick up your toys? Ready. Set. Go!" Then gradually get your kid to beat her own time: "Yesterday, you did five problems in twenty minutes. Do you think you can beat your time?"

LATE-BREAKING NEWS

University of Calgary: A ten-year study by industrial psychologist Piers Steel discovered that those "put it off to the last minute" types tend to be less wealthy and less healthy, and the habit is on the rise.[18] In 1978, 5 percent of Americans considered themselves chronic procrastinators; now it's 26 percent. Three out of four college students are self-proclaimed procrastinators. The reason for the upswing? All those temptations: cell phones, a TV in every room, online video, Web surfing, iPods, video games.

So here's a simple solution to stop your kid from putting things off: *put away those temptations.* She can use the cell phone *after* she takes out the trash. She can watch *American Idol after* she does her homework. She can play Sim City *after* she practices the oboe.

One Parent's Answer

A mom from Scottsdale writes:

My son always dawdled and made me late to work. I pleaded, begged, bribed, and tried waking him up earlier, but nothing worked until I finally had my "Enough" moment. I warned him that if he wasn't dressed, I would take him to school as is (and I do mean "as is"). I gave the principal a "heads up," and he said he'd support me 100 percent. So the next day when Eli was still in his pajamas at eight a.m., I put him in the car and notified the school. When we drove up, there the principal was waiting at the curb (much to the shock of my son, who figured this was all a ploy) and escorted him to class. I know it was extreme, but it sure cured my son's dawdling.

6. *Make your child accountable.* Of course the ultimate goal is for your child to start tasks on her own without your help, so break the habit into baby steps.

Step 1: Be there in the first stage to help her begin that project or chore with a little guidance.

Step 2: Once you are sure your child knows how to do the task, move back as soon as you know she has begun.

Step 3: The minute you know your child has the skills and can start and finish on her own, stop rescuing. And make her suffer the consequence if she doesn't finish on time. Yep, she will get in trouble with her coach for being tardy to practice. She will get a lower grade on her book report for turning it in late. But better she learn those crucial lessons now than later.

WHAT TO EXPECT BY STAGES AND AGES

Preschooler   Kids this age are only beginning to grasp abstract time ("Your playdate is in thirty minutes"), and both understanding the concept of time and telling time are still difficult. They can usually read the hours on a clock, but not minutes and seconds. They usually need reminders as well as an adult to get them started on a task.

School Age   Telling time is part of the school math curriculum; six- or seven-year-olds can read half hours and minutes. School-age kids are ready to learn beginning time management skills, though they still live in the here and now and don't recognize the consequences of putting things off. Although it's normal for kids this age to procrastinate, step in before it becomes a habit. Around fourth grade when the workload increases, dawdling can become a noticeable detriment to academic and social success.

Tween   Dawdling often occurs first thing in the morning because of sleep deprivation; tweens' internal time clocks are in flux due to hormones and physiological changes. They have mastered telling time; they should be expected to set their own alarm clocks and track their daily schedules so that they arrive places on time. Kids this age need to kick the procrastination habit now as their workload increases and expectations mount.

Reading

SEE ALSO: *Boredom, Homework, Overscheduled, Stressed, TV Addiction, Video Games*

THE QUESTION

"My son is really bright; I'm sure of it. But how can he compete with gifted children if he never reads? How can I get him to sit down with a book for fun? I know he'd get a lot out of it and go further in life. How can I persuade him that reading is the source of wisdom and can make you healthy, wealthy, and wise?"

THE ANSWER

Are you hoping your child does well in school, gets good grades and test scores, is accepted to a college, advances in his career, and is a good citizen?[19] If so, then instill a love of reading in your child. Scores of studies cite reading as the key to academic success, and three-quarters of parents chose it as the most important skill for a child to develop.[20]

That's why two recent reports (Scholastic's "Kids and Family Reading Report" and the National Endowment for the Arts' "To Read or Not to Read") should make educators and parents shudder. It appears we have a problem. The percentage of kids who read for enjoyment is dismal at best. Only one in four kids reads for fun every day, and 22 percent rarely, *if ever*, read.[21] The reading decline starts at age eight, continues in a steady downward spiral, and *never picks up again.* Less than one-third of thirteen-year-olds read daily. The percentage of seventeen-year-olds who read nothing for pleasure has doubled in twenty years.[22] It should come as little surprise that our children's reading scores have steadily declined during that same twenty-year period.[23] So why aren't kids reading these days? Their top reasons for not reading: "Too busy," "No time," or just plain "Too tired."

The kid reading crisis is real, the impact is astronomical, and parents are aware there is a problem: 82 percent of parents wish their kids would read more for fun, but don't know ways to get them hooked on words.[24] Here are solutions to help kids read and even enjoy doing so:

- *Get a good resource for kid books.* Both parents *and* kids say a big part of the problem is trouble finding enjoyable books.[25] So treat yourself to a great source that lists kids' top reading choices. Here are four favorite treasuries: *The New Read-Aloud Handbook*, by Jim Trelease; *How to Get Your Child to Love Reading*, by Esmé Raji Codell; *Best Books for Kids Who (Think They) Hate to Read*, by

Laura Backes; and *Great Books for Boys* (and *Great Books for Girls*), by Kathleen Odean. Or talk to a good children's reference librarian or to teachers—but no more excuses!

- *Think outside the book.* The trick is to match your child's reading level and interest to the material. And any age-appropriate reading material is fine to get your kid started—cereal boxes, cartoons, the sports page, baseball cards, the Internet, magazines. Once you find what turns your kid on to the printed page, keep that supply coming. Consider those new graphic (comic book) novels, print out movie reviews, or cut out articles on NASCAR. The literary merit is trivial; getting your kid to feel comfortable with reading is what matters.

- *Carve out reading time.* Kids say the biggest reason they don't read for fun is that there isn't enough time. So find just a few minutes a day. Eliminating one TV show or item from your kid's crammed schedule frees up at least thirty minutes a week. Books in the bathroom, your car, the kitchen, or your kid's backpack are handy to fill in those lulls. Setting aside ten minutes at the same time every night creates a reading routine for *everyone.* If you don't carve out time, reading will get lost in that time-warp shuffle.

- *Create a reading-rich home.* Studies show that the more books you have in your home, the greater the chance your kid will become a reader.[26] So dig out that library card. Attend book fairs at your child's school. Go to library sales. Get your child a subscription to a magazine. You don't have to break the bank, but do have reading material constantly available.

- *Start a book club.* Tweens admit that they worry popular kids won't like them if they read, so help them buck that peer pressure by joining moms of your child's friends and reading together.[27] *The Mother-Daughter Book Club,* by Shireen Dodson, and *The Kids' Book Club Book,* by Judy Gelman and Vicki Levy Krupp, will help you start up a club and find the right books and activities for this unique age group.

- *Become movie critics.* Read a book, then watch the movie based on it. *Charlie and the Chocolate Factory, Because of Winn-Dixie,* or *The Princess Bride* are just a few possibilities. Kids love to be movie critics and debate whether the book or the movie was better. Another version of this idea is to listen to a book on tape during those long carpool rides or while you're on vacation and then reading the "hard copy."

- *Don't stop reading out loud.* Research says that the first drop in kids' reading for fun occurs at around age eight. That is also the age most parents stop reading to their kids. Well, don't stop! Find a book (your kids get to choose) and read out loud—or take turns reading paragraphs.

- *Check that required reading list.* Dig through the bottom of your kid's backpack for his school's required reading list. Then get *two* copies of each requirement: one for your kid and the other for you. You can each read alone, but do discuss *Charlotte's Web, Holes,* or *The Diary of a Young Girl* together. It's a great way to open up a dialogue with a kid.

- *Be a role model.* Studies prove that kids who see their parents read are more likely to read themselves. Let your kids know you value reading and let them see you read and read often. Read from Oprah's book list, join a book club, carry a book with you at all times, or get your friends, neighbors, or town reading. Over 150 American cities and towns are now involved in the Big Read (see http://www.neabigread.org/communities.php). Just read!

- *Get help.* If your child is struggling with reading, then please seek out the advice of trained professionals. Check with your pediatrician to ensure this isn't a vision problem. Talk to his teacher to make sure your child's lack of interest in reading isn't because of a learning disability. And if the struggle continues, don't stop until your child is evaluated and receives the help he deserves.

J. K. Rowling proved that kids do read and love doing so—that is, when you give them the right book. Nearly three out of four kids ages eleven to thirteen have read at least one volume of Rowling's Harry Potter series.[28] But it certainly didn't hurt that parents and kids read the series together. The truth is that the more kids read, the more comfortable they become with the printed page and the more likely it is that they will adopt reading as a lifelong habit. So read, read, and then read more! One of the greatest legacies you can leave your child is to instill a love of books.

Sick Enough to Stay Home

SEE ALSO: *Bullied, Fearful, Lying*

THE QUESTION

"Sometimes I think my son is faking being sick to escape a test, but other times I've sent him and think I should have kept him home. How is a parent to know when their kid really should stay home because he is too sick?"

THE ANSWER

Oh, what kids will do to stay home and avoid that test or the school-yard bully. That's why it's really important to keep tabs on what goes on at school and with your kid's friends, and when those tests and big assignments are due. Then, of course, there is always the possibility that your child really is quite ill and should be under a doctor's care. And oh, the guilt if you do send your child to school—after she pleads to stay home—and an hour later you get that call from the school nurse lecturing you that your child should be home in bed. Here are a few tests to help you decide whether your child is too sick to go to school—or that something else may be going on causing those symptoms:

Fever. A temperature above 100 degrees is grounds for staying home. Use the "Thermometer Test" if you suspect your kid is faking it. Take her temperature and then watch your child (and thermometer) closely. Then *retake* her temperament about ten minutes later to see if it reads the same. Some kids put a thermometer in a hot liquid to boost those degrees.

Contagious condition. An unidentified rash, pink eye, lice, scabies, open sores in the mouth, a phlegm-laden cough, chickenpox, measles, hepatitis A, mumps, whooping cough, impetigo, and strep throat are all stay-at-home conditions.

Inability to participate. Your child doesn't feel well enough to participate in her regular activities or play.[29]

Suffering that *lingers*. Keep your kid home if she has a severe sore throat and trouble swallowing (see how she swallows a favorite drink), wheezing or earache (which worsens when she lays down), a constant cough, difficulty breathing, a stomachache that lasts more than two hours, or repeated bouts of diarrhea, or if she has vomited twice or more in a twenty-four-hour period, and an over-the-counter pain medicine won't alleviate her symptoms.[30]
Take your child to the doctor if an injured body part causes severe pain or is swelling or deformed, or if she avoids using the injured body part.[31]

Attendance guidelines. The school or day-care policy specifies that attendance be forbidden with your child's specific symptoms.

Parental instinct. You really feel that your child is too sick and would be better off at home, simply because she just doesn't "look or act right." Or just ask yourself, *"Would I want my own child near someone else with these same symptoms?*

Symptoms lasting longer than twenty-four hours. Call your doctor ASAP.

If your child is too sick to go to school, she certainly should be too ill to be up and about, play video games, have friends over, or surf the Net. So enforce the "stay in bed" rule, and you'll be less likely to have your kid feign illness. If you discover that your child is "faking it" and really isn't sick at all, then diagnose what's going on that is triggering her "episodes." What is she trying to avoid? Does she seem to be "ill" every Friday when there's also a spelling test? Or is she feigning illness every other Tuesday to avoid undressing for gym? Get to the bottom of it—you may have a whole different kind of symptom to handle.

Teacher Conference

SEE ALSO: *Day Care, Gives Up, Homework, Reading*

THE QUESTION

"I just received a memo from my child's school that my parent-teacher conference has been scheduled. This will be my first one, so what do I ask?"

THE ANSWER

Keep in mind that your child's teacher has scheduled only a set amount of time to talk, so you will want to use every second wisely. Take a few minutes *before* the conference to jot down questions you have, and take them with you so you won't forget to ask. Also ask your child if there is anything the teacher might tell you that you don't already know. (It's always best not to be surprised.) Your goal at the conference is to form a mutually respectful alliance with that teacher as well as to find out how your child is doing and the best ways to support her academic success. Here are a few questions to ask that will help you build that crucial parent-teacher relationship:

Teacher insight: What do you consider my child's strengths and challenges?

Academics: What are her strongest and weakest subjects? How does she compare to the rest of the students? Is she working at grade level? Could she benefit from a tutor? (See "Does Your Child Need a Tutor?" in *Homework*, p. 435.)

Homework: Is there a homework schedule? (See *Homework*, p. 435.) How much homework is she to be doing each night? What if the homework is too difficult? Is there a reading list of books she should be reading at home? What about tests, book reports, or upcoming projects?

Social life: How does she get along with others? Does she know how to socialize respectfully? Who does my child play with? Is there any child you think might be a good friend?

Behavior: How does my child behave around adults? Is she polite and respectful? If there is a behavior problem, what is your discipline approach?

Your role: What can I do at home to support my child (without micromanaging and rescuing!)? Is there anything I can do to help out at school, such as grade papers, go on field trips, help with a project?

Contact: What is the best way and time to reach you (e-mail, phone, note)? How do you prefer to be contacted, and how often?

Problems: If my child is having any kind of problem, how will you let me know? How will I know if things are improving or declining? If things do *not* improve, what would be our "next step"?

After the conference, share what you learned with your child and then commit to doing what you discussed with the teacher. If you feel it is appropriate, write a note to the teacher thanking her for her time and advice. Believe me, she will appreciate it.

The former teacher in me also offers this piece of advice: remember, teachers are trained professionals who for the most part cherish teaching children. So approach your child's teacher as a partner in helping your child be the best she can be. If you see that your child is continuing to struggle academically, behaviorally, or socially and you do not see improvement in two or three weeks, call for another conference. If you still don't get help, then it's time to seek the help of the principal, vice principal, or counselor.

Test Anxiety

SEE ALSO: *Attention Deficit, Fearful, Homework, Pessimistic, Procrastinates, Teacher Conference*

THE QUESTION

"My child has studied hard, has done all his homework, gets his test, and is suddenly hit with a wave of absolute panic. His body freezes and his hands get clammy. Butterflies hit his stomach, and his head is filled with a wave of negative thoughts—"I'm going to flunk," "I'm so dumb"—and then his mind goes completely blank. What can I do to help him do a better job and get rid of his terrible anxiety?"

THE ANSWER

Almost 20 percent of tweens and teens experience test anxiety, but with today's high-stakes testing, the condition is being diagnosed in even our youngest students. And make no mistake, test anxiety can be costly to our children academically, socially, and emotionally. Kids with recurrent bouts are more likely to suffer academically, repeat a grade, perform poorly in activities, require new learning, experience poorer self-esteem, and develop school phobia.[32] There are no quick fixes to the condition, but there are proven solutions that will help reduce the severity and frequency of those bouts as well as improve test scores. The best news is that parents are a big part of the success equation. Here are a few of the best strategies that work to solve this growing problem.

Before the Test

- *Watch how your child responds.* Test jitters are normal, but when performance worries are more severe, the problem is called *test anxiety.* Here are signs to watch for:

   Physical signs: has butterflies, cold or clammy hands, headache, nausea, raised heart rate, perspiration, dry mouth; feels faint, hot or cold, or light-headed

   Emotional signs: feels helpless and pessimistic, wants to cry, fears failure

   Cognitive signs: forgets what she learned, has more trouble than usual concentrating and thinking about test items, is preoccupied with negative thoughts about test performance

- *Stay cool and be accepting.* Stay cool and keep your talks about that upcoming test casual and relaxed. Your child is more likely to open up and share her test concerns if she feels safe to do so. A big kid worry is, "I hope I don't let my parents down," so reaffirm your unconditional love—regardless of that score. Research shows that a warm, accepting parenting style with realistic expectations helps decrease kids' test anxiety.[33]

- *Make a plan for success.* Start by identifying your child's current study habits. Then think of one or two simple solutions to begin helping her improve her test-taking skills. Here are a few ideas:

  - Write each vocabulary word on a flash card so she can review them at her brother's soccer practice.

  - Hire a tutor if necessary.

  - Check in with the teacher so you know the test schedule and can prepare further in advance. Ask also for her perspective and study skill ideas.

  - Reduce activities and responsibilities if your child seems overstretched.

  - Set up a quieter place to study if she seems overwhelmed. (See also *Attention Deficit,* p. 466, and *Homework,* p. 435.)

- *Reframe negative thoughts.* Anxious kids tend to think negative thoughts about their performance, which can affect test taking. So teach your child to challenge each negative idea by finding evidence that it's not *always* true. Here are two examples. *Child:* "I always do badly on tests." *You:* "Practicing your flash cards boosted your spelling grade on Friday." *Child:* "I won't remember anything." *You:* "Eating a good breakfast sure seemed to help improve your memory for your last math test."

- *Teach test-taking strategies.* There are simple skills that help improve test performance as well as reduce kids' anxiety. Here are few tips you can teach your child:

  - *Ask questions.* If you are unsure of the question, raise your hand to get clarification.

  - *Do a "quick flip through."* Get an instant sense of the type of questions and the test length.

  - *Answer what you know.* Respond right away to the questions you know so that you don't forget.

  - *Check answers.* Never turn in a test without first checking to make sure you haven't skipped any questions. Always proofread your answers if you have time.

- *Don't cram.* Test-anxious kids figure they will worry less if they put their studying off and then cram at the last minute. But this approach backfires and instead increases anxiety. She will not only be less likely to know the subject content but also recognize that she's not prepared. So map out a study schedule on a calendar several evenings *before* the test.

- *Set realistic study times.* Study lengths and breaks should be relaxed and geared to your child's attention span.[34] The following are typical study spans for different ages:

  6 to 8 years: 15 minutes

  9 and 10 years: 20 minutes

  11 and 12 years: 30 minutes

  13 years: 30 to 40 minutes

- *Do practice tests.* The more familiar your child is with the test-taking process, the less anxious she will be. So ask the teacher for a few practice tests or purchase one of these manuals: *Dr. Gruber's Essential Guide to Test Taking for Kids: Grades 3, 4, and 5,* by Gary Gruber; *Standardized Test Practice for 4th Grade,* by Charles J. Shields; *Get Ready for Standardized Tests: Grade 6,* by Shirley Vickery. Then help your child apply the new test-taking strategies she's learned as well as those anxiety reducers you're helping her learn by having her take a few practice tests to boost her confidence.

On the Test Day

- *Get enough sleep.* Countless studies find a significant correlation between kids' sleep and test performance. Here are just a few results that confirm your kid needs enough Z's.

  Tel Aviv University: Fourth and sixth graders who got on average thirty-one minutes *less* sleep each night performed *significantly* less well on achievement tests.[35]

  University of Virginia: Elementary students lose an average of seven points on vocabulary tests when they sleep less.[36]

  University of Minnesota: A study of over seven thousand high school students found that "teens who received A's averaged about fifteen more minutes sleep than the B students, who is turn averaged eleven more minutes than the C's and the C's had ten more minutes than the D's."[37]

- *Serve brain food for breakfast.* Don't let your child skip breakfast. Studies prove that a breakfast rich in whole-grain cereals along with a lean protein, such as eggs, helps maintain your child's energy and keeps her more alert during tests.[38]

- *Use anxiety reducers.* Research shows that using a relaxation strategy can reduce test anxiety. Here are three possibilities to teach your child a few weeks before the big test:

  Self-talk. Repeat a relaxing phrase silently. Some examples: "It's only a test." "I don't have to be perfect." "I'll worry later, but I'm going to focus on the test now."

Deep breathing. Take a "three by three": breathe in slowly to a count of three, then exhale slowly to a count of three. Repeat the deep breathing strategy at least three times.

Visualizing a calm scene. Close your eyes and imagine a calm, peaceful place (a park, beach, tree house) that you have experienced and that brings a smile to your face.

Encourage your child to use that strategy during another stressful situation, such as at a sleepover or a family reunion. Model it yourself around your kids, such as when your soufflé isn't rising or the computer won't boot. Or make it a family affair: "Let's practice those deep breaths at bedtime." Practicing in real life will improve the chances that the test-taking strategy will succeed. Besides, the more your child "sees" the strategy working in her life, the more likely she is to use it.

After the Test

- *Review test performance.* During a relaxed time, help your child evaluate her test performance and results. Here are some questions you might ask:

  "Did you feel any different this time?"

  "Did the three-by-three breathing [or other strategy] help?"

  "What part of the test was the easiest? The most difficult?"

  "What things helped that you want to remember to try again?"

  The trick is to help your child recognize *what works* so that she can apply those same strategies again to the next test. You can also determine what still needs correcting or how to form a better test-taking plan.

- *Monitor the situation.* Although it is normal for kids to be anxious before a test, if anxiety persists, increases, or interferes with your child's school performance or life, then it is time to seek help. Talk with your child's teacher to discuss your child's progress and to ensure that she is in the right academic placement; ask whether the teacher advises a tutor. If anxiety mounts or your child continues to struggle, then please seek the counsel of a mental health professional.

The No Child Left Behind act mandates that your child be tested for reading and math every year in grades 3 through 8 and at least once in high school. (That doesn't include all the spelling tests, math tests, history tests, state tests, and on and on and on.) Regardless of how prepared or capable your child, her overriding concern about her performance reduces her ability to focus and to test her best. Considering the emphasis on high-stakes testing, the pressure kids are under to meet higher standards, and the even more rigorous high school tests coming up, it's crucial to help our kids learn successful test-taking and coping strategies early and to nip test anxiety in the bud.

Part 7
Special Needs

OUT OF THE MOUTHS OF BABES
WHY GOD MADE MOMS

Answers given by second-grade schoolchildren to the following question:

What's the difference between moms and dads?

1. Moms work at work and work at home and dads just go to work at work.

2. Moms know how to talk to teachers without scaring them.

3. Dads are taller and stronger, but moms have all the real power 'cause that's who you got to ask if you want to sleep over at your friend's.

4. Moms have magic, they make you feel better without medicine.

Attention Deficit

SEE ALSO: *Angry, Demanding, Homework, Lying, Stressed, Tantrums, Test Anxiety, Won't Listen*

THE PROBLEM

Red Flags

Doesn't pay attention, has trouble concentrating and focusing, interrupts, barrels ahead without thinking, is easily distracted

The Change to Parent For

Your child learns strategies that stretch his ability to focus, recall important information, and pay attention without prompting or help.

Question: "Our son has always been a lively, spontaneous, and rather impulsive kind of kid, but his teacher thinks he has something called Attention Deficit Disorder and should take a drug every day called Ritalin. She complains that he doesn't pay attention and gets so distracted that he can't finish his work. How do we know when to worry because this isn't normal boy behavior?"

Answer: Many kids have trouble paying attention, but far fewer have an actual diagnosable problem such as Attention Deficit Disorder (ADD). Of course, you should work with the teacher to find ways to handle your son's attention problems so that he can succeed in school. But use these three factors to help you decide if your child's behavior really warrants a label:

1. The attention difficulty is clearly noticeable—even extreme—when your child's behavior is compared to other kids the same age and gender.

2. The attention problem has lasted at least six months and is evident in at least two different settings (such as home *and* school, and not just at school).

3. Your child's inability to pay attention *significantly* interferes with his ability to function and thrive in life and is not something your child can control.

   If all these three factors apply to your child, then he is clearly struggling and will be at risk for everything from low self-esteem, school failure, and friendship troubles to drug abuse. It is time to pick up the phone and seek the advice of a trained expert.

LATE-BREAKING NEWS

Limit Early Television Viewing

Children's Hospital and Regional Medical Center, Seattle: A study of over twenty-six hundred children found that each daily hour of television a child one to three years of age watched increased the risk of later attention problems almost 10 percent.[1] What's more, those attention problems, such as trouble focusing and restlessness, didn't show up until around seven years of age. Researchers surmised that those rapid-fire television images impact early brain development and may affect our children's concentration abilities. So consider limiting your child's TV exposure, especially during those early formative years. Doing so may reduce attention problems later in the school-age years.

Why Change?

Let's face it: some kids have a much harder time paying attention, and that inability will probably make their lives a bit more challenging. After all, a big part of getting along as well as learning new information entails tuning in to what we see and hear. But it doesn't mean that we should rush to judgment and assume that our kids have a clinical disorder or need medication if they can't sit still. That said, one in thirty American youngsters between five and nineteen years of age is currently taking the drug Ritalin, and the number over the past two decades has been steadily increasing. Parents currently spend over $1.3 billion each year on the three leading drugs prescribed for kids who have received a diagnosis of ADD.[2] In some U.S. schools, as many as 30 to 40 percent of the children in a typical classroom may be taking prescribed stimulants to control their classroom behavior. Reports say that ADD affects up to 9 percent of school-age children, but even then some people in the medical field fear that only half of those have been properly diagnosed.[3]

Regardless of whether your child is a bit "more spirited" or truly does have an attention deficit, he will need to learn to focus and stay on task longer. The good news is there are simple techniques you can use to increase your child's ability to concentrate, attend longer, and even recall what he hears or sees. In fact, teaching these attention-stretching skills will enhance any child's chances of success, so this entry offers practical solutions to help you start the change for your child.

Signs and Symptoms

Here are common signs of kids who have trouble paying attention:

- *Poor recall.* The child needs to have instructions repeated several times; he can't remember more than one direction at a time. (If you ask him to go to the kitchen for water, he'll go to the kitchen but forget why he went there.)

- *Trouble sustaining attention.* He has trouble focusing on a task for any length; teachers complain that he doesn't pay attention.

- *Distraction.* The child daydreams or always looks around; he is easily sidetracked from the task.

- *Poor attention to detail.* He doesn't give close attention to details and makes careless mistakes.

- *Poor listening skills.* The child does not seem to listen when spoken to directly.

- *Poor organization skills.* He has difficulty arranging or sorting tasks; loses things (toys, school assignments, pencils, books, or tools); and has trouble keeping track of possessions and materials.

- *Avoidance of mental effort.* The child dislikes or is reluctant to engage in tasks requiring prolonged mental exertion.

- *Trouble waiting.* The child fidgets, has difficulty waiting, and interrupts or intrudes on others; he butts into conversations or games.

THE SOLUTION

Step 1. Early Intervention

- *Identify attention stealers.* Most parents assume there must be a clinical reason, such as ADD, for their kid's focusing troubles, but there may be a number of causes. Start instead by identifying possible reasons for your child's attention problems in the following checklist so that you can determine which you can improve on. Here are a few:

  ☐ *Impaired cognitive ability.* Your child has a neurological impairment, a learning disability, seizures.

  ☐ *Auditory or language deficit.* Your child has hearing loss, an ear infection, a language or speech delay, or an auditory processing problem.

  ☐ *Fatigue.* Your child is ill, overtired, sleep deprived, overscheduled with no downtime.

  ☐ *Emotional problem.* Your child is depressed or under stress; has experienced a trauma, such as an accident, divorce, or the death of a loved one; is in a state of tension from bullying; lives with family instability.

  ☐ *Inappropriate expectations.* Instruction or content is not geared to your child's natural learning strengths, internal time table, style, or abilities.

  ☐ *Poor instructions.* Directions are poorly given, or the child is not expected to listen.

  ☐ *Distractions.* The environment is too noisy, too bright, too distracting; there is too much or too little stimulation.

Pay Attention to This!

Could It Be ADHD?

The Diagnostic and Statistical Manual of Mental Disorders, Fourth Edition (DSM-IV-TR) is the official manual published by the American Psychiatric Association that lists all recognized mental and behavioral disorders.[4] Doctors in the United States currently recognize three types of attention deficits:

1. *Inattentive:* The child has difficulty paying attention to tasks or play activities; makes careless mistakes; doesn't seem to listen when spoken to directly; is often easily distracted and forgetful; does not follow instructions; and fails to finish schoolwork, chores, or duties.

2. *Hyperactive:* The child fidgets or squirms in his seat, leaves his seat when he is expected to remain seated, talks excessively, has trouble waiting, appears in perpetual motion, interrupts or intrudes on others, blurts out answers before questions are complete, and is often "on the go" or acts as if "driven by a motor."

3. *Impulsive:* The child often blurts out answers before questions have been finished, has trouble waiting his turn, and interrupts or intrudes on others.

The evaluation is complicated because types of ADHD can also be combined into three different diagnoses: Combined Type (multiple symptoms of inattention, impulsivity, and hyperactivity), Predominately Inattention, and Predominantly Hyperactivity-Impulsivity. Specific factors are also required for each diagnosis. For instance: Inattention or Impulsivity diagnosis requires that the child display *at least six* or more problem behaviors for at least six months, which are *significantly* disruptive and not consistent with normal child development. If you suspect your child has an attention disorder, seek the evaluation *only* of a physician, child neurologist, psychiatrist, psychologist, or pediatric specialist credentialed in child behavior and development.

☐ *Manipulation.* Your child selectively listens only to what he chooses; he uses inattention to avoid what he doesn't want to do; he realizes someone will do the task for him; he is disobedient.

☐ *Genetics.* Although no specific "gene" for attention deficits has been identified, the disorder appears to run in families. One-half of parents with ADHD and 10 to 35 percent of close relatives of children with ADHD have the disorder as well.[5]

What is your best guess as to the cause? Is there one simple solution you can implement?

- *Set appropriate expectations.* Make sure your child's schoolwork matches his appropriate academic capabilities. For instance, if he tests at a 1.5 reading level, don't expect him to read at the 4.2 level. Assignments should be geared only slightly higher than children's ability, otherwise they tune out and will have problems attending. Also make sure that the task isn't set at *too low* of a level so as to cause boredom, which also causes inattentiveness. Your child's teacher can provide you with that information.

- *Watch those labels!* Avoid using any negative labels or derogatory nicknames about your child ("the Attention Deficit Kid," "our absent-minded professor," or "space cadet"). They can become daily reminders of incompetence and turn into self-fulfilling prophecies. What's more, they often stick and become difficult to erase. One good rule to use: *if the nickname does not show respect, it's best not to use it.* And if you hear anyone using a less than flattering term about your child, give it a positive spin. Instead of "He's so hyper," say "Yes, he's really energetic." Or: "She's really spacey." Turn it: "She gets her best ideas daydreaming."

Step 2. Rapid Response

- *Get an accurate picture.* Your first step to a new response is to figure out your kid's true attending capabilities. For instance, what is the usual length of time your kid can focus before he tunes out? Which things does he have no problem attending to? For instance, does he spend hours sorting his hockey cards, playing a certain video game, or skateboarding? Which tasks are most frustrating? And what works to help your child focus best? For instance, giving directions using a quieter tone, repeating them twice, drawing a picture to help him

---

ONE SIMPLE SOLUTION

Change Your Child's Sleep Patterns

In some cases, the solution to your child's attention problems may be simpler than you think. Sleep-deprived kids often have trouble paying attention and display symptoms of impulsivity and hyperactivity.[6] So before jumping to the conclusion that your kid has an attention deficit, try changing his sleep habits to help him get a more restful night's sleep (See *Sleepless*, p. 585.) Research shows that a simple change to your child's bedtime routine, such as tweaking his bedtime, can have great results in stretching his attention span.

remember? Developing an accurate picture of your child's attending capabilities and problems may take time, but is essential. You can also pass on to other caregivers what works best to help your child focus. So take notes and watch to determine which techniques work and which ones don't. Be sure to observe your child in different settings, and do seek the advice of his teacher, coach, and other caregivers.

- *Review your current response.* Experiment until you discover what works best to help your child attend, and then consistently use that new response. Here are few techniques to try:

  - *Get his attention first.* An old teacher rule is always to get the students' attention before giving a direction, thus increasing the likelihood that they *will* pay attention.

  - *Make eye contact.* Get eye to eye with your child to state your directions, or say "Eyes please," which cues your child to look at you and then listen.

  - *Lower your voice.* Use a quiet and calm voice.

  - *Use touch.* Lay your hand gently on your child's shoulder or hand to get his attention.

  - *Be brief.* Keep your directions short and to the point.

  - *Use a visual cue.* Put your hand out like a stop signal as a cue to stop what he's doing and focus instead on the task.

  - *Use a bookmark.* Put your finger on the spot on the paper your child should be focused on, or teach him to use a bookmark to focus on only one line at a time.

- *Keep to a schedule.* Children who have trouble paying attention benefit from routines. Those repetitive schedules create predictability, which reduces stress and helps kids focus. The trick is to find the best time for your child's homework, bed, dinner, and so on, based on *his* attending ability. Warning: the times for these activities may be different from those your other kids. Post those times on the refrigerator or bulletin board as a reminder and stick to the same daily routine as best you can.

- *Reduce distractions.* Kids with short attention spans are distracted easily by noises, smells, and images. So tune in a little more closely to determine what things hinder your child's concentration (for instance, the flickering overhead lights, the cuckoo clock, a barking dog, the neighbor kids yelling) and reduce what you can. Also, turn off the television when it is not being watched. A University of Massachusetts-Amherst study found that the background sound or image on the television reduces children's focusing ability even if the image is viewed in snippets.[7]

- *Set up the ideal work place.* Once you discover what helps your child attend best, set up a study spot that provides his ideal working conditions. Usually it's a smaller, more confined space with no windows, hallways, or sources of noise. Placing the desk against a blank wall can also reduce distractions. Some kids benefit from earplugs, earphones, or even certain types of music. Might these help your child? Involve him in the "discovery process" so that he recognizes what helps him learn; keep experimenting until you find the best options. For example: at his son's suggestion, one dad cut away the side of a refrigerator crate and put a small desk inside. It did the trick.

- *Allow some fidgeting.* A new study from University of Central Florida finds that many ADHD kids use movement to keep themselves alert, especially while performing tasks that challenge their working memory. Researchers recommend that when your child is doing homework, let him fidget, stand up, or chew gum. Unless his behavior is destructive, severely limiting his activity may actually reduce his attending abilities. Experiment with what works to help your child do those math problems or more challenging tasks that require concentration.[8]

- *Offer frequent feedback.* Acknowledge any effort your child makes to stay on task: *"You're getting it!" "Thanks for looking at me to hear what I had to say." "Way to stop and think first."* He needs to hear positive messages. Some kids benefit from a token reinforcement system in which they earn points toward a prize or treat for completed tasks. The trick is to wean the child from the reward system as soon as it is no longer needed. A teacher could help you set up a good behavior modification plan tailored to your child.

- *Get everyone on board.* If at all possible, try to work with your child's teacher (as well as counselor, pediatrician, and so on) to create a positive behavior and academic plan. Ask if a school psychologist should evaluate your child. You will be more successful in reaping positive results if everyone is on the same page and uses the same responses.

- *Get treatment early.* Researchers at Cincinnati Children's Hospital Center studied over three thousand children ages eight to fifteen and found that although almost 9 percent of children meet the criteria for some form of attention deficit, fewer than half receive treatment.[9] Girls in particular are less likely to be recognized. A three-year study found that most kids treated for ADD—whether with medication, behavioral therapy, or both—do improve over time.[10] If you suspect that your child has more than just simple trouble focusing, seek an evaluation from a credentialed specialist. Don't wait! Kids with an attention deficit often suffer from low self-esteem, have trouble with peers, and struggle in school.

Pay Attention to This!

Should You Medicate Your Child?

Medicating kids for attention deficits is a hotly debated issue and should never be taken lightly. To date, medication can be the most effective treatment for children correctly diagnosed with a severe case of ADD or ADHD. Even so, be cautious and seek facts. Here are questions to ask your doctor to help you make the right decision for your child if medication is suggested:

- Why do you advise this medication? How many other children have you prescribed this medication for? Was it helpful? How do you know it was helpful? (Get as many details as possible.)

- How long do you anticipate my child will be on this medication?

- What exact changes should I see in my child? How long will those changes take? (Ask for specifics based on your child's needs. Will this decrease tantrums, help him stay on task, reduce the fidgeting?)

- What is the lowest dose that might be effective? (Ideally use the rule "Start low and go slow.") What happens if he misses a dose? Does he need to take it daily? What about weekends?

- Where do I read about the research and possible side effects of this medication?

- What are the alternatives? What is our next step? How will you monitor my child's progress?

Don't stop with these answers. Get a second medical opinion so that you are confident that your decision about medication is the best option for *your* child. Even then, medication should be only *part* of your child's treatment plan. A three-year study found that most kids treated for attention deficits who received the right treatment—whether with medication or behavior therapy or both—improve greatly within a few years.[11] So don't stop until you get the right treatment!

Step 3. Develop Habits for Change

- *Burn off extra energy.* Research finds that kids with attention deficits are often "calmer, more focused, and more able to follow directions after a time outside, especially in settings like a part or backyard."[12] It seems a brief time in the great outdoors gives kids the chance to burn off excess energy before tackling homework, and actually helps increase attention spans. Look for active outdoor outlets your kid might enjoy that help him work off that "surplus oomph" and help him focus for longer stretches. Possibilities might include gymnastics, tae kwon do, karate, basketball, bike riding, swimming, or skateboarding. Just choose what turns your kid on.

- *Create an organizational system.* Poor organizational skills are common for kids with short attention spans. So help your child learn to organize tasks so that he is less likely to forget assignments. Here's how. First provide a small date book with a page for each school day on which to write assignments. Then purchase a small binder with a *different* colored divider for each school subject plus two additional dividers. Print "To Do" on the front of one divider and "Finished" on another, and then write the name of each subject on the remaining dividers. If your child has trouble reading the terms, create a symbol for each (such as a book to signify "reading" and numbers for "math"). Then, one at a time, teach your child to do these six steps:

  1. *Date.* Write each assignment in the datebook on the due date the minute it is given.

  2. *Store.* Put each assignment in the To Do section.

  3. *Do.* The first homework task is to review the datebook assignments. Then remove your papers from the To Do section.

  4. *Cross off.* As each task is completed, cross off the assignment in the datebook.

  5. *Finish.* Put each completed assignment in the Finished section of the binder.

  6. *Store.* When all assignments are crossed off, put the notebook in the backpack, and place the backpack in the *same* "safe" spot (such as by the front door) to find the next morning.

  The trick is to *teach only one organizational step at a time* and then review the step with your child until it becomes a habit.

- *Chunk the tasks into smaller parts.* Kids with short attention spans often feel overwhelmed with "so much" on a page. If this is your child, "chunk" down tasks into smaller parts to help him stay focused. If he feels overwhelmed even getting started, ask *"What's just the first thing you need to do?"* If the whole math page seems daunting, fold the paper in thirds and tell him to do the top part first (then the middle, then the end). Suggest he do the *most difficult* part of the task first to get it out of the way and reduce the stress.

- *Enhance recall.* Children with attention deficits often focus on the wrong details or have trouble "holding a thought" in their head. These strategies help kids hold a mental representation of important facts and pay closer attention to key ideas or important points:

What's your "keeper"? After your child has read, listened to a story, or watched a documentary, ask, "What's your keeper?" (Which means, "What is the most important thing you want to remember?") Use the question when your child's attention starts to ebb.

Drawing it. Drawing what they hear or read helps some kids stay focused.

Highlighting a fact. Encourage your child to highlight key ideas with a colored highlighting pen as he reads. Tell a younger child that the yellow puts "sunshine" on the most important ideas.

Dinner-hour paraphrasing. Each family member takes a turn briefly describing something that's happened during the day. The next speaker must correctly restate the previous talker's ideas, before contributing his experience. To make it challenging, after everyone's had a turn, see if anyone can identify one important idea from each person's conversation. The game helps kids pay closer attention to a speaker's words.

One-fact note cards. Teach your child to stop at the end of every sentence (or paragraph or page) he reads or hears. He then writes or draws "one fact" on a three-by-five card. When the assignment is finished, help your child review the fact cards and then store them in a recipe-size box. He can later review cards for tests and recall the main ideas.

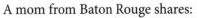

One Parent's Answer

A mom from Baton Rouge shares:

Homework was such a nightly struggle because my son's attention span was so short. I finally figured out the longest time he could focus, and then set mini five-minute study breaks where he could take a drink of water, do a few jumping jacks, or just squeeze a Koosh ball a few times. Those brief breaks seemed to help him refocus and reduced our battles. My next step is to gradually decrease the breaks as his concentration increases. We're using "Slow but sure" as our motto.

WHAT TO EXPECT BY STAGES AND AGES

Preschooler   Typical behaviors—such as not listening, difficulty settling down, and lack of interest in paper tasks—can easily be confused with true attention deficits, but are common with many preschoolers. Doctors generally won't diagnose ADD because most preschoolers can be forgetful, lose their belongings, and be easily distracted to some degree and are unable to sustain attention for long periods (especially boys). So don't jump to the conclusion that your child has a disorder. Pay attention instead to *extreme* behavior patterns: your child is *noticeably* more distracted than other kids, *constantly* in trouble with friends, and *repeatedly* must be asked to listen.

More Helpful Advice

ADHD: Attention-Deficit Hyperactivity Disorder in Children, Adolescents, and Adults, by Paul H. Wender

From Chaos to Calm: Effective Parenting for Challenging Children with ADHD and Other Behavioral Problems, by Sharon Weiss

Parenting Children with ADHD: 10 Lessons That Medicine Cannot Teach, by Vincent J. Monastra

Taking Charge of ADHD: The Complete, Authoritative Guide for Parents, by Russell A. Barkley

The ADD and ADHD Answer Book: Professional Answers to 275 of the Top Questions Parents Ask, by Susan Ashley

The Myth of the A.D.D. Child: 50 Ways to Improve Your Child's Behavior and Attention Span Without Drugs, Labels, or Coercion, by Thomas Armstrong

Treating Huckleberry Finn: A New Narrative Approach to Working with Kids Diagnosed ADD/ADHD, by David Nylund

School Age   More severe symptoms may surface in first and second grade when a child is unable to follow directions and can complete only small quantities of work. Milder attention problems may not surface until third or fourth grade, when kids are expected to function more independently. Symptoms are most likely to be seen at school (the child has greater difficulty completing class work) and at home (homework can take several hours to finish). About 3 to 5 percent of school-age kids are diagnosed with ADD or ADHD, especially boys (by a five-to-one ratio), who tend to have more difficulty focusing.[13]

Tween   Schoolwork and grades can suffer and self-esteem can plummet as workload and academic pressures increase. Stress, peer pressure, bullying, overextended schedules, and lack of sleep peak and can contribute to concentration difficulties as well. Tweens diagnosed with ADD or ADHD are prone to have more problems, including shoplifting, substance abuse, and delinquent and risky behavior that could cause physical injury (especially boys).[14] Of tweens diagnosed with clinical attention deficits, 70 to 80 percent still have symptoms as teens and adults.[15]

Autism Spectrum Disorder

SEE ALSO: *Angry, Attention Deficit, Bullied, Gifted, Impulsive, Insensitive, Learning Disabilities, Rejected, Shy, Teacher Conference, Teased*

THE PROBLEM

Red Flags

Doesn't fit in; displays eccentric behaviors, including compulsive rocking, arm jerking, and repetitive movement; was late talking and has difficulty with speech; is preoccupied with internal monologue, focused on only one thing at a time, and unwilling to be distracted or to engage with others; is socially inept; visibly stands out from the other kids; is excluded or ostracized because of major characteristics that are unlike other kids

The Change to Parent For

Your child learns habits that will help him flourish to the best of his ability in whatever arena he faces. You discover your child's specific emotional, behavioral, and learning needs and find the most appropriate settings to match them.

Question: "My child is just 'different' and noticeably stands out from the rest of the kids. He's never in sync with those darn developmental milestone charts—either way behind or ahead. All he talks and thinks about is meteorology and turns other kids off because he's so obsessive, and he has no friends. His teacher said that he might have Asperger's. Should I get him diagnosed?"

Answer: Although we should celebrate and accept our child's differences, there is a point when parents should seek help. I tell parents to consider these four factors when trying to figure out if their child's quirkiness is normal or too far out and should be checked:

1. *Family factor:* Is your home life compromised? Is everyone walking on eggshells?
2. *Struggle factor:* Is the quirkiness getting in the way of his happiness and ability to function in life? Does your child continue to suffer despite your best parenting efforts?

3. *Instinct factor:* Do you feel deep down that something is just not right? Does your child stand out as obviously different and less developed than other kids his age?

4. *Duration factor:* Has the problem persisted or even increased over time?

If you answered yes to one or more of these questions, then it's time to take this more seriously. The place to begin is by talking to your child's teacher, the school psychologist, and your family doctor to see if they concur with your concerns and think it's time to have your child evaluated.

Why Change?

Of course all kids are different, and thank heavens they are! But the sad truth is that some children are marginalized because other kids consider them "too different." Their unconventional or nonconformist behavior, physical and mental characteristics, and appearance *do* stand out and not always in positive ways. As a result they often experience debilitating rejection and may experience chronic anxiety, depression, low self-esteem, and acute loneliness. Those with Autism Spectrum Disorder are unfortunately pegged as "most different," so they suffer most.

According to the Centers for Disease Control and Prevention, about 1 in 150 kids is now diagnosed with the disorder. That's a tenfold jump in just the past decade, and in fact Autism Spectrum Disorder is considered by mental health professionals as the fastest growing developmental disability in the United States.[16] But that does *not* mean that each of those 1 in 150 children is autistic. There are varying degrees of autism, from very mild and high functioning (usually called Asperger's syndrome or Asperger's Disorder) to severely debilitating and low functioning (or autistic). The most commonly held view among mental health professionals these days is that a child with symptoms *anywhere* on that range—from mild to severe—should be given a diagnosis of Autism Spectrum Disorder (ASD).

At this point there is no accepted cause, no cure, nor any single agreed-on treatment for ASD, though there certainly are dozens of theories. But let me be very clear: Asperger's syndrome and Autism are *neurological* conditions—not psychological or behavioral issues—*and neither of them is caused by "bad parenting."* I emphasize that because two decades ago when I taught autistic kids, the general belief was that a "Refrigerator Mother" brought on the condition. I'm still haunted at the injustice done to those women who were some of the most loving moms I've known—so guilt-ridden believing that horrific notion. You did not bring this on your child, so let's move on to what you can do to help him, and the starting place is acceptance.

Make no mistake: the world needs quirky adults who can think and act "outside the box" (think Sir Isaac Newton, Einstein, van Gogh, Hans Christian Anderson, Mozart,

Bill Gates). But in the here and now, we need to help our children function and succeed more in life. There is one thing that experts do agree on: *early intervention does make a difference.* If you suspect or know that your child lies somewhere on the autism spectrum, this entry describes solutions to help you parent your child's more "eccentric ways" and offer him the best chance for success in life.

Signs and Symptoms

A number of the following symptoms must be prevalent and enduring from a young age for a child to receive a diagnosis of ASD. (Please note: only a trained professional is able to provide an accurate diagnosis.)[17] Where your child fits on the spectrum determines his diagnosis as well as treatment. Here are several signs:

- *Extreme temperament:* unbelievably irritable or needy; chronically frustrated or disturbingly placid

- *Social interaction difficulties:* fails to develop friendships or share enjoyments or achievements with others, lacks social skills; socially awkward; prefers to plays alone; doesn't engage in spontaneous make-believe play or social imitative play appropriate to developmental level

- *Nonverbal behavior difficulties:* avoids eye contact; has difficulties interpreting facial expression, posture, and gesture

- *Lack of emotional intelligence:* has difficulty reading emotions and processing or identifying others' social cues; unaware of others' feelings; understands things very literally, without nuance or ambiguity

- *Lack of ability to show empathy:* unable to see another's perspective; sees things only from his own view

- *Social speech and language variations:* has unusual speech patterns, difficulty initiating or sustaining a conversation; speaks constantly but can't get a point across; talks only about an obsession or not at all

- *Extreme need for routine:* must adhere to rigid routine; transitions or disruptions throw him

- *Repetitive and inappropriate behaviors:* consistently rocks or flaps his hands, has "nuclear" tantrums, generally has no idea he is acting inappropriately

- *Obsession with interests:* has intense, obsessive interests (*all* he talks about is astronomy, *all* she does is play chess)

- *Poor motor skills:* has poor coordination, odd gait when walking or running; physically clumsy

- *Sensory sensitivity:* overly sensitive to sounds, lights, fabrics, textures, or smells

THE SOLUTION

Step 1. Early Intervention

- *Accept your child's difference.* There's no doubt about it: having a child who has extreme needs and is marginalized is one of the tougher parts of parenting. But in order for your child to come to terms with his differences, you *must* accept your child for who he is. He needs your unconditional love and support. Anticipate problems. Identify your child's quirks so that you can find ways to prevent potential problems. For instance, if he *has* to have lunch at a certain time, feed him *before* he goes to the park. Talk to the parent about his fear of balloons popping *before* he goes to the party. If the smell of paste sends him into a tizzy, ask the teacher if he can use a glue stick *before* he does the project. Figure out how long your child can handle a situation *before* he melts down so that you pick him up a half hour earlier and help him save face.

- *Form a partnership with the school.* Become allies with educators at your child's school. Ask for their perspective on how your child is handling the school scene. Talk to the teacher, school psychologist, principal, or counselor and find out what kind of educational and psychological support can be offered. The school may be able to supply additional resources, a dedicated teacher's aide in the classroom, a club tailored to his interests, a quiet place to go when things get tough, names of students with similar interests your child might associate with. Take advantage of the resources available that might serve your child better.

- *Be your child's advocate.* Your kid's quirkiness may raise eyebrows, and you probably will hear negative comments, so you may need to develop thicker skin. Have one great response ready to say when the moment arises: "Thank heavens he's not like the rest of the world," or "We're raising the next Mozart [Einstein, Robin Williams]." Utter it with confidence and then walk on. Your role is to be your child's best advocate and supporter.

- *Empathize and show support.* Some quirky kids are oblivious to their differences and other kids' negative reactions. But if your child is aware of the stares or rejections, acknowledge that the difference will be tough and may continue to be so. *"I know it's really tough to be in a special class." "You're right, it's hard to stop flapping your hands when you're excited." "I know they call you 'retard.' They don't realize how smart you are."* It may help to identify one empathic child in each social setting to look out for your child.

- *Find supportive caregivers.* Your child will need cheerleaders, so connect with those who are directly responsible for your child's care and education. Explain your child's "quirkiness" so that they know this is not intentional or attention-getting behavior. Let them know any special behavior strategies or needs your

Pay Attention to This!

Should Your Child Be in a Special Education Setting?

Most parents with a child on the autism spectrum wrestle with the question of whether or not their child should be in a special classroom setting, be it a gifted program, a special education classroom or program, or a private school specializing in the child's unique interest or needs. Always visit the school and talk to the teacher and administrator, then use these questions to help guide your decision:

- Would my child find friends or fit in with these students?
- Is the class or school a good match for my child's strengths? Does the program accommodate my child's needs?
- Is the staff specially trained to deal with my child's behavior and unique needs? Are they knowledgeable and using the latest proven educational strategies for dealing with ASD?
- Is the program affordable and worth the cost?
- Will there be an individualized plan specific to my child's diagnosis?
- Can I visualize my child in this setting? Would he be happier or more secure in this environment?
- Is my child happy and thriving as best he can in his current placement? Could this new program satisfy his needs significantly more than the other placement? Is it worth the change for my child and my family?

child has that will help him cope. Get to know the other parents, volunteer to help out in class, join the PTA, or become a scout leader. Any way you can engage in the school and community can help your child make friends and fit in.

Step 2. Rapid Response

- *Decide whether to evaluate.* Although there is absolutely nothing wrong with being eccentric, you must weigh whether your child needs special medical, educational, or psychological attention. If he does, that would require an evaluation by a trained mental health professional. Use these as your core questions to guide you as to whether to evaluate and label your child's difficulties:

Would the label help you know whether there is a medical or neurological cause? Many things can cause a child's quirkiness, including ASD. But a child on the autism spectrum often has additional conditions, such as a sensory disorder, attention deficit (ADD or ADHD), depression, Obsessive Compulsive Disorder (OCD), a learning disorder, and giftedness. Without a thorough evaluation, you won't know if your child lies on the autism spectrum or if there are other preexisting conditions.

Would the label help your child secure better treatment? There is no one-size-fits-all treatment for a child with ASD (or any other condition). Each treatment must be based on the right diagnosis (and label). Also, your child won't be able to receive specific treatment or available educational and psychological resources (which can save you hundreds of dollars) without the label.

Would the label help your child function better in life? How happy has your child been in most aspects of his life over the past weeks? Rate your child's overall "happiness quotient" on a scale of 1 to 10 (10 is the highest; 1 the lowest). If he's *generally* happy and in the 6–10 range (every kid has his good and bad days), then you might hold off. If your child is in the 1–5 range, then it's time to look into this further. An evaluation may help your child get along better in life because of specialized remediation. Hint: a child's failure to develop friendships—which can greatly derail the happiness factor—is usually the top reason why parents decide to have their child evaluated.[18]

If you answer yes to even one of these questions, then go for the evaluation. Seek only a credentialed psychologist or psychiatrist who is recommended by sources you trust. You don't have to publicize the results or let others know about your child's specific label, which can be stigmatizing.

- *Get the best treatment.* Once you have evaluated your child, do your research and seek out the best treatment for your child based on his unique issues. A heads-up: professional advice varies greatly depending on the person's training. A pediatric neurologist's opinion will differ from that of an occupational therapist or special education teacher, which means you may end up receiving conflicting advice. Make sure to seek advice only from professionals who are knowledgeable and trained in ASD. Ask for recommendations from your school psychologist, counselor, teacher, and doctor. Call the nearest medical center or university child development center or conduct a thorough Web search. Beware: dozens of treatments (many quite pricey) for ASD profess miraculous "cures." Check the research behind any treatment before signing on the dotted line. Contact the American Medical Association (www.ama-assn.org/), the American Academy of Pediatrics (www.aap.org/), or the American Psychological Association (www.apa.org/) if you are in doubt.

- *Get educated.* Every parent improves her parenting through education, but especially so if your child is diagnosed with ASD. The more you know about your child's condition, the better you can parent. Start by reading a few of the books in the More Helpful Advice box so that you can begin realigning your parenting to an ASD child.

- *Tailor your response to your ASD child.* The fact is that most parenting strategies won't work with ASD kids because their brains are wired differently, so they will respond differently. Here are a few key parenting solutions for ASD kids (pass them on to other caregivers):

  - *Keep emotions in check.* The best way to respond is to be calm, logical, and direct. ASD kids are usually very sensitive and can't manage emotion overload. Stay calm.

  - *Don't force eye contact.* Your child will have a difficult time using eye contact. Just because he isn't looking at you doesn't mean he isn't listening. In fact, forcing him to look at you often makes it more difficult for him to concentrate.

  - *Give step-by-step directions.* ASD kids are rule followers and need to know what is expected. So give clear, simple directions and rules. Speak more slowly, repeat the directions if needed, and give picture cues or hand signals if they help.

  - *Speak literally.* ASD kids often don't read between the lines or have a sense of humor, irony, or ambiguity. They are very concrete.

  - *Be patient.* Your child may take longer to process what you say. So give him time to think. If you interrupt in the middle of his thought, he may have to start all over again.

  - *Keep to routines.* Predictability helps, so stick to a set routine so that he knows what to expect and has a structure he can count on. Also give as much notice as possible if there is a change in the schedule. (A few quiet warnings can help.)

  - *Curb stress.* Researchers at the University of California at San Diego found that too much stress causes temporary memory loss, so ASD kids actually get into a brain-lock mode and can't apply skills or remember information.[19] So reduce stress. Cut back on the loud noises, lights, and chaos, which overstimulate your child. Limit the number of pals and the playdate time. Help him find a quiet place to go when he feels overwhelmed. Go with your child's flow and keep things calm.

  - *Chunk the steps.* ASD kids need to have things broken down into small, understandable steps, whether they're learning to shake hands or say good-bye. Visual cues often help, so draw each step and then practice the skill until your child feels comfortable.

- *Prepare for events.* You can help reduce the stress in a social situation by preparing your child for what might happen at a social event. Let him know how many people will be there, the event theme, how long it lasts, and other details that might help him feel secure.

- *Join a support group.* If you are struggling (which is very common) with your child's diagnosis, then consider finding a parent support group in your area or online, or getting counseling to help you find the inner strength you will need to help you help your child. GRASP is the world's largest support organization for Asperger's and has a list of families to connect with on its Web site (www .grasp.org).

Step 3. Develop Habits for Change

- *Teach new habits to your ASD child.* As I said, normal parenting strategies usually don't work for an ASD child, so you may have to be creative. Think outside the box! For instance:

  Problem: Your child is flapping and waving his hands. **Solution:** Try putting a small wrist weight on his hands to help him keep them down, or put a small toy in each pocket and encourage him to play with the toys and stop the waving.

  Problem: Your child perseverates on the same topic. **Solution:** Try giving him a small box with a lid to "lock away his thoughts." Just show him the box "trick" once and then tell him to remember the box whenever he can't let go of a thought.

  Problem: Your child can't stop moving his legs. **Solution:** Wrap a bungee cord around the legs of chair a few inches off the ground to rest his feet on. The "vibration feel" is often helpful.

One Parent's Answer

A dad from Northridge shares:

My son was diagnosed with Asperger's, but is also gifted. He's always latched on to such obscure interests that he has nothing in common with peers and usually turns the other kids off. He needed some kind of social outlet, so I started looking into what was available in our community by checking the public library, doing a Google search, and leafing through the yellow pages and discovered not only a crossword puzzle club but also a few kids from around the valley who share his passion for ancient history. He finally found a friend and is so much happier.

When you do find a strategy, pass it on to your child's other caregivers.

- *Teach ways to handle a social faux pas.* Getting along with others is often the biggest problem for ASD children. They simply can't read social cues or feel or see emotions the way others do, so they often unintentionally hurt many a person's feelings. So teach your child a few lines to help him say he is sorry. It will take time for him to understand why he should apologize, because he really doesn't realize he did something wrong. But he needs the skill to help him repair relationships. Teach just one line at a time until he can deliver it. Here are a few: *"I'm sorry." "I shouldn't have said that." "I didn't mean to hurt your feelings." "Can I do something to make you feel better?"*

- *Help your child fit in.* The fact is, kids accept or reject you not only because of who you are but also because of how you look. First impressions and how a child looks are not too hard to fix. No matter how different your child is, he can be well groomed, have good hygiene, and dress in a style that fits in with the rest of the kids. Also, are there things your child does that turn kids off? A few basic skills that all kids need and are teachable include taking turns, saying "Excuse me," losing gracefully, and using conversation openers. Richard Lavoie's book *It's So Much Work to Be Your Friend* offers great helpful advice. Just focus on small things you can change so that you can help your child fit in just a bit more.

- *Cultivate a talent.* Children on the autism spectrum generally have a well-developed "splinter skill," such as medieval history, orchids, computers, astronomy, an ant colony, or playing the oboe. Find a way to let your child demonstrate that talent as a way for him to gain appropriate attention and even make a friend.

- *Find a mentor or positive role model.* Consider seeking a possible adult mentor who is empathic and supports your child's interest, whether it is an artist, chess player, cabinetmaker, anthropologist, history buff, or computer expert. It's often helpful for kids to recognize there are many people out there just like them who are happy and hugely successful, and ASD kids often prefer the company of older kids or adults.

- *Find kids with similar interests.* The sad truth is that quirky kids are often rejected, but with a little ingenuity you might be able to help your child find a pal. Ask his teacher for possible suggestions. You can help facilitate a relationship by making your home kid friendly or seeking out places that support your child's natural talents (such as the museum if he's into oil paintings or 4-H if he loves horses). Other kids with similar passions may hang out.

WHAT TO EXPECT BY STAGES AND AGES

Preschooler   Ten percent of kids diagnosed with ASD are identified at age four.[20] Symptoms of ASD first surface because the child's play rituals are noticeably different from those of peers. They often prefer to play by themselves while others play nearby; they are unwilling to acknowledge other kids or join in a group game, and often interact better with adults than with peers. They need adult guidance to initiate and guide relationships. They often collect certain toys or objects but prefer to line them up, count them, or move or organize them in a specific formation instead of playing with them. They may display odd behaviors, such as silliness, excessive loudness, or use of repetitive physical movements, or they may be overly aggressive.

School Age   Social problems become more apparent. At this age, a kid with ASD prefers to isolate himself from social interactions. The child can be excessively bothersome, immature, loud, or meddlesome, causing peers to avoid or reject him. Mid-elementary is when the child may recognize that he doesn't fit in, though he doesn't understand why. Kids with ASD usually display an advanced intellect and reading and vocabulary skills. Fifty percent of kids with Asperger's are diagnosed between five and ten years of age.[21]

LATE-BREAKING NEWS

Fraser Institute, Minnesota: Kim Klein, a pediatric neuropsychologist, and her colleague Pat Pulice headed a study to learn the long-term impact of Asperger's.[22] Although a small number of participants were involved, preliminary results should comfort parents. Here is a sample of how peers without the disorder compared to young adults with Asperger's. The study found that young adults with Asperger's syndrome are

- Equally likely to graduate from high school
- Equally employed, though with fewer hours and more frequent job changes
- Much less likely to have problems with alcohol or drug abuse
- Much less likely to be associated with legal problems

Some areas of difficulty were found as well: 69 percent of young adults with Asperger's needed medication for depression (compared to 39 percent of those study participants without the syndrome). Young adults with Asperger's also required more family support to be successful, were less likely to be in a relationship or married, were more likely to live with their parents, and showed an increased risk for coping problems or poor judgment.

Tween   Friendships and cliques are primary factors, so the social scene can be a jungle for ASD kids lacking the social skills to fit in. Look out for peer teasing, bullying, and rejection. (See *Bullied*, p. 323; *Rejected*, p. 381; *Teased*, p. 415.) Self-esteem can take a nosedive, and depression can become an issue. (See *Depressed*, p. 488.) Twenty percent of kids with Asperger's are diagnosed between ten and twelve years of age.[23]

More Helpful Advice

A Parent's Guide to Asperger Syndrome and High-Functioning Autism: How to Meet the Challenges and Help Your Child Thrive, by Sally Ozonoff, Geraldine Dawson, and James McPartland

The Asperger's Answer Book: The Top 300 Questions Parents Ask, by Susan Ashley

Asperger's Syndrome: A Guide for Parents and Professionals, by Tony Attwood

It's So Much Work to Be Your Friend: Helping the Child with Learning Disabilities Find Social Success, by Richard Lavoie

Nobody Likes Me, Everybody Hates Me: The Top 25 Friendship Problems and How to Solve Them, by Michele Borba

Parenting a Child with Asperger's Syndrome: 200 Tips and Strategies, by Brenda Boyd

Quirky Kids: Understanding and Helping Your Child Who Doesn't Fit In—When to Worry and When Not to Worry, by Perri Klass and Eileen Costello

---

Depressed

SEE ALSO: *Angry, Bullied, Bullying, Dependent, Fearful, Grief, Learning Disabilities, Rejected, Sensitive, Sleepless, Stressed, Teased*

THE PROBLEM

Red Flags

Frequent sadness, tearfulness, or suicidal thoughts; unexplained physical complaints; unprovoked hostility or aggression; fatigue and low energy; extreme sensitivity; loss of enjoyment of previously pleasurable activities; change in eating or sleep habits

The Change to Parent For

Your child begins to enjoy the life he deserves and develops stronger emotional adaptability and coping skills to handle the normal problems of growing up.

Question: "We just moved to a new city and my daughter is having a hard time making friends. She cries and is so moody. How do I know if this is normal or something more serious?"

Answer: Every child feels sad and moody from time to time, but this kind of behavior should have a time limit. To help you see the difference between normal sadness and depression, apply the word "too" in these questions. *Is your child's sadness too deep? Does it last too long or happen too often? Is it interfering with too many other areas of her life such as her home, school, friends?* If so, it could be a sign of clinical depression. If you spot that your child clearly is a "different kid" than she was and there are no physical problems that can explain the symptoms, and if those signs continue over several weeks with no improvement, then it may very well be a depression that needs special help.

Why Change?

Here is what's *not* true about your child and depression: *"She's too young to be depressed." "Don't worry. It's only a phase." "Real depression is something only teens or adults get." "He'll outgrow it."* The sobering reality is that depression does strike kids—and it hits hard.

According to the American Academy of Child and Adolescent Psychiatry, one in twenty children and teens is "significantly" depressed.[24] Not only are the rates of childhood depression increasing, but depression is also impacting younger kids. A kid today is ten times more likely to be seriously depressed compared to a child born in the first third of this century. Almost one-third of thirteen-year-olds have marked depressive symptoms, and by the time kids finish high school, almost 15 percent have had an episode of major depression.[25] Because depression is frequently overlooked, some leading experts predict that almost one in four youngsters will experience a serious episode of depression before his high school graduation.[26]

Clinical depression is *not* a phase or a normal stage of development, nor is it something kids can shrug off. It is a serious and sometimes life-threatening disease, and the long-term consequences are just too severe to ignore. A Yale Medical School study found that depressed youngsters are almost four times more likely to have drug or alcohol problems by their midtwenties.[27] Nearly one in ten kids who develop major depression prior to their puberty commit suicide, and suicide rates for kids and teens have tripled in three decades.[28]

The good news is that when depression is diagnosed early and properly treated, kids almost always can be helped and feel better.[29] And the earlier you seek treatment, the better. Studies show that how we parent can prevent or greatly minimize this debilitating illness. As Marie Kovacs, a leading researcher in the field of childhood depression, points out: "If you want to make a real difference in depression you have to do something before the kids get sick in the first place. The real solution is psychological inoculation."[30] This entry offers some of the proven ways to help your child and get him the help he needs.

Signs and Symptoms

- Your child experiences an increase in physical ailments, such as headaches, stomachaches, nausea, sweaty palms, sleeplessness, or always sleeping, that don't lessen with over-the-counter medication and rest.

- There is a marked, sudden, or intense change in your child's personality, temperament, or behavior that just is not right.

- Your child's symptoms last longer than two weeks, become more intense, or just come and go, and nothing is easing his pain.

- Your child is preoccupied with death or feelings of hopelessness. He is drawing, writing, or asking about death; giving away personal belongings; or saying "What's the use?"

- The sadness interferes with his daily social, academic, or family life.

- Folks who know your child well share their concerns. Don't dismiss their remarks. Listen.

- Your child tells you something is wrong and wants help. Trust him.
- Your instinct says something is not right. Trust your instinct. Chances are, you're right.

If the problem seems to accelerate out of control and your child is saying scary things, or you have any thought that your child is suicidal, DO NOT WAIT. Call the USA National Suicide Hotline: 800-SUICIDE (800-784-2433) or 800-273-8255 and take him to the nearest emergency room immediately. Please.

THE SOLUTION

Step 1. Early Intervention

- *Evaluate the risk factors.* There are specific factors that make kids more vulnerable to depression and put a child more at risk. Look for one-time events or ongoing experiences that diminish your child's self-esteem or reduce emotional resilience and feelings of safety or security. The following is a list of risk factors. Check those that apply to your child and situation:

  ☐ *Genetics.* If a parent or close relative suffers from depression, your child is at increased risk; check your family history.

  ☐ *Previous episode.* Prior episodes of depression increase the chances of reoccurrence.

  ☐ *Problems coping.* Your child lacks resilience, emotional adaptability, or the ability to recover from setbacks.

Pay Attention to This!

Do Not Ignore Depression: Seek Help ASAP to Prevent a Reoccurrence

Oregon Research Institute in Eugene: Peter Lewinsohn, the eminent depression researcher, has followed seventeen hundred children for over a decade. He found that 44 percent of those who developed depression before age eighteen experienced *another* episode by the time they turned twenty-four.[31] Other studies reveal that almost half of kids with untreated depression will suffer another episode within three years.[32] Early diagnosis and treatment can significantly reduce the risk of depression reoccurring. If you suspect your child is depressed, do not wait to get help.

☐ *Stressful life events.* Intense or mounting stresses, such as hospitalization, a parent's death, divorce, discovery of being adopted, loss of a parent's job, or frequent family fighting, can all trigger depression.

☐ *Unstable child rearing.* Your child experiences a dysfunctional parenting and home life.

☐ *Abuse and trauma.* Your child has experienced or is experiencing verbal, emotional, sexual, or physical harassment or abuse.

☐ *Disaster.* A natural or man-made disaster that drastically affects the child's feelings of safety—a hurricane, kidnapping, car accident, terrorist attack (even if not nearby), earthquake, shooting, fire—can set off a depressive episode.

☐ *Peer rejection and bullying.* Your child experiences constant emotional harassment and peer rejection.

☐ *Failure.* Your child has continual experiences of social, academic, or emotional failure.

- *Know your child's "normal" mood level.* Some kids just are a bit moody, restless, or private, and all kids will be sad and angry at times. Your job is to discover what is normal behavior for *your child.* Once you know his typical personality and temperament, you'll be able to spot a marked change in what's normal for your child and then get help for him if you suspect he may be suffering from depression. Watch him more closely in different settings. Ask folks who know and care about your kid for their take. Keep your parenting antenna on alert. Hint: depressed kids are usually more reactive, with more irritability and faster mood swings, than depressed adults.[33] Although it is difficult to diagnose depressed kids, they almost all have a marked increase in anxiety before the depression hits.

- *Become an authority.* The more you understand about childhood depression, the better you'll be able to help your child. So read books. (See the More Helpful Advice box for some suggestions.) Talk to experts. Join a support group. Attend workshops. Refer to these Web sites: the American Academy of Child and Adolescent Psychiatry (www.aacap.org/), the American Psychological Association (www.apa.org/), and the American Academy of Pediatrics (www.aap.org/).

- *Reduce those stressors that you can.* Although stress doesn't cause depression, it can exacerbate it. So take a serious look at your child's calendar, then cut, cut, cut. At this point, nothing matters more than your child's emotional well-being. Lighten that load!

- *Ease up on feeling guilty.* The latest research shows that childhood depression is caused by genetics, biochemistry, or a variety of other factors. In the vast majority of cases, *depression is not caused by poor parenting.* You *did not* bring this illness on your child, so please don't blame yourself. This one is hard, but it's critical for your child's recovery and your peace of mind.

- *Model a positive outlook.* Research shows that depressed kids can "learn" to be depressed or become more depressed just from watching the behavior of those around them. So do some soul searching. What kind of example are you modeling for your child? Ask yourself: How do you handle defeat? How do you act when you don't get that job promotion or have trouble in your relationships? Do you act gloomy, not get out of bed, or take a drink? Watch out. How you handle life's disappointments might just be teaching your child to respond to stress in an unproductive way. Is there any chance that you are depressed or in need of therapy?

Step 2. Rapid Response

- *Love your child.* What your depressed child needs most from you is love, empathy, and acceptance. If you think this is hard for you, see things from your child's side. Imagine his fear ("What is going on?"), feelings of doom ("Why do I hurt so much?"), and despair ("Things will never get better. Why bother?"). Be there. Let him know he did nothing to cause this. Be clear that you're going to do whatever it takes to help him be happy.

- *Boost one-on-one time.* There is no better buffer for depression than a strong, loving bond with your child. It is the foundation for a healthy, positive relationship, and it's what your child needs right now. Find uninterrupted time to be

One Parent's Answer

A mom from St. Louis shares:

My daughter was sad for so long, but I just kept thinking it was just a phase that she'd snap out of. In my mind, she didn't have anything to be so upset about. But my girlfriend convinced me to jot down Laura's mood each day on a calendar. It was only when I saw that Laura was sad not only most of the time but for days on end that I called the doctor. He said that she had major signs of depression and wanted to immediately hospitalize her. This was the most difficult decision I've ever made, but I finally admitted Laura for two weeks, and I am so grateful I did. Those two weeks probably saved her life. The team of doctors said she had been struggling with clinical depression for over a year and was suicidal. They prescribed an antidepressant that she says helps her feel happy again. Laura now sees a therapist who is using "talk therapy" to help her reframe her thoughts and that seems to help as well. It's been an uphill struggle and I know we're not out of the woods, but we're taking things one day at a time. I just wish I would have tracked her behavior sooner.

with your child. If he's not receptive to talking (most depressed kids aren't), then just be there with your presence. Rub his back. Watch a TV show together. Do something you've enjoyed doing before. Read a book. Or just sit in his company so that he knows you care.

- *Stick to a routine.* Structure and routines create predictability and boost feelings of emotional security—and are exactly what your child needs. Maintain a routine as much as you can, such as the same morning and evening rituals and homework, dinnertime, and bedtime schedules. And try to make things *seem* normal even though they probably are not.

- *Take care of yourself.* You have to take care of yourself so you can take care of your child. Find a support group. Exercise. Hire a babysitter so you can get out. Walk around the block. Ask for help. Put a Do Not Disturb sign on your bedroom door.

- *Curb those negatives.* Depressed kids are discouraged and need encouragement. So curb those negative comments: they only discourage kids more. Start by tracking your current ratio of negative to positive statements. Choose a one-hour (or even thirty-minute) time slot when you're together, and count the total number of negative comments. Once you know that number, set a goal to reduce the negative and boost the positive. Ideally a child (especially a depressed one) should hear five positives to every one negative. But what is realistic for you? Start by at least countering every negative with a positive until you change your own response habit. It will make a difference.

- *Keep your tone calm and even.* Depressed kids are hypersensitive. The smallest things set them off. So keep your voice calm. Even lower your voice when talking. Raising it even just a little above normal may set off an overwhelmed child. Hypersensitive kids also have trouble reading emotional cues and assume we're "ticked off" when we're not. If this is your kid, label your emotions so that he doesn't misread them: *"Do you think I'm angry? I'm not upset; I'm just tired."* Also watch your nonverbal cues, such as smirks or raised eyebrows, as they can really trigger a rise in a kid. If needed, take a time-out if emotions get too high.

- *Find a treatment for your child.* The most critical piece of advice for depression is to get help, and the sooner the better. Start with your family physician to rule out any physical causes (such as mononucleosis or an inactive thyroid). The next step is to ask for referrals. Childhood depression is difficult to diagnose, so you will want an evaluation by only those trained and licensed in child and adolescent psychiatry. Ask school psychologists and counselors or your local minister. Take advantage of referral services offered by the Association for the Advancement of Behavior Therapy (www.aabt.org), or call the National Mental Health Association's resource center (800-969-6642) for therapists in your area. Go to a university-affiliated medical center or call the local medical school or

American Psychological Association. You want a doctor or therapist who will not only monitor your child's ongoing progress but also be at the other end of that phone for you if something unexpected happens.

- *Find the best treatment for your child.* Once your child is evaluated, you may need to make difficult choices for your child's treatment: will it involve prescription drugs, ongoing outpatient therapy (in particular cognitive-behavior therapy, "talk therapy," and interpersonal therapy, all of which require specialized training), or even hospitalization. Keep in mind that more than one treatment can work. The more knowledgeable you are about each choice and how they will affect your child, the better you will feel about your decision. So ask specific questions of those professionals about the risks and benefits of all options they recommend, and always ask for a specific treatment plan tailored to your child. Even then, don't be afraid to get a second (or third) opinion. You have one quest: find what works best to help *your* child, and don't stop until you find that answer.

Pay Attention to This!
Should You Medicate Your Child for Depression?

One of the most difficult decisions you may face is whether to medicate your child for depression. Keep in mind that depression is a *life-threatening* disease and that suicide is a possible outcome of untreated depression. Up to 80 percent of youth with clinical depression have thoughts of suicide, and up to 35 percent of youths attempt suicide.[34] So weigh the risks of medicating against the very real danger of ignoring your child's illness. If you do choose medication, consult only with a doctor trained in child and adolescent pharmacology who has conducted a thorough analysis of your child.

Once you start medication, record your child's daily moods and any adverse drug reactions. *Do not stop the medication without your doctor's recommendation.* Doing so can cause the possibility of agitation and increased depression. Contact your physician immediately if your child expresses any thoughts of wanting to die, engages in self-destructive behavior, or shows signs of increased anxiety, agitation, aggressiveness, or impulsivity. Also know that a long-term study found that the most effective treatment for adolescents with major depression was for them to receive antidepressants to reduce their physical symptoms *and* therapy to help them develop new skills to handle their negative emotions.[35]

LATE-BREAKING NEWS

University of Pennsylvania: Research by renowned psychologist Martin Seligman found that helping kids become more optimistic and less negative in their thinking patterns actually helps them be less likely to be depressed as well as better able to bounce back from adversity. Begin to curb your child's negative thinking by countering it with a more balanced view of the world. Suppose your kid didn't make the soccer team, believing "everyone" thinks she's a bad player; you could counter it with a more balanced perspective: *"I know you're disappointed about not making the team. You're a good skier, and you Rollerblade pretty well, too."* Martin Seligman's book *The Optimistic Child* is a must-read for parents and offers a wealth of prevention strategies. Just do remember to check your own negative thinking as well. Your kids are tuning in and copying.

Step 3. Develop Habits for Change

- *Accentuate a positive atmosphere.* Depression not only hurts your child but also can breed negativity in your home. So find ways to accentuate the positive so that other family members won't be affected as well. Consider starting dinners with "Good News Reports" in which each member reports something good that happened during the day. Look for uplifting books and videos to show the good parts of life. Deliberately say more positive messages that your kids overhear. Monitor negative media consumption, such as TV shows, Internet, music lyrics, video games, movies. Cut inspiring articles out of newspapers and magazines and share them with your family. And mandate one family rule to help derail negativism: "One Negative = One Positive." Whenever a family member says a negative comment, the sender must turn it into something positive. Enforcing the rule gradually diminishes negative statements—but you must be consistent.

- *Teach how to relax.* Tiffany Field's research at the University of Miami's Touch Research Institute found that depression dropped in kids who received thirty minutes of a massage twice a week for a month.[36] Watching relaxing videos also seemed to help. Yoga has also been found to be effective in helping beat depression.[37] Help your child discover soothing strategies that take the edge off. Start by sharing what helps you relax, whether it's soaking in a hot tub or going for a bike ride. Then ask your child what might help him, such as shooting baskets, listening to the *Aladdin* soundtrack or relaxation music on his iPod, or writing in his journal. Offer suggestions if needed. Then encourage him to use those activities.

- *Find ways to enjoy life.* This is a tough time for you and your child, but look for ways your child can have fun as best he can. Don't expect him to snap out of it (he can't), but at least help him enjoy life a bit more. Fish at the local pond, play Monopoly, go for batting practice or a baseball game. The trick is to find simple things your child likes to do—and to do them a bit more. Researchers at the Loma Linda University School of Public Health found that watching a comedic video for an hour lowered the anxiety in depressed kids, so don't overlook watching funny movies together.[38]

WHAT TO EXPECT BY STAGES AND AGES

Renowned child and adolescent psychiatrist David Fassler, coauthor with Lynne Dumas of the must-read book *"Help Me, I'm Sad,"* offers these signs of childhood depression:[39]

Preschooler   Verbal skills are limited in kids this age, so they will have trouble describing feelings. Look for loss of pleasure in play[40] as well as frequent and unexplained stomachaches, headaches, and fatigue; overactive and excessive restlessness; irritability or low tolerance for frustration; frequent sadness. Typical preschool behaviors (such as separation anxiety, whining, tantrums, nightmares) are more intense and last several weeks, though usually not at steady intervals.

School Age   In addition to preschooler signs, watch for changes in sleep pattern, significant weight loss or gain, tearfulness, excessive worrying and low self-esteem, unprovoked hostility or aggression, a drop in grades, refusal or reluctance to attend school, loss of interest in playing with peers, and feelings of unworthiness: "Nobody likes me," "I'm no good," "I can't do anything right."

Tween   In addition to school-age signs, look for sleeping longer, feeling hopeless, abusing drugs, drinking or smoking, conduct problems in school, fatigue, loss of enjoyment of previously enjoyable activities, self-destructive behavior, difficulty with relationships, eating-related problems, social isolation, lack of attention to appearance, extreme sensitivity to rejection or failure, physical slowness or agitation, and morbid or suicidal thoughts.

THE DIFFERENCE BETWEEN BOYS AND GIRLS

Although depression is equally common to both genders during childhood, it affects kids at different ages.[41] Younger boys are more likely to be depressed than girls and are more likely to act out their depression by being disruptive, fighting, disobeying, and requiring disciplinary action.[42] Younger girls are more apt to become withdrawn, quiet, or isolated. The trend reverses in the tween years, when girls are twice as likely as boys to be depressed, suffer more severe depression, and have longer first episodes.

More Helpful Advice

Depressed Child: A Parent's Guide for Rescuing Kids, by Douglas A. Riley

"Help Me, I'm Sad": Recognizing, Treating, and Preventing Childhood and Adolescent Depression, by David G. Fassler and Lynne S. Dumas

Lonely, Sad and Angry: How to Help Your Unhappy Child, by Barbara D. Ingersoll

Raising Depression-Free Children: A Parent's Guide to Prevention and Early Intervention, by Kathleen Panula Hockey

The Childhood Depression Sourcebook, by Jeffrey A. Miller

Growing Up Sad: Childhood Depression and Its Treatment, by Leon Cytryn and Donald H. McKnew Jr.

The Optimistic Child: Proven Program to Safeguard Children from Depression and Build Lifelong Resilience, by Martin E. P. Seligman

When a Parent Is Depressed: How to Protect Your Children from the Effects of Depression in the Family, by William R. Beardslee

Eating Disorders

SEE ALSO: *Depressed, Overweight, Peer Pressure, Perfectionist, Picky Eater, Rejected, Stressed, Teased*

THE PROBLEM

Red Flags

Obsesses about weight and appearance; has intense fear of being fat; eats way too much or way too little; wants to eat alone; exercises intensely; buys diet pills, laxatives, and diuretics to purge

The Change to Parent For

Your child realizes that she is likeable at a more normal body weight, develops healthier eating habits, accepts herself as she really is, and recognizes that happiness is not based on clothing size.

Question: "My daughter is only ten but is so frail, eats like a bird, and is so irritable. I think she may have an eating disorder, but everyone tells me she's way too young and it's only hormones kicking in. How do I know when to worry?"

Answer: Children as young as six these days are diagnosed with eating disorders, so it's wise to pay attention to your child's eating habits at any age. That said, it is also difficult to tell the difference between an eating disorder and normal preadolescence, when kids are usually moody and concerned about appearance and weight. So be on the alert for what's not a normal part of your child's development. Here are some examples. She counts calories relentlessly, exercises endlessly, and unrealistically claims to be "too fat." She may usually hide telltale clues like diet pills and laxatives or food packages, or she'll run the shower to disguise vomiting sounds. She may seem depressed or irritable, feel guilty about eating, want to eat alone, or may spend a long time in the bathroom. Every child is different, and you may not see overt signs at the onset.

If you at all suspect an eating disorder, *seek medical advice immediately.* This is a serious, potentially life-threatening illness, and the sooner it is diagnosed, the more effectively it can be treated.

Why Change?

"An eating disorder? Impossible!" "Not my daughter!" Disbelief is usually our first response when we read the headlines about anorexia, bulimia, and bingeing. But the fact is that at least 10 percent of all adolescent girls suffer from eating disorders.[43] Boys now make up about 30 percent of younger children with eating disorders.[44] The disease has no boundaries: male or female, young or old, urban or rural, Catholic or Jewish, black or white. And the rates are only increasing.

Over ten years ago, 34 percent of high school girls thought they were overweight; 90 percent believe they are today.[45] In just five years, diet pill use—including amphetamines, crystal meth, recreational Ritalin, bennies, and other types—has nearly doubled among teen girls; almost 63 percent now use unhealthy weight-control behaviors, such as diet pills, laxatives, vomiting, or skipping meals.[46] But perhaps most disturbing is that children as young as five are now being diagnosed with eating disorders.

Make no mistake: the consequences are *very* serious and can be life threatening. A child with eating disorders is at risk for sleep apnea, asthma, high blood pressure, diabetes, depression, stroke, and heart disease.[47] Anorexia increases a child's risk of premature death by more than *twelve times* the expected rate.[48] Over a thousand women and girls die each year from complications.[49] If you have the slightest suspicion that your child has an eating disorder, *do not wait.* The earlier treatment begins, the greater the likelihood that your child will recover or at least make significant progress. That alone is grounds to make this change. Start now!

Signs and Symptoms

Eating disorders are difficult to detect in the early stages, but here are signs to look for:

- *Constant battles at mealtime:* makes excuses to avoid eating, skips meals, prefers to eat alone. Meal battles aren't really about pickiness in taste or appearance but about taking in another calorie.

- *Bizarre eating behaviors:* spits out food; chews on the same piece of food for an unreasonable and excessive length of time; cuts food into smaller bits; hides food and says it was eaten.

- *Obsessive calorie counting:* constantly weighs self; has an intense fear of being fat; eliminates all sweets, snacks, fat from diet; relentlessly exercises to lose weight; preoccupied with appearance and size.

- *Unrealistic assessment of weight:* describes self as "too fat" though obviously underweight.

- *Halt to menses:* skips periods or menstruation stops altogether.

- *Radical change in temperament:* irritable, depressed; has trouble sleeping; withdraws socially.

- *Physical changes:* has dry skin, puffy face, yellow skin; fine hair on body; brittle fingernails; thin, dry, or brittle hair; swelling feet, achy joints, cold hands.

- *Hoarding or hiding of food:* eats in secret; doesn't eat much at meals or says she's not hungry, but sweets and junk food are missing from cupboards; you find empty food packages around the house.

- *Strange bathroom behaviors:* retreats to the bathroom after eating; flushes toilet frequently, runs water, or turns on shower to cover up vomiting sounds; uses sanitizer sprays or mouthwash excessively.

- *Large changes in weight:* weight fluctuates both up and down; wears bulky clothes to hide body.

- *Extreme dieting methods:* uses laxatives, enemas, water pills (diuretics), or diet pills.

- *Problems with joints, gums, or teeth:* has scraped knuckles from putting fingers down throat to vomit; discolored teeth, gum problems; swollen cheeks from vomiting; sore joints.

- *Compulsive eating:* eats a lot—much more than others would normally eat in a similar situation—when not hungry; no control over eating behavior.

Pay Attention to This!
Beware of Web Sites That Encourage Eating Disorders

Stanford University School of Medicine: Disturbing research found that kids as young as ten are learning weight-loss or purging techniques from Web sites that promote eating disorders.[50] Just a few of those "useful tips" garnered from cyberspace include "Throw up in the shower—it covers up the sound," "Use nail-growth polish so your nails won't look so brittle, and "Fasting makes it easy to overcome bad habits and addictions." The pro-Ana and pro-Mia sites (as in pro-anorexia and pro-bulimia) also provide "thinspiration" by posting photos of bony-thin fashion models. In fact, 96 percent of young patients with eating disorders admit they learn purging and weight-loss methods while logged on.[51] Less than one-third of parents say they have discussed such sites with their kids. The lesson here: *talk to your children and monitor their online activities.*

THE SOLUTION

Step 1. Early Intervention

- *Dig deeper to find the cause.* Researchers studying anorexia in twins deduce that more than half a person's risk for developing eating disorders is biologically determined.[52] Although genes can create a propensity for the disorder, there usually is an environmental issue that ignites it, such as a family issue, a parental response, or a social influence. As you dig deeper to find the reason, focus on those areas you can change. The following is a list of the most common causes of eating disorders. Check those issues that may apply to your child and family situation:

  ☐ *Genetics.* If there is an anorexic child in the family, the sibling is twelve times more at risk of developing anorexia; siblings of bulimics have three times the risk compared to the general population.[53] But remember, even if there is a genetic component, it doesn't mean that the child is going to develop an eating disorder. Environment plays a big role as well.

  ☐ *A stressful trigger.* This can include a breakup with a boyfriend, being cut from a team for being overweight or rejected by peers for being "too fat," an insensitive comment about her weight, or a divorce.

  ☐ *Personality or temperament.* The child is born with a perfectionist-type temperament,[54] is more anxious or impulsive, needs everything to be controlled and ordered, or has poor problem-solving skills.

  ☐ *Highly competitive activities.* The child participates in competitive, aesthetic-type activities, such as gymnastics, cheerleading, ballet, wrestling, boxing, or modeling, where weight and appearance matter; she must exercise excessively and keep to a certain weight.

  ☐ *Low self-esteem.* The child has a poor and unrealistic body image and sense of self; her self-image is based on body shape and weight; she is acknowledged for how she looks, not for who she is.

  ☐ *Peer pressure.* The child feels an intense need to belong, or she is part of a group that worships thinness.

  ☐ *Social influences.* The child consumes a steady stream of media images and "thin is better" messages, idolizing celebrities who are size zero and bony thin.

  ☐ *Unhealthy eating patterns.*[55] Family members model unhealthy eating patterns, including eating irregular meals, eating much more (or less) than normal serving sizes, or abstaining because of guilt, fear, or shame; there is excessive discussion of diet and calorie intake.

  ☐ *Parental eating disorder.* The child's mother is overly concerned with her body image,[56] has an eating disorder,[57] or makes negative comments about the child's and others' weight and appearance.

☐ *Family dynamics.* The parents are less emotionally supportive and empathic;[58] there is a family lack of communication and open expression, and the parents are highly achievement oriented.[59]

☐ *Physical or sexual abuse.* Research shows that almost 60 percent of bulimia sufferers who were hospitalized had experienced physical or sexual abuse, such as incest, rape, or childhood molestation.[60]

Do get a full medical evaluation for your child to rule out medical or emotional problems that might be the cause.

- *Get educated.* A variety of credible health sources and research shows that rates of eating disorders are increasing.[61] Anorexia is a thousand times more prevalent today than it was fifty years ago.[62] As parents, we need to know as much we can, because these diseases are dangerous and life threatening, and the best cure is always prevention. So get educated! The more you are aware of the symptoms and causes of eating disorders, the better able you will be to help your child. Also familiarize yourself with the three most common types of eating disorders:

  Anorexia Nervosa. The child is terrified of weight gain or being fat and severely restricts calories.

  Bulimia Nervosa. The child binges on large quantities of food, then tries to get rid of those calories in unhealthy ways, such as by vomiting, using laxatives, fasting, or exercising compulsively.

  Binge Eating Disorder. This disorder is similar to bulimia, but there is no purging (vomiting or using laxatives).

  See the More Helpful Advice box for resources.

- *Check your attitude.* Kids who see and hear their parents (especially moms) worrying about their weight and appearance may adopt the belief that being thin is the standard to achieve. Although parents do not *cause* eating disorders, they may unintentionally set off their child's genetic susceptibility, or the child will develop a disorder by picking up the parent's attitudes. So watch your comments and tune in to your own behavior. Your child is watching!

- *Build self-esteem.* A positive and well-rounded sense of self-esteem and healthy body image are two of the best means of preventing an eating disorder. So find ways to help your child gain competence in physical, social, and academic endeavors. Praise her for her "inside qualities," not her appearance and accomplishments. Help her discover and nurture her innate strengths and personal qualities. Let her know you love her just because she breathes and exists. Eating disorders aren't just about food but about how kids feel about themselves.

LATE-BREAKING NEWS

Limit Access to Fashion and Diet Magazines

American Academy of Pediatrics: Have you flipped through a fashion or celebrity magazine lately? Only one body type is flaunted: thin, thinner, or thinnest, and those images *do* influence our daughters' eating habits. A five-year study of 2,516 teens found that girls who frequently read those dieting and weight-loss articles are far more likely to fast, vomit, or use laxatives to lose weight.[63] In fact, the data proved that the more frequently a girl reads those fashion magazines, the more likely she is to resort to extreme weight control behaviors. Here are a few "take-aways" from this important study:

- Monitor the media your child consumes a bit more closely, and make sure those bodybuilding magazines do not consume your son as well.

- Limit your child's access to magazines that promote the "thin is better" look and get her a subscription to a healthier alternative.

- Teach your child to be media literate and to resist the ways television, movies, and magazines portray underweight women as glamorous and muscle-bound men as all-powerful.

- Talk frankly about the unglamorous reality of eating disorders (damaged teeth, hair loss, osteoporosis, brittle fingernails, even possible death).

And while you're at it, put down those celebrity and fashion magazines yourself. *Your child is taking notes.*

- *Watch out for aesthetic sports.* Although having your child involved in athletics is generally a healthy, positive outlet, there is a downside. Sports that require *extreme* workouts, constant weigh-ins, food restrictions, and intense competitive efforts can trigger eating disorders.[64] In particular, aesthetic sports that emphasize appearance and weight (such as gymnastics, aerobics, ice skating, dance, and swimming) are found to be more likely to cause five- and seven-year-old girls to be more conscious of their weight (as opposed to girls involved in no sports or in nonaesthetic sports, such as volleyball, soccer, basketball, softball, hockey, tennis, and martial arts). Be ready to address your concerns to your child's coach or find a healthier sport alternative.

- *Watch her friends.* Research on 15,349 adolescents found that eating disorders are contagious and become "transferrable" when girls share their extreme dieting secrets—fasting, bingeing, taking diet pills and laxatives—and glorify their anorexic lifestyles.[65] That contagious effect happens equally among rural, urban, and suburban teens. So tune in a bit more closely to what your daughter's friends are talking about. If the focus is all about dress size and the latest diets, it may be time to steer your child toward others friends with healthier outlooks.

- *Eat regular family meals.* A longitudinal survey of over fifteen hundred adolescents found that girls who regularly ate family meals a few times a week in a structured and positive atmosphere were *one-third less likely to develop an eating disorder.*[66] Girls were also significantly less likely to use extreme dieting measures, such as diet pills, laxatives, or vomiting.[67] If your schedule isn't conducive to family dining, then eat breakfast together instead, but do find time to connect and enjoy each other's company on a regular basis.

Step 2. Rapid Response

- *Determine the severity.* If you have even the slightest inkling that your child's eating disorder could be life threatening, put down this book and drive your child to the nearest hospital or outpatient clinic now. An emergency intervention may be necessary to save your child's life. Your child's doctor can provide names of reputable clinics specializing in eating disorders. If your child balks, ask someone to help accompany you during this ordeal, or dial 911 and law enforcement officers will help you. If you suspect that your child may have an eating disorder and this is not an emergency situation, use the next few steps.

- *Log your child's eating patterns.* Eating disorders are often difficult to spot in the beginning stages. In fact, your child may seem to be on a quest to eat a healthier diet (reducing fat, eating only greens, and so on). But act on your instinct and start making note of your child's daily eating habits: what she eats and how much; whether she's skipping meals; whether she's engaging in symptomatic behaviors, such hiding food, eating alone, and sneaking to the bathroom; and how often and long she exercises. You may need those records to share with a doctor and to confront your child with your concerns. Right now your notes will help assess whether or not your worries are grounded.

- *Share your concerns with your child.* For many parents, the most difficult task is sharing their eating disorder suspicions with their child, but you must so that your child can get help. Gear up by thinking about what you want to say, and then find the best time to voice your concerns in a caring way. Describe the eating or exercise habits that worry you and if necessary share your notes (see previous tip). Then listen carefully to your child and hear where she is coming from. She may sound afraid, feel ashamed, get mad, or even deny the problem—all are normal responses. Some kids are actually relieved that their private

One Parent's Answer

A mom from Colorado Springs shares:

A few moms were so concerned about the rise of eating disorders that we started up a Mother-Daughter Club to strengthen our bond with our girls and help us get them through adolescence with healthy self-esteem. Six of us meet once a month in alternate homes and talk frankly about all kinds of girl issues like puberty, self-image, anorexia, and the media push on thinness. The girls actually look forward to the gatherings. I can't emphasize what a difference it's made: it's kept us close to our daughters and helped us get through some tough times. This is our fourth year, and we're seeing our girls turn into confident young women who enjoy themselves for who they are.

NOTE: An excellent resource to help you join with other moms to begin your own Mother-Daughter Club is *The Mother-Daughter Project: How Mothers and Daughters Can Band Together, Beat the Odds, and Thrive Through Adolescence*, by SuEllen Hamkins and Renee Schultz.

nightmare is finally in the open. If you suspect your child has an eating disorder, make an appointment with a mental health professional. *Do not allow your child to talk you out of it or tell you she's not ready for treatment.* Stress that you love her too much to put her health at risk. Then congratulate yourself: you just carried out the first crucial step toward your child's recovery.

Step 3. Develop Habits for Change

- *Involve your child in the habit change.* The trick to turning your kid's eating habits around is to involve her in the process. Let her help you dump the junk food from those cupboards and shop for healthier options. Get her involved in meal planning or growing a vegetable garden. Teach her how to make simple but good-tasting (and healthier) snacks. Ask her to help you chop up veggies and put them in the fridge. Let your child have a personal stake in what she eats so that she can learn healthy new eating habits.

- *Find positive outlets.* If you notice that your child (and her friends) focus too much on how they look, then find what turns your kid on. Whether it is horseback riding, cello, soccer, knitting, skiing, guitar, or drawing, find a way to nurture your child's natural strengths and support that interest. The experience may ultimately help her realize that who she is, is more important than how she looks.

- *Teach self-monitoring.* One part of successful change is helping a child learn to self-monitor her eating behavior. So if your child is willing, provide her with a record-keeping device, such as a notebook, calendar, or journal, and then encourage her to chart the one behavior she hopes to improve. It might be her eating and exercise habits or even her bingeing and purging. Once they review their records, kids are often surprised at how frequently they binge or skip meals. The recording may be the first baby step in helping your child realize she needs to change. Please note: encouraging your child to weigh herself is *not* part of this tip. (See the One Simple Solution box in this entry.)

- *Find help!* The ideal time to help your child learn new eating and behavior habits is at the *first hint of an eating disorder.* You'll most likely need to find a professional trained in eating disorders to guide you in those new habits. Ask for recommendations from your doctor, school psychologist, counselor, friends, spiritual adviser, or a hospital with an eating disorder unit. The American Psychological Association and the National Association for Anorexia Nervosa and Associated Disorders are also helpful resources. Interview each prospective mental health professional until you find a person you think is right for your child. Look for an individual who has extensive experience and knowledge in eating disorders and a track record of success, who is up-to-date on current treatments, and who you also think will connect with your child.[68]

- *Be patient!* The journey to recovery takes time and hard work. So be patient and continue advocating for your child. She needs you now more than ever. Be particularly available in times of conflict, trauma, or stress, when kids are more vulnerable to eating as a way to cope with problems and avoid issues. Don't

---

ONE SIMPLE SOLUTION

Hide the Scale

University of Minnesota: A study of more than two thousand teens found that those who weighed themselves frequently were more likely to resort to bingeing, skipping meals, taking diet pills, using laxatives, and vomiting.[69] Constantly monitoring those pounds can lead to an unhealthy weight preoccupation, especially for girls who are already concerned about how they look. So put away the scale as the first step to helping kids move away from their obsession to be ultrathin. Over 50 percent of teen girls in the United States say they are unhappy with their weight, and more than a third of normal-weight girls say they are dieting.[70] Enough!

overlook other siblings who can be emotionally affected as well. And please remember to make time for yourself so you can take care of your child. These will be trying times, but you are taking the right steps to help your child.

WHAT TO EXPECT BY STAGES AND AGES

Preschooler   Eating disorders start early: the first signs of anorexia have been spotted in girls as young as four and five. Preschoolers already have well-established routines of familiar, "safe" foods, which make it challenging to have the child try anything new or different, but continue to introduce nutritious food and a balanced lifestyle.

School Age   Media influence pushing the "ultrathin" look begins to take hold: half of girls eight to ten years old and one-third of boys are unhappy with their size;[71] Eighty percent of children have been on a diet by the time they reach the fourth grade.[72] Nurture self-esteem by focusing on your child's inside qualities.

Tween   Peer pressure has a strong influence on children's body image, and the "quest to be thin" escalates at this age. Perfectionism and overachievement escalate with the push to excel and get high grades. Thirty percent of girls ages ten to fourteen are dieting;[73] 12 percent of the 4,746 adolescent girls surveyed reported vomiting or taking diet pills, laxatives, or diuretics to lose weight.[74] Tween girls struggling with low self-esteem are particularly vulnerable to images of thin models and celebrities.

More Helpful Advice

Anorexia Nervosa and Related Eating Disorders in Childhood and Adolescence, by Bryan Lask

Biting the Hand That Starves You: Inspiring Resistance to Anorexia/ Bulimia, by Richard Maisel, David Epston, and Ali Borden

Eating Disorders in Childhood and Adolescence, 3rd Edition, by Bryan Lask and Rachel Bryant-Waugh

Help Your Teenager Beat an Eating Disorder, by James Lock and Daniel le Grange

Treating Bulimia in Adolescents: A Family-Based Approach, by Daniel le Grange and James Lock

When Your Child Has an Eating Disorder: A Step-By-Step Workbook for Parents and Other Caregivers, by Abigail H. Natenshon

SPECIAL NEEDS

Gifted

SEE ALSO: *Angry, Boredom, Depressed, Perfectionist, Reading, Rejected, Sleepless, Stressed*

THE PROBLEM

Red Flags

Perfectionist tendencies or fear of failure; boredom when not challenged; burnout from activity overload; stress from too much acceleration; peer rejection from acting "too different"; hindered social, emotional, or moral development because of overemphasis on the intellectual; sense of entitlement from being labeled "gifted"

The Change to Parent For

Your child recognizes and accepts her unique gifts or talents and receives the right balance of support and challenge to reach her intellectual potential.

Why Change?

I've done dozens of parenting segments on NBC's *Today* show, but none has generated as much interest as "Is Your Child Gifted?" Hundreds of parents flooded my blog requesting the traits of gifted kids—absolutely certain that those traits would apply to their child. Without a doubt, that "gifted" label has become highly coveted among parents these days. Who wouldn't want their child to have a superior intellect? After all, only 2.5 to 3 percent of kids make that mark. How could having a child with extraordinary mental abilities possibly be a problem?

The truth is, there are unique challenges to raising gifted children. For one thing, kids with superior intellectual abilities think and operate differently from "typical" kids, and those distinctions mean we must change our parenting to meet their needs. Gifted kids have boundless enthusiasm for learning, highly developed curiosity, and endless (and I do mean endless) questions about anything and everything. They also can be interested in experimenting, rearranging, and doing things quite differently from the norm. Although certainly positive, those traits can put pressure on parents. Just keeping up with their children's constant desire for more information can be exhausting. There can also be problems at school as parents fight to ensure that their kids are not left with boring busywork while other students try to catch up. Don't be fooled: gifted students do need help to succeed. Without that help and their parents' support, they may become underachievers or even leave school.[75] One surprising fact is that gifted kids drop out at the same rates as nongifted kids: about 5 percent of both populations leave school without graduating. Although most gifted kids have friends and don't turn into the stereotypical "social misfit," they do have unique traits that can cause social and emotional problems.

LATE-BREAKING NEWS

Stretch Your Child's Potential by Nurturing, Not Pushing

University of Chicago: Renowned psychologist Mihaly Csikszentmihalyi and his research team conducted a four-year study of two hundred highly gifted and talented students to see how well they developed their talents as well as to identify factors involved in the loss of their exceptional talent over the years.[76] The team found that those students whose parents guided but did not push them to develop their skills were much more likely to reach their potential.

Here are the subtle but critical differences between pushing and nurturing your child:

Pushing focuses on your interests and is *parent-directed.* Nurturing follows your child's interests and is *kid-directed.*

Pushing tends to rely on a prepackaged curriculum (worksheets, textbooks, flash cards). Nurturing uses real-life lessons and concrete experiences to stretch the child's interest.

Pushing stresses a preset timeline or goal that the parent sticks to. Nurturing is flexible, follows the child's lead, and lets the child focus on the interest at her own pace.

Pushing accelerates too much, too soon, or at too high a level. Nurturing includes watching the child's level of interest and abilities and challenging the child at a level only slightly higher than her abilities.

Pushing emphasizes external motivation, offering rewards and parental reinforcement. Nurturing stresses internal motivation so that the child develops her passion from the inside out.

Pushing a child's talent can rob creativity, produce anxiety, create perfectionism, make the child feel pressured, and turn her off to the joy of learning. Nurturing the talent is more likely to keep a child's interest, instill joy, increase concentration, boost competence, and stretch potential.

Regardless of the challenges, there are solutions to help you parent your gifted child. Here are a few of the best proven strategies to help gifted children reach their intellectual potential and also have fun.

THE SOLUTION

Six Strategies for Change

1. *Determine if your child really is gifted or not.* Truly gifted kids are different. To date, there is no single agreed-on definition. What is agreed is that high intelligence exists and that it may be expressed in many different ways. The driving force of gifted kids is their brain—and it is fundamental to *everything* about them. Here is a list of characteristics of gifted kids, though it's important to note that not *all* characteristics will apply to your child. So look instead for a pattern.

   - *Precociousness:* clearly advanced development in a particular area; abilities are noticeably ahead of peers the same age
   - *Intense interests:* strong, *unforced* interest in reading, science, history, technology, people, music, or some other topic
   - *Extreme curiosity:* interest in experimenting and doing things differently, limitless supply of questions, vivid imagination
   - *Intense concentration:* ability to focus on a single task for long duration; high level of energy
   - *High sensitivity:* intensity in feelings, behavior, and views
   - *Divergent thinking and excellent reasoning:* tendency to put ideas or things together in ways that are unusual and not obvious; elaborate and original thinking; excellent problem-solving skills
   - *Rapid learning:* no need for repetition, practice, being pushed, or skill-and-drill
   - *Excellent memory:* remarkable retention of a great deal of information
   - *Extensive vocabulary:* unusually large vocabulary for age; great comprehension and grasp of the subtleties of language ("gets it" faster)

2. *Decide if you want your child identified as "gifted."* Although parents are usually the first to recognize that their kid is gifted, most gifted programs require the child to be officially identified for enrollment. One of your most important steps is to decide whether you want your child to be tested. Here are a few tips.

   - *Know the identification process.* To be identified as gifted, the child usually is given a standard individual IQ test administered face-to-face (not online) by a certified psychologist. That test is usually given without charge by a school district, or you may pay to have it administered by any certified psychologist in your community. An IQ of 132 is usually used as a cutoff score. Aside from the

IQ test, the school may deem a child as gifted through teacher recommendation, achievement scores, or identified talent in a particular area (such as math or music). Because IQ tests are not considered valid for children younger than four or five, you would wait at least until your child enters school.

- *Weigh the benefits.* Special funds are generally allocated by states and districts to provide gifted children with a more accelerated or enriched education tailored to their intellectual needs. Without that gifted label, your child could not enroll in the program. Would your child really benefit from that program?

- *Talk to the teacher.* If you do decide you want the test, set up a conference to discuss your decision with your child's teacher. Does she see the same potential in your child as you do? Do keep in mind that several studies have shown that teachers identify less than half of students later found to be gifted through individual testing.[77]

- *Figure out your options.* If the teacher declines your request for a test, then you may need to talk to the principal or guidance service in your school district. Ask for the specific name and version of the IQ test your school district uses to identify gifted students. You may also have to hire a credentialed psychologist in your community to test your child. Tests can be pricey, so be prepared.

- *Ask for a test interpretation.* If you do have your child tested, make sure you ask the credentialed psychologist who administered the test to interpret those results and describe those findings for you. Because gifted children are gifted only in certain areas, the results can help you discover where your child's intellectual strengths and weaknesses lie. Ask also what recommendations the psychologist might have for your child's learning. Keep in mind that test results do not have to be shared, and even if your child is identified as gifted, you certainly could decline to place her in a specialized program.

3. *Nurture your child's unique "gift."* Noted educator Benjamin Bloom and a team of researchers at the University of Chicago conducted a five-year study of 120 immensely gifted or talented young people.[78] Among them were exceptional mathematicians and scientists, concert pianists, Olympic swimmers, and accomplished sculptors. Bloom's research found that these world-class talents weren't simply born talented—they were brought up to become talented. Although each child's road to achievement differed slightly, the parents all used remarkably similar practices to nurture their child's gift. As most of us know, the odds that our children will become superstars are remote, but using these parenting practices will help your child live a richer life. Here are the steps to apply Bloom's research to nurture your child's unique gift:

- *Identify the gift.* The parents' first step was to recognize their child's unique talent. Gifted children typically show exceptional talent in one or two areas only—not in everything. So watch for areas in which your child shows intense interest or passion. Be sure it's your child's interest—not yours. Then choose one—and certainly no more than two—talents or strengths at one time so that your child can really explore that interest more in depth and you can discover just how strong the interest is.

- *Emphasize encouragement.* The parents made sure their children's early talent development was positive, fun, and *not pushed.*

- *Make practices enjoyable.* The parents made their practice times *enjoyable* and usually sat with their kids as they practiced.

- *Provide resources to cultivate the talent.* The children's talents improved because parents constantly provided the necessary resources to nurture their skills.

- *Show interest.* Parents attended every major activity to show support, and often learned the skill themselves just so they could spend more time with their child.

- *Stand by your child—win or lose.* Each superstar had an encouraging parent standing by her side, celebrating her wins and cushioning her losses.

- *Focus on the talent.* All parents placed great emphasis on their children's evident talent and spent a tremendous amount of time cultivating it over many years.

4. *Stress "natural" enrichment.* Put down the flash cards and unplug those brainy baby tapes. There is not an ounce of research to prove that all those supposedly IQ-boosting videos work. Besides, flash cards, worksheets, and curriculum guides nurture only academic achievement, not intellect. Gifted kids need rich, real experiences to quench their thirst for learning and satisfy their curiosity. They usually hate the familiar, same-old-route teaching materials and love experimentation. Once they find something that attracts them (the violin, the parts of an alarm clock, dinosaurs, rocks, or whatever!), there's no stopping them. So follow your child's lead in terms of the subjects that interest her at the moment, then find enriching classes or lessons or materials to challenge her learning. Possibilities are endless, including taking your child on field trips or to the museum, subscribing to a magazine that features the interest, checking out videos and books from the library, finding online materials designed for gifted kids, finding someone in your community to mentor your child, or participating in a summer university program designed for gifted tweens.

5. *Find the right educational match for your child.* There is no easy answer in choosing the best school for a gifted child. Just keep in mind that you'll never find the perfect program or classroom, so you will probably have to make some compromises. But these five factors do help gifted kids thrive:

The happy factor: Would your child come home excited about learning? Would she be comfortable with this teacher? Is there a guidance component to help your child "fit in"? Would she feel comfortable with these kids, and would the program help her gain a sense of social competence and learn friendship-making skills?

The identification factor: Does the program use a sound process with which to identify qualified children? Does it allow for teacher recommendations? Does it grant entry only to clearly talented and exceptional kids?

The challenge factor: Is there a challenging curriculum, based on realistic expectations, that stretches your child's mind? Are there enrichment opportunities? Are there acceleration opportunities or any flexibility in letting your child study a topic in depth?[79]

The teacher factor: Does the teacher relate well to gifted children and especially to your kid's unique temperament? Is she regularly trained in addressing the needs of gifted children and in the use of teaching methods that stress the philosophy of gifted education? Does she have a clear plan to help your child reach her potential?

The worth-it factor: Is this placement worth the time, energy, or resources it may take?

6. *Don't label.* "Should I label my child as gifted?" is a question I'm often asked. First, don't assume that gifted kids aren't already aware that they are different, even without the label. As early as three or four years of age, these children often figure out that they "get things quicker" and "think" differently from peers. But if your child is in a program specifically for the "gifted," she will need some kind of explanation. Here are things to consider:

    -   *Watch out for "trophy" status:* A feeling of entitlement ("I'm smarter") is a big turnoff. It's better to stress the idea that "Every kid has special talents that are different but no less valuable."

    -   *Don't use the "G" word.* Most gifted kids hate the term *gifted* because it makes them stand apart when they want to fit in. Most detest serving as "examples" for other kids. So downplay "You're gifted" and stress instead the specific trait in which your child excels.

    -   *Stress effort, not IQ.* A Columbia University study found that regardless of their IQ, those students labeled "smart" received *lower* grades than those kids praised for their effort.[80] So avoid saying the word "smart" (even when you know your child is) and emphasize the effort or interest she exhibits instead. Don't say "You're so smart." Say "You're putting so much effort into your project. It looks great!"

Although those extra IQ points usually make learning and test taking (and getting a higher SAT score) easier, a gifted label far from guarantees a child success. So please don't get so nearsighted that you see only your child's IQ and overlook nurturing her social, emotional, and moral side. The key premise of good parenting is the same regardless of your child's IQ: love your child for who she is—not for what you hope she becomes.

Pay Attention to This!
Traits of Gifted Kids That Might Lead to Potential Problems

Although the needs of gifted kids are for the most part the same as those of other children, there are a few traits that could lead to future problems.[81] No one issue is usually a cause for alarm, so instead look for a pattern. Here are a few warning signs to watch for:

- *Poor peer relations.* Organizing people and things and emphasizing rules cause peer resentment and low self-esteem.[82]

- *Uneven development.* Motor skills (especially fine motor) lag behind cognitive abilities, causing frustration and emotional outbursts.[83]

- *Excessive self-criticism.* Insightfulness can lead gifted kids to set idealistic images of what they might or should be and then criticize themselves when they fall short.[84]

- *Perfectionism.* Setting unrealistically high expectations for themselves significantly hinders their academic potential, boosts anxiety, and causes a fear of failure.[85]

- *Extreme sensitivity.* Emotional intensity makes gifted kids hypersensitive to criticism and vulnerable to peer teasing and bullying.[86]

- *Anxiety.* Overscheduling or a too accelerated curriculum can lead to extreme irritability, stress, sleeplessness, or depression.

WHAT TO EXPECT BY STAGES AND AGES

Preschooler   A child is seen as precocious when development in one area is clearly advanced when compared to that of peers the same age. Gifted kids at this age meet verbal milestones early, have an extensive vocabulary, and may start to read early. They are highly energized about learning and often show intense concentration in one area of interest. They also have the tendency to be bossy; they make their friends stick to rules, or try to organize others.

School Age   IQ tests are most reliable during these ages. Excellent reasoning skills become more noticeable, and a child may dart far ahead of peers in some subjects. If not challenged academically, gifted kids may complain of boredom. Make sure your child is developing necessary friendship-making skills, especially for same-age peers. Extreme sensitivity and insightfulness may cause peer problems or rejection. These kids may prefer to play with older children whose cognitive abilities are closer to theirs.

Tween   Tweens want to fit in, so being seen as "too smart" can be stressful. A social scene pushing "Smart is not cool" can be a nightmare for gifted children, so watch for deliberate attempts to disguise intelligence. Intellectual ability or talent in a particular area becomes more pronounced and may required specialized tutoring, acceleration, or a pull-out program (such

One Parent's Answer

A mom from Vancouver writes:

My son was identified as gifted in the first grade, but I knew it way before. He had an intense curiosity and unlimited supply of questions. I swear the most used word in his vocabulary is "why." While I loved Matt's thirst for knowledge, his insistence to have the answer "right then" was exhausting. And frankly half the time I didn't know the answers. So whenever I didn't know the answer, we would write the question in a journal. I promised that when I had time we would find the answer. Not only did the strategy buy me a bit of time, but Matt loved reviewing all his questions. Best of all, he learned fabulous research skills when we'd search out those answers together online.

as taking math at the high school), especially if the child's IQ is 145 or above. Studies find that when gifted kids are given appropriately challenging environments—even when that means being placed in classes of much older students—they usually adjust well and turn out fine.[87] The real problem lies in failing to offer appropriate acceleration.

Learning Disabilities

SEE ALSO: *Attention Deficit, Gives Up, Homework, Hooked on Rewards, Impulsive, Reading, Teacher Conference, Test Anxiety*

THE QUESTION

"Learning is difficult for my son, and he struggles so in school. How do I know if he has a learning disability and should be tested to see if he needs a special kind of remediation?"

THE ANSWER

One of the harder parts of parenting is watching our children struggle, but the sad truth is that learning isn't easy for some kids, and because so much of their day is spent in school, their self-esteem can take a real nosedive.

"Learning disorders (LD) occur when a child's academic achievement in a specific subject is significantly below what would be expected for their age, school experience, and intellectual ability."[88] Reading difficulties account for about 80 percent of learning disabilities.[89] As a former special education teacher, I'll be the first to tell you that there are no easy answers to the challenges learning disabilities pose; it would take an entire book to describe all the different types of learning disabilities that have been identified and the strategies appropriate to each. But just to give you a quick, introductory view of these problems, here are a few of the key solutions to help you get started:

- *Make the teacher your ally.* As soon as you suspect that your child may have a learning disability, arrange to have a conference with the teacher and try to create a partnership. Your child's teacher is the individual best able to give you the most impartial evaluation of how your child ranks in comparison to his peers. She can tell you whether your concerns are grounded and advise you as to the type of environment and programs that would best help your child. She is also the first connection in the school who can help you find additional learning services for your child. (See *Teacher Conference,* p. 458.)

- *Get learning specifics.* Your child most likely is not struggling in all learning areas. Your task is to discover the subjects or type of work with which your child has the most difficulty and the areas in which he finds success or even enjoyment. Watch a bit more closely as he does his homework. Listen as he talks about school. Ask the teacher what she considers his learning strengths and weaknesses. For instance, which subjects does he enjoy most and least? Then jot down those findings. You will need them to help you develop a learning plan.

- *Know how your child learns best.* Dr. Howard Gardner, of Harvard University, has developed a theory that every child is born with a unique combination of eight intelligences and learns best when he uses those that are his strongest.[90] To help you determine your child's unique strengths, read the descriptions of the eight intelligences Gardner has identified, then try to match your child's strengths with learning strategies that support that strength, so as to reduce his struggle. Your child's teacher should be able to help you. For more information, read *7 Kinds of Smart,* by Thomas Armstrong, and *Frames of Mind,* by Howard Gardner. Here are those eight learning strengths to watch for in your child:

  1. *Linguistic learners* like to read, write, and tell stories. They learn by hearing and seeing words, have advanced vocabularies, memorize facts verbatim, and know unusual amounts of information.

  2. *Bodily/kinesthetic learners* handle their bodies with ease and poise for their age, are adept at using their body for sports or artistic expression, and are skilled in fine motor tasks.

  3. *Intrapersonal learners* have strong self-understanding, are original, enjoy working alone to pursue their own interests and goals, and have a strong sense of right and wrong.

  4. *Interpersonal learners* understand people, lead and organize others, have lots of friends, are looked to by others to make decisions and mediate conflicts, and enjoy joining groups.

  5. *Musical learners* appreciate rhythm, pitch, and melody, and they respond to music. They remember melodies, keep time, may play instruments, and like to sing and hum tunes.

  6. *Logical/mathematical learners* understand numbers, patterns, and relationships, and they enjoy science and math. They categorize, ask questions, do experiments, and figure things out.

  7. *Spatial learners* like to draw, design, and create things, and to daydream and use their imagination. They remember what they see, enjoy reading maps and charts, and work well with colors and pictures.

  8. *Naturalists* like the out-of-doors, are curious, and classify the features of the environment.

- *Rule out potential contributors.* There are a number of factors that can make learning more difficult and reduce your child's ability to focus and attend. So before you get too carried away with testing data, reflect on all those factors that might be upping your child's "struggle quotient" and then reduce those variables. Here are a few factors to consider:

Hearing: Could allergies, a hearing loss, or swimmer's ear be contributing to his inability to hear directions?

Vision: Can your child see the board from far away or read his work close up? Has your child had his vision checked?

Attention: Could your child have ADD or ADHD? (See *Attention Deficit,* p. 466.) Could a prescribed medication be reducing his focusing ability? Ask the pharmacist for a printout of the side effects any medication your child may be taking.

Stress: Is there family conflict, trauma, a recent accident, grief, or bullying happening that could be contributing? (See *Stressed,* p. 303.)

Sleep: Is your child getting restful sleep? (See *Sleepless,* p. 585.)

Eating habits: Is he skipping breakfast or lunch?

Teacher: Does she have a rapport with your child, use best teaching practices, and tailor her expectations so that he can succeed?

Class environment: Is the classroom too noisy, crowded, or busy?

Social scene: Is your child with other students who support and build him up?

- *View test results.* Ask for the results of any standardized achievement tests your child has taken. These results will let you know how well your child is doing academically when compared to peers. Don't be too timid to ask that they been interpreted for you. Also ask to see classroom test results in the teacher's grade book. If those results are consistently too low, then ask the teacher if the work expectations are too high. Is your child in the correct reading or math placement?

- *Consider hiring a tutor.* If homework is a struggle between you and your child and if school tests and grades continue to slide, you may want to hire a tutor. Private tutoring can be pricey, so consider hiring a high school student or even a retired teacher. Also ask the teacher for recommendations. Make sure you work closely with the teacher so that she gives the tutor specific recommendations as to exactly what your child should be studying. (See "Does Your Child Need a Tutor?" in *Homework,* p. 435.)

- *Decide to evaluate your child.* If the struggle continues and your child's grades or test scores do not improve despite your efforts, then it may be time to have your child evaluated for learning disabilities. Do know that in order to determine if your child has a learning disability, he must undergo a series of tests given by a credentialed and trained learning specialist or psychologist. Measures generally include a standardized academic achievement test to assess your child's current age and grade level, and an IQ test to assess intellectual abilities. Usually a learning disability is diagnosed if the child shows a significant difference between his academic achievement and his IQ. Begin at the school level by asking the teacher to see if she will recommend testing. A school psychologist will administer those tests without charge (or you could pay an outside clinician, but only hire someone who is appropriately credentialed and licensed; check with the school psychologist or call your district psychology department).

- *Decide if remediation is needed.* Keep in mind that your child may not qualify for remediation or a special class placement despite the results of the evaluation process. The results must prove that your child's learning struggle warrants special remediation. And those programs vary widely in each school, district, and state. Listen carefully to the options for your child. Most schools are currently implementing what is called Response to Intervention approach to learning disabilities. The school places a struggling student in a remedial class tailored to his difficulties. If that class meets the student's needs, the remediation continues. If the child does not respond, then further testing is done. Other schools use a resource teacher and pull the child out of class for a few hours a week for specialized instruction. If the child's learning disabilities are more severe, a special class or school may be required to help your child. The key is to make sure the teacher is *trained* and *credentialed* in learning disabilities. Retention rarely works to help a struggling child. Your child will need a different type of teaching approach tailored specifically to his unique learning needs.

- *Nurture self-esteem.* Any child struggling with learning needs a boost in confidence. So look for areas in which your child can succeed, and support those interests. Public speaking, music, karate, archery, soccer, art, computer programming—strength possibilities are endless, but the trick is to match your child's natural strengths with an outside interest and then cultivate that area so that he has an opportunity to shine.

Meanwhile, keep empathizing with your child. Learning will not be easy for him, but new teaching strategies for children with learning disabilities are promising. So continue to seek out the best teachers, programs, and strategies that are tailored to your child's specific needs, and never stop advocating for your child.

Overweight

SEE ALSO: *Depressed, Eating Disorders, Grief, Picky Eater, Sleepless, Stressed, TV Addiction, Video Games*

THE PROBLEM

Red Flags

Has poor eating habits, sedentary lifestyle; can't physically keep up with peers; is rejected or teased for weight; uses bulky clothes to hide body; engages in constant mealtime battles

The Change to Parent For

Your child learns a healthier eating regime and becomes more physically active, which helps him slow or stop weight gain as well as develop a healthier lifestyle.

Question: "My son is very large for his age, but my husband wants him to gain so he'll play football and get a scholarship. I worry he'll get picked on and be at risk for health problems. How do I know if my child is overweight or obese or just a big-sized kid?"

Answer: The best way to determine what the normal weight is for your son is to talk to his doctor, who can check growth charts tailored to your child's gender, age, and height. The following are two signs that your child may be at risk for childhood obesity:

1. The child's weight starts to increase at a faster rate than his height after age three. Ask the doctor also to calculate your child's body mass index (BMI, or ratio of height to weight) to see if it is in the healthy range.

2. The child's weight for his height is above the 85th percentile (overweight) or 95th percentile (obese) on standardized growth charts, and his weight is at least 20 percent higher than other kids his gender, age, and height.[91]

   Kids are considered obese when their total body weight is more than 25 percent fat in boys and more than 32 percent in girls.[92] If you are at all concerned, don't wait. The sooner you help your child learn to adopt sensible eating habits, choose food wisely, and get adequate exercise, the better his chances are for long-term health.

Why Change?

Reports from the medical community are almost unanimous: the generation of youth we are raising may well be one of smartest, but also one of the unhealthiest and least active.[93] Childhood obesity now impacts almost one in six of our children, and has more than tripled since 1970.[94] Although the latest research shows that the rate of childhood obesity may be slightly leveling off, about 32 percent of kids and teens are either overweight or obese.[95] Make no mistake: the long-term consequences of obesity are *very* serious. Overweight and obese kids not only have a much higher likelihood of suffering from headaches,[96] sleep apnea, high blood pressure, diabetes, asthma, hypertension, stroke, and heart disease but also face higher rates of peer rejection, low self-esteem, and depression.[97]

This is not an ailment that is fixable with pills or vaccines, but instead involves a total family commitment to a new lifestyle. And the change has far-reaching benefits: it will help your kid grow to be not only physically healthier but also happier and more emotionally healthy. He'll even do better in school: a study at the San Diego State University found that fit kids scored higher on several components of academic achievement.[98] Although not all obese infants become obese adults,[99] there is a greater likelihood that obesity that begins in early childhood will persist throughout life. Beware: most overweight kids *do* grow to become overweight adults.

Although there is a genetic component to obesity, the latest research also shows that parents have a significant and lasting influence on their children's weight as well as health. And your first step to change is recognizing that your child has a weight problem. A study of more than eleven hundred families found that 89 percent of parents of overweight five- to six-year-olds and 63 percent of parents of overweight ten- to twelve-years-olds were unaware that their child was overweight.[100] So what are you waiting for?

LATE-BREAKING NEWS

Limit Television Viewing (or Just Turn It OFF!)

Research finds that *the single most influential factor that helps kids lose weight is reduced TV viewing time.*[101] So turn off the television or at least limit your child's viewing time and then help him find active things to do instead. At least make your kid do jumping jacks through the length of each commercial. The trick is to get your kid up from the couch and moving.

Signs and Symptoms

Every child's body type is different, but here are signs that you need to keep a closer watch on your child's weight, physical activity, and eating habits and perhaps to seek medical advice:

- Describes himself as "too fat" or "too ugly"; obsesses about his appearance; constantly compares himself to others; overriding feeling of shame about his body; expresses concerns about his weight

- Assesses weight unrealistically; says he's "just right" when he's clearly overweight

- Engages in constant food battles; you're always scolding, bribing, or prodding him not to eat so much

- Experiences a rapid weight gain (don't rule out steroids)

- Avoids eating regularly, refuses meals, skips lunch or breakfast as an attempt to drop weight

- Snacks constantly on high-calorie, unhealthy foods or sweets

- Spends large portion of free time watching TV, playing video games, or using the computer

- Is teased by peers for his weight or called names like Fatso, Lard, or Fatty

- Experiences a sudden and uncharacteristic change in personality or behavior: sullen, irritable, depressed; wants to steer clear of school functions or public outings; has a dip in self-esteem

- Has low energy level; weight makes it difficult to keep up with peers in physical activities

Pay Attention to This!
Signs of Binge Eating

Binge eating is the frequent eating of uncontrolled amounts of food, but with no purging (vomiting or using laxatives). It is now the most common eating disorder, and research shows that childhood obesity may be associated with its development,[102] so watch for the signs: uncontrolled eating binges followed by excuses as to where all your food supply went; eating a lot of food quickly and then feeling ashamed or disgusted by the amount eaten; skipping meals and then eating at unusual times, such as late at night; and hiding food wrappers. Kids with this disorder tend to be obese, or they are older girls who diet frequently and then binge. *If you have seen these signs, do not wait to get help.*

THE SOLUTION

Step 1. Early Intervention

- *Find the cause.* There is never one factor that causes kids to be overweight. Your first role is to dig a bit deeper to analyze what may be causing this problem, and then alter what you can fix. The following is a list of possible issues. Check those that may apply to your child or situation. Don't blame the gene pool for your kid's eating habits: they are learned and changeable.

  ☐ *Diet.* Food servings are mainly high in calories and fats; desserts and sweets are daily staples; your child frequently eats out, eats a lot of fast food, eats large portions; school lunches are full of fat.

  ☐ *Food bribes.* "Clean your plate" is your family mantra; your child is praised or rewarded for eating everything, so he doesn't learn to stop eating when full.

  ☐ *Medical condition.* Certain medicines or medical conditions, such as an inactive thyroid, can trigger a chemical imbalance.

  ☐ *Sedentary lifestyle.* Your child's favorite leisure activities—watching television, playing video games, or sitting at the computer—are inactive, so he doesn't burn off calories.

  ☐ *Heredity.* With one obese parent, a child is twice as likely to become overweight.[103]

  ☐ *Limited physical activity.* Recess has been reduced or cut at school; your child is overscheduled, so he has limited time for physical activities; community or housing area is not conducive to physical exercise.

  ☐ *Emotional factors.* Your child overeats to cope with problems or deal with stress, low self-esteem, or boredom.

  ☐ *Food advertising.* Your child is influenced by commercials featuring unhealthy, high-calorie choices.

  ☐ *Unhealthy parental example.* You serve high-calorie food and rarely exercise; healthy eating is not high on your priority list.

  ☐ *Not enough Z's.* Inadequate sleep increases a child's risk of becoming overweight.[104] Each additional hour of sleep reduces a child's chances of becoming overweight or obese by 9 percent. (See *Sleepless,* p. 585, for the recommended amount of sleep per age.)

What is your best guess as to why your child is overweight? What one simple solution can you use to help your child and your family learn healthier eating habits?

- *Look in the mirror.* Take a moment to assess your example when you are with your children. Could your daily eating habits and lifestyle be influencing your child's weight problem? For instance:

Do you talk about dieting, weight gain, dress size?

Do you obsess about how you look or how much you eat?

Do you eat junk food and stock up on those fad diets?

Does your family eat out more than once a week and frequent fast-food restaurants?

Do you serve nutritious and lower-calorie meals consistently to your family?

Do you serve big portions, encourage your child's eating by praising him for finishing everything on his plate, or dish out second helpings of desserts?

Do you criticize your child for his weight and eating habits?

Do you avoid confronting your child about his weight for fear of hurting his self-esteem or creating a conflict? Or are you in denial that your child is overweight?

Do you eat as a way to cope with your own problems?

Are you overweight? Have you been unsuccessful with past diets? Do you pass on your "Diets don't work" or "You can't lose weight" attitude to your child?

Do you have a sedentary lifestyle, watch television often, and exercise infrequently?

Watch out: your example does influence your kids. Is there anything you can do to change your own habits so that you can help your child be healthier and happier?

- *Get a medical assessment.* Talk to your doctor. Make sure there is no physical or emotional reason for a rapid weight gain. Ask her to assess your child's BMI (see the One Simple Solution box) and recommend the best approach to help your child lose weight. New research also shows that when kids become obese, their blood pressure tends to climb along with their weight, putting them at risk for long-term organ damage and other health problems in adulthood.[105] Ask your physician to check your child's blood pressure and to tell you how often your child should be assessed.

Step 2. Rapid Response

- *Don't nag about weight.* Although exercise and healthy eating are critical to weight change, how you respond to your child's eating habits does make a difference. Instead of imposing rigid, calorie-counting rituals on your kid, stress "eating in moderation" and then teach generally healthier eating habits. Nagging, scolding, or criticizing your kid's eating habits will get you nowhere. In fact, doing so is likely to backfire. Studies show that for both boys and girls, being encouraged to diet by a parent roughly triples the likelihood of the child's still being overweight five years later.[106] So halt those "You've had enough!" comments.

- *Limit fast-food intake.* Over half of all families surveyed admitted to eating fast-food meals a couple of times a week.[107] Just know that eating at a restaurant generally means a minimum of two hundred more calories per meal than if you ate at home.[108] Also, kids consume far fewer vegetables, fruits, and milk. When you do eat out, steer your kids towards *healthier* food choices.

- *Be available and build self-esteem.* You play a

ONE SIMPLE SOLUTION

Calculate Your Child's Body Mass Index (BMI) Once a Year

Body mass index (BMI), the ratio of weight to height, is considered one of the most accurate measurements of body fat, and is often used as a screening indicator to identify possible weight problems. The American Academy of Pediatrics recommends that you calculate your child's BMI at least once a year. Just multiply his weight in pounds by 703. Divide that number by his height in inches. Then divide that quotient by his height in inches again. For example, a 55-pound, 50-inch-tall child would have a BMI of about 15. If you can't figure this out, ask your physician to do so. He or she should also tell you what a healthy BMI index would be for your child's age and height.

crucial role not only in helping your child control his weight and have healthier eating habits but also in making him feel accepted and loved. Be sensitive to the possibility that your child is being teased and possibly rejected by his peers, in addition to feeling discouraged about his weight. Make yourself more available and listen carefully to how he feels about his weight and life. Let him know you support him and will help him develop a healthier lifestyle. Don't overlook the possibility that there is an emotional trigger to your child's overeating—a distressing issue or a need for attention.

- *Hide the scale.* A study of more than two thousand teens who weighed themselves frequently found that they were more likely to resort to bingeing, skipping meals, taking diet pills, using laxatives, and vomiting.[109] And instead of losing weight, those who stepped on the scales gained nearly twice as much as those kids who didn't.

- *Watch out for TV food commercials.* The average child is exposed to over forty thousand television commercials per year, and 80 percent of those feature fast food, sugar-laced cereals, and candy.[110] Those ads do influence our kids. In fact, several studies link the dramatic rise in childhood obesity over the past few years to the increase in advertisements for unhealthy foods, sodas, and fast food that are aimed at kids. Don't let TV commercials influence your child's eating habits. Hit the mute button when those commercials air, and encourage family members at least to get off that couch and do jumping jacks until the food advertisement is over. Boost your kid's media literacy; help him recognize that the real aim of those ads is to sell, sell, sell—not to help your child's nutrition intake.

- *Help your child stay active.* University of Minnesota Medical School found that overweight kids who lost weight were successful because they participated in vigorous physical activity.[111] So find an activity your kid enjoys and then encourage him to stick with it until it becomes a habit. Turning this into a family affair will help everyone become healthier and happier together. Here are a few ideas:

  - *Turn your kid on to a fun active hobby.* Skateboarding, karate, weightlifting, boxing, dancing, jumping rope, horseback riding, or whatever meets your kid's fancy.

  - *Use the backyard.* Set up a jungle gym or basketball hoop in your yard.

  - *Find a healthy outlet in your community.* Your child could join a sports team (soccer, baseball, basketball, hockey, or the like); sign him up for gymnastics or swimming at the local community center or for dance classes at the YMCA.

  - *Turn your garage into a gym.* Find a used treadmill, weights, or stationary bike at a garage sale and set them up. Overweight girls who lost weight often participated in weight training and strengthening exercises, so don't overlook those barbells.[112]

  - *Start a mother-daughter exercise club.* Invite another mom and daughter (preferably your child's pal) to join you and your daughter to do Pilates or yoga in your home.

  - *Buy a pedometer.* The American Academy of Pediatrics urges boys to walk at least eleven thousand steps each day and girls at least thirteen thousand.[113] Clipping a pedometer on every family member can turn walking into a fun challenge: Who can walk the most steps today?

  - *Get an exergaming system.* Research finds that activity-oriented videos games that require kids to walk on a treadmill while dancing, kicking, and dodging (such as Dance Dance Revolution and the EyeToy) triples the energy expenditure of mildly obese children.[114] Dance video games that use the exergaming systems increase energy expenditure by a factor of six for more obese kids. Turning on the right video game actually may help kids get in shape.

- *Use books to teach nutrition habits.* Consider using children's literature to teach your child about nutrition and new eating and exercise habits. Here are a few books that help kids learn those lessons in a fun and engaging way: *Too Much,* by Linda T. West; *The Race Against Junk Food,* by Anthony Buono; *Eat Healthy, Feel Great,* by William Sears; *Eating the Alphabet,* by Lois Ehlert; *Showdown at the Food Pyramid,* by Rex Barron.

Step 3. Develop Habits for Change

- *Set realistic goals.* Begin by helping your child set a weight-loss goal of one pound—and no more than two—per month so that he doesn't become discouraged.[115] Then keep in mind that the real goal isn't just to have your kid lose weight but to slow or stop weight gain, learn to eat right, and be more active in order to be healthy. Studies also show that the most effective kid weight management programs usually involve several elements, such as a diet change, an exercise plan, and periodic monitoring by a doctor; they also *include the whole family.*[116] So stress "health" and "exercise," and downplay "diet" and "weight loss" in your plan. And praise any efforts—big or small—your child makes in changing his eating and exercise habits.

- *Change your family's eating habits.* Research shows that those on a diet may actually be *more likely to gain weight over time.* A better approach to changing your kid's weight status is "putting more emphasis on making your home environment healthier and more conducive to healthier weight management."[117] Here are thirteen proven strategies to slowly incorporate healthier eating habits into your lifestyle; they'll help everyone, but especially overweight kids.

ONE SIMPLE SOLUTION

Teach the "Traffic Light" Diet

A proven tool that helps kids significantly change their eating patterns is the "Traffic Light" diet.[118] The colors of a traffic light are assigned to foods based on their nutritional value and fat content. Green "Go" foods, such as broccoli, carrots, and celery sticks, are safe to eat in any quantity; yellow "Caution" foods, such as tuna and low-fat yogurt, are to be eaten in moderation; red "Stop" foods are ones generally to be avoided: french fries, sodas, and donuts. One study found that the diet continued to affect the eating habits of kids five to ten years after treatment began.

1. *Offer smaller portions.* Consider serving food on smaller plates with small portions.

2. *Don't give second helpings.* Serve food once (not family style) and then put food away.

3. *Make healthy snacks handy.* Reduce junk-food eating by preparing healthier snacks.

4. *Don't ban.* Forbidding favorite foods sets kids up for failure; instead serve them "every so often."

5. *Count calories.* Cut higher-calorie items; limit fat intake and sweets; broil and grill instead of frying; serve leaner meats and a variety of protein sources: fish, eggs, beans, and nuts.

6. *Cut sodas.* Replace sodas and other sugary drinks with water and low-fat milk.

7. *Don't rush meals.* You eat more when you eat quickly. Tell everyone to chew slowly.

8. *Eat in moderation.* Encourage kids to stop when they're full instead of urging them to "clean their plate."

9. *Don't single out the overweight kid.* Serve everyone the same food and portions.

10. *Sit, don't stand.* Standing to snack at the kitchen counter increases kids' food intake. To discourage "mindless" eating, insist that everyone eat meals at the table together.

11. *Don't watch TV during meals.* Aside from promoting inactivity, TV is distracting and leads to overeating.

12. *Eat breakfast.* A study of over two thousand teens found that those who ate a daily breakfast consumed a healthier diet and were far less likely to overeat later in the day.[119]

13. *Don't give up!* It often takes ten to fifteen tries for a kid to like a new food. So don't force the food (and create a battle), but do keep serving healthier, lower-calorie food alternatives.

- *Involve your child in the change.* A key to learning new habits is empowering your child in the process so that he has a personal stake in what and how he eats and then is more likely to *want* to change. Have him help you dump that junk food from your cupboards. Get him involved in shopping, meal planning, choosing recipes, or even growing a vegetable garden. Teach him how to make simple but good-tasting and healthier snack options. Ask him to help you chop up veggies and keep them readily available in the fridge. Ask him what kind of exercise program he'd like to start. Encourage him to monitor his own eating habits and keep a log of how many calories he eats.

- *Be patient and steadfast.* Don't expect this to be an overnight process. Be patient and consistent with your plan. Research shows that a critical key to change is a parent's ongoing involvement in helping her child learn healthier eating and exercise habits. So stay the course and know you are making a difference in your child's life for now and the future.

WHAT TO EXPECT BY STAGES AND AGES

Preschooler   Three- to six-year-olds shouldn't weigh more than eight pounds above the average for their height and age.[120] Prevalence of overweight for children ages two to five years old has more than doubled in the past two decades;[121] about 12 percent of kids are obese.[122] This is the best time to start teaching healthy eating habits and to watch weight. Research shows that kids who are overweight as toddlers or preschoolers are more likely to be overweight in early adolescence.[123]

One Parent's Answer

A mom from Tampa shares:

A group of parents were talking one day about how inactive our kids were, and then we realized that most of them are carpooled or bused to school. So on a designated day each week, we now walk our kids to school. My son not only has lost weight but looks forward to meeting the other kids for the walks. And I'm saving money on gas.

NOTE: To organize a walk-to-school program in your town, visit www.cdc .gov/nc/cdphp/dnpa/kidswalk and then start walking!

School Age   Tune in to your child: 90 percent of parents of overweight five- to six-year-olds failed to recognize that their child had a weight problem.[124] Obesity in kids six to eleven years of age has almost tripled in two decades and brings more than a tenfold risk of a youngster growing into an obese adult.[125] After age six, a child shouldn't weigh more than fifteen pounds above average. Television and video game consumption contributes to a sedentary lifestyle and obesity. Five- to seven-year-old girls restricted from eating snacks were more likely to overeat than peers.[126] So don't ban snacks, but offer healthier choices instead—carrot and celery sticks, water, pretzels, and so on.

Tween   Tween girls are more likely to become overweight between the ages of nine and twelve than during their teenage years.[127] Fast-food consumption as well as peer pressure are major influences on eating habits; tweens begin adopting the eating habits of friends instead of heeding parents' dietary advice. Physical activity declines due to overscheduling and heavier homework loads.

SPECIAL NEEDS

More Helpful Advice

A Parent's Guide to Childhood Obesity: A Roadmap to Health, by the American Academy of Pediatrics and Sandra G. Hassink

Conquering Childhood Obesity for Dummies, by Kimberly A. Tessmer, Michelle Hagen, and Meghan Beecher

Overcoming Childhood Obesity, by Colleen Thomason and Ellen Shanley

Secrets of Feeding a Healthy Family, by Ellen Satter

Underage and Overweight: America's Childhood Obesity Epidemic—What Every Parents Needs to Know, by Frances M. Berg

Weight Loss Confidential: How Teens Lose Weight and Keep It Off—and What They Wish Parents Knew, by Anne Fletcher

Part 8
Day to Day

OUT OF THE MOUTHS OF BABES
WHY GOD MADE MOMS

Answers given by second-grade schoolchildren to the following question:

What would it take to make your mom perfect?

1. On the inside she's already perfect.
Outside, I think some kind of plastic surgery.

2. Diet. You know, her hair. I'd diet, maybe blue.

Bathroom Battles

SEE ALSO: *Chores, Dependent*

THE QUESTION

"I know it's important for my child to brush her teeth, but it causes the biggest bathroom battle, and she makes up the most outrageous excuses: 'My toothbrush flew away' and 'There's a hole in the sink.' There has to be some kind of simple solution to get my kid to brush her teeth. Help!"

THE ANSWER

Of course we know that oral health is important, but despite our best efforts, nearly half of parents polled say they experience resistance from their kids to brushing their teeth.[1] And brushing is important. Fifty percent of five- to nine-year-olds will have a cavity or filling.[2] Here are solutions to curb annoying bathroom battles, teach good oral hygiene habits, and even make brushing fun:

- *Set an example.* Kids learn faster if you show the proper way to do a task, so don't overlook taking the time to show your child proper oral hygiene habits. Then model good oral hygiene yourself.

- *Let your child choose.* Seek floss and colorful, fun toothbrushes with playful designs tailored to your child's mouth size. Some kids are sensitive to tastes and smells, so make sure the toothpaste passes *her* taste bud standards. If she still gags, try a tooth brushing powder.

- *Show how.* Teach how to use dab of toothpaste only the size of a pinky finger-nail (too much makes kids gag). Battery-operated toothbrushes ensure that kids brush with the circular motions that are recommended by dentists (but they aren't a must). A young kid can pretend her toothbrush is a train so that she slides her brush over the teeth "tracks" while making fun train noises.[3] If she still rushes, use a child's mouthwash like Listerine Smart Rinse that can provide an extra dose of cavity-fighting fluoride. (It also tints any remaining particles in a child's mouth so that she'll see them when she spits into the sink and realize she needs to do a better cleaning job the next time.)

- *Add "timekeepers."* Most kids don't brush the full dentist-recommended two minutes, so have your kid sing "Happy Birthday" three times, count backwards from 120, or set a timer for two minutes.

- *Create a routine.* Predictability helps kids form habits, so have your child brush at the same time in the morning (such as right after breakfast) and at night (when she puts on her pajamas) so that brushing becomes a ritual. Younger kids love plopping stickers on a chart (or bathroom mirror) each time they brush.

Tooth decay is one of the most common chronic infectious diseases among American kids these days, so do insist that your kid brush.[4] Remember that although bottled water is a great alternative to sodas and fruit drinks, it doesn't have cavity-preventing fluoride like most tap water. And if your child still uses those toothbrush excuses, use the tried-and-true "parent test": insist that she give you a great big breath along with a hug so you can check to see if she really did brush. If not, send her back to the bathroom to try again.

Boredom

SEE ALSO: *Dependent, Fearful, Gives Up, Indecisive, Overscheduled, Procrastinates, Stressed, TV Addiction, Video Games*

THE QUESTION

"'*Mom, I'm bored*' makes most parents go absolutely bonkers. The phrase is as old as the hills and every kid is bound to whine every now and then, but I swear kids today say it far more. How can I deal with my child's constant complaint that she's bored?"

THE ANSWER

I think there are two reasons for the supposed "kid boredom epidemic."

First, much of children's days are structured and adult directed—from playgroups and school to sports, practices, and lessons. (After all, there usually is a teacher, coach, babysitter, or parent at their beck and call to direct, program, or entertain. Right?) So your child may feel that she needs constant direction and doesn't know what to do without it.

Second, parents have bought into a huge myth that kids must be entertained with quality stimulation every waking hour. Not to do so means a certain and irrevocable loss to their mental aptitude. But the research-based truth is that kids' brains *do not* need constant stimulation. (Really truly!) In fact, scientists contend that periodic "unstructured time" exercises a different part of kids' brains that develops their creative side.[5]

But there's another reason to hail the virtues of "having nothing to do": these magnificent kids of ours are among the smartest crop ever raised, but they are also one of the most stressed-out generations. And they are also the first to admit it. A KidsHealth poll found that 41 percent of kids feel stressed most or all of the time because they have *too much* to do.[6] Children need that great commodity called "nothing time" if for nothing more than to decompress, enjoy their own company, and take in the world around them—look at the clouds, feel grass between their toes, watch a ladybug, or just contemplate. And there are proven benefits to learning to deal with boredom and self-entertain. Folks who are ranked low on a "boredom-prone" scale are found to perform better in their education and career and to have a higher degree of self-sufficiency.[7]

Here are a few solutions to help your child (and you) deal with unstructured time:

- *Ease the guilt.* Those unplanned moments help kids recharge and learn crucial life skills—such as creative thinking, resourcefulness, and problem solving—that you can't learn when everything is so programmed and supervised. Research also shows that encouraging "nothing time" or daydreaming helps produce brain waves that boost creativity.[8] So let go of the guilt and get rid of those concerns that you're hindering your kid's brain power if you don't plan every moment with intellectually stimulating and programmed stuff.

- *Set goals in baby steps.* Your job is *not* to play social director for your kids, so don't feel the need to rush in to fill their every waking minute. Set a goal that your child will *slowly* learn to self-entertain. If your child is used to always having someone "show, tell, and solve," this may be a bit of an adjustment. So start by setting aside a short portion of unstructured time tailored to your child's age and maturity, and gradually increase that length as your child increases in her ability to play alone.

- *Identify the real problem.* "I'm bored" is really a catch-all term kids use when they can't put into words what's really bugging them. The biggest challenge is often figuring out what your child means by "bored." The following is a list of common reasons for boredom claims. Check ones that may apply to your child:

  ☐ *Is overscheduled.* Life is so programmed and supervised that there is little downtime, and when there is, your child doesn't know what to do with it.

  ☐ *Is addicted to electronics.* Your child relies on passive forms of entertainment, such as TV, video games, or the computer, so she doesn't know how to respond to an unplugged world.

  ☐ *Lacks outside interests.* Nothing grabs your kid's passion; she lacks a hobby with which to entertain herself.

  ☐ *Tries to avoid tasks.* Your child finds a task too difficult or frustrating and uses boredom as an excuse to get out of completing it.

  ☐ *Has been rescued too often.* Your child is used to your entertaining her and offering suggestions.

  ☐ *Feels neglected or want approval.* Your child hangs around you because she wants attention.

  ☐ *Lacks understanding.* Your child isn't following directions or connecting to the material.[9]

  ☐ *Lacks challenge.* Activities and tasks are too predictable, not stimulating, uninteresting, or too easy.

- *Offer boredom busters.* Although your goal is for your kids to create their own solutions for boredom, they may need a little jump-start if they're used to always being entertained. Try these tips to use as you help your kids gradually become resourceful and rely less on you.

  - *Create a boredom-buster box.* Ask your kids to use paper slips to draw or write down ways to bust boredom; collect the slips in a shoebox. Anytime your kids complain that there's nothing to do, tell them to read their suggestions. You might also add a few boredom-buster ideas that you know your kids enjoy and can do on their own but may be forgetting, such as doing a puzzle, drawing, and reading.

- *Rotate toys and games.* If your child is "bored" with the same toys and games, hide some and then pull them out a few weeks later. They'll seem like brand new. You can also rotate toys with another parent as well.

- *Read.* Give your kids a magazine subscription, check out library books, use books on tape, buy them a cookbook, make the sports page available. Get your kids to read!

- *Extend your child's "boredom threshold."* Today's kids are raised in a culture of instant gratification, constant stimulation, and activity, activity, activity. So downtime or waiting can throw them into a tizzy. If your child is at loose ends, then help her stretch her boredom tolerance. Make her *wait,* without interrupting. Encourage her to do projects that can be stretched to longer than one sitting; for example, she can start with a 25-piece puzzle, then a 100-piece one, then finally one with 1,000 pieces. Or if she loves to draw, then get her a sketchbook so that she can do several drawings instead of just one or two. Insist that your kids sit through the museum lecture or that church session. And don't plan one activity after another. Periodically build in unscheduled time so that your child is forced to handle unplanned moments.

- *Cut back on electronics.* TV and video games can be an easy way out for a kid who can't think of anything to do. They also rob kids of the opportunity to develop creativity and resourcefulness. So set limits on electronic entertainment and then make your kid keep track of daily viewing hours on a paper, or set the timer from your TV's remote for the total minutes allowed per day. (See also *TV Addiction,* p. 618, or *Video Games,* p. 621.)

- *Boost creativity.* Schoolwork stretches academics and your child's cognitive development, but don't forget about helping her learn to think outside the box so that she is also resourceful. Here are ideas to get your kids' creative juices flowing as well as bust those "there's nothing to do" complaints:

  Boxes and sheets. Provide a cardboard box, masking tape, and colored markers and let your child's imagination go wild. The creative possibilities are endless—your kids can build ships, castles, garages, stores, hotels—and best yet, all that fun is free. Put sheets over boxes, chairs, and beds, and kids can create villages and forts. Turning off the lights and giving out flashlights add a whole new dimension.

  Costumes. Fill a bin with old clothes, hats, bath towels (for capes and skirts), and fabrics. Throw in safety pins and encourage your kids to start their own theatre troupe: they can write, direct, and perform plays (for the neighborhood, their family, or certainly Grandma and Grandpa) or just have fun dressing up.

Arts and crafts. Stock a drawer or bin with craft items, such as glue, pipe cleaners, crayons, paper, scissors, and marking pens. Keep recyclable items, such as cereal boxes, paper tubes, Popsicle sticks, magazines, and newspapers. Sidewalk chalk is great for drawing murals on the driveway.

- *Help your child find a passion.* Kids generally have plenty they could do to occupy their time, which is why parents are frustrated when their kids complain that "there's nothing to do." Boredom stems not from lack things to do but from the child's inability to latch on to a specific activity and feel engaged.[10] If your child doesn't have a hobby, it's time for one: guitar, carpentry, knitting, yoga, drawing, photography, macramé, or cooking. Or encourage your child to start a collection, be it rocks, flowers, bugs, coins, or stamps. The trick is to help her find a natural passion that is available during those "do-nothing times," and then give her the tools and skills to support that passion.

- *Listen but don't rescue.* When your kid says, "I'm bored," listen and even agree, "I get bored sometimes myself" or "I can understand," but curb the urge to solve her problem by arranging something to do. Try a broken-record response using sounds not words, such as "Umm," "Ahh," "Ohh," or "Uh-huh," until your kid gets the hint that you're not about to bail her out. If your child continues coming to you for entertainment ideas, ask "What can *you* do?" Remember, the aim is to help your child learn to be resourceful and not have to rely on you as her source of entertainment.

The absolute last thing I'm suggesting you do is to implement all these solutions. But why not try just *one* thing with your kids and then stick to it until you see their boredom threshold increase? And then if one of your kids dares to say "I'm bored!" offer the perfect solution. Point to a list of household chores that you just happen to have taped to the fridge. I bet you anything your child will quickly find something to do.

Chores

SEE ALSO: *Back Talk, Bathroom Battles, Dependent, Hooked on Rewards, Money, Procrastinates*

THE PROBLEM
Red Flags

Resists or refuses to help out; doesn't follow through on tasks; uses deception or argues to avoid work; won't cooperate; doesn't grasp the concept that "we're in this together"

The Change to Parent For

Your child understands that doing chores is an expected part of family membership, and learns habits that nurture responsibility, cooperation, and self-reliance.

Question: "My kids bicker so much about doing their chores that it's easier for me to make their beds or take out the trash myself. How do I get them to do chores without World War III?"

Answer: From this moment on, you must adhere to this parenting commandment: *never do any task for your child that your child can do for himself.* Your kids will never learn to be responsible if they know you'll do their job. Also institute one simple household rule: *chores first, then play,* then follow through with your expectations so that your kids know you really do expect them to chip in and be contributing members of your family.

Why Change?

In a Time/CNN poll, 75 percent of the respondents said that kids today do fewer chores than children did ten or fifteen years ago.[11] Sound familiar? For whatever reason—our hectic pace or their overscheduled lives—we tend to excuse kids from helping. And oh how we rationalize: "His schedule is so tight: he needs time to relax." "It's easier to do it myself." "She works so hard in school; she needs a break."

Let's face it: sometimes it's just easier to put chores low on the priority list. There's so much more to do, right? But there are compelling reasons why you should get your kids to roll up their sleeves and get involved. Research proves just how important it is to involve our kids in those household chores: doing them helps kids learn the skills to take

LATE-BREAKING NEWS

University of Minnesota: Research shows that the best predictor for young adults' success is that they did household chores as kids.[12] Marty Rossmann analyzed how involved children were in household tasks as preschoolers, during their school years, and again as teens. The same group was then interviewed in their midtwenties to discover what kind of adults they had become. Rossmann concluded that doing assigned chores instilled responsibility, competence, self-reliance, and self-worth at a young age—and those qualities remained throughout their lives. And the earlier that parents required their kids to pitch in and lend a hand, the better adjusted the kids were later on.

care of themselves; develop responsibility, empathy, cooperation, and self-reliance; and become better-adjusted young adults.[13] What's more, those studies also show that children who do chores from a young age are more likely to avoid drug use, complete their education, begin a career path, and develop sound relationships with family and friends. Get those kids off the couch and let the chores begin!

Signs and Symptoms

Here are a few signs that it may be time to change your kid's attitude about doing chores:

- *Poor work ethic.* Chores are rarely finished or poorly completed.
- *Home-front battles.* You and your kid are engaged in constant wars and arguing; your child resists or outright refuses to lend a hand.
- *Bribes.* You find yourself resorting to begging, bribery, or nagging to get your kid to do those tasks.
- *Deception.* Your kid says his tasks are finished when he hasn't begun.
- *Rescuing.* Your child expects you to do or redo the chore—and you generally do.
- *Cluelessness.* Your child doesn't have a clue about Life 101, from making a bed to sweeping the floor.
- *Lack of cooperation.* Your child doesn't get the family membership concept: "we're in this together."
- *Irresponsibility.* Your kid rarely takes initiative to do chores on his own; you must remind, coax, or nag.

THE SOLUTION

Step 1. Early Intervention

- *Identify the reason.* Here are some of the most common reasons for kids' resistance or refusal to do chores, along with some simple solutions.

  "It's too hard!" *Solution:* Break the chore down into smaller chunks until your kid has mastered the whole task.

  "I can't do it like you." *Solution:* Don't require perfection, but completion.

  "I don't know how." *Solution:* Model how to do the task and work with your child.

  "Why don't you do it?" *Solution:* Back off and stop rescuing.

  "I don't have time!" *Solution:* Check your child's schedule and allow some latitude. All members could chip in on a weekend morning or reduce daily tasks to essentials.

  "Why do I have to do it?" *Solution:* Explain the significance of the chores and make them matter.

  "I have to meet my friend." *Solution:* Announce a clear deadline for the completion of the task, then stick to it.

  "I don't want to." *Solution:* Attach a consequence to incompletion: no playdate, TV, allowance, or other privilege.

- *Start early.* The earlier in their lives that you expect your kids to take an active role in helping around the house, the easier you'll find it is to get them to lend a hand. Even kids as young as three years old can help out. Though it's never too late for basic training, it's sure easier to begin earlier.[14]

Pay Attention to This!

Research by Dan Kindlon, Harvard psychologist and author of *Too Much of a Good Thing: Raising Children of Character in an Indulgent Age,* found that kids who do not have to do chores or just pitch in and lend a hand around the house are at a greater risk for depression and tend to be self-centered.[15] His studies also found that teens who are not required to regularly help out around the house are more likely to see themselves as spoiled: they know they're getting something for nothing.

ONE SIMPLE SOLUTION

One study found that if kids weren't taught how to do the chore by a parent, they usually gave up in frustration.[16] So introduce each task using three simple steps for mastery:

1. *Teach.* Go through the task, explaining each step, so that your child knows what to do.

2. *Supervise.* Now watch him to ensure that he can handle the job. The first few times he goes solo, have him show you his finished product so that you can make sure the task is done correctly.

3. *Inspect.* Have your child do the chore independently, but make sure he knows to expect surprise inspections from you to ensure that he's still succeeding at the level you expect.

Step 2. Rapid Response

- *Announce expectations.* If you want your kid to be helpful and a contributing family member, then just plain expect him to help out and willingly lend a hand. Hold a family meeting and announce your new expectations. Expect groans and moans. So be it!

- *Specify assignments.* There are many ways to assign chores, so find the solution that works for your family and then stick to it. Each week hold a brief meeting to review assignments. Keep in mind that there is no right or wrong way to assign chores. The secret is to find the solution that works best for you and your family. The following list describes different ways parents assign chores:

    - You assign three simple daily chores and one more time-consuming weekly chore.

    - You assign one easier chore (emptying trash) and one harder one (washing dishes).

    - Your child is responsible for his personal possessions (clothing, toys, bedroom) and one household duty as a contributing family member.

    - Your child chooses one chore he enjoys; you assign the other task.

    - Your child chooses the one task he would like to learn to do that week.

- *Set deadlines.* Instead of saying that chores must be done immediately, set specific time limits for completion ("by bedtime" or "before Saturday"). Special situations, such as birthdays, illnesses, or important upcoming tests, warrant a reprieve.

- *Make them matter.* Give jobs that allow kids to feel that they are contributing to your family. Teach tasks to tweens that will help them handle life on their own in just a few years.

- *Use reminders.* Chore charts that show job assignments and completion dates are helpful. Nonreaders can "read" their chore responsibilities with pictures or photographs.

- *Chunk tasks.* Break down each task into smaller, more manageable parts until your child knows what to do on his own. Be explicit about what you expect.

- *Watch your tone!* A survey found that one-quarter of all responding parents admitted that they constantly nagged their kids about cleaning their room.[17] Stop nagging!

- *Acknowledge efforts.* Don't forget to praise your kids for jobs that are done well and on time. Remember to give yourself a pat on the back when your kid masters a new task.

- *Attach consequences.* Set suitable repercussions for uncompleted tasks, such as the following:

  - *Suffer a logical consequence.* If he doesn't put his dirty clothes in the hamper, he forgoes clean clothes and waits until the next wash cycle.

  - *Withhold allowances.* Never pay kids for work that isn't completed. Although the value of paying kids for doing chores is hotly debated by researchers, if you have decided that your children's allowance is contingent on doing chores, make sure they complete their required tasks before paying them.

  - *Pay the price.* If he doesn't rake the leaves, have someone else do the task, but have your kid pay for it with his allowance.

ONE SIMPLE SOLUTION

Once a week (or day), assign a room or area to each family member to clean (parents included). Hand out brooms, dust rags, and garbage bags. Set a buzzer for five minutes and then encourage each member to dash to his or her designated area and clean things "spick-and-span" before the timer goes off. Kids love to try to "beat the clock." But better yet, it puts the house back in order in minutes and gets every member doing his or her fair share of picking up.

Step 3. Develop Habits for Change

One of our most important roles is to help prepare our kids to handle life without us. To succeed in the adult world, they need to master a number of habits and skills required for basic life know-how. Doing those everyday chores is one of the best ways for them to learn. You will have the most success if you introduce one chore at a time: first show your child exactly how to do the task, then do it with him a few times until he can finally do it alone. Here is a list of age-appropriate chores to get started:

Age-Appropriate Chores and Tasks to Teach Your Children

Age 3: pick up toys and put them into a box; wipe up spills; help set the table; carry pieces of laundry to and from the laundry area; help feed pets; match clean socks so that someone else can fold them; be a "parent's little helper" in a variety of simple household tasks

Ages 4 and 5: all of the above, plus: make their bed by pulling up the comforter; clear dishes from the table; help put silverware on the table; help set the knife, fork, spoon, and napkin; sort clean silverware into proper drawer sections; clean counters with a squirt bottle and sponge; recycle newspapers and stack magazines; empty small wastebaskets; water flowers; bring in the mail or newspaper

Ages 6 and 7: all of the above, plus: set and clear the table; take the dog for a walk; empty dishes from the dishwasher; water grass; help pull weeds; answer the telephone; dust; make snacks; pack their own lunch

Ages 8 and 9: all of the above, plus: put dirty dishes in the dishwasher; vacuum and sweep; make their own lunch; cook simple cold side dishes or desserts; take care of a pet (feed, brush, bathe, clean cages); weed, rake leaves, sweep patio; take care of their own bedroom (dust, pick up possessions, clean closets); clean bathroom sinks and counters; make microwavable snacks; sew buttons; put dirty clothes in hamper; empty hamper

Ages 10 and 11: all of the above, plus: run washer and dryer; fold laundry and it put away, sort lights and darks; take out the heavier trash; put away groceries; cook simple food (while supervised if using stove or oven); help wash the car; mend a seam; babysit (with an adult home)

Ages 12 and 13: all of the above, plus: babysit during the day (with an adult nearby); change sheets; do their own laundry following fabric-care labels, treat simple stains; replace vacuum cleaner bags; wash windows inside and out; change light bulbs; cook a few basic recipes alone; use all household appliances; store food to avoid spoilage; clean shower, toilet, tub; wash car exterior and clean windows; shovel snow; clean out refrigerator; mop; budget their money and balance a checkbook

One Parent's Answer

A mom from Culver City writes:

My kids needed to know I was serious about their chores, so I mandated once-a-week meetings. I'd evaluate each child's chore performance and distribute allowances and accolades for jobs well done or withhold money if jobs were not completed. Not only did our meetings lessen those chore battles and help my kids learn to cooperate but they also became a great time to iron out issues and celebrate my children's individual successes.

WHAT TO EXPECT BY STAGES AND AGES

Preschooler   Keep tasks simple to reduce frustrations. Teach kids exactly how to do the task and even then provide lots of guidance and encouragement. Give them pint-size brooms, dustpans, and tools. Let them put stars or stickers on a chart as tangible reminders of completed tasks.

School Age   Older kids are more likely to cooperate if they have some say in what they have to do: consider letting them negotiate the number of jobs or duties, or even brainstorm a list of possible chores. They are capable of helping out in the household, doing a number of indoor tasks as well as light yard work.

Tween   Kids this age hate being told what to do, so appeal to their quest for independence and avoid a condescending tone. Try giving task choices; ask what they would like to learn, or offer to show them how to do tasks they can use to take care of themselves. Expect battles and resistance, especially if chores haven't been a past requirement, but don't buckle to "the attitude." In a few years they will be on their own, so assign tasks to prepare them for independent living.

More Helpful Advice

Chores Without Wars, 2nd Edition: Turning Housework into Teamwork, by Lynn Lott

Chore Wars: How Households Can Share the Work and Keep the Peace, by James Thornton

Didn't I Tell You to Take Out the Trash?! Techniques for Getting Kids to Do Chores Without Hassles, by Foster W. Cline and Jim Fay

Pick Up Your Socks . . . and Other Skills Growing Children Need, by Elizabeth Crary

Winning the Chore Wars: How to Get Your Child to Do Household Jobs (Effective Parenting Books Series), by Lee Canter and Marlene Canter

Communicating

SEE ALSO: *Argues, Back Talk, Shy, Won't Listen, Yelling*

THE QUESTION

"My son doesn't talk to me. When it comes to communicating, his father and I wind up performing monologues. How can I get him involved in a real conversation?"

THE ANSWER

Talking with a child can sometimes be like walking through a minefield. At any moment you could be asking what you thought was a simple, sincere question, only to find that you just triggered what seems like World War III from your sweet little cherub. Then there's your once cheery, open kid who suddenly gives you the "silent treatment" and has become a closed book. Or your seemingly brilliant tween now speaks in only one-word answers or grunts at best. These are among the most frustrating parenting moments. After all, we know that good communication is what helps keep us connected with our kids and is the basis of a loving parent-child relationship. In fact, research has shown that the number one antidote to risky behavior is a *strong relationship with a parent.* But how do you carry on a dialogue when those everyday talks with your child are just one-sided monologues? How do you begin discussing important topics when your easygoing tween has all of a sudden become moody or sarcastic? How do you even find out what's going on in your child's life when all you get are mumbles and grumbles? Here are a few of the best solutions that help keep those critical communication doors open with your child.

- *Commit to tuning up your listening skills.* Did you know that 35 percent of over a thousand adolescents gave parents D's or F's for listening?[18] So start your solution by grading yourself. On a scale of 1 to 10 (1 being the lowest and 10 the highest), how would you rate your listening skills? What one little thing could you do to improve your score? If you want to keep those talks open, it's critical that you fine-tune your own communication skills. For instance, read a parenting communication classic, such as *P.E.T.: Parent Effectiveness Training,* by Thomas Gordon; *How to Talk So Kids Will Listen and Listen So Kids Will Talk,* by Adele Faber and Elaine Mazlish; or *Between Parent and Child,* by Haim G. Ginott. Take a parenting class or workshop. Or find an adult who your kid says is a great listener, watch his communication style, and pick up a few pointers.

- *Avoid common "talk blockers."* Kids tell us that some adult behaviors are almost guaranteed to halt communication. Here are a few of the top talk blockers to avoid:

  Making nonverbal sounds. Skip the heavy sighs and groans. Be careful: you might even make those sounds without realizing it.

  Acting too hurried. Give your child plenty of time to formulate his thoughts. Don't push.

  Preaching. Beware of sounding "preachy" or coming off as if you're giving a lecture.

  Being long-winded. Kids hate lectures, so use the "One-Minute Rule": if you talk more than a minute, chances are that the kid will tune out. Talk less. Listen more. Besides, the attention span of preschoolers and any tired, stressed-out, sleep-deprived kid is short.

  Not giving full attention. If you want your child to listen, make sure you're willing to do the same. Sit down and make direct eye contact with your child. Kids say eye contact is their way of knowing that we're really listening. In fact, a simple talking tip is *always to look at the color of your child's eyes as you listen.*

  Acting unfriendly. Keep your tone calm, friendly, and conversational. Make sure your child feels that he is being heard and that his point of view is as important as yours. Always ask yourself: *Am I speaking to my child in a tone that I'd use with a friend?*

  Using negative body language. Watch out for nonverbal cues like smirks, shrugs, or raised eyebrows. You may not be using them intentionally, but those subtle signs sure turn kids off and pronto.

  Multitasking. Kids want us to be fully present, so don't multitask during an important conversation. Stop what you're doing and focus on your child with full attentiveness.

  Criticizing. The preschool set doesn't understand nuances, sarcasm, or jokes, and tweens are usually hypersensitive and prone to those hormonal mood swings. So refrain from criticism or sarcasm. Watch out for those sweeping generalities, such as "You always . . . " or "You never . . . , " which are guaranteed talk stoppers.

  Going into a monologue. If you want your kid to talk, give him time to do so. God gave you two ears and one mouth for a reason: *listen* twice as much as you talk.

- *Talk about your child's world.* If communication with your child has shut down a bit, then start with topics that interest and excite him as conversation openers. You can always get to the tougher topics later. For now, try safer subjects to get your kid to open up. Here are a few:

- *Bone up on kid culture.* Use your child's interests for topics, such as TV shows, sports, song lyrics, books, or fashions. For example, read *Teen People* so you can talk about "the latest news" about your daughter's favorite celebrity. Peruse the sports page so you can bring up the batting average of your son's baseball idol. Show interest in your child's world and talk about it!

- *Use your child's expertise.* Ask your child to help you with a problem you're facing for which only he has the answers: "How do I download music to my iPod?" Or ask your kid to teach you how to text. Fifty-three percent of teens say texting has improved their relationship with their parents.[19] Join your child's world.

- *Go to your child's space.* Find the place your child feels most comfortable—the mall, batting cage, tree fort, or Starbucks—and use that place to connect and talk.

- *Talk while doing.* Some kids—especially boys—are more receptive to talking while doing an activity. So try talking while doing an activity your kid enjoys, such as shooting baskets, driving in the car, or building with Lego.

- *Allow time to wait.* Research at Stanford University found that children need "wait time"—or simply more time to think about what they hear—before speaking.[20] So whenever you ask a question or make a request, remember to *wait at least ten seconds* for your child to think about what he heard. He will absorb more information, be more likely to respond, and probably give you a more sophisticated response.

- *Reframe your questions.* If you want your child to open up and talk more, then don't ask questions requiring only a yes or no answer (which produce one-sided conversations). Ask open-ended questions that make it appear that you really do want to listen, and avoid questions that seem trite: "Did you have fun last night?" and "How was school?" don't go over with kids who see them as insincere and "so-o-o predictable." (*"Watch—my mom is going to ask, 'How was your day?' She always does."*) You're likely to get nothing more than "Fine" as a response. Instead ask questions that require specific answers.

- *Use "I messages" to reduce negativity.* Messages starting with "You" generally put the kid on the defensive because of their critical tone: "Don't *you* ever think what you're doing?" "*You* never listen." So begin with "I" instead of "You." Then talk more about your feelings rather than your kid's behavior: "I'm mad . . . ," "I'm upset . . . ," "I'm sad . . . ," or "I'm hurt . . . ," and what he did that led you to feel that way. The simple pronoun switch helps take the bite out of the comment so that your kid is more likely to listen. Give it a try!

- *Choose timing wisely.* Timing is everything, so try to gauge your kid's mood before you talk. It's best to put off that key discussion until his moodiness, fatigue, or frustration subsides. Also figure out at what part of the day your kid is more receptive to talking—and try to make yourself available then. Hint: the two worst times to talk are usually first thing in the morning when the kid is sleep deprived and irritable, and when he first comes home after school when he's usually overwhelmed or exhausted. With one of my sons, I discovered the best time was around five o'clock in front of the refrigerator, and that's where I'd place myself.

- *Don't give up!* Keep trying out new responses and even discussion topics to see what works to restore your relationship and open up a dialogue. If conversations with your kid end up with tears or yelling, then vow to say only positive comments until you can turn things around. Give yourself and your child permission to release steam by walking away if things get too tense. You can always pick up the conversation later. If to preserve your relationship you need to write notes to your child for a while instead of talking, then do so. One mom said there was a period when she and her daughter could communicate only via journal, but it was their way of keeping in touch, and it was what saved their relationship.

Changing habits takes work. Don't give up! It will take time and effort to reap the change you seek, so hang in there. Respectful, open communication with our children is one crucial element of effective parenting. Also, please don't rule out that something else may be triggering the problem, such as stress, alcohol or drugs, puberty, bullying, trauma, grief, or depression. If communication continues to be shut down and your relationship with your child is at stake, then consider seeking the help of a mental health professional.

Disorganized

SEE ALSO: *Attention Deficit, Chores, Homework, Impulsive*

THE QUESTION

"My daughter is sweet and loving, but hopelessly disorganized. I'm always picking up forgotten homework assignments, putting schoolwork into her backpack, and reminding her of her schedule. I worry that she'll need a full-time assistant to help her get through high school. What can I do now to help her be more organized?"

THE ANSWER

There certainly are things you can do to help kids become more organized. And doing so now will help them greatly in the years to come when you're not there to pick up the pieces and be their personal butler or maid. The secret is to take on just one troubling issue at a time, find a simple solution that helps your child, and then stick to it until your organization system becomes a habit. Here are a few of the best solutions:

- *Stop rescuing.* Your first step is often the hardest (but most important). If you really, really want your child to learn how to be better organized, then you must stop being her personal assistant. So take a vow that you will teach your child organization skills; then, once she learns them, you will step back and make her responsible for any consequences (such as missing a deadline, losing a library book, or misplacing sports gear).

- *Create a place for everything.* Your next step is to help your kid organize what she has, so as to make things easier to find and put away. Don't start going crazy here. Just identify the "code red" areas that usually cause the stress and argument, and find a simple solution. For example:

  Problem: Misplaced shoes and jackets. **Solution:** Clean out the closet and then purchase a few inexpensive closet organizers so that she can find and put things away more quickly.

  Problem: Misplaced school papers and supplies. **Solution:** Put a hook by the front door to hang the backpack the second she comes home. All homework comes out and then goes back in that backpack once completed.

Problem: Missing sports gear. **Solution:** In the garage, place small plastic barrels with labels (pictures for younger kids) designating the type of equipment.

- *Reduce clutter.* Kids are more organized when there's less clutter, so go through her drawers, closet, toys, and equipment barrels, and eliminate those unnecessary extras. Throw away all those never used or broken things (and try to do so *at least* every six to eight weeks or even more if your child is a more serious Pig Pen type). Then employ these clutter reducers:

  - *Rotate toys.* Come on—your kid doesn't really play with all those toys, right? So put some of them away and pull them out again in a few weeks. Not only will they seem like brand new, but this tactic will reduce the clutter. Make a rule that when you pull toys out, you always store others in their place.

  - *Hold a garage sale.* Here is a time for your kid to make a little extra cash by selling her old toys, clothes, and books. Put your kids in charge of making flyers, setting up the cash box, and displaying items for sale.

  - *Donate to charity.* Give your child a box and tell her to stock it with gently used possessions. Then help her deliver the box to a Goodwill store or charity of her choice.

  - *Store things under the bed.* For those occasionally used things, get storage bins that can slide under your child's bed. "Out of sight, out of mind" is the organizational strategy. The fewer items seen, the fewer she can mess up and lose.

- *Set a cleanup routine.* Once your child is more organized, the trick is to keep to that system. The best way to do so is by enforcing a quick once- or twice-a-week clean-up policy. Don't expect your child's room to pass a white-glove inspection. Instead, be more realistic: identify those hot spots that need continual upkeep, and ink in clean-up dates on your calendar. For instance: Monday, desk; Tuesday, bedroom; Saturday, sports gear; Sunday, backpack. Then employ the *"first you clean, then you play (or e-mail or call your friends)"* rule. My girlfriend has the two most organized kids in town; she achieved that feat by designating Sunday as "clean the backpack" day. It takes the kids ten minutes to go through their papers, refill notebooks with binder paper, and sharpen their pencils, but the process helps her kids stay organized. Another friend gets her kids motivated by setting an oven timer for ten minutes and encouraging them to play "Beat the Clock."

Please don't expect overnight change in your child, and keep your expectations realistic. You're not going to turn a Pig Pen into a neatnik. But with patience and consistency you will be able to help your child learn how to be more organized and to adopt new organizational habits that she will be able to carry with her the rest of her life.

Money

SEE ALSO: *Chores, Clothes and Appearance, Materialistic, Selfish, Ungrateful*

THE PROBLEM

Red Flags

Is frequently broke and borrowing, spends impulsively, can't save money, doesn't understand the value of money, sometimes tries to avoid dealing with money altogether

The Change to Parent For

Your child learns the value of money, understands basic financial terms, and develops positive spending and saving habits.

Question: "The other moms give their kids allowances. My seven-year-old has trouble sorting his socks. Shouldn't I wait until he at least has his subtraction and addition down pat?"

Answer: It's OK to introduce money to your kids when they are young. Most experts feel that early school age is the best time to start giving allowances, because this family institution teaches money basics. The trick is to give money responsibilities slowly as you explain fundamentals of managing money. Even at seven your child can be responsible for her lunch money, scouting dues, and small candy or toy purchases, and kids are eager to have money of their own. Allowances can also boost your child's math skills as she learns the value of coins and keeps a running total of her "savings." Just be sure you're clear about what you expect her to do with her earnings, and then be consistent with that approach.

Why Change?

Do you feel as if you are your kid's ATM machine? Does your child spend faster than she saves? Do you worry that you'll still be doling out an allowance to your child when she's forty-five years old? If so, you're not alone.

Some of parents' biggest concerns center around their kids' inability to handle money. These are legitimate worries. How a child learns to save and spend in her early years has enormous impact on her future success. And research shows we're not doing such a good job of teaching our kids basic money management skills. Consider these facts about our kids' "money IQ":

- Fewer than half of parents surveyed said they teach their eleven- to fourteen-year-olds how to keep track of their expenses or set a budget.[21]
- One-third of twelve-year-olds don't know that paying by credit card is a form of borrowing (unless you pay your bill in full every month).
- Four out of ten twelve-year-olds don't know that banks charge interest on loans.[22]

The truth is, we can begin to teach our children money management skills when they're as young as three and four years old, and those lessons don't have to be difficult. In fact, the best way for kids to learn them is by taking advantage of simple, everyday, real-life moments—when we're using the ATM machine, paying our bills, balancing our checkbook, deciding on our budget, and talking through our spending decisions. Those lessons will take a bit of patience and persistence, but positive spending habits, financial wisdom, and good money management skills are crucial for life. And that's exactly why we must parent for this kind of change. This entry offers simple solutions to help your child learn good money management habits that will give her a more financially secure future.

Signs and Symptoms

Symptoms of poor money management will vary by a child's age, but here are some signs to watch out for:

- *Blows it.* If your child has it, she spends it. She doesn't think ahead about what she wants or needs; she just buys on a whim whatever she sees.
- *Borrows it.* Your child always needs loans; she expects steady income from your wallet.

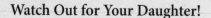

LATE-BREAKING NEWS

Watch Out for Your Daughter!

Nine out of ten of our girls will grow up to be solely responsible for their own finances during at least some part of their lives.[23] But research shows that by the time they're tweens, only half of girls feel as confident about their financial skills as boys do.[24] Don't overlook teaching your daughters about money and empowering them to feel secure about money management!

Pay Attention to This!

Are You Talking to Your Kids About Money? If Not, You'd Better!

Approximately fifteen hundred high school seniors were asked basic facts about personal finance, and the great majority were stumped by those questions: 95 percent scored below a C.[25] So it should be no surprise that another survey found that almost 80 percent of all college freshmen admitted to never having had a conversation with their parents about managing their money.[26] What's more, almost one in four of those teens says it's just fine to blow as much as $500 without checking in with Mom and Pop. If you're concerned about your kids' future spending habits, then start the "money talk" now. Let them know that money doesn't come easy and that you do have clear expectations and limits about their spending (and then tell them what they are).

- *Hoards it.* Your child is becoming an unreformed Scrooge; she saves everything but never spends it, so she never learns how to budget.

- *Loses it.* Your child is not careful with money; she leaves money out and about, and doesn't put cash or coins in a safe place, such as a bank, wallet, or even a drawer.

- *Takes it.* Your child helps herself to money that's left around or in your wallet; she doesn't return extra change to the store clerk.

- *Expects it.* Money *does* grow on trees in your child's eyes because she gets it so easily.

- *Doesn't save it.* Your child's piggy bank never fills to the top; her savings account is always used up.

THE SOLUTION

Step 1. Early Intervention

- *Identify your parenting style.* Here is a quick quiz to see how you are doing to help your kids learn about money management.[27] Check the statements that describe your typical family situation:

  ☐ Do my kids have some money to manage without my interference so that they can make spending mistakes and learn to understand the consequences?

☐ Have I helped my kids set up a spending and saving plan?

☐ Do my kids do regular household chores or jobs to earn money?

☐ Do my kids see a good example in my own behavior in money matters?

☐ Do my kids understand the difference between spending "needs" (essentials) versus "wants" (nonessentials or luxuries)?

☐ Do I encourage my kids to set long-term and short-term spending goals?

☐ Have I taught my kids that loans aren't always an option?

☐ Are my kids taking on increasing financial responsibilities as they get older?

☐ Do I acknowledge my kids when they make wise money decisions?

Your checked answers indicate areas where you are helping your child learn money management skills. Those unchecked statements indicate areas where you may need work on boosting your kids' "money IQ," depending on their ages.

- *Be a good role model.* Kids always look to us as the example to copy. If you are perpetually overdrawn, why expect your son to set a budget? If you buy clothes impulsively, why should you expect your daughter to wait for the sale? If you don't talk about the value of money, don't be surprised when your child thinks that money grows on trees. Be the model of money management you want your kids to copy. They *are* watching.

- *Monitor TV consumption.* Television is the one of the biggest culprits in fueling kids' spending urges, and commercials are relentless in trying to get kids to buy, buy, buy. So limit your kids' exposure to commercials by minimizing their TV viewing. Public television, although not strictly commercial free, offers quality programs with much less advertising.

- *Explain how money works.* Start money lessons when your kids are young. Take them with you to the bank so they see that you have to put money in to take money out. Let them play "store" with toy cash registers and play money. Put price tags on household items, then help your child figure out the cost of "purchasing" each item. Give your preschooler a small, clear jar (baby-food size) that she can use to save coins and "watch them grow." Stress that she can buy something special when the coins reach the top. Let her do simple spending at the store; have her count out the correct amount for the candy or inexpensive toy.

- *Use real-life examples.* Take your child to work. Show your daughter how you balance your checkbook. Talk to your son about how your credit rating is checked before purchasing that car. Show your kids the household bills so that they know how much electricity, gas, water, phone, and cable cost. You don't need to reveal your income or savings, but you should use real opportunities to help your children understand money.

Step 2. Rapid Response

- *Don't give loans.* Kids learn money management by trial and error. So don't bail her out if she overspends and runs out of money needed that week for the movie. So be it! If you do give an advance, consider charging interest. She'll soon figure out that borrowing is pricey. You can discuss pay for extra jobs, such as mowing the lawn or washing the car, especially if the child is saving for a big or special item.

- *Set a cap on the budget.* Allocate a certain amount for expenses like a back-to-school wardrobe. To give her an incentive to be thrifty, explain that if there's money left over, she can pocket it. Make your kid contribute to those nonessential "have to have" items, such as the trendiest sneaks or those pricey jeans. You can pitch in some, but your child has to make up the rest.

- *Give an allowance.* One of the best ways for kids to learn to manage money and keep a budget is by giving them an allowance. Some money experts say an allowance should start when a child is old enough to count, stop swallowing money, and listen to talks about money. Others say it is wiser to wait until school age when kids are more mature. How much to give depends on your comfort level and your child's spending habits and maturity. Here are a few crucial allowance dos and don'ts:

    - *Decide on the amount.* One rule of thumb is to give one dollar for every year of the child's age. Other options: start with a certain amount and increase it by one dollar each year, base the amount on what your child is expected to spend, or survey your friends. Of course, the key deciding factor—particularly in today's troubled economy—should be what is affordable for your family. If money is tight, then have no reservations or guilt about announcing that an allowance is not feasible at present. The average national weekly allowance for ten-year-olds is about $6.00.[28]

ONE SIMPLE SOLUTION

One of the simplest ways to help your kids understand financial concepts is by using money terms in natural settings. At the grocery store: "I need to stay in my budget and spend no more than twenty-five dollars." On a wish list: "If I save fifty dollars for the next six months, I can pay for that stereo system." A partial list of money terms your child should know *before* going off to high school includes *coin, dollar, change, cash, saving, spending, borrowing, balancing, budget, checking account, credit card, debit, savings account, earnings, raise.* Keep your comments short, aim the lesson to your child's level, and use real, in-the-moment examples, and your kids will become little financial wizards in no time.

- *Explain what the allowance has to cover.* Will your child have to pay for school lunches, movie tickets, makeup, and birthday gifts for friends? Or is the allowance simply "mad money" with no strings attached? Be clear.

- *Make it a rite of passage.* Celebrate a first allowance with a dinner or photo op.

- *Add money responsibility.* Gradually make your kid pay for personal items (clothes, candy, movies, scouting dues) as her allowance and age increase.

- *Be consistent.* Allowances should be paid at the same time each week, and the amount shouldn't change unless you've discussed it in advance with your child.

- *Don't tie it to chores.* Once kids have other income (monetary gifts or part-time jobs), they often balk at doing chores because they don't need your cash. This decision is up to you, but do know that 77 percent of parents, along with many child experts, think chores should not be linked to allowance.[29]

- *Don't bail them out.* As mentioned earlier, let them learn from their spending mistakes while they're young and the stakes aren't too high.

- *Don't use it for discipline.* If your child misbehaves, don't withhold allowance money as punishment.

- *Encourage savings.* A study has shown that the more materialistic the kid, the less likely it is that she has a savings account. She's just learned to spend—not save.[30] Here are ways to help kids fight their spending urges and learn to save. Decide on which is the best approach for your family and then stick to it.

  - *Share some.* A portion of her allowance goes to a charity her choice.

ONE SIMPLE SOLUTION

Cut Impulsive Shopping by Teaching Kids to "Think Before Spending"

Set a household rule that your child must write down any pricier intended purchase and postpone buying it for at least twenty-four hours. A younger kid can draw it on her "wish list." The wait time could vary from an hour or day to a week or month depending on the child's age and maturity. If she loses interest before the time is up, even she will agree that she didn't really want that item after all.

- *Fill a piggy bank.* It must be filled or weigh a certain amount before money is spent. A clear container is best because the kid can see her money add up.

- *Give smaller denominations.* Give five $1 bills instead of one $5 bill; break a dollar into four quarters. Offer denominations that support savings.

- *Open a savings account.* Your child can monitor her money just as it's done in the real world.

One Parent's Answer

A mom from Phoenix shares:

My twelve-year-old asked me for so much cash, I was starting to feel like an ATM machine. He never saved a dime, so I decided to provide a little enticement. For any (and I mean any) deposit Zach made, I'd provide a 25 percent incentive in his savings. I also was clear that there would be no more mommy loans. I wanted him to figure out he had to work hard and save for the things he wanted. It took a while for the lesson to sink in, but he now has over $100 in his savings.

- *Give an incentive.* Match a portion of your child's savings with a set contribution (for example, one dollar to every ten saved, or match dollar for dollar).

- *Set a savings goal.* Encourage your kid to save up for a long-range goal (a car, sports gear, a stereo, a college fund).

- *Use the four-jar savings technique.*[31] Give your child four clear jars: one for everyday spending, one for a short-term goal, one for charitable or religious giving, and one for long-term savings. Then help her figure out how to distribute the cash. A younger child can start with two jars: half for spending and half for saving.

- *Have her keep a spending log.* From the time your child can write and count, give her some kind of simple recording book to keep track of her money. A young child can track her earnings (including holiday money gifts); an older child can record her earnings and expenses.

Step 3. Develop Habits for Change

- *Teach smart buying habits.* Encourage your child to read consumer reports online before purchasing that pricey gadget. Ask your daughter to list what she needs before hitting the mall, then have her stick to her list. Tell your son to check the newspaper for sales. Let your child choose among items by comparing prices. Give your child a clothes budget; have her estimate costs, and then insist that she adhere to that budget. Help your kids develop buying habits now to prepare them for the real world later.

- *Encourage an entrepreneurial spirit.* Help your child set up that lemonade stand, print flyers that say he'll mow the neighbors' lawns, babysit, walk the neighbor's dog. Your child can learn from a young age that the way to earn money is through hard work. You'll not only encourage your little entrepreneur but also help her appreciate the value of money.

WHAT TO EXPECT BY STAGES AND AGES

Preschooler   If your child can count to ten, she's ready to learn about money. Introduce coin recognition, counting coins, saving in a piggy bank, exchanging goods and services for money, and the idea that money is the reward for working. By five years of age, most kid's beliefs, values, and expectations regarding money are already well established, so start early.

School Age   Money skills include how to make change, understanding the different denominations of coins and bills and their corresponding values, exchanging money for goods, short-term money saving, and staying within a reasonable budget.

More Helpful Advice

Money Doesn't Grow on Trees: A Parent's Guide to Raising Financially Responsible Children, by Neale Godfrey, Carolina Edwards, and Tad Richards

Allowance Magic: Turn Your Kids into Money Wizards, by David McCurrah

Raising Financially Fit Kids, by Joline Godfrey

Raising Money-Smart Kids: What They Need to Know About Money and How to Tell Them (Kiplinger's Personal Finance), by Janet Bodnar

Tween   This is the time to teach kids how to write checks, balance a checking account, and use a savings account; they should learn such terms as *interest, budget, deficit, borrowing, withdrawal, loan, credit,* and *debit.* Tweens are ready to be responsible for buying their wardrobe, staying within a set budget, paying for all entertainment, doing more demanding chores, and earning money through outside jobs.

Moving

SEE ALSO: *Fearful, Friendship Breakups, Rejected, Stressed*

THE PROBLEM

Red Flags

Clinging, regressive behaviors such as thumb sucking or bedwetting; stomachaches, pervasive worry, oppositional behavior, aggression

The Change to Parent For

Your child gradually learns to adapt to her new environment, acquires new friends, and develops skills that help her fit in, make new friendships, and handle change.

Question: "Our family will be moving next month, and my daughter is so upset. She says I'm ruining her life. I wonder if we made the wrong decision. What effect does moving have on a child?"

Answer: Moving is a stressful event for kids as well as parents. How a child handles the move and "settles in" depends on a number of factors, including her age, temperament, and personality; your attitude; and the circumstances around the move. Some kids see a move as an adventure; others may behave as if you've given them a life sentence, and will take a far longer time to adjust. It is quite normal for a child to display a range of emotions, and it's hard to predict how your child will react. After all, moving to a child is a kind of loss, so she may even respond as though she's experiencing grief. Although it's fine to acknowledge that leaving everything behind will be difficult, don't play into the guilt. Instead, know that there are things that make the transition smoother, so stay focused on what you can do to make a move easier and get your child through this time. Those moving pangs will pass, though it sometimes takes a number of months for a kid to adjust and finally consider her new living environment "home, sweet home."

Why Change?

"What do you mean we're moving?" "But this is my home, and I like it here!" "How will I make new friends? Nobody will like me there." "Thanks a lot, Mom. You just ruined my life!"

Whether your family is moving into the home next door or across the nation, that change can be difficult for one and all. Although moving is a common event that happens to one out of five families each year,[32] just the thought of being uprooted and making such a major change can be unsettling as well as even frightening to a child. It means far more than just fixing up a new bedroom, but also involves changing schools, making new friends, and joining a new team, playgroup, or scout troop, let alone trying to fit in and finding someone to play four-square with or sit next to in the cafeteria. In fact, research shows that a big mistake parents make is not realizing just how upsetting a move can be for kids. It can be traumatic as well as stressful. But there are ways to help guide your children through the moving experience. Using those solutions can help make the experience more positive as well as one that even enhances your child's confidence and social skills and her ability to handle change. Meanwhile, keep this ancient wisdom in mind: "Home is where the heart is." No matter where or why you move, what makes a house a home is always the love shared inside.

Signs and Symptoms

Even the most well adjusted child can have difficulty coping with moving. Tune in a bit more closely and pay attention to these symptoms, especially two weeks before and two weeks after a move, when the stress of a move often peaks and the reality of the change is most likely to sink in.[33]

- *Physical signs:* loss of appetite, insomnia, nightmares, stomachaches, headaches
- *Clinginess and dependency:* reluctance to leave the house or stray far from you or her family
- *Regression:* baby talk, thumb sucking, attention-getting behaviors, bedwetting
- *Outbursts of anger or tears:* tantrums, whining, irritability, aggression, frustration, roller-coaster emotions
- *Stress:* problems sleeping, regular nightmares, trouble concentrating, slipping grades
- *Deviant behavior:* risk taking, lying, stealing, defiance

Although researchers say that children often need as long as sixteen months to make a full adjustment,[34] seek professional help if your child displays intense anxiety signs that last beyond two weeks or increase in intensity, or if you see a marked change in your child that concerns you.

Pay Attention to This!

Of course you don't always have a choice as to whether or not to move, and moving can be challenging at any time or stage in a child's life, but here are five factors that can exacerbate stress and have a stronger negative impact on a move.

1. *Time of year.* A move during the school year—especially midyear—is most difficult; a move during the summer or during a long holiday is preferable because kids have more time to make new friends and adjust before school starts.

2. *Child's age.* Preschoolers and adolescents have the most difficult time moving.[35] Preschoolers are vulnerable to moving-related stress because they haven't developed coping skills and have difficulties handling change. Middle school kids have a tough time with a move because their identity is so tightly wound up with peer acceptance; leaving well-established friendships is hard.

3. *Gender.* Boys moving during junior high years have a more difficult time than girls.[36]

4. *Trauma prior to the move.* A natural disaster (hurricane, fire, tornado), family financial problem or divorce, a parent's death, incarceration, or military deployment for combat—all can contribute to making a move tougher on your children.

5. *Parental attitude.* A parent's negative attitude toward relocation significantly increases an older child's chances of experiencing move-related stress and depression.[37]

Don't think moving across the country is more difficult for kids than moving across the street. Studies show that it is often *more* difficult for children to change schools within a city or school district than to move to another city or district.[38] Dr. Frederic Medway, a professor of psychology at the University of South Carolina and renowned expert on mobility, notes that parents may not recognize that even a "smaller" move is stressful on kids and therefore may not work as hard to help kids adjust. You do make a difference in helping your kids make a smoother transition, regardless of the distance of the move.

DAY TO DAY

THE SOLUTION

Here are the three stages of moving (before, during, and after) as well as specific solutions you can use during each phase to help make the adjustment go more smoothly for your kids and your family.

Step 1. Early Intervention

Here are a few solutions to implement *before* you move to help prepare your children:

- *Anticipate your child's concerns.* Here are the most common kid worries, whether your family is moving across town or across the country. Check those that you feel could apply to your child. If you can predict which issues may concern her, you'll be better able to allay those concerns and boost her confidence.

  - ☐ Won't like the new home, neighborhood, or community
  - ☐ Will lose personal possessions in the move
  - ☐ Won't make new friends, fit in, or be accepted with the group
  - ☐ Won't be able to continue her current sports or hobbies
  - ☐ Will lose touch with old friends
  - ☐ Will suffer from the financial strain of the move
  - ☐ Won't match the new school or class standards (too high or too low academically)
  - ☐ Will once again experience the same social problems (having a poor reputation, being bullied, or feeling rejected)

- *Remain upbeat and calm.* Keep your concerns to yourself and remain as positive about this venture as possible. Your kids will pick up on your moods, which will have a major influence on their outlook.

- *Accentuate advantages.* Explain the benefits to your child so that she has a more positive outlook as well as an explanation to give friends: *"You'll be able to play volleyball like you always wanted!" "We'll be living in a bigger house." "We'll be closer to Grandma."*

- *Give a timeline.* Explain the move step-by-step, tailoring what you say to your child's developmental level. Younger kids have shorter attention spans, so don't offer too many details at once. Older kids want specifics: *Where* are we moving? *How* are we getting there? *When* are we moving? *What* does the new house look like? *When* do I start school? Provide details and make sure the information comes from you or your parenting partner.

- *Anticipate concerns.* Be prepared for resistance and some acting out. Be patient. Answer your kids' questions calmly.

- *Research the new location.* Ask the realtor to send photos and floor plans of your new house. The local chamber of commerce can provide maps of the community and pamphlets of children's activities. Subscribe to the local newspaper so that your family can scope out what's available. Log on to the school and city Web sites for your kids to check out.

- *Gather necessary paperwork.* Contact the new school, day-care facility, sports club, pediatrician, dentist, and veterinarian. Find out what information they need from you and what paperwork you must submit for enrollment. Gather your child's current academic and immunization records to forward to her new school. Also talk to her present teachers and coaches. Do they have any specific recommendations for next year's classes? Do they recommend tutoring to help your child catch up or to make the transition smoother?

- *Include your child in the moving process.* Provide an older child with a floor plan of the house (and especially her bedroom) so that she can arrange in her mind how she wants her furniture placed and can even give directions to the movers. Allowing some choices will help your kid feel more like a participant with control in the process. *"What kind of bedspread would you like? Where should we put the swing in the backyard? What color should we paint your room?"*

One Parent's Answer

A mom from Reno shares:

My son was concerned about fitting in with the kids. So two days before enrolling him, we parked outside his new school to check out how the kids dressed. He was really tuned in to their backpacks, jackets, and shoes. Then we purchased a few similar items, so he had a similar "look." It really helped him feel more comfortable at his new school.

Step 2. Rapid Response

Here are ways to respond to your kids *during* the moving process:

- *Distract your kids.* The actual moving day is bound to be stressful, so reduce the chaos for your children (and you) by having them spend their time elsewhere. Get a babysitter, send your kids to the neighbors, or beg your best girlfriend to watch your kids for the day (or night).

- *Assign moving tasks.* Let your child label (with stickers or marking pens) the boxes filled with her belongings. Assure her that those boxes will be first off the truck (and instruct the movers to ensure that they are). Most cherished personal items (pillow, blanket, action figure, doll, sketchbook and pencils, scrapbook) can be carried by hand in a small backpack.

ONE SIMPLE SOLUTION

Teach Your Children How to Introduce Themselves to Make a New Friend

A simple social skill you can teach a child is how to introduce herself. Tell your kid to use these steps, which might help make a new friend:

1. *Choose a kid you want to meet.* Pick someone who seems friendly and is not too busy doing something, or someone who seems to share your hobbies or interests. Walk confidently toward the kid.

2. *Look the kid in the eye.* Hold your head high. Stand up straight. Smile! If the kid doesn't look at you, it probably means she isn't interested in meeting you. Walk on and find someone else.

3. *Say hello and introduce yourself with a firm, friendly voice.* "Hi, my name is Sara." You might offer your hand to shake. If the kid doesn't give her name, say, "And your name is?"

4. *Say something friendly or ask a friendly question.* "Glad to meet you." "Do you live around here?" "Do you skate here often?" You can also tell something about yourself. "I just moved from Arkansas." "I live in the yellow house." "I like skateboarding, too."

5. *Write down the kid's name, phone number, or e-mail.* Keep a note card and pencil in your pocket or backpack just in case. If you and this other kid seem to hit it off, tell her you'll give her a call or arrange to meet so that you can do something together.

- *Keep essentials handy.* Put one box aside for those essentials you do not want packed or lost in the confusion—for example, your cell phone, medication, diapers and wipes, marking pens, address book, healthy snacks, water bottles, pacifier, bottle, or cup. Also have a few "just in case" small items to occupy your kids' time when you're in a crunch, such as a new coloring or word search book, portable DVD player and a movie, music, story tapes, or a book.

Step 3. Develop Habits for Change

Once you've made the move, it's time to settle in and help your children learn about their new home and community. Here are ways to help your child *after* the move.

- *Tour the house and celebrate new beginnings.* Find a special way or ritual to celebrate your new home and the move. Plant a tree as a new beginning. Take a photo of all of your family to send to all your old friends. Hold a special celebration dinner just for your family to toast one another's health and happiness.

- *Visit the surroundings.* As soon as convenient, let your kids get acquainted with their new community. Go to the local library, park, school, Boys and Girls Club, teen center, soccer club, or pool facilities. Take your child for a visit to preview her new school.

- *Provide continuity.* Stick to your normal family routine especially for those first few days after the move: favorite dinners, TV shows, nighttime stories. It will help your child recognize that although the house is different, basic family routines will remain unchanged.

- *Help your kid blend in.* Clothes, haircuts, shoe styles, and accessories really do matter in helping kids gain peer approval, and communities do have their own cultures. So visit your kid's school (if possible even before the move) and study the appearance of the kids your child is most likely to associate with. Does your kid dress like them? If not, help her revamp her wardrobe so that she blends in.

- *Acknowledge feelings.* If your child doesn't readily share her feelings, you can help her recognize how she feels about the move: *"You must be feeling lonely and miss your old group." "I can see you're worried." "It's tough to join a new team when you don't know any of the kids."* Let her know such feelings are normal. Even if your kid won't talk to you, keep talking to her. *"Is there anything I can do to make you feel more comfortable?" "Do the kids wear or have anything different from the kids back home? Do you need anything?" "Would you like me to talk to your teacher?"* Be patient and understanding. Stress to your child that adjustment takes a while. You might encourage her to write her feelings about the move on paper, put them in a jar and then bury them out back as a time capsule to dig it up to read a year or two from now to realize things really have improved.

- *Befriend other parents.* Be a room parent as soon as you can, offer to carpool, sign up to coach, be the team mom, help out with the church group, meet other camper parents, or attend PTA meetings and other school functions. Introduce yourself to the neighbors. Find out who among your work colleagues, if you have them, have children: it's a way not only to learn about available kid activities but also to find potential new friends for your children (or find a babysitter!).

- *Find outlets for your kid that attract peers.* Look everywhere for opportunities for your child to meet kids—for example, scouting, park and recreation programs, Boys and Girls Clubs, YMCAs, 4-H, teen clubs, church groups, sports teams, library programs, after-school programs, or other youth groups. Pediatricians' offices and libraries often are good places for picking up schedules of upcoming kid events. Your goal is to help your kids find ways to meet new kids. Making the friends is her job—helping her find potential new friends is your role.

LATE-BREAKING NEWS

One study found that 23 percent of children who moved frequently repeated a grade compared with 12 percent of children who never or infrequently moved.[39] Stay in close contact with your child's teacher, especially during those first few weeks after the move—even if your kid tells you, "Everything's fine, Mom. Chill!"

WHAT TO EXPECT BY STAGES AND AGES

Preschooler   Kids this age are closely bonded to their personal possessions (their bed, blanket, swing, toys), so the packing process can be unsettling (especially when their things start disappearing). Using a dollhouse or two shoeboxes—to represent your old and new houses—and a toy truck, role-play with your child how her belongings will be delivered. Show how the truck stops and picks up her things, then moves them to her new house. To make the transition a bit less stressful, pack her bed last. Tantrums and tears are the usual ways preschoolers act out uncertainties, as they can't express their worries in advance. Preschoolers typically go through a period of agitation, generally have difficulty sleeping, and get more upper respiratory infections prior to a move.[40]

School Age   Kids this age are concerned about moving details: *How* will we get our stuff there? *When* will the movers come? *Why* are we moving? Be patient and answer all their questions. School, academic demands, sports or favorite activities, and fitting in are generally their most pressing concerns. Before your move, if possible, try to enroll your child in an activity or sport she loves, and tell her about it. Just make sure your child's abilities match those of the other kids.

More Helpful Advice

For preschoolers: *Melanie Mouse's Moving Day,* by Cyndy Szekeres; *Boomer's Big Day,* by Constance W. McGeorge; *The Berenstain Bears' Moving Day,* by Stan and Jan Berenstain

For school age: *Alexander, Who's Not (Do You Hear Me? I Mean It!) Going to Move,* by Judith Viorst; *I'm Not Moving, Mama!* by Nancy White Carlstrom; *The Lost and Found House,* by Michael Cadnum; *Look Who's Moving to a New Home,* by Susan Bartell and Renee Raab; *Moving Day,* by Tobi Tobias

For tweens: *The Moving Book: A Kid's Survival Guide,* by Gabriel Davis

For parents: *Moving with Children,* by Thomas Olkowski; *Moving with Kids: 25 Ways to Ease Your Family's Transition to a New Home,* by Lori Collins Burgan

Tween   Don't be surprised if your child responds with anger or marked sadness. Tweens often have the toughest time moving and are most resistant. They dread leaving precious close friends and are concerned about fitting in with the new social scene. Help your kid find out about her new school: pick up a handbook or check it out online; get copies of the curriculum, book lists, and activity schedules. You may even be able to access photos of students so that she can see dress styles.

Overscheduled

SEE ALSO: *Dependent, Sleepless, Stressed, Tantrums*

THE QUESTION

"I keep reading that experts say kids are overscheduled, and I'm sure mine are as well. But I also believe that kids thrive on being busy. How do you know when children are *too* scheduled?"

THE ANSWER

Moderate amounts of structured activities are healthy for kids. And some kids do thrive on being busy. Each child differs in terms of whether activities stimulate or paralyze her, so the real challenge is figuring out how much activity is too much for *your* child. The trick is finding the right balance that fits your child's needs, skills, and temperament. Here are eight signs that may indicate that your kid is overscheduled and that it's time to cut down or rethink those activities. Any *one* sign may signal it's time to review her schedule:

1. *Mood shifts.* Your child exhibits sudden mood changes that last more than two weeks and are noticeably different from her typical temperament: for instance she's noticeably *more* whiny, grouchy, irritable, aggressive, defiant, clingy, because of an extended schedule.

2. *Resistance.* Your child digs in her heels or throws a fit when it's time to head to the activity.

3. *Hurry.* She grumbles that she "never has enough time" and is always hurrying to keep up or rushing through daily routines, such as meals, dressing, homework, schoolwork; tasks are left unfinished.

4. *Sleep problems.* Your child sleeps too much or can't get to sleep or stay asleep; she's always tired and yawning.

5. *Health problems.* Your child suddenly has headaches, stomachaches, rashes, frequent colds; she's stressed and unable to focus.

6. *Declining quality of life.* Your child's grades are slipping; she's losing friends, not hanging around buddies; she's forced to give up a sport, passionate interest, or hobby because there is not enough time.

7. *Lack of balance.* A total emphasis on sports or academics or music or tutoring leaves no opportunity to experience other interests or nurture other strengths. Activities should ideally be balanced between those that are adult supervised (sports, scouts, musical instrument) and academically stimulating and those that are unsupervised, social, fun, and relaxed, without the pressure to excel.

8. *Poor family relationships.* Little time is left for you to build a relationship with your child and for her to enjoy being with her family; you feel more like a chauffeur than a parent. Your child's life is on overdrive, with little downtime.

The easiest test is the one we often overlook: Why not ask your child if her load is too much? In a recent KidsHealth survey, almost 80 percent of today's kids say they wish they had more time, and 41 percent admit they feel stressed most of the time because they have too much to do.[41] Typical American kids spend five hours a week in structured activities; 3 to 6 percent of kids spend twenty hours a week; 40 percent of kids ages five to eighteen are not engaged in any activities.[42] What do you think your child would say about her schedule? Most important: Are you ready to trim down that schedule if she says she's too busy and feels overwhelmed?

Every so often, check the pulse of your child's life. List all your kid's activities and add up those hours. The total may well shock you. Are the time, energy, and finances you and your child are putting into the activity really worth the trouble? If not, then consider cutting it from your child's schedule.

Pets

SEE ALSO: *Chores, Dependent, Fearful, Selfish*

THE QUESTION

"My son is begging me to have a pet, but I'm a bit hesitant. How do you know when a child is old enough? Are there really proven benefits to having a pet?"

THE ANSWER

I have to admit I'm a real pet lover, so I'm a little biased. But studies do show that there are clear benefits for kids. Pets can help kids learn important lessons about responsibility as well as birth and death, and can even nurture empathy as children learn to read their animal's emotional signals. Children who are raised with pets have been shown to be more sociable as adults, and even have better communication skills.[43] (Our youngest learned to speak by talking to our giant schnauzer.) Pets also make great therapists: in one study 40 percent of kids said that when they're upset they seek out their pet for comfort![44] Even with all those benefits, weigh things carefully before making a purchase and be sure your child is of the right age and temperament.

Puppies and kittens are not recommended for young children, and if your child is under six years, consider adopting a young adult dog or cat over two years old who arrives already trained. (Read those pet manuals thoroughly for breeds good for children, and pay attention to the animal's temperament. The American Society for the Prevention of Cruelty to Animals also offers helpful advice.)

The American Academy of Child and Adolescent Psychiatry recommends that preschoolers be monitored at all times with a pet because they are easily frustrated.[45] Beware also of allergic reactions triggered by dogs and cats (though new research finds that children raised in homes with two or more cats or dogs during their first year may be less likely to develop allergy and asthma).[46] Kids under the age of ten are unable to care for a cat or dog on their own, but don't rule out a guinea pig, fish, or rat. (On a personal note, my three kids have had snakes, rabbits, guinea pigs, dogs, fish, rabbits—you name it—but the gentlest and easiest to care for by far were rats. We had dozens until we finally realized that Albert was really an Alice.)

Once you decide on a pet, you must take time to teach your kids those critical health and safety tips, such as washing hands with soap and water after handling. Veterinarians caution that kids need to learn to play with and handle pets gently, not to overstimulate them, to stay away when they are hurt, and even to read the pet's body language (what a hiss, an arched back, a growl, or a cower might mean). And then there's that little matter of training the dog, which usually falls on the parent's shoulders.

The real questions are back to you: Do you have the time to supervise your child's interaction with the pet? Are you ready to take on a commitment that could last a number of years? The bottom line: unless your child is a teen or a *very* mature tween, most pets will end up as your responsibility and your child's friend. So be ready!

Picky Eater

SEE ALSO: *Depressed, Eating Disorders, Obesity, Stressed*

THE PROBLEM

Red Flags

Rejects food once liked, is finicky about what she eats, only eats same food repeatedly, refuses to try new foods, engages in constant mealtime battles

The Change to Parent For

Your child becomes less fearful of new foods and more willing to eat what she liked before, enjoys family meals again, and learns that eating can be pleasurable.

Why Change?

Tired of cooking macaroni and cheese night after night or putting only four grapes, three crackers, and a slice of bread on your kid's dinner plate—and making sure they don't touch? Are you just plain worn out from mealtimes that have become brutal battle-grounds, and worried that your child isn't getting all the necessary daily nutrients from those mere teaspoon-size servings? If so, your kid is a member of the Finicky Eater Club along with one in five other kids,[47] but there is a bit of comforting news. Studies show that at least it's not your cooking that's turning your kid off to food.

A University of London study led by Lucy Cooke found that food pickiness is most-ly inherited.[48] Researchers analyzed almost fifty-four hundred pairs of twins between the ages of eight and eleven and found that 78 percent of food pickiness is genetic. But don't surrender too quickly to your kids' DNA. New studies also confirm there really are sim-ple ways to reduce kids' pickiness and help them become more willing to try even their peas and broccoli. Although these strategies certainly won't turn your kid into an instant omnivore or food connoisseur, they are proven to help kids enjoy mealtimes more and even eat more healthily. And those two changes alone are worth the effort.

Pay Attention to This!

Research by the American Academy of Pediatrics and others finds that most kids outgrow their finicky habits and will suffer no adverse consequences.[49] One ten-year study found an increase in eating disorders for those kids with more troublesome early eating patterns, but more research is still needed.[50] Here are six signs that tell you it's time to pay closer attention to your child's finicky eating habits and to seek advice:

1. *Weight loss.* If your child is eating about the same amount and still loses weight or is noticeably underweight for her age and height (according to developmental charts), don't rule out an illness or the onset of anorexia, which can begin as early as six. Watch also for diarrhea, fever, vomiting, or gagging when your child eats any food.

2. *Abrupt appetite change.* Your child may be finicky from the get-go, but if she suddenly becomes picky or even refuses to eat, then something else may be the cause, such as stress, depression, bullying, difficulty in school, or an eating disorder.

3. *Thinning or loss of hair.* This may be a sign that your child is malnourished, anemic, or experiencing stress.

4. *Uncharacteristic behavior change.* Is your child is suddenly experiencing lethargy, anger, inability to concentrate, trouble sleeping, or difficulty keeping up with peers? If so, keep a closer eye on the behavior, which may be triggered by lack of a balanced diet.

5. *Food allergy.* If within minutes (and up to two hours) after eating certain foods your child has such symptoms as coughing, runny nose, itchy skin or eyes, rash, swelling, nausea, diarrhea, gas, cramps, wheezing, crying, or sneezing, she may have a food allergy.

6. *Obsessions in other areas.* If your child's pickiness spills over to other areas besides food (cleaning, dressing, hygiene) and affects her daily life, ask your doctor about Obsessive Compulsive Disorder (OCD).

If you're at all concerned about your child's health, ask for a blood workup to rule out anemia and ease your worries. The solution may be as simple as having your child take a daily multivitamin, but don't ignore such symptoms or your instinct.

THE SOLUTION

Five Strategies for Change

1. *Make mealtime more positive.* The scientific results are unanimous: all kids—especially finicky eaters—benefit from more relaxed mealtimes.[51] In fact, researchers find that picky kids are more likely to eat more vegetables (but not necessarily fruit) and develop more positive attitudes about food when they eat with their families.[52] Your first goal is to make your family meal more relaxed and to avoid five parenting no-no's that increase the battles:

   - *Don't insist on a clean plate.* Coaxing kids to "eat more" will get you nowhere. So don't push food, but do encourage the "One-Bite Rule" (try at least one small bite, but you never have to like it). And when your kid says she's done, believe her!

   - *Don't rush.* Some kids—especially younger ones—take longer to eat, so make mealtime more leisurely. Let your child chew longer if needed, and give her time to eat at her own pace.

   - *Don't be a short-order cook.* Fixing extra substitute meals only teaches finicky eaters that they don't need to eat what's on their plate: "Mom will cook something else." So don't cook individual dishes. Instead provide a less-favorite food along with more popular ones (or at least one item your kid might possibly even swallow), then sit and enjoy your meal.

   - *Don't make food an issue.* Research shows that finicky eaters can become even finickier depending on how we respond. Rewarding kids for eating can backfire and actually *decrease* your child's preference for the food. So forget the lectures, the bargaining and rewarding, the ultimatums and punishments. In fact, the less you say about food the better. Your best response is to stay neutral and calm.

   - *Don't make her eat alone.* Meals should be a family affair. A kid should sit at the table throughout the meal—even if she doesn't eat. But if she doesn't finish, don't make her stay after and eat by herself.

2. *Stick to an eating routine.* You can increase your child's appetite by serving planned meals and snacks at specific times. Just be sure the snack isn't served so close to a meal that it ruins your kid's appetite. Give your child two or three healthy choices, and limit munching on such hunger stealers as fast food, candy, cookies, chips, and dairy products.

3. *Curb appetite stealers.* Watch out for foods that might reduce your kid's appetite. Don't overlook liquid calories, which can fill kids up. A study by the American Academy of Pediatrics warns parents especially about too much milk[53] (surprise!) and soft drinks, which can reduce appetites; serve water instead. If your kid is a "juice-aholic," reduce the sugar intake by adding water to the drink. A few fun books to help your child understand the need for eating more healthily are

D. W. the Picky Eater, by Marc Brown; *Gregory the Terrible Eater,* by Mitchell Sharmat and Jose Aruego; *The Seven Silly Eaters,* by Mary Ann Hoberman and Marla Frazee; *I Will Never Not Ever Eat a Tomato,* by Lauren Child.

4. *Make food with "kid appeal."* Kids do have different taste and food preferences than adults. One trick is to choose foods that are more "kid friendly"; here are some tips:

   - *Get her input.* Try involving her in the buying, planning, preparing, or serving of meals. Give her cookie cutters to make fun shapes out of some items; she can use carrot curls to add hair to her potato, raisins for eyes. Kids are often a bit more willing to eat something they cooked, so just aim for making things fun for the two of you.

   - *Serve small sizes.* "Shrink" the food serving so that it doesn't appear so daunting. Serve smaller portions (even a teaspoon size) on smaller plates.

   - *Follow your kid's lead.* Respect your child's "no foods touching" rule if deemed important and forgo the "Don't play with your food" rule at least for now. Younger kids often touch, smell, and play with new foods.

   - *Go for texture, shape, and color.* Kids enjoy foods that look colorful and appealing and have interesting textures, so take those preferences into consideration in your meal planning. And while you're at it, change your whole focus from how foods taste to just enjoying food. In fact, don't talk about "How does it taste?" Focus instead on "Do you like the texture?" "What a pretty color!" "Don't you love that fun shape?"

   - *Give foods fun names.* A Cornell University study finds that giving vegetables catchy names like X-Ray Vision Carrots, Power Peas, or Dinosaur Broccoli Trees makes picky preschoolers think they will be more fun to eat. What's more, the children continued to be more willing to eat the food the following day.[54]

5. *Keep on trying.* Studies show that *calm,* repeated exposure to a new food (especially vegetables, which are the focus of the studies) daily for five to fourteen days is often effective in getting kids to overcome a food aversion.[55] So don't give up on the food if your kid puts it in the "yuck" category the first time. Instead choose one new item at a time to introduce in small, nonthreatening portions (even a teaspoon is fine). Serving the new item with a couple of familiar staples increases the likelihood that a kid will taste the new food. Do give your child a heads-up as to whether the food will taste sweet, salty, or sour. If all else fails, for the sake of your child's nutrition try disguising a snippet of pureed vegetables in the spaghetti sauce or adding a dash of protein powder to a milk shake. Books offering creative ways to "hide" nutritious foods include *Deceptively Delicious,* by Jessica Seinfeld; *How to Get Your Kid to Eat . . . but Not Too Much,* by Ellyn Satter; *The Sneaky Chef: Simple Strategies for Hiding Healthy Foods in Kids' Favorite Meals,* by Missy Chase Lapine; and *Just Two More Bites! Helping Picky Eaters Say Yes to Food,* by Linda Piette.

Not every kid will like every food, and you can't change someone's eating habits overnight, so be patient. The real goal is to make sure your child has positive eating experiences now that will help promote healthy eating habits for a lifetime. Achieving that goal will also make mealtimes more pleasant for all. Bon appétit!

WHAT TO EXPECT BY STAGES AND AGES

Preschooler   Picky eating is common among young children regardless of sex. Kids generally stop eating a variety of foods around age two—when taste buds start changing and appetites start slowing down—and the behavior can last until around the age of four or five (if not longer). Food jags are common in which the child only wants to eat the same item repeatedly; a natural skepticism toward new foods is a normal part of child development and can last up to a year (or longer). Kids often prefer sweeter and saltier foods and refuse anything that tastes sour or bitter. Drinking too much milk can be an appetite suppressor, particularly at this age.[56]

LATE-BREAKING NEWS

Five Ways Parents Positively Influence Their Kids' Eating Habits

Although genetics plays a large role in finickiness, there is substantial evidence that certain parental responses reduce the odds that a kid will be a picky eater.[57] Studies find that parents of less picky eaters

1. Eat more fruits and vegetables and model good eating habits[58]

2. Expose their kids to an assortment of foods at an early age

3. Continue exposing their kids to the same disliked food item at least ten to fifteen times

4. Don't pressure or use bribes to get their kids to eat ("You get dessert if you eat your peas")

5. Avoid making comments about foods they themselves may or may not enjoy

Beware: your child is watching and will copy your behavior. How are you doing?

School Age   You can extend your kids' tolerance and enjoyment of a variety of foods by making fruits and vegetables available at home and by modeling eating them yourself.[59] Watch out for excessive consumption of sweetened beverages, such as soft drinks and flavored drinks that do not contain 100 percent fruit juice; these increase calorie intake, fill kids up, and don't provide essential nutrients.

Tween   Tweens tend to be less picky, though some kids never get over their earlier childhood eating habits and may still have strong food preferences. Less active kids have decreased appetites. Braces can cause discomfort in chewing certain foods. Peer pressure peaks; studies show that if a kid's classmate or sibling enjoys a particular food, the child is more likely to enjoy it or be enticed to try an undesirable food.[60] So extend a dinner invitation to your child's friend and see if her tastes rubs off on your kid. Food phases (such as vegetarianism or refusal to eat meat products) as well as appetite fluctuations are common at this age, often in response to peer pressure or a budding social consciousness.[61] This is the prime time for the development of eating disorders, so watch out if your child's picky eating habits become more extreme. Look for a sudden drop in weight; critical and demeaning comments or excessive concern about her appearance; obsessive weighing or calorie counting; and physical complaints, such as headache, stomach pain, dizziness, or exhaustion.[62] If you are at all concerned, consult your pediatrician.

One Parent's Answer

A mom from Topeka writes:

My kid was the world's pickiest eater and only ate the same thing for weeks on end. One day I caught her watching the Food Network and it was my "aha moment." I bought her a set of measuring spoons and a kid cookbook, and she started doing simple tasks to fix the meals (washing the grapes, making simple desserts and side dishes) and loved it. Cooking her own food ("like the lady on the Food Network") was what finally got her to try new food. Of course, it didn't hurt that her dad and brother made such a big deal out of her recipes either.

DAY TO DAY

Safety

SEE ALSO: *Bullied, Bullying, Cyberbullying, Dependent, Internet Safety, Intolerant, Peer Pressure, Teased*

THE PROBLEM

Red Flags

Engages in risky or unsafe behaviors, is too trusting, is clueless and unaware of potential danger in situation or surroundings, doesn't know how to recognize suspicious behaviors or ask for help, has poor decision-making skills, is too dependent on you

The Change to Parent For

Your child learns proven age-appropriate tips that will keep him safer in dangerous situations.

Why Change?

Let's face it: raising kids has always been a bit scary, but these days there sure are a number of issues that increase our heart rates, including highly publicized kidnappings, cyberbullying, school shootings, and pedophiles. Those are in addition to all those other worries—tornados, earthquakes, fires, hurricanes, getting hit by a car, or drowning in a swimming pool. Although there are no guarantees of our children's health and well-being, research proves that we can help kids learn simple safety tips and size up unsafe situations so that they will be less likely to be harmed. And we can start boosting our kids' "safety smarts" when they are preschoolers. Although you may fear that talking about such frightening issues will scare the pants off your kids, not to do so is a big mistake. The secret is to bring up such topics in a relaxed way, just as you discuss other daily matters, and not to cover too many skills at once. Just remember to consider your child's age and developmental level, and the kinds of safety know-how he needs at this point in his life. Here are the four most common kid safety issues and parent concerns, along with practical tips. They'll keep your child safer because he'll know what to do "just in case" any type of emergency crops up—and they'll give *you* peace of mind.

THE SOLUTION

Four Most Common Kid Safety Issues, and Strategies for Change

1. *Kidnappings and predators.* Leading the top of parents' safety concerns are stranger abductions, even though the actual threat to your child is extremely small. Regardless of how rare, the issue is one in today's world that can't be ignored. Just do know that a child is far more likely to be abducted by someone the child personally knows. Here are a few critical safety strategies to help prevent a tragedy:

   - *Be proactive.* Don't put your child's name on clothing or belongings for strangers to read. Keep an up-to-date, high-quality photograph; a written physical description including height, weight, eye, and hair color updated every six months; and a medical and dental history of each child handy. Have your child fingerprinted by the police; ask the police to file the prints and keep a copy yourself. Also keep a photo of your child in your wallet at all times in case he gets lost in the park or mall.

   - *Keep close tabs.* Know where your kids are. Know their friends and their friends' parents. Have your tween get into the habit of checking in with you so you know where he is at *all* times. Consider purchasing an inexpensive cell phone with a GPS tracking device for a younger child or a no-frills phone for your tween so that you can monitor his comings and goings.

   - *Teach "not OK" touching.* Teach your kid about "private" body parts and the difference between "OK" and "not-OK" touches. Then teach your child to say "No!" if someone tries to touch him in his bathing suit areas or makes him feel at all afraid, uncomfortable, or confused, and to get away as quickly as possible.

   - *Emphasize "No secrets allowed."* Set a rule: *"If any adult tells you to keep a secret, tell me right away."*

   - *Help your child recognize suspicious behavior.* Experts suggest that instead of scaring (and possibly confusing) your kids with the "Stranger = Danger" approach, you would do better to teach them to recognize suspicious situations. Here are a few adult behaviors to teach your kids to be aware of:

   Asking for help: "I need help finding my child. Please help me!" "Can you help me look for my puppy?"

   Offering treats: "Would you like some candy?" "I have a skateboard in my car. Would you like it?"

   Feigning an emergency: "Hurry! Your mom was in an accident. I'll take you to the hospital."

   Flaunting authority: "I think you're the kid who hurt my son. Come with me, and we'll go find your parents."

Faking friendship with a parent: "I'm an old friend of your dad's. He asked me to come over. Can you take me to your house?"

Role-play suspicious situations such as these with your child so that he'll be more alert and can respond more quickly if the real issue ever arises. Repeatedly remind your child *never* to open the house door to a stranger and never to tell someone that his parents are not home.

- *Establish a family secret code.* Make this your one essential family rule: "Never *leave with* anyone *who can't tell you our family's secret code.*" Choose some simple, memorable word, such as "Geronimo," and stress that the code must remain secret. The *only* ones who know are your family members, a designated family friend or relative who is your emergency contact, or trusted individuals (such as a nanny or ongoing babysitter) who are responsible for your kids in your absence.

- *Forbid meeting online contacts.* Forbid your child ever to divulge personal information, such as his name (or yours), address, birthday, or phone number online. Emphasize that your child should *never, under absolutely any circumstances,* meet anyone he has connected with by phone or online. Explain that someone posing as an eleven-year-old online could actually be a thirty-year-old child molester. (See *Internet Safety,* p. 610.)

- *Teach "drop, yell, and run."* If your child needs to get away quickly, teach him to drop whatever he is carrying (you run faster if you're not carrying something), yell and make a loud scene, and run. If possible, run toward an adult and yell, "Help! This is not my dad!" Tell your child that if he is grabbed, he should fight back, scream, and hold on to anything—such as his bicycle handles or the car door—to make it more difficult for an abductor to take him. Emphasize that you will *never* be upset if your child loses something or hurts someone if he's trying to protect himself.

2. *Public places.* Here are a few tips for teaching your kid how to be safer in public places. (See also *Bullied,* p. 323.)

- *Teach your child to seek help.* Have your child practice saying, "I need help" so that he can assert himself. Tell him that if he is lost, he should walk to the cash register or find an employee wearing the company insignia, a police officer, or a woman (preferably with a child). Tell him *never* to leave the building unless there is a fire or threat of personal injury.

- *Teach your child to stay put.* Teach your child "freeze, look, call out, and wait." As soon as he knows he's lost, your child stops and freezes; looks around from the spot he's standing to see if he can see you; calls out, "Mom!" or "Dad!" and then waits for you to find him. This is critical especially if you are out-of-doors or in a large open place. Teaching your child to call out your actual name instead of Mom or Dad can be helpful in quickly getting your attention in a crowd. Hint: dressing your child in bright colors will help him stand out so that you can spot him quicker.

- *Agree on a meeting spot.* When you are going to be in a crowd, always agree on a place to meet just in case you are separated.

- *Practice safe crossings.* Do not overestimate your child's "safety smarts" when it comes to crossing a street. The National Highway Traffic Safety Administration has found that kids do not master the ability to safely cross a street until they are at least ten years old.[63] Admonish your kids not to play near a street and to tell you if a ball rolls into the street. Practice safe crossing by teaching your child "stop-left-right-left": he should stop at the curb and then look left, right, then left again before crossing; even then he should always keep looking as he crosses. Also teach him to watch for turning vehicles and to try to catch the driver's eye. (Most kids mistakenly assume the driver has seen them.) Preschoolers are impulsive and dash into a street, so insist on one rule when crossing: *"Your hand is glued to Mommy."*

- *Make sure he sticks to places where he can be seen and heard.* Make sure your child knows to walk, skateboard, play, or ride his bike only in well-lit, people-trafficked areas. Teach your child that "safer spots" are places where he can be seen and heard by an adult, such as the middle of a playground or park, the front of a well-lit building, under a lamppost, and the seat behind the bus driver (where the driver can see your child in his rearview mirror). "Unseen and unheard" spots include far corners of a park, unlit areas, the rear of a building, the last restroom stall, and the edge of a parking lot. The "seen and heard" rule is critical because kids are far more likely to fall prey to a bully, kidnapper, or predator in areas unsupervised by adults. Teach that there is safety in numbers and to stick with a buddy.

- *Tell your child to use public restrooms with caution.* Always take your younger child *with you* into a public bathroom. Tell your tween to use the stall closest to the entrance and ask a friend to accompany him.

3. *Firearms and armed violence.* Although schools are still one of the safest places for our children, the rash of school shootings has dramatically heightened the fears of parents and kids alike. But here's your reality check: your child is far more likely to be injured by a firearm while playing at a friend's home or in your own house than he is at school. Here are a few key safety skills:

- *Talk about gun safety.* Seventy-three percent of parents believe it to be extremely unlikely that their own children would handle a gun if they accidentally discovered one,[64] but studies by emergency physicians proved that to be a huge parental misconception.[65] The fact is that kids are frequently finding their parents' guns and hurting people with them, especially themselves. So have serious and repeated talks about gun safety with your child. Stress that weapons are *never* to be touched without your supervision and permission and that he should *always* tell an adult if he comes across one.

- *Lock up firearms.* Unload all firearms, then lock and store guns separately from ammunition in a secure safe. Hide the keys where children cannot find them (and don't tell them where those keys are). Many states hold parents liable for their children's actions, including lack of parental supervision of guns.

- *Query other parents.* More than 40 percent of U.S. households with children have a gun, and in a quarter of those, the weapon is sometimes stored loaded and unlocked.[66] Yet only 30 percent of parents have ever asked their kid whether there are guns in the homes of his friends. This is a potentially life-or-death safety issue, so don't be timid: ask any parent whose house your child visits, "Do you have a gun in your home?" If he or she says yes, ask, "Is it securely locked?" If you feel a bit uncomfortable doing this, just explain that it's a question you always ask every parent. But please ask!

- *Remind your child to report threats.* Teach your children the "Airport Security Rule": take *any* threat seriously, regardless of whether you think the kid may be joking. Your child should tell you or the adult in charge of any event or situation they may have heard about in which someone could be hurt (such as a bomb threat, school shooting, planned violence, suicide, or fight). Stress that it's always "better to be safe than sorry."

- *Teach your child to act quickly.* Tell your child that if he ever hears a gunshot, he should do whatever he can to protect himself: climb out of a second-story window, run zigzag away from the sound, barricade entrances with desks or heavy objects, and take low cover behind something strong, such as an automobile in a parking lot.

- *Encourage your child to use his gut instinct.* Stress to your child that if he ever feels that he could be in danger, he should act on that instinct. Chances are, he's right.

4. *Weather emergencies.* Over the last few years, there appears to be a trend toward more violent weather—tornadoes, hurricanes, floods, typhoons, earthquakes, severe thunderstorms, and lightning. Although of course you always strive to ensure that your child is in the care of a capable and knowledgeable adult, most experts suggest that you teach your child a few preliminary "just in case" guidelines, including these safety tips, in the event of severe weather conditions:

- *Develop a family emergency plan.* Decide where your family members should go in case of a weather emergency. That location will vary depending on what part of the country you live in. For instance, in California, you would prepare for an earthquake; in Kansas, a tornado. Practice going to your chosen location with your children so that if you are ever separated, they will know where to find you.

- *Select a family contact.* Designate a close friend or relative outside your living area as the contact in the event that your children are separated from you. Your children should know the first and last name of the contact, the phone number, and the contact's town and state.

- *Locate emergency supplies.* Show your kids the location of your first-aid kit, flashlight and batteries, wrench, and battery-operated radio. Teach your older child basic first aid and how to operate a fire extinguisher, turn off the water heater and gas lines, and tune to the local radio station for specific weather information (or purchase a weather radio, which alerts you to severe weather and other emergencies twenty-four hours a day).

- *Practice safety responses.* Tell your child that in case of a storm, he should not hold anything metal or stand under a tree, so as not to be struck by lightning. Tell him *not* to use a phone with a cord, take a bath, or shower during a storm. In case of a tornado, earthquake, or explosion, your child should crouch down on his knees under a sturdy table or desk and clasp his hands behind the back of his neck. Stay clear of windows, fireplaces, glass, or fallen objects.

Teach General Safety

Depending on your child's age, teach these general tips and have your kid practice them in case of emergencies:

- Never touch fallen power lines.
- Beware of stray animals. Do *not* approach any animal that is growling or snarling or that appears upset.
- If you smell fire, crawl on the floor to safety. If a door feels warm, do not open it. If possible, cover your head and neck with a wet towel.
- Leave the building immediately if you hear a hissing sound or smell natural gas.

WHAT TO EXPECT BY STAGES AND AGES

Preschooler   Although a major worry for kids this age is that they'll be separated from their parents, they still wander and get lost, so keep your child in your sight at all times. He should be able to verbalize his first and last name (and your last name if it's different) and his phone number with area code; he should know how to dial 911. Insist that he wear a medical bracelet with emergency contact information if he is not capable of

One Parent's Answer

A dad from Tallahassee writes:

We've had a rash of hurricanes these last few years. It just seems that the weather has become more violent. As my kids got older, I had one of those "aha" moments when I realized that my wife and I may not be there when there's a medical emergency. So we decided to enroll all four of us in a CPR class put on by the American Heart Association. It was one of the best things we've ever done. The rules for CPR have changed since I learned them in scouting years ago, so it was a great refresher course. My wife and I now have peace of mind that in case there is an emergency, my kids know what to do to save each other. I write this just as another hurricane is headed for our town. I strongly recommend that every parent visit www.americanheart.org/cpr or call 877-AHA-4CPR for a class near you.

reciting such information. Kids this age should know what to do when lost, how to ask for help, and that they should never leave a building. Teach basic safety skills: a "stranger" is someone we don't know; never say your parents aren't there or answer a door by yourself. Help him identify people to turn to for help in emergency situations, such as a store employee (point out name tags or uniforms), family friends (people Mommy and Daddy have dinner with), or another mommy (a woman with a child). Designate which body parts are "private" and teach "OK" and "not-OK" touches. Enforce the idea that he must never touch a gun and should leave the scene and call you ASAP if someone has one.

School Age   In addition to the preschooler safety skills, teach your children to trust any uncomfortable feelings they have about *someone or a situation,* and to speak up whenever they don't feel safe—even if it seems as if they're talking back to an adult. Emphasize that you will support your child's decision. Help prepare your child for safety issues by playing "What if?" games: "What would you do if . . . *a stranger offered to give you a ride? a friend wanted you to play with his dad's gun? you were outside and heard thunder?*" No matter how "grown up" they think they are, school-age kids are immature and can't make the necessary judgment calls to protect themselves.

Tween   Unsupervised time increases and the urge to "fit in" peaks, so safety issues now include those involving peer pressure, such as alcohol, drugs, prescription medications, smoking, sex, and dare taking. Teach your tween how to make safer, more responsible choices, and practice role-playing risky scenarios with him. Regardless of your child's quest for independence, stay involved and establish clear boundaries and parameters. Know where your kid is *at all times,* especially from three to six o'clock, when this age group is most likely to get in trouble and be unsafe.

Sleepless

SEE ALSO: *Defiant, Depressed, Fearful, Grief, Perfectionist, Rejected, Stressed, Test Anxiety*

THE PROBLEM

Red Flags

Resists or fights going to bed, has trouble falling or staying asleep; lack of sleep has a negative effect on behavior, learning, or emotional or physical health

The Change to Parent For

Your child learns new habits to help her get a more restful night's sleep.

Question: "I know my daughter doesn't always get enough sleep, but how do I know when it's really becoming a problem to be concerned about?"

Answer: Every kid has an occasional sleepless night, but when you notice sleep problems occurring more regularly and affecting your child's behavior, mood, learning, health, or family relationships, then try what I'm recommending in this entry, and if those strategies don't work, it might be time to talk to your doctor.

Why Change?

Chronic sleep difficulties are among the most common childhood problems these days. The American Academy of Sleep Medicine estimates that one in three kids is sleep deprived.[67] What's more, 90 percent of parents believe that their kids are getting enough sleep, even though they're not.[68] The result is children who are cranky, irritable, hyper, moody, unable to focus, headachy, and always lethargic. Sound familiar? If so, your child may be sleep deprived.

Research from the University of Michigan found that as many as 25 percent of kids diagnosed with ADHD have an underlying sleep disorder causing their symptoms.[69] If sleep habits are left unchanged, the resulting sleep deprivation can also stunt growth, ruin grades, lower performance, encourage drug and alcohol use, damage self-esteem, and dramatically increase the likelihood of car accidents (for teens). Kids who get enough sleep are more likely to function better and are less likely to be moody or to act out.

DAY TO DAY

585

Just waiting for your child to grow out of a sleep problem isn't the answer. Sleep is essential for your child's health and growth. Researchers followed school-age children and found that many continued having difficulties falling asleep a year later.[70] But there are proven solutions to end those bedtime battles and help our kids learn better sleep routines that will help them wake up more refreshed and rested.

Signs and Symptoms

Each child responds to sleeplessness differently, but here are possible signs and behaviors to look for on those days that your child is getting less sleep:

- Angers more easily, is more impulsive or defiant
- Is moodier, more irritable and cranky, sadder, more tearful, or anxious
- Has trouble concentrating or focusing, is more distractible and forgetful, has school problems
- Has difficulty waking up, trouble getting out the door; is groggier, late for class
- Yawns frequently, falls asleep during class (talk to her teacher), is tired during the day, needs a regular nap
- Acts out more; has tantrums or meltdowns, more behavior problems
- Needs more attention, is clingier, regresses, sucks thumb, uses baby talk
- Has trouble going to sleep, wakes up at night, has trouble falling back to sleep, has nightmares
- Talks excessively, acts more hyper or "wired," seems "overtired," consumes more caffeinated beverages (cola or energy drinks)

THE SOLUTION

Step 1. Early Intervention

- *Identify the source of the sleeping problem.* Your first change step is to find the reasons your child is losing sleep. Here are eleven causes of sleepless nights. Check those culprits that may be causing your kid to lose a little shut-eye:
  - ☐ *Temperament.* Your child's biological clock is not wired to go to bed early, and trying to get her to adjust will be a struggle. Some kids need more sleep; others less.
  - ☐ *Worries and fears.* Normal fears and stress, whether caused by real-world events, an impending move, or the "boogey man," can cause nightmares and jar the child from a sound sleep.

Pay Attention to This!
The Five Top Sleep Spoilers and Simple Solutions

1. *Nightmares.* Scary dreams are a common and normal part of child development. They usually occur in the early morning hours. The child can recall vivid details of the scary and sometimes terrifying dream and may have trouble going back to sleep. *Solution:* Remain calm, hold your child (if she will allow it), and talk in a soft, reassuring voice until she falls back asleep. It's best not to ask, "What did you dream about?" because it can trigger the fear again. Pressure and worries can bring on nightmares, so assess your child's stress load.

2. *Night terrors.* Your child awakens suddenly from a deep sleep, sits up, stares "glassy eyed," and cries for help. She generally doesn't respond because she is only partially awake, and she probably won't remember a thing the next day. *Solution:* Keep your child safe from injury, but don't try to jar her awake or even comfort her: it could frighten her and make it more difficult to calm down. Night terrors usually go away by themselves and don't indicate emotional difficulties.

3. *Sleepwalking.* Your child wanders around clumsily with eyes open but without fully waking. She usually won't remember anything the next morning. *Solution:* Ensure that the environment is safe; put a gate at the top of the stairs; barricade unsafe areas; gently lead her back to bed.

4. *Restless legs syndrome.* The child experiences uncomfortable sensations like pins and needles in her legs; she kicks repetitively at night to relieve discomfort. *Solution:* Usually exercise and adequate sleep resolve the problem, but if it persists, seek a doctor's advice.

5. *Sleep apnea.* Your child snores, breathes heavily, and gasps with short little breaths; the condition can cause sleepiness during the day and headaches, especially in the morning. *Solution:* Talk to your pediatrician, who may recommend an overnight sleep study, removal of the tonsils or adenoids, or weight loss.

☐ *Sleeping in on weekends.* Staying up later and sleeping in longer upset a kid's internal body clock and create homemade jetlag.[71] Watch out for too many sleepovers!

☐ *Caffeine intake.* Kids who have at least one caffeinated beverage a day lose an average of three-and-a-half hours of sleep per week.[72] Watch out for chocolate, sodas, coffee, energy drinks, coffee-flavored ice cream, cold medicine, pain relievers, and study aids.

☐ *Late-night bedroom activity.* Talking and texting on cell phones, playing videos games, watching TV, and playing with pets can all be overstimulating and keep kids up past their bedtime without parents' knowing; those same things can wake kids up if they have fallen asleep. Sixty-two percent of kids admitted to using cell phones after turning in, and their parents were clueless.[73]

☐ *Daytime sleep.* Too long or unnecessary naps create nighttime sleep disruption; tweens shouldn't nap longer than sixty minutes in the afternoon, or at all in the evening after dinner.

☐ *Inconsistent bedtime routine.* A regular routine conditions the body to expect to go to bed and get up at the same time every day.[74]

☐ *Strenuous activity.* Roughhousing, late-night practices and games, and exercising close to bedtime all overstimulate kids and make it hard for them to relax and wind down.

☐ *Overscheduling and stress.* Stress mounts, exhaustion kicks in, and the body compensates by making extra cortisol; trouble sleeping can be the result.[75]

☐ *Bedroom atmosphere.* Light "wakes up" the brain; too warm a room increases non-REM sleep and changes sleep patterns. A neutral air temperature and darkened room are optimal.

☐ *Illness and discomfort.* Sore teeth, an earache, a stuffy nose, bedwetting, braces, sleep apnea, and restless legs syndrome can rob sleep.

- *Identify your child's particular sleep needs.* As I mentioned earlier, 90 percent of parents polled think their kids get enough sleep—and most are wrong. To parent for change, you must diagnose *your* child's sleep requirements, keep a record of your findings, then create solutions based on *her* needs.

  - *Track a normal sleep schedule.* Each day for a week, write the exact time your child goes to bed and when she finally dozes off. Kids say they have far more difficulty falling asleep than what their parents believe.[76] Do check in to see if she's really asleep.

  - *Check the signs of sleep problems.* Which one of the signs and symptoms (listed earlier) apply to your child? For the real test, ask her first-period teacher.

- *Consult experts.* How much actual shut-eye time does your child require to be her best? Refer to What to Expect by Stages and Ages (p. 592) for guidelines, keeping in mind that each child is unique.

- *Watch for "bed readiness."* Be alert for "sleepy" signs: yawning, rubbing eyes, crankiness, lying down, spacing out, clinginess, her telling you she's tired. If those signals are coming at the same time each night, schedule bedtime accordingly.

ONE SIMPLE SOLUTION

Be Consistent with Your Child's Nightly Sleep Routine

The simplest proven solution for helping kids get a better night's sleep is to follow a nightly routine. One study of 170 kids found that those in white-collar families got to sleep later and rose earlier than those in working-class families, but they actually got a more restful night's sleep.[77] Why? For one simple reason: their bedtimes and wake times were consistent, and they kept to that nighttime ritual. So stick to a bedtime routine until it becomes a habit.

- *Discover nighttime necessities.* Identify what *your child* needs for a restful sleep so that you can make those requirements part of her bedroom routine. A darkened room with the nightlight on? An extra comforter with a sleep tape playing?

- *Rule out medical causes.* Seek a doctor's advice for sleepwalking, restless legs syndrome, sleep apnea, or bedwetting. (See the Pay Attention to This! box, p. 587.)

Step 2. Rapid Response

Your next change step is to create a bedtime routine tailored to your child's unique temperament, body clock, and sleep needs, and *then stick to it.*

- *Set a regular bedtime schedule.* Once you know your child's sleep needs, announce the bedtime hour and stick to it. Research finds that parents who don't enforce a regular bedtime can expect to experience more nighttime disturbances.[78]

- *Sync your child's body clock to the schedule.* Plan ahead to help your child's sleep schedule during vacation get into sync with the upcoming school schedule. If the new bedtime is more than one hour different, you may need to gradually phase in the new sleep time to help your child adjust. Shortening the bedtime by twenty minutes each night might help. The process can take from several days to several weeks.

- *Start bedtime prep earlier.* Begin the "getting ready" process *at least* twenty to thirty minutes before lights-out. The wind-down time helps calm the child and gets you out of the battle. For younger children, try hanging a picture chart showing the sequence of bedtime events (for example, having a light snack, taking a bath, putting on pajamas, brushing teeth, hearing a bedtime story, saying prayers, and saying goodnight). *Stick to that same nightly routine every night until it becomes a habit.*

- *Create wind-down rituals.* Many kids are so wired from stress, exercising, studying, or crowded schedules that it's tough for them to drift off when the lights go out. If your child needs time to wind down, add it into the schedule. Those traditional rituals (taking a warm bath, writing in a journal, taking a shower, reading, sipping warm milk) do help prepare kids' bodies for a better night's sleep.[79] And what about a soothing back rub? The University of Miami School of Medicine finds that a massage not only helps kids fall asleep more easily and sleep more soundly but also reduces stress hormones. The trick is to help your child discover what works for her and then go through the same ritual every night to help her relax.

- *Create positive associations.* Watch out for kids equating bedtime with a power struggle. "If you don't do what I tell you, you're going to bed." Those battles will increase. Instead, your new response is to create positive associations with bedtime that your child will look forward to. *"It's time to snuggle up with a book . . . Let's cuddle a minute together before we turn out the lights . . . Don't wake up until you smell your favorite pancakes cooking . . ."*

- *Stop bed hopping.* Encourage your child to fall asleep on her own. Once kids get used to sleeping with you, they are reluctant to sleep in their own beds. Letting your kid fall asleep in your bed and then moving her to hers can jar her sleep schedule. You can take the firm approach—"You must sleep in your bed"—or you can make the transition more gradual. Set a sleeping bag on the floor next to your bed (not *in* your bed) and drag it gently each night a bit closer to her room until she finally sleeps in her own bed.

- *Respond only once.* You put your kid in bed, all is well, and then the requests start in (for water, a hug, reading the book *again*). Sleep expert Jodi Mindell suggests that you respond to only *one* request and then not return.[80] You can give your younger child a blue block (any object will do) that stands for "one request granted." Once the object is turned in, you no longer comply. You *must* be firm and consistent.

- *Pass the plan on.* Ideally, all adults who supervise your child's bedtime (Grandma, babysitter, your parenting partner) need to be aware of your sleep plan and whatever discoveries you have made to help your child get a more restful night's sleep. Consistency is critical.

ONE SIMPLE SOLUTION

Imagine a Restful Place

First help your kid identify a peaceful place—Grandma's, a tree fort, the beach—and have her re-create the spot in her mind: *"Remember how calm you felt at the lake? Put that picture of that restful place in your mind before you go to sleep."* Guide her to do the visualization while she's breathing deeply, and have her practice doing it until she can pull up the image herself to reduce tension, feel more relaxed, and fall asleep more easily.

Step 3. Develop Habits for Change

Your final step is to help your child learn nightly routines that put her body clock on a regular schedule to get more restful sleep. She will use those same habits at home, on a sleepover, or away at summer camp or college. Here are a few of the best research-proven habits to teach kids:

- *Listen to soothing music.* Research at the University of Taiwan found that listening to relaxing music before bedtime lowers the heart rate and improves sleep 26 percent by the end of the first week.[81] The ideal music is soft and slow—around sixty to eighty beats per minute—such as Mozart, chants, or white noise, but allow your child to choose her selections. She can then bring an MP3 player loaded with the same music whenever she's sleeping away from home.

- *Revise the nighttime schedule.* Educate an older child about sleep stealers and then encourage her to revise her schedule so that she gets a better night's rest. Start by asking, "How many hours do you think you need for a good night's sleep? Okay, then let's think of ways to help you get those hours." You might remind her, "Turn off the computer or TV screen at least a half hour before bedtime. Those flickering lights signal to your brain to stay alert." "Maybe you can practice your dance routine after school? Exercising and rigorous activity too close to bedtime can make you too wired."[82] "Those energy drinks help you now, but they'll also keep you awake at night. What time do you think you should stop drinking that cola?"

- *Teach mental relaxers.* Many kids fall asleep, then wake up in the middle of the night and are unable to drift back to sleep, so teach your child a relaxation exercise. She could try breathing deeply while focusing on a different body part from head to toe and then releasing tension from each area while exhaling; counting backwards from one hundred with her eyes closed; or counting sheep.

One Parent's Answer

A dad from Seattle writes:

We tried all the usual bedtime routines: sipping hot cocoa, taking a bath, reading nighttime stories, but the nightly battles continued with my son. Then one night he asked if I'd play soldiers with him. I figured, what the heck. We played a few minutes and then I tucked him into bed. Eventually playing together was what he looked forward to all day, and the bedtime battles stopped. I guess all he really wanted was a little one-on-one time with me. I just wish I had thought of it a lot sooner!

WHAT TO EXPECT BY STAGES AND AGES

Each child has different sleep needs, and some kids just need more sleep than others. Here are the recommended hours of sleep kids need by age, but always tailor that to your unique child.[83]

Preschooler   Children this age need 11 to 13 hours total, including naps (at age three, 12 hours total; at age four, 11.5 hours total; at age five, 11 hours total). They usually nap one to two hours in the afternoon and stop napping between three and five years of age; only 24 percent of five-year-olds still nap.[84] Imagination flourishes at this age, so nighttime fears and nightmares are common. Sleepwalking and sleep terrors peak during these years.

School Age   School-age kids need 9 to 11 hours total (at ages six and seven, 10 to 11 total hours of nightly sleep; at ages eight and nine, 10 to 10.25 hours; at age ten, 9.75 hours). Sleep difficulties are common among seven- to ten-year-olds because they spend more time in "light sleep" and less in REM.[85] Almost 40 percent of school-age kids suffer from sleep deprivation, which can lead to mood swings and to such behavioral problems as hyperactivity and trouble focusing in school.[86] Activities (social, athletic, and extracurricular) and school demands increase, and stress can mount.

Tween   At age eleven, kids need about 9.5 total hours; at ages twelve and thirteen, they need 9.25 total hours. Internal clocks start to undergo changes, making it more difficult for kids to wake up early and feel refreshed.[87] Kids' sleep needs decrease naturally by about fifteen minutes on average every year.[88] Inadequate sleep can lead to mood swings, irritability, and concentration difficulties, which can have an impact on kids' ability to learn.

More Helpful Advice

Solve Your Child's Sleep Problems, by Richard Ferber

The No-Cry Sleep Solution for Toddlers and Preschoolers: Gentle Ways to Stop Bedtime Battles and Improve Your Child's Sleep, by Elizabeth Pantley

Sleepless in America: Is Your Child Misbehaving or Missing Sleep? by Mary Sheedy Kurcinka

Healthy Sleep Habits, Happy Child, by Marc Weissbluth

Traveling

SEE ALSO: *Boredom, Reading, Sibling Rivalry*

THE QUESTION

"We're taking a car trip with our three kids and would appreciate some sanity savers. They're so used to being electronically entertained, but I'm hoping for alternatives besides having them watching movies the whole time or screaming at each other. Any ideas?"

THE ANSWER

"Aren't we there yet?" "Why do we have to go on this dumb trip?" "Mom, Krista's touching me!" Of course we want to take our kids on road-trip adventures they'll remember all their lives, but then comes reality. Staying in close quarters with kids for a long period of time is bound to spell T-R-O-U-B-L-E. Here are a few "sanity savers" to help you make your car, train, or plane trip more pleasant for you and the kids. The real secret is just a little planning.

- *Set travel rules.* "No hitting or yelling." "Seats are rotated each day." Devise whatever rules you need to maintain sanity and safety. Just lay down those rules before starting off on your trip. Once your kids know you mean business, they usually resolve their problems.

- *Pack rations.* Bring along nonmessy snacks (watch the sugar content) and a small ice chest filled with bottled water or boxed drinks. And if you put that chest *between* two kids, it creates not only a great divider but also a built-in desk to draw or write on.

- *Require personal packing.* Give each child a small backpack to hold *everything* (besides clothes and medicine) she wants to bring (teddy bear, small pillow, book, Etch-a-Sketch, MP3 player, sticker book). It should be able to fit at her feet in the car or be instantly accessible.

- *Do the oldies but goodies.* This is a great time to have your kids learn those old camp songs like "The Wheels on the Bus" or "The Ants Go Marching . . ." Bring along travel bingo cards or a joke book. One child can be your resident "comedian" who teaches the rest of the carload a different joke every fifteen minutes.

- *Hold a scavenger hunt.* Ask your kids to brainstorm the one thing they want to collect each day. The item must be no cost and something they must find. Some examples: a bird feather, a wildflower, a pebble. Give each child a small box or folder to store her mementos.

- *Listen to books.* You can also download books into portable MP3 players or bring along books on tape or CD so that each kid can listen to her own favorite story. Of course, music is always great, but what a memory if you listened to *James and the Giant Peach* or *Charlotte's Web.*

- *Learn geography.* Bring along a map for your kids to mark the family's route with a marking pen and learn map skills as well.

- *Make frequent stops.* Plan for little breaks and fun little outings. A quick game of Frisbee or a relay race can revitalize those kids. But no matter what, stop *at least* every two hours.

When all else fails, consider traveling at night or when your kids are napping, or bring a bottle of aspirin (for yourself). After all, it is your trip as well.

Part 9
Electronics

OUT OF THE MOUTHS OF BABES
WHY GOD MADE MOMS

Answers given by second-grade schoolchildren to the following question:

If you could change one thing about your mom, what would it be?

1. She has this weird thing about me keeping
my room clean. I'd get rid of that.

2. I'd make my mom smarter. Then she would know
it was my sister who did it and not me.

3. I would like for her to get rid of those
invisible eyes on the back of her head.

Cell Phone

SEE ALSO: *Cyberbullying, Internet Safety, Materialistic, Money, Video Games*

THE QUESTION

"We got a cell phone for our ten-year-old so she could phone us when she got to school and was heading home after soccer practice. Now she's talking all day and texting her friends, and our monthly bill has tripled. Worse than that, I caught her looking at Internet pornography on her cell. Her little sister, who's only five years old, wants a phone too. I want our kids to be safe and have friends, but what can I do to control cell phone use and keep the bills down?"

THE ANSWER

Remember those days when you carried a dime in your shoe just in case you had to use the pay phone to call home? Well, those days are gone. Today, kids as young as kindergartners carry cell phones. In fact, between 5 and 10 percent of five-year-olds have a mobile phone; by age ten, fully one-third of American kids have a phone.[1] Within the next three years, more than half of all eight- to twelve-year-olds will have their own mobile phone.[2]

But many parents are agonizing over whether or not to buy their kids a cell phone. Do they take the plunge for the sake of peace of mind? Will they be able to control the monthly bill? How do they keep the kids from texting in class? And how are they to know if their child is ready or if she even needs a cell phone? But there's another problem: the advanced technology of cell phones brings with it such troubling issues as Internet safety, cyberbullying, predators, and access to pornography and adult-content Web sites.

Here are some ways to change and control the way your kids use cell phones:

- *Distinguish between "needs" and "wants."* Every kid wants a cell phone, but there is a big difference between just "having to have one" so she looks cool and really, truly needing one. These factors help you decide if you should make that purchase:

  Safety: Does your child walk home alone or spend any time away from the direct supervision of an adult? Is she being bullied? Does she have an emotional or medical issue?

  Schedule: Do you or your child have schedule conflicts that could lead to her being stranded? Are there after-school, evening, or weekend activities with possible schedule changes?

Peace of mind: Would this help you relax knowing you can connect at any time?

Affordability: Is this purchase something your family can afford?

Responsibility: Is your child reliable and capable of taking care of possessions without reminders?

Weigh those factors carefully; if you have any doubt, delay the purchase. Even though your child may say, "*Everybody* has a cell phone," please note that 54 percent of eight- to ten-year-olds are more likely to borrow their parents' phone (and do so more than three times a week) than own a phone of their own.[3] So put your child on a "test run" and let her borrow your phone first. You can then assess her "responsibility quotient" and whether she can adhere to your expectations.

- *Get educated about a phone's capabilities.* Cell phones now come with all the technology of your home computer, which is why you must get savvy about their features. Here are a few hidden dangers:

  "Video voyeurism." Kids take photos and videos of people in compromising positions (such as girls getting undressed in lockers) and post those images online.

  Cyberbullying. Kids send or receive vicious or lewd text messages, e-mails, or voice messages.

  Electronic cheating. Kids download answers onto the MP3 portion and listen during class, or cheat by texting answers during tests.

  Accessing pornography, adult-themed Web sites, or mature-rated video games. This is easy on many of the newer phones, and you aren't looking over your kid's shoulder.

- *Use these safety measures before putting a phone in your child's hands:*
  - Purchase a phone that does not take pictures or allow Internet access.
  - Add a safety feature (such as Web Guard) that restricts access to adult Internet sites.
  - Restrict incoming calls only to select friends and relatives you know and approve. Ted Thompson, president of the National Association to Prevent Sexual Abuse of Children, warns that sexual predators now use cell phones to "groom" kids by building a relationship and gaining trust over time.[4]
  - Tell your child *never* to meet someone in person whom she has met only through the cell phone (or computer).

- *Set limits on talk time and texting.* Purchase only a basic phone without the pricey bells and whistles and find a carrier with a service plan that limits texting and talk time. T-Mobile's Family Allowance plan has a simple Web-based program that allows you to preset the number of minutes your child can talk or text. A message is sent to your phone alerting you if your child is close to

ELECTRONICS

those limits and then shuts your child's phone service off (except for emergency numbers or to call key family members) so that you don't get caught with those surprise bills. Beware: teens send an average of *922* text messages each month![5] Don't allow your child to access the Web or download fancy ringtones or games, which will send that bill even higher.

- *Set clear phone rules.* Enforce expectations about responsible cell phone use. Any irresponsible phone behavior (such as downloading games or ringtones without your permission, or sending a cruel message to a peer) means loss of the phone. Consider having your child sign a contract agreeing to adhere to your policy. Here are a few rules you might include:

  - *No lending.* Do not lend out your phone. Any friend who borrows, pays the bill.

  - *Grades first.* Do your homework first, then you can use your cell. If grades go down, cell use goes off.

  - *Stick to agreed text and talking time.* Any additional costs, you pay.

  - *Use cell phone etiquette.* Don't text, listen to music, or read messages when you are in a conversation. Turn your phone off (or at least on vibrate) at public gatherings (parties, church, restaurants) and *never* have it on at the dinner table. Use a "three-foot voice" (so that no one more than three feet away can hear you). Set a quieter ringtone.

  - *Abide by your school's rules for cell phones.* You are responsible for obeying your school's policy. (Note: be sure to check the student handbook yourself.)

  The last rule is in your hands: the phone is off after lights-out. Some carriers let parents block their kids' calls at certain times except for emergencies. If your carrier does not have that feature, then take your child's phone out of her bedroom when it's lights-out. Many kids are sleep deprived because of late-night texting and talking.

- *Get your child involved in reviewing the monthly bill.* Those cell phone bills are a great way to teach kids financial responsibility. You might first have your child go online to compare plans offered by different services. Also make her review her monthly bill and compare it to the previous month's. You can then use the bills to negotiate whether she deserves more minutes or if they should be reduced. Insist that she pay for any extra minutes or additional costs, such as downloads or ringtones, from her own piggy bank.

- *Learn to text.* In one survey, more than half the adolescents said that texting actually improved their relationship with their parents.[6] If you don't know how to text, ask your child to teach you. Not only is it a quick way to connect with your child, but it also leaves "no excuse" for your child not to let you know where she is. Tweens also say they feel safer texting rather than phoning (because a peer can't overhear) when they need you to pick them up and give them a ride away from a troubling scene or negative peer pressure. Tell your children that if they ever need you as an excuse, they can text you, and you'll be there no questions asked. In an emergency (such as a natural disaster or other catastrophe), you are also more likely to reach your child by texting, as landlines tend to be blocked with incoming calls. Learn to text!

Cell phones are part of our children's world, and the stats show that even our kindergartners are now mobile phone users. The trick is to stay one step ahead so that you know cell phone technology. Staying savvy is the best way to keep your child safe, help her learn responsibility and money management, and ensure that you don't get any surprise phone bills. Remember, parents are always their children's best firewall. Just make sure to use your influence.

Cyberbullying

SEE ALSO: *Bullied, Bullying, Cliques, Internet Safety, Safety, Teased*

THE PROBLEM

Red Flags

Is threatened or harassed by peers; is hesitant or upset after using the computer, spends unusually long hours online, withdraws from friends, seems depressed

The Change to Parent For

Your child learns what to do if cyberbullied and develops habits that make it less likely that he will be harassed.

Question: "A number of middle school students—including my daughter—are receiving vicious anonymous e-mails and text messages from peers. The school sent a letter home describing the problem as 'cyberbullying.' Playground bullying was bad, but at least the victim knew her tormentor. Isn't there something parents can do to stop this cold-blooded cruelty?"

Answer: "Cold-blooded cruelty" is the perfect descriptor for this digital-age behavior problem called cyberbullying. Let's be clear about the term: cyberbullying is an electronic form of communication to hurt, threaten, embarrass, annoy, blackmail, or otherwise target another minor.[7] Every adult who interacts with kids—parents, educators, librarians, police, pediatricians, coaches, child-care providers—must become educated about this lethal new form bullying so that we can together find ways to stop it. You might start parent book clubs to read and discuss electronic bullying, sponsor school antibullying assemblies, ask the police to speak to kid groups or conduct workshops on Internet safety, or create a newsletter to distribute bullying warning signs in your community. Then please ask kids for their ideas. (Some are listed in Step 3.)

Why Change?

Cyberbullying can be devastating to our children's mental and moral health. (A further clarification: cyberbullying must occur between minors. When an adult becomes involved, the behavior is labeled *cyber harassment* or *cyber stalking*.[8] (See *Internet Safety,*

p. 610.) This intentional form of cruelty has kids using their computers, cell phones, and pagers to send harassing, vile, hateful, and slanderous messages about their peers. It can be anything from excluding a classmate from a buddy list and spreading vicious rumors to posting death threats on a Web site. Although it is most common around the middle school years, the cyberbullying problem is making its way to the younger set, and this insidious trend is increasing. National surveys by online safety expert Parry Aftab estimate that 85 percent of twelve- and thirteen-year-olds have had experience with cyberbullying; 53 percent say they have been bullied online.[9] The U.S. Centers for Disease Control and Prevention show a 50 percent increase during the past five years in the number of kids ages ten to seventeen who said they were cyberbullied via the Internet.[10] It is not surprising that cyber abuse has also caused scathing psychological damage to children who have been victimized. A few of those young victims have actually ended their lives through suicide.

Bullying has always been one of the tougher challenges of growing up; technology just makes inflicting brutality far easier. Worse yet, the target may not be the sole recipient: with just a simple mouse click, dozens if not thousands of other recipients from down the block or across the country can simultaneously receive the same vile message in cyberspace.

Signs and Symptoms

Chances are that your child will not tell you he is being harassed online. Look for these signs of cyberbullying:

- Your child is hesitant to be online and nervous when an instant message, text message, or e-mail appears.

- He is visibly upset after using the computer or cell phone, or suddenly avoids it.

- Your child hides or clears the computer screen or closes his cell phone when you enter.

- He spends longer hours online in a more tense, pensive mood.

- Suspicious phone calls and e-mails are received at your home; suspicious packages arrive.

- Your child withdraws from friends, falls behind in schoolwork, or wants to avoid school.

- He is suddenly sullen, evasive, or withdrawn; there is a marked change in his personality or behavior.

- He loses his appetite, is excessively moody, cries, seems depressed, or has trouble sleeping.

- You may see a drop in your child's academic performance.

THE SOLUTION

Step 1. Early Intervention

- *Keep an open-door policy.* Your goal is to maintain a good ongoing dialogue with your child so that he will feel comfortable telling you if something bad happens online or elsewhere. You are your child's best filter both online and off. Build a relationship of trust and then listen carefully to what your kid says about his online experiences. (See *Communicating,* p. 545.) Also be clear that you want to know if your child receives an inappropriate message (whether online or off).

- *Become computer literate.* If your child has a problem online, you will need to be savvy enough on the computer to be able to give him the best guidance. Go through that tutorial, read the manual, or take a class. Keep up with the capabilities of any new electronic devices your child owns or operates. But keep in mind that the best technology teacher just may be your child. Ask him to give you lessons as well as an online tour of the popular sites he and his classmates frequent most. Believe me, you'll receive a most interesting and informative education. (See *Internet Safety,* p. 610.)

- *Provide electronic guidelines that emphasize respect.* Stress to your child that he should always "think before clicking" and *never* put anything on a Web site or in an e-mail or text message that is hurtful or that he wouldn't want said about him. Point out that schools and law enforcement officers are taking cyber threats seriously, and offenders will be held accountable (and in some cases may even be criminally charged). Be clear that any infringement will result in the loss of the privilege of using the computer.

- *Google your child.* Periodically Google your child's name (as well as yours) on the Web. Just go to the google.com search engine site, insert your child's first and last name in quotation marks, and see what has been posted online about your child. Robin Kowalski, Susan Limber, and Patricia Agatston, authors of the must-read *Cyber Bullying,* suggest that you also use the google.com/alert function to set up regular searches for your child's name.[11] Goggle will send you an e-mail each time your child's name appears online.

- *Check your child's online profile.* Get to know your child's online friends just as you do his offline friends. Ask to see your child's online profile or buddy list. Check to see how many e-mail addresses he has. Some parents allow their children only to e-mail or chat with friends the child has first met offline and whom you have personally met. Your tweens should not be allowed in a chat room or to use such social networking sites as Facebook, Xanga, or MySpace. If you do allow them, however, please be sure you are fully acquainted with the social networking site and confirm that it is appropriate for your child's age and development.

- *Keep passwords handy.* You should have your child's account numbers and passwords at all times. Also have the phone number to your cell phone company and the URL of your computer server handy. You will need those to change your child's password and account in the event that he is harassed.

- *Pay attention to peer relationships.* Get to know your kid's friends. Have them over and befriend them. Watch your child as he interacts with peers. Does he get along well, or could he benefit from learning social skills? (If so, see *Argues*, p. 46; *Cliques*, p. 342; *Peer Pressure*, p. 373; or *Rejected*, p. 381.) You can sometimes (though certainly not always) head off a potential problem online by tuning in to how kids interact face-to-face.

Step 2. Rapid Response

Responses for Less Serious Offenses

If you discover that your child is the victim of cyberbullying, here are the best ways to respond to less serious offenses within the first twenty-four hours.

- *Be empathic and supportive.* If you discover that your child has been bullied online, take it seriously. He needs your empathy. Chances are that your child did *nothing* to bring this on, so support him—but also find out the facts. One survey found that almost half of kids who received abusive messages did *not* know who sent them.[12] Believe your kid if he says he doesn't know who sent it Ask if this has happened before and if so, how frequently. Tell your child to let you know if the problem continues. Cyberbullying generally does not just go away and often becomes a repeated occurrence.

- *Don't be too tough.* A study at Clemson University found that kids often did not tell their parents about cyberbullying for fear of losing online privileges.[13] One study found that almost 60 percent of kids did *not* tell their parents when someone was abusive to them online.[14] So don't overreact or ban him from using the Internet altogether. After all, you want your child to feel comfortable coming to you.

One Parent's Answer

A mom from Denver writes:

I didn't allow my daughter to join any social networking sites so I was shocked when another mother told me my daughter's photo and personal information as well as inflammatory statements were posted on MySpace. I immediately contacted the site and demanded the offensive material be removed. They were very helpful and did so. I discovered MySpace even partnered with WiredSafety. org to provide not only links to report cyberbullying but also safety tips for parents. One of their suggestions was to Google your own kids' names periodically to check to see what is posted online about them, which is exactly what I've been doing lately.

ELECTRONICS

- *Respond according to the severity.* If the first offense is minor, your best response is just to ignore the message by blocking it or just not responding at all. Tell your child to do the same as well, but be clear that you want him to keep you posted if he receives any further messages and to tell you how he is being treated by this kid at school (if he knows who sent the message). It is also a good idea to save the message and print out a copy of it. Monitor your child and your electronic equipment much more closely for the next week or two.

Responses for More Serious or Abusive Messages

If the message has a more serious and threatening tone, then you need to respond to the incident accordingly, taking these next steps:

- *Save evidence.* An online bully's identity can sometimes be determined, and you will need that evidence for authorities or to show the perpetrator's parents. So save any abusive messages to your hard drive and print out a copy as well. A copy of an e-mail with the full header information left intact can provide law enforcement officials with the information needed to trace the sender. Another option for viewing the full header is often located in the Mail Preferences tab of your e-mail browser. Use the Save feature on instant messages. Save any hurtful, slanderous, or hateful message received on a computer or cell phone.

- *Block communication.* Find software that blocks the e-mail address, or report that the address is spam, and most e-mail programs will automatically place further communication from that address into a spam folder. Program your cell phone to block that particular number.

- *Contact your Internet provider.* If your child is cyberbullied, change the phone number, your child's password, and his e-mail account. Contact your Internet service provider (ISP) to report the incident. Look on your ISP's support page for directions as to how to report any abusive e-mails. Forward the e-mail to your provider (and keep a copy for yourself) as soon as possible, as after a certain time period the information may not be traceable.

- *Keep records of cell phone abuse.* If your child receives a vicious text or cell phone message, keep a detailed diary recording the date, time, and caller ID (or note that the number was withheld or not available). If possible, save the message. Report any abusive texts to the mobile phone carrier; the company can trace the phone number. Consider whether to change your child's phone number or buy a new phone.

- *Talk to the teacher and principal.* Do inform the school counselor, teacher, or principal if the bully is your child's classmate or at the school. If the situation warrants it, arrange a meeting with the principal, teacher, or counselor. They can offer emotional support for your child and may be able to offer perspective as to what is going on. Beware that if cyberbullying did not occur on the school campus, school officials will not offer help in tracking down the offender or even disciplining this child.

- *Decide to respond.* Although it is usually recommended that you don't respond to the message, if the abuse continues, you may have little recourse. You might try to reply to the message with *one* stern but nonthreatening note stating that you are aware of the situation, saving all evidence, and will be in contact with authorities if the cyberbullying keeps up. (Keep a copy of your note as well.) Another option is to contact the parent with evidence in hand of their kid's cruel behavior. You may need an impartial third party to accompany you, but such encounters are usually not recommended because they can backfire. Unless you have hard-core evidence, parents often deny the problem, defend their child, and even accuse yours of being the instigator. Tread lightly.

- *Contact the police for safety issues.* Call the police and notify school officials anytime your child's safety is at stake. In particular, call or go to the police if cyberbullying includes threats of physical harm to a child, stalking or harassment, pornographic images, or extortion.[15] Take such threats seriously. If your child receives an e-mail that threatens another child, call the authorities as well. *Do not wait when it comes to threats of violence and extortion: pick up the phone.*

- *Seek professional help.* Cyberbullying can cause severe emotional damage and lead to depression. Please monitor your child carefully. Tune in to his emotional signs right now, but also keep a closer eye on his behavior over the next few weeks. Watch in particular for behaviors that are not typical for your child: a sudden change in mood, sleeping habits, or appetite; inability to focus, or just trouble handling life. (See *Depressed,* p. 488.) Seek the help of a trained mental health professional.

- *Consider if an attorney is required.* If you have contacted the parents (or you don't feel comfortable doing so) and the cyberbullying continues, you may need to hire an attorney to speak for you. Another option is to have an attorney send a certified letter describing possible legal options if the cyberbullying does not stop. In rare cases you may want to press criminal charges. If so, contact a personal injury attorney if your child has been harassed or threatened in such a way as to cause severe emotional or physical damage or his reputation has been severely damaged.[16] In some counties and states, cyberbullying may be considered a criminal act and the parents can be held financially responsible if their child engages in wrongdoing that is due to lack of parental supervision. You can post your legal questions to Parry Aftab, an attorney and authority in cyberbullying, at her Web site, www.wiresafety.org.

Step 3. Develop Habits for Change

- *Ask kids for their ideas.* I've witnessed kids in dozens of communities find the most innovative ways to turn peer cruelty around: Boys and Girls Clubs made placemats with tips to avoid being cyberbullied to distribute to restaurants; a middle school created a Bully Buster program; church groups taught younger kids online safety; scouts plastered "Stop cyberbullying" flyers all over their town; and high school students wrote a weekly news column. Kid cruelty—whether on the playground or in cyberspace—must never be tolerated, but it's going to take a group a committed adults (and kids) to join forces to stop it from spreading.

- *Teach cyberspace safety rules.* Every child needs to learn how to be safe online. Teach the acronym SAFE and these four rules to help your child know what to do in case he is the victim of cyberbullying.

  S – **Stop and don't click.** Never respond to a cyberbully; it only intensifies things. Turn off the monitor, walk away from the computer, and tell an adult. (Don't turn off the computer. You will lose the evidence.)

  A – **Tell an adult.** Don't keep this to yourself. Cyberbullying usually escalates and doesn't go away. Report the threat ASAP to a parent, teacher, or an adult you trust. Your parent needs to get you a new account and password. Even then, periodically change your password.

  F – **Filter out personal information.** Never give out personal information, such as your name (or your parent's name), address, phone number, birth date, Social Security number, or credit card number. Never exchange passwords with even your closest friend or let someone take your place at the computer and pretend to be you.

  E – **Save evidence.** Do not delete the text or phone message. Save the e-mail, blog, or Web page. Print out copies, and show the electronic evidence to an adult. You can use it to track the source and as proof to stop the assault.

- *Stress netiquette.* Many of the rules of the playground also apply to cyberspace. You just need to emphasize that you expect your child to act respectfully both on and off the computer. In addition, teach your child these core computer safety rules: you don't fight, use bad language, copy something that is not yours, or say anything unkind or untrue about someone online. Two sites that teach online safety tips to kids are WiredKids.org and StopCyberbullying.org. (See also *Internet Safety*, p. 610.)

WHAT TO EXPECT BY STAGES AND AGES

Preschooler   Kids this age are too young to be involved with cyberbullying, nor should they be using a computer without adult supervision. Even then, screen time should be limited, as recommended by the American Academy of Pediatrics. Preschoolers can learn beginning Internet safety rules that apply to safety rules off the Internet: *"Say only nice things about people on and off the computer. Never give out your name, address, phone number, or birthday. Use a computer only with an adult."*

School Age   Sending nasty text-messages or voice mails on cell phones is more common than sending e-mails; younger kids usually do so for a "laugh" and don't recognize the consequences. Fourth- and fifth-grade girls begin to send rumors via instant message (IM) or cruel e-mails to another girl for revenge. Cyberbullying can begin as kids become comfortable using a keyboard, so be sure to have "the talk" with your kid.

Tween   Cyberbullying is most prevalent from ages nine to fourteen and usually peaks around age thirteen.[18] The following are the most common ways middle school kids send or receive abusive messages: 67 percent through instant messages (IM), 25 percent in chat rooms, 24 percent through e-mail.[19] Nearly one-third of girls experience cyberbullying and use cyberspace to mock or spread vicious rumors. Ten percent of boys experience cyberbullying and are more likely to post sexually explicit comments. Cell phones can be used to send nasty text messages or take compromising photos of peers in various stages of undress at slumber parties or in locker rooms that are then sent or posted electronically.

More Helpful Advice

Cyber Bullying: Bullying in the Digital Age, by Robin M. Kowalski, Susan P. Limber, and Patricia W. Agatston

Cyberbullying and Cyberthreats: Responding to the Challenge of Online Social Aggression, Threats, and Distress, by Nancy E. Willard

The Parent's Guide to Protecting Your Children in Cyberspace, by Parry Aftab

Some Web sites that offer helpful information on cyberbullying:

Cyber Bully Help (www.cyberbullyhelp.com)

i-SAFE Inc (www.isafe.org)

WiredSafety (www.wiredsafety.org)

NetSmartz (www.netsmartz.org)

Internet Safety

SEE ALSO: *Cheats, Cyberbullying, Fearful, Lying, Safety*

THE PROBLEM

Red Flags

Appears hesitant or upset after using the computer, spends unusually long hours online, withdraws from friends, seems depressed; suspicious phone calls and packages arrive at your home

The Change to Parent For

Your child learns the rules for using the Internet safely as well as what to do in case she is victimized online.

Question: "I'm probably paranoid, but I am worried about letting my daughter log on to the Internet. I read so many horrible stories about pornography, hate sites, and online predators out there. Am I being overly cautious, or is there something else parents can do to keep kids safe?"

Answer: One of the simplest ways to keep kids out of trouble online is not to allow them to find it in the first place. Special software filters not only trail which Internet sites your child is frequenting and monitor her chats, IMs, and e-mails but also can block her from visiting inappropriate ones and even e-mail you reports. Once you have installed the filter, new sites are added and are updated weekly to download. Three of the best filters are Net Nanny, Cybersitter, and 4NetSafety. Even if you install Internet search engine filters, however, they don't always work, so don't rely on them to eliminate the problem completely. The real key is to teach your child clear Internet rules and then monitor her computer. Remember, parents are always the ultimate filter.

Why Change?

Our kids are called the "Net Generation," and rightly so. After all, this is the first group born into the era of iPods, cell phones, text messaging, Web sites, podcasts, and blogs. Technology has transformed our kids' lives, and the largest collection of information in the history of the world is easily accessible at the click of their mouse. But it has also caused many a parent to lose a good night's sleep with images of online sexual predators,

LATE-BREAKING NEWS

What Every Parent Needs to Know About Online Predators

University of New Hampshire: Researchers at the Crimes Against Children Research Center culled data from two surveys of three thousand ten- to seventeen-year-old Internet users as well as two thousand U.S. law enforcement officials and uncovered surprising data.[20] For the most part, online predators use deception to target *specific* children. Predators prey in particular on kids with low self-esteem who lack a strong identity or have a weak social network of their own. Those youth most vulnerable online to a predator

- Have past histories of sexual or physical abuse
- Engage in patterns of risky offline or online behavior
- Frequent chat rooms
- Talk online about sex
- Divulge personal information online
- Lack strong, healthy relationships with their parents
- Are boys who are gay or questioning their sexual orientation

Talk, talk, and talk to your child about healthy versus unhealthy relationships. Nurture your child's self-esteem and identity. The more involved you are in your child's life, the less likely it is that your child will be victimized. The good news is that kids are getting savvier about Internet predators, and none of the victims were under twelve years of age. What's more, two-thirds of twelve- to seventeen-year-olds who have been contacted by strangers online say they've ignored them.[21] But nearly 75 percent of victims who met offenders face-to-face did so more than once. Keep talking to your kids! The message is getting through.

pornography, social networking, cyber stalkers, and scores of inappropriate sites. In fact, a recent survey by *Parents* magazine found that 50 percent of parents are extremely worried about sexual predators on the Internet—the same number that are worried about predators in our neighborhoods.[22] According to one survey, 33 percent of youth Internet users admit they have been exposed to unwanted sexual material online.[23]

Your parenting goal isn't to ban your kids' Internet access. After all, the Internet is here to stay, and the educational benefits for our children are enormous. Instead, we adults need to get a bit savvier about cyberspace and learn what our kids do online so that we can give them the guidance they need to use the Internet safely. We also need to teach them crucial skills to help protect them in cyberspace both now and for the rest of their lives. Here are a few solutions to help your kids navigate the sometimes scary terrain of the wide, wide Web.

Signs and Symptoms

Here are a few signs that your child may not feel safe online or is possibly engaging in inappropriate online behavior:

- Your child spends longer hours online in a more tense, pensive mood.
- She withdraws from friends, falls behind in schoolwork, or wants to avoid school.
- Your credit card statement lists suspicious purchases.
- Your child is suddenly sullen, evasive, or withdrawn; there is a marked change in her personality or behavior.
- She loses her appetite, is excessively moody, cries, seems depressed, or has trouble sleeping.
- Suspicious phone calls and e-mails are received at your home; suspicious packages arrive.
- Your child stops typing, covers the screen, hits Delete, or shuts down the computer when she knows you're close by.

THE SOLUTION

Step 1. Early Intervention

- *Get Internet savvy.* Refer to the More Helpful Advice box for some of the best online safety resources. Look for workshops in your community or at your child's school. Join with other parents to learn cyber safety together. Make sure that when your child goes online at other friends' homes, those parents are monitoring their Internet activity as closely as you would. Also do know your child's passwords, screen names, and account information. Set up a family screen name everyone can use.
- *Set clear rules.* Eighty-seven percent of kids say they are more likely to surf the Web when their parents didn't set clear Internet safety rules (versus 63 percent with parents who did set rules).[24] Set appropriate computer rules (such as the ones in this section) and continue to monitor your kid's online behavior just as you would on the streets or in the park. Post your rules by the computer. A printable online agreement designed for tweens and younger is available

at WiredKids.org. Do talk about *every* new electronic device that enters your home and set clear and appropriate rules for its use. Tech-savvy kids these days log on to computers in Internet cafés or their neighbor's unlocked wireless network, so make sure you are clear that your rules for the Internet are for *any* equipment, *anywhere.*

- *Talk to your child about Internet safety.* Only half of kids surveyed say their parents have warned them of dangerous online behaviors.[25] Explain that someone posing as a twelve-year-old could really be a thirty-five-year-old molester. If your child stares at you in disbelief, tell her that one in five kids ages ten to seventeen has been propositioned online.[26] The best safety program is and always has been committed parents with shared standards and good relationships with their kids. Stress to your child to come to you *anytime* she feels uncomfortable—both on or off the Net.

- *Put the computer in a central location.* Keep the computer only in a central house location that is well traveled. It must be a place you can monitor at all times. And take the computer out of your child's bedroom.

- *Teach the "Walk-By Rule."* Emphasize that if at any time you walk by and see your child covering the screen, switching screens, closing programs, or quickly turning off the computer, you will pull out the plug. End of argument.

- *Learn Internet text lingo.* Kids use their own shorthand to text one another and have at least ten acronyms to warn friends that their parents are in the room. A survey found that 95 percent of parents don't know common chat terms.[27] Learn kid's electronic slang so that you can watch for it. Here are some examples, but keep in mind that kid text lingo changes in a nanosecond, so it behooves you to keep up with the latest texting terms):

 P911: Mom or Dad in room.

 PA: Parent alert.

 POS: Parents over shoulder.

 PIR: Parent in room.

 PAW: Parents are watching.

 143 or 459: I love you.

 420: marijuana.

 LMIRL: Let's meet in real life.

 1, 2, 3, 4, 5: Parent reading the screen.

- *Limit online time.* Monitor your child's online time just as you do TV viewing and video game playing. Don't allow your child to spend unlimited time on the computer. She needs to learn to get along and develop social skills with face-to-face communication. Some parents specify a time limit for e-mailing, surfing, or game playing. Hint: a number of parental control products have Internet time schedulers, which tell you the exact number of minutes your kid has been online.

- *Teach privacy rules.* Make it a rule that your child must *not* register with any online site without your permission. And even if you do give permission, you should read the site's privacy policy.[28] Then remind your child *never* to give out personal information. Explain that sites may try to entice your child to give them her name by offering a free lip gloss or poster. Although most Web sites are now required to get a parent's permission before they collect any personal data from kids twelve and under, you still should take precautions.

- *Steer kids to quality sites.* One way to lessen the likelihood of your child's finding inappropriate material is to steer her to quality sites. One place to start is the American Library Association's Great Sites page (www.ala.org/parentspage/greatsites). Check out each site first (beware that URL owners can change overnight). Bookmark appropriate sites on your toolbar, then set a rule that your kid may go only to those you've preapproved.

- *Google your kids.* Parry Aftab, founder of WiredSafety.org, suggests that you Google your child's name often and set alerts for your child's contact information. The alerts will e-mail you when any of the searched items are recognized; they act as an early warning system to help you spot ways your child's personal information may be exposed to strangers online. Visit InternetSuperHeroes.org for more information. At least once a month, open up files that your kid has downloaded. At least once a week, check the history of sites your child has frequented.

- *Keep your credit card secure.* The safest way to keep your child from entering a pornographic site is by making your credit card number inaccessible. Entry past the home page in most porn sites is governed by the ability to key in a valid card number.[29] Sexually graphic and violent games are also easy for kids to download. All they need is your credit card.

Step 2. Rapid Response

Whether your child comes to tell you about an online predator or you discover he is frequenting pornographic sites, stay calm. (I know, I know. That one is easier said than done, but a cool-parent demeanor is a critical part of your rapid response.) Once you take that slow, deep breath, use these solutions:

- *Open up the dialogue.* Gather as much information as you can. Find out how long this has been going on and if any other kids are involved. If so, notify their parents. If your child's physical safety could be in jeopardy, contact your local police to find out which agencies you should notify or who can help. If your child violated your established computer rules (downloaded X-rated material, used your credit card, or frequented inappropriate sites), set clear consequences.

- *Block your computer.* Monitor your child on your computer or make the Internet inaccessible to your child's use without your presence.

- *Call your server.* Many servers (such as America Online) allow parents to limit incoming e-mail to a specific list of correspondents. You can then quickly scan the senders' addresses to get an idea of the nature of your child's correspondence (and correspondents!). Further, change your child's password and e-mail account. If you are now getting strange unsolicited calls from hate groups or an inappropriate person your child has met online, call your phone company to have the number changed.

- *Call your credit card company.* If your child has been using your credit card to access porn sites or purchase inappropriate material, change your credit card number. You may also want to begin monitoring your credit card account activity online rather than waiting for monthly statements.

- *Check your mail.* Be on the lookout for suspicious packages addressed to your child. If you find yourself on new mailing lists, consider it a sign that your child may be the recipient of unsolicited and inappropriate mail. Monitor incoming mail. You can also open up a post office box, which will eliminate most junk or bulk mail.

- *Monitor your child.* If you notice a sudden and uncharacteristic change in your child (behavior, sleep, appetite, mood, concentration), seek the guidance of a mental health professional.

Pay Attention to This!
What the Kids Say About Online Safety

Boys and Girls Clubs of America surveyed almost six hundred kids and teens about their online views.[30] The findings show we have a lot more parenting to do when it comes to online safety. Here are the percentages of "yes" responses to some of the statements in the survey:

- "It's okay to meet someone I've been 'chatting' with online for a long time": 34 percent

- "It's okay to give my real name in a chat room": 28 percent

- "It's okay to put my address on the Internet": 23 percent

- "It's okay to put my pictures on the Internet": 23 percent

Step 3. Develop Habits for Change

Online predators. Hate sites. Vulgarity. Pornography. Violence. Although there are no guarantees, the best way to keep your child safe online is to set clear rules, put strong filters in place, and then monitor your child's cyber presence. Here are the Seven Cyberspace Don'ts you must teach your child:

1. *Don't go on unapproved sites.* If you don't know which sites are "parent approved" or you're in doubt, ask your parent. (Keep this rule in place until you know your child can be trusted.)

2. *Don't download or buy.* Don't buy anything online without your parents' approval; don't take or give anything to anyone unless your parents say it is okay; don't download anything or install programs without first asking permission.

3. *Don't keep secrets.* If you ever feel uneasy or uncomfortable about an exchange you had with anybody online, or if you ever feel threatened, tell an adult immediately. And then ask your parent if you think you need to get a new account and password. In any case, periodically change your password. And if you log on to an inappropriate site, tell your parents. They can track the history of what sites you've frequented, so admit what happened. Your parents may access and look at any of your files at any time.

4. *Don't give personal information.* Never give out *any* personal information, such as your name or your parent's name, birth date, address, phone number, password, Social Security number, or credit card number. Don't send a photograph over the Internet to someone you don't know personally.

5. *Don't exchange.* Don't give out your passwords to even your closest friend. Don't let someone take your place at the computer and pretend to be you.

6. *Don't respond.* If you feel uncomfortable or the message you're getting feels strange, don't respond. Ever. Hit the Back button, log off right then, and tell your parents.

7. *Don't meet.* Never *ever* meet in person anyone you've met online without your parents present.

WHAT TO EXPECT BY STAGES AND AGES

Preschooler   Preschoolers should not use a computer without adult supervision (and even then daily screen time should be limited). Begin teaching Internet safety rules: *"Never give out your name, address, phone number or birthday. Use a computer* only *with an adult."* Kids this age are impulsive, so boot up the game and have it ready so that waiting isn't involved. Try creativity software or programs that help kids practice prereading and math skills to help her learn beginning keyboard and mouse skills.

School Age   Monitor your child's online behavior: move the computer to a central location, set limits for computer time, check the ratings of all computer games, teach beginning netiquette, and gradually introduce all computer safety rules. Keeping secrets is difficult for kids at this age, so change your password frequently. Stress that your child should never disclose her real name, her parent's name, phone number, address, birth date, or hometown. Teach her to read posted site guidelines about such things as using appropriate language and not cheating. If a kid is too young to turn on the computer, boot up a program, and log off or shut down the computer properly, she is not ready to use the Internet alone.

Tween   The biggest leap in online activity is between the sixth (60 percent) and seventh (82 percent) grades; boys are much less active in Internet use than girls, and girls are more likely to use instant messaging.[31] Teen and adult social networking sites (such as MySpace or Facebook) are not recommended for tweens. More appropriate social networking sites for eight- to thirteen-year-olds include Club Penguin, Imbee, Webkinz, Whyville, Nicktropolis, and Disney XD, but even they should be used only with parental monitoring.

More Helpful Advice

Cyber-Safe Kids, Cyber-Savvy Teens: Helping Young People Learn to Use the Internet Safely and Responsibly, by Nancy E. Willard

How to Protect Your Children on the Internet: A Road Map for Parents and Teachers, by Gregory S. Smith

Growing Up Digital: The Rise of the Net Generation, by Don Tapscott

Me, MySpace and I: Parenting the Net Generation, by Larry Rosen

Totally Wired: What Teens and Tweens Are Really Doing Online, by Anastasia Goodstein

What in the World Are Your Kids Doing Online? How to Understand the Electronic World Your Children Live In, by Susan Shankle and Barbara Melton

Some Web sites that offer helpful information on Internet safety:

FBI's *A Parent's Guide to Internet Safety:* www.fbi.gov/publications/pguide/pguidee.htm

WiredSafety: www.wiredsafety.org

Internet Keep Safe Coalition: www.ikeepsafe.org

GetNetWise: www.getnetwise.org

WebWiseKids: www.webwisekids.org

TV Addiction

SEE ALSO: *Cyberbullying, Homework, Video Games*

THE PROBLEM

Red Flags

TV viewing monopolizes your child's life, becomes a substitute for friends, hobbies, and all other aspects of his life; child experiences withdrawal or behavior flare-ups if he can't watch

The Change to Parent For

Your child learns to be more selective about television watching and finds more proactive outlets for entertainment, creativity, growth, and healthy social development.

Why Change?

"Can't I watch TV just one more hour?" "But there's nothing to do and it's my favorite show!"

It's so easy for kids to fall into the additive habit of spending too much time in front of the boob tube. But the fact is that the more kids watch TV, the more time is lost for nurturing creativity, learning sports or hobbies, playing in the great outdoors, practicing social skills, or just finding ways to entertain and enjoy themselves. Those key "family connecting moments" are lost as well, as are other crucial life lessons.

The statistics are dismal: kids ages six months to six years spend three times as many hours watching TV as they do reading or being read to.[32] One-third of kids ages six and younger have a TV set in their room. The average American kid watches four hours of TV a day.[33] Most of us realize that our kids are in front of that TV more than we'd like, so here are solutions to curb your children's viewing habits and help them find healthier entertainment options (and maybe even save on that electricity bill).

Pay Attention to This!

Stanford University: A study of more than a thousand schoolchildren found that watching real-life violence as displayed on television news programs may have just as powerful an impact on a child as would a personal experience of the incident.[34] So do monitor what your kids watch and switch that TV off anytime your instinct tells you that what is airing is inappropriate.

THE SOLUTION

Five Strategies for Change

1. *Check your whole family's TV viewing habits.* Have you ever really stopped to track how much TV you and your kids watch each day? If not, take the parent challenge: for the next few days, keep a diary of your family's TV habits. Anybody who turns on that TV must log in. Then add those minutes up (or have your kids do the adding—it's a great math lesson). The number just may shock—or delight—you. Just make sure you include your own viewing time as well. That number will fuel your commitment to help break your children's television addiction.

2. *Commit your family to change.* Research shows that the more television our kids watch, the greater their chances of being overweight and having lower grades. But TV addiction can be broken, just like substance addiction, by detox and through strong, consistent commitment. Here are ways to break TV addiction. Do whatever it takes so that your kids know you are serious about breaking this bad habit.

    • Talk to your family about the bad effects of addiction and the good effects of moderation so that they are more likely to buy in to your discussion points.

    • Enforce a policy of 100 percent TV abstinence for at least a month or two (no kidding), and don't give in.

    • Unplug the television sets. Some families actually lock their sets in a closet.

    • Find healthy alternatives and substitute positive activities that your kids can do instead of watching the boob tube. Here are some possibilities: dust off the board games, teach some card games; start music lessons or turn on music; encourage a new hobby, such as knitting, drawing, or yoga; get everyone out of the house and away from the television, go to the gym, put up a basketball hoop, or enroll your kid in a swim program or sports club; how about getting everyone a library card? The trick is to match your child's interests to activity alternatives; the best way to do that is to get them involved in the process, then don't give in.

3. *Set limits on screen time.* Once your kids are weaned from constant viewing, set a limit as to the maximum number of viewing hours each day and then stick to it. Make your kids accountable for staying within the time limits. Here are solutions:

    • Track their viewing hours on a paper taped by the set. Or make them use an inexpensive electronic kitchen timer: the kids punch in their TV time, and the timer must run while they're watching TV. The timer provides an ongoing total of the number of television viewing minutes.

    • Set the timer from your TV's remote for the total minutes allowed each day.

    • Turn off the TV when the show is over.

    • Don't allow channel surfing.

ELECTRONICS

- Establish certain TV-free hours, such as during dinner and from six to eight in the evening when kids usually do homework.

- Specify one night (or all school nights) as a no-TV night. A favorite show that appears during any of these times can be taped and viewed during the weekend. And if you want your child to learn how to get along with other kids, apply the no-TV rule when friends come over.

4. *Be selective as to content.* Insist that your kids select in advance the shows they want to watch, and have them submit a weekly schedule that must be approved. Explain that from now on your children must make an appointment to watch TV so that viewing becomes more of a privilege.

5. *Make the bedroom TV free.* Kids who have a TV in their bedroom watch an average of 286 hours more a year than kids who don't.[35] Research shows that those flickering screens often left on (or turned back on after you've gone to bed) also disrupt kids' sleep.[36] Another study found that children had lower school achievement when they had a TV in their room.[37] It's difficult to monitor what your kid is watching or for how long when he is watching alone in his room. So take that TV out of there right away.

WHAT TO EXPECT BY STAGES AND AGES

Preschooler   Imagination fuels fears among toddlers and preschoolers, so check out what they're watching so as to prevent nightmares. Tune in closely to content and language. Kids copy what they hear, so they'll pick up "sass" talk and inappropriate language from watching certain TV shows.

School Age   Limit exposure especially on school nights, when viewing may push out homework and reading time. Televised violence *by itself* contributes to as much as 15 percent of all of kids' aggressive behaviors,[38] so keep close track of what your kid is watching to be sure that it's in line with your family values.

Tween   Materialism peaks during these ages, and the ubiquitousness of TV commercials boosts it. Review your viewing standards and monitor evening shows in which gratuitous sex, language, and violence are rampant. A top concern for parents of tweens is that the children will see upsetting late-breaking news events without an adult to explain.

One Parent's Answer

A mom from Boise shares:

I realized my kids' life revolved around the TV, so I set strict viewing limits. When they complained there wasn't anything to do, I stocked plastic bins with creative stuff they would enjoy—Lego, clay, craft sticks, glue, marking pens, paper, as well as fun activities for the outdoors. It took a little bit of coaxing, but after two weeks, they don't miss TV and are having a lot more fun discovering an unplugged life.

Video Games

SEE ALSO: *Boredom, Cyberbullying, Homework, Internet Safety, TV Addiction*

THE PROBLEM
Red Flags

Video game playing dominates your child's life, has become a replacement for friends, hobbies, and all other aspects of his life; child experiences withdrawal or behavior flare-ups if he can't play

The Change to Parent For

Your child learns to be more selective about video game playing and finds more proactive outlets for entertainment and healthy social development.

Why Change?

Happen to have a video game lover in your home? If so, you're not alone.[39] But oh, the problems those games can sometimes cause at home, sweet home: "Can't I just play one more hour?" "But there's nuhhhthiiing else to dooo!" "Chill out, Mom. The game is not *that* violent." There's no doubt that video games are a part of the plugged-in generation's lifestyle. Research shows that 99 percent of boys and 94 percent of girls ages twelve to seventeen play computer, Web, portable, or console games.[40] More than 90 percent of kids play video games thirty minutes a day,[41] though boys spend twice as much time playing compared to girls.[42] For some kids, games are "everything." That's why there's also a growing concern among parents about some of the potential hazards of video games: increased aggression, sedentary lifestyles, squelched cognitive development or academic potential. After all, it's very easy for kids to fall into the habit of spending too much time gripping those controllers and staying glued to those screens.

The truth is that regardless of what games your children prefer, *too much* video game playing isn't healthy for anyone and can rob our children of time to experience the great outdoors, read for pleasure, get enough exercise, do their homework, and learn to get along with others. The American Psychological Association has seen a growing trend of kids who are becoming "addicted" to gaming and who play by themselves for hours.

Pay Attention to This!

Here are red flags that may signal that video games are a negative influence on your child:

- *Peer replacement.* Your child is using video games as a substitute for friends or being with other kids.
- *Addiction.* Video games replace other forms of entertainment. If you restrict your child from playing, his behavior flares up and he goes through "video game withdrawal." (Playing video games is all your child wants to do.) This is such a concern of the American Psychological Association that members are hotly debating whether video game addiction should be labeled a mental health disorder.
- *Aggression.* Your child acts out, becomes more impulsive or aggressive after playing.
- *Less caring.* Your child displays less concern or empathy toward others.
- *Sinking grades.* Homework battles increase; grades or test scores decrease.
- *Sleepless.* Your child has trouble falling asleep or staying asleep. (Beware: rapid-fire screen images and aggressive content activate the brain and can keep kids awake.)
- *Couch-potato lifestyle.* Your child is too sedentary; his game playing is interfering with his getting enough exercise, and he's gaining weight.
- *Credit card charges.* Your credit card shows unexplained spending. Online gaming networks charge to play; video games are easily purchased online using a parent's credit card.

But don't rush to judgment too quickly. Over the last decade, video game makers have come a long way. Playing some of those games actually benefits our kids' learning and motor dexterity; some even help keep them in better shape. Here are solutions to help you wade through those tough choices and know whether that video game is actually aiding or hindering your child's development.

THE SOLUTION

Eight Strategies for Change

1. *Know your child.* For my two cents, I don't think it's healthy for any kid to be playing violent video games. But don't get me wrong: playing one video game is not going to cause irrevocable damage. Just please know that *some* children *are* influenced by aggressive content. A review by the University of Michigan of over eighty-five studies found that "video games increase aggressive thoughts and angry feelings,

aggressive behaviors and decrease helping behavior."[43] Kids who are more sensitive, have an aggressive or "hyper" temperament, or are predisposed to aggression caused by witnessing or experiencing it are also more likely to be aggressive after playing certain video games.[44] Nearly two-thirds of teens who play games report seeing or hearing "people being mean and overly aggressive while playing," and 49 percent say they see "people being hateful, racist, or sexist while playing."[45] But you don't need research to prove that to you. Just monitor your child's behavior more closely. If you notice that he becomes more wound up or aggressive and you think it's due to his playing that game, the solution is simple: take away that game and stay abreast of late-breaking research so that you can make responsible parenting decisions as to what is best for your child. A great book to help you understand the research is *Grand Theft Childhood: The Surprising Truth About Violent Video Games and What Parents Can Do,* by Lawrence Kutner and Cheryl Olson.

2. *Set acceptable rules and limits that fit your kid.* Be clear as to not only which games are off-limits but also how long your kid is allowed to play. Here are some ideas:

- *Set reasonable rules.* Your child can play for half an hour on weekdays or two hours on weekends. *"Homework first, then video games."*

- *Adapt rules to your child.* If he has trouble falling or staying asleep, the rule is: *"No playing at least two hours before bedtime."* If grades suffer because of too much playing, then pull the power source, pronto!

LATE-BREAKING NEWS

Video Games May Decrease Your Child's Capability to Feel for Others

University of Toronto: A study with 150 fourth and fifth graders found that those spending the most time playing violent video games were also most likely to agree with such statements as "People with guns or knives are cool" and "Parents should tell their kids to fight if they have to."[46] Those same kids are also more likely to disagree with such statements as "When I'm mean to someone I generally feel bad about it later" or "I'm happy when my teacher says my friend did a good job." Many child experts (myself included) are concerned that playing violent video games may decrease your child's ability to empathize, that glorious capacity to feel for another. The long and the short on video games is that there needs to be more research to determine the long-range impact on our children. Meanwhile, keep a closer eye on your child's behavior.

- *Use as reward.* Use video game playing as a reward for meeting a certain requirement. *"You may play for half an hour after you read for half an hour."*

- *Be consistent.* Once you set your rules, consistently reinforce them.

- *Limit accessibility.* Game consoles and computers may not be in your child's bedroom. All inappropriate games owned by older family members (including your spouse) are inaccessible not only to your child but also to his friends.

- *Use timekeepers.* To make sure your child doesn't exceed your playing time limit, tell him he must set an oven timer. Once it buzzes, the controls go away. The oven timer works far more effectively than nagging.

3. *Be selective as to content.* Set clear parameters as to which games you will allow your kids to play. Ratings established by the Entertainment Software Rating Board (ESRB) are prominently labeled on the outside of each video game box. (By the way, game raters include child development experts, retired school principals, teachers, and parents.) Teach your kid these ratings so that there are no questions or arguments:[47]

EC (Early Childhood; ages 3+): contains no inappropriate or objectionable material

E (Everyone; ages 6+): may contain minimal violence, some comic mischief or crude language

T (Teen; ages 13+): may contain violent content, mild or strong language, and suggestive themes

M (Mature; ages 17+): may include more intense violence or language, mature sexual themes

AO (Adult Only; ages 18+): may include graphic depictions of sex and violence

4. *Watch the whole game.* Many games appear mild at the lowest skill level but grow increasingly violent as the player's skill increases. So if the box with the rating is missing, watch what your child is playing all the way through to the end or ask your child to give you a demo. These games' appearance can be deceiving. One of the biggest sellers, Grand Theft Auto, begins as a fast-paced racing game, but as players move up in the competition (and later into the game), they earn points for knocking a policeman off his motorcycle and running down a pedestrian.[48] Players can also hire a prostitute, have sex with her, then knock her out and get their money back. Yes, such games are rated for adults, but kids say they can gain access to them easily, and many parents never watch beyond the first scenes, not realizing how inappropriate the content of following scenes might be. And a recent study found that nearly 80 percent of E-rated violent games contain some violence.[49]

5. *Take time for friends.* UCLA studies find that although certain video games can increase kids' IQ, they do so at the expense of kids' learning crucial social skills. So don't let video game playing detract from being with friends. You may also want to put limits on game playing when friends come over or restrict video game playing

altogether. Keep in mind, though, that gaming is considered a social experience for kids. Don't be surprised when once you set limits for video playing in your home, your kid decides to spend more time at his friend's house. If the friend's parents are allowing unlimited video playing, it may be time to speak with them and share your own policy. They just may decide to adopt a one-hour limit as well.

6. *Offer enticing alternatives.* If you want to have your child cut back on video game playing or you notice that game playing has become an addiction, then what do you want him to do instead? The key is to find options that will entice *your* child. A new hobby? A sport? Bike riding? Setting up an outdoor basketball hoop or weights? A musical instrument? Sudoku or crossword puzzles? Starting a bug collection? Reading? Keep in mind that many kids say they play video games because they are bored (even though I'm sure there are dozens of available options in your home). So consider having a box with a few "just-in-case" options if your kid is going through video game withdrawal. (See also *Boredom,* p. 534.)

7. *Find ways to make play beneficial.* Don't throw out those video controllers just yet. Studies show there are benefits to video gaming. Playing video games is found to help kids develop teamwork, decision-making and problem-solving skills, the ability to strategize, mental dexterity, and creativity, and even learn the infrastructure and government of civilizations.[50] The secret is to find the *right* games and then use them the *right* way. Here are three strategies to do so:

   • *Go violence free.* A UCLA study found that playing games that challenge kids to decode puzzles, solve problems, and test hypotheses actually increases their nonverbal IQ scores.[51] Look for fantasy or adventure games that are nonviolent (check the ratings), political strategy games like Sim City, history and geography teaching games like Carmen Sandiego, or games that teach economic principles like Lemonade Stand.

   • *Play with them.* One study found that the more time kids spend playing video games *with* their parents, the more time they spend with them in other activities as well.[52] Games that use puzzles, games based on classic board games, and trivia quiz games can all be great family fun.

   • *Require movement.* Mayo Clinic researchers in Rochester, Minnesota, found that activity-oriented video games (playing football, baseball, bowling, and so on) that use "exergaming" systems actually inspire kids to get in shape.[53] What's more, video games that require kids to move, dance, kick, or dodge while playing (such as Dance Dance Revolution and EyeToy) triple the energy expenditure of lean and mildly obese children—and they like to do it. Those dance video games increase energy expenditure by a factor of six for more obese kids. If you want your kids to shed a extra few pounds, turning on the right video game may actually help. Why not get the whole family involved?

ELECTRONICS

8. *Teach anger management.* A study of 1,254 tweens found that a big reason they play video games is to manage their feelings, including anger and stress.[54] Make sure your child knows about healthy ways to release anger: exercise, healthier eating, writing in a journal about upset feelings, talking to someone about his upset thoughts, and doing deep breathing exercises or meditation. Then encourage your child to use those strategies to get his anger out.

One Parent's Answer

A mom from Salt Lake City shares:

I'm now much more vigilant about what my child plays and thoroughly check not only the ratings but also the content. I made the mistake of buying Conker's Bad Fur Day, a Nintendo game about a squirrel, expecting it to be family friendly like Donkey Kong or Mario, and discovered it was anything but. A cute little squirrel gets drunk at a bar, throws up and then blacks out while swearing profusely—and that's just for starters. It was my wakeup call. I made a new house rule: "No purchase unless I read the game and rating description from the Internet" (my son has to print it off for me), and I read the back cover description and game rating. And even after a purchase I ask my kid to give me a demo.

WHAT TO EXPECT BY STAGES AND AGES

Preschooler   Kids this age cannot easily distinguish between real life and fantasy, so violent images may seem real and can even traumatize young children and cause nightmares. Limit games to those with an EC (Early Childhood) rating. Be aware that over a thousand studies find that kids exposed to violent programming at a young age have a higher tendency for more aggressive and violent behavior later in life.[55] Tune in to your child's behavior!

School Age   Video game playing begins to increase, especially with boys, and becomes part of their pop culture; 60 percent of boys in the fourth through sixth grade say they play video or computer games daily.[56]

Tween   Video game playing reaches a peak at eighth grade, when boys spend the most time playing video games, averaging twenty-three hours a week; girls spend twelve hours a week.[57] Almost half of over nine hundred tweens surveyed said their favorite electronic games involve violence.[58] Their top choice is the M-rated Grand Theft Auto. Other boys' favorite game choices include fighters; shooters; and sports, fantasy role-playing, action adventure, and strategy games. Girls prefer classic board games, card or dice games, trivia quiz games, and puzzles.

Notes

Introduction

1. In a Public Agenda nationwide telephone survey ("A Lot Easier Said Than Done") of 1,607 parents or guardians of children ages five to seventeen, 76 percent of parents said that raising kids today is a whole lot harder than it was for their own parents; six in ten rated parents "fair" or "poor" at raising their kids: Public Agenda, "From Self-Control to Good Eating Habits: Parents in New Survey Report Limited Success Teaching Their Kids 'Absolutely Essential'" (New York: Public Agenda, 2002), http://www.publicagenda.org/press-releases/self-control-good-eating-habits-parents-new-survey-report-limited-success-teaching-their-kids-absolutely-essentia; in a survey by the Pew Research Center, 71 percent of women said it is more difficult to be a mother today than it was twenty to thirty years ago; eight out of ten women ages fifty to sixty-four agree: Pew Research Center, *Today's Parents Have Tougher Job, Less Success,* May 25, 2007, http://www.marketingcharts.com/topics/men/survey-todays-parents-have-tougher-job-less-success-471/.
2. Public Agenda, "From Self-Control to Good Eating Habits."
3. P. McGraw, *Family First: Your Step-by-Step Plan for Creating a Phenomenal Family* (New York: Free Press, 2004), 14.
4. An excellent summary of the crisis is found in R. Kadison and T. F. DiGeronimo, *College of the Overwhelmed: The Campus Mental Health Crisis and What to Do About It* (San Francisco: Jossey-Bass, 2004).
5. *Parenting* magazine survey results reported on the *Today* show Nov. 24, 2007, available at http://micheleborba.ivillage.com/parenting/archives/2007/04/.
6. S. Begley and J. Interlandi, "The Dumbest Generation? Don't Be Dumb," *Newsweek,* June 2, 2008, 43–44.
7. Research from McGill University cited in C. Honore, *Under Pressure: Rescuing Childhood from the Culture of Hyper-Parenting* (Toronto: Knopf, 2008).
8. Rates of childhood depression are increasing, and depression is affecting younger kids; a child today is ten times more likely to be seriously depressed compared to a child born in the first third of this century: P. Lewinsohn, P. Rohde, J. Seeley, and S. Fischer, "Age-Cohort Changes in the Lifetime Occurrence of Depression and Other Mental Disorders," *Journal of Abnormal Psychology* 102 (1993): 110–120; about 5 percent of American kids under the age of eighteen are seriously depressed: American Academy of Child and Adolescent Psychiatry, *Facts for Families: The Depressed Child,* July 2004, http://www.aacap.org/cs/root/facts_for_families/the_depressed_child.
9. In a survey by the Center for a New American Dream, 70 percent of parents said they believe kids are too focused on buying things: cited in K. Kelly and L. Kulman, "Kid Power," *U.S. News & World Report,* Sept. 13, 2004, 48.
10. A 2006 personality survey found signs of "elevated narcissism" in nearly two-thirds of the 16,475 U.S. college students interviewed, a 30 percent jump from 1982: J. M. Twenge, *Generation*

Me: Why Today's Young Americans Are More Confident, Assertive, Entitled—and More Miserable Than Ever Before (New York: Free Press, 2006).

11. J. S. Dacey and L. B. Fiore, *The Safe Child Handbook: How to Protect Your Family and Cope with Anxiety in a Threat-Filled World* (San Francisco: Jossey-Bass, 2006).

12. Between 8 and 10 percent of U.S. kids are now seriously troubled by stress and stress symptoms: J. S. Dacey and L. B. Fiore, *Your Anxious Child* (San Francisco: Jossey-Bass, 2000), 2–3; a national survey of 875 kids by KidsHealth found that 41 percent of nine- to thirteen-year-olds feel stressed most or all of the time: KidsHealth, *What Kids Say About: Handling Stress,* Oct. 2005, http://www.kidshealth.org/parent/emotions/feelings/kids_stress.html; one in three U.S. children suffers from chronic stress symptoms: G. Witkin, *KidStress* (New York:Viking, 1999), 3.

13. A nationwide survey found that 93 percent of responding adults believe that parents have failed to teach kids honesty, respect, and responsibility; the study, titled "Kids These Days: What Americans Really Think About the Next Generation," was conducted by the nonpartisan group Public Agenda for the Advertising Council and Ronald McDonald House charities in June 1997: cited in P. Applebome, "Children Score Low in Adults' Esteem, a Study Finds," *New York Times,* June 26, 1997, A12.

14. Kadison and DiGeronimo, *College of the Overwhelmed.*

15. J. Warner, *Perfect Madness: Motherhood in the Age of Anxiety* (New York: Penguin Books, 2005).

16. Perhaps the earliest published citing of the term *helicopter parent* (defined as a "nosy grown-up who's always hovering around. Quick to offer a teacher unwanted help") appears in N. Zeman, "Buzzwords," *Newsweek,* Sept. 9, 1991; Glen Egelman, M.D., used the term *snowplow parenting* in S. C. Caufield, "Ninth Leadership Forum: Student Health 2010: What Changes Will the Next Five Years Bring?" *Student Health Spectrum,* Feb. 2006, 4–18.

17. D. E. Levin and J. Kilbourne, *So Sexy So Soon: The New Sexualized Childhood and What Parents Can Do to Protect Their Kids* (New York: Ballantine Books, 2008), 66.

18. H. E. Marano, *A Nation of Wimps: The High Cost of Invasive Parenting* (New York: Broadway Books, 2008); A. Quart, *Hothouse Kids: How the Pressure to Succeed Threatens Childhood* (New York: Penguin, 2006).

19. R. M. Scheffler, S. P. Hinshaw, S. Modrek, and P. Levine, "The Global Market for ADHD Medications," *Health Affairs* 26, no. 2 (Mar.-Apr. 2007): 450–456.

20. Survey conducted by Synocate in 2004, cited in Honore, *Under Pressure,* 33.

21. P. Tyre, J. Scelfo, and B. Kantrowitz, "The Power of No," *Newsweek,* Sept. 13, 2004, 43.

22. N. Gibbs, "Who's in Charge Here?" *Time,* Aug. 6, 2001, 42.

23. The term *paranoid parenting* is attributed to F. Furedi, *Paranoid Parenting: Why Ignoring the Experts May Be Best for Your Child* (Chicago: Chicago Review Press, 2002).

24. The school knapsack called "My Child's Pack" retails for $175 and was designed by two fathers: "Back-to-School Armor," *Time,* Aug. 27, 2007, 17.

25. Dacey and Fiore, *Safe Child Handbook.*

26. Levin and Kilbourne, *So Sexy So Soon,* 66.

27. V. Rideout and E. Hamel, *The Media Family: Electronic Media in the Lives of Infants, Toddlers, Preschools and Their Parents* (Menlo Park, Calif.: Kaiser Family Foundation, 2006).

28. A. Lenhart and others, *Teens, Video Games, and Civics: Teens' Gaming Experiences Are Diverse and Include Significant Social and Civil Engagement* (Washington, D.C.: Pew Internet and American Life Project, 2008).

29. D. F. Roberts, U. G. Foehr, and V. Rideout, *Generation M: Media in the Lives of 8–18 Year-Olds* (Menlo Park, Calif.: Kaiser Family Foundation, 2005).

30. Over a quarter of all these under-twos have TVs in the bedrooms: V. Rideout, E. A. Vandewater, and E. A. Wartella, *Zero to Six: Electronic Media in the Lives of Infants, Toddlers and Preschoolers* (Menlo Park, Calif.: Kaiser Family Foundation, 2003).

31. Quote by Benjamin Spock cited in A. Stoddard, *Mothers: A Celebration* (New York: Avon Books, 1996), 6.

32. A. E. Kazdin with C. Rotella, *The Kazdin Method for Parenting the Defiant Child* (New York: Houghton Mifflin, 2008), 38.

33. Kazdin with Rotella, *The Kazdin Method*, 7.

The Parents Magazine "Joys of Motherhood Survey"

1. Survey questions were written by Michele Borba; survey design and analysis were by Consumer Insights, Meredith Corporation. The study was conducted among the Meredith Reader Panels of *Parents* and *American Baby* from October 3 to October 17, 2006. Of the 9,792 females who read, subscribe to, or buy *Parents* on the newsstand who were surveyed, a total of 2,140 completed the survey, an overall response rate of 22 percent. The bulk of survey respondents are ages twenty-five to thirty-nine (86 percent), have some college or more formal education (27 percent have completed some college, 40 percent have a college degree, and 21 percent have some postgrad work), and live in two-parent households (96 percent). More than half (54 percent) of these households have just one parent employed outside the home; in 42 percent of the households, both parents work. The majority (59 percent) of respondents live in a suburban area, with the remainder divided among those living in small towns (19 percent), urban areas (12 percent), or rural areas (10 percent). Half (50 percent) of the respondents have one child, 34 percent have two, and 17 percent have three or more children. A third of the respondents (33 percent) have a child under one year of age, 65 percent have a child one to two, and 35 percent have a child three to five.

Part 1: Family

ADOPTED

1. David Brodzinsky, professor emeritus from Rutgers University, cited in M. Trudeau, "Adopted Teens Face Higher Risk for ADHD," National Public Radio, Oct. 4, 2008, http://www.npr/org/templates/story/story.php?storyId=90184184.

2. P. L. Benson, A. R. Sharma, and E. C. Roehlkepartain, *Growing Up Adopted: A Portrait of Adolescents and Their Families* (Minneapolis: Search Institute, 1994).

3. Peter L. Benson quoted in C. Wetzstein, "Verdict on Teens Adopted at Birth: The Kids Are Alright," News World Communications, Aug. 8, 1994, http//findarticles.com/p/articles/mi_m1571/is_n32_v10/ai_15716056/print?tag=artBody;col1.

4. J. Greco, "Growing Up Adopted," foreverparents.com, Apr. 20, 2008, www.zimbio.com/Adoptive+Parents/articles/68/Growing+Up+Adopted.

5. Benson, Sharma, and Roehlkepartain, *Growing Up Adopted*.

6. Wetzstein, "Verdict on Teens Adopted at Birth."

7. M. Keyes and others, "The Mental Health of US Adolescents Adopted in Infancy," *Archives of Pediatrics and Adolescent Medicine* 162, no. 5 (May 2008): 419–425.

8. D. M. Brodzinsky, L. S. Singer, and A. M. Braff, "Children's Understanding of Adoption," *Child Development* 55 (June 1984): 869–878.

DIVORCE

9. R. Bauserman, "Child Adjustment in Joint-Custody Versus Sole-Custody Arrangements: A Meta-Analytic Review," *Journal of Family Psychology* 16, no. 1 (2002): 91–102, http://www.apa.org/journals/releases/fam16191.pdf.

10. American Psychological Association, *Briefing Sheet: An Overview of the Psychological Literature on the Effects of Divorce on Children,* May 2004, http://www.apa.org/ppo/issues/divorcechild.html.

11. "The Mom Exchange: Mom Debate," *Parenting,* July 2007, 24.

12. National Institute of Mental Health, "Preventive Sessions After Divorce Protect Children into Teens," Oct. 15, 2002, http://www.nimh.nih.gov/science-news/2002/preventive-sessions-after-divorce-protect-children-into-teens.shtml.

13. H. E. Marano, *A Nation of Wimps* (New York: Random House, 2008), 81.

14. Marano, *Nation of Wimps,* 80.

15. J. S. Wallerstein, J. M. Lewis, and S. Blakeslee, *The Unexpected Legacy of Divorce: The 25 Year Landmark Study* (New York: Hyperion, 2001).

16. Wallerstein, Lewis, and Blakeslee, *The Unexpected Legacy of Divorce.*

17. M. Gary Neuman, author of *Helping Kids Cope with Divorce the Sandcastles Way,* cited in D. Gehrke-White, "Divorced Couples Urged to Ensure Their Kids Flourish," *Desert Sun,* Sept. 17, 2002, D3.

18. Y. Sun and Y. Li, "Stable Postdivorce Family Structures During Late Adolescence and Socioeconomic Consequences in Adulthood," *Journal of Marriage and Family* 70, no. 1 (Jan. 2008): 129–143. Data are from the National Education Longitudinal Study, which surveyed 6,954 students across the country beginning in eighth grade in 1988, when they were about fourteen years old. They were surveyed again in 1990, 1992, and then again in 2000, when they were about twenty-six years old.

19. Bauserman, "Child Adjustment."

20. American Psychological Association, *Briefing Sheet.*

MIDDLE CHILD

21. W. Cole, "The New Science of Siblings," *Time,* July 2, 2006, http://www.time.com/time/magazine/article/0,9171,1209949-1,00.html.

22. K. J. Conger, R. D. Conger, and L. V. Scaramella, "Parents, Siblings, Psychological Control, and Adolescent Adjustment," *Journal of Adolescent Research* 12, no. 1 (1997): 113–138; F. Romeo, "A Child's Birth Order: Educational Implications," *Journal of Instructional Psychology* 21 (1994): 155–161; R. Travis and V. Kohli, "The Birth Order Factor: Ordinal Position, Social Strata and Educational Achievement," *Journal of Social Psychology* 135 (1995): 499–508.

23. D. Gellene, "Firstborns Surge Ahead on IQ Points," *Los Angeles Times,* June 23, 2007.

OLDEST CHILD

24. S. E. Black, P. J. Devereux, and K. G. Salvanes. "The More the Merrier? The Effect of Family Size and Birth Order on Children's Education," *Quarterly Journal of Economics* 120, no. 2 (2005): 669–700.

25. Petter Kristenson study on firstborn sons cited in K. Mishra, "Your Older Sibling Really Is Smarter, Study Says: More Time with Adults May Be a Major Factor," *San Francisco Chronicle,* June 22, 2007, http://www.sfgate.com/cgi-bin/article.cgi?f=/c/a/2007/06/22/MNGJQQJVQR1.DTL.

26. V. J. Hotz, L. Hao, and G. Z. Jin, "Games Parents and Adolescents Play: Risky Behaviour, Parental Reputation and Strategic Transfers," *Economic Journal* 118, no. 28 (Mar. 2008): 515–555.

27. M. K. Ounsted and A. M. Hendrick, "The First-Born Child: Patterns of Development," *Developmental Medicine and Child Neurology* 19 (1977): 445–453.

28. T. L. Frederick, P. J. Hartung, D. Goh, and M. Gaylor, "Appraising Birth Order in Career Assessment: Linkages to Holland's and Super's Models," *Journal of Career Assessment* 9, no. 1 (2001): 25–39.

29. K. Ninomiya, "Birth Order Health," Kent Ninomiya Health & Happiness, Jan. 23, 2008, http://ninomiya-kent.blogspot.com/2008/01/birth-order-health-kent-ninomiya.html.

ONLY CHILD

30. H. Richards and R. Goodman, "Are Only Children Different? A Study of Child Psychiatric Referrals. A Research Note," *Journal of Child Psychology and Psychiatry* 37, no. 6 (Sept. 1996): 753–757. Study compared 683 only children to 2,364 children from two-child families from the age of five years and found no difference between the two groups.

31. J. Chang and S. Holmberg, "The Only Child Myth: Many Believe Lack of Siblings Leads to Selfish, Spoiled Kids," *ABC News,* Aug. 17 2007, http:abcnews.go.com/2020Story?id=3488411&page=1.

32. D. F. Polit and T. Falbo, "Only Children and Personality Development: A Quantitative Review," *Journal of Marriage and the Family* 49 (1987): 309–325.

33. Studies by Douglas Downey, professor of sociology at Ohio State University, cited in K. Deveny, "Why Only-Children Rule," *Newsweek,* June 2, 2008, http://www.newsweek.com/id/138538.

34. D. Downey and D. J. Condron, "Playing Well with Others in Kindergarten: The Benefits of Siblings at Home," *Journal of Marriage and Family* 66 (2004): 333–350.

SIBLING RIVALRY

35. W. Cole, "The New Science of Siblings," *Time,* July 2, 2006, http://www.time.com/time/magazine/article/0,9171,1209949-1,00.html.

36. Katherine Conger's research on favoritism cited in Cole, "New Science of Siblings."

37. Information from the Gesell Institute cited in R. Lavoie, *It's So Much Work to Be Your Friend: Helping the Child with Learning Disabilities Find Social Success* (New York: Touchstone Books, 2005), 176–184.

38. Research by Laurie Kramer, professor of applied family studies at the University of Illinois at Urbana-Champaign, cited in Cole, "New Science of Siblings."

TWINS AND MULTIPLES

39. J. E. Moore, "Multiple Births: The Art and Science of Caring for Twins, Triplets, and More," *Pediatrics in Review* 28 (2007): e9–e15.

40. K.-V. Le-Bucklin, *Twins 101: 50 Must-Have Tips from Pregnancy Through Early Childhood* (San Francisco: Jossey-Bass, 2008), 159–161.

41. P. Malmstrom and E. Davis, "Encouraging Individuality in Twins," iVillage, http://parenting.ivillage.com/baby/bmultiples/0,,43x4,00.html.

42. C. Fiedorowicz and others, "Neurobiological Basis of Learning Disabilities: An Overview," *Learning Disabilities: A Multidisciplinary Journal* 11, no. 2 (Spring 2001): 61–74.

43. Photo by Chris Christo in "The Rescuing Hug," *Worcester Telegram & Gazette,* Nov. 18, 1995.

YOUNGEST CHILD

44. A study from University of Toyama in Japan found that the risk of being overweight in boys in particular was significantly lower with increasing numbers of elder siblings or a sister: cited in R. Dobson, "Why First-Born Children Have Higher IQs," *Times Online,* Apr. 11, 2008, http://www.timesonline.co.uk/tol/life_and_style/health/article3729274.ece.

45. Research by W. Karmaus cited in "First-Born Babies' Higher Asthma and Allergy Rates Due to Pregnancy Conditions," *ScienceDaily,* May 21, 2008, http://www.sciencedaily.com/releases/2008/05/080520090453.htm.

46. Kristenson study cited in K. Mishra, "Your Older Sibling Really Is Smarter, Study Says: More Time with Adults May Be a Major Factor," *San Francisco Chronicle,* June 22, 2007.

47. J. Price, "Parent-Child Quality Time: Does Birth Order Matter?" *Journal of Human Resources* 43, no. 1 (Winter 2008): 240–265.

48. Research cited in R. Kelley, "Getting Away with It," *Newsweek,* Apr. 30, 2008, http://www.newsweek.com/id/134920.

49. S. E. Black, P. J. Devereux, and K. G. Salvanes, "The More the Merrier? The Effect of Family Size and Birth Order on Children's Education," *Quarterly Journal of Economics,* 120, no. 2 (2005): 669–700.

50. R. W. Richardson and L. A. Richardson, *Birth Order and You* (North Vancouver, B.C.: Self-Counsel Press, 1990); C. Ernst and J. Angst, *Birth Order* (Berlin: Springer-Verlag, 1983).

Part 2: Behavior

ARGUES

1. G. Spivack and M. B. Shure, "Interpersonal Cognitive Problem-Solving and Clinical Theory," in vol. 5 of *Advances in Child Clinical Psychology,* ed. B. Lahey and A. E. Kazdin (New York: Plenum, 1982), 323–373.

2. M. Gurian and P. Henley, *Boys and Girls Learn Differently: A Guide for Teachers and Parents* (San Francisco: Jossey-Bass, 2002), 36.

3. National survey by the Josephson Institute of Ethics and CHARACTER COUNTS! Coalition, *1998 Report Card on the Ethics of American Youth,* Oct. 19, 1998, www.josephsoninstitute.or/98-Survey/violence/98survey.htm.

4. N. Drew, *The Kids' Guide to Working Out Conflicts: How to Keep Cool, Stay Safe, and Get Along* (Minneapolis: Free Spirit, 2004), 21.
5. Drew, *Kids' Guide*, 7.

BACK TALK
6. A. Siegler, "What a Nice Kid," *Child* (1997), cited in R. Taffel, *Nurturing Good Children Now* (New York: Golden Books, 1999).

BITING
7. C. M. Todd, "When Children Bite," National Network for Child Care, http://www.nncc .porg/Guidance/dc16_children.bite.html.
8. American Academy of Child and Adolescent Psychiatry, *Facts for Families: Fighting and Biting,* May 2001, http://www.aacap.org/cs/root/facts_for_families_fighting_and_biting.
9. American Academy of Child and Adolescent Psychiatry, *Facts for Families.*
10. L. Gierer, "Children Who Bite Are Sending Signals, Experts Say," *Desert Sun,* Mar. 18, 2002, D3.

BOSSY
11. S. R. Asher and G. A. Williams, "Children Without Friends, Part 2: The Reasons for Peer Rejection," *Day Care Center Connections* 3, no. 1 (1993): 3–5.
12. Research by W. Thomas Boyce cited in M. Elias, "Bossier Preschool Kids Are Healthier," *USA Today,* Mar. 8, 2000, 6D.
13. R. Lavoie, *It's So Much Work to Be Your Friend: Helping the Child with Learning Disabilities Find Social Success* (New York: Touchstone Books, 2005), 330.
14. P. Mussen, E. Rutherford, S. Harris, and C. Keasey, "Honesty and Altruism Among Preadolescents," *Developmental Psychology* 3 (1970): 169–194; R. B. Hampton, "Adolescent Prosocial Behavior: Peer Group and Situational Factors Associated with Helping," *Journal of Personality and Social Psychology* 46 (1970): 153–162.

BRAGS
15. E. Jones and S. Berglas, "Control of the Attributions About the Self Through Self-Handicapping Strategies," in *The Self in Social Psychology,* ed. R. Baumeister (Philadelphia: Psychology Press, 1999).

DEFIANT
16. All box information is from P. Applebome, "Children Score Low in Adults' Esteem, a Study Finds," *New York Times,* June 26, 1997, A12, A17. Survey conducted by the nonpartisan group Public Agenda for the Advertising Council and Ronald McDonald House Charities in June 1997.
17. American Psychiatric Association cited in J. Bernstein, *10 Days to a Less Defiant Child: The Breakthrough Program for Overcoming Your Child's Difficult Behavior* (New York: De Capo Press, 2006), 4–5.
18. N. I. Bernstein, *Treating the Unmanageable Adolescent: A Guide to Oppositional Defiant and Conduct Disorders* (Northvale, N.J.: Aronson, 1996), 6–7.

HOOKED ON REWARDS

19. Interview with Alfie Kohn cited in D. J. Heiss, "Rewards Can Be as Bad as Punishments," *Redlands Daily Facts,* Nov. 15, 2007.

20. D. Rowe, J. Parker, and J. Stimpson, *Raising Happy Children* (London: Hodder & Stoughton, 1999), 189.

21. J. Reid Holman, "Are You Using the Right Rewards?" *Better Homes and Gardens,* Nov. 1997, 112–114.

22. Study by Elizabeth Newson, University of Nottingham, cited in Rowe, Parker, and Stimpson, *Raising Happy Children,* 190.

23. T. Amabile and J. Gitomer, "Children's Artistic Creativity: Effects of Choice in Task Materials," *Personality and Social Psychology Bulletin* 10 (1984): 209–215.

IMPULSIVE

24. T. Armstrong, "To Empower! Not Control! A Holistic Approach to ADHD," *Pathways,* Oct. 2008, 14–17.

25. M. Schulman and E. Mekler, *Bringing Up a Moral Child* (Reading, Mass.: Addison-Wesley, 1985), 20; STAR (Stop, Think, Act Right) developed by M. Borba, *Building Moral Intelligence* (San Francisco: Jossey-Bass, 2004).

26. M. Frith, "Computer Games May Help Kids with ADHD," *Sydney Morning Herald,* Aug. 26, 2007.

27. Armstrong, "To Empower! Not Control!"

28. E. L. Schor, ed., *Caring for Your School-Age Child: Ages 5 to 12* (New York: Bantam Books, 1999), 269–270.

SWEARS

29. E. L. Schor, ed., *Caring for Your School-Age Child: Ages 5 to 12* (New York: Bantam, 2004), 237.

30. From a survey conducted for American Demographics in 2003, cited in S. M. Llana, "Can a $103 Fine Stop Students from Swearing?" *Christian Science Monitor,* Dec. 7, 2005.

31. J. Elish, "Cover Your Ears! Profanity on the Rise in Prime Time," Florida State University, Nov. 30, 2004, FSU.com.

32. N. Hellmich, "Today's Schools Cursed by an Increase in Swearing," *USA Today,* May 20, 1997, D4.

33. Llana, "Can a $103 Fine Stop Students from Swearing?"

34. Results from national survey reported on *ABC Nightly News,* June 2, 2000.

35. Schor, *Caring for Your School-Age Child,* 239.

36. D. Debrovner, "Parents Report," *Parents,* Aug. 2007, 155.

TANTRUMS

37. E. L. Schor, ed., *Caring for Your School-Age Child: Ages 5 to 12* (New York: Bantam, 2004), 232.

38. T. B. Brazelton, *Touchpoints: Your Child's Emotional and Behavioral Development* (Reading, Mass.: Addison-Wesley, 1992).

39. M. T. Stein, "Difficult Behavior, Temper Tantrums to Conduct Disorders," in *Rudolph's Pediatrics,* 21st ed., ed. C. D. Rudolph and others (New York: McGraw-Hill, 2003), 444–450.

TIME-OUT

40. E. L. Schor, ed., *Caring for Your School-Age Child: Ages 5 to 12* (New York: Bantam, 2004), 213.
41. Schor, *Caring for Your School-Age Child*, 213.

WHINING

42. Research cited in J. S. Chatsky, "Parties Without the Presents," *USA Weekend*, Apr. 6, 2003, 22.
43. National poll of 750 youth conducted by the Center for a New American Dream, cited in M. Irvine, "Nagging the Norm for Many Youth," *Desert Sun*, June 18, 2002, A4.
44. A. Ricker and C. Crowder, *Whining: 3 Steps to Stopping It Before the Tears and Tantrums Start* (New York: Simon & Schuster, 2000).

WON'T LISTEN

45. *Parents* magazine poll cited in L. Lambert, "From Chaos to Cooperation: A 21 Day Discipline Makeover," *Parents*, Oct. 2000, 142–145.
46. P. Kramaer, "Now Hear This!" *Parents*, Feb. 2007, 105.
47. Statement by the *Journal of the American Medical Association* that 14.9 percent of school-age children have some degree of hearing loss cited in A. Gordon-Langbein, "How Can I Tell If My Child Has a Problem Hearing?" *New York Daily News*, Apr. 16, 2001.
48. R. Morell, "Ability to Listen to Two Things at Once Is Largely Inherited, Says Twin Study," July 17, 2007, http://www.nih.gov/news/pr/jul2007/nidcd-17.htm. This article summarizes research sponsored by the National Institute on Deafness and Other Communication Disorders, which was published in *Human Genetics*, Aug. 2007.

YELLING

49. Murray A. Straus's study concerning increase in parental yelling cited in R. Sobel, "Wounding with Words," *U.S. News & World Report*, Aug. 28, 2000, 53.

Part 3: Character

BAD MANNERS

1. Poll of 1,005 adults conducted by KRC Research & Consulting with assistance from *U.S. News* pollsters, cited in J. Marks, "The American Uncivil Wars," *U.S. News Online*, Apr. 22, 1996, http://www.usnews.com/usnews/issue/civil.htm.
2. J. Johnson and S. Farkas, *Kids These Days: What Americans Really Think About the Next Generation* (Washington, D.C.: Public Agenda, 1997).
3. H. Cho, "Take a Class on Class: College Students Learn How to Act in the Business World," *Baltimore Sun*, Dec. 11, 2006, 41.
4. Etiquette tips for the different stages and ages provided by Cindy Handler (Etiquette and Leadership Institute in Athens, Georgia), telephone interview, Dec. 5, 2007.

CHEATS

5. U. Bronfenbrenner and others, *The State of Americans: This Generation and the Next* (New York: Free Press, 1969).

6. Josephson Institute of Ethics, *The Ethics of America's Youth: A Warning and a Call to Action* (Marina del Rey, Calif.: Josephson Institute of Ethics, 1990), cited in T. Lickona, *Educating for Character: How Our Schools Can Teach Respect and Responsibility* (New York: Bantam Books, 1991), 14.

7. S. Laidlaw, "Kids in Organized Sports More Likely to Cheat, Study Shows," *Toronto Star,* Mar. 5, 2007.

8. Don McCabe's work on percentage of seventh graders who cheat cited in C. Kleiner and M. Lord, "The Cheating Game: 'Everyone's Doing It,' from Grade School to Graduate School," *U.S. News & World Report,* Nov. 22, 1999, http://www.softwaresecure.com/pdf/TheCheating Game_USNews11-99_.pdf.

9. Study by Public Agenda cited in A. M. Chaker, "The New Cheating Epidemic," *Redbook,* Apr. 2003, 151–154.

10. Kleiner and Lord, "Cheating Game."

11. Don McCabe's interview of five hundred high school students in New Jersey cited in K. Thomas, "Net Makes Cheating as Easy as ABC," *USA Today,* Mar. 20, 2001, D3.

12. W. Kalyn, "Is Your Child Cheating?" *Good Housekeeping,* Apr. 2004, 109.

13. Chaker, "New Cheating Epidemic."

14. Educational Testing Service/Ad Council Campaign to Discourage Academic Cheating, *Academic Cheating Fact Sheet,* http://www.glass-castle.com/clients/www-nocheating-org/ adcouncil/research/cheatingfactsheet.html.

15. MassGeneral Hospital for Children, *Cheating,* June 8, 2008, www.massgeneralforchildren.org.

16. Educational Testing Service/Ad Council Campaign to Discourage Academic Cheating, *Academic Cheating Fact Sheet.*

17. In a nationwide survey of thirty thousand middle and high school students conducted by the Josephson Institute of Ethics, 64 percent said they had cheated on an exam in the last twelve months (38 percent did so two or more times): Josephson Institute and CHARAC-TER COUNTS! Coalition, *The Ethics of American Youth—2008 Summary,* Nov. 2008, http://charactercounts.org/programs/reportcard.

INSENSITIVE

18. S. A. Denham, *Emotional Development in Young Children* (New York: Guilford Press, 1998), 34–39.

19. S. Nowicki and M. P. Duke, *Helping the Child Who Doesn't Fit In* (Atlanta: Peachtree Press, 1992).

20. J. L. Singer, D. G. Singer, and W. S. Rapacznskyi, "Family Patterns and Television Viewing as Predictors of Children's Beliefs and Aggression," *Journal of Communication* 43, no. 2 (1984): 73–89.

21. R. Coles, *The Moral Intelligence of Children* (New York: Random House, 1997).

22. M. Schulman and E. Mekler, *Bringing Up a Moral Child* (Reading, Mass.: Addison-Wesley, 1985), 55.

23. M. Hoffman, "Development of Prosocial Motivation: Empathy and Guilt," in *The Development of Prosocial Behavior,* ed. N. Eisenberg (Orlando, Fla.: Academic Press, 1983).

INTOLERANT

24. Research data cited in L. Duvall, *Respecting Our Differences: A Guide to Getting Along in a Changing World* (Minneapolis: Free Spirit Press, 1994), 154.

25. G. Allport, *The Nature of Prejudice: 25th Anniversary Edition* (New York: Basic Books, 1979).

26. Dr. Melanie Killen, associate director for the Center for Children, Relationships, and Culture at the University of Maryland, cited in S. Jain, "No Pride in Prejudice," *Parent Wise Austin*, Feb. 2008, 8.

27. I. Chang, "Race Matters," *Working Mother*, June-July 2008, 142.

28. Ideas adapted from C. W. Ford, *We Can All Get Along: Fifty Steps You Can Take to Help End Racism* (New York: Dell, 1994), 79.

29. M. A. Wright, *I'm Chocolate, You're Vanilla: Raising Healthy Black and Biracial Children in a Race-Conscious World* (San Francisco: Jossey-Bass, 1998), 266–267.

LYING

30. C. Kleiner and M. Lord, "The Cheating Game," *U.S. News and World Report*, Nov. 22, 1999, 55–61.

31. Kleiner and Lord "Cheating Game."

32. N. Darling, K. Hames, and P. Cumsille, "When Parents and Adolescents Disagree: Disclosure Strategies and Motivations," presented at the biennial meeting of the Society for Research in Adolescence, 2000, http://www.oberlin.edu/faculty/ndarling/lab/stratdis.pdf.

33. P. Bronson, "Learning to Lie," *New York Magazine*, Feb. 10, 2008, http://nymag.com/news/features/43893/.

34. American Academy of Child and Adolescent Psychiatry, *Facts for Families: Conduct Disorder*, July 2004, http://www.aacap.org/cs/root/facts_for_families/conduct_disorder.

35. K. Lang, V. Talwar, N. Bala, and R.C.L. Lindsay, "Children's Lie-Telling to Conceal a Parent's Transgression: Legal Implications," *Law and Human Behavior* 28, no. 4 (Aug. 2004), http://www.talwarresearch.com/files/talwar_lee_1.pdf.

36. Study by Victoria Talwar at McGill University cited in "Kids Lie to Test the Limits," *CBC News*, Aug. 9, 2006, http://www.cbc.ca/health/story/2006/08/09/lie-children.html.

37. From an NBC poll of two thousand parents conducted online by iVillage and reported by the author on the *Today* show, Oct. 18, 2007.

38. Bronson, "Learning to Lie."

39. V. Talwar and K. Lee, "Development of Lying to Conceal a Transgression: Children's Control of Expressive Behaviour During Verbal Deception," *International Journal of Behavioral Development* 26, no. 5 (2002), 436–444.

40. Talwar, "Kids Lie to Test the Limits."

41. Bronson, "Learning to Lie."

42. M. Price, "Liar, Liar, Neurons Fire," *Monitor on Psychology* 39, no. 1 (Jan. 2008), http://www.apa.org/monitor/jan08/liar.html.

43. Bronson, "Learning to Lie."

44. Nancy Darling's research cited in J. Chang, C. Strathmann, L. Owens, and I. Ibanga, "Why Do Kids Lie?" ABC News, Feb. 12, 2008, http://abcnews.go.com/GMA/story?id=4277319&page=1.

MATERIALISTIC

45. J. B. Schor, "Those Ads Are Enough to Make Your Kids Sick," *Washington Post,* Sept. 12, 2004, B4.

46. N. Robinson and others, "Effects of Reducing Television Viewing on Children's Requests for Toys," *Developmental and Behavioral Pediatrics* 229, no. 3 (2001); M. Buijzen and P. M. Valkenburg, "The Effects of Television Advertising on Materialism, Parent-Child Conflict, and Unhappiness: A Review of Research," *Applied Developmental Psychology* 24, no. 4 (2003), 437–456.

47. "Children 'Damaged' by Materialism," *BBC News,* Feb. 26, 2008, http://news.bbc.co.uk/2/hi/uk_news/7262936.stm.

48. J. B. Schor, *Born to Buy: The Commercialized Child and the New Consumer Culture* (New York: Scribner, 2005).

49. L. N. Chaplin and D. R. John, "Growing Up in a Material World: Age Differences in Materialism in Children and Adolescents, *Journal of Consumer Research* 34, no. 4 (2007): 480–493.

50. Schor, *Born to Buy,* 13.

51. New American Dream, *New American Dream Survey Report,* Sept. 2004, http://www.newdream.org/about/pdfs/Finalpollreport.pdf.

52. Study cited in M. Elias, "Ads Targeting Kids," *USA Today,* Mar. 22, 2000, D5.

53. Study of 206 middle and high school children in rural Midwest: T. Kasser, "Psychometric Development of Brief Measures of Frugality, Generosity, and Materialism for Use in Children and Adolescents," in *Conceptualizing and Measuring Indicators of Positive Development: What Do Children Need to Flourish?* ed. K. Moore and L. Lippman (New York: Kluwer/Plenum, 2005), 357–373.

54. D. R. John, "Consumer Socialization of Children: A Retrospective Look at Twenty-Five Years of Research," *Journal of Consumer Research* 26 (1999): 183–213.

55. M. E. Goldberg, G. J. Gorn, L. A. Peracchio, and G. Bamossy, "Understanding Materialism Among Youth," *Journal of Consumer Psychology* 13, no. 3 (2003): 278–288.

56. Goldberg and others, "Understanding Materialism Among Youth."

57. Chaplin and John, "Growing Up in a Material World."

58. Chaplin and John, "Growing Up in a Material World"; survey for the Children's Society by the GfK NOP, a leading market research company based in London, cited in "Children 'Damaged' by Materialism."

59. Schor, *Born to Buy.*

60. Chaplin and John, "Growing Up in a Material World."

61. Chaplin and John, "Growing Up in a Material World."

62. Schor, *Born to Buy.*

63. Study by Martin Lindstrom citing Millward Brown global market research agency, cited in Schor, "Those Ads Are Enough."

64. Survey of 991 kids about peer pressure cited in A. Goldstein, "Paging All Parents," *Time,* July 3, 2000, 47.

NOT KNOWING RIGHT FROM WRONG

65. C. Dweck, *Mindset: The New Psychology of Success* (New York: Ballantine Books, 2007).

66. *Newsweek* poll cited in M. Medved and D. Medved, *Saving Childhood: Protecting Our Children from the National Assault on Innocence* (New York: HarperPerennial, 1998), 172.

67. P. Applebome, "Children Score Low in Adults' Esteem, a Study Finds," *New York Times,* June 26, 1997, A12; S. Farkas and J. Johnson, *Kids These Days: What Americans Really Think About the Next Generation* (New York: Public Agenda, 1997).

68. American Academy of Child and Adolescent Psychiatry, *Facts for Families: Conduct Disorder,* July 2004, http://www.aacap.org/cs/root/facts_for_families/conduct_disorder.

69. N. Eisenberg, *The Caring Child* (Cambridge, Mass.: Harvard University Press, 1992), 96.

70. T. Lickona, *Raising Good Children* (New York: Bantam, 1983), 128.

71. Characteristics of conscience and moral growth are derived from the work of Thomas Lickona, Lawrence Kohlberg, and William Damon.

72. N. W. Hall, "Do the Right Thing!" *Parents,* July 1999, 155–156.

POOR SPORT

73. National Association of Sports Officials concerns reported by S. Smith, "Is the Choice Sportsmanship or Death?" Knight Ridder/Tribune Information Services, July 23, 2000, http://www.youthdevelopment.org.

74. National Institute on Drug Abuse, *NIDA InfoFacts: High School and Youth Trends,* June 2003, http://www.drugabuse.gov/Infofax/HSYouthtrends.html.

75. "Cheating Abundant in Youth Sports, Study Suggests," National Public Radio, Dec. 3, 2005, http://www.npr.org/templates/story/story.php?storyId=5037483.

76. K. S. Lombardi, "When Little League Becomes Hardball," *New York Times,* Mar. 24, 1996, http://query.nytimes.com/gst/fullpage.html?res=9801E0DC1439F937A15750C0A9609582 60&sec=&spon=&pagewanted=2.

SELFISH AND SPOILED

77. M. Alias, "Ads Targeting Kids," *USA Today,* Mar. 22, 2000, D5.

78. AOL/Time Warner poll cited in N. Gibbs, "Who's in Charge Here?" *Time,* Aug. 6, 2001, 46.

79. E. Hallowell, *The Childhood Roots of Adult Happiness* (New York: Ballantine Books, 2003).

80. J. B. Schor, *Born to Buy: The Commercialized Child and the New Consumer Culture* (New York: Scribner, 2005).

81. M. Hoffman, "Development of Prosocial Motivation: Empathy and Guilt," in *The Development of Prosocial Behavior,* ed. N. Eisenberg (Orlando, Fla.: Academic Press, 1983).

82. M. Duke and S. Nowicki, *Helping the Child Who Doesn't Fit In* (Atlanta: Peachtree Press, 1992), 129–144.

83. Time/CNN poll: "Are Your Kids Spoiled?" *CNNMoney,* July 30, 2001, http://money.cnn.com/2001/07/30/living/v_smart_assets.

84. Study conducted by Penn State Smeal College of Business, cited in M. E. Goldberg, G. J. Gorn, L.A. Peracchio, and G. Bamossy, "Understanding Materialism Among Youth," *Journal of Consumer Psychology* 13, no. 3 (2001): 278–288.

85. Survey cited in J. S. Chatsky, "Parties Without the Presents," *USA Weekend,* Apr. 6, 2003, 22.

86. E. Staub, *The Development of Prosocial Behavior in Children* (Morristown, N.J.: General Learning Press, 1975).

87. Staub, *Development of Prosocial Behavior in Children.*

STEALS

88. New York-Presbyterian Hospital, *Lying and Stealing,* http://nyp.org/health/pediatrics_lying.html.

89. D. K. Daeg de Mott, "Stealing," in *Gale Encyclopedia of Childhood and Adolescence,* ed. J. Kagan and S. B. Gall (Detroit: Gale Research, 1998).

90. Survey cited in Goldstein, "Paging All Parents," *Time,* July 3, 2000, 47.

91. The Josephson Institute of Ethics and CHARACTER COUNTS! *1998 Report Card on the Ethics of American Youth,* Oct. 19, 1998, www.josephsoninstitute.org/98-Survey/98survey.htm.

92. J. Whalen, *A Senseless and Preventable Mistake That Could Cost* YOUR *Child Their Dignity, Pride and Big Dream for the Future,* 2006, http://stopyourkidsfromshoplifting.com.

UNGRATEFUL

93. R. A. Emmons and M. E. McCullough, "Counting Blessings Versus Burdens: Experimental Studies of Gratitude and Subjective Well-Being in Daily Life," *Journal of Personality and Social Psychology* 84 (2003): 377–389.

94. Cindy Handler (Etiquette and Leadership Institute at Athens, Georgia), telephone interview, Dec. 5, 2007.

Part 4: Emotions

ANGRY

1. American Academy of Pediatrics, *Joint Statement on the Impact on Entertainment Violence on Children. Congressional Public Health Summit,* July 26, 2000, http://www.aap.org/advocacy/releases/jstmtevc.htm.

2. Josephson Institute Center for Youth Ethics, *The Ethics of American Youth: 2000,* http://charactercounts.org/programs/reportcard/2000/index.html.

DEPENDENT

3. Data from U.S. Census Bureau cited in P. Tyre, "Bringing Up Adultolescents," *Newsweek,* Mar. 25, 2002, 39; an online survey by MonsterTRAK.com, a job-search firm, found that 60 percent of college students plan to live at home after graduation: cited in Tyre, "Bringing Up Adultolescents."

4. Four-step process to teach a new skill adapted from R. Lavoie, *It's So Much Work to Be Your Friend: Helping the Child with Learning Disabilities Find Social Success* (New York: Touchstone Books, 2005), 280.

5. L. Kutner, "Kids' Behavior," *Parents,* Oct. 2006, 195.

FEARFUL

6. J. S. Dacey and L. B. Fiore, *Your Anxious Child* (San Francisco: Jossey-Bass, 2000), 2–3.

7. Dacey and Fiore, *Your Anxious Child.*

8. American Academy of Child and Adolescent Psychiatry, *Facts for Families: Panic Disorder in Children and Adolescents,* Nov. 2004, www.aacap.org/cs/root/facts_for_families/panic_disorder_in_children_and_adolescents.

9. "Parenting Style May Foster Anxiety," *Psychology Today,* Sept.-Oct. 2004, http://www.psychologytoday.com/articles/pto-19940901-000013.html.

10. Research by Richard Davidson cited in D. Goleman, *Social Intelligence* (New York: Bantam Books, 2006), 185.

11. R. Schachter and C. S. McCauley, *When Your Child Is Afraid* (New York: Fireside, 1988); Dacey and Fiore, *Your Anxious Child,* 14–15.

12. A national survey of seven- to ten-year-olds found that 71 percent worry about getting shot or stabbed; 63 percent worry that they might die young: cited in G. Witkin, *KidStress* (New York: Viking, 1999), 3.

GRIEF

13. Study conducted by Bella DePaula, a social psychologist at the University of California at Santa Barbara, cited in S. Vedantam, "Almost Everyone Lies, Often Seeing It as a Kindness," *Washington Post,* Feb. 19, 2007, A02, http://www.washingtonpost.com/wp-dyn/content/article/2007/02/18/AR2007021800915.html.

14. American Academy of Pediatrics Committee on Psychosocial Aspects of Child and Family Health, "The Pediatrician and Childhood Bereavement," *Pediatrics* 105 (2000): 445–447, http://aappolicy.aappublications.org/cgi/content/full/pediatrics;105/2/445.

15. E. A. Grollman, *Explaining Death to Children* (Boston: Beacon Press, 1967), 18–20.

16. J. E. Baker, M. D. Shaffer, G. Wasserman, and M. Davies, "Psychological Tasks for Bereaved Children," *American Journal of Orthopsychiatry* 62, no. 11 (1992): 105–116.

17. Committee on Psychosocial Aspects of Child and Family Health, "The Pediatrician and Childhood Bereavement," *Pediatrics* 89 (1992): 516–518.

18. Information on the stages of children's understanding of death are from Hospice of Southeastern Connecticut Bereavement Program, http://sids-network.org/sibling/sibunderstanding.html; and M. Nagy, "The Child's View of Death," in *The Meaning of Death,* ed. Herman Feifel (New York: McGraw-Hill, 1959).

19. L. P. Barakat, R. Sills, and S. Labagnara, "Management of Fatal Illness and Death in Children or Their Parents," *Pediatric Review* 16 (1995): 419–424.

20. M. B. Gibbons, "A Child Dies, a Child Survives: The Impact of Sibling Loss," *Journal of Pediatric Health Care* 6 (1992): 65–72.

HOMESICK

21. C. A. Thurber, "The Experience and Expression of Homesickness in Preadolescent and Adolescent Boys," *Child Development* 66 (1995): 1162–1178.

22. C. A. Thurber, "The Phenomenology of Homesickness in Boys," *Journal of Abnormal Child Psychology* 27 (1999): 125–139.

23. C. A. Thurber, "New Thinking Needed on Helping Kids Avoid or Cope with Homesickness," University of Michigan Health System, Jan. 3, 2007, http://www.health78.com/health-news/New-Thinking-Needed-On-Helping-Kids-Avoid-Or-Cope-With-Homesickness/50651.

24. Thurber, "New Thinking Needed."

25. C. A. Thurber, E. Walter, and the Council on School Health, "Preventing and Treating Homesickness," *Pediatrics* 119, no. 1 (Jan. 2007): 192–201.

26. Thurber, Walter, and the Council on School Health, "Preventing and Treating Homesickness."

27. B. K. Britton and A. D. Pellegrini, eds., *Narrative Thought and Narrative Language* (Hillsdale, N.J.: Erlbaum, 1990); C. A. Thurber, "The Digital Umbilical," *Camping* 79 (2006): 44–51.

28. Thurber, Walter, and the Council on School Health, "Preventing and Treating Homesickness."

29. Survey conducted by Sesame Street, cited in N. Kalish, "Decisions: Sleepover Start-Up," *Working Mother,* Dec.-Jan. 2004, 80.

30. Thurber, Walter, and the Council on School Health, "Preventing and Treating Homesickness."

PERFECTIONIST

31. "Perfectionism Can Lead to Imperfect Health: High Achievers More Prone to Emotional, Physical and Relationship Problems," *ScienceDaily,* June 14, 2004, http://www.sciencedaily.com/releases/2004/06/040614074620.htm.

32. Walter Kaye, psychiatrist at the University of Pittsburgh, notes that perfectionism is not a side effect of anorexia but a personality trait that puts the child at risk for the eating disorder: cited in "Persistent Perfectionists," *Psychology Today,* May-June 1996, http://www.psychologytoday.com/articles/pto-19960501-000007.html.

33. M. Cook, "Lab Probes Perfectionism for Links with Depression," *USC Reports* 48, no. 2 (Jan. 24, 2002), http://www.publicaffairs.ubc.ca/ubcreports/2002/02jan24/perfectionism.html.

34. P. L. Hewitt's research cited in "Perfectionism Can Lead to Imperfect Health."

35. M. H. Kernis, "Self-Esteem as a Multifaceted Construct," in *Understanding Early Adolescent Self and Identity: Applications and Interventions,* ed. T. M. Brinthaupt and R. P. Lipka (Albany: State University of New York Press, 2002), 57–88.

PESSIMISTIC

36. M. Seligman, *The Optimistic Child: A Revolutionary Program That Safeguards Children Against Depression and Builds Lifelong Resilience* (New York: Houghton Mifflin, 1995).

37. Seligman, *The Optimistic Child,* 8.

SENSITIVE

38. E. N. Aron, *The Highly Sensitive Child: Helping Our Children Thrive When the World Overwhelms Them* (New York: Broadway, 2002).

39. Aron's characteristics of highly sensitive children cited in T. Goodwell, "Parenting a Highly Sensitive Child," *Mothering,* 2002, http://www.mothering.com/articles/growing_child/child_health/highly-sensitive.html.

40. San Diego State University study by Robert McGivern reported by R. Ward, "Why Teens Are Moody," *Psychology Today,* Mar.-Apr. 2003, http://www.psychologytoday.com/articles/PTO-20030521-000001.html.

41. M. P. Duke, S.Nowicki, and E. Q. Martin, *Teaching Your Child the Language of Social Success* (Atlanta: Peachtree Press, 1996), 60.

42. F. Virtro of Texas Woman's University cited in J. S. Freedman, *Easing the Teasing: Helping Your Child Cope with Name-Calling, Ridicule and Verbal Bullying* (New York: McGraw-Hill, 2002), 14.

43. Research conducted by Kaoru Yamamoto, University of Colorado, cited in E. McCoy, *What to Do When Kids Are Mean to Your Child* (Pleasantville, N.Y.: Reader's Digest Press, 1997), 15.

SHY

44. Jerome Kagan's statistics on shyness cited in D. Goleman, *Social Intelligence* (New York: Bantam Books, 2006), 11; Kagan quoted in J. Kluger, "Secrets of the Shy," *Time*, Mar. 28, 2005, http://www.time.com/time/magazine/article/0,9171,1042458,00.html.

45. "The Shy Brain," *Psychology Today*, Nov.-Dec. 1995, www.psychologytoday.com/articles/pto-19951101-000031.html.

46. C. Jozefowicz, "Once Shy, Always Shy?" *Psychology Today*, June 23, 2003, www.psychology today.com/articles/pto-20031022-000011.html.

47. Jerilyn Ross, president of Anxiety Disorders Association of America, quoted in B. Markway and G. Markway, *Nurturing the Shy Child: Practical Help for Raising Confident and Socially Skilled Kids and Teens* (New York: St. Martin's Press, 2004), 11.

48. Carl Schwartz and Jerome Kagan of Harvard University cited in Kluger, "Secrets of the Shy."

49. American Psychiatric Association, *Diagnostic and Statistical Manual of Mental Disorders*, 4th ed. (Washington, D.C.: American Psychiatric Association).

50. P. Jaret, "How Shy Is Too Shy?" *Los Angeles Times*, Feb. 21, 2005, F1.

51. Marco Battaglia study cited in Kluger, "Secrets of the Shy."

52. Jerome Kagan studies cited in C. Millstone, "How to Help Your Shy Child," *National Post*, Mar. 3, 2004, A11.

53. Regina Pally of UCLA urges parents to respond to children's timid behavior with empathy, taking care not to equate being anxious with being bad: cited in Kluger, "Secrets of the Shy."

STRESSED

54. Poll of one thousand parents posted on the iVillage community the week of Nov. 3 through Nov. 10, 2007, asking "Do you think today's kids are more stressed out than kids were when you were young?"

55. J. S. Dacey and L. B. Fiore, *Your Anxious Child* (San Francisco: Jossey-Bass, 2000), 2–3.

56. E. H. Parlapiano, "Stress in Kids," *Parents*, Feb. 2004, 134.

57. G. Witkin, *KidStress* (New York: Viking, 1999), 3.

58. Research led by Mary Caserta, University of Rochester Medical Center, cited in "Children Under Stress Develop More Fevers," *ScienceDaily*, Mar. 7, 2007, http://www.sciencedaily.com/releases/2007/03/070305202905.htm.

59. Signs of when to worry are based on a personal conversation with David Fassler, child and adolescent psychiatrist, New York, Nov. 6, 2007.

60. Study in 2003 of 649 college students by sociologists Heather Turner and Melissa Butler at the University of New Hampshire found that childhood stress was a significant factor in young adult depression: cited in P. J. Kiger, "What's Wrong with This Picture? The Stressed-Out American Family, Part Four," *Ladies Home Journal*, June 2004.

61. Johns Hopkins research cited in T. E. Chansky, *Freeing Your Child from Anxiety* (New York: Broadway Books, 2004).

62. KidsHealth, *What Kids Say About: Handling Stress*, Oct. 2005, http://www.kidshealth.org/parent/emotions/feelings/kids_stress.html.

WORRIED ABOUT THE WORLD

63. Poll by Knowledge Networks for AP and MTV involved online interviews conducted from Apr. 16 to Apr. 23 with 1,280 people ages thirteen to twenty-four: cited in J. Noveck and T. Tompson, "AP/MTV Poll: Happiness for America's Young People Often Means Ties, Faith, Belonging," *Associated Press National Wire,* Aug. 19, 2007, http://www.socialtechnologies. com/FileView.aspx?filename=AP1.pdf.

64. Boys and Girls Clubs of America, *Youth Report to America: 2005 National TEENSupreme Keystone Project Report* (Atlanta: Boys and Girls Clubs of America, 2005).

65. Children Now poll cited in L. Garisto Pfaff, "In the News," *Parents,* Mar. 2004, 205–206.

66. "The 'Mean-World' Syndrome," *Oregonian,* July 22, 2002, http://www.oregonlive.com/special/ girls/index.ssf?.special/oregonian/girls/072202_ed.html.

Part 5: Social Scene

BAD FRIENDS

1. Chris Knoester's research was based on data from the National Longitudinal Study of Adolescent Health, including interviews from a national sample of 11,483 seventh to twelfth graders and parents; cited in "Parents Can Help Teens Choose 'Good' Friends, Study Finds," *Ohio State Research News,* Aug. 13, 2005, http://researchnews.osu.edu/archive/adolfrnd.htm.

2. P. Bearman and others, "Peer Potential: Making the Most of How Teens Influence Each Other," National Campaign to Prevent Teen Pregnancy, 2004, cited in A. M. Smith, "The Power of Peers," Institute for Youth Development, http://www.youthdevelopment.org/articles/ fp109901.htm.

BULLIED

3. S. Fitzgerald, "Nearly 1 in 3 Students Either a Bully or Victim," *Seattle Times,* Apr. 25, 2001, available at http://www.peace.ca/bullyorvictim.htm; R. Rubin, "Study: Bullies and Their Victims Tend to Be More Violent," *USA Today,* Apr. 15, 2003, 9D. The cited study was published in *Archives of Pediatric and Adolescent Medicine,* based on a nationally representative sample of 15,686 students in grades 6 through 10. The study showed that those who bullied or were bullied were more likely to be involved in violent behavior.

4. PTA survey cited in J. Zaslow, "Tough Kids, Tough Calls," *Time,* Apr. 22, 2002, 76.

5. Joseph Wright, associate professor of pediatrics, emergency medicine, and prevention and community health at Children's National Medical Center, cited in L. Little, "Bullying Increasing: First Boys, Now Girls," *WebMD,* FoxNews.com, Oct. 12, 2005, http://www.foxnews.com/ story/0,2933,172055,00.html.

6. U.S. Department of Justice statistic cited by how-to-stop-bullying.com, http://how-to-stop -bullying.com/bullyingstatistics.html.

7. Research by the National Education Association cited in S. Fried and P. Fried, *Bullies and Victims* (New York: Evans, 1996), xii.

8. R. Arce, "Study: Kids Rate Bullying and Teasing as 'Big Problem': Survey Finds Children Don't Think Parents Hear Their Safety Concerns," CNN.com, Mar. 8, 2001, http://archives. cnn.com/2001/US/03/08/violence.survey/.

9. "Bullying Among Sixth Graders a Daily Occurrence, UCLA Study Finds," *ScienceDaily*, Apr. 11, 2005, http://www.sciencedaily.com/releases/2005/04/050411100940.htm.

10. N. R. Crick, "Relational and Overt Forms of Peer Victimization: A Multiinformant Approach," *Journal of Consulting and Clinical Psychology* 66, no. 2 (Mar. 26, 1998): 337–347.

11. J. C. Rusby, K. K. Forrester, A. Biglan, and C. W. Metzler, "Relationships Between Peer Harassment and Adolescent Problem Behaviors," *Journal of Early Adolescence* 25, no. 4 (2005): 453–477.

12. "Girls Twice as Likely as Boys to Remain Victims of Bullying, Study Finds," *ScienceDaily*, Jan. 13, 2009, http://www.sciencedaily.com/releases/2009/01/090112093509.htm.

13. Statistic cited in A. Mulrine, "Once Bullied, Now Bullies—with Guns," *U.S. News & World Report,* May 3, 1999, 24.

14. S. Ziegler and M. Rosenstein-Manner, *Bullying at School: Toronto in an International Context* (Toronto: Toronto Board of Education, 1999), 22.

15. Arce, "Study: Kids Rate Bullying."

16. H. E. Marano, "Fending Off Bullies: Quit Picking on Me! Self-Confidence Is the Best Way to Fight Bullies," *Psychology Today,* May-June 1998, http://www.psychologytoday.com/articles/pto-19980501-000011.html.

17. Rubin, "Study: Bullies."

18. Center for School Mental Health Assistance, "Bullying Resource Packet," University of Maryland, 2002, http://csmh.umaryland.edu/resources.html/resource_packets/download_files/bullying_2002.pdf.

19. "Boy-Girl Bullying in Middle Grades More Common Than Previously Thought," *ScienceDaily,* Dec. 10, 2008, http://www.sciencedaily.com/releases/2008/12/081209221711.htm.

20. Center for School Mental Health Assistance, "Bullying Resource Packet."

21. Boys experience two physical harassments every three days; girls report one incident of physical harassment every four days: Rusby and others, "Relationships Between Peer Harassment and Adolescent Problem Behaviors."

22. Rubin, "Study: Bullies."

BULLYING

23. Cited in K. Zarzour, *Facing the Schoolyard Bully* (Buffalo, N.Y.: Firefly Books, 2000), 10.

24. Study prepared for the American Psychological Association cited in J. Turley, "Bullying's Day in Court," *USA Today,* July 15, 2008, 7D.

25. KidsHealth survey cited in Turley, "Bullying's Day in Court."

26. P. C. Rodkin, T. W. Farmer, R. Pearl, and R. Van Acker, "Heterogeneity of Popular Boys: Antisocial and Prosocial Configurations," *Developmental Psychology* 36, no. 1. (Jan. 2000): 14–21.

27. D. Olweus, "Bully/Victim Problems Among Schoolchildren: Basic Facts and Effects of a School-Based Intervention Program," in *The Development and Treatment of Childhood Aggression,* ed. D. Pepler and K. Rubin (Hillsdale, N.J.: Erlbaum, 1991), 441–448.

28. D. Olweus, "Bully/Victim Problems in School: Facts and Intervention," *European Journal of Psychology of Education* 9, no. 4 (1997): 495–510.

29. Survey of 13,936 boys and 9,497 girls in Australia cited in K. Rigby, "What Children Tell Us About Bullying in Schools," *Children Australia* 22, no. 2 (1997): 28–34, http:www.kenrigby.net/childtelus.htm.

30. A. Dickinson, "Bad Boys Rule: A New Study Shows Some of the Most Popular Kids in School Are 'Extremely Antisocial,'" *Time,* Jan. 31, 2000, 77.

31. University of Michigan study by Leonard Eron cited in Z. Lazar, "Bullying: A Serious Business," *Child,* Feb. 2001, 78–84.

32. Committee on Communications, American Academy of Pediatrics, "Media Violence," *Pediatrics* 95 (1995): 949–951.

33. American Psychological Association, "Summary Report of the American Psychological Association Commission on Violence and Youth," in vol. 1 of *Violence and Youth: Psychology's Response* (Washington, D.C.: American Psychological Association, 1993).

34. S. Denham, *Emotional Development in Young Children* (New York: Guilford Press, 1998).

35. S. Bernadette-Shapiro, D. Ehrensaf, and J. L. Shapiro, "Father Participation in Childcare and the Development of Empathy in Sons: An Empirical Study," *Family Therapy* 23, no. 2 (1996): 77–93.

36. Rigby, "What Children Tell Us."

37. Statistic based on a 2001 Kaiser Foundation study done in conjunction with Nickelodeon TV network and Children Now, cited in B. Coloroso, *The Bully, the Bullied, and the Bystander* (New York: HarperCollins, 2002), 12.

CLIQUES

38. D. Prothrow-Stith and H. R. Spivak, *Sugar and Spice and No Longer Nice: How We Can Stop Girls' Violence* (San Francisco: Jossey-Bass, 2005), 23–32.

39. Girls Incorporated, "Girls and Violence in the United States," June 2008, www.girls-inc.org/downloads/GirlsandViolence.pdf.

40. M. A. Zah and others, "Violence by Teenage Girls: Trends and Context," cited in J. Robert Flores, "Girls Study Group: Understanding and Responding to Girls' Delinquency," U.S. Department of Justice, May 2008, http://www.ncjrs.gov/pdffiles1/ojjdp/218905.pdf.

41. A. Gershon, L. K. Gowen, L. Compian, and C. Hayward, "Gender-Stereotyped Imagined Dates and Weight Concerns in Sixth-Grade Girls," *Sex Roles: A Journal of Research* 50, nos. 7–8 (2004), available at http://findarticles.com/p/articles/mi_m2294/is_7-8_50/ai_n6079186.

42. C. C. Giannetti and M. Sagarese, *Cliques: 8 Steps to Help Your Child Survive the Social Jungle* (New York: Broadway Books, 2001), 19–20.

43. R. Lavoie, *It's So Much Work to Be Your Friend: Helping the Child with Learning Disabilities Find Social Success* (New York: Touchstone Books, 2005), 330.

CLOTHES AND APPEARANCE

44. S. Weiner, "Goodbye to Girlhood," *Washington Post,* Feb. 20, 2007, HE01, http://www.washingtonpost.com/wp-dyn/content/article/2007/02/16/AR2007021602263.html.

45. S. Lamb and L. M. Brown, *Packaging Girlhood* (New York: St. Martin's Griffin, 2006), 25.

CRUSHES

46. J. G. Job, "Young Love," *Parents,* Feb. 2002, 145–146.

47. T. Sharples, "Young Love," *Time,* Jan. 28, 2008, 93–96.

48. Sharples, "Young Love."

DRINKING

49. U.S. Department of Health and Human Services, "Underage Drinking," Alcohol Alert No. 67, Jan. 2006, http://pubs.niaaa.nih.gov/publications/AA67/AA67.htm.

50. Statistics about fourth through sixth graders are from a University of Michigan survey cited in C. L. Mithers, "Teens Too Soon," *Ladies' Home Journal,* Mar. 2002, 60–68; additional data on grade school drinking habits gathered by University of Pittsburgh researcher John Donovan from survey of twenty-five thousand students, cited in M. Hitti, "Underage Drinking Hits Grade School," *CBS News,* Aug. 31, 2007, http://www.cbsnews.com/stories/2007/08/31/health/webmd/main3224978.shtml?source=search_story.

51. L. D. Johnson, P. M. O'Malley, J. G. Bachman, and J. E. Schulenberg, *Monitoring the Future National Survey Results on Adolescent Drug Use: Overview of Key Findings, 2007,* NIH Publication No. 08-6418 (Bethesda, Md.: National Institute on Drug Abuse, 2008), table 3, http://www.monitoringthefuture.org/pubs/monographs/overview2007.pdf.

52. G. Newes-Adeyi, C. M. Chen, G. D. Williams, and V. B. Faden, *Surveillance Report #74: Trends in Underage Drinking in the United States, 1991–2003* (Washington, D.C.: National Institute on Alcohol Abuse and Alcoholism, Oct. 2005), http://pubs.niaaa.nih.gov/publications/surveillance74/Underage%2074.pdf.

53. R. B. Noll, R. A. Zucker, and G. S. Greenberg, "Identification of Alcohol by Smell Among Preschoolers: Evidence for Early Socialization About Drugs Occurring in the Home," *Child Development* 61 (1990): 1520–1527.

54. M. E. Dunn and M. S. Goldman, "Empirical Modeling of an Alcohol Expectancy Memory Network in Elementary School Children as a Function of Grade," *Experimental and Clinical Psychopharmacology* 4 (1996): 209–217.

55. William Damon, director of the Stanford University Center on Adolescence, quoted in B. Kantrowitz and A. Underwood, "The Teen Drinking Dilemma," *Newsweek,* June 25, 2007, 36.

56. U.S. Department of Health and Human Services, "Alcohol Alert."

57. "More Teens Are Binge Drinking," CBS News, Jan. 2, 2007, http://www.cbsnews.com/stories/2007/01/2/eveningnews.

58. "CASA 2000 Teen Survey: Teens with 'Hands-Off' Parents at Four Times Greater Risk of Smoking, Drinking and Using Illegal Drugs as Teens with 'Hands-On' Parents," *Columbia News,* Feb. 2001, http://www.columbia.edu/cu/news/01/02/CASA_survey.html.

59. B. Kantrowitz and A. Underwood, "The Teen Drinking Dilemma," *Newsweek,* June 25, 2007, 37.

60. Dunn and Goldman, "Empirical Modeling."

61. Research led by Brian A. Primack cited in "One of Every Three Popular Songs Contains References to Substance Use," *ScienceDaily,* Nov. 11, 2007, http://www.sciencedaily.com/releases/2007/11/071109210416.htm.

62. S. A. Brown and S. F. Tapert, "Health Consequences of Adolescent Alcohol Involvement," in *Reducing Underage Drinking: A Collective Responsibility, Background Papers* [CD-ROM], ed. R. J. Bonnie and M. E. O'Connell (Washington, D.C.: National Academies Press, 2004), 383–401.

63. G. Hastings, S. Anderson, E. Cooke, and R. Gordon, "Alcohol Advertising and Marketing and Young People's Drinking: A Review of the Research," *Journal of Public Health Policy* 26 (2005): 296–311.

64. E. W. Austin and C. Knaus, "Predicting the Potential for Risky Behavior Among Those 'Too Young' to Drink as a Result of Appealing Advertising," *Journal of Health Communications* 5 (2000): 13–27.

65. "Teen Drinking: Key Findings," a summary of surveys conducted for the American Medical Association by Teen Research Unlimited and Harris Interactive, Spring 2005, http://www.confidentialtreatment.com/pub/files/3571/Teen_Drinking_Key_Findings-AMA.pdf.

66. Telephone survey of 1,297 twelve- to seventeen-year-olds and 562 parents conducted for the National Center on Addiction and Substance Abuse at Columbia University, cited D. Leinwand, "Survey: Parents Clueless on Booze, Drugs at Teen Parties," *USA Today,* Aug. 17, 2006, 8A.

67. Survey of 991 kids ages nine to fourteen cited in A. Goldstein, "Paging All Parents," *Time,* July 3, 2000, 47.

68. L. Graeber, "Stop Preteen Drinking Before It Starts," *Parents,* Jan. 2000, 143–144.

FRIENDSHIP BREAKUPS

69. Z. Rubin, *Children's Friendships* (Cambridge, Mass.: Harvard University Press, 1980), 89.

70. M. Brenton, "When Best Friends Part," *Parents,* May 1998, 45.

71. University of Maryland survey of six hundred kids found that they consider five traits critical to close friendships: cited in K. H. Rubin with A. Thompson, *The Friendship Factor: Helping Our Children Navigate Their Social World—and Why It Matters for Their Success and Happiness* (New York: Viking, 2002).

72. F. Frankel, *Good Friends Are Hard to Find: Help Your Child Find, Make and Keep Friends* (Los Angeles: Perspective, 1996), 147.

73. C. E. Schaefer and T. F. DiGeronimo, *Ages and Stages: A Parent's Guide to Normal Childhood Development* (Hoboken, N.J.: Wiley, 2000), 191.

GROWING UP TOO FAST

74. *Parents* magazine hired Global Strategy Group to conduct a phone survey of one thousand moms and dads across the country; results reported in "What Keeps Parents Up at Night," *Parents,* Jan. 2008, 20.

75. K. Deveny with R. Kelley, "Girls Gone Wild: What Are Celebs Teaching Kids?" *Newsweek,* Feb. 12, 2007, 40–47.

76. J. D. Brown and J. R. Steels, *Sex and the Mass Media* (Menlo Park, Calif.: Kaiser Family Foundation, 1995).

77. S. Weiner, "Goodbye to Girlhood," *Washington Post,* Feb. 20, 2007, http://www.washingtonpost.com/wp-dyn/content/article/2007/02/16/AR2007021602263.html.

78. From study by the Kaiser Family Foundation, cited in C. L. Mithers, "Teens Too Soon," *Ladies' Home Journal,* Mar. 2002, 60–68.

79. Weiner, "Goodbye to Girlhood."

80. Study in *Pediatrics* cited in Deveny with Kelley, "Girls Gone Wild."

81. Weiner, "Goodbye to Girlhood."

82. University of Michigan study cited in J. Newman, "How to Let Kids Be Kids," *Redbook,* Aug. 2008, 188–195.

83. Alvin Rosenfeld, M.D., former head of the child psychiatry training program at Stanford University and author of *The Overscheduled Child,* cited in Newman, "How to Let Kids Be Kids," 190.

84. M. E. Herman-Giddens and others, "Secondary Sexual Characteristics and Menses in Young Girls Seen in Office Practice: A Study from the Pediatric Research in Office Settings Network," *Pediatrics* 99, no. 4 (Apr. 1997): 505–512.

85. J. Noveck and T. Tompson, "Poll: Family Ties Key to Youth Happiness, *Washington Post,* Aug. 20, 2007, http://www.washingtonpost.com/wp-dyn/content/article/2007/08/20/AR200708 2000451.html; actual poll results available at http://www.mtv.com/thinkmtv/about/pdfs/ APMTV_happinesspoll.pdf.

86. Study by Reed Larson surveyed 483 adolescents with the beeper method: fifty-five families recorded their feelings and activities for one week whenever prompted at random intervals by a beeper: R. Larson and M. H. Richards, *Divergent Realities: The Emotional Lives of Mothers, Fathers, and Adolescents* (New York: Basic Books, 1995).

87. Survey from *Advertising Age* cited in B. Gardiner, "Technology for Kids," *nwa WorldTraveler,* 2008, 74.

PEER PRESSURE

88. Boys and Girls Clubs of America, *Youth Report to America: 2005 National TEENSupreme Keystone Project Report* (Atlanta: Boys and Girls Clubs of America, 2005).

89. Survey cited in A. Goldstein, "Paging All Parents," *Time,* July 3, 2000, 47.

90. "CASA 2000 Teen Survey: Teens with 'Hands-Off' Parents at Four Times Greater Risk of Smoking, Drinking and Using Illegal Drugs as Teens with 'Hands-On' Parents," *Columbia News,* Feb. 23, 2001, http://www.columbia.edu/cu/news/01/02/CASA_survey.html.

91. R. Bock, "Parents' Involvement Helps Kids Overcome Peer Influence on Smoking," National Institutes of Health, Dec. 23, 2002, www.nih.gov/news/pr/dec2002/nichd-23.htm.

REJECTED

92. E. McCoy, *What to Do . . . When Kids Are Mean to Your Child: Real Solutions from Experts, Parents, and Kids* (Pleasantville, N.Y.: Reader's Digest, 1997), 50.

93. D. Newsdale and A. Lambert, "Effects of Experimentally Manipulated Peer Rejection on Children's Negative Affect, Self-Esteem, and Maladaptive Social Behavior," *International Journal of Behavioral Development* 31, no. 2 (2007): 111–122.

94. Research reported in M. Fox, "A Snub Really Does Feel Like a Kick in the Gut," *USA Today,* Oct. 13, 2003, 7D.

95. Research from Jacqueline Mize and Gregory Petit, Alabama Auburn University, reported in H. E. Marano, "Why Johnny Can't Play," *Psychology Today,* Sept.-Oct. 1997, http://www .psychologytoday.com/articles/pto-19970901-000020.html.

96. Long-term study of four hundred children by the University of Illinois Pathways Project, directed by G. Ladd and funded with grants from the National Institutes of Health, cited in "Kids Who Don't Get Along with Others Also Less Likely to Learn," *ScienceDaily,* Sept. 8, 1998, http://sciencedaily.com/releases/1998/09/980908073710.htm.

97. S. P. Keane, A. J. Conger, and J. Vogel, "Dyadic Interactions in Accepted and Rejected Children," *Journal of Psychopathology and Behavioral Assessment* 6, no. 3 (1984): 171–188.

98. B. N. Vosk, R. Forehand, and R. Figueroa, "Perception of Emotions by Accepted and Rejected Children," *Journal of Psychopathology and Behavioral Assessment* 5, no. 2 (June 1983): 151–160.

99. A. Cillessen, W. M. Bukowski, and G. Haselager, *Stability of Sociometric Categories* (San Francisco: Jossey-Bass, 2000).

100. J. Gottman, "Toward a Definition of Social Isolation in Children," *Child Development* 48 (1977): 513–517; K. H. Rubin and M. L. Clark, "Preschool Teachers' Ratings of Behavioral Problems: Observational, Sociometric, and Sociocognitive Correlates," *Journal of Abnormal Child Psychology* 11 (1983): 273–286.

101. Vanderbilt University study cited in L. Kutner, "If Your Child Is Rejected by Peers," http://www.drkutner.com/parenting/articles/rejected.html.

102. Study in which preteens and teens voice in on who is most likely to be rejected, cited in R. Lavoie, *It's So Much Work to Be Your Friend: Helping the Child with Learning Disabilities Find Social Success* (New York: Touchstone Books, 2005), 329–333.

ROLE MODELS

103. K. Deveny with R. Kelley, "Girls Gone Wild: What Are Celebs Teaching Kids?" *Newsweek,* Feb. 12, 2007, 40–47.

104. American Psychological Association, Task Force on the Sexualization of Girls, *Report of the APA Task Force on the Sexualization of Girls* (Washington, D.C.: American Psychological Association, 2007), http://www.apa.org/pi/wpo/sexualizationrep.pdf.

105. Fifty-seven percent of teens say that professional athletes influenced their decision to use steroids; 63 percent said pro athletes influenced their friends' decisions to use them: J. Stenson, "Kids on Steroids Willing to Risk It All for Success," MSNBC, Mar. 3, 2008, http://www.msnbc.msn.com/id/222984780.

106. MTV-AP survey cited in J. Noveck and T. Thompson, "Poll: Young Often Draw Happiness from Family, Pals," *Desert Sun,* Aug. 20, 2007, A3.

107. Search Institute survey cited in S. Johnson, "Cheating Is Not the Problem," *San Jose Mercury News,* Feb. 6, 2004, available at http://www.scu.edu/ethics/publications/ethicalperspectives/stopping_cheating.html.

108. A national online survey of twenty-seven hundred girls ages eight to twelve conducted Dec. 1999, cited in W. Roban, *Teens Before Their Time* (New York: Girl Scouts of the USA, 2000).

109. A. K. Yancey, J. M. Siegel, and K. L. McDaniel, "Role Models, Ethnic Identity, and Health-Risk Behavior in Urban Adolescents," *Archives of Pediatrics and Adolescent Medicine* 156 (2002): 55–61.

SEX

110. J. D. Brown and others, "Sexy Media Matter: Exposure to Sexual Content in Music, Movies, Television, and Magazines Predicts Black and White Adolescents' Sexual Behavior," *Pediatrics* 117, no. 4 (Apr. 2006): 1018–1027.

111. Statistic reported by the Centers for Disease Control and Prevention, cited in Associated Press, "Trend Ends," *Desert Sun,* June 21, 2008, A11.

112. K. Paulsen, "Familiar Reality Requires Common-Sense Sex Ed," *USA Today,* Sept. 3, 2008, A14.

113. S. Reinberg, "Many Teens Don't Keep Virginity Pledges," *U.S. News & World Report,* Dec. 29, 2008, http://health.usnews.com/articles/health/healthday/2008/12/29/many-teens-dont-keep-virginity-pledges.html.

114. Findings of the Centers for Disease Control and Prevention cited in S. Jayson, "Teens Define Sex in New Ways," *USA Today,* Oct. 10, 2005, http://www.usatoday.com/news/health/2005 -10-18-teens-sex_x.htm.

115. T. Lewin, "Teens Dispute What Constitutes Sex," *Desert Sun,* Dec. 20, 2000, F5.

116. Research by the American Academy of Pediatrics cited in Jayson, "Teens Define Sex in New Ways."

117. Research at University of Minnesota cited in "Closeness to Mother Can Delay First Instance of Sexual Intercourse Among Younger Teens," *ScienceDaily,* Sept. 11, 2002, http://www.science daily.com/releases/2002/09/020911073512.htm; Children Now and the Kaiser Family Foundation, "Talking with Kids About Sex and Relationships," http://www.talkingwithkids.org/ sex.html

118. Associated Press, "Teens Most Often Have Sex at Home," *USA Today,* Sept. 26, 2002, available at http://www.thenationalcampaign.org/media/PDF/2005_old/MSNBC_9_26_02.pdf.

119. J. Mahoney, "Teens' Sex Habits Linked to Self-Esteem," *Globe and Mail,* May 4, 2005.

120. Mahoney, "Teens' Sex Habits."

121. Children Now and the Kaiser Family Foundation, "Talking with Kids."

122. Mahoney, "Teens' Sex Habits"; E. L. Zurbriggen and others, *Report of the APA Task Force on the Sexualization of Girls* (Washington, D.C.: American Psychological Association, 2007), http://www.apa.org/pi/wpo/sexualizationrep.pdf.

SHARING

123. T. Berry Brazelton cited in "Doctor Urges Parents to Teach Kids to Share," *Desert Sun,* June 7, 2000.

124. A. Rogers-Warren and D. M. Baer, "Correspondence Between Saying and Doing: Teaching Preschoolers to Share and Praise," *Journal of Applied Behavior Analysis* 9, no. 3 (1976): 335–354.

125. T. R. Shepherd and J. Keberstein, "Books, Puppets and Sharing: Teaching Preschool Children to Share," *Psychology in the Schools* 26, no. 3 (1989): 311–316.

126. Z. Rubin, *Children's Friendship* (Cambridge, Mass.: Harvard University Press, 1980), 16–17.

STEROIDS

127. A. D. Faigenbaum, L. D. Zaichkowsky, D. E. Gardner, and L. J. Micheli, "Anabolic Steroid Use by Male and Female Middle School Students," *Pediatrics* 101 (1998): e6.

128. A. Manning, "Kids, Steroids, Don't Mix, *USA Today,* July 9, 2002, http://www.usatoday.com/ educate/college/healthscience/casestudies/20020916-steroids.pdf.

129. D. L. Moore, "School Tackles Alarming Subject: Steroid Use," May 4, 2005, http://www.usa today.com/sports/preps/2005-05-04-hs-steroids-cover_x.htm.

130. Manning, "Kids, Steroids, Don't Mix."

131. CBS Broadcasting, "Steroid Use Becomes Growing Problem Among Teens," May 2, 2008, http://cbs11tv.com/health/teen.steroid.use.2.714164.html.

132. J. Stenson, "Kids on Steroids Willing to Risk It All for Success," MSNBC, Mar. 3, 2008, http:// www.msnbc.msn.com/id/22984780/.

133. Stenson, "Kids on Steroids."

134. Stenson, "Kids on Steroids."

TATTLES

135. J. Piaget, *The Moral Judgment of the Child* (Old Tappan, N.J.: Macmillan, 1965).

136. Survey cited in "For the Record," *Time,* Apr. 22, 2002, 18.

TEASED

137. National Education Association report cited in S. Fried and P. Fried, *Bullies and Victims: Helping Your Child Through the Schoolyard Battlefield* (New York: Evans, 1996).

138. K. Kumpulainen and others, "Bullying and Psychiatric Systems Among Elementary School-Age Children," *Child Abuse and Neglect* 22, no. 7 (1988): 705–717; E.V.E. Hodges and D. G. Perry, "Victims of Peer Abuse: An Overview," *Journal of Emotional and Behavioral Problems* 5 (1996): 23–28.

139. Research from S. Joseph at the University of Warwick cited in "New Research Dispels Popular Myth That a Bully's Words Will Never Hurt You," *ScienceDaily,* Apr. 17, 2003, http://www.sciencedaily.com/releases/2003/04/030417080610.htm.

140. Survey by T. R. Warm of 250 children and adolescents, cited in E. McCoy, *What to Do When Kids Are Mean to Your Child* (Pleasantville, N.Y.: Reader's Digest Press, 1997), 21.

141. M. Fox, "A Snub Really Does Feel Like a Kick in the Gut," *USA Today,* Oct. 13, 2003, 7D.

142. McCoy, *What to Do.*

143. B. M. Levy, *Behavior Problems: Name-Calling and Teasing: Strategies for Parents and Teachers* (Bethesda, Md.: National Association of School Psychologists, 2004).

144. R. Kowalski, "I Was Only Kidding: Victim and Perpetrators' Perceptions of Teasing," *Personality and Social Psychology Bulletin* 26 (2000): 231–241.

145. J. S. Freedman, *Easing the Teasing: Helping Your Child Cope with Name-Calling, Ridicule, and Verbal Bullying* (New York: McGraw-Hill, 2002), 15.

Part 6: School

DAY CARE

1. Ten-year study by the National Institute of Child Health and Human Development of eleven hundred children in ten American cities, cited in B. Kantrowitz, "A New Battle Over Day Care," *Newsweek,* Apr. 30, 2001, available at http://www.encyclopedia.com/doc/1G1-73626738.html; B. Carey, "Poor Behavior Is Linked to Time in Day Care," *New York Times,* Mar. 26, 2007, http://www.nytimes.com/2007/03/26/us/26center.html.

GIVES UP

2. H. W. Stevenson, and J. W. Stigler, *The Learning Gap* (New York: Simon & Schuster, 1992).

3. L. S. Blackwell, C. S. Dweck, and K. H. Trzesniewski, "Implicit Theories of Intelligence Predict Achievement Across an Adolescent Transition: A Longitudinal Study and an Intervention," *Child Development* 78, no. 1 (Feb. 7, 2007): 246–263.

HOMEWORK

4. Public Agenda research cited in M. Mohler, "So Much Homework, So Little Time," *Family Circle,* Sept. 2007, 86–94, http://www.parents.com/teens-tweens/school-college/school-college/so-much-homework-so-little-time/.

5. Research by Harris Cooper cited in Mohler, "So Much Homework."

6. Research by Harris Cooper on the effect of homework in H. Cooper, *Homework* (White Plains, N.Y.: Longman, 1989), cited in J. Bempechat, *Getting Our Kids Back on Track: Educating Children for the Future* (San Francisco: Jossey-Bass, 2001), 66.

7. Recommendation of the National Education Association and PTA and finding of the University of Michigan study cited in R. Bacher, "End Homework Hassles," *Parents,* Oct. 2006, 205–206.

8. Mohler, "So Much Homework."

9. "Early Eye Exams," *Parents,* Dec. 2004, 80.

10. Harris Poll Online survey of 1,814 seventh- and eighth-grade students conducted for the National Association of Secondary School Principals and Phi Delta Kappa, cited in T. Wong Briggs and A. Gonzalez, "Middle-School Homework Gender Gap," *USA Today,* Aug. 27, 2007, D1.

LEADERSHIP

11. National online survey of 2,475 girls and 1,514 boys between the ages of eight and seventeen, fielded from June 22, 2007, to June 29, 2007: Girl Scout Research Institute, *Change It Up! What Girls Say About Redefining Leadership* (New York: Girls Scouts of the USA, 2008), 38.

12. Girl Scout Research Institute, *Change It Up!* 31.

13. The need for single-sex, safe environments for girls to confide in trusting adults and other girls is noted in Girl Scout Research Institute, *Feeling Safe* (New York: Girls Scouts of the USA, 2003).

14. K. Mishra, "Your Older Sibling Really Is Smarter, Study Says: More Time with Adults May Be a Major Factor," *San Francisco Chronicle,* June 22, 2007, http://www.sfgate.com/cgi-bin/article.cgi?f=/c/a/2007/06/22/MNGJQQJVQR1.DTL.

15. Girl Scout Research Institute, *Feeling Safe,* 20.

ORGANIZED SPORTS

16. American Academy of Pediatrics, "AAP Parenting Corner Q & A: Sports and Your Child," Mar. 2007, http://www.aap.org/publiced/BR_Sports.htm.

PROCRASTINATES

17. Research by Pamela Thacher, St. Lawrence University, cited in "All-Nighters Equal Lower Grades," *ScienceDaily,* Dec. 1, 2007, http://www.sciencedaily.com/releases/2007/11/071130162518.htm.

18. Piers Steel's research cited in S. Borenstein, "Study Is a Put Off: Scientists Research Why Procrastination Is Getting Worse," *USA Today,* Jan. 12, 2007, http://www.usatoday.com/tech/science/2007-01-12-procrastination-study_x.htm.

READING

19. Literary readers were found to be twice as likely as nonreaders to volunteer or do charity work: National Endowment for the Arts, *The Arts and Civil Engagement: Involved in Arts, Involved in Life* (Washington, D.C.: National Endowment for the Arts, 2006).

20. National survey of five hundred children ages five to seventeen years old and of one parent or primary guardian per child, in twenty-five major cities: Scholastic, *The Kids and Family Reading Report* (New York: Scholastic, 2006), http://www.scholastic.com/aboutscholastic/news/press_07252006_CP.htm.

21. Scholastic, *2008 Kids and Family Reading Report: Reading in the 21st Century: Turning the Page with Technology* (New York: Scholastic, 2008), http://www.scholastic.com/aboutscholastic/news/kfrr08web.pdf.

22. National Endowment for the Arts, *To Read or Not to Read: A Question of National Consequence* (Washington, D.C.: National Endowment for the Arts, 2007), 7, http://www.nea.gov/research/ToRead.pdf; a summary is available at http://www.nea.gov/news/news07/TRNR.html.

23. National Endowment for the Arts, *To Read or Not to Read,* 14.

24. Scholastic, *2008 Kids and Family Reading Report.*

25. Scholastic, *2008 Kids and Family Reading Report.*

26. A. N. Greco and R. M. Wharton, *Book Industry TRENDS 2007* (New York: Book Industry Study Group, 2007).

27. V. Hallett, "The Power of Potter: Can the Teenage Wizard Turn a Generation of Halfhearted Readers into Lifelong Bookworms?" *U.S. New & World Report,* July 25, 2005, http://www.usnews.com/usnews/culture/articles/050725/25read.htm.

28. Hallett, "The Power of Potter."

SICK ENOUGH TO STAY HOME

29. Recommendation from the Mayo Clinic cited in S. Rudavsky, C. Midey, and L. Donno, "How Sick Is Too Sick for School?" *USA Today,* Sept. 6, 2006, 7D, http://www.usatoday.com/news/health/2006-09-05-sick-kids_x.htm.

30. Rudavsky, Midey, and Donno, "How Sick Is Too Sick."

31. C. Tobin, "Stay or Go? Whether to Send Your Child to School," *Today's Parent,* Sept. 2007, http://www.todaysparent.com/healthsafety/schoolage/article.jsp?content=20070803_100626_6120&page=4; Rudavsky, Midey, and Donno, "How Sick Is Too Sick."

TEST ANXIETY

32. R. Hembree, "Correlates, Causes, Effects, and Treatment of Test Anxiety," *Review of Educational Research* 58, no. 1 (Spring 1988): 47–77.

33. N. R. Thergaonkar and A. J. Wadkar, "Relationship Between Test Anxiety and Parenting Style," *Journal of Indian Association for Child and Adolescent Mental Health* 2, no. 4 (2007): 10–12.

34. D. Binkley, "Help Children Succeed in School," University of Illinois Extension, Urban Programs Resource Network, 2008, http://www.urbanext.uiuc.edu/succeed/06-test.html.

35. A. Sadeh, R. Gruber, and A. Raviv, "The Effects of Sleep Restriction and Extension on School-Age Children: What a Difference an Hour Makes," *Child Development* 74, no. 2 (Mar. 2003): 444–445.

36. P. M. Suratt and others, "Reduced Time in Bed and Obstructive Sleep-Disordered Breathing in Children Are Associated with Cognitive Impairment," *Pediatrics* 119, no. 2 (Feb. 2007): 320–329.

37. Survey of seven thousand Minnesota high schoolers showed that more sleep reaps higher grades, cited in K. Wahlstrom, *Adolescent Sleep Needs and School Starting Times* (Bloomington, Ind.: Phi Delta Kappa International, 1999); for more research correlating sleep and academic achievement, refer to P. Bronson, "Snooze or Lose," *New York,* Oct. 8, 2007, http://nymag.com/news/features/38951/.

38. Research by Reremoana Theodore from University of Otago showing that what kids eat makes them smarter featured in "What to Feed Your Kids to Make Them Smarter," *Sunday Star Times,* Jan. 18, 2009, www.stuff.co.nz/sundaystartimes/4822142a6005.html; L. M. Staub, "The Correlation Between Eating Breakfast and School Performance," Missouri Western State University, 2008, http://clearinghouse.missouriwestern.edu/manuscripts/203.asp.

Part 7: Special Needs

ATTENTION DEFICIT

1. D. A. Christakis, F. J. Zimmerman, D. L. DiGiuseppe, and C. A. McCarty, "Early Television Exposure and Subsequent Attentional Problems in Children," *Pediatrics* 113, no. 4 (Apr. 2004): 708–713.

2. Top three prescriptions for kids diagnosed with ADD per year: $490 million on Concerta; $430 million on Strattera; $410 million on Adderall, based on 2004 Medical Expenditure Panel Survey, from the Agency for Healthcare Research and Quality and National Center for Health Statistics, 2004: cited in T. W. Briggs and M. E. Mullins, "Prescriptions for Kids," *USA Today,* Nov. 13, 2007, D1.

3. K. Painter, "Lofty Hopes for ADHD Kids," *USA Today,* Sept. 17, 2007, 6D.

4. All information in this box is from American Psychiatric Association, *Diagnostic and Statistical Manual of Mental Disorders,* 4th ed. (Washington, D.C.: American Psychiatric Association, 1994); specific topics: inattention, 83–84; hyperactivity, 84; impulsivity, 84.

5. S. Ashley, *The ADD and ADHD Answer Book: The Top 275 Questions Parents Ask* (Naperville, Ill.: Sourcebooks, 2005), 13.

6. Ivanhoe Broadcast Service, "What Parents Think May Be ADHD, May Not," News 8 Austin Story, Apr. 1, 2008, http://www.news8austin.com/content/headlines/?ArID=204389&SecID=2.

7. Daniel Anderson, a psychologist at the University of Massachusetts-Amherst, conducted a study on TV distractions in which fifty children ages one to three were observed for an hour at a time as they played alone with a variety of toys while a small TV aired a taped episode of *Jeopardy;* Anderson's results were published in *Child Development,* July 15, 2008, and reported in G. Toppo, "Just Having TV on Can Distract Kids," *USA Today,* July 15, 2008, 7D.

8. Research by Mark D. Rapport, University of Central Florida, cited in "Hyperactivity Enables Children with ADHD to Stay Alert: Teachers Urged Not to Severely Limit That Activity," *ScienceDaily,* Mar. 9, 2009, http://www.sciencedaily.com/releases/2009/03/090309105038.htm.

9. Research led by T. E. Froehlich and published in *Archives of Pediatrics and Adolescent Medicine* 161, no. 9 (2007): 857–864; key findings available at "Nine Percent of US Children Age 8 to 15 Meet Criteria for Having ADHD, Study Suggests," *ScienceDaily,* http://www.sciencedaily.com/releases/2007/09/070903204843.htm.

10. Three-year study led by Peter Jensen, director of the Center for the Advance of Children's Mental Health at Columbia University, reported in Painter, "Lofty Hopes."

11. Study reported in K. Painter, "Attention Deficit Treatments Help Kids over Time, Study Finds," *Desert Sun,* July 20, 2007, A5.

12. Cited in K. Painter, "Send Your Kids Outside—Now," *USA Today,* Mar. 20, 2006, 4D.

13. Ashley, *ADD and ADHD Answer Book,* 26.

14. K. R. Stern, "A Treatment Study of Children with Attention Deficit Hyperactivity Disorder," no. 20 (Washington, D.C.: U.S. Department of Justice, May 2001).

15. Painter, "Lofty Hopes."

AUTISM SPECTRUM DISORDER

16. R. Mishori, "What Do We Know About Autism?" *Parade,* Jan. 27, 2008, http://www.parade .com/articles/editions/2008/edition_01-27-2008/Is_There_Hope_For_Autism.

17. American Psychiatric Association, *Diagnostic and Statistical Manual of Mental Disorders,* 4th ed. (Washington, D.C.: American Psychiatric Association, 1994).

18. S. Ashley, *The Asperger's Answer Book: The Top 300 Questions Parents Ask* (Naperville, Ill.: Sourcebooks, 2007), 79.

19. E. Courschesne, R. Carper, and N. Akshoomoff, "Evidence of Brain Overgrowth in the First Year of Life in Autism," *Journal of the American Medical Association* 290 (2003): 337–344.

20. Ashley, *Asperger's Answer Book,* 16.

21. Ashley, *Asperger's Answer Book,* 16.

22. "Fraser Researches Effects of Asperger's Disorder on Lives of Young Adults," Fall 2008, http://www.fraser.org/newsletters/FIF_fall08.pdf.

23. Ashley, *Asperger's Answer Book,* 16.

DEPRESSED

24. Cited in M.E.P. Seligman, *The Optimistic Child* (New York: Houghton Mifflin, 1995).

25. P. Lewinsohn, P. Rohde, J. Seeley, and S. Fischer, "Age-Cohort Changes in the Lifetime Occurrence of Depression and Other Mental Disorders," *Journal of Abnormal Psychology* 102 (1993): 110–120; C. Garrison and others, "Major Depressive Disorder and Dysthymia in Young Adolescents," *American Journal of Epidemiology* 135 (1992): 792–802.

26. D. G. Fassler and L. S. Dumas, *"Help Me, I'm Sad": Recognizing, Treating, and Preventing Childhood and Adolescent Depression* (New York: Viking, 1997), 12.

27. Yale Medical School study cited in M. Elias, "Kids and Depression: Are Drugs the Answer?" *USA Today,* Nov. 30, 1999, 2A.

28. Elias, "Kids and Depression."

29. W. R. Beardless and Stuart Goldman, "Living Beyond Sadness," *Newsweek,* Sept. 22, 2003, 70.

30. Marie Kovacs, psychologist at Western Psychiatric Institute and Clinic in Pittsburgh, quoted in Fassler and Dumas, *"Help Me, I'm Sad,"* xii.

31. Lewinsohn and others, "Age-Cohort Changes."

32. Fassler and Dumas, *"Help Me, I'm Sad,"* 37.

33. B. Kantrowitz, "It's Hard for Parents to Understand," *Newsweek,* Oct. 7, 2002, 60–61.

34. A. Haavisto and others, "Suicidal Ideation and Suicide Attempts Among Child and Adolescent Psychiatric Inpatients in Finland," *Journal of Affective Disorders* 76, no. 1 (2003): 211–221; D. D. Hallfors and others, "Adolescent Depression and Suicide Risk: Association with Sex and Drug Behavior," *American Journal of Preventive Medicine* 27 (2004): 224–231.

35. National Institute of Mental Health study cited in "Depressed Adolescents Respond Best with Psychotherapy and Antidepressants Combined," *ScienceDaily,* Oct. 7, 2007, http://www.sciencedaily.com/releases/2007/10/071001172838.htm.

36. Research on massage cited in C. Kalb, "Coping with Anxiety," *Newsweek,* Feb. 24, 2003, 51–52.

37. A. Weintraub, "Yoga: Not Just an Exercise: Yoga Can Help You Beat Depression. How Hatha Yoga Saved the Life of One Manic Depressive," *Psychology Today,* Nov.-Dec. 2000, http://www.psychologytoday.com/articles/pto-20001101-000022.html.

38. Research cited in Kalb, "Coping with Anxiety."

39. Fassler and Dumas, *"Help Me, I'm Sad,"* 50, 55, 59.

40. Joan Luby of Washington University School of Medicine identified depression through play by having preschoolers watch two puppets discussing their emotions, then asking kids to point to the one that sounded most like them; cited in C. Kalb, "Troubled Souls," *Newsweek,* Sept. 22, 2003, 69.

41. B. Birmaher and others, "Childhood and Adolescent Depression: A Review of the Past 10 Years. Part I," *Journal of the American Academy of Child and Adolescent Psychiatry* 35, no. 11 (1996): 1427–1439.

42. Fassler and Dumas, *"Help Me, I'm Sad,"* 17.

EATING DISORDERS

43. D. Schlass Saliman, "Catch It Early," *Working Mother,* Oct. 2007, 228–231.

44. C. Poirot, "Too-Thin Kids: Eating Disorders Are Striking Younger Children," *Fort-Worth Star-Telegram,* Sept. 19, 2002, http://www.accessmylibrary.com/coms2/summary_0286-8951094_ITM.

45. H. Brubach, "Biblio File: Starved to Perfection," *New York Times,* Apr. 15, 2007, http://query.nytimes.com/gst/fullpage.html?res=9B0CE3DF153FF936A25757C0A9619C8B63&fta=y

46. Research from the University of Minnesota cited in "New Study Shows Teenage Girls' Use of Diet Pills Doubles Over Five-Year Span," *ScienceDaily,* Nov. 1, 2006, http://www.sciencedaily.com/releases/2006/10/061030143332.htm.

47. L. H. Epstein, R. R. Wing, R. Koeske, and A. Valoski, "Long-Term Effects of Family-Based Treatment of Childhood Obesity," *Journal of Consulting and Clinical Psychology* 55, no. 1 (1987): 91–95.

48. Poirot, "Too-Thin Kids."

49. S. Chollar, "How to Spot an Eating Disorder," CNN.com, Apr. 28, 2000, http://archives.cnn.com/2000/HEALTH/diet.fitness/04/28/anorexia.sidebar.wmd/index.html

50. S. Song, "Starvation on the Web," *Time,* July 11, 2005.

51. A. Voiland, "Teens Health: Web Sites That Promote Eating Disorders," *U.S. News & World Report,* Dec. 6, 2006, http:health.usnews.com/usnews/health/articles/061206/6healt.anorexia_print.htm.

52. T. Whitmire, "'Study' Genes May Cause Risk for Anorexia," *USA Today,* Mar. 15, 2006, http://www.usatoday.com/tech/science/genetics/2006-03-15-anorexia-study_x.htm.

53. Poirot, "Too-Thin Kids."

54. E. P. Nobel, quoted in "Research Links Single Gene to Addictive Behaviors," *Chicago Tribune,* Mar. 15, 1994.

55. S. Makin, *More Than Just a Meal: The Art of Eating Disorders* (London: Kingsley, 2000).

56. A. Moreno and N. H. Thalen, "Parental Factors Related to Bulimia Nervosa," *Addictive Behaviors* 18 (1993): 681–689.

57. J. R. Blitzer, N. Rollins, and A. Blackwell, "Children Who Starve Themselves: Anorexia Nervosa," *Psychosomatic Medicine* 23 (1961): 369–383.

58. H. Steiger, K. Liquornik, J. Chapman, and N. Hassain, "Personality and Family Disturbances in Eating-Disorder Patients: Comparison of 'Restrictor' and 'Binger' to Normal Controls," *International Journal of Eating Disorders* 10 (1991): 510–512.

59. S. Stern and others, "Family Environment in Anorexia Nervosa and Bulimia," *International Journal of Eating Disorders* 8 (1989): 25–31.

60. C. Johnson, *Psychodynamic Treatment of Anorexia Nervosa and Bulimia* (New York: Guilford Press, 1991), 278.

61. K. Boutelle and others, "Weight Control Among Obese, Over-Weight and Non-Overweight Adolescents, " *Journal of Pediatric Psychology* 27 (2002): 531–540; National Institute of Mental Health, "Eating Disorders," 2005, www.nimh.nih.gov/publicat/eatingdisorders.cfm.

62. H. H. Goldman, *Review of General Psychiatry* (Los Altos, Calif.: Lange Medical Publications, 1984), 464.

63. P. van den Berg, D. Neumark-Sztainer, P. J. Hannan, and J. Haines, "Is Dieting Advice from Magazines Helpful or Harmful? Five-Year Associations with Weight-Control Behaviors and Psychological Outcomes in Adolescents," *Pediatrics* 119 (2007): 30–37.

64. K. K. Davidson, M. B. Earnest, and L. L. Birch, "Participation in Aesthetic Sports and Girls' Weight Concerns at Ages 5 and 7 Years," *International Journal of Eating Disorders* 31, no. 3 (Apr. 2002): 312–317.

65. V. L. Forman-Hoffman and C. L. Cunningham, "Eating Disorders May Be Contagious," *International Journal of Eating Disorders,* Apr. 2008, cited by Reuters Health, *Huffington Post,* Apr. 18, 2008, http://www.huffingtonpost.com/2008/04/18/are-eating-disorders-cont_n_97463.html.

66. Research by Dianne Neumark-Sztainer, University of Minnesota School of Public Health, cited in "Regular Family Meals Promote Healthy Eating Habits," *ScienceDaily,* Nov. 18, 2004, http://www.sciencedaily.com/releases/2004/11/041116232104.htm.

67. Five year longitudinal study of 2,516 adolescents at 31 Minnesota schools: D. Neumark-Sztainer, "Disordered Eating Less Common Among Teen Girls Who Regularly Eat Family Meals," *Archives of Pediatric and Adolescent Medicine* 162, no. 1 (2008): 17–22.

68. A. H. Natenshon, *When Your Child Has an Eating Disorder* (San Francisco: Jossey-Bass, 1999), 135.

69. Research led by Dianne Neumark-Sztainer, University of Minnesota School of Public Health, cited in "Promoting Self-Weighing in Teens Is Not Helpful to Weight Management, Study Shows," *ScienceDaily,* Dec. 6, 2006, http://www.sciencedaily.com/releases/2006/12/061206093643.htm.

70. K. Boutelle and others, "Weight Control."

71. Half of girls eight to ten years old and one-third of boys are unhappy with their size; 40 percent of fourth graders have been on a "diet" once in a while: M. Maine, *Body Wars: Making Peace with Women's Bodies* (Carlsbad, Calif.: Gurze Books, 2000).

72. C. Orenstein, "The Dialectic of Fat," *Ms.,* Summer 2005, http://www.msmagazine.com/summer2005/womenandfat.asp.

73. S. Proudfoot, "Warning: Viewing These Images Is Bad for Your Body Esteem," *Ottawa Citizen,* Apr. 2, 2007, A12.

74. D. Neumark-Sztainer and others, "Weight-Related Concerns and Behaviors Among Overweight and Non-Overweight Adolescents: Implications for Preventing Weight-Related Disorders," *Archives of Pediatric and Adolescent Medicine* 156 (2002): 171–178.

GIFTED

75. J. Cloud, "Are We Failing Our Geniuses?" *Time,* Aug 16, 2007.

76. M. Csikszentmihalyi, K. Rathunde, and S. Whalen, *Talented Teenagers: The Roots of Success and Failure* (New York: Cambridge University Press, 1997).

77. J. T. Webb, E. A. Meckstroth, and S. S. Tolan, *Guiding the Gifted Child: A Practical Source for Parents and Teachers* (Dayton, Ohio: Ohio Psychology Press, 1994), 46–47.

78. B. Bloom, *Developing Talent in Young People* (New York: Ballantine, 1985).

79. Cloud, "Are We Failing Our Geniuses?"

80. Columbia University study cited in C. Dweck, *Mindset: The New Psychology of Success* (New York: Random House, 2006).

81. J. T. Webb, "Nurturing Social-Emotional Development of Gifted Children: What Are the Social-Emotional Needs of Gifted Children?" (Washington, D.C.: ERIC, 2006), http://www.education.com/print/Ref_Nurturing_Social/.

82. Webb, "Nurturing Social-Emotional Development."

83. J. T. Webb and P. A. Kleine, "Assessing Gifted and Talent Children," in *Testing Young Children,* ed. J. Culbertson and D. Willis (Austin, Tex.: Pro-Ed, 1993), 383–407.

84. P. M. Powell and T. Haden, "The Intellectual and Psychosocial Nature of Extreme Giftedness." *Roper Review* 6, no. 3 (1984): 131–133.

85. M. Adderholt-Elliot, *Perfectionism: What's So Bad About Being Good?* (Minneapolis: Free Spirit, 1989).

86. Webb, Meckstroth, and Tolan, *Guiding the Gifted Child,* 18.

87. Cloud, "Are We Failing Our Geniuses?"

LEARNING DISABILITIES

88. S. Ashley, *The Asperger's Answer Book* (Naperville, Ill.: Sourcebooks, 2007), 67.

89. Ashley, *Asperger's Answer Book,* 67.

90. H. Gardner, *Frames of Mind: The Theory of Multiple Intelligences* (New York: Basic Books, 1983).

OVERWEIGHT

91. How to determine BMI: J. Sheehan, "The Obesity Epidemic: Is Your Child at Risk?" *Parents,* July 1999, 62–65.

92. T. G. Lohman, "The Use of Skinfolds to Estimate Body Fatness on Children and Youth," *Journal of Physical Education, Recreation and Dance* 58, no. 9 (1987): 98–102.

93. Headline of article published in *U.S. News & World Report,* cited in D. Hughes, "Health and Your Family," *USA Weekend,* Mar. 14–16, 2008, 9.

94. K. Springer, "Not Hungry? No Problem," *Newsweek,* Jan. 29, 2007, 68.

95. N. Hellmich, "Childhood Obesity Levels Off," *USA Today,* May 28, 2008, 5D.

96. Study led by Andrew Hershey, pediatric neurologist at Cincinnati Children's Hospital Medical Center, cited in "Study: Headaches Worse in Obese Kids," *Desert Sun,* Sept. 17, 2008, A5.

97. L. H. Epstein, R. R. Wing, R. Koeske, and A. Valoski, "Long-Term Effects of Family-Based Treatment of Childhood Obesity," *Journal of Consulting and Clinical Psychology* 55, no. 1 (1987): 91–95.

98. San Diego State University study cited in C. Fuller, "Fit Bodies, Sharp Minds," *Family Circle,* Sept. 1998, 76.

99. Epstein and others, "Long-Term Effects."

100. Research by Deakin University cited in "Parents Fail to Recognize Their Children's Weight," *ScienceDaily,* Feb. 5, 2007, http://www.sciencedaily.com/releases/2007/02/070205111728.htm.

101. Research led by K. Boutelle, University of Minnesota Medical School, cited in "What It Takes for Teens to Lose Weight," *ScienceDaily,* Mar. 28, 2007, http://www.sciencedaily.com/releases/2007/03/070327113649.htm.

102. C. M. Morgan and others, "Loss of Control Over Eating, Adiposity, and Psychopathology in Overweight Children," *International Journal of Eating Disorders* 31 (May 2002): 430–441.

103. Sheehan, "Obesity Epidemic."

104. X. Chen, M. A. Beydoun, and Y. Wang, "Is Sleep Duration Associated with Childhood Obesity? A Systematic Review and Meta-Analysis," *Obesity (Silver Spring)* 16, no. 2 (Feb. 2008): 265–274.

105. "The Year in Medicine from A to Z," *Time,* Dec. 3, 2007, 74.

106. K. Stacy, "Parents Can Hinder Teen Weight Loss," *WebMD,* June 4, 2008, http://www.cbsnews.com/stories/2008/06/04/health/webmd/main4152902.shtml.

107. Research by K. Boutelle, University of Minnesota Medical School, cited in "Fast Food as Family Meals Limits Healthy Food Intake, Increases Obesity Risk," Jan. 9, 2007, *ScienceDaily,* http://www.sciencedaily.com/releases/2007/01/070108114306.htm.

108. S. A. French, M. Story, and R. W. Jeffery, "Environmental Influences on Eating and Physical Activity," *Annual Review of Public Health* 22 (May 2001): 337–353.

109. Longitudinal five-year study of two thousand adolescents conducted by lead author D. Neumark-Sztainer, University of Minnesota, cited in "Promoting Self-Weighing in Teens Is Not Helpful to Weight Management, Study Shows," *ScienceDaily,* Dec. 6, 2006, http://sciencedaily.com/releases/2006/12/061206093643.htm.

110. K. N. Horgen, M. Choate, and K. D. Brownell, "Television Food Advertising: Targeting Children in a Toxic Environment," in *Handbook of Children and Media,* ed. D. G. Singer and J. L. Singer (Thousand Oaks, Calif.: Sage, 2001), 447–461.

111. Boutelle, "What It Takes."

112. Boutelle, "What It Takes."

113. K. Miller Stacy, "Step It Up to Avoid Obesity," *WebMD Medical News,* Apr. 16, 2008, http://children.webmd.com/news/20080417/step-it-up-to-avoid-childhood-obesity.

114. Research by Mayo Clinic cited in "Adding Activity to Video Games Fights Obesity, Study Shows," *ScienceDaily,* Jan. 10, 2007, http://www.sciencedaily.com/releases/2007/01/070104144703.htm.

115. C. L. Williams, L. A. Campanaro, M. Squillace, and M. Bollella, "Management of Childhood Obesity in Pediatric Practice," *Annals of the New York Academy of Sciences* 817 (1997): 225–240.

116. M. Golan and S. Crow, "Targeting Parents Exclusively in the Treatment of Childhood Obesity: Long-Term Results," *Obesity Research* 12 (2004): 357–361.

117. Anne Harding, "'Do More, Talk Less' to Help Heavy Teens Slim Down," Reuters, June 4, 2008, http://www.reuters.com/article/healthNews/idUSCOL46234220080604.

118. L. H. Epstein and others, "Effects of Diet Plus Exercise on Weight Change in Parents and Children," *Journal of Consulting and Clinical Psychology* 52 (1984): 429–437; L. H. Epstein and others, "A Five-Year Follow-Up of Family-Based Behavioral Treatments for Childhood Obesity," *Journal of Consulting and Clinical Psychology* 58 (1990): 661–664.

119. Research from the University of Minnesota School of Public Health cited in "Teens Who Eat Breakfast Daily Eat Healthier Diets Than Those Who Skip Breakfast," *Pediatrics,* Mar. 3, 2008, http://www.sciencedaily.com/releases/2008/03/080303072640.htm.

120. Sheehan, "Obesity Epidemic."

121. Centers for Disease Control and Prevention, National Center for Chronic Disease Prevention and Health Promotion, "Childhood Overweight," May 22, 2007, www.cdc.gov/needphp/dnpa/obesity/childhood.

122. Findings reported in the *Journal of the American Medical Association* cited in Hellmich, "Childhood Obesity Levels Off."

123. Research funded by the National Institute of Child Health and Human Development cited in "Overweight in Early Childhood Increases Chances for Obesity at Age 12," *ScienceDaily,* Sept 7. 2006, http://www.sciencedaily.com/releases/2006/09/060905084731.htm.

124. M. Cohen, "Would You Know If Your Kid Was Overweight?" *Redbook,* June 2008, 205.

125. The proportion of obese six- to eleven-year-olds increased from 6.5 percent to 18.8 percent in two decades: "Help Kids Lose Weight," *Parents,* May 2007, 40.

126. Study published in the *American Journal of Clinical Nutrition,* 2002, cited in Springer, "Not Hungry?"

127. Research published in the *Journal of Pediatrics,* Jan. 2007, cited in L. Neegaard, "Study: Tween Girls More at Risk of Weight Gain," *Desert Sun,* Jan. 8, 2007, A7.

Part 8: Day to Day

BATHROOM BATTLES

1. Survey of parents with children ages six to twelve conducted by Strategy One and Harris Interactive, cited in Johnson & Johnson, "The Disappearing Toothbrush: Survey Reveals Kids' Top Excuses to Avoid Brushing," http://www.jnj.com/connect/news/product/20080310_172614.

2. Centers for Disease Control and Prevention, "Children's Oral Health," Mar. 3, 2009, http://www.cdc.gov/OralHealth/topics/child.htm.

3. E. Pantley, *The No-Cry Discipline Solution* (New York: McGraw-Hill, 2007), 279.

4. Centers for Disease Control and Prevention, "Children's Oral Health."

BOREDOM

5. C. Schweich Handler, "The Importance of Doing Nothing," *Parenting,* May 1999, 100–105.

6. KidsHealth, *What Kids Say About: Handling Stress,* Oct. 2005, http://www.kidshealth.org/parent/emotions/feelings/kids_stress.html.

7. J. D. Watt and S. J. Vodanovich, "Boredom Proneness and Psychosocial Development," *Journal of Psychology* 133 (1999): 303–314.

8. A. P. Murphy, "The Benefits of Boredom," *USA Weekend,* Sept. 3, 2006.

9. M. Csikszentmihalyi, *Flow: The Psychology of Optimal Experience* (New York: HarperPerennial, 1999).

10. Wikipedia, "Boredom," http://en.wikipedia.org/wiki/Boredom; C. D. Fisher, "Boredom at Work: A Neglected Concept," *Human Relations* 46 (1993): 395–417.

CHORES

11. Poll results cited in J. L. Pricer, "Time to Do Chores," *Desert Sun,* May 2002.

12. Research by M. Rossmann cited in "Involving Children in Household Tasks: Is It Worth the Effort?" *ResearchWORKS,* College of Education and Human Development, University of Minnesota, Sept. 2002, http://cehd.umn.edu/pubs/ResearchWorks/Rossmann.html.

13. L. Wolf, "The Value of Chores for Children," Parenthood.com, Sept. 2002, http:/www.parenthood.com/articles.html?article_id-6266.

14. Study by Sampson Lee Blair cited in L. Summerill, "The Chore of Chores," *ASU Research,* Summer 2001, http://researchmag.asu.edu/stories/chores.html.

15. D. Kindlon, *Too Much of a Good Thing: Raising Children of Character in an Indulgent Age* (New York: Talk Miramax Books, 2001), 206.

16. Study on chores from E. Crary, *Pick Up Your Socks . . . and Other Skills Growing Children Need* (Seattle: Parenting Press, 1990).

17. "Involving Children."

COMMUNICATING

18. National survey cited in E. Portillo, "Teens Give Adults Low Grades on Ruling World," *Desert Sun,* June 18, 2005, A17.

19. Samsung Texting Survey, conducted Mar. 2008, cited in S. E. Pfeffer, "Family Time," *Family Circle,* Sept. 2008, 53.

20. M. B. Rowe, "Wait-Time: Slowing Down May Be a Way of Speeding Up!" *Journal of Teacher Education* 31, no. 1 (1986): 43–50.

MONEY

21. Survey of parents by the American Savings Education Council in Washington, D.C., cited in S. Garland, "Mom, I Need Money!" *Parents,* May 2002, 193–194.

22. *Consumer Reports* survey cited in D. Harris, "How to Help Your Kids Live as Well as (or Better Than) You," *Parenting,* Dec.-Jan. 1999, 233.

23. Research by the National Center for Women and Retirement Research.

24. Harris, "How to Help Your Kids," 241.

25. Survey by the JumpStart Coalition cited in Harris, "How to Help Your Kids," 234.

26. S. Mahoney, "Is Your Teen $$$ Smart?" *Family Circle,* Feb. 2008, 66.

27. Quiz adapted from A. M. Morrow, *Money Sense for Your Children* (Corvallis: EM/Oregon State University Extension Service, 1991).

28. R. Immerman, "Dollars and Sense," *Parents,* Aug. 2002, 177–178.

29. Poll by parents.com cited in Immerman, "Dollars and Sense."

30. M. E. Goldberg, G. J. Gorn, L. A. Peracchio, and G. Bamossy, "Understanding Materialism Among Youth," *Journal of Consumer Psychology* 13, no. 3 (2003): 278–288.

31. The four-jar technique was recommended by Julie Kletzman, president of MoneyMentors. net, and cited in Immerman, "Dollars and Sense."

MOVING

32. W. Steele and C. H. Sheppard, "Moving Can Become Traumatic," *Trauma and Loss: Research and Interventions* 3, no. 1 (2003), http://www.tlcinst.org/Moving.html.

33. L. Oesterreich, *Understanding Children: Moving to a New Home,* National Network for Child Care, 2008, http:www.nncc.org/Child.Dev/movenew.html.

34. Oesterreich, *Understanding Children.*

35. K. H. Marchant and F. J. Medway, "Adjustment and Achievement Associated with Mobility in Military Families," *Psychology in the Schools* 24 (1987): 289–347; American Academy of Child and Adolescent Psychiatry, *Facts for Families: Children and Family Moves,* Nov. 2002, http://www.aacap.org/cs/root/facts_for_families/children_and_family_moves.

36. L. Kutner, "Parent and Child," *New York Times,* Jan. 18, 1990.

37. B. C. Norford and F. J. Medway, "Adolescents' Mobility Histories and Present Social Adjustment," *Psychology in the Schools* 39, no. 1 (Dec. 2001): 51–62.

38. Research by Frederic J. Medway cited in Kutner, "Parent and Child."

39. D. Conley, *The Pecking Order: Which Siblings Succeed and Why* (New York: Pantheon, 2004), 181.

40. Research by Tiffany Field of the Department of Pediatrics at the University of Miami Medical School, cited in L. Kutner, *Insights for Parents: Handling the Stress of a Family Move,* www.drkutner.com/parenting/articles/family_move.html.

OVERSCHEDULED

41. KidsHealth, *What Kids Say About: Handling Stress,* Oct. 2005, http://www.kidshealth.org/parent/emotions/feelings/kids_stress.html.

42. Data from the Society for Research in Child Development cited in D. McGinn, "The Benefits of Busy," *Newsweek,* Oct. 2, 2006, 43.

PETS

43. *Dogs and Kids,* 2008, http://www.purina.co.uk/Home/All+About+Dogs/Living+Together +Dog/Get+More+Out+Of+Life+Dog/Dogs+and+Kids.htm.

44. Study by June McNicholas, University of Warwick, cited in S. O'Malley, "AR-News: (UK) How Children Benefit from Their Pets," Oct. 14, 2003, http://lists.envirolink.org/pipermail/ar-news?week-of-Mon-20031033/008091.html.

45. American Academy of Child and Adolescent Psychiatry, *Facts for Families: Pets and Children,* May 2008, http://www.aacap.org/cs/root/facts_for_families/pets_and_children.

46. D. R. Ownby and others, "Exposure to Dogs and Cats in the First Year of Life and Risk of Allergic Sensitization at 6 to 7 Years of Age," *Journal of the American Medical Association* 288, no. 8 (2002): 963–972.

PICKY EATER

47. C. W. Wright, K. N. Parkinson, D. Shipton, and R. F. Drewett, "How Do Toddler Eating Problems Relate to Their Eating Behavior, Food Preferences, and Growth?" *Pediatrics* 120 (2007): e1069–e1075.

48. L. J. Cooke, C.M.A. Haworth, and J. Wardle, "Genetic and Environmental Influences on Children's Food Neophobia," *American Journal of Clinical Nutrition* 86, no. 2 (Aug. 2007): 428–433.

49. Wright and others, "How Do Toddler Eating Problems Relate"; a study of 426 eight- to twelve-year-olds and their primary caregivers found that picky eating is not associated with disordered eating: C. Jacobi, G. Schmitz, W. S. Agras, "Is Picky Eating an Eating Disorder?" *International Journal of Eating Disorders* 41, no. 7 (Nov. 2008): 626–634, http://www.labmeeting .com/paper/28476636/is-picky-eating-an-eating-disorder.

50. M. Marchi and P. Cohen, "Early Childhood Eating Behaviors and Adolescent Eating Disorders," *Journal of the American Academy of Child and Adolescent Psychiatry* 29, no. 1 (1990): 112–117.

51. Research by Dianne Neumark-Sztainer, University of Minnesota School of Public Health, cited in "Regular Family Meals Promote Healthy Eating Habits," *ScienceDaily,* Nov. 18, 2004, http://www.sciencedaily.com/releases/2004/11/041116232104.htm.

52. L. J. Cooke and others, "Demographic, Familial and Trait Predictors of Fruit and Vegetable Consumption by Pre-School Children," *Public Health Nutrition* 7, no. 2 (Apr 2004): 295–302; abstract available at http://www.ncbi.nlm.nih.gov/pubmed/15003137.

53. Wright and others, "How Do Toddler Eating Problems Relate."

54. Cornell University study cited in "Eat Your Vegetables: Preschoolers Love Vegetables with Catchy Names Like 'X-Ray Vision Carrots' and 'Tomato Bursts,'" *ScienceDaily,* Mar. 4, 2009, http://www.sciencedaily.com/releases/2009/03/090302120019.htm.

55. J. Wardle and others, "Increasing Children's Acceptance of Vegetables: A Randomized Trial of Parent-Led Exposure," *Appetite* 40, no. 2 (Apr. 2003): 155–162.

56. Wright and others, "How Do Toddler Eating Problems Relate."

57. A. K. Ventura and L. L. Birch, "Does Parenting Affect Children's Eating and Weight Status?" *International Journal of Behavioral Nutrition and Physical Activity* 5 (Mar. 17, 2008): 15.

58. A. T. Galloway, L. Fioritto, Y. Lee, and L. L. Birch, "Parental Pressure, Dietary Patterns and Weight Status Among Girls Who Are 'Picky Eaters,'" *Journal of the American Dietetic Association* 105, no. 4 (Apr. 2005): 541–548.

59. K. W. Cullen and others, "Availability, Accessibility, and Preferences for Fruit, 100% Fruit Juice and Vegetables Influence Children's Dietary Behavior," *Health Education Behavior* 30, no. 5 (2003): 615–626; D. Neumark-Sztainer and others, "Family Meal Patterns: Associations with Sociodemographic Characteristics and Improved Dietary Intake Among Adolescents," *Journal of the American Dietetic Association* 103, no. 3 (2003): 317–322

60. Peer pressure research by Leanne Birch at Penn State cited in A. Krieg, "Why Kids Are Picky Eaters," *ABC News,* Nov. 23, 2007, http://www.pediatricservices.com/parents/pc-33.htm.

61. M. D. Rosen, "I Don't Eat That!" *Parents,* July 2004, 161.

62. Rosen, "I Don't Eat That," 162.

SAFETY

63. National Highway Traffic Safety Administration cited in Liberty Mutual, "Child Safety Guide," *Libertylines* 12, no. 2 (Summer 2008).

64. P. Doskoch, "Playdates with Guns?" *Parents,* Mar. 1999, 163.

65. F. Baxley and M. Miller, "Parental Misperceptions About Children and Firearms," *Archives of Pediatrics and Adolescent Medicine* 160 (May 30, 2006): 542–547.

66. C. A. Okoro and others, "Prevalence of Household Firearms and Firearm-Storage Practices in the 50 States and the District of Columbia: Findings from the Behavioral Risk Factor Surveillance System, 2002," *Pediatrics* 116, no. 3 (Sept. 2005): e370–e376, http://pediatrics.aappublications.org/cgi/content/full/116/3/e370

SLEEPLESS

67. J. M. Adams, "Is Your Child Getting Enough Sleep?" *Parenting,* June 2005, 106–111.

68. Research by M. A. Carskadon cited in "The Science of Lost Sleep in Teens," *ScienceDaily,* Mar. 29, 2006, http://www.sciencedaily.com/releases/2006/03/060328081509.htm.

69. R. D. Chervin and others, "Inattention, Hyperactivity, and Symptoms of Sleep-Disordered Breathing," *Pediatrics* 109 (2002): 449–456.

70. L. Fricke-Oerkermann and others, "Prevalence and Course of Sleep Problems in Childhood," *Sleep* 30, no. 10 (2007): 1371–1377.

71. Study by S. J. Crowley cited in "Late Weekend Sleep Among Teens May Lead to Poor Academic Performance," *Medical News Today,* June 17, 2007, http://www.medicalnewstoday.com/articles/74097.php.

72. Caffeine data from "Sleep in America" poll conducted by the National Sleep Foundation: cited in Adams, "Is Your Child Getting Enough Sleep?"

73. J. R. Beck, "Kid's Health," *Family Circle,* Nov. 29, 2007.

74. A. Merryman, "How to Get Kids to Sleep More," *New York,* Oct. 8, 2007, http://nymag.com/news/features/38979/.

75. Merryman, "How to Get Kids to Sleep More."

76. Fricke-Oerkermann and others, "Prevalence and Course of Sleep Problems."

77. Merryman, "How to Get Kids to Sleep More."

78. Study from the Brown University School of Medicine cited in P. Kruger, "It's 10 PM, Why Are Your Kids Awake?" *Parenting,* Dec.-Jan. 1999, 94.

79. L. Epstein and S. Mardon, "Homeroom Zombies," *Newsweek,* Sept. 17, 2007, 64–65.

80. Jodi Mindell cited in "Bedtime Don'ts," *Parents,* June 2006, 150.

81. Hui-Ling Lai's research at the University of Taiwan cited in "Listen to Music to Help You Sleep," *BBC News,* Feb. 2, 2005, http://news.bbc.co.uk/1/hi/health/4228707.stm.

82. Gary Zammit, director of the Sleep Disorders Institute at St. Luke's-Roosevelt Hospital Center in New York City, cited in E. Young, "I Can't Sleep," *Parents,* Dec. 1998, 139–140.

83. R. Ferber, *Solve Your Child's Sleep Problems* (New York: Fireside, 2006).

84. J. Owens and J. Mindell, *Take Charge of Your Child's Sleep: The All-in-One Resource for Solving Sleep Problems in Kids and Teens* (Cambridge, Mass.: Da Capo Press, 2005).

85. Alan Williams, child psychologist and associate professor of pediatrics at Mercer University Medical School, cited in Young, "I Can't Sleep," 139.

86. Research led by Judith Owens, Brown University, cited in "Study Finds Host of Sleep-Related Problems Among School-Age Kids," *ScienceDaily,* http://www.sciencedaily.com/releases/2000/02/000215064317.htm

87. "Science of Lost Sleep in Teens."

88. M. Lundstrom, "Help Kids Sleep All Night," *Redbook,* Jan. 2007, 138.

Part 9: Electronics

CELL PHONES

1. P. Carson, "Handsets as 'Must-Have': Preteens Demand Social Connectivity," *RCR Wireless News,* Sept. 23, 2008, http://rcrwireless.com/section/infrastructure_award/.

2. Online poll by computer review site CNET.com, 2006, cited in L. E. Shapiro, "When Is the Right Age to Get a Child a Cell Phone?" http://Ezine Articles.com/?expert=Lawrence E. Shapiro.

3. E. Woyke, "Tweens Hooked on Phones," Forbes.com, Sept. 10, 2008, http://www.forbes.com/2008/09/10/tweens-cell-phone-tech-personal-cx_ew_0910tweens.html.

4. Ted Thompson cited in J. Wilson, "What to Know Before Buying Your Kid a Cell Phone," CNN.com, Aug. 31, 2008, http://www.cnn.com/2008/TECH/ptech/08/11/cellphones.kids/index.html?eref=rss_latest.

5. Samsung Texting Survey, Mar. 2008, cited in S. E. Pfeffer, "Family Time," *Family Circle,* Sept. 8, 2008, 53.

6. Samsung Texting Survey, cited in Pfeffer, "Family Time."

CYBERBULLYING

7. P. Aftab, "The STOPcyberbullying Toolkit Guide for Parents," 2008, http://wireforsafety.

8. Distinction made by Parry Aftab, a lawyer specializing in Internet safety, executive director of WiredSafety.org, and author of *The Parent's Guide to Protecting Your Children in Cyberspace* (New York: McGraw Hill, 1999).

9. Based on personal conversations with Parry Aftab, New York City, June 2-3, 2008.

10. U.S. Centers for Disease Control and Prevention cited in M. Fox, "Teens Take Bullying to the Internet, Study Finds," Reuters, Nov. 27, 2007.

11. R. M. Kowalski, S. P. Limber, and P. W. Agatston, *Cyber Bullying: Bullying in the Digital Age* (Malden, Mass.: Blackwell, 2008), 121.

12. Survey cited in Kowalski, Limber, and Agatston, *Cyber Bullying,* 74.

13. Study by Patricia Agatston and colleagues at Clemson University in South Carolina, cited in M. Fox, "Teens Take Bullying to the Internet, Study Finds," Reuters, Nov. 27, 2007, http:www.reuters.com/articlePrint?articleid=USN2750833620071127.

14. Survey by iSafe.org cited in M. Wilde, "Get the FAQ About Cyberbullying," www.greatschools.net/cgi-bin/showarticle/551.

15. Kowalski, Limber, and Agatston, *Cyber Bullying,* 105.

16. Kowalski, Limber, and Agatston, *Cyber Bullying,* 105; their suggestions are based on the work of N. Willard, *A Parent's Guide to Cyberbullying and Cyberthreats: Addressing Online Social Cruelty,* Center for Responsible Internet Use, http://www.cyberbully.org/docs/cbct.parents.pdf.

17. J. Swartz, "Schoolyard Bullies Get Nastier Online," *USA Today,* Mar. 7, 2005, 1, http://www
    .usatoday.com/tech/news/2005-03-06-cover-cyberbullies_x.htm

18. Swartz, "Schoolyard Bullies."

19. R. M. Kowalski and S. P. Limber, "Electronic Bullying Among Middle School Students,"
    Journal of Adolescent Health 41 (2004): S22–S30.

INTERNET SAFETY

20. Research from the University of New Hampshire cited in T. Pearce, "Few Pedophiles Pos-
    ing as Youths Online," *Globe and Mail,* Feb. 2008, http://www.theglobeandmail.com/servlet/
    story/RTGAM.20080220.wpredator20/BNStory/Technology/home.

21. A. Lenhart and M. Madden, *Teens, Privacy and Online Social Networks: How Teens Manage
    Their Online Identities and Personal Information in the Age of MySpace* (Washington, D.C.:
    Pew Internet and American Life Project, Apr. 18, 2007), http://www.pewinternet.org/pdfs/
    PIP_Teens_Privacy_SNS_Report_Final.pdf.

22. Nationwide phone survey of one thousand parents by Global Strategy Group; all respon-
    dents had at least one child age twelve or under, and nearly 80 percent had a child younger
    than age six: cited in "What Keeps Parents Up at Night?" *Parents,* Jan. 2008, 20.

23. J. Moore, "Help Your Kids Stay Cyber-Safe," *Redbook,* June 2008, 206.

24. 87 percent of kids surf Webs without parental rules vs. 63 percent with rules; only half of
    children warned by parents of online dangers: D. Smiroldo, "Children and Decision-Making
    in Cyberspace," *Genesee Valley Parent,* Oct. 2007, 30–34.

25. Smiroldo, "Children and Decision-Making in Cyberspace."

26. Department of Justice survey cited in S. Brenna, "The Sexual Predator Threat," *Parents,* May
    2007, 153–154.

27. P. Olsen, "Up on Teen Text Lingo?" *USA Weekend,* Jan. 13, 2008, http://www.netlingo.com/
    news/Up_on_teen_text_lingo.pdf.

28. R. Furger, "It's a Wide, Wide Web," *Parenting,* May 1999, 126.

29. D. Okrent, "Raising Kids Online: What Can Parents Do?" *Time,* May 10, 1999, 38–43.

30. Boys and Girls Club of America survey of 565 kids ages six to eighteen, cited in L. Joseph
    and S. Ward, "USA Today Snapshots, Youth Views on Online Safety," *USA Today,* Aug. 15,
    2002, 1.

31. A. Lenhart, M. Madden, and P. Hitlin, *Teens and Technology: Youth Are Leading the Transi-
    tion to a Fully Wired and Mobile Nation,* July 27, 2005, http://www.pewinternet.org.

TV ADDICTION

32. "Kids, Parents and 'Screen Time,'" *Chicago Tribune,* 2003, http://www.hyper-parenting.
    com/chicagotrib4.htm.

33. K. Horsch, "Breaking the TV Habit," *Parents,* Apr. 2006, 153–154.

34. Stanford University study cited in G. Witkin, *KidStress* (New York: Viking, 1999), 2.

35. Horsch, "Breaking the TV Habit."

36. TV causes sleep disturbances in young children: K. Doheny, "TV Could Be Disrupting Your
    Kid's Sleep," *U.S. News & World Report,* Mar. 7, 2009, http://health.usnews.com/usnews/health/
    healthday/080225/tv-could-be-disrupting-your-kids-sleep.htm; study on effect of television

viewing habits and sleep disturbances in kindergarteners through fourth graders: J. Owens and others, "Television-Viewing Habits and Sleep Disturbance in School Children," *Pediatrics* 104, no. 3 (Sept. 1999): e27, http://pediatrics.aappublications.org/cgi/content/full/104/3/e27; Carole Marcus, MD, director of the Sleep Center at Children's Hospital of Philadelphia, says television in bedroom can rob sleep: cited by A. Cahill, "Back to Sleep," *Philadelphia,* Sept. 2008, http://www.phillymag.com/articles/web_original_health_back_to_sleep/.

37. D.L.G. Borzekowsky and T. N. Robinson, "The Remote, the Mouse, and the No. 2 Pencil: The Household Media Environment and Academic Achievement Among Third Grade Students," *Archives of Pediatrics and Adolescent Medicine* 159, no. 7 (2005): 607–613, http://archpedi.ama-assn.org/cgi/content/abstract/159/7/607?maxtoshow=&HITS=10&hits=10&RESULTFORMAT=&fulltext=television+bedrooms&searchid=1120595127674_1281&stored_search=&FIRSTINDEX=0&journalcode=archpedi

38. American Psychological Association, "Summary Report of the American Psychological Association Commission on Violence and Youth," in vol. 1 of *Violence and Youth: Psychology's Response* (Washington, D.C.: American Psychological Association, 1993), quoted in J. Garbarino, *Lost Boys* (New York: Free Press, 1999), 198.

VIDEO GAMES

39. $11 billion industry; games in 80 percent of homes with children: B. Greenberg, "Children Spend More Time Playing Video Games Than Watching TV, MSU Survey Shows," Michigan State University, Apr. 2, 2004, http://news.msu.edu/story/466/.

40. A. Lenhart and others, *Teens, Video Games, and Civics: Teens' Gaming Experiences Are Diverse and Include Significant Social and Civil Engagement* (Washington, D.C.: Pew Internet and American Life Project, 2008).

41. Michigan State University research shows that playing violent video games leads to a brain activity pattern that may be characteristic for aggressive thoughts: "Violent Video Games Lead to Brain Activity Characteristics of Aggression," *ScienceDaily,* Oct. 12, 2005, http://www.sciencedaily.com/releases/2005/10/051012082710.htm.

42. Greenberg, "Children Spend More Time."

43. University of Michigan review by Brad Bushman cited in Laidman, "Impact of Violent Video Games."

44. A Swinburne University of Technology study of 120 kids ages eleven to fifteen found that those children prone to worrying, neurotic behavior, and predisposed to aggression were likely to be more aggressive after playing violent video games: cited in "Most Kids 'Unaffected' by Violent Games," *Sydney Morning Herald,* Apr. 1, 2007, http://www.smh.com.au/news/National/Most-kids-unaffected-by-violent-games/2007/04/01/1175366055463.html.

45. Lenhart and others, *Teens.*

46. University of Toronto study published in *Journal of Adolescence,* cited in J. Laidman, "Impact of Violent Video Games on Young Children Examined in New Study," *Toledo Blade,* Feb. 14, 2004.

47. Video game ratings established by the Entertainment Software Rating Board cited by "How the Entertained Are Warned," *USA Today,* May 4, 1999, 6D.

48. Laidman, "Impact of Violent Video Games."

49. P. Abrams, "Making Peace with Video Games," *Parents*, Sept. 2002, 169–170.

50. Patricia Greenfield's research at UCLA cited in J. Quittner, "Are Video Games Really So Bad?" *Time* 153, no. 18 (May 10, 1999), http://www.time.com/time/magazine/article/0,9171 ,990921,00.html.

51. Quittner, "Are Video Games Really So Bad?"

52. Joint study by the University of Michigan, Ann Arbor, and the University of Texas, Austin, of 1,491 ten- to nineteen-year-olds during the school year: H. M. Cummings and E. A. Vandewater, "Relation of Adolescent Video Game Play to Time Spent in Other Activities," *Archives of Pediatrics and Adolescent Medicine* 161, no. 7 (July 2007): 684–689.

53. Mayo Clinic research cited in "Adding Activity to Video Games Fights Obesity, Study Shows," *ScienceDaily*, Jan. 10, 2007, http://sciencedaily.com/releases/2007/01/070104144703.htm.

54. Study of 1,254 preteens from two states conducted by Massachusetts General Hospital: C. K. Olson and others, "Factors Correlated with Violent Video Game Use by Adolescent Boys and Girls," *Journal of Adolescent Health* 41, no. 1 (July 2007): 77–83.

55. Studies gathered from the Surgeon General's office and the National Institute of Mental Health: American Academy of Pediatrics, *Joint Statement on the Impact of Entertainment Violence on Children*, July 26, 2000, www.aap.org/advocacy/releases/jstmtevc.htm.

56. The "Kids' Takes on Media" survey, a study of fifty-seven hundred students in grades 3 to 10, was conducted in 2003 by Erin Research for the Canadian Teachers' Federation: cited in J. Edmiston, "What Are They Watching?" *Today's Parent*, Dec.-Jan. 2004.

57. Greenberg, "Children Spend More Time."

58. J. Leo, "When Life Imitates Video," *U.S. News & World Report*, May 3, 1999, 14.

About the Author

Michele Borba, Ed.D., is an internationally renowned educator who is recognized for her practical, solution-based strategies to strengthen children's behavioral, social, and moral development. A sought-after motivational speaker, she has presented workshops to over one million participants worldwide and has been an educational consultant to hundreds of schools.

Dr. Borba is a contributor for NBC's *Today* show and frequently appears as a guest expert on television and radio, including *Oprah and Friends, Dr. Phil, The Tyra Banks Show, Geraldo and Friends, The View, CNN Headline News, The Early Show, Fox Headline News, Fox & Friends, MSNBC's Countdown, CNN American Morning, Inside Edition,* and *Canada AM.* She has been interviewed in hundreds of publications, including *Redbook, People, Newsweek, U.S. News & World Report,* the *Chicago Tribune,* and the *Los Angeles Times;* she is an iVillage contributor and writes the Parenting Solutions blog. She also serves as an advisory board member for *Parents* magazine.

She is the award-winning author of twenty-two books, including *12 Simple Secrets Real Moms Know; Nobody Likes Me, Everybody Hates Me; Don't Give Me That Attitude!; No More Misbehavin': 38 Difficult Behaviors and How to Stop Them; Building Moral Intelligence,* cited by *Publisher's Weekly* as "among the most noteworthy of 2001"; *Parents Do Make a Difference,* selected by *Child* magazine as an "Outstanding Parent Book of 1999"; and *Esteem Builders,* used by over 1.5 million students worldwide.

Dr. Borba's numerous awards include the National Educator Award, presented by the National Council of Self-Esteem. Her proposal to end school violence (SB1667) was signed into California law in 2002. She has served as a consultant or spokesperson for the U.S. Office of Education, McDonalds' Global Mom's Panel, Office Depot, Learning Curve West, Galderma, Johnson & Johnson, Splenda, Wal-Mart, and T-Mobile. She lives in Palm Springs, California, with her husband, and has three grown sons.

To contact Dr. Borba regarding her work or media availability, or to schedule a keynote or workshop for your organization, go to www.micheleborba.com.

Index

munication, 163; rapid response to, 164, 163; reason to change, 160; resources for, 167; signs and symptoms of, 160; signs and symptoms of, 160

Instant message (IM), 609, 617

Internal motivation, 89–90

Internet, and cheating, 154

Internet safety: desired change for, 610; early intervention with, 612–614; habits for change with, 616; indications of need for change in, 610; and parental rules, 667n24; rapid response to, 614; reason for change around, 610–612; resources for, 617; and seven cyberspace don'ts, 616; signs and symptoms around, 612; and what every parent needs to know about online predators, 611; and what kids say about online safety, 615; what to expect by stages and ages with, 616–617

InternetSuperHeroes.org, 614

Intolerance: desired change for, 168; expectations by stages and ages with, 171; five strategies for changing, 169–171; indications of need for change in, 168; reason for changing, 168; what to do if your child is victim of, 172

Intervention, xxx

Involvement without evidence, 34

IQ scores, 510–512, 514; and birth order, 23; and firstborns, 20, 25; in twins and multiples, 39; and youngest children, 42

Irresponsibility, 539

Irritability: and defiant behavior, 78; and sleeping problems, 592

It's a Wonderful Life (movie), xxxv

It's So Much Work to Be Your Friend (Lavoie), 485

iVillage online community, xvi, xxv, 303

J

James and the Giant Peach (CD), 594–595

Jealousy: and biting, 61; and bragging behavior, 72; and defiant behavior, 79

Johns Hopkins University, 42

Jokes, 106

Jolie, Angelina, 392

Jordan, Michael, 201, 281, 432

Josephson Institute of Ethics (Los Angeles), 152, 239

Journal of Child Psychology and Psychiatry, 631

"Joys of Motherhood Survey," xxxiii, 629n1; and motherhood experience, xxxv; and motherhood stress, xxxiv; and qualities moms want most in child, xxxiii–xxxiv; and use of new child-rearing research, xxxiv; and what one tip or piece of advice would have made better mom, xxxv–xxxvi; and where moms seek advice, xxxiv

K

Kagan, Jerome, 292, 295

Kalish, Nancy, 440

Karr-Morse, Robin, 5

Keilburger, Craig, 392

Kennedy, Edward, 41

Keyes, Margaret, 6

"Kids and Family Reading Report" Scholastic, 453

Kid's Book Club Book (Gelman and Krupp), 454

KidsHealth poll, 534

Kindlon, Dan, 540

King, Martin Luther, Jr., 376, 392

Klein, Kim, 486

Knoester, Chris, 315

Kovacs, Marie, 489

Kowalski, Robin, 604

Kristenson, Petter, 23

Krupp, Vicki Levy, 454

Kutner, Lawrence, 623

L

Labels: and attention deficit, 470; and Autism Spectrum Disorder, 482; and gifted child, 512; and sensitivity, 287; and shyness, 294,